KWIKSCAN™

New Testament

COMPLETE AUTHORIZED KING JAMES VERSION

KWIKSCAN™ EDITORIAL STAFF

Micro-Books, Incorporated
Windermere, Florida 32786

Library of Congress Cataloging - in - Publication Data:
BS2085 1986.w56 1987 220.5'2034 87-1515

ISBN 0-941485-02-1

Published in the United States of America

HOW **KWIKSCAN™** BENEFITS YOU

Try a simple experiment and immediately you will see the tremendous benefits of **KWIKSCAN™.** First, read every word in the text below. Secondly, go back through the text reading only those words in bold type. Once you read a couple of columns, you will never want to read anything printed the traditional way again.

KWIKSCAN™ words (The words printed in bold type) **comprise about 50% of a** total **Text,** and often much less. **And,** as you are about to find out, **by reading the bold words only, you** will **reduce reading time by up to Two Thirds!** (Much less time for some people and a little more for others.) **This is true because** of two reasons. The first is obvious. **You simply eliminate** the necessity of **reading about half the words** – words that can be left out without changing the overall meaning of the text. **Secondly,** and less obvious until you think about it, **you eliminate left to right head and or eye movement – a big problem** many have **in reading and** also **a consumer of** large chunks of your valuable **time. Besides** the benefits of **saving** huge amounts of **time, KWIKSCAN™** also **increases** the **understanding** of most readers **by making the text** less complicated and **easier to follow. It helps retention too.** (You will remember more of what you read!) **If right now, you are reading just the bold words** when you finish, **you will read only 119 out of** a total of **256 words,** and you will do it **in about one-third the time required to read the entire text. Yes, after** reading the exciting new **KWIKSCAN™** way, **you will never want to go back to the old** and ordinary **ways of reading** and you will know why KWIKSCAN™ is called "The greatest step forward in reading since the invention of the printing press."

TABLE OF CONTENTS

IMPORTANT MESSAGE TO THE READERS

"All scripture is given by inspiration of God..." (II Timothy 3:16).

The text of the KWIKSCAN™ New Testament includes every word of The Authorized King James Version. Not a single word has been eliminated or altered. Highlighting (placing certain words in bold faced type), does not indicate that they have greater importance. Rather, the bold words assist readers in quickly reviewing the text. For a thorough understanding of the scripture, readers should study the complete text. However, the SCAN represents thousands of hours of intensive research and work by dedicated Bible scholars, proof editors, computer systems analyst, and typesetting specialists, all of whom are committed to assisting readers in understanding the Holy Scriptures.

THE GOSPEL ACCORDING TO MATTHEW

BACKGROUND INFORMATION

Author – Matthew, a tax collector who became **one of The Twelve Disciples** of Jesus.
Date Written – probably **between 61** and **70** A.D.

Number of:
Verses - 1,071
Chapters - 28
Total Words - 23,684
Scan Words - 11,770
Scan Words represent 49 % of Total Words.

Theme – showing that **Jesus Christ is the Fulfillment of** The Old Testament **prophecies** concerning the promised Messiah.

OUTLINE OF THE GOSPEL

I. **The birth and childhood** of Jesus Christ.
Chapters 1:1—2:23
II. **The beginning of the ministry** of Jesus Christ.
Chapters 3:1—4:11
III. **The public ministry** of Jesus Christ in fulfillment of Old Testament prophecy.
Chapters 4:12—25:46
IV. **The passion** of Jesus Christ in fulfillment of Old Testament prophecy.
Chapters 26:1—27:66
V. **The resurrection** of Jesus Christ.
Chapter 28:1—20

CHAPTER 1

1. **The book** of the generation
of Jesus Christ,
the son of David,
the son of Abraham.
2. Abraham begat Isaac; and Isaac
begat Jacob; and Jacob begat Judas
and his brethren;
3. And Judas begat Phares and Zara
of Thamar; and Phares begat Esrom;
and Esrom begat Aram;
4. And Aram begat Aminadab; and
Aminadab begat Naasson; and
Naasson begat Salmon;
5. And Salmon begat Booz of Rachab;
and Booz begat Obed of Ruth; and
Obed begat Jesse;
6. And Jesse begat David the king;
and David the king begat Solomon of
her *that had been the wife* of Urias;
7. And Solomon begat Roboam; and
Roboam begat Abia; and
Abia begat Asa;
8. And Asa begat Josaphat; and
Josaphat begat Joram; and Joram
begat Ozias;
9. And Ozias begat Joatham; and
Joatham begat Achaz; and Achaz
begat Ezekias;
10. And Ezekias begat Manasses;
and Manasses begat Amon; and
Amon begat Josias;
11. And Josias begat Jechonias and
his brethren, about the time they were
carried away to Babylon:
12. And after they were brought to
Babylon, Jechonias begat Salathiel;
and Salathiel begat Zorobabel;
13. And Zorobabel begat Abiud; and
Abiud begat Eliakim; and Eliakim
begat Azor;
14. And Azor begat Sadoc; and Sadoc
begat Achim; and Achim begat Eliud;
15. And Eliud begat Eleazar; and
Eleazar begat Matthan; and Matthan
begat Jacob;
16. And Jacob begat Joseph the
husband of Mary, of whom was born
Jesus, who is called Christ.
17. So all the generations
from Abraham to David
***are* fourteen generations;**
and from David until the
carrying away into
Babylon *are* fourteen
generations; and from
the carrying away into
Babylon unto Christ *are*
fourteen generations.
18. **Now** the birth of Jesus Christ
was on this wise:
When as his mother
Mary was espoused to
Joseph, before they came
together, she was found
with child of the
Holy Ghost.
19. **Then Joseph** her husband,
being a just *man*, and not willing
to make her a public example,
was minded to put her
away privily.
20. **But** while he thought on these
things, behold,
the angel of the LORD
appeared unto him in a dream,
saying, Joseph,
thou son of David,
fear not to take unto thee
Mary thy wife:
for that which is conceived
in her is of the Holy Ghost.
21. **And she shall bring forth**
a son, and thou shalt
call his name JESUS: for he
shall save his people
from their sins.
22. **Now all this** was done, that it
might be fulfilled which
was spoken of the Lord
by the prophet, saying,
23. **Behold, a virgin shall**
be with child, and shall
bring forth a son, and they
shall call his name
Emmanuel, which
being interpreted
is, God with us.
24. **Then Joseph** being raised
from sleep did as the angel of the Lord
had bidden him, and
took unto him his wife:
25. **And knew her not till she**
had brought forth her firstborn
son: and he called his name
JESUS.

CHAPTER 2

1. **Now** when Jesus was born in Bethlehem of Judaea
in the days of Herod
the king, behold,
there came wise men from
the east to Jerusalem,
2. **Saying, Where is he** that is
born King of the Jews? for
we have seen his star
in the east,
and are come to
worship him.
3. **When Herod** the king had
heard *these things,*
he was troubled,
and all Jerusalem with him.
4. **And when he had**
gathered all the chief
priests and scribes
of the people together,
he demanded of them
where Christ should
be born.
5. **And they said** unto him,
In Bethlehem of Judaea:
for thus it is written
by the prophet,
6. And thou Bethlehem, *in* the land of Juda, art not the least among the princes of Juda: for out of thee shall come a Governor, that shall rule my people Israel.
7. **Then Herod,** when he had
privily called the wise men,
inquired of them diligently
what time the
star appeared.
8. **And he** sent them to
Bethlehem, and
said, Go and search diligently
for the young child;
and when ye have found *him* ,
bring me word again,
that I may come and
worship him also.
9. When they had heard the king,
they departed; and, lo, the
star, which they saw in the east,
went before them, till it came
and stood over
where the young
child was.
10. When they saw the star, they rejoiced with exceeding great joy.
11. **And** when they were come into the house,
they saw the young
child with Mary his mother,
and fell down,
and worshipped him: and
when they had opened their
treasures, they
presented unto him
gifts; gold, and
frankincense and myrrh.
12. **And being warned of**
God in a dream that they
should not return to
Herod, they departed into
their own country another way.
13. **And** when they were
departed, behold,
the angel of the Lord
appeareth to Joseph in a
dream, saying, Arise, and
take the young child and
his mother, and flee into
Egypt, and be thou there
until I bring thee word:
for Herod will seek
the young child
to destroy him.
14. When he arose,
he took the young child
and his mother by night,
and departed into Egypt:
15. And was there until
the death of Herod:
that it might be fulfilled
which was spoken of
the Lord by
the prophet, saying, Out of
Egypt have I called my son.
16. **Then Herod,** when he saw that
he was mocked of the wise men, was
exceeding wroth, and sent forth, and
slew all the children that were
in Bethlehem, and in all the
coasts thereof,
from two years old
and under,
according to the time which he had
diligently inquired of the wise men.
17. **Then was fulfilled that**
which was

spoken by Jeremy
the prophet, saying,
18. **In Rama was** there a voice
heard, lamentation, and weeping,
and great
mourning, Rachel weeping
***for* her children,** and would not
be comforted, because they are not.
19. **But when Herod was**
dead, behold,
an angel of the Lord
appeareth in a dream
to Joseph in Egypt,
20. **Saying,** Arise, and
take the young child and
his mother, and go into
the land of
Israel: for they are dead which
sought the young child's life.
21. And he arose, and took the young
child and his mother, and came into
the land of Israel.
22. **But when he heard that**
Archelaus did reign in
Judaea in the room of
his father Herod,
he was afraid
to go thither: notwithstanding,
being warned of God
in a dream,
he turned aside into
the parts of
Galilee:
23. And he came
and dwelt in a city called
Nazareth: that it might
be fulfilled
which was spoken by the prophets,
He shall be called
a Nazarene.

CHAPTER 3

1. **In those days came John**
the Baptist, preaching
in the wilderness of Judaea,
2. **And saying, Repent ye:**
for the kingdom of heaven
is at hand.
3. **For this is he** that was
spoken of by the prophet
Esaias, saying, The voice
of one crying in the
wilderness, Prepare ye the
way of the Lord,
make his paths straight.
4. And the same John had his raiment
of camel's hair, and a leathern girdle
about his loins; and his meat was
locusts and wild honey.
5. **Then went out to him**
Jerusalem, and all
Judaea, and all
the region round about
Jordan,
6. **And were baptized**
of him in Jordan,
confessing their sins.
7. **But when he saw** many of
the Pharisees and
Sadducees come to his baptism,
he said unto them,
O generation of vipers,
who hath warned you to
flee from the wrath
to come?
8. **Bring forth** therefore
fruits meet
for repentance:
9. **And think not**
to say within yourselves,
We have Abraham to *our*
father: for I say unto you, that
God is able of these
stones to raise up children
unto Abraham.
10. And now also the axe is laid unto
the root of the trees: therefore every
tree which bringeth not forth good fruit
is hewn down, and cast into the fire.
11. **I indeed baptize you**
with water unto repentance.
but he that cometh after me
is mightier than I, whose
shoes I am not worthy to
bear: he shall baptize you
with the Holy Ghost, and *with*
fire:
12. Whose fan *is* in his hand, and he
will throughly purge his floor, and
gather his wheat into the garner; but
he will burn up the chaff with
unquenchable fire.
13. **Then cometh Jesus**
from Galilee to Jordan
unto John, to be baptized
of him.

14. **But John forbad him,**
saying, I have need to be baptized of
thee, and comest thou to me?
15. **And Jesus** answering
said unto him,
Suffer *it to be so*
now: for thus it becometh us
to fulfil all righteousness.
Then he suffered him.
16. **And Jesus, when he was**
baptized, went up straightway
out of the water: and, lo, the
heavens were
opened unto him,
and he saw the Spirit of
God descending like a
dove, and lighting
upon him:
17. **And lo a voice from**
heaven, saying, This is my
beloved Son, in whom I am
well pleased.

CHAPTER 4

1. **Then was Jesus** led up of the
Spirit into the wilderness to be
tempted of the devil.
2. **And when he had fasted**
forty days and forty
nights, he was afterward an
hungered.
3. And when
the tempter came to him, he
said, If thou be the Son of
God, command that these
stones be made bread.
4. **But he answered** and said,
It is written, Man shall not
live by bread alone, but by
every word
that proceedeth out of the mouth
of God.
5. **Then the devil** taketh him up
into the holy city, and
setteth him on a pinnacle of
the temple,
6. **And saith**
unto him, If thou be the Son of God,
cast thyself down: for it is
written, He shall give his
angels charge concerning thee:
and in *their* hands they
shall bear thee up, lest at any
time thou dash thy foot
against a stone.
7. **Jesus said** unto him,
It is written again, Thou
shalt not tempt the Lord thy
God.
8. **Again, the devil taketh**
him up into an exceeding
high mountain, and
sheweth him all the
kingdoms of the world,
and the glory of them;
9. **And saith** unto him,
All these things will
I give thee, if thou wilt
fall down and
worship me.
10. **Then saith Jesus** unto him,
Get thee hence, Satan: for it
is written, Thou shalt
worship the Lord thy God,
and him only shalt thou serve.
11. **Then the devil leaveth**
him, and, behold,
angels came and
ministered unto him.
12. **Now when Jesus had**
heard that John was cast
into prison, he departed
into Galilee;
13. And leaving Nazareth, he came
and dwelt in Capernaum, which is
upon the sea coast, in the borders of
Zabulon and Nephthalim:
14. That it might be fulfilled which
was spoken by Esaias the
prophet, saying,
15. The land of Zabulon, and the
land of Nephthalim, *by* the way of the
sea, beyond Jordan, Galilee of
the Gentiles;
16. The people which sat in darkness
saw great light; and to them which sat
in the region and shadow of death light
is sprung up.
17. **From that time Jesus**
began to preach, and to say,
Repent: for the kingdom of
heaven is at hand.
18. **And Jesus,**
walking by the sea of Galilee,
saw two brethren, Simon called
Peter, and Andrew his

■ **brother,** casting a net into the sea:
for they were fishers.
■ 19. **And he saith** unto them,
■ **Follow me, and I will make**
■ **you fishers of men.**
■ 20. **And they**
straightway left *their* nets, and
■ **followed him.**
■ 21. **And** going on from thence,
■ **he saw** other two brethren,
■ **James** *the son* of Zebedee,
■ **and John his brother,**
in a ship with Zebedee their father,
mending their nets;
■ **and he called them.**
■ 22. **And they immediately**
left the ship and their father, and
■ **followed him.**
■ 23. **And Jesus went about**
■ **all Galilee, teaching in their**
■ **synagogues,** and
■ **preaching** the gospel
of the kingdom,
■ **and healing all** manner of
■ **sickness and all** manner of
■ **disease** among the people.
24. And his fame went
throughout all Syria:
■ **and they brought** unto him
■ **all sick people** that were taken
with divers diseases and torments,
■ **and those** which were
■ **possessed with devils,**
■ **and those which**
■ **were lunatic,**
and those that had the palsy;
■ **and he healed them.**
■ 25. **And there followed him**
■ **great multitudes** of people from
Galilee, and *from* Decapolis, and *from*
Jerusalem, and *from* Judaea, and *from*
beyond Jordan.

CHAPTER 5

■ 1. **And seeing the**
■ **multitudes, he went up into**
■ **a mountain:** and when he was
set, his disciples came unto him:
■ 2. **And** he opened his mouth, and
■ **taught them, saying,**
■ 3. **Blessed are the poor in**
■ **spirit: for theirs is the**
■ **kingdom** of heaven.
■ 4. **Blessed are they that**
■ **mourn: for they shall**
■ **be comforted.**
■ 5. **Blessed are the meek: for**
■ **they shall inherit the earth.**
■ 6. **Blessed are they which**
■ **do hunger and thirst after**
■ **righteousness: for they**
■ **shall be filled.**
■ 7. **Blessed are the merciful:**
■ **for they shall obtain mercy.**
■ 8. **Blessed are the pure in**
■ **heart: for they shall**
■ **see God.**
■ 9. **Blessed are the**
■ **peacemakers: for they**
■ **shall be called the children**
■ **of God.**
■ 10. **Blessed are they which**
■ **are persecuted for**
■ **righteousness' sake: for**
■ **theirs is the kingdom**
of heaven.
■ 11. **Blessed are ye, when**
■ ***men* shall revile you, and**
■ **persecute *you*, and** shall
■ **say** all manner of
■ **evil against you falsely,**
■ **for my sake.**
■ 12. **Rejoice,**
and be exceeding glad:
■ **for great *is* your reward**
in heaven: for so persecuted they the
prophets which were before you.
■ 13. **Ye are the salt of the**
■ **earth: but if the salt have**
■ **lost his savour,**
wherewith shall it be salted?
■ **it is** thenceforth
■ **good for nothing,**
but to be cast out, and to be trodden
under foot of men.
■ 14. **Ye are the light of the**
■ **world.** A city that is set on an hill
cannot be hid.
15. Neither do men light a candle, and
put it under a bushel, but on a
candlestick; and it giveth light unto all
that are in the house.
■ 16. **Let your light so shine**
■ **before men, that they may**
■ **see your good works, and**
■ **glorify your Father**

which is in heaven.
17. **Think not that I am come**
to destroy the law,
or the prophets:
I am not come to destroy,
but to fulfil.
18. For verily I say unto you,
Till heaven and earth pass,
one jot
or one tittle
shall in no wise pass
from the law,
till all be fulfilled.
19. **Whosoever therefore**
shall break one of these
least commandments, and
shall teach men so, he
shall be called the
least in the kingdom
of heaven:
but whosoever shall do
and teach *them*, the same
shall be called great
in the kingdom of heaven.
20. For I say unto you, That
except your righteousness
shall exceed *the*
***righteousness* of the**
scribes and Pharisees, ye
shall in no case enter into
the kingdom of heaven.
21. **Ye have heard**
that it was said by them of old time,
Thou shalt not kill;
and whosoever shall kill shall be in
danger of the judgment:
22. **But I say** unto you, That
whosoever is angry with
his brother without a cause
shall be in danger of the
judgment: and whosoever shall
say to his brother, Raca, shall be in
danger of the council: but
whosoever shall say, Thou
fool, shall be in danger of
hell fire.
23. **Therefore if thou bring**
thy gift to the altar, and there
rememberest that thy
brother hath aught
against thee;
24. **Leave there thy gift**
before the altar,
and go thy way;
first be reconciled
to thy brother,
and then come and offer thy gift.
25. **Agree with thine**
adversary quickly, whiles
thou art in the way with him; lest at
any time the adversary deliver thee to
the judge, and the judge deliver thee
to the officer, and thou be
cast into prison.
26. Verily I say unto thee, Thou shalt
by no means come out thence, till
thou hast paid the uttermost farthing.
27. **Ye have heard** that it was
said by them of old time,
Thou shalt not
commit adultery:
28. **But I say** unto you, That
whosoever looketh on a
woman to lust after her
hath committed adultery
with her already
in his heart.
29. **And if thy right eye**
offend thee, pluck it out,
and cast *it* from thee:
for it is profitable for thee
that one of thy members
should perish, and not *that*
thy whole body should be
cast into hell.
30. And if thy right hand offend thee,
cut it off, and cast *it* from thee: for it is
profitable for thee that one of thy
members should perish, and not *that*
thy whole body should be
cast into hell.
31. It hath been said, Whosoever
shall put away his wife, let him give
her a writing of divorcement:
32. But I say unto you, That
whosoever shall put away
his wife, saving for
the cause of
fornication, causeth her to
commit adultery: and
whosoever shall marry her
that is divorced
committeth adultery.
33. **Again, ye have heard** that
it hath been said by them of old time,
Thou shalt not forswear

thyself, but shalt perform
unto the Lord thine oaths:
34. **But I say** unto you,
Swear not at all; neither by
heaven; for it is God's throne:
35. Nor by the earth; for it is his
footstool: neither by Jerusalem; for it
is the city of the great King.
36. Neither shalt thou swear by thy
head, because thou canst not make
one hair white or black.
37. **But let your communica-**
tion be, Yea, yea; Nay, nay:
for whatsoever is more
than these
cometh of evil.
38. **Ye have heard**
that it hath been said,
An eye for an eye,
and a tooth for a tooth:
39. **But I say** unto you, That ye
resist not evil: but
whosoever shall smite thee
on thy right cheek, turn to
him the other also.
40. **And if any man will sue**
thee at the law,
and take away thy coat, let
him have *thy* cloak also.
41. **And whosoever shall**
compel thee to go a mile,
go with him twain.
42. **Give to him that asketh**
thee, and from him that
would borrow of thee
turn not thou away.
43. **Ye have heard**
that it hath been said,
Thou shalt love thy
neighbour, and hate
thine enemy.
44. **But I say** unto you,
Love your enemies,
bless them that curse you, do good to
them that hate you, and pray for them
which despitefully use you, and
persecute you;
45. **That ye may be the**
children of your Father
which is in heaven:
for he maketh his sun to
rise on the evil and on the
good, and sendeth rain on the just
and on the unjust.
46. **For if ye love them which**
love you, what reward have ye?
do not even the publicans
the same?
47. **And if ye salute your**
brethren only, what do ye
more *than others?*
do not even the publicans so?
48. **Be ye therefore perfect,**
even as your Father
which is in heaven
is perfect.

CHAPTER 6

1. Take heed that ye
do not your alms before
men, to be seen of them:
otherwise ye have no
reward of your Father which
is in heaven.
2. Therefore when thou doest *thine*
alms, do not sound a trumpet before
thee, as the hypocrites do in the
synagogues and in the streets, that
they may have glory of men. Verily I
say unto you, They have their reward.
3. **But when thou doest**
alms, let not thy left hand
know what thy right
hand doeth:
4. That thine alms may be in secret:
and thy Father which seeth
in secret himself
shall reward thee openly.
5. **And when thou prayest,**
thou shalt not be as the
hypocrites *are:* for they love to
pray standing in the synagogues and
in the corners of the streets, that they
may be seen of men. Verily I say unto
you, They have their reward.
6. But thou,
when thou prayest, enter
into thy closet,
and when thou hast shut thy door,
pray to thy Father which is
in secret; and thy Father
which seeth in secret
shall reward thee openly.
7. But when ye pray,
use not vain repetitions,
as the heathen *do* : for they think that

they shall be heard for their
much speaking.
8. Be not ye therefore
like unto them: for
your Father
knoweth what things
ye have
need of, before ye ask him.
9. **After this manner** therefore
pray ye: Our Father which
art in heaven, Hallowed be
thy name.
10. **Thy kingdom come, Thy**
will be done in earth, as *it is*
in heaven.
11. **Give us this day our**
daily bread.
12. **And forgive us our**
debts, as we forgive
our debtors.
13. **And lead us not into**
temptation, but deliver us
from evil: For thine is the
kingdom, and the power,
and the glory, for ever.
Amen.
14. **For if ye forgive men**
their trespasses,
your heavenly Father will
also forgive you:
15. But if ye forgive not men their
trespasses, neither will your Father
forgive your trespasses.
16. **Moreover when ye fast,**
be not, as the hypocrites,
of a sad countenance: for
they disfigure their faces, that they
may appear unto men to fast. Verily I
say unto you, They have their reward.
17. **But** thou, when thou fastest,
anoint thine head, and
wash thy face;
18. **That thou appear not**
unto men to fast, but unto thy
Father which is in secret:
and thy Father, which seeth
in secret, shall reward
thee openly.
19. **Lay not up for**
yourselves treasures upon
earth, where moth and rust doth
corrupt, and where thieves break
through and steal:
20. **But lay up** for yourselves
treasures in heaven,
where neither moth nor rust doth
corrupt, and where thieves do not
break through nor steal:
21. **For where your treasure**
is, there will your heart
be also.
22. The light of the body is the eye: if
therefore thine eye be single, thy
whole body shall be full of light.
23. But if thine eye be evil, thy whole
body shall be full of darkness. If
therefore the light that is in thee be
darkness, how great *is* that darkness!
24. **No man can serve two**
masters: for either he will hate the
one, and love the other; or else he will
hold to the one, and despise the
other.
Ye cannot serve God
and mammon.
25. **Therefore I say unto you,**
Take no thought for your
life, what ye shall
eat, or what ye shall
drink; nor yet for your body,
what ye shall
put on. Is not the life more than
meat, and the body than raiment?
26. **Behold the fowls**
of the air: for
they sow not, neither do
they reap, nor gather into barns;
yet your heavenly
Father feedeth them. Are ye
not much better than they?
27. **Which of you by taking**
thought can add one cubit
unto his stature?
28. **And why take** ye
thought for raiment?
Consider the lilies
of the field, how they grow;
they toil not, neither do they spin:
29. **And yet**
I say unto you, That even
Solomon in all his glory
was not arrayed
like one of these.
30. **Wherefore, if God so**
clothe the grass of the field,
which to-day is, and to-morrow is cast

into the oven,
***shall he* not much more**
***clothe* you, O ye**
of little faith?
31. **Therefore take no**
thought, saying, What shall
we eat? or, What shall we
drink? or, Wherewithal
shall we be clothed?
32. (For after all these things do the
Gentiles seek:) for
your heavenly
Father knoweth that
ye have need of all these things.
33. **But seek ye first the**
kingdom of God, and his
righteousness; and all
these things shall be
added unto you.
34. **Take therefore no**
thought for the morrow:
for the morrow shall take thought for
the things of itself. Sufficient unto the
day *is* the evil thereof.

CHAPTER 7

1. **Judge not, that ye be**
not judged.
2. For with what judgment ye judge, ye
shall be judged: and with what
measure ye mete, it shall be
measured to you again.
3. **And why beholdest** thou
the mote that is
in thy brother's eye, but
considerest not the beam
that is
in thine own eye?
4. Or how wilt thou say to thy brother,
Let me pull out the mote out of thine
eye; and, behold, a beam *is* in thine
own eye?
5. **Thou hypocrite, first cast**
out the beam out
of thine own eye; and then
shalt thou see clearly to
cast out the mote out
of thy brother's eye.
6. Give not that which is holy unto the
dogs, neither cast ye your pearls
before swine, lest they trample them
under their feet, and turn again and
rend you.
7. **Ask, and it shall be given**
you;
seek, and ye shall find;
knock, and it shall be
opened unto you:
8. For every one that asketh
receiveth; and he that seeketh
findeth; and to him that knocketh it
shall be opened.
9. **Or what man**
is there of you, whom
if his son ask bread, will he
give him a stone?
10. Or if he ask a fish, will he give
him a serpent?
11. **If ye then, being evil,**
know how to give good
gifts unto your children,
how much more shall your
Father which is in heaven
give good things to them
that ask him?
12. Therefore all things
whatsoever ye would that
men should do to you, do
ye even so
to them: for this is the law
and the prophets.
13. **Enter ye in at the strait**
gate: for wide *is* the gate,
and broad *is* the way, that
leadeth to destruction, and
many there be which go in thereat:
14. **Because strait *is* the**
gate, and narrow *is* the
way, which leadeth unto
life, and few there be that
find it.
15. **Beware of false**
prophets, which come to you
in sheep's clothing, but
inwardly they
are ravening
wolves.
16. **Ye shall know them by**
their fruits. Do men gather grapes
of thorns, or figs of thistles?
17. Even so every good tree bringeth
forth good fruit; but a corrupt tree
bringeth forth evil fruit.
18. **A good tree cannot bring**
forth evil fruit, neither *can* a
corrupt tree bring forth good fruit.

19. Every tree that bringeth not forth
good fruit is hewn down, and cast into
the fire.
20. Wherefore by their fruits ye shall
know them.
21. **Not every one that saith**
unto me, Lord, Lord, shall
enter into the kingdom
of heaven;
but he that doeth the will of
my Father which is in heaven.
22. **Many will say**
to me in that day,
Lord, Lord, have we not
prophesied in thy name?
and in thy name have
cast out devils? and in thy
name done many wonderful works?
23. **And then will I profess**
unto them, I never knew
you: depart from me,
ye that work iniquity.
24. **Therefore whosoever**
heareth these sayings
of mine,
and doeth them, I will liken
him
unto a wise man, which
built his house upon
a rock:
25. **And the rain** descended,
and the
floods came,
and the
winds blew, and
beat upon that house;
and it fell not:
for it was founded upon a rock.
26. **And every one that**
heareth these sayings
of mine,
and doeth them not,
shall be likened unto a
foolish man, which built his
house upon the sand:
27. **And the rain** descended,
and the
floods came,
and the
winds blew, and
beat upon that house;
and it fell: and great was
the fall of it.

28. **And** it came to pass, when Jesus
had ended these sayings,
the people were
astonished at his doctrine:
29. **For he taught** them
as *one* having authority,
and not as the scribes.

CHAPTER 8

1. **When he was come down**
from the mountain, great
multitudes followed him.
2. **And,** behold, there came
a leper and
worshipped him, saying,
Lord, if thou wilt,
thou canst make me clean.
3. **And Jesus**
put forth *his* hand, and
touched him, saying, I will;
be thou clean. And
immediately
his leprosy was cleansed.
4. **And Jesus saith** unto him,
See thou tell no man; but go
thy way,
shew thyself to the priest,
and offer the gift that Moses
commanded,
for a testimony unto them.
5. **And when Jesus** was
entered into
Capernaum, there came
unto him
a centurion, beseeching him,
6. And
saying, Lord,
my servant lieth at home
sick of the
palsy, grievously tormented.
7. **And Jesus saith** unto him,
I will come and heal him.
8. **The centurion** answered and
said, Lord, I am not worthy
that thou shouldest come
under my roof: but speak
the word only, and my
servant shall be healed.
9. For I am a man under authority,
having soldiers under me: and I say to
this *man*, Go, and he goeth; and to
another, Come, and he cometh; and to
my servant, Do this, and he doeth *it*.

10. **When Jesus heard *it*,**
he marvelled, and
said to them that followed,
Verily I say unto you
I have not found so great
faith, no, not in Israel.
11. And I say unto you, That many
shall come from the east and west,
and shall sit down with Abraham, and
Isaac, and Jacob, in the
kingdom of heaven.
12. But the children of the kingdom
shall be cast out into outer darkness:
there shall be weeping and gnashing
of teeth.
13. **And Jesus said unto the**
centurion, Go thy way; and
as thou hast believed, *so*
be it done unto thee.
And his servant was
healed in the selfsame hour.
14. **And when Jesus was**
come into Peter's house, he
saw his wife's mother
laid, and
sick of a fever.
15. **And he touched her**
hand, and the fever left
her: and she arose, and ministered
unto them.
16. When the even was come, they
brought unto him many that were
possessed with devils:
and he cast out the spirits
with *his* word, and healed
all that were sick:
17. **That it might be fulfilled**
which was spoken by Esaias the
prophet, saying,
Himself took our infirmities,
and bare *our* sicknesses.
18. Now when Jesus saw great
multitudes about him, he gave
commandment to depart unto
the other side.
19. **And a certain scribe**
came, and
said unto him, Master,
I will follow thee
whithersoever thou goest.
20. **And Jesus saith**
unto him, The foxes have holes, and
the birds of the air *have* nests; but
the Son of man hath not
where to lay *his* head.
21. **And another** of his disciples
said unto him,
Lord, suffer me first to go
and bury my father.
22. **But Jesus said**
unto him, Follow me; and
let the dead bury
their dead.
23. **And when he was**
entered into
a ship, his disciples
followed him.
24. **And, behold, there**
arose a great tempest
in the sea, insomuch that the ship
was covered with the waves:
but he was asleep.
25. **And his disciples**
came to *him*, and
awoke him, saying, Lord,
save us: we perish.
26. **And he saith**
unto them, Why are ye fearful,
O ye of little faith? Then he
arose, and
rebuked the winds
and the sea;
and there was a
great calm.
27. **But the men marvelled,**
saying, What manner of
man is this, that
even the winds and the
sea obey him!
28. **And when he was come**
to the other side
into the country of the
Gergesenes, there met him
two possessed with devils,
coming out of the tombs, exceeding
fierce, so that no man might pass by
that way.
29. **And, behold, they cried**
out, saying, What have we
to do with thee, Jesus, thou
Son of God? art thou come
hither
to torment us before
the time?
30. And there was a good way off from
them an herd of many swine feeding.

31. So the devils besought him,
saying, If thou cast us out,
■ **suffer us to go** away
■ **into the herd of swine.**
■ 32. **And he said** unto them,
■ **Go. And** when they were come out,
■ **they went into the herd**
of swine:
■ **and,** behold, the whole herd of swine
■ **ran violently down**
a steep place
■ **into the sea, and perished**
in the waters.
■ 33. **And they that kept**
■ **them fled,**
and went their ways into the city,
■ **and told every thing,**
and what was befallen to the
possessed of the devils.
■ 34. **And, behold, the whole**
■ **city came** out to meet Jesus:
■ **and** when they saw him, they
■ **besought *him* that he would**
■ **depart** out of their coasts.

CHAPTER 9

■ 1. **And he** entered into a ship, and
passed over, and
■ **came into his own city.**
■ 2. **And,** behold,
■ **they brought** to
■ **him a man sick of** the
■ **palsy,** lying on a bed:
■ **and Jesus seeing their faith**
■ **said** unto the sick of the palsy;
■ **Son,** be of good cheer;
■ **thy sins be forgiven** thee.
■ 3. **And, behold,** certain of
■ **the scribes said within**
■ **themselves, This *man***
■ **blasphemeth.**
■ 4. **And Jesus knowing their**
■ **thoughts said, Wherefore**
■ **think ye evil** in your hearts?
■ 5. **For whether is easier, to**
■ **say, *Thy* sins be forgiven**
thee;
■ **or** to say,
■ **Arise, and walk?**
■ 6. **But that ye may know** that
■ **the Son** of man
■ **hath power** on earth
■ **to forgive sins, (then saith**
■ **he to the sick** of the palsy,)
■ **Arise,** take up thy bed, and go unto
thine house.
■ 7. **And he arose,**
and departed to his house.
8. But when the multitudes saw *it,* they
marvelled, and glorified God, which
had given such power unto men.
■ 9. **And as Jesus passed**
forth from thence,
■ **he saw** a man, named
■ **Matthew,** sitting at the
receipt of custom:
■ **and he saith** unto him,
■ **Follow me. And he** arose, and
■ **followed him.**
■ 10. **And** it came to pass,
■ **as Jesus sat at meat**
■ **in the house,** behold,
■ **many publicans and**
■ **sinners** came and
■ **sat down with him**
and his disciples.
■ 11. **And when the Pharisees**
■ **saw *it,* they said**
unto his disciples,
■ **Why eateth your Master**
■ **with** publicans and
■ **sinners?**
■ 12. **But** when
■ **Jesus** heard *that,* he
■ **said** unto them,
■ **They that be whole need**
■ **not a physician,**
but they that are sick.
13. But go ye and learn what *that*
meaneth, I will have mercy, and not
sacrifice: for
■ **I am not come to call the**
■ **righteous, but sinners to**
■ **repentance.**
■ 14. **Then came** to him
■ **the disciples of John,**
■ **saying, Why do we and the**
■ **Pharisees fast** oft,
■ **but thy disciples fast not?**
■ 15. **And Jesus said** unto them
■ **Can the children of the**
■ **bridechamber mourn, as**
■ **long as the bridegroom is**
■ **with them?** but the days will come,
when the bridegroom shall be taken
from them, and then shall they fast.

16. No man putteth a piece of new cloth unto an old garment, for that which is put in to fill it up taketh from the garment, and the rent is made worse.
17. Neither do men put new wine into old bottles: else the bottles break, and the wine runneth out, and the bottles perish: but they put new wine into new bottles, and both are preserved.
18. **While he spake** these things unto them, behold, **there came a certain ruler, and worshipped him, saying, My daughter is** even now **dead: but come** and lay thy hand upon her, **and she shall live.**
19. And Jesus arose, and followed him, and *so did* his disciples.
20. **And, behold, a woman,** which was diseased **with an issue of blood** twelve years, came behind *him,* and **touched** the hem of **his garment:**
21. **For she said** within herself, **If I may but touch his garment, I shall be whole.**
22. **But Jesus turned** him about, **and** when he saw her, he **said, Daughter,** be of good comfort; **thy faith hath made thee whole.** And the woman was made whole from that hour.
23. **And when Jesus came into the ruler's house,** and saw the minstrels and the people making a noise,
24. **He said** unto them, Give place: for **the maid is not dead, but sleepeth. And they laughed him to scorn.**
25. **But** when the people were put forth, **he** went in, and **took her by the hand, and the maid arose.**
26. And the fame hereof went abroad into all that land.
27. **And when Jesus departed** thence, **two blind men followed him,** crying, and saying, *Thou* son of David, have mercy on us.
28. And when he was come **into the house,** the blind men came to him: **and Jesus saith** unto them, **Believe ye that I am able to do this? They said** unto him, **Yea, Lord.**
29. **Then touched he their eyes, saying, According to your faith be it unto you.**
30. **And their eyes were opened;** and Jesus straitly charged them, saying, See *that* no man know *it* .
31. But they, when they were departed, spread abroad his fame in all that country.
32. **As they went out,** behold, **they brought** to him **a dumb man possessed with a devil.**
33. **And when the devil was cast out, the dumb spake:** and the multitudes marvelled, saying, It was never so seen in Israel.
34. **But the Pharisees said, He casteth out devils through the prince of the devils.**
35. **And Jesus went about** all the cities and villages, **teaching** in their synagogues, **and preaching** the gospel of the kingdom, **and healing** every sickness and every disease among the people.
36. **But when he saw the multitudes, he was moved with compassion** on them, **because they** fainted, and **were** scattered abroad, **as sheep having no shepherd.**
37. **Then saith he** unto his disciples, **The harvest truly *is* plenteous, but the**

labourers *are* few;
38. **Pray ye** therefore
the Lord of the harvest,
that he will send forth
labourers into his harvest.

CHAPTER 10

1. **And** when he had called
unto *him*
his twelve disciples, he
gave them
power *against* unclean
spirits, to cast them out,
and to heal all manner of
sickness and all
manner of disease.
2. Now the names of the twelve
apostles are these; The first, Simon,
who is called Peter, and Andrew his
brother; James *the son* of Zebedee,
and John his brother;
3. Philip, and Bartholomew; Thomas,
and Matthew the publican; James *the*
son of Alphaeus, and Lebbaeus,
whose surname was Thaddaeus;
4. Simon the Canaanite, and Judas
Iscariot, who also betrayed him.
5. **These twelve Jesus**
sent forth, and
commanded them,
saying, Go not into the way of
the Gentiles, and into
any city of
the Samaritans enter ye not:
6. **But go rather to the lost**
sheep of the house
of Israel.
7. **And** as ye go,
preach, saying, The
kingdom of heaven
is at hand.
8. **Heal** the sick, cleanse the lepers,
raise the dead, cast out
devils: freely ye have
received, freely give.
9. **Provide neither gold,**
nor silver, nor brass in
your purses,
10. Nor scrip for *your* journey,
neither two coats, neither
shoes, nor yet staves: for
the workman is worthy of
his meat.
11. **And into whatsoever city**
or town
ye shall enter,
inquire who in it
is worthy; and there abide
till ye go thence.
12. And when ye come into an house,
salute it.
13. **And if the house be**
worthy, let your peace
come upon it: but if it be not
worthy, let your peace return to you.
14. **And whosoever shall**
not receive you,
nor hear your words,
when ye depart
out of that house or city,
shake off the dust of
your feet.
15. Verily I say unto you,
It shall be more tolerable
for the land of
Sodom and Gomorrha in
the day of judgment, than
for that city.
16. **Behold, I send you forth**
as sheep in the midst of
wolves: be ye therefore
wise as serpents, and
harmless as doves.
17. **But beware** of men: for
they will deliver you up to the
councils, and they will
scourge you
in their synagogues;
18. **And ye shall be brought**
before governors and
kings for my sake,
for a testimony
against them and the Gentiles.
19. But when they deliver you up,
take no thought how or
what ye shall speak:
for it shall be given you
in that same hour what ye shall speak.
20. **For it is** not ye that speak, but
the Spirit of your Father
which speaketh in you.
21. **And the brother shall**
deliver up the
brother to death, and the
father the child: and the
children shall rise up against

***their* parents, and cause them to be put to death.**

22. **And ye shall be hated** of all *men* **for my name's sake: but he that endureth** to the end **shall be saved.**

23. But when they persecute you in this city, flee ye into another: for verily I say unto you, Ye shall not have gone over the cities of Israel, till the Son of man be come.

24. The disciple is not above *his* master, nor the servant above his lord.

25. It is enough for the disciple that he be as his master, and the servant as his lord. If they have called the master of the house Beelzebub, how much more *shall they call* them of his household?

26. **Fear them not therefore: for there is nothing** covered, **that shall not be revealed;** and hid, that shall not be known.

27. **What I tell you in darkness,** *that* speak ye in light: and what ye hear in the ear, ***that* preach ye upon the housetops.**

28. **And fear not them which kill the body,** but are not able to kill the soul: **but rather fear him which is able to destroy both soul and body in hell.**

29. **Are not two sparrows sold for a farthing? and one of them shall not fall** on the ground **without your Father.**

30. **But the very hairs of your head are all numbered.**

31. **Fear ye not** therefore, **ye are of more value** than many sparrows.

32. **Whosoever** therefore **shall confess me before men, him will I confess also before my Father** which is in heaven.

33. **But whosoever shall deny me** before men, **him will I also deny before my Father** which is in heaven.

34. **Think not that I am come to send peace** on earth: I came not to send peace, **but a sword.**

35. **For I am come to set a man** at variance **against his father, and** the **daughter against** her **mother,** and the daughter in law against her mother in law.

36. And a man's foes *shall be they* of his own household.

37. **He that loveth father or mother more than me is not worthy of me: and he that loveth son or daughter more than me is not worthy** of me.

38. **And he that taketh not his cross,** and followeth after me, **is not worthy of me.**

39. He that findeth his life shall lose it: and **he that loseth his life for my sake shall find it.**

40. **He that receiveth you receiveth me, and he that receiveth me receiveth him that sent me.**

41. He that receiveth a prophet in the name of a prophet shall receive a prophet's reward; and he that receiveth a righteous man in the name of a righteous man shall receive a righteous man's reward.

42. And whosoever shall give to drink unto one of these little ones a cup of cold *water* only in the name of a disciple, verily I say unto you, he shall in no wise lose his reward.

CHAPTER 11

1. And it came to pass, when Jesus had made an end of commanding his twelve disciples, he departed thence to teach and to preach in their cities.

2. **Now when John had heard** in the prison **the works of Christ, he sent two of his disciples,**

3. **And said** unto him,

Art thou he that should
come, or do we look for another?
4. **Jesus answered**
and said unto them,
Go and shew John again
those things which ye do
hear and see:
5. The blind receive their sight, and
the lame walk, the lepers are
cleansed, and the deaf hear, the dead
are raised up, and the poor have the
gospel preached to them.
6. **And blessed is *he,***
whosoever shall not be
offended in me.
7. **And** as they departed,
Jesus began to say unto
the multitudes concerning
John, What went ye
out into the wilderness
to see?
A reed shaken with the wind?
8. But what went ye out for to see? A
man clothed in soft raiment? behold,
they that wear soft *clothing* are in
kings' houses.
9. But what went ye out for to see?
A prophet? yea, I say unto you,
and more than a prophet.
10. **For this is *he*, of whom it**
is written, Behold, I send
my messenger before thy face,
which shall prepare thy
way before thee.
11. Verily I say unto you, Among them
that are born of women
there hath not risen a
greater than John the
Baptist: notwithstanding he
that is least in the kingdom
of heaven
is greater than he.
12. And from the days of John the
Baptist until now the kingdom of
heaven suffereth violence, and the
violent take it by force.
13. For all the prophets and the law
prophesied until John.
14. **And if ye will receive *it,***
this is Elias, which was for
to come.
15. He that hath ears to hear,
let him hear.

16. **But whereunto shall I**
liken this generation?
It is like unto children sitting in the
markets, and calling unto
their fellows,
17. And saying, We have piped unto
you, and ye have not danced; we
have mourned unto you, and ye have
not lamented.
18. **For John came neither**
eating nor drinking, and
they say, He hath a devil.
19. **The Son of man came**
eating and drinking, and
they say, Behold a man
gluttonous, and a winebibber,
a friend of publicans and
sinners. But wisdom is justified of
her children.
20. Then began he to upbraid the
cities wherein most of his mighty
works were done, because they
repented not:
21. **Woe unto thee,**
Chorazin! woe unto thee,
Bethsaida! for if the mighty
works, which were done in you, had
been done in Tyre and Sidon, they
would have repented long ago in
sackcloth and ashes.
22. But I say unto you,
It shall be more tolerable
for Tyre and Sidon at the
day of
judgment, than for you.
23. **And thou, Capernaum,**
which art exalted unto heaven, shalt
be brought down to hell: for
if the mighty works, which
have been done in thee,
had been done in Sodom, it
would have remained
until this day.
24. **But** I say unto you, That
it shall be more tolerable
for the land of
Sodom in the day of
judgment, than for thee.
25. **At that time Jesus**
answered and
said, I thank thee, O Father,
Lord of heaven and earth,
because thou hast hid

these things
from the wise
and prudent,
and hast
revealed them unto babes.
26. Even so, Father: for so it seemed
good in thy sight.
27. **All things are delivered**
unto me of my Father:
and no man knoweth
the Son, but the Father; neither
knoweth any man
the Father, save the Son,
and *he* to whomsoever the
Son will reveal *him*.
28. **Come unto me,** all *ye* that
labour and are heavy laden,
and I will give you rest.
29. **Take my yoke** upon you,
and learn of me;
for I am meek and lowly in heart:
and ye shall find rest
unto your souls.
30. **For** my yoke *is* easy, and
my burden is light.

CHAPTER 12

1. At that time
Jesus went on the sabbath
day through the corn; and
his disciples
were an hungered, and
began to pluck the ears of
corn and to eat.
2. **But when the Pharisees**
saw *it*, they said
unto him, Behold,
thy disciples do that which
is not lawful to do
upon the sabbath day.
3. **But he said**
unto them, Have ye not read what
David did, when he was an
hungered, and they that
were with him;
4. How he entered into the house of
God, and
did eat the shewbread,
which was not lawful for
him to eat,
neither for them which were with him,
but only for the priests?
5. Or have ye not read in the law, how
that on the sabbath days the priests
in the temple profane the sabbath,
and are blameless?
6. **But** I say unto you, That
in this place is *one* greater
than the temple.
7. But if ye had known what *this*
meaneth, I will have mercy, and not
sacrifice, ye would not have
condemned the guiltless.
8. **For the Son** of man
is Lord even
of the sabbath day.
9. And when he was departed thence,
he went into their synagogue:
10. **And, behold, there was**
a man which had *his* hand
withered. And they asked
him, saying,
Is it lawful to heal on the
sabbath days? that they
might accuse him.
11. **And he said** unto them,
What man
shall there be among you, that
shall have one sheep,
and if it
fall into a pit on the
sabbath day,
will he
not lay hold on it, and
lift *it* out?
12. **How much then is a man**
better than a sheep?
Wherefore it is lawful to do well on the
sabbath days.
13. **Then saith he to the man,**
Stretch forth thine hand. And
he stretched *it* forth;
and it was restored
whole, like as the other.
14. **Then the Pharisees**
went out, and
held a council against him,
how they might
destroy him.
15. **But** when Jesus knew *it*,
he withdrew himself from thence:
and great multitudes
followed him,
and he healed them all;
16. **And charged them that**
they should not make him

known:
17. **That it might be fulfilled**
which was spoken by
Esaias the prophet, saying,
18. **Behold my servant,**
whom I have chosen;
my beloved, in
whom my
soul is well pleased:
I will put my spirit upon
him, and he shall shew judgment to
the Gentiles.
19. He shall not strive, nor cry;
neither shall any man hear his voice in
the streets.
20. A bruised reed shall he not break,
and smoking flax shall he not
quench, till he send forth judgment
unto victory.
21. **And in his name shall the**
Gentiles trust.
22. **Then was brought** unto him
one possessed
with a devil, blind, and
dumb: and he healed him,
insomuch that the blind and dumb
both spake and saw.
23. And all the people were amazed,
and said, Is not this the son of David?
24. **But when the Pharisees**
heard *it,*
they said, This *fellow* doth
not cast out devils,
but by Beelzebub
the prince of the devils.
25. **And Jesus knew their**
thoughts, and said
unto them, Every kingdom divided
against itself is brought to desolation;
and every city or house divided
against itself shall not stand:
26. **And if Satan cast out**
Satan, he is divided
against himself;
how shall then his
kingdom stand?
27. And if I by Beelzebub cast out
devils, by whom do your children cast
them out? therefore they shall be
your judges.
28. **But if I cast out devils by**
the Spirit of God, then the
kingdom of God is come
unto you.
29. Or else how can one enter into a
strong man's house, and spoil his
goods, except he first bind the strong
man? and then he will spoil his house.
30. **He that is not with me is**
against me;
and he that gathereth not with me
scattereth abroad.
31. Wherefore I say unto you,
All manner of sin and
blasphemy shall be
forgiven unto men:
but the blasphemy *against*
the *Holy* Ghost
shall not be forgiven unto men.
32. **And whosoever**
speaketh a word
against the Son of man, it
shall be forgiven him:
but whosoever speaketh
against the Holy Ghost, it
shall not be forgiven
him, neither
in this world, neither in the
world to come.
33. Either make the tree good, and his
fruit good; or else make the tree
corrupt, and his fruit corrupt: for the
tree is known by *his* fruit.
34. **O generation of vipers,**
how
can ye, being evil, speak
good things?
for out of the abundance of the heart
the mouth speaketh.
35. A good man out of the good
treasure of the heart bringeth forth
good things: and an evil man out of
the evil treasure bringeth
forth evil things.
36. **But I say** unto you,
That every idle word
that men shall
speak, they shall give
account thereof in the
day of judgment.
37. **For by thy words thou**
shalt be justified, and
by thy words thou shalt be
condemned.
38. **Then certain**
of the scribes and of the

Pharisees answered, saying,
Master, we would see a
sign from thee.
39. **But he answered**
and said unto them,
An evil and adulterous
generation seeketh after
a sign; and there shall no
sign be given to it,
but the sign of the prophet
Jonas:
40. **For as Jonas was three**
days and three nights in the
whale's belly;
so shall the Son of man be
three days and three nights
in the heart of the earth.
41. **The men of Nineveh shall**
rise in judgment with this
generation, and
shall condemn it:
because they repented at the
preaching of Jonas; and,
behold, a greater than
Jonas *is* here.
42. The queen of the south shall rise
up in the judgment with this
generation, and shall condemn it: for
she came from the uttermost parts of
the earth to hear the wisdom of
Solomon; and, behold, a greater than
Solomon *is* here.
43. **When the unclean spirit**
is gone out of a man, he
walketh through dry places,
seeking rest, and
findeth none.
44. **Then he saith, I will return**
into my house
from whence I came out;
and when he is come,
he findeth *it* empty,
swept, and garnished.
45. **Then goeth he, and**
taketh with himself
seven other spirits
more wicked than himself,
and they enter in and dwell there:
and the last *state* of that
man is worse than the first.
Even so shall it be also
unto this wicked
generation.
46. While he yet talked to the people,
behold, *his* mother and his brethren
stood without, desiring to
speak with him.
47. **Then one said** unto him,
Behold, thy mother and thy
brethren stand without,
desiring to speak
with thee.
48. But he answered and said unto
him that told him, Who is my mother?
and who are my brethren?
49. **And he stretched forth**
his hand toward his
disciples, and said,
Behold my mother
and my brethren!
50. **For whosoever shall do**
the will of my Father
which is in heaven,
the same is my brother, and
sister, and mother.

CHAPTER 13

1. **The same day** went Jesus out
of the house, and sat by the sea side.
2. And great multitudes were gathered
together unto him, so that
he went into a ship, and sat;
and the whole multitude
stood on the shore.
3. **And he spake**
many things unto them in
parables, saying, Behold,
a sower went forth to sow;
4. **And when he sowed,**
some *seeds* fell by the way
side, and the
fowls came and
devoured them up:
5. **Some fell upon stony**
places, where they had not much
earth: and forthwith they sprung up,
because they had no
deepness of earth:
6. **And when the sun**
was up, they were
scorched; and because
they had no root, they
withered away.
7. **And some fell among**
thorns; and the thorns
sprung up, and

■ **choked them:**
■ 8. **But other fell into good**
■ **ground, and brought forth**
■ **fruit,** some an hundredfold, some
sixtyfold, some thirtyfold.
9. Who hath ears to hear, let him hear.
■ 10. **And the disciples**
came, and
■ **said** unto him,
■ **Why speakest thou unto**
■ **them in parables?**
■ 11. **He answered**
and said unto them,
■ **Because it is given** unto
■ **you to know the mysteries**
of the kingdom of heaven,
■ **but to them it is not** given.
■ 12. **For whosoever hath, to**
■ **him shall be given,** and he
shall have more abundance:
■ **but whosoever hath not,**
■ **from him shall be taken**
away even that he hath.
■ 13. **Therefore speak I** to them
■ **in parables: because they**
■ **seeing see not; and**
■ **hearing they hear not,**
neither do they understand.
■ 14. **And in them is fulfilled**
■ **the prophecy of Esaias,**
which saith,
■ **By hearing ye shall hear,**
■ **and** shall
■ **not understand; and**
■ **seeing ye** shall see, and
■ **shall not perceive:**
■ 15. **For this people's heart is**
■ **waxed gross,** and
■ ***their* ears are dull** of hearing,
■ **and their eyes** they have
■ **closed;** lest at any time they
should see with *their* eyes, and hear
with *their* ears, and should understand
with *their* heart, and should be
converted, and I should heal them.
■ 16. **But blessed *are* your**
■ **eyes,** for they see:
■ **and** your
■ **ears,** for they hear.
■ 17. **For** verily I say unto you, That
■ **many** prophets and righteous *men*
■ **have desired to see** *those*
■ ***things* which ye see,**
and have not seen *them;*
■ **and to hear** *those*
■ ***things* which ye hear**
and have not heard *them.*
18. Hear ye therefore the parable of
the sower.
■ 19. **When any one heareth**
■ **the word** of the kingdom,
■ **and understandeth *it* not,**
then cometh
■ **the wicked *one,*** and
■ **catcheth away that which**
■ **was sown** in his heart.
■ **This is he** which received seed
■ **by the way side.**
■ 20. **But he that received the**
■ **seed into stony places,**
the same
■ **is he that heareth the word,**
■ **and** anon with joy receiveth it;
■ 21. **Yet hath he not root** in
himself, but dureth for a while:
■ **for when tribulation**
or persecution
■ **ariseth** because of the word,
by and by
■ **he is offended.**
■ 22. **He also that received**
■ **seed among the thorns**
is he that heareth the word;
■ **and the care of this world,**
■ **and** the deceitfulness of
■ **riches, choke the word,**
and he becometh unfruitful.
■ 23. **But he that received**
■ **seed into** the
■ **good ground is he that**
■ **heareth** the word,
■ **and understandeth**
it; which also
■ **beareth fruit, and bringeth**
■ **forth,** some
■ **an hundredfold,**
some sixty, some thirty.
24. Another parable put he forth unto
them, saying,
■ **The kingdom** of heaven
■ **is likened unto a man**
■ **which sowed good seed**
in his field:
■ 25. **But** while men slept,
■ **his enemy came and**
■ **sowed tares** among the wheat,

and went his way.
26. But when the blade was sprung
up, and brought forth fruit, then
appeared the tares also.
27. **So the servants**
of the householder came and
said unto him,
Sir, didst not thou sow
good seed in thy field?
from whence then
hath it tares?
28. **He said** unto them,
An enemy hath done this.
The servants said unto him, Wilt thou
then that we go and gather them up?
29. But he said, Nay; lest while ye
gather up the tares, ye root up also
the wheat with them.
30. **Let both grow together**
until the harvest: and in
the time of
harvest I will say
to the reapers,
Gather ye together
first the tares, and
bind them in bundles to
burn them: but gather the
wheat into my barn.
31. **Another parable put he**
forth unto them,
saying, The kingdom
of heaven
is like to
a grain of
mustard seed, which a
man took, and
sowed in his field:
32. **Which indeed is** the
least of all seeds: but when
it is
grown, it is the
greatest among herbs, and
becometh a tree,
so that the birds of the air come and
lodge in the branches thereof.
33. Another parable
spake he unto them;
The kingdom of heaven
is like unto
leaven, which a woman
took, and
hid in three measures of
meal, till the whole
was leavened.
34. **All these things spake**
Jesus unto the multitude in
parables; and without a parable spake
he not unto them:
35. **That it might be fulfilled**
which was spoken by the
prophet, saying,
I will open my mouth
in parables; I will
utter things which have
been kept secret from the
foundation of the world.
36. Then Jesus sent the multitude
away, and went into the house: and
his disciples came unto him,
saying, Declare unto us
the parable of the tares
of the field.
37. **He answered**
and said unto them,
He that soweth the good seed
is the Son of man;
38. **The field is the world; the**
good seed are the children
of the kingdom; but the
tares are the children of the
wicked *one;*
39. **The enemy** that sowed them
is the devil; the harvest is
the end of the world;
and the reapers are
the angels.
40. **As therefore the tares**
are gathered and burned
in the fire;
so shall it be in the end
of this world.
41. **The Son of man shall**
send forth
his angels, and they shall
gather out of his kingdom
all things that offend, and them
which do iniquity;
42. **And shall cast them into**
a furnace of fire: there shall be
wailing and gnashing of teeth.
43. **Then shall the righteous**
shine forth as the sun in the
kingdom of their Father. Who hath
ears to hear, let him hear.
44. **Again, the kingdom**
of heaven

is like unto treasure hid in a
field; the which when a man
hath found, he hideth, and
for joy thereof goeth and
selleth all that
he hath,
and buyeth that field.
45. **Again, the kingdom**
of heaven
is like unto
a merchant man,
seeking goodly
pearls:
46. **Who,** when he had
found one pearl of great
price, went and
sold all that
he had, and bought it.
47. **Again, the kingdom**
of heaven
is like unto a net, that was
cast into the sea, and
gathered of every kind:
48. Which, when it was full, they drew
to shore, and sat down,
and gathered the good
into vessels,
but cast the bad away.
49. **So shall it be at the end**
of the world:
the angels shall come forth, and
sever the wicked from among
the just,
50. **And shall cast them into**
the furnace of
fire: there shall be wailing and
gnashing of teeth.
51. Jesus saith unto them, Have ye
understood all these things? They say
unto him, Yea, Lord.
52. Then said he unto them, Therefore
every scribe *which is* instructed unto
the kingdom of heaven is like unto a
man *that is* an householder, which
bringeth forth out of his treasure
things new and old.
53. **And** it came to pass, *that* when
Jesus had finished these
parables, he
departed thence.
54. **And when he was come**
into his own country, he
taught them in their synagogue,
insomuch that they were
astonished, and said,
Whence hath this *man* this
wisdom, and these mighty
works?
55. **Is not this the**
carpenter's son? is not his
mother called Mary? and his brethren,
James, and Joses,
and Simon, and Judas?
56. And his sisters, are they not all
with us? Whence then hath this *man* all
these things?
57. **And they were offended**
in him.
But Jesus said unto them,
A prophet is not without
honour, save in his own
country, and in his own house.
58. And he did not many mighty works
there because of their unbelief.

CHAPTER 14

1. At that time
Herod the tetrarch heard of
the fame of Jesus,
2. **And said** unto his servants,
This is John the Baptist; he is
risen from the dead; and therefore
mighty works do shew forth
themselves in him.
3. **For Herod had** laid hold on
John, and bound him, and
put *him* in prison for
Herodias' sake, his brother
Philip's wife.
4. **For John said unto him, It**
is not lawful for thee to
have her.
5. And when he would have put him to
death, he feared the multitude,
because they counted him as a
prophet.
6. **But when Herod's**
birthday was kept, the
daughter of Herodias
danced before them,
and pleased Herod.
7. **Whereupon he promised**
with an oath to give
her whatsoever she
would ask.
8. **And she, being** before

■ **instructed of her mother,**
■ **said, Give me** here
■ **John Baptist's head**
in a charger.
■ 9. **And the king** was sorry:
nevertheless for the oath's sake, and
them which sat with him at meat,
he commanded *it* to be given *her.*
10. And he sent, and
■ **beheaded John** in the prison.
■ 11. **And his head was**
■ **brought in a charger,**
and given to the damsel: and she
brought *it* to her mother.
■ 12. **And his disciples came,**
■ **and took** up
■ **the body, and buried it,**
■ **and** went and
■ **told Jesus.**
■ 13. **When Jesus heard** *of it,*
■ **he departed** thence
■ **by ship into a**
■ **desert place** apart:
■ **and** when the
■ **people** had heard *thereof,* they
■ **followed him on foot**
out of the cities.
■ 14. **And Jesus** went forth, and
saw a great multitude, and was
■ **moved with compassion**
toward them, and he
■ **healed their sick.**
15. And when it was evening,
■ **his disciples came** to him,
■ **saying, This is a desert**
■ **place,** and the time is now past;
■ **send the multitude away,**
■ **that they may**
go into the villages, and
■ **buy themselves victuals.**
■ 16. **But Jesus said**
unto them, They need not depart;
■ **give** ye
■ **them to eat.**
■ 17. **And they say** unto him,
■ **We have** here
■ **but five loaves,**
■ **and two fishes.**
18. He said, Bring them hither to me.
■ 19. **And he** commanded the
multitude to sit down
on the grass, and
■ **took the five loaves, and**
■ **the two fishes, and**
looking up to heaven,
■ **he blessed, and** brake, and
■ **gave the loaves to *his***
■ **disciples, and the**
■ **disciples to the multitude.**
■ 20. **And they did all eat,**
and were filled: and they took up of
the fragments that remained twelve
baskets full.
21. And they that had eaten were
■ **about five thousand men,**
■ **beside women**
■ **and children.**
■ 22. **And straightway Jesus**
■ **constrained his disciples**
■ **to get into a ship,** and to go
before him unto the other side, while
he sent the multitudes away.
■ 23. **And when he had sent**
■ **the multitudes away, he**
■ **went** up into a mountain apart
■ **to pray:** and when the evening was
come, he was there
■ **alone.**
■ 24. **But the ship was**
now in the midst of the sea,
■ **tossed with waves:**
for the wind was contrary.
■ 25. **And** in the fourth
watch of the night
■ **Jesus went unto them,**
■ **walking on the sea.**
■ 26. **And when the disciples**
■ **saw** him walking on the sea,
■ **they were troubled,**
■ **saying, It is a spirit;**
and they cried out for fear.
■ 27. **But straightway**
■ **Jesus spake**
unto them, saying, Be of good cheer;
■ **it is I; be not afraid.**
■ 28. **And Peter** answered him and
■ **said, Lord,** if it be thou,
■ **bid me come unto thee**
on the water.
■ 29. **And he said, Come. And**
when
■ **Peter** was come down
out of the ship, he
■ **walked on the water,**
to go to Jesus.
■ 30. **But when he saw the**

wind boisterous,
he was afraid; and
beginning to sink, he cried,
saying,
Lord, save me.
31. **And immediately Jesus**
stretched forth *his* hand, and
caught him, and said
unto him,
O thou of little faith,
wherefore didst thou doubt?
32. And when they were come into the
ship, the wind ceased.
33. **Then they**
that were in the ship came and
worshipped him, saying,
Of a truth
thou art the Son of God.
34. **And** when they were gone over,
they came into the land of
Gennesaret.
35. **And** when the men of that place
had knowledge of him,
they sent out into all that country
round about, and
brought unto him all that
were diseased;
36. **And besought him that**
they might only touch
the hem of
his garment: and
as many as touched
were made perfectly
whole.

CHAPTER 15

1. **Then came** to Jesus
scribes and Pharisees,
which were of Jerusalem,
saying,
2. **Why do thy disciples**
transgress the tradition of
the elders? for they wash not their
hands when they eat bread.
3. **But he answered**
and said unto them,
Why do ye also transgress
the commandment of God
by your tradition?
4. For God commanded, saying,
Honour thy father and mother: and, He
that curseth father or mother, let him
die the death.
5. But ye say, Whosoever shall say to
his father or *his* mother, *It is* a gift, by
whatsoever thou mightest be profited
by me;
6. And honour not his father or his
mother, *he shall be free.* Thus have ye
made the commandment of God of
none effect by your tradition.
7. ***Ye* hypocrites, well did**
Esaias prophesy of you,
saying,
8. **This people** draweth nigh unto
me with their mouth, and
honoureth me with *their*
lips; but their heart is far
from me.
9. But in vain they do worship me,
teaching *for* doctrines the
commandments of men.
10. **And he called the**
multitude, and said
unto them, Hear, and understand:
11. **Not that which goeth into**
the mouth defileth a man;
but that which cometh out
of the mouth, this
defileth a man.
12. **Then came his disciples,**
and said
unto him, Knowest thou that
the Pharisees
were offended,
after they heard this saying?
13. **But he answered** and said,
Every plant, which my
heavenly
Father hath not planted,
shall be rooted up.
14. **Let them alone: they be**
blind leaders of the blind.
And if the blind lead the
blind, both shall fall
into the ditch.
15. Then answered Peter and said
unto him, Declare unto us this
parable.
16. **And Jesus said,** Are ye also
yet without understanding?
17. Do not ye yet understand, that
whatsoever entereth in at
the mouth goeth into the belly, and
is cast out into
the draught?

18. **But those things which**
proceed out of the mouth
come forth
from the heart; and they defile
the man.
19. **For out of the heart**
proceed evil thoughts, murders,
adulteries, fornications, thefts, false
witness, blasphemies:
20. These are *the things*
which defile a man:
but to eat with unwashen
hands defileth not a man.
21. **Then Jesus went**
hence, and departed
into the coasts of
Tyre and Sidon.
22. **And, behold, a woman**
of Canaan
came out of the same coasts, and
cried unto him, saying,
Have mercy on me,
O Lord, *thou* son of David;
my daughter ***is*** grievously
vexed with a devil.
23. **But he answered her not**
a word.
And his disciples came and
besought him, saying,
Send her away;
for she crieth after us.
24. **But he answered** and said,
I am not sent but unto
the lost sheep of the house of
Israel.
25. **Then came she and**
worshipped him, saying,
Lord, help me.
26. **But he answered** and said,
It is not meet to take the
children's bread, and to
cast ***it*** **to dogs.**
27. **And she said,** Truth, Lord:
yet the dogs eat of the
crumbs which fall from their
masters' table.
28. **Then Jesus** answered and
said unto her, O woman,
great ***is*** **thy faith: be it**
unto thee even
as thou wilt. And her
daughter was made whole
from that very hour.

29. **And Jesus**
departed from thence, and
came nigh
unto the sea of
Galilee; and went up
into a mountain,
and sat down there.
30. **And great multitudes**
came unto him, having with them
those that were lame, blind, dumb,
maimed, and many others, and cast
them down at Jesus' feet;
and he healed them:
31. Insomuch that the multitude
wondered, when they saw the dumb to
speak, the maimed to be whole, the
lame to walk, and the blind to see:
and they glorified the God
of Israel.
32. **Then Jesus** called his
disciples *unto him,* and
said, I have compassion
on the multitude, because they
continue with me now three days, and
have nothing to eat:
and I will not send them
away fasting,
lest they faint in the way.
33. And his disciples say unto him,
Whence should we have so much
bread in the wilderness, as to fill so
great a multitude?
34. And Jesus saith unto them,
How many loaves have
ye? And they said, Seven,
and a few little
fishes.
35. And he commanded the multitude
to sit down on the ground.
36. **And he took the seven**
loaves and the
fishes, and gave thanks,
and brake *them,*
and gave to his disciples,
and the disciples to
the multitude.
37. **And they did all eat,**
and were filled:
and they took up of the broken
meat that was
left seven baskets full.
38. **And they that did eat**
were four thousand men,

beside women
and children.
39. **And he** sent away the multitude,
and took ship, and
came into the coasts of
Magdala.

CHAPTER 16

1. **The Pharisees** also
with the Sadducees came,
and
tempting desired
him that he would
shew them a sign from heaven.
2. **He answered** and said unto
them, When it is evening, ye say, *It*
will be fair weather: for the sky is red.
3. And in the morning, *It will be* foul
weather to-day: for the sky is red and
lowering.
O *ye* hypocrites, ye can
discern the face of the sky;
but can ye
not *discern*
the signs of the times?
4. **A wicked** and adulterous
generation seeketh after a
sign; and there shall no
sign be given unto it,
but the sign of the prophet
Jonas. And he left them,
and departed.
5. **And when his disciples**
were come to the other side,
they had forgotten to take
bread.
6. **Then Jesus said**
unto them, Take heed and
beware of the leaven of the
Pharisees and of the
Sadducees.
7. **And they reasoned**
among themselves,
saying, *It is* because we
have taken no bread.
8. ***Which* when Jesus**
perceived, he said unto them,
O ye of little faith, why reason ye
among yourselves, because ye have
brought no bread?
9. Do ye not yet understand, neither
remember the five loaves of the five
thousand, and how many baskets ye
took up?
10. Neither the seven loaves of the
four thousand, and how many baskets
ye took up?
11. How is it that ye
do not understand that
I spake *it* not to you
concerning bread, that ye
should beware of the leaven of the
Pharisees and of the Sadducees?
12. **Then understood they** how
that he bade *them* not
beware of the leaven of bread, but
of the doctrine of the
Pharisees and of the
Sadducees.
13. **When Jesus came into**
the coasts of
Caesarea Philippi, he
asked his disciples, saying,
Whom do men say that I
the Son of man
am?
14. **And they said, Some *say***
that thou art
John the Baptist: some,
Elias; and
others, Jeremias,
or one of the prophets.
15. **He saith** unto them,
But whom say ye that I am?
16. **And** Simon
Peter answered and
said, Thou art the Christ,
the Son of the living God.
17. **And Jesus answered**
and said unto him,
Blessed art thou,
Simon Barjona:
for flesh and blood
hath not revealed *it* unto thee,
but my Father
which is in heaven.
18. And I say also unto thee, That
thou art Peter, and upon
this rock I will build my
church; and the gates
of hell shall not
prevail against it.
19. **And I will give unto thee**
the keys of the kingdom
of heaven:
and whatsoever thou shalt

bind on earth shall be
bound in heaven: and
whatsoever thou shalt
loose on earth shall be
loosed in heaven.
20. Then charged he his disciples that
they should tell no man that he was
Jesus the Christ.
21. **From that time** forth
began Jesus to shew unto
his disciples, how that
he must go unto Jerusalem, and
suffer many things of the elders and
chief priests and scribes,
and be killed, and be
raised again the third day.
22. **Then Peter** took him, and
began to rebuke him,
saying, Be it far from thee,
Lord: this shall not be
unto thee.
23. **But he** turned, and
said unto Peter, Get thee
behind me, Satan:
thou art an offence unto me: for thou
savourest not the things that be of
God, but those that be of men.
24. **Then said Jesus**
unto his disciples,
If any *man* will
come after me, let him deny
himself, and take up his
cross, and follow me.
25. **For whosoever will save**
his life shall lose it: and
whosoever will lose his life
for my sake shall find it.
26. **For what is a man**
profited, if he shall
gain the whole
world, and lose his own
soul? or what shall a man give in
exchange for his soul?
27. **For the Son of man shall**
come in the glory of his
Father with his angels;
and then he shall reward
every man according
to his works.
28. Verily I say unto you, There be
some standing here, which shall not
taste of death, till they see the Son of
man coming in his kingdom.

CHAPTER 17

1. **And after six days Jesus**
taketh Peter, James,
and John
his brother, and bringeth them up
into an high mountain apart,
2. **And was transfigured**
before them: and his face did
shine as the sun, and his raiment was
white as the light.
3. **And, behold, there**
appeared unto them
Moses and Elias talking
with him.
4. **Then answered Peter,**
and said unto Jesus,
Lord, it is good for us to be here: if
thou wilt,
let us make here
three tabernacles; one
for thee, and one for
Moses, and one for
Elias.
5. **While he yet spake,** behold,
a bright
cloud overshadowed
them: and behold
a voice out of the cloud,
which
said, This is my beloved
Son, in whom I am well
pleased; hear ye him.
6. And when the disciples heard *it,*
they fell on their face,
and were sore afraid.
7. **And Jesus** came and
touched them, and said,
Arise, and
be not afraid.
8. **And** when they had
lifted up their eyes,
they saw no man, save
Jesus only.
9. And as they came down from the
mountain, Jesus charged them,
saying, Tell the vision to no man, until
the Son of man be risen again from the
dead.
10. **And his disciples asked**
him, saying,
Why then
say the scribes that Elias
must first come?

11. **And Jesus answered**
and said unto them, Elias truly shall
first come, and restore all things.
12. But I say unto you, That
Elias is come already,
and they knew him not, but have done
unto him whatsoever they listed.
Likewise shall also the Son of man
suffer of them.
13. **Then the disciples**
understood that
he spake unto them
of John the Baptist.
14. **And** when they were
come to the multitude,
there came to him
a *certain*
man, kneeling down to him,
and saying,
15. **Lord, have mercy on my**
son: for he is lunatic,
and sore vexed: for ofttimes he falleth
into the fire, and oft into the water.
16. **And I brought him to thy**
disciples, and they could
not cure him.
17. Then Jesus answered and said, O
faithless and perverse generation,
how long shall I be with you? how long
shall I suffer you?
bring him hither to me.
18. **And Jesus rebuked the**
devil; and he departed out of him:
and the child was cured
from that very hour.
19. **Then came the disciples**
to Jesus apart,
and said, Why could not
we cast him out?
20. **And Jesus said** unto them,
Because of your unbelief:
for verily I say unto you,
If ye have faith as a grain of
mustard seed, ye shall say
unto this mountain,
Remove hence to yonder place;
and it shall remove; and
nothing shall be
impossible unto you.
21. **Howbeit this kind goeth**
not out but
by prayer and fasting.
22. **And while** they abode
in Galilee, Jesus said
unto them,
The Son of man shall be
betrayed into the hands of men:
23. **And they shall kill him,**
and the third day he shall
be raised again.
And they were exceeding sorry.
24. **And when they were**
come to Capernaum, they
that received tribute *money*
came to Peter, and said,
Doth not your master
pay tribute?
25. **He saith, Yes. And when**
he was come into the
house, Jesus prevented
him, saying, What thinkest
thou, Simon? of whom do
the kings of the earth
take custom or
tribute? of their own
children, or of
strangers?
26. **Peter saith** unto him,
Of strangers. Jesus saith
unto him,
Then are the children free.
27. **Notwithstanding, lest we**
should offend them,
go thou
to the sea, and
cast an hook,
and take up
the fish that first cometh up;
and when thou hast
opened his mouth, thou
shalt find a piece of
money: that
take, and give unto them
for me and thee.

CHAPTER 18

1. **At the same time came the**
disciples unto Jesus,
saying, Who is the greatest
in the kingdom of heaven?
2. **And Jesus called a little**
child unto him, and set him in the
midst of them,
3. **And said,** Verily I say unto you,
Except ye be converted,
and become as little

children, ye shall not enter
into the kingdom of heaven.
4. **Whosoever therefore**
shall humble himself as
this little child, the same is
greatest in the kingdom
of heaven.
5. **And whoso shall receive**
one such little
child in my name
receiveth me.
6. **But whoso shall offend**
one of these little ones
which believe in me, it were
better for him that
a millstone were hanged
about his neck, and *that* he
were drowned
in the depth of the sea.
7. Woe unto the world because of
offences! for it
must needs be that offences
come; but woe to that
man by whom the
offence cometh!
8. **Wherefore if thy hand or**
thy foot offend thee, cut
them off, and cast *them* from thee:
it is better for thee
to enter into
life halt or
maimed, rather than
having two hands or two feet
to be cast into
everlasting fire.
9. And if thine eye offend thee, pluck
it out, and cast *it* from thee: it is better
for thee to enter into life with one eye,
rather than having two eyes to be cast
into hell fire.
10. Take heed that ye despise not one
of these little ones; for I say unto you,
That in heaven their angels do always
behold the face of my Father which is
in heaven.
11. **For the Son** of man
is come to save that which
was lost.
12. How think ye?
if a man have an hundred
sheep, and one of them
be gone astray,
doth he not leave the ninety
and nine,
and goeth into the mountains,
and seeketh that which is
gone astray?
13. **And if** so be that
he find it, verily I say unto you,
he rejoiceth more of that *sheep,*
than of the ninety and nine
which went not astray.
14. **Even so it is not the will**
of your Father which is in heaven
that one of these little ones
should perish.
15. **Moreover if thy brother**
shall trespass against
thee, go and tell him his fault
between thee and him alone:
if he shall hear thee,
thou hast gained thy
brother.
16. **But if he will not hear**
thee, then
take with thee
one or two more,
that in the mouth of two or three
witnesses every word
may be established.
17. **And if he** shall
neglect to hear them, tell
it unto
the church: but if he neglect
to hear the church,
let him be unto thee as
an heathen man and a publican.
18. Verily I say unto you,
Whatsoever ye shall bind
on earth shall be bound in
heaven: and whatsoever
ye shall
loose on earth
shall be loosed in heaven.
19. Again I say unto you, That
if two of you
shall agree on earth
as touching any thing that
they shall
ask, it shall be done for them
of my Father which is in heaven.
20. **For where two or three**
are gathered together
in my name, there am I
in the midst of them.
21. **Then came Peter** to him,

and said, Lord,
how oft shall my brother
sin against me,
and I forgive him? till
seven times?
22. **Jesus saith**
unto him, I say not unto thee, Until
seven times: but, Until
seventy times seven.
23. **Therefore is the kingdom**
of heaven
likened unto a certain
king, which would
take account of
his servants.
24. And when he had begun to reckon,
one was brought unto him, which
owed him ten thousand
talents.
25. But forasmuch as he had not to
pay,
his lord commanded
him to be sold, and his wife, and
children, and all that he had, and
payment to be made.
26. **The servant** therefore
fell down, and worshipped him,
saying, Lord,
have patience with me,
and I will pay thee all.
27. **Then the lord** of that servant
was moved with
compassion, and loosed him,
and forgave him
the debt.
28. **But the same servant**
went out, and
found one of his fellow-
servants, which owed him
an hundred pence:
and he laid hands on him, and
took *him* by the throat,
saying, Pay me that thou owest.
29. **And his fellow-servant**
fell down
at his feet, and besought him,
saying, Have patience
with me,
and I will pay thee all.
30. **And he would not: but**
went and
cast him into prison,
till he should pay the debt.
31. **So when his fellow-**
servants saw what was done,
they were very sorry, and came and
told unto
their lord all that was done.
32. **Then his lord,**
after that he had called him,
said unto him, O
thou wicked servant, I
forgave thee all that debt,
because thou desiredst me:
33. **Shouldest not thou also**
have had compassion on
thy fellow-servant,
even as I had pity on thee?
34. **And his lord** was wroth, and
delivered him to the
tormentors, till he should
pay all that was due unto him.
35. **So likewise shall my**
heavenly
Father do also uno you,
if ye from your hearts
forgive not every one his brother
their trespasses.

CHAPTER 19

1. **And** it came to pass, *that* when
Jesus had finished these sayings,
he departed from Galilee, and
came into the coasts of
Judaea beyond Jordan;
2. And great multitudes followed him;
and he healed them there.
3. **The Pharisees also came**
unto him, tempting him, and
saying unto him,
Is it lawful for a man to put
away his wife for
every cause?
4. **And he answered**
and said unto them,
Have ye not read, that he
which made *them* at the beginning
made them male and female,
5. And
said, For this cause shall a man
leave father and mother, and shall
cleave to his wife: and
they twain shall be
one flesh?
6. **Wherefore** they are no more
twain, but one flesh.

What therefore
God hath joined together,
let not man put asunder.
7. **They say** unto him,
Why did Moses
then command to
give a writing of
divorcement,
and to put her away?
8. **He saith** unto them,
Moses because of the
hardness of your hearts
suffered you to put away
your wives: but
from the beginning it was not so.
9. And I say unto you,
Whosoever shall put away
his wife, except *it be*
for fornication, and shall
marry another, committeth
adultery: and whoso marrieth her
which is put away doth
commit adultery.
10. **His disciples say**
unto him, *If* the case of the man be so
with *his* wife,
it is not good to marry.
11. **But he said** unto them,
All *men* cannot receive this
saying, save *they* to whom
it is given.
12. For there are some eunuchs,
which were so born from *their* mother's
womb: and there are some eunuchs,
which were made eunuchs of men:
and there be eunuchs, which have
made themselves eunuchs for the
kingdom of heaven's sake.
He that is able to receive *it,*
let him receive *it.*
13. **Then were there brought**
unto him
little children, that he should put
his hands on them, and pray:
and the disciples
rebuked them.
14. **But Jesus said, Suffer**
little children,
and forbid them not,
to come unto me: for of
such is the kingdom
of heaven.
15. And he laid *his* hands on them,
and departed thence.
16. **And, behold, one** came and
said unto him,
Good Master, what good
thing shall I do, that I may
have eternal life?
17. **And he said** unto him,
Why callest thou
me good? *there is* none
good but one, *that is,*
God: but if thou wilt enter
into
life, keep the
commandments.
18. **He saith** unto him,
Which? Jesus said, Thou
shalt do no murder,
Thou shalt
not commit adultery,
Thou shalt
not steal, Thou shalt
not bear false witness,
19. **Honour thy father and** *thy*
mother: and, Thou shalt
love thy neighbour
as thyself.
20. **The young man saith**
unto him,
All these things
have I kept from my youth up:
what lack I yet?
21. **Jesus said**
unto him, If thou wilt be perfect,
go *and* sell that thou hast,
and give to the poor, and thou
shalt have treasure in heaven:
and come *and*
follow me.
22. **But when the young man**
heard that saying,
he went away sorrowful:
for he had great
possessions.
23. **Then said Jesus** unto his
disciples, Verily I say unto you, That a
rich man shall hardly enter into the
kingdom of heaven.
24. And again I say unto you,
It is easier for a camel to
go through the eye of a
needle, than for a rich man
to enter into the kingdom
of God.

25. **When his disciples**
heard *it,*
they were exceedingly
amazed, saying, Who then
can be saved?
26. **But Jesus** beheld *them,* and
said unto them, With men this is
impossible; but
with God all things
are possible.
27. **Then answered Peter** and
said unto him, Behold,
we have forsaken all, and
followed thee; what shall
we have therefore?
28. **And Jesus said** unto them,
Verily I say unto you, That ye which
have followed me, in the regeneration
when the Son of man shall sit in the
throne of his glory,
ye also
shall sit upon twelve
thrones, judging
the twelve tribes of
Israel.
29. **And every one that hath**
forsaken houses, or
brethren, or
sisters, or
father, or
mother, or
wife, or
children, or lands, for my
name's sake, shall receive
an hundredfold, and shall
inherit everlasting life.
30. But many *that are* first shall be
last; and the last *shall be* first.

CHAPTER 20

1. **For the kingdom** of heaven
is like unto a man
that is an householder,
which went out early
in the morning
to hire labourers
into his vineyard.
2. And when he had
agreed with the labourers
for a penny a day,
he sent them into his vineyard.
3. **And** he went out
about the third hour, and
saw others standing idle
in the marketplace,
4. **And said** unto them;
Go ye also
into the vineyard, and
whatsoever is right I will
give you. And they went their way.
5. **Again he went out about**
the sixth and ninth hour,
and did likewise.
6. **And about the eleventh**
hour he went out, and
found others standing idle,
and saith unto them,
Why stand ye here all the day
idle?
7. **They say** unto him, Because
no man hath hired us. He
saith unto them,
Go ye also
into the vineyard; and
whatsoever is right, *that*
shall ye receive.
8. **So when even was come,**
the lord of the vineyard
saith unto his steward,
Call the labourers, and
give them *their* hire,
beginning from the last unto the first.
9. **And when they came that**
***were hired* about the**
eleventh hour, they re-
ceived every man a penny.
10. **But when the first came,**
they supposed that they
should have received
more; and they likewise re-
ceived every man a penny.
11. **And** when they had received *it,*
they murmured against the
goodman of the house,
12. **Saying, These last have**
wrought *but* one hour, and
thou hast made them equal
unto us, which have borne the burden
and heat of the day.
13. **But he answered**
one of them, and said, Friend, I do
thee no wrong:
didst not thou agree with
me for a penny?
14. Take *that* thine *is,* and go thy way:
I will give unto this last,

even as unto thee.
15. **Is it not lawful** for me
to do what I will with mine
own? Is thine eye evil,
because I am good?
16. **So the last shall be first,**
and the first last:
for many be called,
but few chosen.
17. **And Jesus**
going up to Jerusalem
took the twelve disciples
apart in the way,
and said unto them,
18. **Behold, we go** up
to Jerusalem; and the Son
of man
shall be betrayed unto the
chief priests and unto the scribes,
and they shall condemn
him to death,
19. **And shall deliver him**
to the Gentiles to mock,
and to scourge, and
to crucify *him:* and the third
day
he shall rise again.
20. **Then came** to him
the mother of Zebedees
children with her sons,
worshipping *him,* and desiring a
certain thing of him.
21. **And** he said unto her,
What wilt thou?
She saith unto him,
Grant that these
my two sons may sit, the
one on thy right hand, and
the other on the left,
in thy kingdom.
22. **But Jesus answered**
and said, Ye know not what ye ask.
Are ye able to drink of the
cup that I shall drink
of, and to be baptized with the
baptism that I am baptized with?
They say unto him,
We are able.
23. **And he saith** unto them,
Ye shall drink indeed
of my cup, and be baptized with the
baptism that I am baptized with:
but to sit on my right hand,
and on my left, is not mine
to give, but *it shall be given to them*
for whom it is prepared of my Father.
24. **And when the**
ten heard *it,*
they were moved with
indignation
against the two brethren.
25. **But Jesus**
called them unto *him,* and
said, Ye know that the princes of
the Gentiles exercise dominion over
them, and they that are great exercise
authority upon them.
26. But it shall not be so
among you: but
whosoever will be great
among you, let him be
your minister;
27. And whosoever will be chief
among you, let him be your servant:
28. **Even as the Son** of man
came not to be ministered
unto, but to minister, and to
give his life a ransom
for many.
29. And as they departed from
Jericho, a great multitude
followed him.
30. **And, behold, two blind**
men sitting by the way side, when
they heard that Jesus passed by,
cried out, saying,
Have mercy on us,
O Lord, *thou* son of David.
31. **And the multitude**
rebuked them, because they
should hold their peace:
but they cried the more,
saying, Have mercy on us, O Lord,
thou son of David.
32. **And Jesus**
stood still, and called them, and
said, What will ye that I
shall do unto you?
33. **They say** unto him, Lord,
that our eyes may
be opened.
34. **So Jesus**
had compassion *on them,* and
touched their eyes: and
immediately
their eyes received sight,

and they followed him.

CHAPTER 21

1. **And when they** drew nigh unto
Jerusalem, and
were come to Bethphage,
unto the mount of Olives,
then sent Jesus two
disciples,
2. **Saying** unto them,
Go into the village over against you,
and straightway
ye shall find an ass tied,
and a colt
with her: loose *them,* and
bring *them* unto me.
3. And if any *man* say aught unto you,
ye shall say, The Lord hath need of
them; and straightway
he will send them.
4. **All this** was done, that it might be
fulfilled which
was spoken by the
prophet, saying,
5. Tell ye the daughter of Sion,
Behold,
thy King cometh
unto thee, meek, and
sitting upon an ass,
and a colt the foal of an ass.
6. **And the disciples** went, and
did as Jesus commanded
them,
7. **And brought the ass,**
and the colt, and put on them
their clothes,
and they set *him* thereon.
8. **And a very great**
multitude spread their
garments in the way;
others cut down
branches from the trees,
and strawed *them*
in the way.
9. **And** the multitudes that went
before, and that followed,
cried, saying,
Hosanna to the son of David:
Blessed *is* he that cometh in
the name of the Lord;
Hosanna in the highest.
10. And when he was come into
Jerusalem, all the city was moved,
saying, Who is this?
11. And the multitude said, This is
Jesus the prophet of Nazareth
of Galilee.
12. **And Jesus went into the**
temple of God,
and cast out all them
that sold and bought
in the temple,
and overthrew the tables
of the moneychangers, and the seats
of them that sold doves,
13. **And said** unto them,
It is written, My house shall
be called the house of
prayer; but ye have made it
a den of thieves.
14. **And the blind and the**
lame came to him in the temple;
and he healed them.
15. **And when the chief**
priests and scribes saw
the wonderful
things that
he did, and the children
crying in the temple, and saying,
Hosanna to the son of David;
they were sore
displeased,
16. **And said** unto him,
Hearest thou
what these say? And
Jesus saith unto them,
Yea; have ye never read,
Out of the mouth of babes
and sucklings
thou hast
perfected praise?
17. **And he left** them,
and went out of the city
into Bethany; and he
lodged there.
18. **Now in the morning**
as he returned into the city,
he hungered.
19. **And when he saw a fig**
tree in the way, he came to it,
and found nothing thereon,
but leaves only,
and said unto it,
Let no fruit grow on thee
henceforward for ever.
And presently

the fig tree withered away.
20. **And when the disciples**
saw it, they
marvelled, saying, How soon is
the fig tree withered away !
21. **Jesus answered** and said
unto them, Verily I say unto you,
If ye have faith, and doubt not,
ye shall not only do this *which is done*
to the fig tree, but also if
ye shall say unto this
mountain, Be thou
removed, and be thou cast into
the sea;
it shall be done.
22. And all things,
whatsoever ye shall ask
in prayer,
believing, ye shall receive.
23. **And when he was come**
into the temple, the chief
priests and the elders of the people
came unto him
as he was teaching, and
said, By what authority
doest thou these things?
and who gave thee this authority?
24. **And Jesus answered**
and said unto them,
I also will ask you one
thing, which if ye tell me, I in like
wise will tell you by what authority I do
these things.
25. **The baptism of John,**
whence was it? from
heaven, or of men? And
they reasoned
with themselves, saying,
If we shall
say, From heaven;
he will say unto us,
Why did ye not then
believe him?
26. **But if we shall say, Of**
men; we fear the people;
for all hold John as a
prophet.
27. **And they answered**
Jesus, and said,
We cannot tell. And he said
unto them,
Neither tell I you
by what authority I do these things.

28. **But what think ye? A** *certain*
man had two sons; and he
came to the first, and
said, Son,
go work to day in my
vineyard.
29. **He answered** and said,
I will not: but afterward
he repented, and
went.
30. **And he came to the**
second, and said likewise.
And he answered and said,
I *go,* sir: and went not.
31. **Whether** of them twain
did the will of *his* father?
They say unto him,
The first. Jesus saith
unto them, Verily I say unto you, That
the publicans and the
harlots go into the kingdom
of God
before you.
32. For John came unto you in the way
of righteousness, and ye believed him
not: but the publicans and the harlots
believed him: and ye, when ye had
seen *it,* repented not afterward, that
ye might believe him.
33. Hear another parable:
There was a certain
householder, which
planted a vineyard, and
hedged it round about, and digged a
winepress in it, and built a tower,
and let it out
to husbandmen,
and went into a far country:
34. **And when** the time of
the fruit drew near, he sent
his
servants to
the husbandmen, that they might
receive the fruits of it.
35. **And the husbandmen**
took his servants, and
beat one, and
killed another,
and stoned another.
36. **Again, he sent other**
servants more than the first:
and they did unto them
likewise.

37. **But last** of all
he sent unto them
his son, saying, They will
reverence my son.
38. **But when the**
husbandmen saw the son,
they said among themselves, This is
the heir; come, let us kill him, and let
us seize on his inheritance.
39. And they caught *him* , and cast *him*
out of the vineyard, and
slew *him.*
40. **When the lord** therefore
of the vineyard cometh,
what will he do
unto those husbandmen?
41. **They say** unto him,
He will miserably
destroy those wicked men
and will let out *his* vineyard
unto other husbandmen,
which shall render him the fruits in
their seasons.
42. **Jesus saith** unto them,
Did ye never read
in the scriptures,
The stone which the
builders rejected, the same
is become the head of the
corner: this is the Lord's doing, and
it is marvellous in our eyes?
43. **Therefore say I unto you,**
The kingdom of God
shall be taken from you,
and given to a nation
bringing forth the
fruits thereof.
44. **And whosoever shall**
fall on this stone shall be
broken: but on whomsoever it shall
fall, it will grind him to powder.
45. And when the chief priests and
Pharisees had heard his parables,
they perceived that he
spake of them.
46. But when they sought to lay hands
on him, they feared the multitude,
because they took him for a prophet.

CHAPTER 22

1. **And Jesus** answered and
spake unto them
again by parables, and said,
2. The kingdom of heaven is like unto
a certain
king, which
made a marriage
for his son,
3. **And sent** forth his
servants to call them
that were
bidden to the wedding: and
they would not come.
4. **Again, he sent forth** other
servants, saying, Tell them
which are bidden, Behold,
I have prepared my dinner:
my oxen and *my* fatlings *are* killed,
and all things *are* ready:
come unto the marriage.
5. **But they made light of *it,***
and went their ways, one to
his farm, another to his merchandise:
6. **And the remnant took**
his servants,
and entreated *them* spitefully,
and slew *them.*
7. **But when the king heard**
thereof, he was wroth: and
he sent forth
his armies, and destroyed
those murderers,
and burned up their city.
8. **Then saith he to his**
servants, The wedding is
ready, but they which were bidden
were not worthy.
9. **Go** ye therefore
into the highways, and as
many as ye shall
find, bid to the marriage.
10. **So those servants**
went out into the highways, and
gathered together all
as many as they found,
both bad and good:
and the wedding was
furnished with guests.
11. **And when the king came**
in to see the guests,
he saw there
a man which had not on a
wedding garment:
12. **And he saith** unto him, Friend,
how camest thou in hither
not having a wedding

■ **garment? And he**
■ **was speechless.**
■ 13. **Then said the king**
■ **to the servants,**
Bind him hand and foot, and
■ **take him** away,
■ **and cast *him* into outer**
■ **darkness,** there shall be weeping
and gnashing of teeth.
■ 14. **For many are called, but**
■ **few** *are*
■ **chosen.**
■ 15. **Then went the Pharisees,**
■ **and took counsel how they**
■ **might entangle him** in *his* talk.
■ 16. **And they sent** out unto him
■ **their disciples**
with the Herodians,
■ **saying,** Master,
■ **we know that thou art true,**
and teachest the way of God in truth,
neither carest thou for any *man:* for
thou regardest not the person of men.
■ 17. **Tell us** therefore,
What thinkest thou?
■ **Is it lawful to give tribute**
■ **unto Caesar,** or not?
■ 18. **But Jesus** perceived their
wickedness, and
■ **said, Why tempt ye me,**
■ ***ye* hypocrites?**
■ 19. **Shew me the tribute**
■ **money. And they brought**
unto him
■ **a penny.**
■ 20. **And he saith** unto them,
■ **Whose *is* this image**
and superscription?
■ 21. **They say** unto him,
■ **Caesar's. Then saith he**
unto them,
■ **Render** therefore
■ **unto Caesar the things**
■ **which are Caesar's; and**
■ **unto God the things**
■ **that are God's.**
22. When they had heard *these words,*
they marvelled, and left him,
and went their way.
■ 23. **The same day came** to him
■ **the Sadducees, which say**
that
■ **there is no resurrection,**
■ **and asked** him,
24. Saying, Master,
■ **Moses said, If a man die,**
■ **having no children, his**
■ **brother shall marry his**
■ **wife, and raise up seed**
unto his brother.
■ 25. **Now there were** with us
■ **seven brethren:** and
■ **the first,** when he had married a
wife, deceased, and,
■ **having no issue, left his**
■ **wife unto his brother:**
■ 26. **Likewise the second**
also, and the third,
■ **unto the seventh.**
27. And last of all the
woman died also.
■ 28. **Therefore in the**
■ **resurrection whose wife**
■ **shall she be** of the seven?
for they all had her.
■ 29. **Jesus answered**
and said unto them,
■ **Ye do err, not knowing the**
■ **scriptures, nor the power**
■ **of God.**
■ 30. **For in the resurrection**
■ **they neither marry,**
nor are given in marriage,
■ **but are as the angels** of God
in heaven.
■ 31. **But as touching the**
■ **resurrection** of the dead,
■ **have ye not read** that which
was spoken unto you by God, saying,
■ 32. **I am the God of**
■ **Abraham, and** the God of
■ **Isaac, and** the God of
■ **Jacob? God is** not
■ **the God** of the dead, but
■ **of the living.**
33. And when the multitude heard *this,*
they were astonished at his doctrine.
■ 34. **But when the Pharisees**
■ **had heard** that he had put the
Sadducees to silence, they were
gathered together.
■ 35. **Then one of them,** *which was*
■ **a lawyer, asked** *him a question,*
tempting him, and saying,
■ 36. **Master, which *is* the**
■ **great commandment**

in the law?
37. **Jesus said** unto him,
Thou shalt love the Lord thy
God with all thy heart, and with all
thy soul, and with all thy mind.
38. This is the first
and great commandment.
39. **And the second *is***
like unto it,
Thou shalt love thy
neighbour as thyself.
40. **On these** two commandments
hang all the law and
the prophets.
41. While the Pharisees were
gathered together,
Jesus asked them,
42. **Saying, What think ye of**
Christ? whose son is he?
They say unto him,
***The son* of David.**
43. **He saith** unto them,
How then doth David in spirit
call him Lord, saying,
44. The LORD said unto my Lord, Sit
thou on my right hand, till I make thine
enemies thy footstool?
45. **If David then call him**
Lord, how is he his son?
46. **And no man was able to**
answer him a word, neither durst
any *man* from that day forth ask him
any more *questions* .

CHAPTER 23

1. **Then spake Jesus** to the
multitude, and to his disciples,
2. **Saying The** scribes and the
Pharisees sit in
Moses' seat:
3. All therefore
whatsoever they bid you
observe, that observe and do;
but do not ye after their
works: for they say, and do not.
4. **For they bind heavy**
burdens and grievous to be borne,
and lay *them* on men's
shoulders; but they
***themselves* will not move**
them with
one of their fingers.
5. But all their works
they do for
to be seen of men: they make
broad their phylacteries, and enlarge
the borders of their garments,
6. **And love** the uppermost rooms
at feasts, and the chief seats
in the synagogues,
7. And greetings in the markets, and
to be called of men,
Rabbi, Rabbi.
8. **But be not ye called**
Rabbi: for
one is your Master, *even*
Christ; and all ye are brethren.
9. **And call no *man*** your
father upon the earth:
for one is
your Father, which
is in heaven.
10. Neither be ye called masters: for
one is your Master, *even* Christ.
11. **But he that is greatest**
among you
shall be your servant.
12. And whosoever shall exalt himself
shall be abased; and he that shall
humble himself shall be exalted.
13. **But woe unto you,**
scribes and
Pharisees, hypocrites!
for ye shut up the kingdom
of heaven
against men: for ye neither go in
yourselves, neither suffer ye them
that are entering to go in.
14. Woe unto you, scribes and
Pharisees, hypocrites! for
ye devour widows' houses,
and for a pretence
make long prayer:
therefore ye shall receive
the greater damnation.
15. Woe unto you, scribes and
Pharisees, hypocrites! for
ye compass sea and land to
make one proselyte, and
when he is made, ye
make him twofold
more the child of hell
than yourselves.
16. **Woe unto you,**
ye blind guides,
which say, Whosoever

shall swear by the temple,
it is nothing; but whosoever
shall swear by the gold
of the temple, he
is a debtor!
17. *Ye* fools and blind:
for whether is greater, the
gold, or the temple that
sanctifieth the gold?
18. **And, Whosoever shall**
swear by the altar, it is
nothing; but whosoever
sweareth by the gift that is
upon it, he
is guilty.
19. ***Ye* fools and blind:**
for whether *is* greater, the gift, or the
altar that sanctifieth the gift?
20. **Whoso therefore shall**
swear by the altar,
sweareth by it, and by all
things thereon.
21. And whoso shall swear by the
temple, sweareth by it, and by him
that dwelleth therein.
22. And he that shall swear by
heaven, sweareth by the throne of
God, and by him that sitteth thereon.
23. **Woe unto you,**
scribes and Pharisees,
hypocrites! for ye pay tithe
of mint and anise and cummin,
and have omitted
the weightier *matters* of the law,
judgment, mercy, and faith:
these ought ye to have done, and not
to leave the other undone.
24. ***Ye*** blind guides, which
strain at a gnat, and
swallow a camel.
25. Woe unto you, scribes and
Pharisees, hypocrites! for
ye make clean the outside
of the cup and of the platter,
but within they are full of
extortion and excess.
26. *Thou* blind Pharisee,
cleanse first that *which is*
within the cup and platter,
that the outside of them
may be clean also.
27. Woe unto you, scribes and
Pharisees, hypocrites! for
ye are like unto
whited sepulchres,
which indeed appear beautiful
outward, but are within
full of dead *men's* bones,
and of all uncleanness.
28. Even so ye also outwardly appear
righteous unto men, but within
ye are full of hypocrisy
and iniquity.
29. Woe unto you, scribes and
Pharisees, hypocrites! because
ye build the tombs of the
prophets, and garnish the
sepulchres of the righteous,
30. **And say,** If we had been in the
days of our fathers,
we would not have been
partakers with them
in the blood of
the prophets.
31. Wherefore ye be witnesses unto
yourselves, that
ye are the children of them
which killed the prophets.
32. Fill ye up then the
measure of your fathers.
33. ***Ye* serpents,**
ye generation of vipers,
how can ye escape
the damnation of
hell?
34. **Wherefore, behold, I**
send unto you prophets,
and wise men, and scribes:
and *some* of them ye shall
kill and crucify;
and *some* of them shall ye
scourge in your synagogues,
and persecute
them from city to city:
35. **That upon you may**
come all the righteous
blood shed upon the earth,
from the blood of righteous Abel unto
the blood of Zacharias son of
Barachias, whom ye slew between the
temple and the altar.
36. Verily I say unto you,
All these things shall come
upon this generation.
37. **O Jerusalem,** Jerusalem,
***thou* that killest the**

prophets, and stonest them which are sent unto thee,
how often would I have gathered thy children together, even
as a hen gathereth her chickens under *her* wings,
and ye would not!
38. Behold, your house is left unto you desolate.
39. For I say unto you, Ye shall not see me henceforth, till ye shall say, Blessed *is* he that cometh in the name of the Lord.

CHAPTER 24

1. **And Jesus** went out, and **departed** from the temple:
and his disciples came to *him* for to
shew him the buildings of the temple.
2. **And Jesus said** unto them, See ye not all these things? verily I say unto you,
There shall not be left here **one stone upon another,** that shall not be thrown down.
3. **And as he sat** upon the mount of Olives,
the disciples came unto him privately,
saying, Tell us,
when shall these things be?
and what *shall be*
the sign of thy coming, and of the end of the world?
4. **And Jesus answered** and said unto them,
Take heed that no man deceive you.
5. **For many shall come** in my name,
saying, I am Christ; and shall deceive many.
6. **And ye shall hear of wars** and rumours of wars: see that ye
be not troubled: for all *these things* must come to pass, but
the end is not yet.
7. **For nation shall rise against nation,** and kingdom against kingdom:
and there shall be famines, and
pestilences, and earthquakes, in divers places.
8. **All these *are* the beginning of sorrows.**
9. **Then shall they** deliver you up to be afflicted, and shall
kill you: and ye shall be hated of all nations
for my name's sake.
10. **And then shall many** be offended, and shall
betray one another, and shall hate one another.
11. **And many false prophets** shall rise, and
shall deceive many.
12. **And** because iniquity shall abound
the love of many shall wax cold.
13. **But he that shall endure** unto the end, the same
shall be saved.
14. **And this gospel** of the kingdom
shall be preached in all the world for a witness unto all nations;
and then shall the end come.
15. **When ye therefore shall see the abomination of desolation,** spoken of by Daniel the prophet, stand in the holy place, (whoso readeth, let him understand:)
16. Then let them which be in Judaea
flee into the mountains:
17. Let him which is on the housetop not come down to take any thing out of his house:
18. Neither let him which is in the field return back to take his clothes.
19. And woe unto them that are with child, and to them that give suck in those days!
20. But pray ye that your flight be not in the winter, neither on the sabbath day:
21. **For then shall be great tribulation, such as was not since the beginning** of the world to this time, no,

nor ever shall be.
22. **And except those days**
should be shortened, there
should no flesh be saved:
but for the elect's sake those days
shall be shortened.
23. **Then if any man** shall
say unto you,
Lo, here *is* Christ, or there;
believe *it* not.
24. **For there shall arise**
false Christs,
and false prophets,
and shall
shew great
signs and wonders;
insomuch that, if *it were*
possible, they shall
deceive the very
elect.
25. Behold, I have told you before.
26. **Wherefore if they** shall
say unto you,
Behold, he is in the desert;
go not forth: behold,
he is in the secret chambers;
believe *it*
not.
27. **For as the lightning**
cometh out of the east, and
shineth even unto the west;
so shall also the coming
of the Son of man
be.
28. For wheresoever the carcase is,
there will the eagles be gathered
together.
29. **Immediately after the**
tribulation of those days shall the
sun be darkened, and the moon shall
not give her light, and the stars shall
fall from heaven, and the powers of
the heavens shall be shaken:
30. And then shall appear the sign of
the Son of man in heaven: and then
shall all the tribes of the
earth mourn, and
they shall see the Son of
man coming
in the clouds of heaven
with power and
great glory.
31. **And he shall send his**
angels with a great sound of a
trumpet,
and they shall gather together
his elect from the four winds, from
one end of heaven to the other.
32. **Now learn** a parable
of the fig tree; When his
branch is yet
tender, and putteth
forth leaves,
ye know that
summer *is* nigh:
33. **So likewise** ye,
when ye shall see all these
things, know that it is near,
even at the doors.
34. Verily I say unto you,
This generation shall not pass,
till all these things be fulfilled.
35. **Heaven and earth shall**
pass away,
but my words shall not
pass away.
36. **But of that day** and hour
knoweth no *man,* no, not the
angels of heaven,
but my Father only.
37. **But as the days of Noe**
***were,* so shall also the**
coming of the Son of man
be.
38. For as in the days that were
before the flood they were
eating and drinking,
marrying and giving in marriage,
until the day that
Noe entered into the ark,
39. **And** knew not until
the flood came, and
took them all away;
so shall also the coming
of the Son of man
be.
40. **Then shall two be in the**
field; the one shall be
taken, and the other left.
41. Two *women shall be* grinding at the
mill; the one shall be taken, and the
other left.
42. **Watch** therefore: for
ye know not what hour your
Lord doth come.
43. But know this, that if the goodman

of the house had known in what watch
the thief would come, he would have
watched, and would not have suffered
his house to be broken up.
44. Therefore be ye also ready:
for in such an hour as ye
think not the Son of man
cometh.
45. Who then is a faithful and wise
servant, whom his lord hath made
ruler over his household, to give them
meat in due season?
46. **Blessed *is* that servant,**
whom his lord when he
cometh shall find so
doing.
47. Verily I say unto you, That
he shall make him ruler
over all his goods.
48. **But** and if
that evil servant shall say
in his heart,
My lord delayeth
his coming;
49. And shall begin to smite *his* fellow
servants, and to eat and drink
with the drunken;
50. **The lord** of that servant
shall come in a day
when he looketh not for
him, and in an hour that he is not
aware of,
51. **And shall cut him**
asunder, and appoint *him* his
portion with the hypocrites:
there shall be weeping and
gnashing of teeth.

CHAPTER 25

1. Then shall the kingdom of heaven
be likened unto
ten virgins, which
took their
lamps, and went forth
to meet the bridegroom.
2. **And five** of them
were wise, and five
***were* foolish.**
3. **They that *were* foolish**
took their lamps, and took
no oil with them:
4. **But the wise took oil**
in their vessels with their lamps.
5. **While the bridegroom**
tarried, they all slumbered and
slept.
6. **And at midnight there was**
a cry made,
Behold, the bridegroom
cometh; go ye out to meet him.
7. **Then all those virgins**
arose, and
trimmed their
lamps.
8. **And the foolish said unto**
the wise, Give us of your
oil; for our lamps are gone
out.
9. **But the wise answered,**
saying,
Not so; lest there be not enough for
us and you:
but go ye rather to them that sell,
and buy for yourselves.
10. **And while they went to**
buy, the bridegroom came;
and they that were ready
went in with him to the marriage:
and the door was shut.
11. **Afterward came also the**
other virgins, saying, Lord,
Lord,
open to us.
12. **But he answered**
and said, Verily I say unto you,
I know you not.
13. **Watch therefore, for ye**
know neither the day nor
the hour wherein
the Son of man
cometh.
14. For *the kingdom of heaven is* as
a man travelling into a far
country, *who*
called his own servants,
and delivered unto them his goods.
15. **And unto one he gave**
five talents, to another two,
and to another one; to every
man according to his several ability;
and straightway
took his journey.
16. **Then he that had**
received the five talents went
and traded with the same, and
made *them* other

five talents.
17. **And likewise he that *had***
***received* two,** he also
gained other
two.
18. **But he that had received**
one went and
digged in the earth, and hid
his lord's money.
19. **After a** long
time the lord of those servants
cometh, and reckoneth
with them.
20. **And so he that had**
received five talents
came and
brought other five talents,
saying, Lord, thou deliveredst unto
me five talents: behold,
I have gained beside them
five talents more.
21. **His lord said** unto him,
Well done,
thou good and faithful servant:
thou hast been faithful over
a few things, I will make
thee ruler over many things:
enter thou into the joy of thy lord.
22. **He also that had**
received two talents came
and said, Lord, thou deliveredst
unto me two talents: behold,
I have gained two other
talents beside them.
23. **His lord said** unto him,
Well done, good and
faithful servant; thou hast been
faithful over a few things, I will make
thee ruler over many things: enter
thou into the joy of thy lord.
24. **Then he which had**
received the one talent
came and said, Lord,
I knew thee that
thou art an
hard man, reaping where thou hast
not sown, and gathering where thou
hast not strawed:
25. **And I was afraid, and**
went and
hid thy talent in the earth: lo,
there thou hast *that is* thine.
26. **His lord answered**
and said unto him,
***Thou* wicked and slothful**
servant, thou knewest that I reap
where I sowed not, and gather where I
have not strawed:
27. **Thou oughtest therefore**
to have put my money to
the exchangers, and *then*
at my coming
I should have received
mine own with
usury.
28. **Take therefore the talent**
from him, and give *it* unto
him which hath ten talents.
29. **For unto every one that**
hath shall be given,
and he shall have abundance:
but from him that hath not
shall be taken away
even that which he hath.
30. **And cast ye the**
unprofitable servant into
outer darkness: there shall be
weeping and gnashing of teeth.
31. **When the Son** of man
shall come in his glory,
and all the holy angels with him,
then shall he
sit upon the throne of his
glory:
32. **And before him shall be**
gathered all nations: and
he shall separate them
one from another,
as a shepherd divideth *his*
sheep from the goats:
33. **And he shall set the**
sheep on his right hand,
but the goats on the left.
34. **Then shall the King say**
unto them on his right hand,
Come, ye blessed of my Father,
inherit the kingdom
prepared for you from the foundation
of the world:
35. **For I was an hungered,**
and ye gave me meat: I
was thirsty, and ye gave
me drink:
I was a stranger, and ye took me in:
36. Naked, and ye clothed me: I was
sick, and ye visited me: I was in

prison, and ye came unto me.
37. **Then shall the righteous answer** him, saying, Lord, **when saw we thee** an hungred, and fed *thee?* or thirsty, and gave *thee* drink?
38. When saw we thee a stranger, and took *thee* in? or naked, and clothed *thee?*
39. Or when saw we thee sick, or in prison, and came unto thee?
40. **And the King shall answer** and say unto them, Verily I say unto you, **inasmuch as ye have done *it* unto one of the least of these my brethren, ye have done *it* unto me.**
41. **Then shall he say also unto them on the left hand, Depart from me, ye cursed,** into everlasting fire, prepared for the devil and his angels:
42. **For I was an hungered, and ye gave me no meat: I was thirsty, and ye gave me no drink:**
43. I was a stranger, and ye took me not in: naked, and ye clothed me not: sick, and in prison, and ye visited me not.
44. Then shall they also answer him, saying, Lord, when saw we thee an hungred, or athirst, or a stranger, or naked, or sick, or in prison, and did not minister unto thee?
45. Then shall he answer them, saying, Verily I say unto you, Inasmuch as ye did *it* not to one of the least of these, ye did *it* not to me.
46. **And these shall go away into everlasting punishment:** but the righteous into life eternal.

CHAPTER 26

1. And it came to pass, **when Jesus had finished** all these sayings, **he said** unto his disciples,
2. Ye know that **after two days** is *the feast of* the passover, and **the Son** of man **is betrayed to be crucified.**
3. **Then assembled together the chief priests,** and the **scribes, and** the **elders** of the people, **unto the palace of** the high priest, who was called **Caiaphas,**
4. **And consulted that they might take Jesus** by subtilty, **and kill *him.***
5. But they said, Not on the feast *day,* lest there be an uproar among the people.
6. **Now when Jesus was in Bethany,** in the house of Simon the leper,
7. **There came** unto him **a woman having** an alabaster box of very precious **ointment, and poured it on his head,** as he sat *at meat.*
8. **But when his disciples saw** *it,* **they had indignation,** saying, To what purpose *is* this waste?
9. **For this ointment might have been sold** for much, **and given to the poor.**
10. **When Jesus understood** *it,* **he said** unto them, Why trouble ye the woman? for **she hath wrought a good work** upon me.
11. For ye have the poor always with you; but me ye have not always.
12. **For** in that **she hath poured this ointment on my body,** she did *it* **for my burial.**
13. Verily I say unto you, **Wheresoever this gospel shall be preached** in the whole world, ***there* shall also this, that this woman hath done, be told for a memorial of her.**
14. **Then** one of the twelve, called **Judas** Iscariot, **went unto the chief priests,**

■ 15. **And said** *unto them,*
■ **What will ye give** me,
■ **and I will deliver him**
unto you?
■ **And they covenanted**
with him for
■ **thirty pieces of silver.**
16. And from that time he sought
opportunity to betray him.
17. Now the first *day* of the *feast of*
unleavened bread
■ **the disciples came to**
■ **Jesus, saying** unto him,
■ **Where wilt thou that we**
■ **prepare for** thee to eat
■ **the passover?**
■ 18. **And he said, Go into the**
■ **city to** such
■ **a man, and say** unto him,
■ **The Master saith,**
My time is at hand;
■ **I will keep the passover at**
■ **thy house** with my disciples.
19. And the disciples did as Jesus
had appointed them; and they made
ready the passover.
■ 20. **Now** when the even was come,
■ **he sat down with**
■ **the twelve.**
■ 21. **And** as they did eat,
■ **he said,** Verily I say unto you, that
■ **one of you shall betray me.**
■ 22. **And they were** exceeding
■ **sorrowful, and began**
every one of them
■ **to say** unto him,
■ **Lord, is it I?**
■ 23. **And he answered** and said,
■ **He that dippeth** *his* hand
■ **with me** in the dish,
■ **the same shall betray me.**
24. The Son of man goeth as it is
written of him: but woe unto that man
by whom the Son of man is betrayed!
it had been good for that man if he had
not been born.
■ 25. **Then Judas,** which betrayed
him, answered and
■ **said,** Master,
■ **is it I? He said** unto him,
■ **Thou hast said.**
26. And as they were eating,
■ **Jesus took bread, and**
■ **blessed** *it,*
■ **and brake** ***it,*** **and**
gave *it* to the disciples, and
■ **said, Take, eat;**
■ **this is my body.**
■ 27. **And he took the cup, and**
■ **gave thanks,** and gave *it* to them,
■ **saying, Drink** ye all of
■ **it;**
■ 28. **For this is my blood**
of the new testament, which is
■ **shed for** many for
■ **the remission of sins.**
29. But I say unto you, I will not drink
henceforth of this fruit of the vine,
until that day when I drink it new with
you in my Father's kingdom.
■ 30. **And when they had sung**
an hymn
■ **they went out**
into the mount of Olives.
■ 31. **Then saith Jesus** unto them,
■ **All ye shall be offended**
■ **because of me this night:**
for it is written, I will smite the
shepherd, and the sheep of the flock
shall be scattered abroad.
■ 32. **But after I am risen**
■ **again, I will go before you**
■ **into Galilee.**
■ 33. **Peter answered**
and said unto him,
■ **Though all** *men* shall
■ **be offended** because of thee,
■ ***yet*** **will I never be offended.**
■ 34. **Jesus said** unto him, Verily I
say unto thee, That this night,
■ **before the cock crow, thou**
■ **shalt deny me thrice.**
35. Peter said unto him, Though I
should die with thee, yet will I not deny
thee. Likewise also said
all the disciples.
■ 36. **Then cometh Jesus with**
■ **them unto** a place called
■ **Gethsemane, and saith**
unto the disciples,
■ **Sit** ye here,
■ **while I go and pray** yonder.
■ 37. **And he took** with him
■ **Peter and the two sons of**
■ **Zebedee,** and began to be
sorrowful and very heavy.

38. **Then saith he** unto them,
My soul is exceeding
sorrowful, even unto death:
tarry ye here,
and watch with me.
39. **And he went** a little
farther, and fell on his face,
and prayed, saying, O my
Father, if it be possible, let
this cup pass from me:
nevertheless not as I will,
but as thou *wilt*.
40. **And he cometh**
unto the disciples,
and findeth them asleep,
and saith unto Peter, What,
could ye not watch with me
one hour?
41. Watch and pray, that ye enter not
into temptation:
the spirit indeed
***is* willing, but the flesh**
***is* weak.**
42. **He went** away again
the second time, and
prayed, saying, O my Father,
if this cup may not pass
away from me,
except I drink it,
thy will be done.
43. **And he** came and
found them asleep again:
for their eyes were heavy.
44. **And he** left them, and went
away again, and
prayed the third time, saying
the same words.
45. **Then cometh he to his**
disciples, and saith
unto them,
Sleep on now, and take *your*
rest: behold, the hour is at hand, and
the Son of man is betrayed into the
hands of sinners.
46. Rise, let us be going: behold, he is
at hand that doth betray me.
47. **And while he yet spake,**
lo,
Judas, one of the twelve,
came, and
with him a great multitude
with swords and staves,
from the chief priests
and elders of the people.
48. **Now he** that betrayed him
gave them a sign, saying,
Whomsoever I shall kiss,
that same
is he: hold him fast.
49. **And forthwith he** came to
Jesus, and said, Hail, master; and
kissed him.
50. And Jesus said unto him, Friend,
wherefore art thou come?
Then came
they, and
laid hands on Jesus and
took him.
51. **And, behold, one**
of them which were
with Jesus
stretched out *his* hand, and
drew his sword, and struck
a servant of the high
priest's, and smote
off his ear.
52. **Then said Jesus** unto him,
Put up again thy sword
into his place:
for all
they that take the sword
shall perish with the sword.
53. **Thinkest thou that I**
cannot now pray to my
Father, and he shall presently
give me more than
twelve legions of angels?
54. **But how then shall the**
scriptures be fulfilled, that
thus it must be?
55. In that same hour said Jesus to
the multitudes, Are ye come out as
against a thief with swords and staves
for to take me? I sat daily with you
teaching in the temple, and ye laid no
hold on me.
56. But all this was done, that the
scriptures of the prophets
might be fulfilled.
Then all the disciples
forsook him, and
fled.
57. **And they**
that had laid hold on Jesus
led *him* away
to Caiaphas the high

priest, where the scribes and the
elders were assembled.
58. **But Peter followed** him
afar off unto the high priest's
palace, and went in,
and sat with the servants,
to see the end.
59. **Now** the chief priests, and
elders, and all
the council, sought false
witness against Jesus,
to put him to death;
60. **But found none:**
yea, though many false witnesses
came, yet found they none.
At the last came two false
witnesses,
61. **And said, This *fellow***
said, I am able to destroy
the temple of God,
and to
build it in three days.
62. **And the high priest**
arose, and
said unto him, Answerest
thou nothing? what *is it which*
these witness against thee?
63. **But Jesus held his**
peace, And the high priest
answered and
said unto him, I adjure thee
by the living God, that thou
tell us whether thou be the
Christ, the Son of God.
64. **Jesus saith**
unto him,Thou hast said:
nevertheless I say unto you,
Hereafter shall ye see the
Son of man
sitting on the right hand of
power, and coming in the
clouds of heaven.
65. **Then the high priest rent**
his clothes, saying, He hath
spoken blasphemy;
what further need have we of
witnesses? behold, now ye have
heard his blasphemy.
66. **What think ye? They**
answered and
said, He is guilty of death.
67. **Then** did
they spit in his face, and
buffeted him; and others
smote *him*
with the palms of their hands,
68. **Saying, Prophesy unto**
us, thou Christ, Who is he that
smote thee?
69. **Now Peter sat**
without in the palace:
and a damsel came unto him,
saying, Thou also
wast with Jesus of Galilee.
70. **But he denied** before *them* all,
saying, I know not what thou sayest.
71. **And** when he was gone out into
the porch,
another *maid* saw him, and
said unto them that were there,
This *fellow* was also
with Jesus of Nazareth.
72. **And again he denied**
with an oath, I do not know the man.
73. **And** after a while came unto *him*
they that stood by, and
said to Peter,
Surely thou also
art *one* of them; for
thy speech bewrayeth thee.
74. **Then began he to**
curse and to
swear, *saying,* I know not
the man. And immediately
the cock crew.
75. **And Peter remembered**
the word of Jesus, which said
unto him, Before the cock crow, thou
shalt deny me thrice.
And he went out,
and wept bitterly.

CHAPTER 27

1. When the morning was come, all
the chief priests and elders
of the people
took counsel against
Jesus to put him to death:
2. **And** when they had bound him,
they led *him* away, and
delivered him to Pontius
Pilate the governor.
3. **Then Judas,** which had
betrayed him, when he saw that he
was condemned,
repented himself,

■ **and brought** again
■ **the** thirty pieces of
■ **silver to the chief priests**
and elders,
■ 4. **Saying, I have**
sinned in that I have
■ **betrayed the innocent**
■ **blood. And they said, What**
■ ***is that* to us?** see thou *to that.*
■ 5. **And he cast down the**
pieces of
■ **silver** in the temple, and departed,
■ **and** went and
■ **hanged himself.**
■ 6. **And the chief priests took**
■ **the silver** pieces, and said, It is
not lawful for to put them into the
treasury, because it is the
price of blood.
7. And they took counsel,
■ **and bought** with them
■ **the** potter's
■ **field,** to bury strangers in.
8. Wherefore that field was
■ **called, The field of blood,**
unto this day.
■ 9. **Then was fulfilled that**
■ **which was spoken by**
■ **Jeremy** the prophet, saying, And
they took the thirty pieces of silver,
the price of him that was valued,
whom they of the children of
Israel did value;
10. And gave them for the potter's
field, as the Lord appointed me.
■ 11. **And Jesus stood before**
■ **the governor: and the**
■ **governor asked him,** saying,
■ **Art thou the King of the**
■ **Jews? And Jesus said**
unto him,
■ **Thou sayest.**
■ 12. **And when he**
■ **was accused**
of the chief priests and elders,
■ **he answered nothing.**
13. Then said Pilate unto him, Hearest
thou not how many things they
witness against thee?
■ 14. **And** he answered him to never a
word; insomuch that
■ **the governor marvelled**
greatly.

■ 15. **Now at *that* feast the**
■ **governor was wont to**
■ **release** unto the people
■ **a prisoner,** whom they would.
16. And they had then a notable
prisoner, called Barabbas.
17. Therefore when they were
gathered together,
■ **Pilate said** unto them,
■ **Whom will** ye that
■ **I release** unto you?
■ **Barabbas, or Jesus**
which is called Christ?
18. For he knew that for envy they had
delivered him.
19. When he was set down on the
judgment seat,
■ **his wife sent unto him,**
■ **saying, Have** thou
■ **nothing to do with that just**
■ **man:** for
■ **I have suffered**
many things this day
■ **in a dream because of him.**
■ 20. **But the chief priests**
and elders
■ **persuaded the multitude**
■ **that they should ask**
■ **Barabbas, and**
■ **destroy Jesus.**
21. The governor answered and said
unto them, Whether of the twain will ye
that I release unto you?
They said, Barabbas.
■ 22. **Pilate saith** unto them,
■ **What shall I do then with**
■ **Jesus** which is called Christ?
■ ***They* all say** unto him,
■ **Let him be crucified.**
■ 23. **And the governor said,**
■ **Why, what evil hath he**
■ **done? But they cried**
■ **out** the
■ **more, saying, Let him**
■ **be crucified.**
■ 24. **When Pilate saw that he**
■ **could prevail nothing,** but
that rather a tumult was made,
■ **he** took water, and
■ **washed *his* hands**
before the multitude,
■ **saying, I am innocent of the**
■ **blood of this just person:**

see *ye to it.*
25. **Then** answered all
the people, and
said, His blood *be* on us,
and on
our children.
26. Then released he
Barabbas unto them:
and when he had scourged
Jesus, he delivered *him* to
be crucified.
27. **Then the soldiers**
of the governor
took Jesus into the common hall,
and gathered unto him the whole band
of soldiers.
28. **And they stripped him,**
and put on him a
scarlet robe.
29. **And** when they had platted
a crown of thorns, they put *it*
upon his head,
and a reed in his right hand:
and they
bowed the knee before him,
and mocked him,
saying, Hail, King
of the Jews!
30. **And they spit upon him,**
and took the reed,
and smote him on the head.
31. **And after that**
they had mocked him,
they took the robe off from him, and
put his own raiment on him,
and led him away to
crucify *him.*
32. **And** as they came out,
they found
a man of Cyrene,
Simon by name: him
they compelled to
bear his cross.
33. **And when they were**
come unto a place called
Golgotha, that is to say, a place
of a skull,
34. **They gave him vinegar**
to drink mingled
with gall: and
when he had tasted *thereof,*
he would not drink.
35. **And they crucified him,**
and parted his garments,
casting lots: that it might be
fulfilled which was
spoken by the prophet,
They parted my garments among
them, and upon my vesture did they
cast lots.
36. And sitting down they
watched him there;
37. **And set up over his head**
his accusation written, THIS
IS JESUS THE KING
OF THE JEWS.
38. **Then were there two**
thieves crucified with him,
one on the right hand,
and another on the left.
39. **And they that passed by**
reviled him, wagging their heads,
40. **And saying,** Thou that
destroyest the temple, and buildest *it*
in three days, save thyself.
If thou be the Son of God,
come down from the cross.
41. **Likewise also the chief**
priests mocking
him, with the scribes and elders,
said,
42. He saved others; himself he
cannot save.
If he be the King of Israel,
let him now come down
from the cross,
and we will believe him.
43. He trusted in God; let him deliver
him now, if he will have him: for he
said, I am the Son of God.
44. The thieves also, which were
crucified with him, cast the
same in his teeth.
45. Now from the sixth hour there was
darkness over all the land unto the
ninth hour.
46. **And about the ninth hour**
Jesus cried with a loud voice,
saying, Eli, Eli, lama sabachthani?
that is to say,
My God, my God, why hast
thou forsaken me?
47. Some of them that stood there,
when they heard *that,* said, This *man*
calleth for Elias.
48. **And straightway one**

of them ran, and
took a sponge, and
filled *it*
with vinegar, and
put *it* on a reed, and
gave him to drink.
49. **The rest said,** Let be,
let us see whether Elias will
come to
save him.
50. **Jesus, when he had**
cried again
with a loud voice, yielded
up the ghost.
51. **And, behold, the veil of**
the temple was rent
in twain from the top to the bottom;
and the earth did quake,
and the rocks rent;
52. **And** the graves were
opened; and
many bodies of the saints
which slept
arose,
53. **And came out of the**
graves after his resurrection, and
went into the holy city,
and appeared unto many.
54. **Now when the centurion,**
and they that were
with him, watching Jesus,
saw the earthquake, and
those things that were done,
they feared greatly,
saying, Truly this was the
Son of God.
55. **And many women were**
there beholding afar off, which
followed Jesus from Galilee,
ministering unto him:
56. Among which was Mary
Magdalene, and Mary the mother of
James and Joses, and the mother of
Zebedees children.
57. When the even was come,
there came
a rich man of Arimathaea,
named Joseph, who also
himself was Jesus' disciple:
58. **He went to Pilate, and**
begged the body of Jesus.
Then Pilate commanded the body to
be delivered.
59. **And when Joseph had**
taken the body, he
wrapped it in a clean
linen cloth,
60. **And laid it in his own** new
tomb, which he had hewn
out in the rock:
and he rolled a great
stone to the door of the
sepulchre, and departed.
61. And there was Mary Magdalene,
and the other Mary, sitting over
against the sepulchre.
62. **Now the next day,** that
followed the day of the preparation,
the chief priests and
Pharisees came together
unto Pilate,
63. **Saying, Sir, we remem-**
ber that that deceiver said,
while he was yet alive,
After three days I will rise
again.
64. **Command therefore that**
the sepulchre be made
sure until the third day,
lest his disciples
come by night, and
steal him away, and say unto
the people, He is risen from the dead:
so the last error shall be worse
than the first.
65. **Pilate said** unto them,
Ye have a watch: go your way,
make ***it*** **as sure as ye can.**
66. **So they went,**
and made the sepulchre sure,
sealing the stone, and
setting a watch.

CHAPTER 28

1. In the end of the sabbath, as it
began to dawn toward
the first ***day*** **of the week,**
came Mary Magdalene
and the other Mary to see
the sepulchre.
2. **And, behold, there was a**
great earthquake: for the
angel of the Lord
descended
from heaven, and came
and rolled back the stone

from the door, and sat upon it.
3. His countenance was like lightning,
and his raiment white as snow:
4. **And for fear** of him
the keepers did shake, and
became as dead *men*.
5. **And the angel** answered and
said unto the women, Fear
not ye: for I know that
ye seek Jesus,
which was crucified.
6. **He is not here: for he is**
risen, as he said. Come, see the
place where the Lord lay.
7. **And go quickly, and tell**
his disciples
that he is risen from the dead;
and, behold, he goeth
before you into Galilee;
there shall ye see him: lo,
I have told you.
8. **And they** departed quickly from
the sepulchre with fear
and great joy; and
did run to bring his
disciples word.
9. **And as they went to tell**
his disciples, behold,
Jesus met them, saying, All hail.
And they
came and held him by the feet, and
worshipped him.
10. Then said Jesus unto them, Be
not afraid: go tell my brethren that
they go into Galilee, and there shall
they see me.
11. **Now** when they were
going, behold,
some of the watch came
into the city,
and shewed unto
the chief priests all
the things that were done.
12. **And** when they were
assembled with
the elders, and had taken
counsel, they
gave large
money unto the soldiers,
13. **Saying, Say ye, His**
disciples came by night, and
stole him *away*
while we slept.
14. And if this come to the governor's
ears, we will persuade him, and
secure you.
15. **So they** took the money, and
did as they were taught:
and this saying is commonly reported
among the Jews until this day.
16. **Then the eleven** disciples
went away into Galilee,
into a mountain where Jesus had
appointed them.
17. And when they saw him, they
worshipped him: but some doubted.
18. **And Jesus came and**
spake unto them,
saying, All power is given
unto me in heaven and in earth.
19. **Go** ye therefore,
and teach all nations,
baptizing them in the name of
the Father, and of the Son, and of the
Holy Ghost:
20. **Teaching them to**
observe all things
whatsoever I have
commanded you:
and, lo, I am with
you alway, *even*
unto the end
of the world.
Amen.

THE GOSPEL ACCORDING TO MARK

BACKGROUND INFORMATION

Author – Mark, a missionary
Date Written – probably **between 57** and **65** A.D.

Number of:
Verses - 678
Chapters - 16
Total Worlds -15,171
Scan Words -7,290
Scan Words represent 48 % of Total Words.

Theme – written to Christians to inform them of the ministry of Jesus on earth as the Son of God.

OUTLINE OF THE GOSPEL

I. **Christ's early ministry,** baptism and temptation, including healings, conflicts with Pharisees and early travels.
Chapters 1—8

II. **Christ's predictions of his death,** doctrine of discipleship **and transfiguration.**
Chapters 8—10

III. **Christ's** entry into Jerusalem and **Crucifixion.**
Chapters 10—16

IV. **Christ's Resurrection** and appearances to his disciples.
Chapters 16—20

CHAPTER 1

1. **The beginning of the**
gospel of Jesus Christ,
the Son of God;
2. **As it is written**
in the prophets, Behold, I send
my messenger
before thy face, which
shall prepare thy way
before thee.
3. **The voice of one crying in**
the wilderness, Prepare ye
the way of the Lord,
make his paths straight.
4. **John did baptize**
in the wilderness,
and preach the baptism of
repentance for the remission
of sins.
5. **And there went out** unto him
all the land of
Judaea, and they of
Jerusalem, and were all
baptized of him in the
river of Jordan,
confessing their sins.
6. **And John was clothed**
with camel's hair, and with a
girdle of a skin about his loins; and he
did eat locusts and wild honey;
7. **And preached, saying,**
There cometh one mightier
than I after me, the latchet of
whose shoes I am not
worthy to
stoop down and
unloose.
8. I indeed have baptized you with
water: but
he shall baptize you with
the Holy Ghost.
9. **And** it came to pass in those
days, that
Jesus came from Nazareth of
Galilee, and
was baptized of John
in Jordan.
10. **And straightway coming**
up out of the water, he saw
the heavens opened, and
the Spirit like a dove
descending upon him:
11. **And there came a voice**
from heaven,
***saying,* Thou art my**
beloved Son,
in whom I am well pleased.
12. **And immediately the**
spirit driveth him into
the wilderness.
13. And he was there in
the wilderness forty days,
tempted of Satan;
and was with the wild beasts;
and the angels ministered
unto him.
14. **Now after that John was**
put in prison, Jesus came
into Galilee,
preaching the gospel
of the kingdom of God,
15. **And saying,** The time is
fulfilled, and the kingdom of
God is at hand:
repent ye, and believe
the gospel.
16. **Now** as he walked by the sea of
Galilee, he saw
Simon and Andrew his brother
casting a net into the sea: for they
were fishers.
17. **And Jesus said** unto them,
Come ye after me,
and I will make you to become
fishers of men.
18. **And straightway they**
forsook their nets, and
followed him.
19. **And** when he had gone a little
farther thence,
he saw James
the *son* of Zebedee,
and John his brother, who also
were in the ship
mending their nets.
20. **And straightway he**
called them: and they left
their father Zebedee in
the ship with the hired servants,
and went after him.
21. **And** they went into
Capernaum; and straightway
on the sabbath day he
entered into the
synagogue, and taught.
22. And they were astonished at his

doctrine: for he taught them
as one that had authority,
and not as the scribes.
23. **And** there was in their
synagogue
a man with an unclean
spirit; and he
cried out,
24. **Saying, Let *us* alone;** what
have we to do with thee,
thou Jesus of Nazareth? art
thou come to destroy us? I know thee
who thou art, the Holy One of God.
25. **And Jesus rebuked him,**
saying, Hold thy peace, and
come out of him.
26. **And when the unclean**
spirit had torn him, and
cried with a loud voice,
he came out of him.
27. **And they were all**
amazed, insomuch that they
questioned among themselves,
saying, What thing is this? what
new doctrine *is* this? for with
authority commandeth he
even the unclean spirits,
and they do
obey him.
28. **And immediately his**
fame spread abroad
throughout all the region
round about Galilee.
29. **And** forthwith, when they were
come out of the synagogue,
they entered into the house
of Simon and Andrew, with
James and John.
30. **But Simon's wife's**
mother lay sick of a fever, and
anon they tell him of her.
31. **And he** came and took her by
the hand, and
lifted her up; and immediately
the fever left her, and she
ministered unto them.
32. **And** at even,
when the sun did set,
they brought unto him
all that were diseased, and
them that were
possessed with devils.
33. And all the city was gathered
together at the door.
34. **And he healed many** that
were sick of divers diseases, and
cast out many devils; and suffered
not the devils to speak, because they
knew him.
35. **And in the morning,**
rising up a great while
before day, he went
out, and departed
into a solitary place, and
there prayed.
36. **And Simon and they that**
were with him followed
after him.
37. **And when they had**
found him, they said unto him,
All *men* seek for thee.
38. **And he said** unto them,
Let us go into the next towns,
that I may preach there also:
for therefore came I forth.
39. **And he preached**
in their synagogues
throughout all Galilee,
and cast out devils.
40. **And there came a leper**
to him, beseeching him, and kneeling
down to him, and
saying unto him, If thou wilt,
thou canst make me clean.
41. **And Jesus,** moved with
compassion, put forth *his* hand, and
touched him, and saith
unto him, I will;
be thou clean.
42. **And** as soon as he had spoken,
immediately the leprosy
departed from him, and
he was cleansed.
43. **And he** straitly charged him,
and forthwith
sent him away;
44. **And saith** unto him, See thou
say nothing to any man:
but go thy way, shew thyself
to the priest, and offer
for thy cleansing
those things which Moses
commanded, for a
testimony unto them.
45. **But he** went out, and
began to publish *it* much, and

to blaze abroad the matter,
insomuch that Jesus could
no more openly enter into
the city, but
was without in desert places: and
they came to him
from every quarter.

CHAPTER 2

1. **And again he entered into**
Capernaum after *some* days;
and it was noised that he
was in the house.
2. **And straightway many**
were gathered
together, insomuch that there was no
room to receive *them,* no, not so much
as about the door:
and he preached the
word unto them.
3. **And** they come unto him,
bringing one sick of the
palsy, which was borne of four.
4. And when
they could not come
nigh unto him
for the press,
they uncovered the roof
where he was:
and when they had
broken *it* up, they
let down the bed wherein the
sick of the palsy lay.
5. **When Jesus saw their**
faith, he said
unto the sick of the palsy,
Son, thy sins be
forgiven thee.
6. **But** there was certain of
the scribes sitting there, and
reasoning in their hearts,
7. Why doth this *man* thus speak
blasphemies?
who can forgive sins but
God only?
8. And immediately
when Jesus perceived
in his spirit
that they so reasoned
within themselves,
he said unto them, Why reason ye
these things in your hearts?
9. **Whether is it easier to say**
to the sick of the palsy,
***Thy* sins be forgiven thee;**
or to say,
Arise, and take up thy bed,
and walk?
10. **But that ye may know**
that the Son of man
hath power on earth
to forgive sins, (he saith to the
sick of the palsy,)
11. **I say** unto thee,
Arise, and take up thy bed, and go
thy way into thine house.
12. **And immediately he**
arose, took up the bed,
and went forth before them all;
insomuch that
they were all amazed, and
glorified God, saying, We never
saw it on this fashion.
13. And he went forth again by the sea
side; and all the multitude resorted
unto him, and he taught them.
14. **And** as he passed by,
he saw Levi the *son* of Alphaeus
sitting at the receipt of
custom, and said unto him,
Follow me. And he arose and
followed him.
15. **And** it came to pass, that,
as Jesus sat at meat
in his house, many
publicans and sinners sat
also together
with Jesus and his disciples:
for there were many, and they
followed him.
16. **And when the scribes**
and Pharisees saw him eat
with publicans and sinners,
they said unto his disciples,
How is it that
he eateth and drinketh with
publicans and sinners?
17. **When Jesus heard** *it,*
he saith unto them, They that are
whole have no need of the physician,
but they that are sick:
I came not to call the
righteous, but sinners to
repentance.
18. **And** the disciples of John and of
the Pharisees used to fast: and

they come and
say unto him, Why do the
disciples of John and of the Pharisees
fast, but
thy disciples fast not?
19. **And Jesus said** unto them,
Can the children of the bridechamber
fast, while the bridegroom is
with them?
as long as they have the
bridegroom with them,
they cannot fast.
20. **But** the days will come,
when the bridegroom shall
be taken away from them, and
then shall they fast
in those days.
21. **No man also seweth**
a piece of
new cloth on an old
garment: else
the new piece that filled it up
taketh away from the old,
and the rent is made worse.
22. **And no man putteth new**
wine into old bottles: else
the new wine doth burst the
bottles, and the wine is spilled, and
the bottles will be marred:
but new wine must be put
into new bottles.
23. **And** it came to pass, that
he went through the corn
fields on the sabbath day;
and his disciples began,
as they went,
to pluck the ears of
corn.
24. **And the Pharisees said**
unto him, Behold,
why do they on the sabbath day
that which is not lawful?
25. **And he said** unto them,
Have ye never read what
David did, when he
had need, and was an
hungered, he, and they that
were with him?
26. **How he went into the**
house of God in the days of
Abiathar the high priest,
and did eat the
shewbread, which is not
lawful to eat but for the priests, and
gave also to them which
were with him?
27. And he said unto them, The
sabbath was made for man, and not
man for the sabbath:
28. Therefore
the Son of man is Lord also
of the sabbath.

CHAPTER 3

1. And he entered again into the
synagogue; and
there was a man there
which had a
withered hand.
2. **And they watched him,**
whether he would heal him
on the sabbath day;
that they might accuse him.
3. **And he saith unto the man**
which had the withered hand,
Stand forth.
4. And he saith unto them,
Is it lawful to do good on
the sabbath days, or to do
evil? to save life, or to kill? But they
held their peace.
5. **And** when he had looked round
about on them
with anger, being grieved
for the hardness of their
hearts, he saith unto the
man, Stretch forth thine
hand. And he stretched *it* out:
and his hand was restored
whole as the other.
6. **And the Pharisees**
went forth, and straightway
took counsel
with the Herodians against him,
how they might
destroy him.
7. **But Jesus withdrew**
himself with his disciples
to the sea:
and a great multitude from Galilee
followed him, and from Judaea,
8. And from Jerusalem, and from
Idumaea, and *from* beyond Jordan;
and they about Tyre and Sidon, a
great multitude,
when they had heard what

■ **great things he did, came**
■ **unto him.**
■ 9. **And he spake to his**
■ **disciples, that a small ship**
■ **should wait on him**
because of the multitude,
■ **lest they should throng him.**
■ 10. **For he had healed many;**
insomuch that they pressed upon him
for to touch him,
as many as had plagues.
■ 11. **And unclean spirits,**
when they saw him,
■ **fell down before him,**
and cried,
■ **saying, Thou art the**
■ **Son of God.**
■ 12. **And he straitly charged**
■ **them that they should not**
■ **make him known.**
■ 13. **And he goeth up into a**
■ **mountain,** and calleth *unto him*
whom he would: and they
came unto him.
■ 14. **And he ordained twelve,**
■ **that they should be with**
■ **him, and that he might send**
■ **them forth to preach,**
■ 15. **And** to have power
■ **to heal** sicknesses,
■ **and to cast out devils:**
16. And Simon he surnamed Peter;
17. And James the *son* of Zebedee,
and John the brother of James; and
he surnamed them Boanerges, which
is, The sons of thunder:
18. And Andrew, and Philip, and
Bartholomew, and Matthew, and
Thomas, and James the *son* of
Alphaeus, and Thaddaeus, and Simon
the Canaanite,
19. And Judas Iscariot, which also
betrayed him: and they went into an
house.
■ 20. **And the multitude**
■ **cometh together again,** so
that they could not so much
as eat bread.
■ 21. **And** when
■ **his friends** heard *of it,* they
■ **went out to lay hold on him:**
■ **for they said, He is**
■ **beside himself.**

■ 22. **And the scribes** which came
down from Jerusalem
■ **said,** He hath Beelzebub, and
■ **by the prince of the devils**
■ **casteth he out devils.**
■ 23. **And he** called them
unto him, and
■ **said** unto them
■ **in parables, How can**
■ **Satan cast out Satan?**
24. And if a kingdom be divided
against itself, that kingdom
cannot stand.
25. And if a house be divided against
itself, that house cannot stand.
■ 26. **And if Satan** rise up against
himself, and
■ **be divided, he cannot**
■ **stand,** but hath an end.
■ 27. **No man can enter** into
■ **a strong man's house,**
and spoil his goods,
■ **except he will first bind the**
■ **strong man;** and then he will spoil
his house.
28. Verily I say unto you,
■ **All sins shall be forgiven**
unto the sons of men, and
blasphemies wherewith soever they
shall blaspheme:
■ 29. **But he that shall**
■ **blaspheme against the**
■ **Holy Ghost hath never**
■ **forgiveness, but** is in danger of
■ **eternal damnation.**
30. Because they said, He hath an
unclean spirit.
31. There came
■ **then his brethren and his**
■ **mother,** and, standing without,
■ **sent** unto him,
■ **calling him.**
■ 32. **And the multitude** sat about
him, and they
■ **said** unto him, Behold,
■ **thy mother and thy brethren**
without
■ **seek for thee.**
33. And he answered them, saying,
Who is my mother, or my brethren?
■ 34. **And he looked** round about
■ **on them which sat about**
■ **him, and said, Behold my**

mother and my brethren!
35. **For whosoever shall do**
the will of God, the same
is my brother, and my
sister, and mother.

CHAPTER 4

1. **And he** began again to teach by
the sea side: and there was gathered
unto him a great multitude, so that he
entered into a ship,
and sat in the sea;
and the whole
multitude was by the sea
on the land.
2. **And he taught them**
many things
by parables, and said
unto them in his doctrine,
3. Hearken; Behold,
there went out a
sower to sow:
4. **And** it came to pass, as he sowed,
some fell by the way side,
and the fowls of the air came and
devoured it up.
5. **And some fell on stony**
ground, where it had
not much earth;
and immediately it sprang up,
because it had no depth
of earth:
6. But when
the sun was up, it was
scorched; and
because it had no root,
it withered away.
7. **And some fell among**
thorns, and the thorns
grew up, and
choked it, and it yielded no fruit.
8. **And other fell on good**
ground, and did yield fruit
that sprang up and increased; and
brought forth, some thirty, and some
sixty, and some an hundred.
9. And he said unto them, He that hath
ears to hear, let him hear.
10. **And when** he was
alone, they that were about him
with the twelve
asked of him the parable.
11. **And he said** unto them,
Unto you it
is given to know
the mystery of the kingdom
of God: but unto them
that are without, all *these*
things are done
in parables:
12. **That seeing they may**
see, and
not perceive; and hearing
they may hear, and
not understand; lest
at any time
they should
be converted, and *their* sins
should be forgiven them.
13. And he said unto them,
Know ye not
this parable? and how then will
ye know all parables?
14. **The sower soweth**
the word.
15. **And these** are they
by the way side, where the word
is sown; but
when they have
heard, Satan cometh
immediately,
and taketh away the word
that was sown in their hearts.
16. **And these**
are they likewise which are
sown on stony ground; who,
when they have heard
the word, immediately
receive it with gladness;
17. **And have no root**
in themselves, and
so endure but for a time: afterward,
when affliction or
persecution ariseth for the
word's sake, immediately
they are offended.
18. **And these** are they which are
sown among thorns; such as
hear the word,
19. **And the cares** of this world,
and the deceitfulness of
riches, and the lusts of other things
entering in,
choke the word,
and it becometh unfruitful.
20. **And these** are they which are

■ **sown on good ground;**
such as hear the word, and
■ **receive *it,* and bring forth**
■ **fruit,** some thirtyfold, some sixty,
and some an hundred.
■ 21. **And he said** unto them,
■ **Is a candle** brought to be
■ **put under a bushel, or**
under a bed? and not to be
■ **set on a candlestick?**
■ 22. **For there is nothing hid,**
which shall not be manifested;
■ **neither** was any thing
■ **kept secret, but that it**
■ **should come abroad.**
23. If any man have ears to hear,
let him hear.
24. And he said unto them, Take heed
what ye hear: with what measure ye
mete, it shall be measured to you: and
■ **unto you that hear shall**
■ **more be given.**
■ 25. **For he that hath,** to him
■ **shall be given: and he that**
■ **hath not,** from him
■ **shall be taken**
even that which he hath.
26. And he said,
■ **So is the kingdom of God,**
as
■ **if a man** should
■ **cast seed into the ground;**
■ 27. **And should sleep,**
and rise night and day,
■ **and the seed should**
spring and
■ **grow up, he knoweth**
■ **not how.**
■ 28. **For the earth bringeth**
■ **forth fruit of herself;** first the
blade, then the ear, after that the full
corn in the ear.
■ 29. **But** when the fruit is
brought forth,
■ **immediately he putteth in**
■ **the sickle, because the**
■ **harvest is come.**
30. And he said,
■ **Whereunto shall we liken**
■ **the kingdom** of God? or with what
comparison shall we compare it?
■ 31. ***It is* like a grain of**
■ **mustard seed, which,** when it
is sown in the earth,
■ **is less than all the seeds**
that be in the earth:
■ 32. **But when it is sown,**
it groweth up, and
■ **becometh greater than all**
■ **herbs,** and shooteth out great
branches; so that the fowls of the air
may lodge under the shadow of it.
■ 33. **And with** many such
■ **parables spake he the**
■ **word** unto them, as they were able
to hear *it.*
34. But without a parable spake he not
unto them:
■ **and when they were alone,**
■ **he expounded** all things
■ **to his disciples.**
■ 35. **And** the same day, when the
even was come, he
■ **saith** unto them,
■ **Let us pass over unto the**
■ **other side.**
■ 36. **And** when they had sent away
the multitude, they took him even as
he was
■ **in the ship.** And there were also
■ **with** him
■ **other little ships.**
37. And
■ **there arose a great storm**
of wind, and the waves beat into the
ship, so that it was now full.
■ 38. **And he was** in the hinder part
of the ship,
■ **asleep** on a pillow:
■ **and they awake him, and**
■ **say** unto him, Master,
■ **carest thou not that**
■ **we perish?**
■ 39. **And he** arose, and
■ **rebuked the wind,** and said
unto the sea, Peace, be still.
And the wind ceased,
■ **and there was a**
■ **great calm.**
■ 40. **And he said** unto them,
■ **Why** are ye so fearful? how
■ **is it that ye have no faith?**
■ 41. **And they feared**
■ **exceedingly, and said**
one to another,
■ **What manner of man is this,**

■ **that even the wind and the**
■ **sea obey him?**

CHAPTER 5

■ 1. **And they came**
over unto the other side of the sea,
■ **into the country of**
■ **the Gadarenes.**
■ 2. **And** when he was come out of the
ship, immediately
■ **there met him out of the**
■ **tombs a man with an**
■ **unclean spirit,**
■ 3. **Who** had *his* dwelling among the
tombs; and
■ **no man could bind**
him, no, not with chains:
4. Because that he had been often
bound with fetters and chains, and the
chains had been plucked asunder by
him, and the fetters broken in pieces:
■ **neither could any *man***
■ **tame him.**
■ 5. **And always,** night and day, he
was in the mountains,
and in the tombs,
■ **crying, and cutting himself**
■ **with stones.**
■ 6. **But when he saw Jesus**
afar off,
■ **he ran and**
■ **worshipped him,**
7. And cried with a loud voice,
■ **and said, What have I to do**
■ **with thee, Jesus, *thou* Son**
■ **of** the most high
■ **God?** I adjure thee
by God, that thou
■ **torment me not.**
8. For he said unto him, Come out of
the man, *thou* unclean spirit.
■ 9. **And he asked him, What**
■ ***is* thy name? And he**
■ **answered,** saying, My name *is*
■ **Legion: for we are many.**
■ 10. **And he besought him**
much that he would
■ **not send them away out of**
■ **the country.**
■ 11. **Now there was** there nigh
unto the mountains
■ **a great herd of**
■ **swine feeding.**

■ 12. **And all the devils**
■ **besought him,** saying,
■ **Send us into the swine,**
that we may enter into them.
13. And forthwith
■ **Jesus gave them leave.**
And the unclean spirits went out, and
entered into the swine:
■ **and the herd ran violently**
down a steep place
■ **into the sea,**
(they were about two thousand;)
■ **and were choked** in the sea.
■ 14. **And they**
that fed the swine fled, and
■ **told *it* in the city, and** in the
■ **country. And they went out**
■ **to see** what it was that was done.
15. And they come to
■ **Jesus, and see him that**
was possessed with the devil, and
■ **had the legion, sitting,**
and clothed,
■ **and in his right mind:**
and they were afraid.
16. And they that saw *it* told them how
it befell to him that was possessed
with the devil, and *also* concerning the
swine.
■ 17. **And they began** to pray him
■ **to depart** out of their coasts.
■ 18. **And** when he was
come into the ship,
■ **he that had been**
■ **possessed** with the devil
■ **prayed him that he might**
■ **be with him.**
19. Howbeit
■ **Jesus** suffered him not, but
■ **saith unto him, Go home**
to thy friends,
■ **and tell them how great**
■ **things the Lord hath done**
for thee, and hath had
compassion on thee.
■ 20. **And he** departed, and
■ **began to publish** in Decapolis
■ **how great things Jesus had**
■ **done** for him:
■ **and all *men* did marvel.**
■ 21. **And** when
■ **Jesus** was
■ **passed** over again

by ship unto the other side,
much people gathered unto him: and
he was nigh unto the sea.
22. **And,** behold, there cometh
one of the rulers
of the synagogue,
Jairus by name; and when
he saw him, he
fell at his feet,
23. And besought him greatly,
saying, My little daughter
lieth at the point of death:
I pray thee,
come and lay thy hands on her,
that she may be healed;
and she shall live.
24. **And *Jesus* went with him;**
and much people followed him, and
thronged him.
25. **And a certain woman,**
which had an issue of
blood twelve years,
26. **And had suffered many**
things of many physicians, and had
spent all that she had, and was nothing bettered, but rather grew worse,
27. **When she had heard of**
Jesus, came in the press behind,
and touched his garment.
28. For she said, If I may touch but his
clothes, I shall be whole.
29. **And straightway** the
fountain of her blood was dried up;
and she felt in *her* body that
she was healed of that plague.
30. **And Jesus,** immediately
knowing in himself
that virtue had gone
out of him,
turned him about in the press, and
said, Who touched
my clothes?
31. **And his disciples said**
unto him,
Thou seest the multitude
thronging thee, and sayest thou,
Who touched me?
32. **And he looked round**
about
to see her that had done this
thing.
33. **But the woman fearing**
and trembling, knowing what was done
in her,
came and fell down before him,
and told him all the truth.
34. **And he said**
unto her, Daughter,
thy faith hath made thee
whole; go in peace, and be
whole of thy plague.
35. **While he yet spake, there**
came from the ruler of the
synagogue's *house certain*
which said, Thy daughter is
dead: why troublest thou the
Master any further?
36. **As soon as Jesus heard**
the word that was spoken,
he saith
unto the ruler of the synagogue,
Be not afraid, only believe.
37. And he suffered no man to follow
him, save Peter, and James, and
John the brother of James.
38. **And he cometh to the**
house of the ruler of the
synagogue, and seeth the tumult, and
them that wept and wailed greatly.
39. **And** when he was come in, he
saith unto them,
Why make ye this ado, and
weep? the damsel is not
dead, but sleepeth.
40. **And they laughed**
him to scorn.
But when he had put them
all out, he taketh the father
and the mother of the damsel,
and them that were with him,
and entereth in where the
damsel was lying.
41. **And he took the damsel**
by the hand, and said
unto her, Talitha cumi; which is,
being interpreted,
Damsel, I say unto
thee, arise.
42. **And straightway the**
damsel arose, and walked; for
she was *of the age* of twelve years.
And they were astonished
with a great astonishment.
43. **And he** charged them straitly
that no man should know it; and
commanded that

something should be given
her to eat.

CHAPTER 6

1. **And he** went out from thence, and
came into his own country;
and his disciples follow him.
2. **And** when the sabbath
day was come,
he began to teach in the
synagogue: and many
hearing *him* were
astonished, saying, From
whence hath this *man* these things?
and what wisdom *is* this which is given
unto him, that even such mighty
works are wrought by his hands?
3. **Is not this the carpenter,**
the son of Mary, the brother of
James, and Joses, and of Juda, and
Simon? and are not his sisters here
with us?
And they were offended
at him.
4. **But Jesus, said** unto them,
A prophet is not without
honour, but in his own
country, and among his own kin,
and in his own house.
5. **And he could** there
do no mighty work, save
that he laid his hands
upon a few sick folk,
and healed *them.*
6. **And he marvelled**
because of their unbelief.
And he went round about
the villages, teaching.
7. **And he called** *unto him*
the twelve, and began to
send them forth by two and
two; and gave them power
over unclean spirits;
8. **And commanded them**
that they should take
nothing for *their* journey,
save a staff only; no scrip, no bread,
no money in *their* purse:
9. But *be* shod with sandals; and not
put on two coats.
10. **And he said** unto them, In
what place soever ye enter into an
house, there abide till ye depart from
that place.
11. **And whosoever shall**
not receive you, nor hear you,
when ye depart thence,
shake off the dust under
your feet for a testimony
against them.
Verily I say unto you,
It shall be more tolerable
for Sodom and Gomorrha
in the day of judgment,
than for that city.
12. **And they** went out, and
preached that men
should repent.
13. **And they cast out many**
devils, and anointed with
oil many that were
sick, and healed *them.*
14. **And king Herod** heard *of*
him; (for his name was spread
abroad:) and he
said, That John the Baptist
was risen from the dead, and
therefore mighty works do shew forth
themselves in him.
15. **Others said, That it is**
Elias. And others said,
That it is a prophet,
or as
one of the prophets.
16. **But** when
Herod heard *thereof,* he
said, It is John,
whom I beheaded:
he is risen from the dead.
17. **For Herod himself had**
sent forth and laid
hold upon John, and
bound him in prison for
Herodias' sake, his brother
Philip's wife: for he had married her.
18. **For John had said**
unto Herod,
It is not lawful for thee
to have thy brother's wife.
19. **Therefore Herodias** had a
quarrel against him, and
would have killed him; but
she could not:
20. **For Herod feared John,**
knowing that he was a just man and an
holy, and observed him; and when he

heard him, he did many things, and
heard him gladly.
21. **And** when a convenient day was
come, that
Herod on his birthday
made a supper
to his lords, high captains,
and chief *estates* of Galilee;
22. **And when the daughter**
of the said
Herodias came in, and
danced, and pleased
Herod and them that sat with him,
the king said unto the damsel,
Ask of me
whatsoever thou wilt, and I
will give *it* thee.
23. And he sware unto her,
Whatsoever thou shalt ask of me, I
will give *it* thee, unto the half
of my kingdom.
24. **And she went** forth, and said
unto her mother, What shall
I ask? And she said, The
head of John the Baptist.
25. **And she came** in straightway
with haste unto the king,
and asked, saying, I will that thou
give me by and by in a charger
the head of
John the Baptist.
26. **And the king was** exceeding
sorry; *yet* for his oath's
sake, and for their sakes which sat
with him,
he would not reject her.
27. **And** immediately
the king sent
an executioner,
and commanded his head to be
brought: and he went and
beheaded him in the prison,
28. **And brought his head** in a
charger, and gave it to the damsel:
and the damsel gave it to
her mother.
29. And when his disciples heard *of it,*
they came and took up his corpse,
and laid it in a tomb.
30. **And the apostles**
gathered themselves together
unto Jesus, and told him
all things, both
what they had done,
and what they had taught.
31. **And he said** unto them,
Come ye yourselves
apart into a desert place,
and rest a while: for there were
many coming and going, and they had
no leisure so much as to eat.
32. **And they departed** into a
desert place
by ship privately.
33. **And the people saw**
them departing, and many knew him,
and ran afoot thither out of all
cities, and outwent them,
and came together
unto him.
34. **And Jesus,** when he came
out, saw much people, and
was moved with
compassion toward them,
because they were as
sheep not having a
shepherd: and he began to teach
them many things.
35. **And when the day was**
now far spent, his
disciples came unto him, and
said, This is a desert
place, and now the
time *is* far passed:
36. **Send them away, that**
they may go into the country round
about, and into the villages, and
buy themselves
bread: for they have
nothing to eat.
37. **He answered**
and said unto them,
Give ye them to eat. And
they say unto him,
Shall we go and buy
two hundred pennyworth of
bread, and give them to eat?
38. **He saith** unto them,
How many loaves have
ye? go and see.
And when they knew,
they say, Five,
and two fishes.
39. **And he commanded**
them to make all
sit down by companies upon the

green grass.
40. And they sat down
in ranks,
by hundreds, and by fifties.
41. **And when he had taken**
the five loaves and the two
fishes, he
looked up to heaven, and
blessed, and brake the loaves,
and gave *them*
to his disciples to set before
them; and the two fishes divided he
among them all.
42. **And they** did all eat, and
were filled.
43. **And they took up twelve**
baskets full of the
fragments, and of the fishes.
44. **And they that did eat**
of the loaves
were about five
thousand men.
45. **And straightway he**
constrained his disciples
to get into the ship, and to
go to the other side before unto
Bethsaida, while he sent
away the people.
46. **And** when he had
sent them away,
he departed into a
mountain to pray.
47. And when even was come, the
ship was in the midst of the sea, and
he alone on the land.
48. **And he saw them toiling**
in rowing; for the wind was
contrary unto them:
and about the fourth
watch of the night
he cometh unto them,
walking upon the sea, and
would have passed by
them.
49. **But** when they saw him walking
upon the sea,
they supposed it had been
a spirit, and
cried out:
50. For they all saw him,
and were troubled.
And immediately he
talked with them, and
saith unto them,
Be of good cheer: it is I;
be not afraid.
51. **And he went** up unto them
into the ship; and the wind
ceased: and they were
sore amazed in themselves
beyond measure, and wondered.
52. For they considered not *the*
miracle of the loaves: for their heart
was hardened.
53. **And** when they had passed over,
they came into the land
of Gennesaret,
and drew to the shore.
54. **And when they**
were come out of the ship,
straightway they knew him,
55. And ran through that whole region
round about, and
began to carry about in
beds those that were sick,
where they heard he was.
56. And whithersoever he entered,
into villages, or cities, or country,
they laid the sick in the
streets, and besought him
that they might touch
if it were but the border of
his garment: and
as many as touched him
were made whole.

CHAPTER 7

1. **Then came** together unto him
the Pharisees, and
certain of the
scribes,
which came from Jerusalem.
2. **And** when they
saw some of
his disciples eat bread
with defiled, that is to say,
with unwashen hands,
they found fault.
3. **For the Pharisees,**
and all the Jews,
except they wash
their hands oft,
eat not,
holding the tradition of the elders.
4. **And *when they*** *come* from the
market, except they wash, they eat

not. And many other things there be,
which they have received to hold, *as*
the washing of cups, and pots, brasen
vessels, and of tables.
5. Then the Pharisees and scribes
asked him, Why walk not
thy disciples according to
the tradition of the elders,
but eat bread with
unwashen hands?
6. **He answered** and said unto
them, Well hath Esaias prophesied of
you hypocrites, as
it is written, This people
honoureth me with *their*
lips, but their heart is far
from me.
7. **Howbeit in vain do they**
worship me, teaching *for*
doctrines the commandments of men.
8. **For** laying aside the commandment
of God, ye hold the tradition of men,
as the washing of pots and cups: and
many other such like things ye do.
9. And he said unto them, Full well
ye reject the command-
ment of God, that ye may
keep your own tradition.
10. **For Moses said, Honour**
thy father and thy mother;
and, Whoso curseth father or mother,
let him die the death:
11. **But ye say,** If a man shall say
to his father or mother,
It is Corban, that is to say,
a gift, by whatsoever
thou mightest be profited
by me; *he shall be free.*
12. **And** ye suffer him
no more to do aught for his
father or his mother;
13. **Making the word of God**
of none effect through your
tradition, which ye have delivered:
and many such like things do ye.
14. **And when he had called**
all the people *unto him,*
he said unto them,
Hearken unto me every one *of you,*
and understand:
15. **There is nothing from**
without a man, that
entering into him
can defile him: but the
things which come out of
him, those are they that
defile the man.
16. If any man have ears to hear,
let him hear.
17. And when he was entered into the
house from the people,
his disciples asked him
concerning the parable.
18. **And he saith** unto them, Are
ye so without understanding also? Do
ye not perceive, that
whatsoever thing from
without entereth into the
man, *it* cannot defile him;
19. **Because it entereth**
not into his heart, but
into the belly, and goeth
out into the draught,
purging all meats?
20. **And he said, That which**
cometh out of the man, that
defileth the man.
21. **For from within,** out of the
heart of men,
proceed evil thoughts,
adulteries, fornications, murders,
22. Thefts, covetousness,
wickedness, deceit, lasciviousness,
an evil eye, blasphemy,
pride, foolishness:
23. All these evil things come from
within, and defile the man.
24. **And** from thence
he arose, and
went into the borders of
Tyre and Sidon, and entered
into an house,
and would have no man
know *it:* but he could
not be hid.
25. **For a *certain* woman,**
whose young daughter had an
unclean spirit, heard of him, and came
and fell at his feet:
26. The woman was a Greek,
a Syrophenician
by nation; and she
besought him that he would
cast forth the devil out of
her daughter.
27. **But Jesus said** unto her, Let

the children first be filled: for
it is not meet to take the
children's bread, and to
cast *it* unto the dogs.
28. **And she answered** and
said unto him, Yes, Lord:
yet the dogs under the table
eat of the children's
crumbs.
29. **And he said** unto her,
For this saying go thy way;
the devil is gone out
of thy daughter.
30. And when she was come to her
house, she found the devil gone out,
and her daughter laid upon the bed.
31. **And** again, departing from the
coasts of Tyre and Sidon,
he came unto the sea of Galilee,
through the midst of the coasts of
Decapolis.
32. **And they bring unto**
him one that was deaf,
and had an impediment
in his speech;
and they beseech him to
put his hand upon him.
33. **And he took him aside**
from the multitude,
and put his fingers into his
ears, and he spit, and
touched his tongue;
34. And looking up to heaven,
he sighed,
and saith unto him,
Ephphatha, that is,
Be opened.
35. **And straightway his**
ears were opened, and the
string of his tongue was loosed,
and he spake plain.
36. **And he charged them**
that they should tell no
man: but the more he charged
them, so much the more a great deal
they published *it;*
37. **And were** beyond measure
astonished, saying, He hath
done all things well:
he maketh both
the deaf to hear,
and the dumb
to speak.

CHAPTER 8

1. In those days the multitude being
very great, and having nothing to eat,
Jesus called his disciples
unto him,
and saith unto them,
2. I have compassion on
the multitude, because they
have now been with me
three days, and
have nothing to eat:
3. **And if I send them away**
fasting to their own houses,
they will faint by the way: for
divers of them came from far.
4. **And his disciples**
answered him,
From whence can a man
satisfy these *men* with
bread here in the wilderness?
5. **And he asked** them,
How many loaves have
ye? And they said, Seven.
6. And he commanded the people to
sit down on the ground: and
he took the seven loaves,
and gave thanks, and
brake, and gave to his disciples to
set before *them;*
and they did
set *them* before the people
7. And they had a few small fishes:
and he blessed, and commanded to
set them also before *them.*
8. **So they** did eat, and
were filled: and they took up of
the broken
***meat* that was left**
seven baskets.
9. **And they** that had eaten
were about four thousand:
and he sent them away.
10. **And** straightway
he entered into
a ship with his disciples,
and came into the parts of
Dalmanutha.
11. **And the Pharisees came**
forth, and began
to question with
him, seeking of him
a sign from heaven,
tempting him.

12. **And he** sighed deeply in his
spirit, and
saith, Why doth this generation
seek after a sign?
verily I say unto you,
There shall no sign be
given unto this generation.
13. **And he** left them, and entering
into the ship again
departed to the other side.
14. **Now *the disciples* had**
forgotten to take bread,
neither had they in the ship with them
more than one loaf.
15. **And he charged them,**
saying, Take heed,
beware of the leaven of the
Pharisees, and *of* the leaven of
Herod.
16. **And they reasoned**
among themselves, saying,
***It is* because we have**
no bread.
17. And when
Jesus knew *it,* he
saith unto them,
Why reason ye, because ye
have no bread?
perceive ye not yet, neither
understand? have ye your heart
yet hardened?
18. Having eyes, see ye not? and
having ears, hear ye not? and
do ye not remember?
19. **When I brake the five**
loaves among five
thousand, how many baskets full
of fragments took ye up? They say
unto him, Twelve.
20. **And** when the
seven among four
thousand, how many baskets full
of fragments took ye up? And they
said, Seven.
21. **And he said unto them,**
How is it that ye do
not understand?
22. **And he cometh to**
Bethsaida; and they bring
a blind man unto him, and
besought him to touch him.
23. **And he** took the blind man by
the hand, and led him out of the town;
and when he had
spit on his eyes, and put his
hands upon him, he
asked him
if he saw aught.
24. **And he** looked up, and
said, I see men
as trees, walking.
25. **After that he put *his***
hands again upon his
eyes, and made him look up:
and he was restored, and
saw every man clearly.
26. And he sent him away to his
house, saying, Neither go into the
town, nor tell *it* to any in the town.
27. **And Jesus** went out, and his
disciples, into the towns of Caesarea
Philippi: and by the way he
asked his disciples, saying
unto them,
Whom do men say
that I am?
28. And
they answered, John the
Baptist; but some *say,*
Elias; and others, One of
the prophets.
29. **And he saith** unto them,
But whom say ye that I am?
And Peter answereth
and saith unto him,
Thou art the Christ.
30. And he charged them that they
should tell no man of him.
31. **And he began to teach**
them, that the Son of man
must suffer many things, and be
rejected of the elders, and *of* the chief
priests, and scribes,
and be killed, and after
three days rise again.
32. And he spake that saying openly.
And Peter took him, and
began to rebuke him.
33. **But** when he had turned about
and looked on his disciples,
he rebuked Peter, saying,
Get thee behind me, Satan:
for thou savourest not the things that
be of God, but the things
that be of men.
34. **And when he had called**

the people *unto him* with his
disciples also,
he said unto them,
Whosoever will come after
me, let him deny himself,
and take up his cross, and
follow me.
35. For whosoever will save his life
shall lose it; but whosoever shall lose
his life for my sake and the gospel's,
the same shall save it.
36. **For what shall it profit a**
man, if he shall gain the
whole world, and lose his
own soul?
37. **Or what shall a man give**
in exchange for his soul?
38. **Whosoever** therefore
shall be ashamed of me and
of my words in this adulterous and
sinful generation;
of him also shall the Son of
man be ashamed, when he
cometh in the glory of his Father with
the holy angels.

CHAPTER 9

1. **And he said** unto them,
Verily I say unto you, That
there be some
of them that stand
here, which shall not taste
of death, till they have seen
the kingdom of God come
with power.
2. And after six days
Jesus taketh *with him*
Peter, and James, and
John, and leadeth them up
into an high mountain
apart by themselves:
and he was transfigured
before them.
3. **And his raiment became**
shining, exceeding
white as snow; so as no fuller on
earth can white them.
4. **And there appeared**
unto them
Elias with Moses:
and they were
talking with Jesus.
5. **And Peter answered**
and said to Jesus,
Master, it is good for
us to be here: and
let us make three
tabernacles; one for thee, and
one for Moses, and one for Elias.
6. For he wist not what to say; for they
were sore afraid.
7. **And** there was
a cloud that
overshadowed them: and
a voice came out of the cloud,
saying, This is my beloved
Son: hear him.
8. **And suddenly,**
when they had looked round about,
they saw no man any more, save
Jesus only with themselves.
9. **And** as they came down
from the mountain,
he charged them that they
should tell no man what things
they had seen,
till the Son of man were
risen from the dead.
10. **And they**
kept that saying with themselves,
questioning one with
another what the rising
from the dead
should mean.
11. And they
asked him, saying,
Why say the scribes that
Elias must first come?
12. **And he answered**
and told them,
Elias verily cometh first,
and restoreth all things;
and how it is written of
the Son of man, that he
must suffer many things,
and be set at nought.
13. **But I say** unto you, That
Elias is indeed come, and
they have done unto him
whatsoever they listed, as it
is written of him.
14. **And when he came to *his***
disciples, he saw
a great multitude about them, and
the scribes questioning
with them.

15. And straightway all the people,
when they beheldd him, were greatly
amazed, and running
to *him* saluted him.
16. **And he asked** the scribes,
What question ye with them?
17. **And one** of the multitude
answered and said, Master,
I have brought unto thee
my son, which hath a
dumb spirit;
18. And wheresoever he taketh him,
he teareth him: and he foameth, and
gnasheth with his teeth,
and pineth away:
and I spake to thy
disciples that they should
cast him out; and they
could not.
19. **He answereth** him, and saith,
O faithless generation, how long shall
I be with you? how long shall
I suffer you?
bring him unto me.
20. And they brought him unto him:
and when he saw him,
straightway
the spirit tare him; and he
fell on the ground,
and wallowed foaming.
21. **And he asked his father,**
How long is it ago
since this came unto him?
And he said, Of a child.
22. And ofttimes it hath cast him into
the fire, and into the waters, to
destroy him:
but if thou canst do any
thing, have compassion on us, and
help us.
23. **Jesus said** unto him, If thou
canst believe,
all things *are* possible to
him that believeth.
24. And straightway
the father of the child
cried out, and said with tears,
Lord, I believe;
help thou mine unbelief.
25. **When Jesus saw** that
the people
came running together,
he rebuked the foul spirit,
saying unto him,
***Thou* dumb and deaf spirit,**
I charge thee,
come out of him,
and enter no more into him.
26. **And *the spirit***
cried, and rent him sore, and
came out of him: and he
was as one dead; insomuch
that many said, He is dead.
27. **But Jesus**
took him by the hand, and
lifted him up; and he arose.
28. And when he was
come into the house,
his disciples asked
him privately,
Why could not we
cast him out?
29. **And he said** unto them,
This kind can come forth by
nothing, but by prayer
and fasting.
30. And they departed thence, and
passed through Galilee;
and he would not that any
man should know *it.*
31. **For he taught his**
disciples, and said unto them,
The Son of man is delivered
into the hands of men, and
they shall kill him; and
after that he is killed,
he shall rise the third day.
32. But they understood not that
saying, and were afraid to ask him.
33. **And he** came to Capernaum:
and being in the house he
asked them, What was it
that ye disputed among
yourselves by the way?
34. But they held their peace:
for by the way
they had disputed
among themselves,
who *should be*
the greatest.
35. **And he** sat down, and called the
twelve, and
saith unto them, If any man
desire to be first, *the same*
shall be last of all, and
servant of all.

■ 36. **And he took a child, and**
set him in the midst of them: and when
he had taken him in his arms, he
■ **said** unto them,
■ 37. **Whosoever shall**
■ **receive one** of such children
■ **in my name, receiveth me:**
■ **and** whosoever shall receive me,
receiveth not me, but
■ **him that sent me.**
■ 38. **And John answered** him,
saying, Master,
■ **we saw one casting out**
■ **devils in thy name,** and he
followeth not us:
■ **and we forbad him,**
■ **because he followeth**
■ **not us.**
■ 39. **But Jesus said, Forbid**
■ **him not:** for there is no man which
shall do a miracle in my name, that
can lightly speak evil of me.
40. For he that is not against us is on
our part.
■ 41. **For whosoever shall**
■ **give** you a cup of
■ **water** to drink
■ **in my name,** because ye belong
to Christ, verily I say unto you, he
■ **shall not lose his reward.**
■ 42. **And whosoever shall**
■ **offend** one of
■ ***these*** **little ones**
that believe in me,
■ **it is better** for him that a millstone
were hanged about his neck, and
■ **he were cast into the sea.**
■ 43. **And if thy hand offend**
■ **thee, cut it off: it is better**
for thee
■ **to enter into life maimed,**
■ **than having two hands to**
■ **go into hell,** into the fire that
never shall be quenched:
44. Where their worm dieth not, and
the fire is not quenched.
■ 45. **And if thy foot offend**
■ **thee, cut it off: it is better**
for thee to enter halt into life,
■ **than having two feet to be**
■ **cast into hell,** into the fire that
never shall be quenched:
46. Where their worm dieth not, and
the fire is not quenched.
■ 47. **And if thine eye offend**
■ **thee, pluck it out: it is better**
for thee to enter into the kingdom of
God with one eye,
■ **than having two eyes to be**
■ **cast into hell fire:**
■ 48. **Where their worm dieth**
■ **not, and the fire is**
■ **not quenched.**
49. For every one shall be salted with
fire, and every sacrifice shall be
salted with salt.
50. Salt *is* good: but if the salt have
lost his saltness, wherewith will ye
season it? Have salt in yourselves,
and have peace one with another.

CHAPTER 10

■ 1. **And** he arose from thence, and
cometh into the coasts of Judaea
■ **by the** farther side of
■ **Jordan:** and the people resort unto
him again; and, as he was wont,
■ **he taught** them again.
■ 2. **And the Pharisees**
came to him, and
■ **asked him, Is it lawful for a**
■ **man to put away** ***his*** **wife?**
tempting him.
■ 3. **And he answered**
and said unto them,
■ **What did Moses**
■ **command you?**
■ 4. **And they said,**
Moses suffered
■ **to write a bill**
■ **of divorcement,**
and to put *her* away.
■ 5. **And Jesus answered**
and said unto them,
■ **For the hardness of your**
■ **heart he wrote** you this precept.
■ 6. **But from the beginning**
of the creation
■ **God made them male**
■ **and female.**
7. For this cause shall a man leave his
father and mother,
and cleave to his wife;
■ 8. **And they twain shall be**
■ **one flesh:** so then they are no
more twain, but one flesh.

9. **What therefore God hath
joined together, let not man
put asunder.**
10. And in the house his disciples
asked him again of the same *matter.*
11. **And he saith** unto them,
**Whosoever shall put away
his wife, and marry
another, committeth
adultery** against her.
12. **And if a woman shall put
away her husband, and be
married to another, she
committeth adultery.**
13. **And they brought young
children** to him, that he should
touch them:
**and *his* disciples rebuked
those that brought *them.***
14. **But** when
Jesus saw *it,* he was much
displeased, and
said unto them,
**Suffer the little children to
come unto me,**
and forbid them not:
for of such is the kingdom
of God.
15. Verily I say unto you,
**Whosoever shall not
receive the kingdom** of God
**as a little child, he shall not
enter** therein.
16. **And he** took them up in his
arms, put *his* hands upon them, and
blessed them.
17. And when he was gone
forth into the way,
there came one
running, and kneeled to him,
and asked him, Good Master,
**what shall I do that I may
inherit eternal life?**
18. **And Jesus said** unto him,
Why callest thou me good? *there is*
none good but one, *that is,* God.
19. Thou knowest the
commandments,
Do not commit adultery,
Do not
kill, Do not
steal, Do not
**bear false witness, Defraud
not, Honour thy father
and mother.**
20. **And he** answered and
said unto him,
**Master, all these have I
observed** from my youth.
21. **Then Jesus**
beholding him loved him, and
said unto him,
One thing thou lackest:
go thy way,
**sell whatsoever thou hast,
and give to the poor,**
and thou shalt have treasure in
heaven: and come, take up the cross,
and follow me.
22. **And he was sad** at that
saying, and went away grieved:
**for he had great
possessions.**
23. **And Jesus**
looked round about, and
saith unto his disciples, How hardly
shall they that have riches enter into
the kingdom of God!
24. And the disciples were astonished
at his words. But Jesus answereth
again, and saith unto them, Children,
**how hard is it for them that
trust in riches to enter into
the kingdom of God!**
25. It is easier for a camel to go
through the eye of a needle, than for a
rich man to enter into
the kingdom of God.
26. **And they were
astonished** out of measure,
saying among themselves,
Who then can be saved?
27. **And Jesus** looking upon them
**saith, With men *it is*
impossible, but**
not with God: for
**with God all things
are possible.**
28. **Then Peter** began to
say unto him, Lo,
**we have left all, and have
followed thee.**
29. **And Jesus answered**
and said, Verily I say unto you,
**There is no man that hath
left house, or brethren,**

or sisters, or father, or mother,
or wife, or children,
or lands, for my sake,
and the gospel's,
30. **But he shall receive an**
hundredfold now in this
time, houses, and brethren, and
sisters, and mothers,
and children, and lands,
with persecutions; and in
the world to come
eternal life.
31. But many *that are* first shall be
last; and the last first.
32. **And** they were
in the way going up
to Jerusalem; and Jesus went
before them: and they were amazed;
and as they followed, they were
afraid. And
he took again the twelve, and
began to tell them what
things should happen
unto him,
33. ***Saying,*** Behold, we go up to
Jerusalem; and
the Son of man shall be
delivered unto the chief
priests, and unto the
scribes; and they shall
condemn him to death,
and shall deliver him to the Gentiles:
34. And they shall mock him, and shall
scourge him, and shall spit upon him,
and shall kill him:
and the third day he shall
rise again.
35. **And James and John,**
the sons of Zebedee,
come unto him,
saying, Master,
we would that thou shouldest
do for us whatsoever we
shall desire.
36. **And he said** unto them,
What would ye that I
should do for you?
37. **They said** unto him,
Grant unto us
that we may sit, one
on thy right hand,
and the other on thy
left hand, in thy glory.

38. **But Jesus said** unto them,
Ye know not what ye ask:
can ye drink of the cup that
I drink of? and be baptized with
the baptism that I am baptized with?
39. **And they said** unto him,
We can.
And Jesus said unto them,
Ye shall indeed drink of the
cup that I drink of; and with the
baptism that I am baptized withal shall
ye be baptized:
40. **But to sit on my right** hand
and on my
left hand is not mine to
give; but *it shall be given*
***to them* for whom**
it is prepared.
41. And when
the ten heard *it*, they
began to be much
displeased with
James and John.
42. **But Jesus**
called them *to him,* and
saith unto them, Ye know that they
which are accounted to rule over the
Gentiles exercise lordship over them;
and their great ones exercise
authority upon them.
43. But so shall it not be
among you: but
whosoever will be great
among you, shall be
your minister:
44. **And** whosoever of you will be
the chiefest, shall be
servant of all.
45. **For even the Son of man**
came not to be ministered unto, but
to minister, and to give his
life a ransom for many.
46. **And they came to**
Jericho: and as he went out of
Jericho with his disciples and a great
number of people,
blind Bartimaeus,
the son of Timaeus,
sat by the highway
side begging.
47. **And** when he heard that it was
Jesus of Nazareth,
he began to cry out, and say,

Jesus, *thou* son of David,
have mercy on me.
48. And many charged him that he
should hold his peace: but he cried
the more a great deal, *Thou* son of
David, have mercy on me.
49. **And Jesus** stood still, and
commanded him to be
called. And they call the blind man,
saying unto him, Be of good comfort,
rise; he calleth thee.
50. **And he,** casting away his
garment, rose, and
came to Jesus.
51. **And Jesus** answered and
said unto him,
What wilt thou that I should
do unto thee?
The blind man said unto him,
Lord, that I might receive
my sight.
52. **And Jesus said**
unto him, Go thy way;
thy faith hath made
thee whole.
And immediately he
received his sight,
and followed Jesus in the way.

CHAPTER 11

1. **And when they came nigh**
to Jerusalem, unto Bethphage and
Bethany, at
the mount of Olives, he
sendeth forth
two of his
disciples,
2. **And saith** unto them,
Go your way
into the village over against you:
and as soon as ye be entered into it,
ye shall find a colt tied,
whereon never man sat;
loose him, and bring *him.*
3. And if any man say unto you, Why
do ye this? say ye that the Lord hath
need of him; and straightway he will
send him hither.
4. **And they** went their way, and
found the colt tied by the door
without in a place
where two ways met;
and they loose him.
5. **And certain** of them
that stood there said
unto them,
What do ye, loosing the colt?
6. **And they said** unto them
even as Jesus had
commanded: and they
let them go.
7. **And they brought the colt**
to Jesus, and cast their
garments on him;
and he sat upon him.
8. **And many spread their**
garments in the way:
and others cut down
branches off the trees,
and strawed *them*
in the way.
9. **And they** that went before,
and they that followed,
cried, saying,
Hosanna; Blessed *is* he
that cometh in the name
of the Lord:
10. Blessed *be* the kingdom of our
father David, that cometh in the name
of the Lord: Hosanna in the highest.
11. **And Jesus entered** into
Jerusalem, and
into the temple: and
when he had
looked round
about upon all things,
and now the eventide was come, he
went out
unto Bethany with the twelve.
12. **And on the morrow,**
when they were come from Bethany,
he was hungry:
13. **And seeing a fig tree**
afar off having leaves,
he came, if haply he might find any
thing thereon:
and when he came to it, he
found nothing but leaves;
for the time of figs was not *yet.*
14. **And Jesus** answered and
said unto it, No man eat
fruit of thee hereafter
for ever. And his disciples heard *it.*
15. **And they come to**
Jerusalem: and Jesus
went into the temple, and

began to cast out them that
sold and bought in the
temple, and overthrew the tables of
the moneychangers, and the seats of
them that sold doves;
16. And would not suffer that any man
should carry *any* vessel
through the temple.
17. **And he taught, saying**
unto them, Is it not written,
My house shall be called
of all nations
the house of prayer? but ye
have made it a den
of thieves.
18. **And the scribes and**
chief priests heard *it,* and
sought how they might
destroy him: for they
feared him, because all the
people were astonished
at his doctrine.
19. And when even was come, he
went out of the city.
20. **And in the morning,**
as they passed by,
they saw the fig tree dried
up from the roots.
21. **And Peter**
calling to remembrance
saith unto him,
Master, behold,
the fig tree which thou
cursedst is withered away.
22. **And Jesus** answering
saith unto them,
Have faith in God.
23. **For** verily I say unto you, That
whosoever shall say unto
this mountain,
Be thou removed, and
be thou cast into the sea;
and shall not doubt in his
heart, but shall believe that those
things which he saith shall come to
pass; he
shall have whatsoever
he saith.
24. **Therefore I say** unto you,
What things soever ye
desire, when ye pray,
believe that ye receive *them,*
and ye shall have *them.*
25. **And when** ye stand
praying, forgive, if ye have
aught against any: that your Father
also which is in heaven may forgive
you your trespasses.
26. **But if ye do not forgive,**
neither will your Father
which is in heaven
forgive your trespasses.
27. **And they come again to**
Jerusalem: and
as he was walking in the temple,
there come to him
the chief priests, and the
scribes, and the elders,
28. **And say** unto him,
By what authority doest
thou these things? and who
gave thee this authority
to do these things?
29. **And Jesus answered**
and said unto them,
I will also ask of you one
question, and answer me, and I
will tell you by what authority I do
these things.
30. **The baptism of John,**
was *it* from heaven, or of
men? answer me.
31. **And they reasoned** with
themselves, saying,
If we shall say, From
heaven; he will say, Why
then did ye not
believe him?
32. **But if we shall say, Of**
men; they feared the people:
for all *men* counted John,
that he was
a prophet indeed.
33. **And they answered**
and said unto Jesus,
We cannot tell. And Jesus
answering saith unto them,
Neither do I tell you by what
authority I do these things.

CHAPTER 12

1. **And he began to speak**
unto them
by parables. A *certain*
man planted a vineyard,
and set an hedge about *it,*

and digged *a* *place for* the
winevat and built a tower,
and let it out
to husbandmen,
and went into a far country.
2. **And** at the season
he sent to the husbandmen
a servant, that he might
receive from the husbandmen of
the fruit of the vineyard.
3. **And they** caught *him,* and
beat him, and sent *him*
away empty.
4. **And again he sent** unto them
another servant; and at him
they cast stones, and
wounded *him* in the head,
and sent *him* away
shamefully handled.
5. **And again he sent**
another; and him they
killed, and many others;
beating some, and
killing some.
6. **Having** yet therefore
one son, his wellbeloved,
he sent him also last unto them,
saying, They will
reverence my son.
7. **But those husbandmen**
said among themselves,
This is the heir; come,
let us kill him, and the
inheritance shall be our's.
8. **And they** took him, and
killed *him,* and cast *him*
out of the vineyard.
9. **What shall therefore the**
lord of the vineyard do? he
will come and
destroy the husbandmen,
and will give the vineyard
unto others.
10. And have ye not read this
scripture; The stone which the
builders rejected is become the head
of the corner:
11. This was the Lord's doing, and it is
marvellous in our eyes?
12. **And they sought to lay**
hold on him,
but feared the people:
for they knew that he had
spoken the parable
against them:
and they left him, and went their way.
13. **And they send**
unto him certain of the
Pharisees and of the Herodians,
to catch him in *his* words.
14. **And** when they were come,
they say unto him,
Master, we know that thou
art true, and carest for no man: for
thou regardest not the person of men,
but teachest the way of God in truth:
Is it lawful to give tribute to
Caesar, or not?
15. Shall we give, or shall we not give?
But he, knowing their
hypocrisy, said unto them,
Why tempt ye me? bring me
a penny, that I may see *it.*
16. **And they brought *it.* And**
he saith unto them,
whose *is* this image and
superscription? And they
said unto him,
Caesar's.
17. **And Jesus** answering
said unto them,
Render to Caesar the
things that are Caesar's,
and to God the things that
are God's.
And they marvelled at him.
18. **Then come** unto him
the Sadducees,
which say there is no resurrection;
and they asked him, saying,
19. **Master, Moses wrote**
unto us,
If a man's brother die, and
leave *his*
wife *behind him,*
and leave
no children, that his
brother should take his
wife, and raise up seed
unto his brother.
20. **Now there were seven**
brethren: and the first took a wife,
and dying left no seed.
21. And the second took her, and
died, neither left he any seed: and the
third likewise.

22. **And the seven had her,**
and left no seed: last of all the
woman died also.
23. **In the resurrection**
therefore, when they shall rise,
whose wife shall she be of
them? for the seven had her to wife.
24. **And Jesus answering** said
unto them, Do ye not therefore err,
because ye know not the scriptures,
neither the power of God?
25. For
when they shall rise
from the dead,
they neither marry, nor are
given in marriage; but are
as the angels
which are in heaven.
26. **And as touching the**
dead, that they rise:
have ye not read in the book of
Moses, how in the bush God spake
unto him, saying, I *am* the God of
Abraham, and the God of Isaac, and
the God of Jacob?
27. **He is not the God of the**
dead, but the God
of the living:
ye therefore do greatly err.
28. **And one of the scribes**
came, and having heard them
reasoning together, and perceiving
that he had answered them well,
asked him, Which is the
first commandment of all?
29. **And Jesus answered** him,
The first of all the commandments *is*,
Hear, O Israel;
The Lord our God
is one Lord:
30. **And thou shalt love the**
Lord thy God with all thy
heart, and with all thy
soul, and with all thy
mind, and with all thy
strength: this
is the first commandment.
31. **And the second *is***
like, *namely* this,
Thou shalt love thy
neighbour as thyself.
There is none other commandment
greater than these.
32. **And the scribe said**
unto him, Well, Master,
thou hast said the truth: for
there is one God;
and there is none other but he:
33. **And to love him** with all the
heart, and with all the understanding,
and with all the soul,
and with all the strength,
and to love *his* neighbour
as himself,
is more than all whole
burnt offerings and sacrifices.
34. And when
Jesus saw that he answered
discreetly, he
said unto him,
Thou art not far from the
kingdom of God. And no man after
that durst ask him *any question*.
35. **And Jesus** answered and
said, while he taught in the temple,
How say the scribes that
Christ is the son of David?
36. **For David** himself
said by the Holy Ghost,
The LORD said to my Lord,
Sit thou on my right hand, till
I make thine enemies thy footstool.
37. **David** therefore himself
calleth him Lord; and
whence is he *then*
his son? And the common
people heard him gladly.
38. **And he said**
unto them in his doctrine,
Beware of the scribes,
which love to go in long
clothing, and *love*
salutations in the marketplaces,
39. **And the chief seats**
in the synagogues,
and the uppermost
rooms at feasts:
40. **Which devour widows'**
houses, and for a pretence
make long prayers: these
shall receive greater
damnation.
41. **And Jesus sat**
over against the treasury,
and beheld how the people
cast money into the

■ **treasury:** and many that were rich
cast in much.
42. And there came
■ **a certain poor widow,**
and she
■ **threw in two mites,**
which make a farthing.
■ 43. **And he** called *unto him* his
disciples, and
■ **saith** unto them,
Verily I say unto you, That
■ **this poor widow hath cast**
■ **more in, than all** they which
have cast into the treasury:
■ 44. **For all *they* did cast in of**
■ **their abundance; but she**
of her want did
■ **cast in all that she had,**
even all her living.

CHAPTER 13

■ 1. **And** as he went out of the temple,
■ **one of his disciples saith**
unto him,
■ **Master, see what manner**
■ **of** stones and what
■ **buildings** *are here!*
■ 2. **And Jesus answering**
■ **said** unto him,
■ **Seest thou these great**
■ **buildings? there shall not**
■ **be left one stone upon**
■ **another,** that shall
not be thrown down.
3. And as he sat upon the mount of
Olives over against the temple,
■ **Peter and James and John**
■ **and Andrew asked him**
privately,
■ 4. **Tell us, when shall these**
■ **things be?** and what *shall be* the
sign when all these things
shall be fulfilled?
■ 5. **And Jesus** answering them
■ **began to say,** Take heed lest
any *man* deceive you:
■ 6. **For many shall come in**
■ **my name,** saying, I am *Christ;*
■ **and shall deceive many.**
■ 7. **And when ye shall hear of**
■ **wars** and rumours of wars,
■ **be ye not troubled: for** *such*
things must needs be; but
■ **the end *shall* not *be* yet.**
■ 8. **For nation shall rise**
■ **against nation,** and kingdom
against kingdom:
■ **and there shall be**
■ **earthquakes** in divers places,
■ **and** there shall be
■ **famines** and troubles:
■ **these *are* the beginnings**
■ **of sorrows.**
■ 9. **But take heed** to yourselves:
■ **for they shall deliver you**
■ **up to councils;** and in the
synagogues ye shall be beaten: and
ye shall be brought before
rulers and kings
■ **for my sake,**
for a testimony against them.
■ 10. **And the gospel must first**
■ **be published among**
■ **all nations.**
■ 11. **But** when they shall lead *you,*
and deliver you up,
■ **take no thought** beforehand
■ **what ye shall speak,** neither
do ye premeditate: but whatsoever
shall be given you in that hour,
that speak ye:
■ **for it is not ye that speak,**
■ **but the Holy Ghost.**
■ 12. **Now the brother shall**
■ **betray the brother** to death,
and the father the son;
■ **and children** shall rise up against
■ ***their* parents, and shall**
■ **cause them to be**
■ **put to death.**
■ 13. **And ye shall be hated**
of all *men*
■ **for my name's sake: but he**
■ **that shall endure**
unto the end, the same
■ **shall be saved.**
■ 14. **But when ye shall see the**
■ **abomination of**
■ **desolation,** spoken of by Daniel
the prophet, standing where it ought
not, (let him that readeth understand,)
■ **then** let them that be in Judaea
■ **flee to the mountains:**
■ 15. **And let him that is on the**
■ **housetop not go down** into
the house, neither enter *therein,* to

take any thing out of his house:
16. **And let him that is in the field not turn back again for** to take up **his garment.**
17. **But woe to them** that are **with child,** and to them that give suck in those days!
18. **And pray** ye that **your flight be not in the winter.**
19. **For *in* those days shall be affliction,** such as was not from the beginning of the creation which God created unto this time, neither shall be.
20. **And except that the Lord had shortened those days, no flesh should be saved:** but for the elect's sake, whom he hath chosen, he hath shortened the days.
21. And then **if any man** shall **say** to you, Lo, **here *is* Christ;** or, lo, *he is* there; **believe *him* not:**
22. **For false Christs** and false prophets **shall rise,** and shall shew signs and wonders, **to seduce, if *it were* possible, even the elect.**
23. But take ye heed: behold, **I have foretold you all things.**
24. **But** in those days, **after that tribulation, the sun shall be darkened,** and the moon shall not give her light,
25. **And the stars** of heaven **shall fall, and the** powers that are in **heaven** shall be **shaken.**
26. **And then shall they see the Son of man coming** in the clouds with great power and glory.
27. **And** then shall he send **his angels,** and **shall gather** together **his elect** from the four winds, from the uttermost part of the earth to the uttermost part of heaven.
28. **Now learn a parable of the fig tree; When her branch** is yet tender, and **putteth forth leaves,** ye know that **summer is near:**
29. **So ye in like manner, when ye shall see these things** come to pass, **know that it is nigh,** *even* at the doors.
30. **Verily I say** unto you, that **this generation shall not pass, till all these things be done.**
31. **Heaven and earth shall pass away: but my words shall not** pass away.
32. **But of that day and** *that* **hour knoweth no man,** no, not the angels which are in heaven, **neither the Son, but the Father.**
33. Take ye heed, watch and pray: for ye know not when the time is.
34. ***For the Son of Man is* as a man taking a far journey, who** left his house, and **gave** authority to his servants, and **to every man his work,** and commanded the porter to watch.
35. **Watch ye therefore: for ye know not when the master** of the house **cometh,** at even, or at midnight, or at the cockcrowing, or in the morning:
36. **Lest coming suddenly he find you sleeping.**
37. And what I say unto you I say unto all, Watch.

CHAPTER 14

1. **After two days was** *the feast of* **the passover,** and of unleavened bread: **and the chief priests and the scribes sought how they might** take him by craft, and **put *him* to death.**
2. But they said, Not on the feast *day,* lest there be an uproar of the people.
3. **And being in Bethany**

in the house of Simon the leper,
as he sat at meat,
there came a woman
having an alabaster box of
ointment of spikenard very
precious; and she brake the box,
and poured *it* on his head.
4. And there were
some that had indignation
within themselves, and
said, Why was this waste of
the ointment made?
5. **For it might have**
been sold
for more than three hundred pence,
and have been
given to the poor.
And they murmured against her.
6. **And Jesus said,**
Let her alone; why trouble ye her?
she hath wrought a good
work on me.
7. **For ye have the poor**
with you
always, and whensoever ye will ye
may do them good:
but me ye have not always.
8. She hath done what she could:
she is come aforehand
to anoint my body
to the burying.
9. **Verily I say** unto you,
Wheresoever this gospel
shall be preached throughout
the whole world,
this also that she hath done
shall be spoken of for a
memorial of her.
10. **And Judas Iscariot,**
one of the twelve,
went unto the chief priests,
to betray him unto them.
11. **And** when they heard *it,*
they were glad, and
promised to give
him money. And he sought how
he might conveniently betray him.
12. **And the** first day of unleavened
bread, when they killed
the passover, his
disciples said unto him,
Where wilt thou that we
go and
prepare that thou mayest eat
the passover?
13. **And he sendeth forth two**
of his disciples, and saith
unto them,
Go ye into the city, and there shall
meet you
a man bearing
a pitcher of water:
follow him.
14. **And** wheresoever he shall go in,
say ye to the goodman of the house,
The Master saith,
Where is the
guestchamber, where I
shall eat the passover with
my disciples?
15. **And he will shew you a**
large upper room
furnished *and* prepared:
there make ready for us.
16. And his disciples went forth, and
came into the city, and found as he
had said unto them: and they made
ready the passover.
17. **And in the evening**
he cometh with the twelve.
18. And as
they sat and did eat, Jesus
said, Verily I say unto you,
One of you which eateth with me
shall betray me.
19. **And they began**
to be sorrowful, and
to say
unto him one by one,
***Is* it I?** and another *said, Is* it I?
20. **And he answered**
and said unto them,
***It is* one** of the twelve,
that dippeth with me
in the dish.
21. The Son of man indeed goeth,
as it is written of him: but
woe to that man by whom the
Son of man is betrayed!
good were it for that man
if he had never been born.
22. **And** as they did eat,
Jesus took bread, and
blessed, and brake *it,*
and gave to them,
and said, Take, eat:

this is my body.
23. **And he took the cup, and**
when he had given thanks,
he gave *it* to them: and
they all drank of it.
24. **And he said** unto them,
This is my blood
of the new testament,
which is shed for many.
25. **Verily** I say unto you,
I will drink no more
of the fruit of the vine,
until that day that
I drink it new in the
kingdom of God.
26. **And when they had sung**
an hymn, they went out into
the mount of Olives.
27. **And Jesus saith** unto them,
All ye shall be offended
because of me this night: for
it is written, I will smite the shepherd,
and the sheep shall be scattered.
28. But after that I am risen, I will go
before you into Galilee.
29. **But Peter said** unto him,
Although all shall be
offended, yet *will* not I.
30. **And Jesus saith** unto him,
Verily I say unto thee, That this day,
even in
this night, before the cock
crow twice, thou shalt deny
me thrice.
31. But he spake the more
vehemently, If I should die with thee, I
will not deny thee in any wise.
Likewise also said they all.
32. **And they came to**
a place which was named
Gethsemane: and he saith
to his disciples,
Sit ye here, while
I shall pray.
33. **And he taketh** with him
Peter and James and John,
and began to be sore amazed, and to
be very heavy;
34. **And saith** unto them,
My soul is exceeding
sorrowful unto death:
tarry ye here, and watch.
35. **And he went forward**
a little,
and fell on the ground, and
prayed that, if it were possible, the
hour might pass from him.
36. And he said, Abba,
Father, all things
are possible unto thee;
take away this cup from
me: nevertheless not what I
will, but what thou wilt.
37. **And he cometh, and**
findeth them sleeping, and
saith unto Peter, Simon,
sleepest thou?
couldest not thou watch
one hour?
38. **Watch ye and pray,** lest ye
enter into temptation. The spirit truly
is ready, but the flesh *is* weak.
39. **And again he** went away, and
prayed, and spake
the same words.
40. **And when he returned,**
he found them asleep
again, (for their eyes were heavy,)
neither wist they what to answer him.
41. **And he cometh the third**
time, and saith unto them,
Sleep on now, and take *your*
rest: it is enough,
the hour is come; behold, the
Son of man is betrayed into the hands
of sinners.
42. Rise up, let us go; lo,
he that betrayeth me
is at hand.
43. **And immediately,**
while he yet spake,
cometh Judas,
one of the twelve,
and with him a great
multitude with swords and staves,
from the chief priests and the scribes
and the elders.
44. **And he** that betrayed him
had given them a token,
saying, Whomsoever I
shall kiss, that same is he;
take him,
and lead *him* away safely.
45. **And** as soon as he was come,
he goeth straightway
to him, and

saith, Master, master; and
kissed him.
46. **And they**
laid their hands on him, and
took him.
47. **And one** of them that stood by
drew a sword, and smote a
servant of the high priest,
and cut off his ear.
48. **And Jesus** answered and
said unto them,
Are ye come out, as
against a thief,
with swords and *with* staves
to take me?
49. **I was daily** with you
in the temple teaching,
and ye took me not:
but the scriptures
must be fulfilled.
50. **And they all** forsook him, and
fled.
51. And there followed him a certain
young man, having a linen cloth cast
about *his* naked *body;* and the young
men laid hold on him:
52. And he left the linen cloth, and fled
from them naked.
53. **And they led Jesus**
away to the high priest: and
with him were assembled all the chief
priests and the elders
and the scribes.
54. **And Peter followed him**
afar off, even into the palace of the
high priest:
and he sat with the
servants, and warmed
himself at the fire.
55. **And the chief priests** and
all the council
sought for witness against
Jesus to put him to death;
and found none.
56. **For many bare false**
witness against him,
but their witness agreed
not together.
57. **And there arose certain,**
and bare false witness against him,
saying,
58. **We heard him say, I will**
destroy this temple that is
made with hands,
and within three days I will
build another made
without hands.
59. But neither so did their witness
agree together.
60. **And the high priest**
stood up in the midst, and
asked Jesus, saying,
Answerest thou nothing?
what *is it which* these
witness against thee?
61. **But he held his peace,**
and answered nothing.
Again the high priest asked
him, and said unto him,
Art thou the Christ,
the Son of the Blessed?
62. **And Jesus said, I am:**
and ye shall see the Son of
man sitting on the right
hand of power, and
coming in the clouds
of heaven.
63. **Then the high priest rent**
his clothes, and saith, What
need we any further witnesses?
64. **Ye have heard the**
blasphemy: what think ye?
And they all condemned
him to be guilty of
death.
65. **And some began** to spit on
him, and to cover his face, and
to buffet him, and to say unto
him, Prophesy:
and the servants did
strike him
with the palms of their hands.
66. **And** as Peter was beneath in the
palace, there cometh
one of the maids of
the high priest:
67. And when she
saw Peter warming himself,
she looked upon him,
and said, And
thou also
wast with Jesus of Nazareth.
68. **But he denied,** saying, I know
not, neither understand I what thou
sayest. And he went out
into the porch;

and the cock crew.
69. **And a maid saw him**
again, and began to say to them
that stood by,
This is *one* of them.
70. **And he denied it again.**
And a little after,
they that stood by said
again to Peter,
Surely thou art *one* of them:
for thou art a Galilaean, and thy
speech agreeth *thereto.*
71. **But he began to curse**
and to swear,
***saying,* I know not this man**
of whom ye speak.
72. **And the second time the**
cock crew. And Peter
called to mind the word
that Jesus said unto him, Before
the cock crow twice, thou shalt deny
me thrice.
And when he thought thereon,
he wept.

CHAPTER 15

1. **And** straightway in the morning
the chief priests
held a consultation with the
elders and scribes
and the whole council, and
bound Jesus,
and carried *him* away,
and delivered *him*
to Pilate.
2. **And Pilate asked** him,
Art thou the King of the
Jews? And
he answering
said unto him,
Thou sayest *it.*
3. **And the chief priests**
accused him of many
things: but he answered nothing.
4. And Pilate asked him again, saying,
Answerest thou nothing? behold how
many things they witness
against thee.
5. **But Jesus** yet
answered nothing; so
that Pilate marvelled.
6. **Now at *that* feast he**
released unto them
one prisoner, whomsoever
they desired.
7. **And there was *one***
named Barabbas, *which lay*
bound with them that had made
insurrection with him,
who had committed
murder in the insurrection.
8. And the multitude crying aloud
began to desire *him to do* as he had
ever done unto them.
9. But
Pilate answered them, saying,
Will ye that I release unto you
the King of the Jews?
10. For he knew that the chief priests
had delivered him for envy.
11. **But the chief priests**
moved the people, that he
should rather
release Barabbas unto them.
12. **And Pilate answered** and
said again unto them,
What will ye then that I shall
do *unto* *him* whom ye call
the King of the Jews?
13. **And they cried** out again,
Crucify him.
14. **Then Pilate said** unto them,
Why, what evil hath he
done? And they cried out
the more exceedingly,
Crucify him.
15. **And *so* Pilate,**
willing to content the people,
released Barabbas
unto them,
and delivered Jesus, when
he had scourged *him,* to be crucified.
16. **And the soldiers led him**
away
into the hall, called
Praetorium; and they call
together the whole band.
17. **And they clothed him**
with purple, and platted a
crown of thorns, and put it
about his *head,*
18. And began to salute him, Hail,
King of the Jews!
19. And they smote him on the head
with a reed, and did spit upon him, and
bowing *their* knees worshipped him.

20. **And when they had**
mocked him, they took off the
purple from him, and put his own
clothes on him, and
led him out to crucify him.
21. **And they compel one**
Simon a Cyrenian, who passed
by, coming out of the country, the
father of Alexander and Rufus,
to bear his cross.
22. **And they bring him unto**
the place
Golgotha, which is, being
interpreted, The place of a skull.
23. **And they gave him** to drink
wine mingled with myrrh:
but he received *it* not.
24. **And when they had**
crucified him, they parted
his garments, casting lots
upon them, what every
man should take.
25. **And** it was the third hour, and
they crucified him.
26. **And the superscription**
of his accusation
was written over,
THE KING OF THE JEWS.
27. **And with him they crucify**
two thieves; the one on his right
hand, and the other on his left.
28. **And the scripture was**
fulfilled, which saith, And
he was numbered with
the transgressors.
29. **And they that passed by**
railed on him,
wagging their heads, and
saying, Ah, thou that destroyest
the temple, and buildest *it* in
three days,
30. **Save thyself, and come**
down from the cross.
31. **Likewise also the chief**
priests mocking said
among themselves with the scribes,
He saved others; himself
he cannot save.
32. Let Christ the King of Israel
descend now from the cross, that we
may see and believe. And they that
were crucified with him reviled him.
33. And when
the sixth hour was come,
there was darkness over
the whole land until the
ninth hour.
34. **And at the ninth hour**
Jesus cried with a loud voice,
saying, Eloi, Eloi, lama sabachthani?
which is, being interpreted,
My God, my God, why hast
thou forsaken me?
35. And some of them that stood by,
when they heard *it,* said, Behold, he
calleth Elias.
36. **And one ran and filled a**
sponge full of vinegar,
and put *it* on a reed,
and gave him to drink,
saying, Let alone;
let us see whether Elias will
come to
take him down.
37. **And Jesus cried with a**
loud voice, and gave up
the ghost.
38. **And the veil of the temple**
was rent in twain
from the top to the bottom.
39. **And when the centurion,**
which stood over against him,
saw that he so
cried out, and gave up the ghost,
he said, Truly this man was
the Son of God.
40. **There were also women**
looking on afar off:
among whom was
Mary Magdalene, and
Mary the mother of James
the less and of
Joses, and Salome;
41. **(Who** also, when he was in
Galilee,
followed him, and
ministered unto him;)
and many other women which came up
with him unto Jerusalem.
42. And now when the even was
come, because it was the preparation,
that is, the day before the sabbath,
43. **Joseph** of Arimathaea,
an honourable counsellor,
which also waited for the kingdom of
God, came, and

went in boldly
unto Pilate, and craved the
body of Jesus.
44. **And Pilate** marvelled if he were
already dead: and calling *unto him* the
centurion, he asked him whether he
had been any while dead.
45. And when he knew *it* of the
centurion, he
gave the body to Joseph.
46. **And he bought fine linen,**
and took him down,
and wrapped him in the linen,
and laid him in a sepulchre
which was hewn out of a rock,
and rolled a stone unto the
door of the sepulchre.
47. And Mary Magdalene and Mary *the*
mother of Joses beheld where
he was laid.

CHAPTER 16

1. And when the sabbath was past,
Mary Magdalene, and
Mary the *mother* of James,
and Salome, had bought sweet
spices, that they might come and
anoint him.
2. And very early in the morning the
first *day* of the week, they
came unto the sepulchre
at the rising of the sun.
3. **And they said**
among themselves,
Who shall roll us away the
stone from the door
of the sepulchre?
4. **And** when they looked,
they saw that the stone was
rolled away:
for it was very great.
5. **And entering**
into the sepulchre,
they saw a young man
sitting on the right side,
clothed in a long white
garment; and they were affrighted.
6. **And he saith** unto them,
Be not affrighted:
Ye seek Jesus
of Nazareth, which was crucified:
he is risen; he is not here:
behold the place where they laid him.
7. But go your way,
tell his disciples and Peter
that he goeth before you
into Galilee: there shall ye
see him, as he said unto you.
8. **And they went**
out quickly,
and fled from the sepulchre; for they
trembled and were amazed: neither
said they any thing to any *man;*
for they were afraid.
9. Now when
Jesus was risen early the first *day* of
the week, he
appeared first to Mary
Magdalene, out of whom he had
cast seven devils.
10. ***And* she** went and
told them that had
been with him,
as they mourned and wept.
11. **And they,** when they had heard
that he was alive, and had
been seen of her,
believed not.
12. **After that he appeared in**
another form unto two of
them, as they walked,
and went into the country.
13. **And they** went and
told *it* unto
the residue: neither
believed they them.
14. **Afterward he appeared**
unto the eleven
as they sat at meat,
and upbraided them with their
unbelief and hardness of heart,
because they believed not
them which had seen him
after he was risen.
15. **And he said** unto them,
Go ye into all the world,
and preach the gospel to
every creature.
16. **He that believeth**
and is baptized
shall be saved; but he that
believeth not shall be damned.
17. And these
signs shall follow them that
believe; In my name shall they
cast out devils; they shall speak with

new tongues;
18. They shall take up serpents; and if they drink any deadly thing, it shall not hurt them; they shall lay hands on the sick, and they shall recover.
19. **So then after the Lord had spoken** unto them, **he was received up** into heaven, **and sat on the right hand of God.**
20. **And they went forth,** and **preached every where, the Lord** working with *them,* and **confirming the word with signs** following. **Amen.**

THE GOSPEL ACCORDING TO LUKE

BACKGROUND INFORMATION

Author – Luke, physician and Gentile companion of Paul
Date Written – probably **between 60** and **80** A.D.

Number of:
Verses - 1,151
Chapters - 24
Total Words - 25,944
Scan Words - 12,707
Scan Words represent 48 % of Total Words.

Theme – written to reveal that Jesus is **The Son of God** in a way that would appeal **to the Gentile world.**

OUTLINE OF THE GOSPEL

I. **Christ's birth narratives** and early years.
Chapters 1—2
II. **Christ's preparation for his ministry.**
Chapters 3—4
III. **Christ's Galilaean ministry** including sermon at Nazareth.
Chapters 4—9
IV. **Christ's journey to Jerusalem** including resurrection of Lazarus and conversion of Zacchaeus.
Chapters 9—19
V. **Christ's crucifixion, resurrection, and ascension.**
Chapters 19—24

CHAPTER 1

1. **Forasmuch as many**
have taken in hand to
set forth in order
a declaration of those
things which are most surely
believed among us,
2. **Even** as they delivered
them unto us,
which from the beginning
were eyewitnesses, and
ministers of the word;
3. **It seemed good** to me also,
having had perfect understanding of
all things from the very first,
to write unto thee in order,
most excellent Theophilus,
4. **That thou mightest know**
the certainty of those
things, wherein thou hast
been instructed.
5. **There was** in the days of Herod,
the king of Judaea,
a certain priest named
Zacharias, of the course of Abia:
and his wife *was* of the daughters
of Aaron, and her name *was*
Elisabeth.
6. **And they were both**
righteous before God, walking in
all the commandments and
ordinances of the Lord blameless.
7. **And** they had no child,
because that
Elisabeth was barren, and
they both were *now*
well stricken in years.
8. **And** it came to pass, that
while he executed the
priest's office before God in the
order of his course,
9. According to the custom of the
priest's office,
his lot was to burn incense
when he went into the
temple of the Lord.
10. **And the whole multitude**
of the people
were praying without
at the time of incense.
11. **And there appeared**
unto him
an angel of the Lord standing on
the right side of the altar of incense.
12. **And when Zacharias**
saw *him*, he was troubled, and
fear fell upon him.
13. **But the angel said** unto him,
Fear not, Zacharias: for thy prayer
is heard; and
thy wife Elisabeth shall
bear thee a son, and thou
shalt call his name John.
14. **And** thou shalt have joy and
gladness; and
many shall rejoice
at his birth.
15. **For he shall be great**
in the sight of the Lord, and shall drink
neither wine nor strong drink;
and he shall be
filled with the Holy Ghost,
even from his mother's womb.
16. **And many**
of the children of Israel
shall he turn to the Lord
their God.
17. **And he shall go before**
him in the spirit and power
of Elias, to turn the hearts of the
fathers to the children, and the
disobedient to the wisdom of the just;
to make ready a people
prepared for the Lord.
18. **And Zacharias said**
unto the angel,
Whereby shall I know this?
for I am an old man, and my wife well
stricken in years.
19. **And the angel** answering
said unto him,
I am Gabriel, that stand in the
presence of God;
and am sent to speak
unto thee, and to shew thee
these glad tidings.
20. **And, behold, thou shalt**
be dumb, and not able to speak,
until the day that these things
shall be performed,
because thou believest not
my words, which shall be fulfilled
in their season.
21. **And the people**
waited for Zacharias, and
marvelled that he tarried

so long in the temple.
22. **And when he came out,**
he could not speak unto them: and
they perceived that he had
seen a vision in the temple:
for he beckoned unto them,
and remained speechless.
23. And it came to pass, that, as soon
as the days of his ministration were
accomplished, he departed to his own
house.
24. **And** after those days his wife
Elisabeth conceived, and
hid herself five months,
saying,
25. Thus hath the Lord dealt with me in
the days wherein he looked on *me*, to
take away my reproach among men.
26. **And in the sixth month**
the angel
Gabriel was sent from God
unto a city of Galilee, named
Nazareth,
27. **To a virgin** espoused to a man
whose name was Joseph, of the
house of David; and the virgin's
name *was* Mary.
28. **And the angel**
came in unto her, and
said, Hail, *thou that art* highly
favoured, the Lord *is* with thee:
blessed *art* thou
among women.
29. **And** when she saw *him*,
she was troubled at his
saying, and cast in her mind what
manner of
salutation this should be.
30. **And the angel said**
unto her,
Fear not, Mary: for thou
hast found favour
with God.
31. **And,** behold,
thou shalt conceive
in thy womb,
and bring forth a son, and
shalt call his name JESUS.
32. **He shall be** great, and shall be
called the Son of the
Highest: and the Lord God shall
give unto him the throne
of his father David:
33. **And** he shall reign over the
house of Jacob for ever; and
of his kingdom there shall
be no end.
34. **Then said Mary**
unto the angel,
How shall this be, seeing I
know not a man?
35. **And the angel answered**
and said unto her,
The Holy Ghost shall come
upon thee, and the power of the
Highest shall overshadow thee:
therefore also
that holy thing
which shall be born of thee
shall be called the Son of
God.
36. **And, behold, thy cousin**
Elisabeth, she
hath also conceived
a son in her old age: and this is the
sixth month with her,
who was called barren.
37. For with God nothing
shall be impossible.
38. **And Mary said,** Behold the
handmaid of the Lord;
be it unto me according to
thy word. And the angel
departed from her.
39. **And Mary arose**
in those days,
and went into the hill country
with haste, into a city of
Juda;
40. **And entered** into
the house of Zacharias,
and saluted Elisabeth.
41. **And** it came to pass, that,
when Elisabeth heard the
salutation of Mary, the
babe leaped in her womb;
and Elisabeth was filled
with the Holy Ghost:
42. **And she spake**
out with a loud voice, and said,
Blessed *art* thou
among women,
and blessed *is* the fruit of thy womb.
43. **And whence *is* this to me,**
that the mother of my Lord
should come to me?

44. For, lo, as soon as the voice of thy
salutation sounded in mine ears, the
babe leaped in my womb for joy.
45. And blessed *is* she that believed:
for there shall be a performance of
those things which were told her from
the Lord.
46. **And Mary said, My soul**
doth magnify the Lord,
47. **And my spirit hath**
rejoiced in God
my Saviour.
48. For he hath regarded the low
estate of his handmaiden: for, behold,
from henceforth all
generations shall
call me blessed.
49. For he that is mighty hath done to
me great things; and holy *is* his name.
50. **And his mercy *is* on them**
that fear him
from generation to generation.
51. He hath shewed strength with his
arm; he hath scattered the proud in
the imagination of their hearts.
52. **He hath** put down the mighty
from *their* seats, and
exalted them of
low degree.
53. He hath filled the hungry
with good things;
and the rich he hath sent
empty away.
54. He hath holpen his servant Israel,
in remembrance of *his* mercy;
55. As he spake to our fathers, to
Abraham, and to his seed for ever.
56. **And Mary abode with**
her about three months,
and returned to her own house.
57. **Now Elisabeth's full time**
came that she should be delivered;
and she brought
forth a son.
58. **And her neighbours**
and her cousins heard how the Lord
had shewed great mercy upon her;
and they
rejoiced with her.
59. *And* it came to pass, that
on the eighth day they
came to circumcise the
child; and they
called him Zacharias,
after the name of his father.
60. **And his mother**
answered and
said, Not *so;* but he shall
be called John.
61. And they said unto her, There is
none of thy kindred that is
called by this name.
62. **And they made signs to**
his father, how he would
have him called.
63. **And he asked for a**
writing table, and wrote,
saying,
His name is John.
And they marvelled all.
64. **And his mouth was**
opened immediately, and his
tongue *loosed,*
and he spake,
and praised God.
65. **And** fear came on all that dwelt
round about them: and all
these sayings were noised
abroad throughout
all the hill country of
Judaea.
66. And all they that heard *them* laid
them up in their hearts, saying,
What manner of child shall
this be! And the hand
of the Lord was with him.
67. **And** his father
Zacharias was filled with
the Holy Ghost, and
prophesied, saying,
68. **Blessed *be* the Lord**
God of Israel;
for he hath visited and
redeemed his people,
69. **And hath raised up an**
horn of salvation for us in the
house of his servant David;
70. **As he spake by** the mouth of
his holy prophets, which have
been since the world began:
71. **That we should be**
saved from our enemies, and from
the hand of all that hate us;
72. To perform the mercy
promised to our fathers,
and to remember

his holy covenant;
73. The oath which he sware to our
father Abraham,
74. That he would grant unto us,
that we being delivered out of the
hand of our enemies
might serve him
without fear,
75. **In holiness and**
righteousness before him,
all the days of our life.
76. **And thou, child,**
shalt be called the prophet of the
Highest: for thou
shalt go before the face of
the Lord to prepare
his ways;
77. **To give knowledge of**
salvation unto his people
by the remission of
their sins,
78. Through the tender mercy of our
God; whereby the dayspring from on
high hath visited us,
79. **To give light to them** that sit
in darkness and
in the shadow of death,
to guide our feet
into the way of peace.
80. **And the child grew, and**
waxed strong in spirit, and
was in the deserts till
the day of
his shewing unto Israel.

CHAPTER 2

1. **And** it came to pass in those
days, that
there went out a decree
from Caesar Augustus that
all the world should
be taxed.
2. (*And* this taxing was first made
when Cyrenius was governor of
Syria.)
3. **And all went to be taxed,**
every one
into his own city.
4. **And Joseph also went**
up from Galilee, out of the city of
Nazareth, into Judaea,
unto the city of
David, which is called
Bethlehem; (because he was of
the house and lineage of David:)
5. **To be taxed with Mary**
his espoused wife,
being great with child.
6. **And** so it was, that,
while they were
there, the days were
accomplished that
she should be delivered.
7. And she
brought forth her
firstborn son, and wrapped him
in swaddling clothes,
and laid him in a manger;
because there was no
room for them in the inn.
8. **And there were**
in the same country
shepherds abiding in the field,
keeping watch over their
flock by night.
9. **And, lo, the angel of the**
Lord came upon them, and
the glory of the Lord shone round
about them: and they
were sore afraid.
10. **And** the angel
said unto them,
Fear not: for, behold,
I bring you good tidings
of great joy,
which shall be to all people.
11. **For unto you is born**
this day in the city of David
a Saviour,
which is Christ the Lord.
12. **And** this *shall be* a sign unto you;
Ye shall find the babe
wrapped in swaddling clothes,
lying in a manger.
13. **And suddenly**
there was with the angel a multitude of
the heavenly host praising
God, and saying,
14. **Glory to God in the**
highest, and on earth
peace, good
will toward men.
15. **And** it came to pass, as the
angels were gone away from them into
heaven,
the shepherds said

one to another,
Let us now go
even unto Bethlehem,
and see this thing
which is come to pass,
which the Lord hath made
known unto us.
16. **And they came** with haste,
and found Mary, and Joseph, and
the babe lying in a manger.
17. **And** when they had seen *it,*
they made known abroad
the saying which was
told them concerning
this child.
18. **And all they that heard *it***
wondered at those things which
were told them by the shepherds.
19. **But Mary kept all these**
things, and pondered *them*
in her heart.
20. **And the shepherds**
returned, glorifying and
praising God for all the things
that they had heard and seen, as it
was told unto them.
21. **And when eight days**
were accomplished for the
circumcising of the child,
his name was called
JESUS, which was so named
of the angel before he was
conceived in the womb.
22. **And** when the days of her
purification according to the law of
Moses were accomplished,
they brought him to
Jerusalem, to present *him*
to the Lord;
23. (As it is written in the law of the
LORD, Every male that openeth the
womb shall be called holy to the Lord;)
24. **And to offer a sacrifice**
according to that which
is said in the law
of the Lord,
A pair of turtledoves, or
two young pigeons.
25. **And, behold, there was**
a man in Jerusalem, whose
name *was* Simeon; and the
same man *was* just and devout,
waiting for the consolation of Israel:
and the Holy Ghost was upon him.
26. And it was revealed unto him by
the Holy Ghost, that he should not
see death, before he had seen the
Lord's Christ.
27. **And he came by the**
Spirit into the temple: and
when the parents brought
in the child Jesus, to do for him
after the custom of the law,
28. **Then took he him up in**
his arms, and blessed
God, and said,
29. **Lord, now lettest thou thy**
servant depart in peace,
according to thy word:
30. **For mine eyes have seen**
thy salvation,
31. Which thou hast prepared before
the face of all people;
32. A light to lighten the Gentiles, and
the glory of thy people Israel.
33. **And Joseph and his**
mother marvelled at those
things which were spoken of him.
34. **And Simeon**
blessed them, and
said unto Mary his mother,
Behold, this *child* is set for
the fall and rising again of
many in Israel; and for a sign which
shall be spoken against;
35. (Yea, a sword shall pierce through
thy own soul also,)
that the thoughts of many
hearts may be revealed.
36. **And there was one Anna,**
a prophetess, the daughter of
Phanuel, of the tribe of Aser: she was
of a great age, and had lived with
an husband seven years from
her virginity;
37. And she *was* a widow of about
fourscore and four years,
which departed not from
the temple, but served *God*
with fastings and prayers
night and day.
38. **And she** coming in that instant
gave thanks
likewise unto the Lord,
and spake of him to all
them that looked for

redemption in Jerusalem.
39. **And** when they had performed
all things according to the law
of the Lord,
they returned into Galilee,
to their own city Nazareth.
40. **And the child grew, and**
waxed strong in spirit,
filled with wisdom:
and the grace of God
was upon him.
41. Now his parents went to
Jerusalem every year at the feast of
the passover.
42. **And when he was twelve**
years old, they went
up to Jerusalem
after the custom of the feast.
43. **And** when they had fulfilled the
days, as they returned, the child
Jesus tarried behind
in Jerusalem;
and Joseph and his
mother knew not *of it*.
44. **But they,** supposing him to have
been in the company,
went a day's journey; and
they
sought him among *their* kinsfolk
and acquaintance.
45. **And** when they
found him not, they turned back
again to Jerusalem, seeking him.
46. **And** it came to pass, that
after three days they found
him in the temple, sitting in
the midst of the doctors,
both hearing them,
and asking
them questions.
47. And all that heard him were
astonished at his understanding
and answers.
48. **And** when they saw him,
they were amazed: and his
mother said unto him,
Son, why hast thou
thus dealt with us?
behold, thy father and
I have sought
thee sorrowing.
49. **And he said** unto them,
How is it that ye sought me?
wist ye not that I
must be about my
Father's business?
50. **And they understood not**
the saying which he spake unto them.
51. **And he went down**
with them, and came
to Nazareth, and was
subject unto them:
but his mother kept all these
sayings in her heart.
52. **And Jesus increased in**
wisdom and stature, and in
favour with God and man.

CHAPTER 3

1. **Now in the fifteenth year**
of the reign of Tiberius
Caesar, Pontius Pilate being
governor of Judaea, and Herod being
tetrarch of Galilee, and his brother
Philip tetrarch of Ituraea and of the
region of Trachonitis, and Lysanias
the tetrarch of Abilene,
2. Annas and Caiaphas
being the high priests,
the word of God came unto
John the son of Zacharias
in the wilderness.
3. **And he came**
into all the country
about Jordan, preaching
the baptism of repentance
for the remission of sins;
4. **As it is written**
in the book of the words of
Esaias the prophet, saying,
The voice of one crying in
the wilderness, Prepare ye
the way of the Lord,
make his paths straight.
5. Every valley shall be filled, and
every mountain and hill shall be
brought low; and the crooked shall be
made straight, and the rough ways
shall be made smooth;
6. **And all flesh shall see the**
salvation of God.
7. **Then said he to the**
multitude that came forth
to be baptized of him,
O generation of vipers,
who hath warned you to flee from the

wrath to come?
8. **Bring forth** therefore
fruits worthy of repentance,
and begin not to say within
yourselves, We have Abraham
to *our* father:
for I say unto you, That God is able
of these stones to raise up children
unto Abraham.
9. And now also the axe is laid unto
the root of the trees:
every tree therefore which
bringeth not forth good fruit
is hewn down, and cast
into the fire.
10. **And the people asked**
him, saying,
What shall we do then?
11. **He answereth**
and saith unto them,
He that hath two coats,
let him
impart to him that hath
none; and he that hath meat,
let him do likewise.
12. **Then came also**
publicans to be baptized,
and said unto him,
Master, what shall we do?
13. **And he said** unto them,
Exact no more than that
which is appointed you.
14. **And the soldiers**
likewise demanded
of him, saying, And
what shall we do? And he
said unto them,
Do violence to no man,
neither accuse *any* falsely; and be
content with your wages.
15. **And as the people were**
in expectation, and all men
mused in their hearts of John,
whether he were the Christ,
or not;
16. **John answered,** saying
unto *them* all, I indeed baptize
you with water; but
one mightier than I cometh,
the latchet of
whose shoes I am not
worthy to unloose: he shall
baptize you with the Holy
Ghost and with fire:
17. Whose fan *is* in his hand,
and he will
throughly purge his floor, and will
gather the wheat into his
garner; but the chaff he will
burn with fire unquenchable.
18. And many other things in his
exhortation preached
he unto the people.
19. **But Herod** the tetrarch,
being reproved by him for
Herodias
his brother Philip's wife,
and for all the
evils which Herod had
done,
20. Added yet this above all, that he
shut up John in prison.
21. **Now** when all the people
were baptized,
it came to pass, that Jesus
also being baptized,
and praying, the
heaven was
opened,
22. **And the Holy Ghost**
descended in a bodily shape
like a dove upon him, and
a voice came from heaven, which
said, Thou art my beloved
Son; in thee I am
well pleased.
23. And Jesus himself began to be
about thirty years of age, being (as
was supposed) the son of Joseph,
which was *the son* of Heli,
24. Which was *the son* of Matthat,
which was *the son* of Levi, which was
the son of Melchi, which was *the son*
of Janna, which was *the son* of
Joseph,
25. Which was *the son* of Mattathias,
which was *the son* of Amos, which was
the son of Naum, which was *the son* of
Esli, which was *the son* of Nagge,
26. Which was *the son* of Maath,
which was *the son* of Mattathias,
which was *the son* of Semei, which
was *the son* of Joseph, which was *the*
son of Juda,
27. Which was *the son* of Joanna,
which was *the son* of Rhesa, which

was *the son* of Zorobabel, which was *the son* of Salathiel, which was *the son* of Neri,
28. Which was *the son* of Melchi, which was *the son* of Addi, which was *the son* of Cosam, which was *the son* of Elmodam, which was *the son* of Er,
29. Which was *the son* of Jose, which was *the son* of Eliezer, which was *the son* of Jorim, which was *the son* of Matthat, which was *the son* of Levi,
30. Which was *the son* of Simeon, which was *the son* of Juda, which was *the son* of Joseph, which was *the son* of Jonan, which was *the son* of Eliakim,
31. Which was *the son* of Melea, which was *the son* of Menan, which was *the son* of Mattatha, which was *the son* of Nathan, which was *the son* of David,
32. Which was *the son* of Jesse, which was *the son* of Obed, which was *the son* of Booz, which was *the son* of Salmon, which was *the son* of Naasson,
33. Which was *the son* of Aminadab, which was *the son* of Aram, which was *the son* of Esrom, which was *the son* of Phares, which was *the son* of Juda,
34. Which was *the son* of Jacob, which was *the son* of Isaac, which was *the son* of Abraham, which was *the son* of Thara, which was *the son* of Nachor,
35. Which was *the son* of Saruch, which was *the son* of Ragau, which was *the son* of Phalec, which was *the son* of Heber, which was *the son* of Sala,
36. Which was *the son* of Cainan, which was *the son* of Arphaxad, which was *the son* of Sem, which was *the son* of Noe, which was *the son* of Lamech,
37. Which was *the son* of Mathusala, which was *the son* of Enoch, which was *the son* of Jared, which was *the son* of Maleleel, which was *the son* of Cainan,
38. Which was *the son* of Enos, which was *the son* of Seth, which was *the son* of Adam, which was *the son* of God.

CHAPTER 4

■ 1. **And Jesus** being full of the Holy Ghost returned from Jordan, and
■ **was led by the**
■ **Spirit into**
■ **the wilderness,**
■ 2. **Being forty days tempted**
■ **of the devil. And**
in those days he
■ **did eat nothing: and**
when they were ended,
■ **he** afterward
■ **hungered.**
■ 3. **And the devil said** unto him,
■ **If thou be the Son of God,**
■ **command this stone** that it
■ **be made bread.**
■ 4. **And Jesus answered**
him, saying, It is written, That
■ **man shall not live by bread**
■ **alone, but by every**
■ **word of God.**
■ 5. **And the devil,** taking him up
into an high mountain,
■ **shewed** unto
■ **him all the kingdoms of the**
■ **world** in a moment of time.
■ 6. **And the devil said** unto him,
■ **All this power will I give**
■ **thee,** and the glory of them: for that
is delivered unto me; and to
whomsoever I will I give it.
■ 7. **If thou therefore wilt**
■ **worship me,** all shall be thine.
■ 8. **And Jesus answered**
and said unto him,
■ **Get thee behind me, Satan:**
■ **for** it is written,
■ **Thou shalt worship the**
■ **Lord thy God,** and him
■ **only** shalt thou serve.
■ 9. **And he brought him to**
■ **Jerusalem,** and set him
■ **on a pinnacle of the**
■ **temple, and said** unto him,
■ **If thou be the Son of God,**
■ **cast thyself down** from hence:
■ 10. **For** it is written,
■ **He shall give his angels**
■ **charge over thee,** to keep thee:
■ 11. **And** in *their* hands
■ **they shall bear thee up,**
lest at any time thou dash thy foot

against a stone.
12. **And Jesus**
answering said unto him, It is
said, Thou shalt not tempt
the Lord thy God.
13. **And when the devil had**
ended all the temptation,
he departed
from him for a season.
14. **And Jesus returned**
in the power of the Spirit
into Galilee: and there went
out a fame of him
through all the region round about.
15. And he taught in their
synagogues, being glorified of all.
16. **And he came to**
Nazareth,
where he had been brought up:
and, as his custom was, he
went into the synagogue on
the sabbath day,
and stood up for to read.
17. **And there was delivered**
unto him
the book of the prophet
Esaias. And when he had opened
the book, he found the place
where it was written,
18. **The Spirit of the Lord**
is upon me, because he
hath anointed me to
preach the gospel
to the poor; he hath sent me
to heal the brokenhearted, to
preach deliverance to the captives,
and recovering of sight to
the blind, to set at liberty
them that are bruised,
19. To preach the acceptable year of
the Lord.
20. **And he closed the book,**
and he gave *it* again to the minister,
and sat down. And the eyes of
all them that were in the synagogue
were fastened on him.
21. **And he began to say**
unto them,
This day is this scripture
fulfilled in your ears.
22. **And all bare him**
witness, and wondered at
the gracious words which proceeded
out of his mouth. And they said,
Is not this Joseph's son?
23. And he said unto them, Ye will
surely say unto me this proverb,
Physician, heal thyself: whatsoever
we have heard done in Capernaum, do
also here in thy country.
24. **And he said,**
Verily I say unto you,
No prophet is accepted in
his own country.
25. **But** I tell you of a truth,
many widows were in
Israel in the days of Elias,
when the heaven was shut up three
years and six months,
when great famine was
throughout all the land;
26. **But unto none of them**
was Elias sent, save unto
Sarepta, *a city* of Sidon, unto
a woman *that was* a widow.
27. **And many lepers**
were in Israel in the time of
Eliseus the prophet;
and none of them was
cleansed, saving Naaman
the Syrian.
28. **And all they in**
the synagogue,
when they heard these things,
were filled with wrath,
29. **And** rose up, and thrust him out
of the city, and
led him unto the brow of the
hill whereon their city was built,
that they might cast him
down headlong.
30. **But he passing through**
the midst of them
went his way,
31. **And came** down
to Capernaum, a city of
Galilee, and taught
them on the sabbath days.
32. **And they were**
astonished at his doctrine:
for his word was with power.
33. **And** in the synagogue there was
a man, which had a spirit of
an unclean devil, and
cried out with a loud voice,
34. **Saying, Let *us* alone;**

what have we to do with thee,
thou Jesus of Nazareth? art thou
come to destroy us? I know thee who
thou art; the
Holy One of God.
35. **And Jesus rebuked him,**
saying,
Hold thy peace, and come
out of him. And when the devil
had thrown him in the midst,
he came out of him,
and hurt him not.
36. **And they were all**
amazed, and spake
among themselves,
saying, What a word *is* this!
for with authority and power
he commandeth the
unclean spirits, and they
come out.
37. And the fame of him went
out into every place of the
country round about.
38. **And he** arose out of the
synagogue, and
entered into Simon's
house. And Simon's wife's
mother was taken with
a great fever;
and they besought him for her.
39. **And he** stood over her, and
rebuked the fever;
and it left her:
and immediately she
arose and ministered
unto them.
40. **Now when the sun was**
setting, all they that had
any sick with divers diseases
brought them unto him; and
he laid his hands on every one of
them, and
healed them.
41. **And devils also came**
out of many, crying out,
and saying,
Thou art Christ the Son of God.
And he rebuking *them*
suffered them not to speak:
for they knew that he was Christ.
42. **And** when it was day,
he departed and went
into a desert place: and the
people sought him, and
came unto him, and stayed
him, that he should not
depart from them.
43. **And he said** unto them,
I must preach
the kingdom of God
to other cities also: for
therefore am I sent.
44. And he preached in the
synagogues of Galilee.

CHAPTER 5

1. **And** it came to pass, that,
as the people pressed
upon him to hear the word of God,
he stood by the lake
of Gennesaret,
2. **And saw two ships**
standing by the lake: but the
fishermen were gone out of them,
and were washing *their* nets.
3. **And he entered**
into one of the ships, which was
Simon's, and prayed him
that he would thrust out
a little from the land.
And he sat down, and
taught the people out
of the ship.
4. **Now when he had left**
speaking, he said unto
Simon, Launch out
into the deep,
and let down your nets
for a draught.
5. **And Simon answering**
said unto him,
Master, we have toiled all
the night, and have taken
nothing: nevertheless at thy
word I will let down the net.
6. **And** when they had this done,
they enclosed a great
multitude of fishes:
and their net brake.
7. **And they beckoned** unto
***their* partners,** which were
in the other ship, that they
should come and help them.
And they came, and
filled both the ships,
so that they began to sink.

8. **When Simon Peter saw** it,
he fell down at Jesus'
knees, saying, Depart
from me; for
I am a
sinful man, O Lord.
9. **For he was astonished,**
and all that were with him, at the
draught of the fishes which
they had taken:
10. **And so** *was* also James, and
John, the sons of Zebedee, which
were partners with Simon.
And Jesus said unto Simon,
Fear not; from henceforth
thou shalt catch men.
11. **And** when they had brought their
ships to land,
they forsook all, and
followed him.
12. **And** it came to pass, when he
was in a certain city, behold
a man full of leprosy: who
seeing Jesus fell on *his* face, and
besought him, saying,
Lord, if thou wilt, thou canst
make me clean.
13. **And he** put forth *his* hand, and
touched him, saying, I will:
be thou clean. And
immediately
the leprosy departed
from him.
14. **And he charged him to**
tell no man: but go,
and shew thyself
to the priest, and offer
for thy cleansing,
according as Moses
commanded, for a
testimony unto them.
15. But so much the more went there a
fame abroad of him:
and great multitudes came
together to hear, and to be
healed by him
of their infirmities.
16. And he withdrew himself into the
wilderness, and prayed.
17. And it came to pass on a certain
day, as he was teaching, that there
were Pharisees and doctors of the law
sitting by, which were come out of
every town of Galilee, and Judaea,
and Jerusalem: and the power of the
Lord was *present* to heal them.
18. **And, behold, men**
brought in a bed a man
which was taken
with a palsy: and they
sought *means* to bring him in, and
to lay *him* before him.
19. And when they could not find
by what *way* they might
bring him in because of the
multitude, they went upon
the housetop, and let him
down through the tiling
with *his* couch into the midst
before Jesus.
20. **And when he saw their**
faith, he said unto him,
Man, thy sins are
forgiven thee.
21. **And the scribes and the**
Pharisees began to
reason, saying, Who is this which
speaketh blasphemies?
Who can forgive sins, but
God alone?
22. **But when Jesus**
perceived their thoughts,
he answering
said unto them, What reason
ye in your hearts?
23. **Whether is easier, to**
say, Thy sins be forgiven
thee; or to say,
Rise up and walk?
24. **But** that ye may
know that the Son of man
hath power upon earth
to forgive sins, (he said
unto the sick of the palsy,)
I say unto thee,
Arise, and take up thy couch,
and go into thine house.
25. **And** immediately
he rose up before them, and took
up that whereon he lay,
and departed
to his own house, glorifying God.
26. **And they were all**
amazed, and they glorified God,
and were filled with fear, saying, We
have seen strange things to-day.

27. **And** after these things
he went forth, and saw
a publican, named
Levi, sitting at the receipt of
custom: and he
said unto him,
Follow me.
28. **And he left all,** rose up,
and followed him.
29. **And Levi made him a**
great feast in his own house:
and there was a great company of
publicans and of others that
sat down
with them.
30. **But their scribes and**
Pharisees murmured
against his disciples,
saying, Why do ye eat
and drink
with publicans and
sinners?
31. **And Jesus** answering
said unto them, They that are whole
need not a physician; but they that
are sick.
32. **I came not to call the**
righteous, but sinners
to repentance.
33. **And they said** unto him,
Why do the disciples of
John fast often, and make
prayers, and likewise *the disciples* of
the Pharisees;
but thine eat and drink?
34. **And he said** unto them,
Can ye make
the children of the
bridechamber fast, while
the bridegroom is
with them?
35. **But** the days will come, when
the bridegroom shall be
taken away from them, and
then shall they fast
in those days.
36. **And he spake also a**
parable unto them;
No man putteth a piece of a
new garment upon an old;
if otherwise, then both the new
maketh a rent, and the piece that
was *taken* out of
the new agreeth not
with the old.
37. **And no man putteth new**
wine into old bottles; else the
new wine will burst the bottles, and be
spilled, and the bottles shall perish.
38. But new wine must be put into new
bottles; and both are preserved.
39. **No man also having**
drunk old *wine* straightway
desireth new:
for he saith, The old is better.

CHAPTER 6

1. **And** it came to pass on the
second sabbath after the first, that
he went through the corn
fields; and his disciples
plucked the ears of
corn, and did eat,
rubbing *them* in *their* hands.
2. **And** certain of
the Pharisees said unto them,
Why do ye that which is not
lawful to do
on the sabbath days?
3. **And Jesus answering**
them said,
Have ye not read
so much as this,
what David did,
when himself was an hungred, and
they which were with him;
4. **How he went into the**
house of God, and did take
and eat
the shewbread, and gave also
to them that were with him;
which it is not lawful to eat
but for the priests alone?
5. And he said unto them, That
the Son of man is Lord also
of the sabbath.
6. **And** it came to pass also on
another sabbath, that he entered into
the synagogue and taught: and
there was a man whose
right hand was withered.
7. **And the scribes and**
Pharisees watched him,
whether he would heal on
the sabbath day; that they
might find an accusation against him.

8. **But he** knew their thoughts, and
said to the man
which had the withered hand,
Rise up, and stand forth in the
midst. And he arose and stood forth.
9. **Then said Jesus unto**
them, I will ask you one thing;
Is it lawful on the sabbath
days to do good, or to do
evil? to save life, or to destroy *it*?
10. **And** looking round about
upon them all,
he said unto the man,
Stretch forth thy hand.
And he did so:
and his hand was restored
whole as the other.
11. **And they**
were filled with madness; and
communed one with another
what they might do to
Jesus.
12. **And** it came to pass in those
days, that
he went out into a mountain
to pray,
and continued all night in
prayer to God.
13. **And when it was day, he**
called *unto him*
his disciples: and of them he
chose twelve, whom also
he named apostles;
14. **Simon,** (whom he also
named Peter,)
and Andrew his brother,
James and John, Philip
and Bartholomew,
15. **Matthew and Thomas,**
James the *son* of Alphaeus,
and Simon called Zelotes,
16. **And Judas *the brother***
of James, and Judas
Iscariot, which also was
the traitor.
17. **And** he came down
with them, and stood in the plain,
and the company of
his disciples, and
a great multitude of people out
of all Judaea and Jerusalem, and from
the sea coast of Tyre and Sidon,
which
came to hear him, and to
be healed of their diseases;
18. And they that were vexed with
unclean spirits: and they were healed.
19. **And the** whole
multitude sought to touch
him: for there went virtue
out of him, and healed
***them* all.**
20. **And he** lifted up his eyes on his
disciples, and
said, Blessed *be ye* poor:
for yours is the kingdom
of God.
21. **Blessed *are ye* that**
hunger now:
for ye shall be filled.
Blessed *are ye* that weep
now:
for ye shall laugh.
22. **Blessed are ye, when**
men shall hate you, and when they
shall separate you
from their company, and
shall reproach *you*,
and cast out your name as evil,
for the Son of man's sake.
23. **Rejoice** ye in that day, and leap
for joy: for, behold,
your reward *is* great in
heaven: for in the like manner did
their fathers unto the prophets.
24. **But woe unto you that**
are rich! for
ye have received
your consolation.
25. **Woe unto you that**
are full! for
ye shall hunger. Woe unto
you that laugh now! for
ye shall mourn and weep.
26. **Woe unto you, when** all
men shall
speak well of you! for so
did their fathers to the
false prophets.
27. **But I say** unto you which hear,
Love your enemies,
do good to them which hate you,
28. **Bless** them that curse you,
and pray for them which
despitefully use you.
29. **And unto him that**

smiteth thee on the *one*
cheek offer also
the other; and him that
taketh away
thy cloak forbid not *to take*
***thy* coat also.**
30. **Give to every man that**
asketh of thee; and of him that
taketh away thy goods
ask *them* not again.
31. **And as ye would that**
men should
do to you, do ye also to
them likewise.
32. **For if ye love them**
which love you, what thank have ye?
for sinners also love those
that love them.
33. **And** if ye
do good to them which do
good to you, what
thank have ye?
for sinners also do even the same.
34. **And if ye lend *to them* of**
whom ye hope to receive,
what thank have ye? for
sinners also lend to sinners,
to receive as much again.
35. **But love ye your**
enemies, and do good, and lend,
hoping for nothing again;
and your reward shall be
great, and ye shall be the children
of the Highest: for he is kind unto the
unthankful and *to* the evil.
36. **Be ye therefore merciful,**
as your Father also is merciful.
37. **Judge not, and**
ye shall not be judged:
condemn not,
and ye shall not be condemned:
forgive, and ye shall
be forgiven:
38. **Give, and it shall be**
given unto you; good
measure, pressed down,
and shaken together,
and running over,
shall men give into your bosom.
For with the same measure
that ye mete withal
it shall be measured to you
again.

39. **And he spake a parable**
unto them,
Can the blind lead the
blind? shall they not both
fall into the ditch?
40. **The disciple is not**
above his master:
but every one that is perfect shall be
as his master.
41. **And why beholdest thou**
the mote that is in thy
brother's eye, but perceivest
not the beam that is
in thine own eye?
42. Either how canst thou say to thy
brother, Brother, let me pull out the
mote that is in thine eye, when thou
thyself beholdest not the beam that is
in thine own eye? Thou hypocrite,
cast out first
the beam out
of thine own eye, and then
shalt thou see clearly to
pull out the mote
that is
in thy brother's eye.
43. **For a good tree** bringeth not
forth corrupt fruit; neither
doth a corrupt tree
bring forth good fruit.
44. **For every tree is known**
by his own fruit. For of thorns
men do not gather figs, nor of a
bramble bush gather they grapes.
45. **A good man**
out of the good treasure of his heart
bringeth forth that which is
good; and an evil man
out of the evil treasure of his heart
bringeth forth
that which is evil: for of the
abundance of the heart his
mouth speaketh.
46. And why call ye me, Lord, Lord,
and do not the things which I say?
47. **Whosoever**
cometh to me, and
heareth my sayings,
and doeth them,
I will shew you to whom he is like:
48. **He is like a man which**
built an house, and digged
deep, and laid the foundation

on a rock: and when
the flood arose, the stream
beat vehemently upon that house,
and could not shake it: for it
was founded upon a rock.
49. **But he that heareth, and**
doeth not, is like a man that
without a foundation
built an house upon the
earth; against which
the stream did beat
vehemently, and immediately
it fell; and the ruin of that house
was great.

CHAPTER 7

1. **Now** when he had ended all his
sayings in the audience of the people,
he entered into
Capernaum.
2. **And a certain centurion's**
servant, who was dear unto him,
was sick, and ready to die.
3. **And when he heard of**
Jesus, he sent
unto him the elders of the Jews,
beseeching him that he
would come and
heal his servant.
4. **And when** they came to
Jesus, they besought him instantly,
saying, That he was worthy for whom
he should do this:
5. For he loveth our nation, and he
hath built us a synagogue.
6. Then Jesus went with them.
And when he
was now not far from the
house, the centurion sent
friends to him,
saying unto him, Lord,
trouble not thyself:
for I am not worthy that
thou shouldest enter
under my roof:
7. Wherefore neither thought I myself
worthy to come unto thee:
but say in a word, and my
servant shall be healed.
8. For I also am a man set under
authority, having under me soldiers,
and I say unto one, Go, and he goeth;
and to another, Come, and he cometh;
and to my servant, Do this,
and he doeth *it*.
9. **When Jesus heard**
these things,
he marvelled
at him, and turned him about,
and said unto the people that
followed him, I say unto you,
I have not found so great
faith, no, not
in Israel.
10. **And they** that were sent,
returning to the house,
found the servant whole
that had been sick.
11. **And** it came to pass
the day after, that
he went into a city called
Nain; and many of his disciples
went with him, and much people.
12. **Now when he came nigh**
to the gate of the city, behold,
there was a dead man
carried out, the only son of
his mother, and she was
a widow: and much people of the
city was with her.
13. **And when the Lord saw**
her, he had compassion
on her, and said unto her,
Weep not.
14. **And he** came and
touched the bier: and they that
bare *him* stood still.
And he
said, Young man,
I say unto thee,
Arise.
15. **And he** that was dead
sat up, and began to
speak. And he delivered
him to his mother.
16. **And** there came a fear on all: and
they glorified God, saying,
That a great prophet is
risen up among us;
and, That God hath visited his people.
17. **And this rumour of him**
went forth
throughout all Judaea,
and throughout all
the region round about.
18. **And the disciples of**

■ **John shewed him** of all
■ **these things.**
■ 19. **And John calling** *unto him*
■ **two** of his
■ **disciples sent** ***them*** **to**
■ **Jesus,** saying, Art thou he that
should come? or look we for another?
■ 20. **When the men were**
■ **come** unto him,
■ **they said,** John Baptist hath sent
us unto thee, saying,
■ **Art thou he that should**
■ **come? or look**
■ **we for another?**
■ 21. **And** in that same hour
■ **he cured many of** ***their***
■ **infirmities and** plagues, and of
■ **evil spirits; and unto many**
■ ***that were*** **blind he**
■ **gave sight.**
■ 22. **Then Jesus** answering
■ **said** unto them,
■ **Go** your way, and
■ **tell John what** things
■ **ye have seen and heard;**
how that the blind see, the lame walk,
the lepers are cleansed, the deaf
hear, the dead are raised, to the poor
the gospel is preached.
23. And blessed is *he*, whosoever
shall not be offended in me.
■ 24. **And when the**
■ **messengers of John** were
■ **departed, he began to**
■ **speak** unto the people
■ **concerning John, What**
■ **went ye out into the**
■ **wilderness for to see?**
A reed shaken with the wind?
25. But what went ye out for to see?
■ **A man clothed in soft**
■ **raiment? Behold, they**
which are gorgeously apparelled,
and live delicately,
■ **are in kings' courts.**
26. But what went ye out for to see? A
prophet? Yea, I say unto you, and
much more than a prophet.
27. This is *he*, of whom it is written,
■ **Behold, I send my**
■ **messenger** before thy face,
■ **which shall prepare thy**
■ **way before thee.**

■ 28. **For** I say unto you,
■ **Among those** that are
■ **born of women there is not**
■ **a greater prophet than**
■ **John** the Baptist:
■ **but he that is least in the**
■ **kingdom of God is greater**
■ **than he.**
■ 29. **And all the people that**
■ **heard** *him*, and the publicans,
■ **justified God, being**
■ **baptized** with the baptism
■ **of John.**
■ 30. **But the Pharisees**
and lawyers
■ **rejected the counsel**
of God against themselves,
■ **being not baptized of him.**
■ 31. **And the Lord said,**
Whereunto then shall I liken the men
of this generation? and to what are
they like?
■ 32. **They are like** unto
■ **children** sitting
■ **in the marketplace,**
and calling one to another, and
■ **saying, We have piped**
unto you,
■ **and ye have not danced;**
■ **we** have
■ **mourned** to you,
■ **and ye have not wept.**
■ 33. **For John** the Baptist
■ **came neither eating** bread
■ **nor drinking wine; and ye**
■ **say, He hath a devil.**
■ 34. **The Son of man is come**
■ **eating and drinking; and ye**
■ **say, Behold a gluttonous**
■ **man,** and
■ **a winebibber, a friend of**
publicans and
■ **sinners!**
35. But wisdom is justified
of all her children.
■ 36. **And one of the Pharisees**
■ **desired him that he would**
■ **eat with him.** And he went into the
Pharisee's house, and sat down to
meat.
■ 37. **And, behold, a woman**
in the city,
■ **which was a sinner,**

when she knew that *Jesus* sat at meat
in the Pharisee's house,
brought an alabaster box of
ointment,
38. **And** stood at his feet behind *him*
weeping, and
began to wash his feet with
tears, and did
wipe *them* with the hairs of
her head, and kissed
his feet,
and anointed *them*
with the ointment.
39. **Now when the Pharisee**
which had bidden him
saw *it*, he spake within
himself,
saying, This man, if he were
a prophet, would have
known who and what manner of
woman *this is* that toucheth him: for
she is a sinner.
40. **And Jesus** answering
said unto him,
Simon, I have somewhat to say
unto thee. And he saith,
Master, say on.
41. **There was a certain**
creditor which had two
debtors: the one owed five
hundred pence, and the
other fifty.
42. **And** when they had
nothing to pay,
he frankly
forgave them both.
Tell me therefore,
which of them will
love him most?
43. **Simon answered**
and said, I suppose that
***he*, to whom he forgave**
most. And he said unto him,
Thou hast rightly judged.
44. **And he**
turned to the woman, and
said unto Simon, Seest
thou this woman?
I entered into thine house,
thou gavest me no water
for my feet: but she hath
washed my feet with tears,
and wiped *them* with the
hairs of her head.
45. **Thou gavest me no kiss:**
but this woman
since the time I came in
hath not ceased to kiss
my feet.
46. My head with oil thou didst not
anoint: but this woman hath anointed
my feet with ointment.
47. **Wherefore** I say unto thee,
Her sins, which are many,
are forgiven; for she loved
much: but to whom little is forgiven,
the same loveth little.
48. And he said unto her,
Thy sins are forgiven.
49. **And they that sat at meat**
with him
began to say within themselves,
Who is this that forgiveth
sins also?
50. **And he said to the**
woman, Thy faith hath
saved thee; go in peace.

CHAPTER 8

1. And it came to pass afterward, that
he went throughout every city and
village, preaching and shewing the
glad tidings of the kingdom of God:
and the twelve *were* with him,
2. And certain women, which had been
healed of evil spirits and infirmities,
Mary called Magdalene,
out of whom went seven devils,
3. And Joanna the wife of Chuza
Herod's steward, and Susanna,
and many
others, which
ministered unto him of
their substance.
4. **And when much people**
were gathered together, and
were come to him out of every city,
he spake by a parable:
5. **A sower went out to sow**
his seed:
and as he sowed,
some fell by the way side;
and it was trodden down,
and the fowls of the air
devoured it.
6. **And some fell upon a**

rock; and
as soon as it was sprung up,
it withered away,
because it lacked
moisture.
7. **And some fell among**
thorns; and the thorns
sprang up with it, and
choked it.
8. **And other fell on good**
ground, and sprang up,
and bare fruit an
hundredfold. And when he had
said these things, he cried, He that
hath ears to hear, let him hear.
9. **And his disciples asked**
him, saying,
What might this parable
be?
10. **And he said,** Unto you it is
given to know the mysteries of the
kingdom of God: but to others in
parables; that seeing they might not
see, and hearing they might not
understand.
11. **Now the parable is this:**
The seed is the word of God.
12. **Those by the way side**
are they that hear; then
cometh
the devil, and
taketh away the word out
of their hearts, lest they
should
believe and be saved.
13. **They on the rock**
are they, which, when they hear,
receive the word with joy;
and these
have no root,
which for a while believe,
and in time of temptation
fall away.
14. **And that which fell**
among thorns are they, which,
when they have heard, go forth, and
are choked with cares and
riches and pleasures of
***this* life, and bring no fruit**
to perfection.
15. **But that on the good**
ground are they, which in an
honest and good heart, having heard
the word, keep *it*, and
bring forth fruit
with patience.
16. **No man, when he hath**
lighted a candle, covereth
it with a vessel,
or putteth *it* under a bed;
but setteth *it* on a
candlestick, that they
which enter in
may see the light.
17. **For nothing is** secret, that
shall not be made manifest; neither
any thing
hid, that shall not be known
and come abroad.
18. Take heed therefore how ye hear:
for whosoever hath, to him
shall be given; and
whosoever hath not, from
him shall be taken even that
which he seemeth to have.
19. **Then came** to him
his mother and his
***brethren*,** and could not come at
him for the press.
20. **And it was told him**
by certain which said,
Thy mother and thy
brethren stand without,
desiring to see thee.
21. **And he answered**
and said unto them,
My mother and my brethren
are these which hear the
word of God,
and do it.
22. **Now** it came to pass on a certain
day, that
he went into a ship
with his disciples:
and he
said unto them,
Let us go over
unto the other side
of the lake. And they launched forth.
23. **But as they sailed he fell**
asleep: and there came
down
a storm of wind on the lake;
and they were filled *with*
***water*,** and were in jeopardy.
24. **And they came to him,**

and awoke him,
saying, Master, master,
we perish. Then he arose, and
rebuked the wind and the
raging of the water: and they ceased,
and there was a calm.
25. **And he said** unto them,
Where is your faith? And
they being afraid
wondered, saying
one to another,
What manner of man is this!
for he commandeth
even the winds and water,
and they
obey him.
26. **And** they arrived
at the country of
the Gadarenes,
which is over against Galilee.
27. And when he went forth to land,
there met him out of the city
a certain
man, which had devils
long time,
and ware no clothes, neither
abode in *any* house, but in
the tombs.
28. **When he saw Jesus, he**
cried out, and
fell down before him, and
with a loud voice
said, What have I to do with thee,
Jesus, ***thou*** **Son of God**
most high? I beseech thee,
torment me not.
29. (For he had commanded the
unclean spirit to come out of the man.
For oftentimes it had caught him: and
he was kept bound with
chains and in fetters;
and he brake the bands,
and was driven of the devil
into the wilderness.)
30. **And Jesus asked**
him, saying,
What is thy name? And he
said, Legion: because
many devils were entered
into him.
31. And they besought him that he
would not command them to go out
into the deep.

32. **And there was**
there an herd of
many swine feeding
on the mountain:
and they besought him
that he would suffer them
to enter into them.
And he suffered them.
33. **Then** went
the devils out of the man, and
entered into
the swine: and the herd
ran violently down a steep place
into the lake, and were choked.
34. **When they that fed** ***them***
saw what was done,
they fled, and went
and told ***it*** **in the city**
and in the country.
35. **Then they went out to see**
what was done; and came to
Jesus, and found
the man, out of whom the
devils were departed,
sitting at the feet of Jesus,
clothed, and in his right
mind: and they were afraid.
36. **They also** which saw *it*
told them by what means
he that was possessed of the devils
was healed.
37. **Then the whole multitude**
of the country of the
Gadarenes round about
besought him to depart
from them;
for they were taken with
great fear: and he went up into the
ship, and returned back again.
38. **Now the man** out of whom the
devils were departed
besought him that he might
be with him: but Jesus sent
him away, saying,
39. **Return to thine own**
house, and shew how great things
God hath done unto thee.
And he went his way,
and published
throughout the whole city
how great things Jesus
had done unto him.
40. **And** it came to pass, that,

when Jesus was returned,
the people
gladly received him: for they
were all
waiting for him.
41. **And,** behold,
there came a man named
Jairus, and he was
a ruler of the synagogue:
and he fell down at Jesus' feet, and
besought him that he would
come into his *house*:
42. **For he had one** only
daughter,
about twelve years of age,
and she lay a-dying. But as
he went the people thronged him.
43. **And a woman having an**
issue of blood twelve
years, which had spent all her living
upon physicians, neither could be
healed of any,
44. **Came behind *him*, and**
touched the border of
his garment: and
immediately her issue of
blood stanched.
45. **And Jesus said, Who**
touched me? When all denied,
Peter and they that were with him
said, Master, the multitude
throng thee and press *thee*,
and sayest thou, Who
touched me?
46. **And Jesus said,**
Somebody hath touched me: for
I perceive that virtue is
gone out of me.
47. **And when the woman**
saw that
she was not hid, she came
trembling,
and falling down before him, she
declared unto him
before all the people
for what cause she had
touched him, and how she
was healed immediately.
48. **And he said** unto her,
Daughter, be of good comfort:
thy faith hath made thee
whole; go in peace.
49. **While he yet spake, there**
cometh one from the ruler
of the synagogue's *house*,
saying to him,
Thy daughter is dead; trouble
not the Master.
50. **But when Jesus heard *it*,**
he answered him, saying,
Fear not: believe only, and
she shall be made whole.
51. **And when he came into**
the house, he suffered no man to
go in, save Peter, and James, and
John, and the father and the mother of
the maiden.
52. And all wept, and bewailed her: but
he said, Weep not; she
is not dead, but
sleepeth.
53. **And they laughed him to**
scorn, knowing that she was dead.
54. **And he** put them all out, and
took her by the hand,
and called,
saying, Maid, arise.
55. **And** her spirit came again, and
she arose straightway: and he
commanded to give her meat.
56. And her parents were astonished:
but he charged them that they should
tell no man what was done.

CHAPTER 9

1. **Then he called his twelve**
disciples together,
and gave them power
and authority over all devils,
and to cure diseases.
2. **And he sent them to**
preach the kingdom of God,
and to heal the sick.
3. **And he said** unto them,
Take nothing for *your*
journey, neither staves, nor scrip,
neither bread, neither money; neither
have two coats apiece.
4. **And whatsoever house**
ye enter into,
there abide, and thence depart.
5. **And whosoever will not**
receive you,
when ye go out of that city,
shake off the very
dust from your feet for a

testimony against them.
6. **And they** departed, and
went through the towns,
preaching the gospel, and
healing every where.
7. **Now Herod** the tetrarch heard
of all that was done by him: and he
was perplexed,
because that
it was said of some,
that John was risen
from the dead;
8. And of some, that Elias had
appeared; and of others, that one of
the old prophets was risen again.
9. **And Herod said, John**
have I beheaded: but who
is this, of whom I hear such things?
And he desired to see him.
10. **And the apostles, when**
they were
returned, told him
all that
they had done. And he took
them, and went aside
privately into a desert
place belonging to the
city called Bethsaida.
11. **And the people,**
when they knew *it,*
followed him: and he
received them, and
spake unto them of the
kingdom of God, and
healed them
that had need of healing.
12. **And** when the day
began to wear away,
then came the twelve,
and said unto him,
Send the multitude away,
that they may go into the towns
and country round about,
and lodge, and get
victuals: for we are here in a
desert place.
13. **But he said** unto them,
Give ye them to eat. And
they said, We have no more
but five loaves and two
fishes; except we should go and
buy meat for all this people.
14. **For they were about five**
thousand men. And he said
to his disciples,
Make them sit down
by fifties in a company.
15. And they did so, and made them
all sit down.
16. **Then he took the five**
loaves and the two fishes,
and looking up to heaven, he
blessed them, and brake,
and gave to the disciples to
set before the multitude.
17. **And they did eat,**
and were all filled:
and there
was taken up of fragments that
remained to them
twelve baskets.
18. **And** it came to pass,
as he was alone
praying, his disciples were
with him: and he asked
them, saying,
Whom say the people
that I am?
19. **They** answering
said, John the Baptist; but
some *say*, Elias; and
others *say*, that
one of the old
prophets is risen again.
20. **He said** unto them,
But whom say ye that I am?
Peter answering said,
The Christ of God.
21. **And he**
straitly charged them, and
commanded *them* to tell no
man that thing;
22. **Saying, The Son of man**
must suffer many things, and be
rejected of the elders and chief
priests and scribes,
and be slain, and be
raised the third day.
23. **And he said** to *them all,*
If any *man* will come after
me, let him deny himself, and
take up his cross daily,
and follow me.
24. For whosoever will save his life
shall lose it: but whosoever will lose
his life for my sake, the same

shall save it.
25. **For what is a man**
advantaged, if he gain the
whole world, and lose
himself, or be cast away?
26. **For whosoever shall be**
ashamed of me
and of my words, of him
shall the Son of man be
ashamed, when he shall
come in his own glory, and *in*
his Father's, and of the holy angels.
27. But I tell you of a truth, there be
some standing here, which shall not
taste of death, till they see the
kingdom of God.
28. **And** it came to pass about an
eight days after these sayings,
he took Peter and John and
James, and went up
into a mountain to pray.
29. **And** as he prayed,
the fashion of his
countenance was altered,
and his raiment
was white *and* glistering.
30. **And, behold, there**
talked with him
two men, which were
Moses and Elias:
31. **Who** appeared in glory, and
spake of his decease
which he should
accomplish at Jerusalem.
32. **But Peter and they that**
were with him
were heavy with sleep: and when
they were awake, they
saw his glory, and the two
men that stood with him.
33. **And** it came to pass,
as they departed from him,
Peter said unto Jesus, Master, it
is good for us to be here: and
let us make three
tabernacles; one for thee,
and one for
Moses, and one for
Elias: not knowing what he said.
34. **While he thus spake,**
there came
a cloud, and
overshadowed them:
and they feared as they
entered into the cloud.
35. **And there came a voice**
out of the cloud,
saying, This is my beloved
Son: hear him.
36. And when the voice was past,
Jesus was found alone.
And they kept *it* close, and
told no man in those days
any of those things
which they had seen.
37. **And** it came to pass,
that on the next day,
when they were come down
from the hill,
much people met him.
38. **And, behold, a man**
of the company
cried out, saying,
Master, I beseech thee,
look upon my son: for he is mine
only child.
39. **And, lo, a spirit taketh**
him, and he suddenly crieth out;
and it
teareth him
that he foameth again, and
bruising him
hardly departeth from him.
40. **And I besought thy**
disciples to cast him out;
and they could not.
41. **And Jesus** answering
said, O faithless and perverse
generation, how long shall
I be with you, and suffer you?
Bring thy son hither.
42. **And** as he was yet a-coming,
the devil threw him down,
and tare *him.*
And Jesus rebuked the
unclean spirit, and healed
the child,
and delivered him again to his father.
43. **And they were all**
amazed at the mighty
power of God.
But while they wondered
every one at all things which
Jesus did, he
said unto his disciples,
44. Let these sayings sink

down into your ears: for
the Son of man shall be
delivered into the hands
of men.
45. But they understood not
this saying, and it was hid from them,
that they perceived it not:
and they
feared to ask him
of that saying.
46. Then there arose a
reasoning among them,
which of them
should be greatest.
47. And Jesus, perceiving the
thought of their heart,
took a child, and set him by him,
48. And said unto them,
Whosoever shall receive
this child in my name
receiveth me:
and whosoever shall receive me
receiveth him that sent me:
for he that is least
among you all, the same
shall be great.
49. And John answered and
said, Master,
we saw one casting out
devils in thy name; and we
forbad him,
because he followeth not with us.
50. And Jesus said unto him,
Forbid *him* not: for he that
is not against us is for us.
51. And it came to pass,
when the time was come
that he should be received
up, he stedfastly
set his face to
go to Jerusalem,
52. And sent messengers
before his face: and they went,
and entered
into a village of the
Samaritans, to make
ready for him.
53. And they did not receive
him, because his face was as
though he would go to Jerusalem.
54. And when his disciples
James and John
saw *this*, they said, Lord,
wilt thou that we command
fire to come down
from heaven, and consume
them, even as Elias did?
55. But he turned, and
rebuked them, and said,
Ye know not what manner
of spirit ye are of.
56. For the Son of man is not
come to destroy men's
lives, but to save *them*.
And they went to another village.
57. And it came to pass,
that, as they went in the way,
a certain *man* said unto him,
Lord, I will follow thee
whithersoever thou goest.
58. And Jesus said
unto him, Foxes have holes, and
birds of the air *have* nests; but
the Son of man hath not
where to lay *his* head.
59. And he said unto
another, Follow me. But he
said, Lord, suffer me first to
go and
bury my father.
60. Jesus said unto him,
Let the dead bury their
dead: but go thou
and preach the kingdom of God.
61. And another also
said, Lord, I will follow thee;
but let me first go
bid them farewell, which
are at home
at my house.
62. And Jesus said unto him,
No man, having put his
hand to the plough, and
looking back, is fit for the
kingdom of God.

CHAPTER 10

1. After these things the
LORD appointed other
seventy also,
and sent them
two and two before his face
into every city and place,
whither he himself
would come.
2. Therefore said he unto them,

■ **The harvest** truly
■ ***is* great, but the labourers**
■ ***are* few: pray** ye therefore
■ **the Lord** of the harvest,
■ **that he** would
■ **send forth labourers**
into his harvest.
■ 3. **Go** your ways: behold,
I send you forth
■ **as lambs among wolves.**
■ 4. **Carry neither purse, nor**
■ **scrip,** nor shoes: and
salute no man by the way.
■ 5. **And into whatsoever**
■ **house ye enter, first say,**
■ **Peace *be* to this house.**
6. And if the son of peace be there,
your peace shall rest upon it: if not, it
shall turn to you again.
■ 7. **And** in the same house
■ **remain, eating and**
■ **drinking such things as**
■ **they give: for the labourer**
■ **is worthy of his hire.**
Go not from house to house.
■ 8. **And into whatsoever city**
■ **ye enter,** and they receive you,
■ **eat** such
■ **things** as are
■ **set before you:**
■ 9. **And heal the sick**
that are therein,
■ **and say** unto them,
■ **The kingdom of God is**
■ **come nigh unto you.**
■ 10. **But into whatsoever city**
■ **ye enter, and they receive**
■ **you not,** go your ways out into
the streets of the same, and
■ **say,**
■ 11. **Even the very dust of**
■ **your city,** which cleaveth on us,
■ **we** do
■ **wipe off against you:**
notwithstanding be ye sure of
this, that the kingdom of God is
come nigh unto you.
12. But I say unto you, that it shall be
more tolerable in that day for Sodom,
than for that city.
13. Woe unto thee, Chorazin!
woe unto thee, Bethsaida!
■ **for if the mighty works had**
■ **been done in Tyre and**
■ **Sidon, which have been**
■ **done in you, they had**
a great while ago
■ **repented,**
sitting in sackcloth and ashes.
■ 14. **But it shall be more**
■ **tolerable for Tyre and**
■ **Sidon at the judgment, than**
■ **for you.**
15. And thou, Capernaum, which art
exalted to heaven, shalt be thrust
down to hell.
16. He that heareth you heareth me;
and he that despiseth you despiseth
me; and he that despiseth me
despiseth him that sent me.
■ 17. **And the seventy returned**
again with joy,
■ **saying, Lord, even the**
■ **devils are subject unto us**
■ **through thy name.**
■ 18. **And he said** unto them,
■ **I beheld Satan as lightning**
■ **fall from heaven.**
■ 19. **Behold, I give unto you**
■ **power** to tread on serpents
and scorpions, and over all
the power of the enemy:
■ **and nothing shall**
by any means
■ **hurt you.**
20. Notwithstanding in this
■ **rejoice not, that the spirits**
■ **are subject unto you; but**
■ **rather** rejoice,
■ **because your names are**
■ **written in heaven.**
■ 21. **In that hour Jesus**
rejoiced in spirit, and
■ **said, I thank thee, O Father,**
Lord of heaven and earth,
■ **that thou hast hid these**
■ **things from the wise and**
■ **prudent, and hast revealed**
■ **them unto babes:**
even so, Father; for so it
seemed good in thy sight.
■ 22. **All things are delivered**
■ **to me of my Father:**
and no man knoweth who the
Son is, but the Father; and
who the Father is, but the Son,

and *he* to whom the
Son will reveal *him*.
23. **And he turned** him
unto *his* disciples,
and said privately,
Blessed *are* the eyes which
see the things that ye see:
24. **For** I tell you, that many
prophets and kings have
desired to see those things
which ye see, and have not seen
them; and to hear those things which
ye hear, and have not heard *them*.
25. **And, behold, a** certain
lawyer stood up, and
tempted him, saying, Master,
what shall I do to inherit
eternal life?
26. **He said** unto him,
What is written
in the law? how readest thou?
27. **And he answering** said,
Thou shalt love the Lord thy
God with all thy heart,
and with all thy
soul, and with all thy
strength, and with all thy
mind; and thy
neighbour as thyself.
28. **And he said** unto him,
Thou hast answered right:
this do, and thou shalt live.
29. **But he, willing to justify**
himself, said unto Jesus, And
who is my neighbour?
30. **And Jesus answering**
said,
A certain *man* went down
from Jerusalem to Jericho,
and fell among thieves,
which stripped him
of his raiment,
and wounded *him*,
and departed,
leaving *him* half dead.
31. And by chance there came down
a certain priest that way: and
when he saw him, he
passed by on the other side.
32. **And likewise a Levite,**
when he was at the place, came
and looked *on him*, and
passed by on the other side.

33. **But a certain Samaritan,**
as he journeyed, came
where he was: and when he
saw him,
he had compassion *on him*,
34. **And** went to *him*, and
bound up
his wounds, pouring in oil and
wine, and set him on his own beast,
and brought him to an inn,
and took care of him.
35. **And on the morrow**
when he departed,
he took out two pence,
and gave *them* to the host,
and said unto him,
Take care of him; and
whatsoever thou
spendest more,
when I come again,
I will repay thee.
36. **Which** now of these
three, thinkest thou,
was neighbour unto him
that fell among the thieves?
37. **And he said, He that**
shewed mercy on him.
Then said Jesus unto him,
Go, and do thou
likewise.
38. **Now** it came to pass,
as they went, that
he entered into a certain
village: and a certain
woman named
Martha received him into
her house.
39. **And** she had a sister called
Mary, which
also sat at Jesus' feet, and
heard his word.
40. **But Martha was**
cumbered about much
serving, and came to him,
and said, Lord, dost thou not
care that
my sister hath left me to
serve alone? bid her
therefore that she
help me.
41. **And Jesus answered**
and said unto her, Martha,
Martha, thou art careful and

troubled about
many things:
42. **But** one thing is needful: and
Mary hath chosen that
good part, which shall not
be taken away from her.

CHAPTER 11

1. **And** it came to pass, that,
as he was praying
in a certain place, when he ceased,
one of his disciples said
unto him,
Lord, teach us to pray,
as John also taught his disciples.
2. **And he said** unto them,
When ye pray, say, Our
Father which art in heaven,
Hallowed be thy name.
Thy kingdom come. Thy
will be done, as
in heaven, so in earth.
3. **Give us** day by day
our daily bread.
4. **And forgive us our sins;**
for we also forgive
every one that is indebted to us.
And lead us not into
temptation; but deliver
us from evil.
5. **And he said** unto them,
Which of you shall have a
friend, and shall go unto
him at midnight, and say
unto him, Friend,
lend me three loaves;
6. For a friend of mine in his
journey is come to me, and I have
nothing to set before him?
7. **And he** from within
shall answer and say,
Trouble me not: the door
is now shut, and my children are
with me in bed;
I cannot rise and give thee.
8. **I say** unto you,
Though he will not rise
and give him,
because he is his friend,
yet because of his
importunity he will rise and
give him as many as he needeth.
9. **And I say** unto you,
Ask, and it shall be given
you;
seek, and ye shall find;
knock, and it shall be
opened unto you.
10. For every one that asketh
receiveth; and he that seeketh
findeth; and to him that knocketh it
shall be opened.
11. **If a son** shall
ask bread of any of you that is
a father, will he give him
a stone? or if *he ask*
a fish, will he for a fish
give him
a serpent?
12. Or if he shall ask an egg, will he
offer him a scorpion?
13. **If ye then, being evil,**
know how to
give good gifts
unto your children:
how much more
shall *your* heavenly Father
give the Holy Spirit to them
that ask him?
14. **And he was casting out**
a devil, and it was dumb.
And it came to pass,
when the devil was gone
out, the dumb spake;
and the people wondered.
15. **But some** of them
said, He casteth out devils
through Beelzebub
the chief of the devils.
16. **And others,** tempting *him,*
sought of him
a sign from heaven.
17. **But he,** knowing their thoughts,
said unto them,
Every kingdom divided
against itself is brought to desolation;
and a house *divided* against a house
falleth.
18. **If Satan also be divided**
against himself,
how shall his kingdom
stand? because ye say that I cast
out devils through Beelzebub.
19. And if I by Beelzebub cast out
devils, by whom do your sons cast
them out? therefore shall they be your

judges.
20. **But if I with the finger of**
God cast out devils, no
doubt the kingdom of God
is come upon you.
21. **When a strong man** armed
keepeth his palace, his
goods are in peace:
22. **But when a stronger**
than he shall come upon him, and
overcome him, he taketh
from him
all his armour wherein
he trusted, and divideth
his spoils.
23. **He that is not with me is**
against me: and he that
gathereth not with me scattereth.
24. **When the unclean spirit**
is gone out of a man,
he walketh through dry places,
seeking rest; and finding none,
he saith, I will return unto
my house whence I came out.
25. **And** when he cometh,
he findeth *it* swept
and garnished.
26. **Then goeth he, and**
taketh *to him*
seven other spirits
more wicked than himself; and they
enter in, and dwell there:
and the last *state* of that man
is worse than the first.
27. And it came to pass,
as he spake these things,
a certain
woman of the company
lifted up her voice, and
said unto him,
Blessed *is* the womb that
bare thee, and the paps which
thou hast sucked.
28. **But he said,** Yea
rather, blessed *are* they
that hear the word of God,
and keep it.
29. And when the people were
gathered thick together, he began
to say,
This is an
evil generation: they
seek a sign; and there shall
no sign be given it, but the
sign of Jonas the prophet.
30. **For as Jonas was a sign**
unto the Ninevites, so shall
also the Son of man be
to this generation.
31. The queen of the south shall rise
up in the judgment with the men of this
generation, and condemn them: for
she came from the utmost parts of the
earth to hear the wisdom of Solomon;
and, behold, a greater than Solomon
is here.
32. **The men of Nineve**
shall rise up in the judgment with
this generation, and shall condemn
it: for they
repented at the preaching
of Jonas; and, behold,
a greater than Jonas *is*
here.
33. **No man, when he hath**
lighted a candle, putteth *it*
in a secret place, neither
under a bushel, but on a
candlestick, that they
which come in
may see the light.
34. **The light of the body is**
the eye: therefore
when thine eye is single, thy
whole body also is full of light;
but when *thine eye* is evil, thy body
also *is* full of darkness.
35. Take heed therefore that the light
which is in thee be not darkness.
36. If thy whole body therefore *be* full
of light, having no part dark, the whole
shall be full of light,
as when the bright shining of a
candle doth give thee light.
37. **And** as he spake,
a certain
Pharisee besought him to
dine with him: and he went in,
and sat down to meat.
38. **And** when the Pharisee saw *it*,
he marvelled that he had
not first
washed before dinner.
39. **And the Lord said** unto him,
Now do ye Pharisees make
clean the outside

of the cup and the platter;
but your inward part is full
of ravening and
wickedness.
40. ***Ye* fools, did not he that**
made that which is without
make that which is within
also?
41. But rather give alms of such
things as ye have; and, behold, all
things are clean unto you.
42. **But woe unto you,**
Pharisees! for ye tithe
mint and rue and all manner of herbs,
and pass over judgment and
the love of God:
these ought ye to have done,
and not to leave the other undone.
43. Woe unto you, Pharisees! for
ye love the uppermost
seats in the synagogues,
and greetings in
the markets.
44. **Woe unto you,**
scribes and Pharisees,
hypocrites! for ye are as graves
which appear not, and the men that
walk over *them* are not aware of *them.*
45. **Then answered one of**
the lawyers, and said unto him,
Master, thus saying thou
reproachest us also.
46. **And he said, Woe unto**
you also, *ye* lawyers!
for ye lade men with
burdens grievous to be borne,
and ye yourselves
touch not the burdens with
one of
your fingers.
47. Woe unto you! for
ye build the sepulchres of
the prophets, and your
fathers killed them.
48. Truly ye bear witness that
ye allow the deeds of your fathers:
for they indeed killed them,
and ye build their sepulchres.
49. Therefore also said the
wisdom of God,
I will send them prophets
and apostles, and *some*
of them
they shall slay
and persecute:
50. **That the blood of all the**
prophets, which was shed from
the foundation of the world,
may be required of this
generation;
51. From the blood of Abel unto the
blood of Zacharias which perished
between the altar and the temple:
verily I say unto you, It shall be
required of this generation.
52. **Woe unto you, lawyers!**
for ye have taken away the
key of knowledge:
ye entered not in yourselves,
and them that were entering
in ye hindered.
53. **And as he said these**
things unto them,
the scribes and the
Pharisees began to urge
him vehemently, and to provoke him
to speak of many things:
54. Laying wait for him, and
seeking to catch something
out of his mouth,
that they might accuse him.

CHAPTER 12

1. In the mean time, when there were
gathered together an innumerable
multitude of people, insomuch that
they trode one upon another,
he began to say unto his
disciples first of all,
Beware ye of the leaven of
the Pharisees, which is
hypocrisy.
2. **For there is nothing** covered,
that shall not be revealed; neither hid,
that shall not be known.
3. Therefore whatsoever ye have
spoken in darkness shall be heard in
the light; and that which ye have
spoken in the ear in closets shall be
proclaimed upon the housetops.
4. **And I say** unto you my friends,
Be not afraid of them that
kill the body, and after that have
no more that they can do.
5. **But** I will forewarn
you whom ye shall fear:

Fear him, which
after he hath killed
hath power to cast into
hell; yea, I say unto you, Fear him.
6. **Are not five sparrows**
sold for two farthings,
and not one of them
is forgotten before God?
7. **But even the** very
hairs of your head are all
numbered. Fear not therefore:
ye are of more value than
many sparrows.
8. Also I say unto you,
Whosoever shall confess
me before men, him shall
the Son of man also
confess before the angels
of God:
9. But he that denieth me before
men shall be denied before the
angels of God.
10. **And whosoever shall**
speak a word against the
Son of man, it shall be
forgiven him:
but unto him that
blasphemeth against
the Holy Ghost it shall not
be forgiven.
11. **And when they bring you**
unto the synagogues, and *unto*
magistrates, and powers,
take ye no thought how or
what thing
ye shall answer,
or what ye shall say:
12. **For the Holy Ghost shall**
teach you in the same hour
what *ye* ought
to say.
13. **And one** of the company
said unto him,
Master, speak to my
brother, that he divide the
inheritance with me.
14. **And he said** unto him, Man,
who made me a judge or a
divider over you?
15. And he said unto them,
Take heed, and
beware of covetousness:
for a man's life consisteth
not in the abundance of
the things which
he possesseth.
16. **And he spake a parable**
unto them, saying,
The ground of a certain
rich man brought
forth plentifully:
17. **And he thought** within
himself, saying, What shall I do,
because
I have no room where
to bestow my fruits?
18. And he said, This will I do:
I will pull down my barns,
and build greater;
and there will I bestow all my
fruits and my goods.
19. **And I will say to my soul,**
Soul, thou hast much goods laid up for
many years;
take thine ease, eat, drink,
***and* be merry.**
20. **But God said** unto him,
***Thou* fool, this night thy soul**
shall be required of thee:
then whose shall those things be,
which thou hast provided?
21. **So *is* he that layeth up**
treasure for himself,
and is not rich toward God.
22. And he said unto his disciples,
Therefore I say unto you,
Take no thought for your
life, what ye shall eat;
neither for the body,
what ye shall put on.
23. **The life is more than**
meat, and the body *is more* than
raiment.
24. **Consider the ravens:** for
they neither sow nor reap;
which neither have storehouse
nor barn; and
God feedeth them:
how much more
are ye better than the
fowls?
25. **And which of you**
with taking thought
can add to his stature
one cubit?
26. If ye then be not able to do that

thing which is least, why take ye thought for the rest?

27. **Consider the lilies how they grow: they toil not,** they spin not; and **yet** I say unto you, that **Solomon** in all his glory **was not arrayed like** one of **these.**

28. **If then God so clothe the grass,** which is to day in the field, and to-morrow is cast into the oven; **how much more *will he clothe* you,** O ye of little faith?

29. **And seek not ye what ye shall eat, or** what ye shall **drink,** neither be ye of doubtful mind.

30. For all these things do the nations of the world seek after: and **your Father knoweth that ye have need** of these things.

31. **But rather seek ye the kingdom of God; and all these** things **shall be added** unto you.

32. **Fear not,** little flock; for **it is your Father's good pleasure to give you the kingdom.**

33. **Sell that ye have, and give alms; provide yourselves** bags which wax not old, **a treasure in the heavens that faileth not,** where no thief approacheth, neither moth corrupteth.

34. **For where your treasure is, there will your heart be also.**

35. Let your loins be girded about, and *your* lights burning;

36. And ye yourselves like unto men that wait for their lord, when he will return from the wedding; that when he cometh and knocketh, they may open unto him immediately.

37. **Blessed *are* those** servants, **whom the lord when he cometh shall find watching:** verily I say unto you, that he shall gird himself, and make them to sit down to meat, and will come forth and serve them.

38. And if he shall come in the second watch, or come in the third watch, and find *them* so, blessed are those servants.

39. And this know, that if the goodman of the house had known what hour the thief would come, he would have watched, and not have suffered his house to be broken through.

40. **Be ye therefore ready** also: **for the Son of man cometh** at an hour **when ye think not.**

41. Then Peter said unto him, Lord, speakest thou this parable unto us, or even to all?

42. And the Lord said, **Who** then **is that faithful and wise steward, whom *his* lord shall make ruler over his household,** to give *them their* portion of meat in due season?

43. Blessed *is* that servant, whom his lord when he cometh shall find so doing.

44. Of a truth I say unto you, that he will make him ruler over all that he hath.

45. **But and if that servant say** in his heart, **My lord delayeth his coming; and shall begin** to beat the menservants and maidens, and **to eat and drink,** and to be drunken;

46. **The lord** of that servant **will come** in a day when he looketh not for *him*, and at an hour when he is not aware, and will cut him in sunder, **and will appoint him his portion with the unbelievers.**

47. **And that servant, which knew his lord's will, and prepared not** *himself*, neither did according to his will, **shall be beaten with many**

stripes.
48. **But he that knew not, and did** commit
things worthy of stripes, shall be beaten with few *stripes.* For unto
whomsoever much is given, of him
shall be much required: and to whom men have committed much, of him they will ask the more.
49. I am come to send fire on the earth; and what will I, if it be already kindled?
50. But I have a baptism to be baptized with; and how am I straitened till it be accomplished!
51. **Suppose ye that I am come to give peace** on earth? I tell you,
Nay; but rather division:
52. For from henceforth there shall be five in one house divided, three against two, and two against three.
53. **The father shall be divided against the son,** and the son against the father;
the mother against the daughter, and the daughter against the mother; the mother in law against her daughter in law, and the daughter in law against her mother in law.
54. **And he said** also to the people,
When ye see a cloud rise out of the west, straightway
ye say, There cometh a shower; and so it is.
55. And when *ye see* the south wind blow, ye say, There will be heat; and it cometh to pass.
56. *Ye* hypocrites,
ye can discern the face of the
sky and of the
earth; but how is it that
ye do not discern this time?
57. Yea, and why even of yourselves judge ye not what is right?
58. **When thou goest with thine adversary to the magistrate,** *as thou art* in the way,
give diligence that thou mayest
be delivered from him;
lest he hale thee to the judge, and the judge deliver thee to the officer, and the officer
cast thee into prison.
59. I tell thee, thou shalt not depart thence,
till thou hast paid the very last mite.

CHAPTER 13

1. **There were** present at that season
some that told him of the Galilaeans, whose blood Pilate had mingled with their sacrifices.
2. **And Jesus answering** said unto them,
Suppose ye that these Galilaeans were sinners above all the Galilaeans,
because they suffered such things?
3. I tell you, Nay: but, except ye repent, ye shall all likewise perish.
4. **Or those** eighteen,
upon whom the tower in Siloam fell, and slew them, think ye
that they were sinners above all men that dwelt in Jerusalem?
5. **I tell you, Nay: but, except ye repent, ye shall all likewise perish.**
6. **He spake also this parable; A certain *man* had a fig tree** planted in his vineyard;
and he came and
sought fruit thereon, and found none.
7. **Then said he unto the dresser** of his vineyard, Behold, these three years I come seeking fruit on this fig tree, and find none:
cut it down; why cumbereth it the ground?
8. **And he answering said**

unto him,
Lord, let it alone this year
also,
till I shall dig about it, and
dung ***it*****:**
9. **And if it bear fruit,** ***well*****:** and
if not, ***then*** after that thou shalt
cut it down.
10. **And** he was teaching
in one of the synagogues
on the sabbath.
11. And, behold, there was
a woman which had a
spirit of infirmity
eighteen years,
and was bowed together,
and could in no wise lift up *herself*.
12. **And when Jesus saw**
her, he called *her to him*, and
said unto her,
Woman, thou art loosed
from thine infirmity.
13. **And** he laid *his* hands
on her: and immediately
she was made straight,
and glorified God.
14. **And the ruler**
of the synagogue
answered with indignation,
because that
Jesus had
healed on the sabbath day,
and said unto the people,
There are six days in which
men ought to work: in them
therefore come and be healed, and
not on the sabbath day.
15. **The Lord then answered**
him, and said,
Thou **hypocrite, doth not**
each one of you on the
sabbath loose his ox or ***his***
ass from the stall,
and lead ***him*** away
to watering?
16. **And ought not this**
woman, being a daughter of
Abraham, whom Satan hath bound, lo,
these eighteen years,
be loosed from this bond
on the sabbath day?
17. **And** when he
had said these things,
all his adversaries were
ashamed: and all the people
rejoiced for all the glorious things
that were done by him.
18. **Then said he, Unto what**
is the kingdom of God like?
and whereunto shall I resemble it?
19. **It is like a grain of**
mustard seed, which a man
took, and
cast into his garden; and it
grew, and waxed a great
tree; and the fowls of the air lodged
in the branches of it.
20. **And again** he said, Whereunto
shall I liken the kingdom of God?
21. **It is like leaven,**
which a woman took and
hid in three measures of
meal, till the whole
was leavened.
22. And he went through the cities
and villages, teaching,
and journeying toward Jerusalem.
23. **Then said one**
unto him, Lord,
are there few that be
saved? And he said
unto them,
24. **Strive to enter** in at
the strait gate: for many,
I say unto you,
will seek to enter in,
and shall not be able.
25. **When once the master**
of the house is risen up, and
hath shut to
the door, and ye
begin to stand without, and to
knock at the door, saying,
Lord,
Lord, open unto us; and he
shall answer and say unto you,
I know you not whence ye are:
26. **Then shall ye** begin to
say, We have eaten and
drunk in thy presence,
and thou hast taught in our streets.
27. **But he shall say,** I tell you,
I know you not whence ye are;
depart from me, all
ye **workers of iniquity.**
28. **There shall be weeping**

■ **and gnashing of teeth,**
when ye shall see Abraham, and
Isaac, and Jacob, and all the
prophets, in the kingdom of God, and
you yourselves thrust out.
■ 29. **And they shall come**
■ **from the east,** and *from* the
■ **west,** and from the
■ **north, and** *from* the
■ **south, and shall sit down**
■ **in the kingdom** of God.
30. And, behold, there are last which
shall be first, and there are first which
shall be last.
■ 31. **The same day** there
■ **came** certain of
■ **the Pharisees, saying**
unto him, Get thee out, and
■ **depart** hence:
■ **for Herod will kill thee.**
■ 32. **And he said** unto them,
■ **Go** ye, and
■ **tell that fox,** Behold,
■ **I cast out devils, and I do**
■ **cures** to-day and to-morrow,
■ **and the third day I shall**
■ **be perfected.**
■ 33. **Nevertheless I must walk**
■ **to-day, and to-morrow,**
and the *day* following:
■ **for it cannot be that a**
■ **prophet perish out of**
■ **Jerusalem.**
■ 34. **O Jerusalem,** Jerusalem,
which killest the prophets, and
stonest them that are sent unto thee;
■ **how often would I have**
■ **gathered thy children**
■ **together,** as a hen *doth gather*
her brood under *her* wings,
■ **and ye would not !**
■ 35. **Behold, your house is**
left unto you
■ **desolate: and**
verily I say unto you,
■ **Ye shall not see me, until**
the time come when
■ **ye** shall
■ **say, Blessed *is***
■ **he that cometh**
■ **in the**
■ **name of**
■ **the Lord.**

CHAPTER 14

■ 1. **And** it came to pass, as
■ **he went into the house of**
■ **one of the chief Pharisees**
■ **to eat** bread
■ **on the sabbath**
day, that they watched him.
■ 2. **And, behold,**
■ **there was a** certain
■ **man** before him
■ **which had the dropsy.**
■ 3. **And Jesus** answering
■ **spake** unto the lawyers and
Pharisees, saying,
■ **Is it lawful to heal on the**
■ **sabbath** day?
■ 4. **And they held their**
■ **peace. And he** took *him*, and
■ **healed him,** and let him go;
5. And answered them, saying, Which
of you shall have an ass or an ox
fallen into a pit, and will not
straightway pull him out on the
sabbath day?
6. And they could not answer him
again to these things.
■ 7. **And he put forth a**
■ **parable** to those which
were bidden,
■ **when he marked how they**
■ **chose** out
■ **the chief rooms;**
saying unto them.
■ 8. **When thou art bidden**
of any *man*
■ **to a wedding, sit not down**
■ **in the highest room; lest a**
■ **more honourable man**
than thou
■ **be bidden** of him;
■ 9. **And he** that bade thee and him
■ **come and say** to thee,
■ **Give this man place; and**
■ **thou** begin with shame to
■ **take the lowest room.**
■ 10. **But** when thou art bidden,
■ **go and sit** down
■ **in the lowest room; that**
when he that bade thee cometh,
■ **he may say** unto thee,
■ **Friend, go up higher: then**
■ **shalt thou have worship**
in the presence

of them that sit at meat
with thee.
11. For whosoever exalteth himself
shall be abased; and
he that humbleth himself
shall be exalted.
12. **Then said he**
also to him that bade him,
When thou makest a dinner
or a supper,
call not thy friends, nor *thy*
brethren, neither thy kinsmen,
nor *thy*
rich neighbours; lest
they also bid thee again, and
a recompence be made
thee.
13. **But** when thou makest a feast,
call the poor, the maimed,
the lame, the blind:
14. **And thou shalt be**
blessed; for they cannot
recompense thee:
for thou shalt be
recompensed at the
resurrection of the just.
15. And when one of them that sat at
meat with him heard these things, he
said unto him, Blessed *is* he that shall
eat bread in the kingdom of God.
16. **Then said he** unto him,
A certain
man made a great supper,
and bade many:
17. **And sent his servant**
at supper time
to say to them that were bidden,
Come; for all things are
now ready.
18. **And they** all with one *consent*
began to make excuse. The
first said unto him, I have bought a
piece of ground, and I must needs go
and see it: I pray thee have me
excused.
19. And another said, I have bought
five yoke of oxen, and I go to prove
them: I pray thee have me excused.
20. And another said, I have married a
wife, and therefore I cannot come.
21. **So that servant** came, and
shewed his lord these
things. Then the master
of the house
being angry said
to his servant,
Go out quickly
into the streets and lanes
of the city,
and bring in hither
the poor, and the maimed,
and the halt, and the blind.
22. **And the servant said,**
Lord,
it is done as thou
hast commanded, and
yet there is room.
23. **And the lord said**
unto the servant,
Go out into the highways
and hedges, and compel
them to come in, that my house
may be filled.
24. **For I say** unto you,
That none of those
men which were
bidden shall taste of my
supper.
25. And there went great multitudes
with him: and he turned, and said unto
them,
26. If any *man* come to me, and hate
not his father, and mother, and wife,
and children, and brethren, and
sisters, yea, and his own life also, he
cannot be my disciple.
27. **And whosoever doth not**
bear his cross, and come
after me, cannot be
my disciple.
28. **For which of you,**
intending to build a tower,
sitteth not down
first, and
counteth the cost, whether he
have *sufficient* to finish *it.*
29. **Lest haply,** after
he hath laid the foundation, and
is not able to finish it,
all that behold *it* begin to mock him,
30. Saying, This man began to build,
and was not able to finish.
31. **Or what king, going to**
make
war against another king,
sitteth not down

first, and
consulteh wether he be
able with ten thousand
to meet him that cometh
against him
with twenty thousand?
32. **Or else,** while the other is
yet a great way off,
he sendeth an ambassage,
and desireth conditions of
peace.
33. **So likewise,** whosoever
he be of you
that forsaketh not all
that he hath, he
cannot be my disciple.
34. **Salt is good: but if the**
salt have lost his savour,
wherewith shall it be seasoned?
35. **It is** neither fit for the land, nor
yet for the dunghill; *but* men
cast it
out. He that hath ears to hear, let
him hear.

CHAPTER 15

1. **Then drew near** unto him all
the publicans and sinners
for to hear him.
2. **And the Pharisees and**
scribes murmured, saying,
This man receiveth sinners,
and eateth with them.
3. **And he spake this**
parable unto them, saying,
4. **What man** of you,
having an hundred sheep,
if he lose one of them,
doth not leave the ninety and nine
in the wilderness, and
go after that which is lost,
until he find it?
5. **And** when he hath found *it*, he
layeth it on his shoulders,
rejoicing.
6. **And** when he cometh home, he
calleth together his friends and
neighbours, saying unto them,
Rejoice with me; for I have
found my sheep
which was lost.
7. **I say** unto you, that likewise
joy shall be in heaven over
one sinner that repenteth,
more than over ninety and nine just
persons, which need no repentance.
8. **Either what woman**
having ten pieces of
silver, if she lose one
piece, doth not light a candle,
and sweep the house, and
seek diligently till
she find it?
9. And when she hath found *it*, she
calleth *her* friends and *her* neighbours
together, saying, Rejoice with me; for
I have found the piece
which I had lost.
10. **Likewise,** I say unto you,
there is joy in the presence
of the angels of
God over one sinner
that repenteth.
11. **And he said, A** certain
man had two sons:
12. **And the younger** of them
said to *his* father,
Father, give me the portion
of goods that falleth to me.
And he divided unto them *his* living.
13. **And** not many days after
the younger son
gathered all together, and
took his journey into a far
country, and there wasted
his substance with
riotous living.
14. **And** when he had spent all,
there arose a mighty
famine in that land;
and he began to
be in want.
15. **And he went**
and joined himself
to a citizen of that country;
and he sent him into his fields
to feed swine.
16. **And he** would fain have
filled his belly with the
husks that the swine did
eat: and no man
gave unto him.
17. **And when he came to**
himself, he said, How many
hired servants of my father's have
bread enough and to spare, and

I perish with hunger!
18. **I will** arise and
go to my father, and will
say unto him, Father,
I have sinned
against heaven, and before thee,
19. And am no more worthy to be
called thy son:
make me as one of thy
hired servants.
20. **And he arose,**
and came to his father.
But when he was yet a great
way off, his father saw him,
and
had compassion, and ran,
and fell on his neck,
and kissed him.
21. **And the son said**
unto him, Father,
I have sinned against heaven,
and in thy sight, and am no more
worthy to be called thy son.
22. **But the father said**
to his servants,
Bring forth the best robe,
and put *it* on him;
and put a ring on his hand,
and shoes on his feet:
23. **And** bring hither the
fatted calf, and kill *it*; and
let us eat, and be merry:
24. **For this my son**
was dead, and is alive again; he
was lost, and is found.
And they began to be merry.
25. **Now his elder son**
was in the field: and as he
came and
drew nigh to the house, he
heard music and dancing.
26. **And** he called
one of the servants, and
asked what these
things meant.
27. **And he said** unto him,
Thy brother is come; and
thy father hath killed the
fatted calf, because he hath
received him safe and sound.
28. **And he was angry, and**
would not go in: therefore came his
father out, and entreated him.
29. And he answering
said to his father, Lo, these
many years do I serve
thee, neither
transgressed I at any time
thy commandment: and yet
thou never gavest me a kid,
that I might make merry
with my friends:
30. **But** as soon as
this thy son was come,
which hath devoured thy
living with harlots, thou
hast killed for him the
fatted calf.
31. **And he said** unto him,
Son, thou art ever with me, and
all that I have is thine.
32. It was meet that
we should make merry,
and be glad:
for this
thy brother was dead, and
is alive again; and was lost, and is
found.

CHAPTER 16

1. **And he said also unto his**
disciples, There was a
certain
rich man, which had a
steward; and
the same was accused
unto him
that he had wasted
his goods.
2. **And he** called him, and
said unto him, How is it that
I hear this of thee?
give an account of thy
stewardship; for thou
mayest be no longer steward.
3. **Then the steward said**
within himself, What shall I
do? for my lord taketh away from me
the stewardship: I cannot dig; to beg I
am ashamed.
4. **I am resolved what to do,**
that, when I am put out of the
stewardship, they may receive me
into their houses.
5. **So he called** every one of
his lord's debtors *unto him,*

and said unto the first,
How much owest thou unto
my lord?
6. **And he said, An hundred**
measures of oil. And he
said unto him,
Take thy bill,
and sit down quickly,
and write fifty.
7. **Then said he to another,**
And
how much owest thou?
And he said,
An hundred measures of
wheat. And he said unto him,
Take thy bill, and
write fourscore.
8. **And the lord commended**
the unjust steward,
because he had done wisely:
for the children of this
world are in their generation
wiser than the children
of light.
9. **And I say** unto you,
Make to yourselves
friends of the mammon of
unrighteousness; that,
when ye fail, they may
receive you
into everlasting habitations.
10. **He that is faithful in that**
which is least is faithful
also in much: and he that is
unjust in the least is unjust also in
much.
11. **If therefore ye have not**
been faithful
in the unrighteous mammon,
who will commit to your
trust the true riches?
12. And if ye have not been faithful in
that which is another man's, who shall
give you that which is your own?
13. **No servant can serve**
two masters: for either he will
hate the one, and love the other; or
else he will hold to the one, and
despise the other.
Ye cannot serve God
and mammon.
14. **And the Pharisees**
also, who were covetous,
heard all these things:
and they
derided him.
15. **And he said** unto them, Ye
are they which justify yourselves
before men; but
God knoweth your hearts:
for that which is highly
esteemed among men
is abomination in the sight
of God.
16. **The law and the**
prophets were until John:
since that time the kingdom
of God is preached,
and every man presseth into it.
17. **And it is easier for**
heaven and earth to pass,
than one tittle of the
law to fail.
18. **Whosoever putteth**
away his wife, and
marrieth another,
committeth adultery:
and whosoever marrieth
her that is put away
from *her* husband
committeth adultery.
19. **There was a certain rich**
man, which was clothed in purple
and fine linen, and fared sumptuously
every day:
20. **And** there was
a certain
beggar named Lazarus,
which was
laid at his gate, full of sores,
21. **And desiring to be fed**
with the crumbs which fell
from the rich man's table:
moreover the dogs came and licked
his sores.
22. **And** it came to pass, that
the beggar died, and was
carried by the angels
into Abraham's bosom: the
rich man also died,
and was buried;
23. **And in hell he lift**
up his eyes, being
in torments, and seeth
Abraham afar off,
and Lazarus in his bosom.

24. **And he cried** and said,
Father Abraham,
have mercy on me, and
send Lazarus, that
he may dip the tip of
his finger in water, and
cool my tongue; for I am
tormented in this flame.
25. **But Abraham said,**
Son, remember that
thou in thy lifetime
receivedst thy good things,
and likewise
Lazarus evil things: but
now he is comforted, and
thou art tormented.
26. **And beside** all this,
between us and you
there is a great gulf fixed:
so that they which would pass
from hence to
you cannot; neither can they
pass to us, that *would come* from
thence.
27. **Then he said,** I pray thee
therefore, father, that thou wouldest
send him to my
father's house:
28. **For I have five brethren;**
that he may testify unto them,
lest they also come into
this place of torment.
29. **Abraham saith** unto him,
They have Moses and the
prophets; let them hear them.
30. **And he said,**
Nay, father Abraham: but
if one went unto them
from the dead, they
will repent.
31. **And he said** unto him,
If they hear not Moses and
the prophets, neither will
they be persuaded, though
one rose from the dead.

CHAPTER 17

1. **Then said he unto the**
disciples, It is impossible but that
offences will come: but
woe unto him, through
whom they come!
2. **It were better** for him
that a millstone were hanged
about his neck, and
he cast into the sea, than
that he should
offend one of these
little ones.
3. Take heed to yourselves:
If thy brother trespass
against thee,
rebuke him; and if he
repent, forgive him.
4. **And if he trespass**
against thee
seven times in a day, and
seven times in a day turn again to
thee, saying, I
repent; thou shalt
forgive him.
5. **And the apostles said**
unto the Lord,
Increase our faith.
6. **And the Lord said, If ye**
had faith as a grain of
mustard seed, ye might
say unto this sycamine
tree, Be thou plucked
up by the root, and be
thou planted in the sea;
and it should obey you.
7. But which of you, having a servant
plowing or feeding cattle, will say unto
him by and by, when he is come from
the field, Go and sit down to meat?
8. And will not rather say unto him,
Make ready wherewith I may sup, and
gird thyself, and serve me, till I have
eaten and drunken; and afterward
thou shalt eat and drink?
9. Doth he thank that servant
because he did the things that were
commanded him? I trow not.
10. So likewise ye, when ye shall have
done all those things which are
commanded you, say, We are
unprofitable servants: we have done
that which was our duty to do.
11. **And** it came to pass,
as he went to Jerusalem,
that he passed
through the midst of
Samaria and Galilee.
12. And as he entered into
a certain village,

there met him ten men that were
lepers, which stood afar off:
13. **And they**
lifted up *their* voices, and
said, Jesus, Master,
have mercy on us.
14. **And** when he saw *them,*
he said unto them,
Go shew yourselves unto
the priests. And
it came to pass, that,
as they went, they
were cleansed.
15. **And one of them,**
when he saw that he was healed,
turned back, and
with a loud voice
glorified God,
16. **And fell** down on *his* face
at his feet, giving him
thanks: and he was a Samaritan.
17. **And Jesus** answering
said, Were there not ten
cleansed? but
where are the nine?
18. **There are not** found that
returned to give glory to God,
save this stranger.
19. **And he said** unto him,
Arise, go thy way:
thy faith hath made
thee whole.
20. **And when he was**
demanded of the
Pharisees, when the
kingdom of God
should come, he answered
them and said, The kingdom of God
cometh not with observation:
21. Neither shall they say, Lo here! or,
lo there! for, behold
the kingdom of
God is within you.
22. **And he said unto the**
disciples, The days will
come, when ye shall desire
to see one of the days of
the Son of man,
and ye shall not see *it.*
23. And they shall say to you, See
here; or, see there: go not after *them,*
nor follow *them.*
24. **For as the lightning,** that
lighteneth out of the one *part*
under heaven,
shineth unto the other *part*
under heaven;
so shall also
the Son of man be
in his day.
25. **But first must he suffer**
many things,
and be rejected
of this generation.
26. **And as** it was
in the days of Noe, so shall
it be also
in the days of the Son of man.
27. **They did eat,** they
drank, they
married wives,
they were given in marriage,
until the day that
Noe entered into
the ark, and the flood
came, and
destroyed them all.
28. **Likewise also as** it was in
the days of Lot; they did eat, they
drank, they bought, they sold, they
planted, they builded;
29. But the same day that
Lot went out of Sodom it
rained fire and brimstone
from heaven, and
destroyed them all.
30. **Even thus shall it be**
in the day
when the Son of man
is revealed.
31. **In that day, he which**
shall be upon
the housetop,
and his stuff in the house,
let him not come down
to take it away: and he that is in the
field, let him likewise not return back.
32. Remember Lot's wife.
33. Whosoever shall seek to save his
life shall lose it; and whosoever shall
lose his life shall preserve it.
34. **I tell you,** in that night
there shall be two men
in one bed; the
one shall be taken, and the
other shall be

left.
35. Two *women* shall be grinding
together; the one shall be taken, and
the other left.
36. Two *men* shall be in the field; the
one shall be taken, and the other left.
37. **And they** answered and
said unto him,
Where, Lord? And he said
unto them,
Wheresoever the body is,
thither will the eagles be
gathered together.

CHAPTER 18

1. **And he spake a parable**
unto them to *this* end,
that men ought always to
pray, and not to faint;
2. **Saying, There was** in a city
a judge, which feared not
God, neither regarded man:
3. **And** there was
a widow in that city; and she
came unto him, saying,
Avenge me of
mine adversary.
4. **And he would not** for a while:
but afterward he
said within himself, Though I
fear not God, nor regard man;
5. Yet because this widow
troubleth me,
I will avenge her, lest by her
continual coming she
weary me.
6. **And the Lord said,**
Hear what the unjust judge saith.
7. **And shall not God**
avenge his own elect,
which cry day and night
unto him, though he bear
long with them?
8. I tell you that he will avenge them
speedily. Nevertheless when the Son
of man cometh, shall he find faith on
the earth?
9. **And he spake this**
parable unto certain which
trusted in themselves
that they were righteous,
and despised others:
10. **Two men went**
up into the temple
to pray; the one
a Pharisee, and the other
a publican.
11. **The Pharisee** stood and
prayed thus with himself,
God, I thank thee, that I am
not as other men
are, extortioners, unjust, adulterers,
or even as this publican.
12. **I fast** twice in the week,
I give tithes of all that I possess.
13. **And the publican,**
standing afar off,
would not lift up so much as
his eyes unto heaven, but
smote upon his breast,
saying, God be
merciful to me a sinner.
14. I tell you,
this man went down
to his house justified *rather*
than the other: for every one that
exalteth himself shall be abased; and
he that humbleth himself
shall be exalted.
15. **And they brought**
unto him also
infants, that he would touch
them: but when
his disciples saw *it*, they
rebuked them.
16. **But Jesus**
called them *unto him*, and
said, Suffer little children
to come unto me,
and forbid them not:
for of such is the kingdom
of God.
17. Verily I say unto you,
Whosoever shall not
receive the kingdom of God
as a little
child shall in no wise enter
therein.
18. **And a certain ruler**
asked him, saying, Good Master,
what shall I do to inherit
eternal life?
19. **And Jesus said**
unto him, Why callest thou me good?
none *is* good, save one, *that is*, God.
20. Thou knowest the

commandments,
Do not commit adultery,
Do not
kill, Do not
steal, Do not
bear false witness, Honour
thy father and thy mother.
21. **And he said, All these**
have I kept from my youth up.
22. **Now when Jesus heard**
these things,
he said unto him,
Yet lackest thou one thing:
sell all that thou hast, and
distribute unto the poor,
and thou shalt have
treasure in heaven: and
come, follow me.
23. **And** when he heard this,
he was very
sorrowful: for he
was very rich.
24. **And when Jesus saw**
that he was very sorrowful,
he said, How hardly shall
they that have riches enter
into the kingdom of God!
25. **For it is easier for a**
camel to go through a
needle's eye, than for a rich man
to enter into the kingdom of God.
26. **And they that heard it**
said, Who then can
be saved?
27. **And he said, The things**
which are
impossible with men are
possible with God.
28. **Then Peter said,** Lo,
we have left all, and
followed thee.
29. **And he said** unto them,
Verily I say unto you,
There is no man that hath
left house, or parents, or
brethren, or wife, or
children, for the kingdom of
God's sake,
30. **Who shall not receive**
manifold more
in this present time,
and in the world to come
life everlasting.

31. **Then he took** *unto him*
the twelve, and said
unto them, Behold,
we go up to Jerusalem,
and all things that are
written by the prophets
concerning the Son of man
shall be accomplished.
32. **For he shall be delivered**
unto the Gentiles,
and shall be mocked, and spitefully
entreated, and spitted on:
33. **And they shall**
scourge *him*, and
put him to death: and the
third day he shall rise again.
34. And they understood none of
these things: and this saying was hid
from them, neither knew they the
things which were spoken.
35. **And** it came to pass, that
as he was come nigh
unto Jericho, a certain
blind man sat by the way side
begging:
36. And hearing the multitude pass
by, he asked what it meant.
37. And they told him, that Jesus of
Nazareth passeth by.
38. **And he cried,** saying,
Jesus, *thou* son of David,
have mercy on me.
39. **And they** which went before
rebuked him, that he should
hold his peace: but he cried so much
the more, *Thou* son of David,
have mercy on me.
40. **And Jesus** stood, and
commanded him to be
brought unto him: and when he was
come near, he asked him,
41. **Saying, What wilt thou**
that I shall do unto thee?
And he said, Lord, that I
may receive my sight.
42. **And Jesus said** unto him,
Receive thy sight: thy faith
hath saved thee.
43. **And immediately he**
received his sight, and
followed him, glorifying God: and all
the people, when they *saw it*, gave
praise unto God.

CHAPTER 19

1. And *Jesus* entered and passed
through Jericho.
2. And, behold, *there was*
a man
named Zacchaeus, which was
the chief among the
publicans, and he
was rich.
3. **And he sought to see**
Jesus who he was;
and could not for the press,
because he was little
of stature.
4. **And he** ran before, and
climbed up into a
sycomore tree to see him:
for he was to pass that *way*.
5. **And when Jesus came**
to the place,
he looked up, and saw him,
and said unto him,
Zacchaeus, make haste, and
come down; for to-day
I must abide at thy house.
6. **And he** made haste, and
came down, and
received him joyfully.
7. **And when they saw** it,
they all murmured, saying,
That he was gone to be guest
with a man that is a sinner.
8. **And Zacchaeus** stood, and
said unto the Lord:
Behold, Lord, the
half of my goods I give to
the poor; and if I have
taken any thing from any
man by false accusation,
I restore him fourfold.
9. **And Jesus said** unto him,
This day is salvation come
to this house, forsomuch as he
also is a son of Abraham.
10. **For the Son of man is**
come to seek and
to save that which
was lost.
11. **And** as they heard these things,
he added and
spake a parable, because he
was nigh to Jerusalem, and because
they thought that the kingdom of God
should immediately appear.
12. He said therefore,
A certain nobleman went
into a far country to receive
for himself
a kingdom, and to return.
13. **And he called his ten**
servants, and
delivered them
ten pounds, and said
unto them,
Occupy till I come.
14. But his citizens hated him, and
sent a message after him, saying, We
will not have this *man* to reign over us.
15. **And** it came to pass, that
when he was
returned, having received
the kingdom, then
he commanded these
servants to be called unto
him, to whom he had given the money,
that he might know how
much every man had
gained by trading.
16. **Then came the first,**
saying, Lord, thy pound
hath gained ten pounds.
17. **And he said** unto him,
Well, thou good servant:
because thou hast been
faithful in a very little,
have thou authority over
ten cities.
18. **And the second** came,
saying, Lord, thy pound hath
gained five pounds.
19. **And he said** likewise to him,
Be thou also over
five cities.
20. **And another came,**
saying, Lord, behold,
here is thy pound, which I have
kept laid up in a napkin:
21. **For I feared thee,**
because thou art an
austere man: thou takest up that
thou layedst not down, and reapest
that thou didst not sow.
22. **And he saith** unto him, Out of
thine own mouth will I judge thee,
thou wicked servant. Thou
knewest that I was an austere man,

taking up that I laid not down, and
reaping that I did not sow:
23. **Wherefore then gavest
not thou my money into the
bank, that** at my coming
I might have
required mine own with
usury?
24. And he said unto them
that stood by,
Take from him
**the pound, and give it to
him that hath ten pounds.**
25. (And they said unto him, Lord, he
hath ten pounds.)
26. **For I say** unto you,
**That unto every one which
hath shall be given;**
and from him that hath not, even that
he hath shall be taken away from him.
27. **But those mine enemies,**
which would not that I should reign
over them,
bring hither, and slay them
before me.
28. And when he had thus spoken, he
went before, ascending up to
Jerusalem.
29. **And** it came to pass,
when he was come nigh
to Bethphage and Bethany,
at the mount called
**the mount of Olives, he sent
two** of his
disciples,
30. **Saying, Go ye into the
village** over against *you* ; in the
which at your entering
ye shall find a colt tied,
whereon yet never man sat: loose
him, and
bring him hither.
31. **And if any man ask** you,
Why do ye loose him?
thus shall ye
say unto him, Because
the Lord hath need of him.
32. And they that were sent went their
way, and found even as he had said
unto them.
33. And as they were loosing the colt,
the owners thereof said unto them,
Why loose ye the colt?
34. And they said, The Lord hath need
of him.
35. **And they brought him**
to Jesus:
and they
**cast their garments upon
the colt, and they set Jesus
thereon.**
36. **And** as he went, they
**spread their clothes in the
way.**
37. **And** when he was come nigh,
even now at the descent of the mount
of Olives,
the whole multitude
of the disciples
began to rejoice and
praise God with a loud voice
**for all the mighty works that
they had seen;**
38. Saying, Blessed *be* the King that
cometh in the name of the Lord: peace
in heaven, and glory in the highest.
39. **And some of the
Pharisees** from among
the multitude
said unto him, Master,
rebuke thy disciples.
40. **And he answered**
and said unto them, I tell you that,
**if these should hold their
peace, the stones would**
immediately
cry out.
41. **And** when he was come near,
**he beheld the city, and
wept over it,**
42. **Saying, If thou hadst
known,** even thou, at least in this
thy day,
the things *which belong*
**unto thy peace! but now
they are hid** from thine eyes.
43. **For** the days shall come upon
thee, that
thine enemies shall
cast a trench about thee, and
compass thee round,
and keep thee in on every side,
44. **And shall lay thee even
with the ground,**
and thy children within thee;
and they shall not leave

in thee
one stone upon another;
because thou knewest not
the time of
thy visitation.
45. **And he went into the**
temple, and began to cast
out them that sold therein,
and them that
bought;
46. **Saying** unto them,
It is written, My house is the
house of prayer: but ye
have made it a den
of thieves.
47. **And** he taught daily
in the temple. But
the chief priests and the
scribes and the chief of the people
sought to destroy him,
48. And could not find what they might
do: for all the people were very
attentive to hear him.

CHAPTER 20

1. And it came to pass, *that* on one of
those days, as he taught the people in
the temple,
and preached the gospel,
the chief priests and the
scribes came
upon *him* with the elders,
2. And spake unto him,
saying, Tell us, by what
authority doest thou these
things? or who is he that gave thee
this authority?
3. **And he answered and**
said unto them, I will also ask you
one thing; and answer me:
4. **The baptism of John, was**
it from heaven, or of men?
5. **And they reasoned**
with themselves,
saying, If we shall say,
From heaven; he will say,
Why then believed ye
him not?
6. **But and if we say,**
Of men; all
the people will stone us:
for they be persuaded that
John was a prophet.
7. **And they answered, that**
they could not tell
whence *it was.*
8. **And Jesus said** unto them,
Neither tell I you by what
authority I do these things.
9. **Then began he to speak**
to the people
this parable; A certain
man planted a vineyard,
and let it forth
to husbandmen, and went
into a far country
for a long time.
10. **And** at the season
he sent a servant
to the husbandmen,
that they should give him of
the fruit of the vineyard:
but the husbandmen beat
him, and sent *him* away empty.
11. **And again he sent**
another servant:
and they beat him also, and
entreated *him* shamefully, and sent
him away empty.
12. **And again he sent a**
third: and they wounded
him also, and cast *him* out.
13. **Then said the lord**
of the vineyard, What shall I do?
I will send my beloved son:
it may be they will reverence *him* when
they see him.
14. **But** when the husbandmen
saw him,
they reasoned
among themselves, saying,
This is the heir: come,
let us kill him, that the
inheritance may be ours.
15. So they cast him out of the
vineyard, and killed *him.*
What therefore shall the
lord of the vineyard
do unto them?
16. **He shall** come and
destroy these
husbandmen, and shall
give the vineyard to others.
And when they heard *it*, they said,
God forbid.
17. **And he** beheld them, and

said, What is this then that is
written,
The stone which the
builders rejected, the same
is become the head of
the corner?
18. Whosoever shall fall upon that
stone shall be broken; but on
whomsoever it shall fall, it will grind
him to powder.
19. **And the** chief
priests and the scribes
the same hour sought to lay hands
on him; and they feared the people:
for they
perceived that he had
spoken this parable
against them.
20. **And they watched**
him, and sent forth spies, which
should feign themselves just men,
that they might take hold of
his words, that
so they might deliver him
unto the power and authority of
the governor.
21. **And they asked him,**
saying,
Master, we know that thou
sayest and teachest rightly, neither
acceptest thou the person *of any*, but
teachest the way of
God truly:
22. **Is it lawful** for us
to give tribute unto Caesar,
or no?
23. **But he** perceived their
craftiness, and
said unto them,
Why tempt ye me?
24. **Shew me a penny.**
Whose image and superscription
hath it? They answered
and said,
Caesar's.
25. **And he said** unto them,
Render therefore
unto Caesar the things
which be Caesar's, and
unto God the things which
be God's.
26. **And they** could not take hold of
his words before the people: and they
marvelled at his answer,
and held their peace.
27. **Then came** to him certain of
the Sadducees, which deny
that there is
any resurrection;
and they asked him,
28. **Saying, Master, Moses**
wrote unto us,
If any man's brother die,
having a wife, and he die
without children, that his
brother should take his
wife, and raise up seed
unto his brother.
29. **There were** therefore
seven brethren: and the
first took a wife, and died
without children.
30. And the second took her to wife,
and he died childless.
31. **And** the third took her; and
in like manner the seven
also: and they
left no children, and died.
32. **Last of all the woman**
died also.
33. **Therefore in the**
resurrection whose wife
of them
is she? for seven had her to wife.
34. **And Jesus answering**
said unto them,
The children of this world marry,
and are given in marriage:
35. **But they which shall**
be accounted worthy to
obtain that world, and
the resurrection from the dead,
neither marry, nor are
given in marriage:
36. **Neither can they die**
any more: for they are
equal unto the angels;
and are the children of
God, being the children of the
resurrection.
37. Now that the dead are raised,
even Moses shewed at the bush,
when he calleth the Lord the God of
Abraham, and the God of Isaac, and
the God of Jacob.
38. **For he is not a God of the**

dead, but of the living:
for all live unto him.
39. **Then** certain of
the scribes answering
said, Master,
thou hast well said.
40. And after that they durst not ask
him any *question at all.*
41. **And he said** unto them,
How say they that Christ is
David's son?
42. **And David** himself
saith in the book of Psalms,
The Lord said unto
my Lord, Sit thou
on my right hand,
43. Till I make thine enemies
thy footstool.
44. **David therefore calleth**
him Lord, how is he
then his son?
45. **Then** in the audience
of all the people
he said unto his disciples,
46. **Beware of the scribes,**
which desire to walk in long robes, and
love greetings in the markets, and the
highest seats in the synagogues, and
the chief rooms at feasts;
47. **Which devour widows'**
houses, and for a shew
make long prayers: the
same shall receive
greater damnation.

CHAPTER 21

1. **And he** looked up, and
saw the rich men casting
their gifts into the treasury.
2. **And** he saw also
a certain
poor widow casting in thither
two mites.
3. **And he said,** Of a truth
I say unto you, that
this poor widow hath cast
in more than they all:
4. **For all these have of their**
abundance cast in
unto the offerings of God:
but she of her penury
hath cast in all the living
that she had.

5. **And as some spake of**
the temple, how it was adorned
with goodly stones and gifts,
he said,
6. *As for* these things which ye
behold, the days will come, in the
which
there shall not be left one
stone upon another,
that shall not be thrown down.
7. **And they asked** him,
saying, Master, but when shall
these things be? and
what sign will there be when
these things shall come to pass?
8. **And he said,** Take heed
that ye be not deceived: for
many shall come in my
name, saying, I am Christ;
and the time draweth near:
go ye
not therefore
after them.
9. **But when ye shall hear of**
wars and commotions,
be not terrified: for these things
must first come to pass;
but the end is not by and by.
10. Then said he unto them,
Nation shall rise against
nation, and kingdom against
kingdom:
11. **And great earthquakes**
shall be in divers places,
and famines,
and pestilences; and fearful sights
and great signs shall there
be from heaven.
12. **But before all these, they**
shall lay their hands on you, and
persecute you, delivering *you* up
to the synagogues, and into prisons,
being brought before kings and rulers
for my name's sake.
13. **And it shall turn to you**
for a testimony.
14. **Settle it** therefore in your hearts,
not to meditate before what
ye shall answer:
15. **For I will give you**
a mouth and
wisdom, which all your
adversaries shall not be able to

gainsay nor resist.

16. **And ye shall be betrayed** both by parents, and brethren, and kinsfolks, and friends; **and some** of you **shall** they cause to **be put to death.**

17. **And ye shall be hated** of all *men* **for my name's sake.**

18. **But there shall not an hair of your head perish.**

19. In your patience possess ye your souls.

20. **And when ye shall see Jerusalem compassed with armies, then know that the desolation** thereof **is nigh.**

21. **Then let them** which are **in Judaea flee** to the mountains; and let them which are in the midst of it depart out; and let not them that are in the countries enter thereinto.

22. **For these be the days of vengeance, that all** things which are written **may be fulfilled.**

23. But woe unto them that are with child, and to them that give suck, in those days! for **there shall be great distress** in the land, and wrath upon this people.

24. And they shall fall by the edge of the sword, and shall be led away captive into all nations: **and Jerusalem shall be trodden down** of the Gentiles, **until the times of the Gentiles be fulfilled.**

25. **And there shall be signs in the sun,** and in the **moon, and** in the **stars; and upon the earth distress of nations,** with perplexity; the sea and the waves roaring;

26. **Men's hearts failing them for fear,** and for looking after those things which are coming on the earth: for the powers of heaven shall be shaken.

27. **And then shall they see the Son of man coming** in a cloud with power and great glory.

28. **And when these things** begin to **come to pass, then look up,** and lift up your heads; **for your redemption draweth nigh.**

29. **And he spake** to them **a parable; Behold the fig tree,** and all the trees;

30. **When they now shoot forth, ye** see and **know** of your own selves **that summer is** now **nigh** at hand.

31. **So likewise ye, when ye see these things** come to pass, **know** ye **that the kingdom of God is** nigh **at hand.**

32. Verily I say unto you, **This generation shall not pass away, till all be fulfilled.**

33. **Heaven and earth shall pass away: but my words shall not** pass away.

34. **And take heed** to yourselves, **lest** at any time **your hearts be overcharged with** surfeiting, and drunkenness, and **cares of this life, and so that day come upon you unawares.**

35. For as a snare shall it come on all them that dwell on the face of the whole earth.

36. **Watch** ye therefore, **and pray** always, **that ye may be accounted worthy** to escape all these things that shall come to pass, and **to stand before the Son** of man.

37. And in the day time he was teaching in the temple; and at night he went out, and abode in the mount that is called *the mount* of Olives.

38. And all the people came early in
the morning to him in the temple, for to
hear him.

CHAPTER 22

1. **Now the feast of**
unleavened bread drew
nigh, which is called the Passover.
2. **And the** chief
priests and scribes sought
how they might kill him;
for they feared the people.
3. **Then entered Satan into**
Judas surnamed Iscariot,
being of the number of the twelve.
4. **And he went** his way,
and communed with the
chief priests and captains,
how he might betray him
unto them.
5. **And they** were glad, and
covenanted to give
him money.
6. **And he** promised, and
sought opportunity to
betray him unto them in the
absence of the multitude.
7. **Then came the day of**
unleavened bread, when
the passover must be killed.
8. **And he sent Peter and**
John, saying, Go and
prepare us the passover,
that we may eat.
9. And they said unto him, Where wilt
thou that we prepare?
10. And he said unto them, Behold,
when ye are entered into the city,
there shall a man meet you, bearing
a pitcher of water; follow him into the
house where he entereth in.
11. And ye shall say unto the
goodman of the house, The Master
saith unto thee, Where is the
guestchamber, where I shall eat the
passover with my disciples?
12. And he shall shew you a large
upper room furnished: there make
ready.
13. **And they went, and** found
as he had said unto them: and they
made ready the passover.
14. **And** when the hour was come,
he sat down, and the
twelve apostles with him.
15. **And he said**
unto them, With desire
I have desired to eat this
passover with you before
I suffer:
16. **For** I say unto you,
I will not any more eat
thereof,
until it be fulfilled in the
kingdom of God.
17. **And he took the cup, and**
gave thanks, and said,
Take this, and divide *it*
among yourselves:
18. **For** I say unto you,
I will not drink of the fruit
of the vine,
until the kingdom of God
shall come.
19. **And he took bread,** and
gave thanks, and brake ***it*****,**
and gave unto them,
saying, This is my body
which is
given for you: this do in
remembrance of me.
20. **Likewise also the cup**
after supper,
saying, This cup ***is*** **the new**
testament in my blood,
which is shed for you.
21. **But,** behold, the hand of
him that betrayeth me ***is***
with me on the table.
22. **And truly the Son of man**
goeth, as it was determined:
but woe unto that man by
whom he is betrayed!
23. **And they began to**
inquire among themselves,
which of them it was that
should do this thing.
24. **And there was also a**
strife among them, which
of them
should be accounted
the greatest.
25. **And he said** unto them, The
kings of the Gentiles exercise
lordship over them; and they that
exercise authority upon them are

called benefactors.
26. But ye *shall* not *be* so: but
he that is greatest among you,
let him be as the younger; and he
that is chief, as he that doth
serve.
27. For whether *is* greater, he that
sitteth at meat, or he that serveth? *is*
not he that sitteth at meat? but
I am among you as he
that serveth.
28. **Ye** are they which
have continued with me
in my temptations.
29. **And I appoint** unto
you a kingdom, as my Father
hath appointed unto me;
30. **That ye may eat** and drink
at my table in my kingdom,
and sit on thrones
judging the twelve tribes
of Israel.
31. **And the Lord said,**
Simon, Simon, behold,
Satan hath desired *to have*
you, that he may sift *you* as wheat:
32. **But I have prayed** for thee,
that thy faith fail not:
and when thou art converted,
strengthen thy brethren.
33. **And he said** unto him,
Lord, I am ready to go with
thee, both into prison, and
to death.
34. **And he said,** I tell thee,
Peter, the cock shall not
crow this day,
before that thou shalt thrice
deny that thou knowest
me.
35. And he said unto them, When I
sent you without purse, and scrip, and
shoes, lacked ye any thing? And they
said, Nothing.
36. Then said he unto them, But now,
he that hath a purse, let him take *it*,
and likewise *his* scrip: and he that
hath no sword, let him sell his
garment, and buy one.
37. For I say unto you, that this that is
written must yet be accomplished in
me, And he was reckoned among the
transgressors: for the things
concerning me have an end.
38. And they said, Lord, behold, here
are two swords. And he said unto
them, It is enough.
39. **And he came**
out, and went, as he was wont,
to the mount of Olives; and
his disciples also followed
him.
40. And when he was at the place, he
said unto them, Pray that ye enter not
into temptation.
41. **And he was withdrawn**
from them about a stone's cast,
and kneeled down,
and prayed,
42. **Saying, Father,**
if thou be willing,
remove this cup from me:
nevertheless not my will,
but thine, be done.
43. **And there appeared an**
angel unto him
from heaven,
strengthening him.
44. **And being in an agony**
he prayed more earnestly: and
his sweat was as it were
great drops of blood
falling down
to the ground.
45. **And when he**
rose up from prayer, and
was come to his disciples,
he found them sleeping
for sorrow,
46. **And said** unto them,
Why sleep ye?
rise and pray, lest ye enter
into temptation.
47. **And** while he yet spake,
behold a multitude, and
he that was called
Judas, one of the twelve,
went before them, and
drew near unto
Jesus to kiss him.
48. **But Jesus said** unto him,
Judas, betrayest thou the
Son of man
with a kiss?
49. When they which were about him
saw what would follow, they said unto

him, Lord, shall we smite with the
sword?
50. **And one** of them
smote the servant of the
high priest, and cut off his
right ear.
51. **And Jesus** answered and said,
Suffer ye thus far. And he
touched his ear, and
healed him.
52. **Then Jesus said**
unto the chief priests, and captains of
the temple, and the elders,
which were come to him,
Be ye come out,
as against a thief, with
swords and staves?
53. When I was daily with you in the
temple, ye stretched forth no hands
against me: but this is your hour, and
the power of darkness.
54. **Then took they him,**
and led *him,*
and brought him into the
high priest's house. And
Peter followed afar off.
55. **And when they had**
kindled a fire in the midst of the
hall, and were set down together,
Peter sat down
among them.
56. **But a certain maid**
beheld him as he sat by the fire,
and earnestly looked upon him,
and said, This man was
also with him.
57. **And he denied** him, saying,
Woman, I know him not.
58. **And** after a little while
another saw him, and
said, Thou art also of them.
And Peter said, Man,
I am not.
59. And about the space
of one hour after
another confidently
affirmed, saying, Of a truth
this *fellow* also
was with him:
for he is a Galilaean.
60. **And Peter said,** Man,
I know not what thou
sayest. And immediately,
while he yet spake,
the cock crew.
61. **And the Lord** turned, and
looked upon Peter. And Peter
remembered the word of the Lord, how
he had said unto him, Before the cock
crow, thou shalt deny me thrice.
62. **And Peter went out, and**
wept bitterly.
63. **And the men that held**
Jesus mocked him,
and smote *him.*
64. **And when they had**
blindfolded him, they
struck him
on the face, and asked him,
saying, Prophesy, who
is that
smote thee?
65. **And** many other things
blasphemously spake they
against him.
66. **And** as soon as it was day,
the elders of the people and the
chief priests and the scribes came
together, and
led him into their
council, saying,
67. **Art thou the Christ?** tell us.
And he said unto them,
If I tell you, ye will
not believe:
68. And if I also ask *you*, ye will not
answer me, nor let *me* go.
69. **Hereafter shall the Son**
of man sit on the right hand
of the power of God.
70. **Then said they** all,
Art thou then the Son of
God? And he said unto them,
Ye say that I am.
71. **And they said,** What
need we any further
witness? for we ourselves
have heard of his
own mouth.

CHAPTER 23

1. **And the whole multitude**
of them arose, and
led him unto Pilate.
2. And they began to accuse him,
saying, We found this

fellow perverting the nation, and
forbidding to give tribute to
Caesar, saying that
he himself
is Christ a King.
3. **And Pilate asked**
him, saying,
Art thou the King of the
Jews? And he answered him and
said, Thou sayest *it*.
4. **Then said Pilate** to the chief
priests and *to* the people,
I find no fault in this man.
5. **And they were the more**
fierce, saying, He stirreth
up the people, teaching
throughout all Jewry, beginning
from Galilee to this place.
6. **When Pilate heard**
of Galilee, he asked whether
the man were a Galilaean.
7. And as soon as he knew
that he belonged unto
Herod's jurisdiction, he
sent him to Herod, who himself
also was at Jerusalem at that time.
8. **And when Herod saw**
Jesus, he was exceeding
glad: for he was desirous to see him
of a long *season*,
because he had heard
many things of him;
and he
hoped to have seen some
miracle done by him.
9. **Then he questioned** with
him in many words;
but he answered him
nothing.
10. **And the chief priests and**
scribes stood and
vehemently accused him.
11. **And Herod** with his
men of war set him at nought,
and mocked *him*, and arrayed
him in a gorgeous robe, and
sent him again to Pilate.
12. And the same day Pilate and
Herod were made friends together: for
before they were at enmity between
themselves.
13. **And Pilate,** when he had
called together
the chief priests and
the rulers and the people,
14. **Said** unto them,
Ye have brought this man
unto me,
as one that perverteth the
people: and, behold,
I, having examined *him* before you,
have found no fault in
this man touching those things
whereof ye accuse
him:
15. No, nor yet Herod: for I sent you to
him; and, lo, nothing worthy of death
is done unto him.
16. **I will therefore chastise**
him, and release *him*.
17. (**For** of necessity
he must release one
unto them
at the feast.)
18. **And they cried** out all at
once, saying, Away with this *man*, and
release unto us
Barabbas:
19. (**Who for** a certain
sedition made in the city,
and for
murder, was cast
into prison.)
20. **Pilate** therefore,
willing to release Jesus,
spake again to them.
21. **But they cried,**
saying, Crucify *him*,
crucify him.
22. **And he said** unto them
the third time, Why, what
evil hath he done? I have
found no cause of death in him: I will
therefore chastise him, and let *him* go.
23. **And they** were instant
with loud voices, requiring that
he might be crucified. And the voices
of them and of the chief priests
prevailed.
24. **And Pilate gave**
sentence that it should be
as they required.
25. **And** he released unto them
him that for sedition and murder
was cast into prison, whom they had
desired; but he

delivered Jesus to
their will.
26. **And** as they led him away, they
laid hold
upon one
Simon, a Cyrenian, coming out
of the country, and on him
they laid the cross, that he
might bear *it* after Jesus.
27. **And** there followed him
a great company
of people, and of women, which also
bewailed and
lamented him.
28. **But Jesus** turning unto them
said, Daughters of Jerusalem,
weep not for me, but weep
for yourselves,
and for your children.
29. **For, behold, the days**
are coming, in the
which they shall say,
Blessed *are* the barren, and
the wombs that never bare, and the
paps which never gave suck.
30. **Then shall they** begin to
say to the mountains, Fall
on us; and to the hills,
Cover us.
31. For if they do these things in a
green tree, what shall be done in the
dry?
32. **And there were also two**
other,
malefactors, led with him
to be put to death.
33. **And when they were**
come to the place, which is called
Calvary, there
they crucified him, and the
malefactors, one
on the right hand,
and the other on
the left.
34. **Then said Jesus, Father,**
forgive them; for they know
not what they do. And they
parted his raiment, and
cast lots.
35. **And the people**
stood beholding. And the rulers
also with them
derided *him*, saying, He
saved others; let him save
himself, if he be Christ,
the chosen of God.
36. **And the soldiers also**
mocked him, coming to him, and
offering him vinegar,
37. And saying, If thou be the king of
the Jews, save thyself.
38. **And a superscription** also
was written over him in letters
of Greek, and Latin, and Hebrew,
THIS IS THE KING OF THE
JEWS.
39. **And one of the**
malefactors which were hanged
railed on him,
saying, If thou be Christ,
save thyself and us.
40. **But the other** answering
rebuked him, saying, Dost
not thou fear God, seeing thou
art in the same condemnation?
41. And we indeed justly; for
we receive the due reward
of our deeds: but this man
hath done nothing amiss.
42. **And he said** unto Jesus,
Lord, remember me when
thou comest into
thy kingdom.
43. **And Jesus said**
unto him, Verily I say unto thee,
To-day shalt thou be with
me in paradise.
44. **And** it was about
the sixth hour, and
there was a darkness
over all the earth
until the ninth hour.
45. And the sun was darkened,
and the veil of the temple
was rent in the midst.
46. **And when Jesus had**
cried with a loud voice, he said,
Father, into thy hands I
commend my spirit:
and having said thus,
he gave up the ghost.
47. **Now when the centurion**
saw what was done,
he glorified God, saying,
Certainly
this was a righteous man.

48. And all the people that came
together to that sight, beholding the
things which were done, smote their
breasts, and returned.
49. And all his acquaintance, and the
women that followed him from Galilee,
stood afar off, beholding these things.
50. **And,** behold, *there was* a man
named
Joseph, a counsellor; *and he was* a
good man, and a just:
51. (The same had not consented to
the counsel and deed of them;) *he
was*
of Arimathaea, a city of the
Jews: who also himself waited for the
kingdom of God.
52. This *man* went unto Pilate, and
begged the body of Jesus.
53. **And he** took it down, and
**wrapped it in linen, and
laid it in a sepulchre** that was
hewn in stone, wherein never man
before was laid.
54. And that day was the preparation,
and the sabbath drew on.
55. **And the women** also, which
came with him from Galilee, followed
after, and beheld the sepulchre, and
how his body was laid.
56. And they returned, and
**prepared spices and
ointments;** and rested the
sabbath day according to the
commandment.

CHAPTER 24

1. **Now upon the first *day* of
the week,**
very early in the morning,
**they came unto the
sepulchre, bringing the
spices** which they had prepared,
and certain *others* with them.
2. **And they found the stone
rolled away** from the sepulchre.
3. **And they** entered in, and
**found not the body of the
Lord Jesus.**
4. **And** it came to pass, as they were
much perplexed thereabout, behold,
**two men stood by them in
shining garments:**
5. **And** as they were afraid,
and bowed down *their* faces to the
earth, they
said unto them,
**Why seek ye the living
among the dead?**
6. **He is not here, but is
risen: remember how he
spake** unto you when he was
yet in Galilee,
7. **Saying, The Son of man
must be** delivered into the
hands of sinful men, and be
**crucified, and the third day
rise again.**
8. **And they remembered**
his words,
9. **And returned**
from the sepulchre,
and told all these things unto
the eleven, and to all the rest.
10. It was Mary Magdalene and
Joanna, and Mary *the mother* of
James, and other *women that were*
with them, which told these things
unto the apostles.
11. **And their words seemed**
to them
**as idle tales, and they
believed them not.**
12. **Then arose Peter, and
ran unto the sepulchre; and**
stooping down, he
**beheld the linen clothes
laid by themselves,**
and departed, wondering in himself
at that which was come to pass.
13. **And, behold, two of them
went** that same day
to a village called
Emmaus, which was from
Jerusalem *about* threescore furlongs.
14. **And they talked** together
of all
**these things which
had happened.**
15. **And** it came to pass, that,
while they communed *together*
and reasoned,
Jesus himself drew near,
and went with them.
16. **But their eyes were
holden that they should not**

know him.
17. **And he said** unto them,
What manner of
communications *are* these
that ye have one to another, as
ye walk, and are sad?
18. **And the one** of them,
whose name was Cleopas,
answering
said unto him,
Art thou only a stranger
in Jerusalem,
and hast not known the
things which are come to
pass there in these days?
19. **And he said** unto them,
What things? And they said
unto him,
Concerning Jesus
of Nazareth, which was
a prophet mighty in deed
and word
before God and all the people:
20. **And how the chief**
priests and our rulers
delivered him to be
condemned to death, and have
crucified him.
21. **But we trusted**
that it had been
he which
should have redeemed
Israel: and beside all this, to-day is
the third day since these
things were done.
22. **Yea, and certain women**
also of our company made us
astonished, which were
early at the sepulchre;
23. And when they
found not his body,
they came,
saying, that they had also
seen a vision of angels,
which said that he
was alive.
24. And certain of them which were
with us went to the sepulchre, and
found *it* even so as the women had
said: but him they saw not.
25. **Then he said** unto them,
O fools, and slow of heart
to believe all that
the prophets have spoken:
26. **Ought not Christ to have**
suffered these things,
and to
enter into his glory?
27. **And beginning at Moses**
and all the prophets,
he expounded unto them in all
the scriptures the things
concerning himself.
28. And they drew nigh unto the
village, whither they went: and he
made as though he would have gone
further.
29. But they constrained him, saying,
Abide with us: for it is toward evening,
and the day is far spent. And he went
in to tarry with them.
30. **And** it came to pass,
as he sat at meat with them,
he took bread, and
blessed *it*, and brake,
and gave to them.
31. **And their eyes** were
opened, and they knew
him; and he vanished
out of their sight.
32. **And they said**
one to another,
Did not our heart burn
within us, while he talked
with us by the way, and
while he opened to
us the scriptures?
33. **And they**
rose up the same hour, and
returned to Jerusalem, and
found the eleven
gathered together, and them
that were with them,
34. Saying, The Lord is risen indeed,
and hath appeared to Simon.
35. **And they told** what things
were done in the way, and
how he was known of them
in breaking of bread.
36. **And** as they thus spake,
Jesus himself
stood in the midst of them,
and saith unto them,
Peace *be* unto you.
37. **But they were terrified**
and affrighted,

■ **and supposed that they**
■ **had seen a spirit.**
■ 38. **And he said** unto them,
■ **Why are ye troubled?** and
why do thoughts arise in your hearts?
■ 39. **Behold**
my hands and my feet, that
■ **it is I** myself:
■ **handle me, and see; for a**
■ **spirit hath not flesh and**
■ **bones,** as ye see me have.
■ 40. **And** when he had thus spoken,
■ **he shewed** them
■ ***his* hands and *his***
■ **feet.**
■ 41. **And while they yet**
■ **believed not for joy,**
and wondered,
■ **he said** unto them,
■ **Have ye here any meat?**
■ 42. **And they gave him**
a piece of a broiled
■ **fish, and** of an
■ **honeycomb.**
43. And he took *it*, and did
eat before them.
■ 44. **And he said** unto them,
■ **These *are* the words which**
■ **I spake** unto you,
while I was yet with you,
■ **that all** things must
■ **be fulfilled,** which were written in
the law of Moses, and *in* the prophets,
and *in* the psalms,
■ **concerning me.**
■ 45. **Then opened he their**
■ **understanding,** that they might
understand the scriptures,
■ 46. **And said** unto them,
■ **Thus it is written, and** thus
■ **it behoved Christ to suffer,**
■ **and to rise** from the dead
■ **the third day:**
■ 47. **And that repentance**
and remission of sins
■ **should be preached in his**
■ **name** among all nations,
beginning at Jerusalem.
■ 48. **And ye are witnesses**
of these things.
■ 49. **And, behold, I send the**
■ **promise of my Father**
upon you:
■ **but tarry ye in** the city of
■ **Jerusalem, until ye be**
■ **endued with power**
from on high.
■ 50. **And he led them out**
as far as
■ **to Bethany, and**
he lifted up his hands, and
■ **blessed them.**
■ 51. **And** it came to pass, while he
blessed them, he
■ **was** parted from them, and
■ **carried up into heaven.**
■ 52. **And they worshipped**
■ **him,** and returned to Jerusalem with
great joy:
53. And were continually in the
temple,
■ **praising and**
■ **blessing God.**
■ **Amen.**

THE GOSPEL ACCORDING TO JOHN

BACKGROUND INFORMATION

Author – John, one of The Twelve Disciples of Jesus
Date written – probably **between 70** and **85** A.D.

Number of:
Versus - 879
Chapters - 21
Total Words - 19,099
Scan Words -9,115
Scan Words represent 47 % of Total Words.

Theme – The Eternal Word of God who **became a human** being in order **that we might have** the gift of **eternal life** through Him.

OUTLINE OF THE GOSPEL

I. **The Introduction.** Chapter 1
II. **Christ's glory and power** revealed. Chapters 2—6
III. **Christ's conflicts** as He taught and continued to perform miracles. Chapter 7—12
IV. **Christ's special revelations** to his disciples. Chapters 13—17
V. **Christ's arrest, trial, crucifixion and resurrection.** Chapters 18—20
VI. **Christ's appearance to His disciples.** Chapter 21

CHAPTER 1

1. **In the beginning was the**
Word, and the Word was
with God, and the Word
was God.
2. The same was in the
beginning with God.
3. **All things were made by**
him; and without him was not any
thing made that was made.
4. **In him was life; and**
the life was
the light of men.
5. **And the light shineth**
in darkness;
and the darkness
comprehended it not.
6. There was a man sent from God,
whose name *was*
John.
7. The same came for a witness, to
bear witness of the Light, that all
men through him might believe.
8. He was not that Light, but
was sent **to bear witness of**
that Light.
9. *That* was
the true Light, which lighteth
every man that cometh into the world.
10. **He was in the world,**
and the world was made by him,
and the world
knew him not.
11. He came unto his own,
and his own received
him not.
12. **But as many as received**
him, to them gave he power
to become the sons of
God, *even* to them that
believe on his name:
13. **Which were born,**
not of blood,
nor of the will of the flesh,
nor of the will of man,
but of God.
14. **And the Word was made**
flesh, and dwelt among us,
(and we beheld his glory, the glory as
of the only begotten of the Father,)
full of grace and truth.
15. **John bare witness**
of him, and cried,
saying, This was he
of whom I spake, He that
cometh after me is
preferred before me:
for he was before me.
16. And of his fulness have all we
received, and grace for grace.
17. For the law was given by Moses,
but grace and truth
came by Jesus Christ.
18. **No man hath seen God**
at any time;
the only begotten Son, which
is in the bosom of the Father, he
hath declared *him.*
19. **And this is the record of**
John, when the Jews sent
priests and Levites from Jerusalem to
ask him, Who art thou?
20. **And he confessed,**
and denied not; but confessed,
I am not the Christ.
21. **And they asked**
him, What then? Art thou Elias?
And he saith, I am not.
Art thou that prophet?
And he answered, No.
22. **Then said they** unto him,
Who art thou? that we may give
an answer to them that sent us. What
sayest thou of thyself?
23. **He said, I *am* the voice**
of one crying in the
wilderness, Make
straight the way of the Lord,
as said the prophet Esaias.
24. And they which were sent
were of the Pharisees.
25. **And they asked him,**
and said unto him,
Why baptizest thou then,
if thou be not that Christ, nor Elias,
neither that prophet?
26. **John answered**
them, saying,
I baptize with water: but
there standeth one among
you, whom ye know not;
27. He it is, who coming after me is
preferred before me,
whose shoe's latchet I am
not worthy to unloose.
28. These things were done in

Bethabara beyond Jordan, where
John was baptizing.
29. **The next day John seeth
Jesus coming** unto him,
**and saith, Behold the Lamb
of God, which taketh away
the sin of the world.**
30. **This is he** of whom I said, After
me cometh a man which is
preferred before me:
for he was before me.
31. And I knew him not: but that he
should be made manifest to Israel,
therefore am I come
baptizing with water.
32. **And John bare record,
saying, I saw the Spirit
descending** from heaven
like a dove, and it abode
upon him.
33. And I knew him not: but
he that sent me
to baptize with water, the same
said unto me,
**Upon whom thou shalt see
the Spirit descending, and
remaining** on him
the same is he which
**baptizeth with the
Holy Ghost.**
34. And I saw, and bare record that
this is the Son of God.
35. **Again the next day after
John stood, and two
of his disciples;**
36. **And looking upon Jesus**
as he walked,
**he saith, Behold the Lamb
of God!**
37. **And the two disciples**
heard him speak, and they
followed Jesus.
38. **Then Jesus** turned, and saw
them following, and
**saith unto them, What seek
ye? They said** unto him, Rabbi,
(which is to say, being
interpreted, Master,)
where dwellest thou?
39. **He saith** unto them,
Come and see. They came
and saw where he dwelt,
**and abode with him that
day:** for it was about the tenth hour.
40. **One of the two** which heard
John *speak,* and followed him,
was Andrew,
Simon Peter's brother.
41. **He first findeth his own
brother Simon, and saith**
unto him,
**We have found the
Messias,** which is, being
interpreted, the Christ.
42. **And he brought him to
Jesus.** And when
Jesus beheld him, he
said, Thou art Simon
the son of Jona:
**thou shalt be
called Cephas,**
which is by interpretation,
A stone.
43. **The day following Jesus**
would go forth into Galilee, and
findeth Philip, and saith
unto him,
Follow me.
44. Now Philip was of Bethsaida, the
city of Andrew and Peter.
45. **Philip findeth Nathanael,
and saith** unto him,
**We have found him, of
whom Moses** in the law,
**and the prophets, did
write,** Jesus of Nazareth,
the son of Joseph.
46. **And Nathanael said**
unto him,
**Can there any good thing
come out of Nazareth?
Philip saith** unto him,
Come and see.
47. **Jesus saw Nathanael**
coming to him,
and saith of him, Behold
an Israelite indeed,
in whom is no guile!
48. **Nathanael saith** unto him,
**Whence knowest thou me?
Jesus answered** and said unto
him, Before that Philip called thee,
**when thou wast under the
fig tree, I saw thee.**
49. **Nathanael answered** and
saith unto him,

Rabbi, thou art the Son of God; thou art the King of Israel.
50. **Jesus answered** and said unto him,
Because I said unto thee,
I saw thee under the fig tree, believest thou? thou shalt see greater things than these.
51. And he saith unto him, Verily, verily, I say unto you,
Hereafter ye shall see heaven open, and the angels of God ascending and descending upon the Son of man.

CHAPTER 2

1. And the third day
there was a marriage in Cana of Galilee;
and the mother of Jesus was there:
2. And both Jesus was called, and his disciples, to the marriage.
3. And when they wanted wine,
the mother of Jesus saith unto him, They have no wine.
4. Jesus saith unto her, Woman, what have I to do with thee? mine hour is not yet come.
5. **His mother saith unto the servants, Whatsoever he saith** unto you,
do *it*.
6. **And there were** set there
six waterpots of stone, after the manner of the purifying of the Jews, containing two or three firkins apiece.
7. **Jesus saith** unto them,
Fill the waterpots with water.
And they filled them up to the brim.
8. **And** he saith unto them,
Draw out now, and bear unto the governor of the feast. And they bare *it*.
9. **When the ruler** of the feast had **tasted the water** that was made wine, and knew not whence it was: (but the servants which drew the water knew;)
the governor of the feast **called the bridegroom,**
10. **And saith** unto him,
Every man at the beginning doth set forth good wine;
and when men have well drunk, then that which is worse:
***but* thou hast kept the good wine until now.**
11. **This beginning of miracles did Jesus in Cana of Galilee,** and manifested forth his glory; and his disciples believed on him.
12. After this he went down to Capernaum, he, and his mother, and his brethren, and his disciples: and they continued there not many days.
13. **And the Jews' passover was at hand, and Jesus went up to Jerusalem.**
14. **And found in the temple those that sold**
oxen and sheep and doves,
and the changers of money sitting:
15. **And when he had made a scourge**
of small cords,
he drove them all out of the temple, and the sheep, and the oxen; and poured out the changers' money,
and overthrew the tables;
16. **And said** unto them that sold doves, Take these things hence;
make not my Father's house an house of merchandise.
17. And his disciples remembered that it was written, The zeal of thine house hath eaten me up.
18. **Then answered the Jews** and said unto him,
What sign shewest thou unto us,
seeing that thou doest these things?
19. **Jesus answered** and said unto them,
Destroy this temple, and in three days I will raise it up.
20. Then said the Jews, Forty and six years was this temple in building, and

wilt thou rear it up in three days?
21. **But he spake of the**
temple of his body.
22. **When therefore he was**
risen from the dead,
his disciples remembered
that he had said this unto them;
and they believed the
scripture, and the word which Jesus
had said.
23. **Now** when he was in Jerusalem
at the passover,
in the feast day,
many believed in his name,
when they saw the miracles
which he did.
24. **But Jesus did not**
commit himself unto them,
because he knew all *men,*
25. And needed not that any should
testify of man: for
he knew what was in man.

CHAPTER 3

1. There was a man of
the Pharisees, named
Nicodemus, a ruler
of the Jews:
2. The same
came to Jesus by night,
and said unto him,
Rabbi, we know that
thou art a teacher come
from God: for no man can
do these miracles
that thou doest,
except God be with him.
3. **Jesus** answered and
said unto him, Verily, verily,
I say unto thee,
Except a man be born
again, he cannot see the
kingdom of God.
4. **Nicodemus saith** unto him,
How can a man be born
when he is old? can he enter
the second time into his
mother's womb, and be born?
5. **Jesus answered,**
Verily, verily, I say unto thee,
Except a man be born of
water and *of* the Spirit, he
cannot enter into the
kingdom of God.
6. **That which is born of the**
flesh is flesh; and that
which is
born of the Spirit is spirit.
7. **Marvel not that**
I said unto thee,
Ye must be born again.
8. **The wind bloweth**
where it listeth,
and thou hearest the sound
thereof, but
canst not tell whence it
cometh, and whither it
goeth: so is every
one that is
born of the Spirit.
9. **Nicodemus answered**
and said unto him,
How can these things be?
10. **Jesus answered** and said
unto him, Art thou a master of Israel,
and knowest not these things?
11. Verily, verily, I say unto thee,
We speak that we do know,
and testify that we have seen; and ye
receive not our witness.
12. If I have told you earthly things,
and ye believe not, how shall
ye believe, if I tell you
of heavenly things?
13. And no man hath ascended up to
heaven, but he that came down from
heaven, *even* the Son of man which is
in heaven.
14. **And as Moses lifted up**
the serpent in the
wilderness, even so must
the Son of man be lifted up:
15. **That whosoever**
believeth in him should not
perish, but have eternal life.
16. **For God so loved the**
world, that he gave his only
begotten Son, that
whosoever believeth in him
should not perish, but have
everlasting life.
17. **For God sent not his Son**
into the world
to condemn the world;
but that the world through
him might be saved.

18. He that believeth on
him is not condemned:
**but he that believeth not is
condemned already,
because he hath not
believed in the name of the
only begotten Son of God.**
19. **And this is the
condemnation, that light is
come** into the world,
and men loved darkness
rather than light,
**because their
deeds were evil.**
20. For every one that doeth evil
hateth the light, neither cometh to the
light, lest his deeds
should be reproved.
21. **But he that doeth truth
cometh to the light,** that his
deeds may be made manifest, that
they are wrought in God.
22. **After these things came
Jesus** and his disciples
into the land of
Judaea; and there he tarried with
them, and baptized.
23. **And John also was
baptizing in Aenon** near to
Salim, because there was much water
there: and they came,
and were baptized.
24. For John was not yet
cast into prison.
25. **Then there arose a
question** between *some* of John's
disciples and the Jews
about purifying.
26. **And they came unto
John, and said** unto him, Rabbi,
he that was with thee
beyond Jordan,
**to whom thou barest
witness, behold,** the same
baptizeth, and
all *men* come to him.
27. **John answered** and said, A
man can receive nothing, except it be
given him from heaven.
28. Ye yourselves bear me witness,
that I said,
I am not the Christ, but that I
am sent before him.
29. **He that hath the bride is
the bridegroom: but the
friend of the bridegroom,**
which standeth and heareth him,
rejoiceth greatly because of the
bridegroom's voice: this
my joy therefore is fulfilled.
30. **He must increase, but I
must decrease.**
31. **He that cometh from
above is above all:** he that is
of the earth is earthly, and speaketh
of the earth: he that cometh from
heaven is above all.
32. And what he hath seen and heard,
that he testifieth; and no man
receiveth his testimony.
33. **He that hath received his
testimony hath set to his
seal that God is true.**
34. For he whom God hath sent
speaketh the words of God:
for God giveth not the Spirit by
measure *unto him.*
35. **The Father loveth the
Son, and hath given all
things into his hand.**
36. **He that believeth on the
Son hath everlasting life:
and he that believeth not**
the Son shall not see life; but
**the wrath of God abideth
on him.**

CHAPTER 4

1. When therefore the LORD knew
how the Pharisees had heard that
Jesus made and baptized more
disciples than John,
2. (Though Jesus himself baptized
not, but his disciples,)
3. He left Judaea, and
**departed again
into Galilee.**
4. And he must needs go
through Samaria.
5. **Then cometh he to a city**
of Samaria, which is
called Sychar, near to the parcel
of ground that Jacob gave
to his son Joseph.
6. **Now Jacob's well was
there. Jesus** therefore, being

wearied with *his* journey,
sat thus on the well: *and*
it was about the sixth hour.
7. **There cometh a woman**
of Samaria
to draw water: Jesus saith
unto her,
Give me to drink.
8. (For his disciples were gone away
unto the city to buy meat.)
9. **Then saith the woman**
of Samaria unto him,
How is it that thou, being
a Jew, askest drink of
me, which am
a woman of Samaria? for the
Jews have no dealings
with the Samaritans.
10. **Jesus answered**
and said unto her,
If thou knewest
the gift of God, and
who it is that saith to thee,
Give me to drink; thou
wouldest have asked of
him, and he would have
given thee living water.
11. **The woman saith**
unto him, Sir,
thou hast nothing to draw
with, and the well is deep: from
whence then hast thou
that living water?
12. Art thou greater than our father
Jacob, which gave us the well, and
drank thereof himself, and his
children, and his cattle?
13. **Jesus answered**
and said unto her,
Whosoever drinketh of this
water shall thirst again:
14. **But whosoever drinketh**
of the water that I
shall give him
shall never thirst;
but the water that
I shall give him shall be in him
a well of water springing up
into everlasting life.
15. **The woman saith** unto him,
Sir, give me this water, that I
thirst not, neither come hither to draw.
16. **Jesus saith** unto her, Go,
call thy husband,
and come hither.
17. **The woman** answered and
said, I have no husband.
Jesus said unto her,
Thou hast well said,
I have no husband:
18. **For thou hast had five**
husbands; and he whom thou now
hast is not thy husband: in that saidst
thou truly.
19. **The woman saith**
unto him, Sir, I perceive that
thou art a prophet.
20. **Our fathers worshipped**
in this mountain; and ye
say, that in Jerusalem is
the place where men ought
to worship.
21. **Jesus saith** unto her, Woman,
believe me, the hour cometh, when ye
shall neither in this mountain, nor yet
at Jerusalem, worship the Father.
22. **Ye worship ye know not**
what: we know what we worship: for
salvation is of the Jews.
23. **But the hour** cometh, and
now is, when the true
worshippers shall worship
the Father in spirit and in
truth: for the Father seeketh such to
worship him.
24. **God *is* a Spirit: and they**
that worship him must
worship *him* in spirit
and in truth.
25. **The woman saith** unto him,
I know that Messias
cometh, which is called Christ:
when he is come, he
will tell us all things.
26. **Jesus saith** unto her,
I that speak unto thee
am *he.*
27. An upon this came his disciples,
and marvelled that he talked with
the woman: yet no man said, What
seekest thou? or, Why talkest thou
with her?
28. **The woman**
then left her waterpot, and
went her way
into the city, and saith

to the men,
29. **Come, see a man, which**
told me all things that ever
I did: is not this the Christ?
30. Then they went out of the city, and
came unto him.
31. **In the mean while his**
disciples prayed him,
saying, Master, eat.
32. **But he said** unto them,
I have meat to eat that ye
know not of.
33. **Therefore said the**
disciples one to another,
Hath any man brought him
***aught* to eat?**
34. **Jesus saith** unto them,
My meat is to do the will of
him that sent me,
and to finish his work.
35. **Say not ye, There are yet**
four months, and *then*
cometh harvest?
behold, I say unto you,
Lift up your eyes, and look on
the fields; for they
are white already
to harvest.
36. **And he that reapeth**
receiveth wages, and
gathereth fruit unto life
eternal: that both he that soweth
and he that reapeth
may rejoice together.
37. And herein is that saying true,
One soweth, and another reapeth.
38. I sent you to reap that whereon ye
bestowed no labour: other men
laboured, and ye are entered
into their labours.
39. **And many of the**
Samaritans of that city
believed on him
for the saying of the
woman, which testified,
He told me all that ever I did.
40. So when
the Samaritans
were come unto him, they
besought him that he would
tarry with them:
and he abode
there two days.
41. **And many**
more believed
because of his own word;
42. **And said unto the**
woman, Now we believe,
not because of thy saying:
for we have heard *him*
ourselves, and know that
this is indeed the Christ,
the Saviour of the world.
43. **Now** after two days
he departed thence, and
went into Galilee.
44. **For Jesus himself**
testified, that a prophet
hath no honour in
his own country.
45. **Then** when he
was come into Galilee,
the Galilaeans received
him, having seen all the
things that he did at
Jerusalem at the feast: for they
also went unto the feast.
46. **So Jesus came again**
into Cana
of Galilee, where he made
the water wine.
And there was
a certain nobleman, whose
son was sick at Capernaum.
47. When he heard that Jesus was
come out of Judaea into Galilee, he
went unto him, and
besought him that
he would come down, and
heal his son: for he was
at the point of death.
48. Then said Jesus unto him, Except
ye see signs and wonders,
ye will not believe.
49. **The nobleman saith**
unto him,
Sir, come down ere
my child die.
50. **Jesus saith**
unto him, Go thy way;
thy son liveth. And the man
believed the word that Jesus had
spoken unto him, and
he went his way.
51. **And** as he was now going down,
his servants met him,

and told *him*,
saying, Thy son liveth.
52. Then inquired he of them the hour
when he began to amend. And they
said unto him, Yesterday at the
seventh hour the fever left him.
53. So the father knew that *it was* at
the same hour, in the which Jesus
said unto him, Thy son liveth: and
himself believed, and his
whole house.
54. **This *is* again the second**
miracle *that* Jesus did,
when he was come out of
Judaea into Galilee.

CHAPTER 5

1. **After this** there was a feast of
the Jews; and
Jesus went up
to Jerusalem.
2. Now there is at Jerusalem
by the sheep *market*
a pool, which is
called in the Hebrew tongue
Bethesda, having five
porches.
3. **In these lay** a great multitude of
impotent folk,
of blind, halt, withered,
waiting for the moving
of the water.
4. **For an angel went down**
at a certain season
into the pool, and troubled
the water: whosoever then
first after the troubling of
the water stepped in
was made whole
of whatsoever disease he had.
5. **And a certain man**
was there, which
had an infirmity thirty and
eight years.
6. **When Jesus saw him**
lie, and knew that he had been now a
long time *in that case,*
he saith unto him,
Wilt thou be made whole?
7. **The impotent man**
answered him, Sir,
I have no man,
when the water is troubled,
to put me into the pool: but
while I am coming, another steppeth
down before me.
8. **Jesus saith** unto him,
Rise, take up thy bed,
and walk.
9. **And immediately the man**
was made whole, and took up
his bed, and walked: and on the same
day was the sabbath.
10. **The Jews therefore said**
unto him that was cured,
It is the sabbath day: it is
not lawful for thee to
carry *thy* bed.
11. **He answered** them,
He that made me whole,
the same
said unto me,
Take up thy bed, and walk.
12. **Then asked they him,**
What man is that which said unto
thee, Take up thy bed, and walk?
13. **And he** that was healed
wist not who it was: for Jesus
had conveyed himself away, a
multitude being in *that* place.
14. **Afterward Jesus findeth**
him in the temple,
and said unto him, Behold,
thou art made whole: sin
no more,
lest a worse thing come unto thee.
15. **The man** departed, and
told the Jews that it was
Jesus, which had made him whole.
16. **And** therefore did
the Jews persecute Jesus, and
sought to slay him,
because he had done
these things
on the sabbath day.
17. **But Jesus answered** them,
My Father worketh hitherto,
and I work.
18. **Therefore the Jews**
sought the more to kill him,
because he not only had broken
the sabbath, but
said also that
God was his Father,
making himself equal with God.
19. **Then answered Jesus** and

said unto them, Verily, verily,
I say unto you,
The Son can do nothing of
himself, but what he seeth
the Father do: for what things
soever he doeth, these also doeth the
Son likewise.
20. **For the Father loveth the**
Son, and sheweth him all
things that himself doeth:
and he will shew him greater works
than these, that ye may marvel.
21. **For as the Father raiseth**
up the dead,
and quickeneth *them;*
even so the Son quickeneth
whom he will.
22. **For the Father**
judgeth no man, but
hath committed all
judgment unto the Son:
23. That all *men* should honour the
Son, even as they honour the Father.
He that honoureth not the
Son honoureth
not the Father
which hath sent him.
24. Verily, verily, I say unto you,
He that heareth my word,
and believeth
on him that sent me,
hath everlasting life, and
shall not come into condemnation; but
is passed from death
unto life.
25. Verily, verily, I say unto you,
The hour
is coming, and
now is, when the dead
shall hear the voice of the
Son of God:
and they that hear
shall live.
26. For as the Father hath life in
himself; so hath he given to the Son
to have life in himself;
27. And hath given him authority to
execute judgment also, because he is
the Son of man.
28. Marvel not at this: for
the hour is coming, in the
which all that are in
the graves shall
hear his voice,
29. **And shall come forth;**
they that have done good,
unto the resurrection of life;
and they that have done evil, unto
the resurrection of
damnation.
30. **I can** of mine own self
do nothing: as I hear, I
judge: and my judgment is just;
because I seek not mine own will, but
the will of the Father which
hath sent me.
31. **If I bear witness of**
myself, my witness
is not true.
32. **There is another that**
beareth witness of me; and I
know that the witness which he
witnesseth of me is true.
33. **Ye sent unto John, and**
he bare witness unto the truth.
34. But I receive not testimony from
man: but these things I say, that ye
might be saved.
35. **He was** a burning and
a shining light: and ye were
willing for a season to
rejoice in his light.
36. **But I have greater**
witness than *that* of
John: for the works which the
Father hath given me to finish,
the same works that I do,
bear witness of me, that the
Father hath sent me.
37. **And the Father** himself, which
hath sent me,
hath borne witness of me.
Ye have neither heard his voice at any
time, nor seen his shape.
38. **And ye have not his**
word abiding in you:
for whom he hath sent, him
ye believe not.
39. **Search the scriptures;**
for in them ye think ye have eternal
life: and
they are they which
testify of me.
40. And ye will not come to me, that ye
might have life.
41. I receive not honour from men.

42. **But** I know you, that **ye have not the love of God** in you.

43. **I am come in my Father's name, and ye receive me not:** if another shall come in his own name, him ye will receive.

44. How can ye believe, which receive honour one of another, and seek not the honour that *cometh* from God only?

45. **Do not think that I will accuse you** to the Father: **there is *one* that accuseth you, *even* Moses,** in whom ye trust.

46. For had ye believed **Moses,** ye would have believed me; for he **wrote of me.**

47. **But if ye believe not his writings, how shall ye believe my words?**

CHAPTER 6

1. After these things **Jesus went over the sea of Galilee,** which is *the sea* of Tiberias.

2. **And a great multitude followed him, because they saw his miracles** which he did on them that were diseased.

3. **And Jesus went up into a mountain,** and there he sat with his disciples.

4. And the passover, a feast of the Jews, was nigh.

5. **When Jesus** then lifted up *his* eyes, and **saw a great company come** unto him, **he saith unto Philip, Whence shall we buy bread,** that these may eat?

6. **And this he said to prove him:** for he himself knew what he would do.

7. **Philip answered him, Two hundred pennyworth of bread is not sufficient** for them, that every one of them may take a little.

8. One of his disciples, **Andrew,** Simon Peter's brother, **saith** unto him,

9. There is **a lad** here, which **hath five barley loaves, and two small fishes:** but what are they among so many?

10. **And Jesus said, Make the men sit down.** Now there was much grass in the place. So the men sat down, **in number about five thousand.**

11. **And Jesus took the loaves; and when he had given thanks, he distributed** to the disciples, and the disciples to them that were set down; **and likewise of the fishes** as much as they would.

12. **When they were filled, he said** unto his disciples, **Gather up** the fragments that remain, **that nothing be lost.**

13. **Therefore they gathered** *them* together, and filled **twelve baskets with the fragments** of the five barley loaves, **which remained** over and above unto them that had eaten.

14. **Then those men, when they had seen the miracle** that Jesus did, **said, This is** of a truth **that prophet that should come** into the world.

15. **When Jesus** therefore **perceived that they would** come and take him by force, to **make him a king, he departed** again into a mountain himself alone.

16. **And** when even was *now* come, **his disciples went** down unto the sea,

17. **And entered into a ship, and went** over the sea **toward Capernaum.** And it

was now dark, and Jesus was not
come to them.
18. **And the sea arose**
by reason
of a great wind that blew.
19. **So when they had rowed**
about five and twenty or
thirty furlongs, they see
Jesus walking on the sea,
and drawing nigh unto the ship:
and they were afraid.
20. **But he saith** unto them,
It is I; be not afraid.
21. **Then they willingly**
received him into the ship:
and immediately
the ship was at the land
whither they went.
22. The day following, when the
people which stood on the other side
of the sea saw that there was none
other boat there, save that one
whereinto his disciples were entered,
and that Jesus went not with his
disciples into the boat, but *that* his
disciples were gone away alone;
23. (Howbeit there came other boats
from Tiberias nigh unto the place
where they did eat bread, after that
the Lord had given thanks:)
24. **When the people** therefore
saw that Jesus was not
there, neither his disciples,
they also took shipping, and
came to Capernaum,
seeking for Jesus.
25. **And when they**
had found him
on the other side of the sea
they said unto him, Rabbi,
when camest thou hither?
26. **Jesus answered** them and
said, Verily, verily, I say unto you,
Ye seek me, not because ye saw
the miracles, but
because ye did eat of the
loaves, and were filled.
27. **Labour** not for the meat which
perisheth, but
for that meat which
endureth unto everlasting
life, which the Son of man
shall give unto you: for him hath
God the Father sealed.
28. **Then said they** unto him,
What shall we do, that we might
work the works of God?
29. **Jesus answered** and said
unto them,
This is the work of God, that
ye believe on him whom he
hath sent.
30. **They said** therefore unto him,
What sign shewest thou then,
that we may see, and believe thee?
what dost thou work?
31. **Our fathers did eat**
manna in the desert;
as it is written, He gave
them bread from heaven
to eat.
32. **Then Jesus said** unto them,
Verily, verily, I say unto you,
Moses gave you not that
bread from heaven; but my
Father giveth you the true
bread from heaven.
33. **For the bread of God is**
he which cometh down
from heaven,
and giveth life unto the world.
34. **Then said they**
unto him, Lord, evermore
give us this bread.
35. **And Jesus said** unto them,
I am the bread of life:
he that cometh to me shall never
hunger; and he that believeth on me
shall never thirst.
36. **But** I said unto you, That
ye also have seen me, and
believe not.
37. **All that the Father giveth**
me shall
come to me; and him that cometh
to me I will in no wise cast out.
38. **For I came** down from heaven,
not to do mine own will, but
the will of him that sent me.
39. And this is the Father's will which
hath sent me, that of all which he hath
given me I should lose nothing, but
should raise it up again
at the last day.
40. **And** this is the will of him that
sent me, that

every one which seeth the
Son, and believeth on him,
may have everlasting life:
and I will raise him up
at the last day.
41. **The Jews then murmured**
at him,
because he said, I am the
bread which came down
from heaven.
42. **And they said, Is not this**
Jesus, the son of Joseph,
whose father and mother we know?
how is it then that
he saith, I came down
from heaven?
43. **Jesus therefore**
answered and said unto them,
Murmur not among yourselves.
44. **No man can come to me,**
except the Father which hath
sent me draw him: and I will raise him
up at the last day.
45. It is written in the prophets, And
they shall be all taught of God.
Every man therefore that
hath heard, and
hath learned of the Father,
cometh unto me.
46. Not that any man hath seen the
Father, save he which is of God, he
hath seen the Father.
47. Verily, verily, I say unto you,
He that believeth on me
hath everlasting life.
48. **I am that bread of life.**
49. **Your fathers did eat**
manna in the wilderness,
and are dead.
50. This is the bread which cometh
down from heaven, that a man may
eat thereof, and not die.
51. **I am the living bread** which
came down from heaven:
if any man eat of this bread,
he shall live for ever: and
the bread that I will give is
my flesh, which I will give for the
life of the world.
52. **The Jews therefore**
strove among themselves,
saying, How can this man
give us ***his*** **flesh to eat?**

53. **Then Jesus said** unto them,
Verily, verily, I say unto you,
Except ye eat the flesh of
the Son of man, and drink
his blood, ye have no life
in you.
54. **Whoso eateth my flesh,**
and drinketh my blood,
hath eternal life; and
I will raise him up at the last day.
55. For my flesh is meat indeed, and
my blood is drink indeed.
56. He that eateth my flesh, and
drinketh my blood,
dwelleth in me, and I in him.
57. As the living Father
hath sent me, and
I live by the Father: so he
that eateth me, even he
shall live by me.
58. This is that bread which came
down from heaven: not as your
fathers did eat manna, and are dead:
he that eateth of this bread
shall live forever.
59. These things said he in the
synagogue, as he taught
in Capernaum.
60. **Many therefore of**
his disciples,
when they had heard *this,*
said, This is an hard
saying; who can hear it?
61. **When Jesus knew**
in himself that
his disciples murmured at it,
he said unto them,
Doth this offend you?
62. *What* and if ye shall see the Son of
man ascend up where he was before?
63. **It is the spirit that**
quickeneth; the flesh
profiteth nothing:
the words that I speak
unto you, *they*
are spirit, and *they* are
life.
64. **But** there are
some of you that
believe not. For Jesus
knew from the beginning
who they were that
believed not, and who

should betray him.
65. **And he said,** Therefore said I
unto you, that
no man can come unto me,
except it were given unto him
of my Father.
66. **From that *time* many of**
his disciples went back, and
walked no more with him.
67. **Then said Jesus unto the**
twelve, Will ye also
go away?
68. Then Simon
Peter answered him, Lord,
to whom shall we go? thou
hast the words
of eternal life.
69. **And we believe** and are sure
that thou art that Christ,
the Son of the living God.
70. **Jesus answered** them,
Have not I chosen you twelve, and
one of you is a devil?
71. **He spake of Judas**
Iscariot *the son* of Simon: for he it
was that should betray him, being one
of the twelve.

CHAPTER 7

1. After these things
Jesus walked in Galilee:
for he would not walk in Jewry,
because the Jews sought
to kill him.
2. Now the Jew's feast of tabernacles
was at hand.
3. **His brethren therefore**
said unto him, Depart hence, and
go into Judaea, that thy
disciples also may see the works that
thou doest.
4. **For *there is* no man *that***
doeth any thing in secret,
and he himself seeketh to be known
openly. If thou do these things,
shew thyself to the world.
5. For neither did his brethren
believe in him.
6. **Then Jesus said** unto them,
My time is not yet come:
but your time is alway ready.
7. The world cannot hate you; but me
it hateth, because I testify of it, that
the works thereof are evil.
8. **Go ye up unto this feast:**
I go not up yet unto this feast:
for my time is not yet full come.
9. **When he had said these**
words unto them,
he abode *still* in Galilee.
10. **But** when his
brethren were gone up,
then went he also up unto the
feast, not openly, but as it were
in secret.
11. **Then the Jews**
sought him at the feast, and
said, Where is he?
12. **And there was much**
murmuring among the people
concerning him: for
some said, He is a good
man: others said, Nay;
but he deceiveth the people.
13. **Howbeit no man spake**
openly of him
for fear of the Jews.
14. **Now** about the midst of the feast
Jesus went up into the
temple, and taught.
15. **And the Jews marvelled,**
saying, How knoweth this
man letters, having
never learned?
16. **Jesus answered**
them, and said,
My doctrine is not mine, but
his that sent me.
17. **If any man will do his**
will, he shall know
of the doctrine,
whether it be of God,
or *whether* I speak of myself.
18. He that speaketh of himself
seeketh his own glory: but he that
seeketh his glory that sent him, the
same is true, and no unrighteousness
is in him.
19. **Did not Moses give you**
the law, and *yet* none of you
keepeth the law? Why go ye
about to kill me?
20. **The people answered**
and said,
Thou hast a devil:
who goeth about to kill thee?

21. **Jesus answered**
and said unto them
I have done one work,
and ye all marvel.
22. Moses therefore gave unto you
circumcision; (not because it is of
Moses, but of the fathers;)
and ye on the sabbath day
circumcise a man.
23. **If a man on the sabbath**
day receive circumcision,
that the law of Moses
should not be broken; are
ye angry at me, because I
have made a man every whit
whole on the
sabbath day?
24. Judge not according to the
appearance, but judge
righteous judgment.
25. **Then said some**
of them of Jerusalem,
Is not this he, whom they
seek to kill?
26. **But, lo,** he speaketh boldly, and
they say nothing unto him.
Do the rulers know indeed that
this is the very
Christ?
27. Howbeit we know this man whence
he is: but when Christ cometh, no man
knoweth whence he is.
28. **Then cried Jesus in the**
temple as he taught, saying, Ye
both know me, and ye know
whence I am: and
I am not come of myself,
but he that sent me is true,
whom ye know not.
29. **But I know him:**
for I am from him,
and he hath sent me.
30. **Then they sought to take**
him: but no man laid hands
on him, because his hour was not
yet come.
31. **And many** of the people
believed on him,
and said, When Christ
cometh, will he do more
miracles than these which this
man hath done?
32. The Pharisees heard that the
people murmured such things
concerning him; and
the Pharisees and the chief
priests sent officers
to take him.
33. **Then said Jesus** unto them,
Yet a little while am I with you, and
then I go unto him that sent me.
34. **Ye shall seek me, and**
shall not find *me:* and
where I am, *thither*
ye cannot come.
35. **Then said the Jews**
among themselves,
Whither will he go, that we shall
not find him? will he go unto the
dispersed among the Gentiles, and
teach the Gentiles?
36. What *manner of* saying is this that
he said, Ye shall seek me, and shall
not find *me*: and where I am, *thither ye*
cannot come?
37. **In the last day, that great**
***day* of the feast, Jesus**
stood and
cried, saying, If any man
thirst, let him come unto
me, and drink.
38. **He that believeth on me,**
as the scripture hath said,
out of his belly shall flow
rivers of living water.
39. **(But this spake he of the**
Spirit, which they that believe on
him should receive: for the Holy Ghost
was not yet *given*; because that
Jesus was not yet glorified.)
40. **Many of the people**
therefore, when they
heard this saying,
said, Of a truth
this is the Prophet.
41. **Others said, This is the**
Christ. But some said, Shall
Christ come out of Galilee?
42. **Hath not the scripture**
said, That Christ cometh
of the seed of David, and
out of the town of
Bethlehem, where
David was?
43. **So there was a division**
among the people

because of him.
44. And some of them would
have taken him; but no man
laid hands on him.
■ 45. **Then came the officers**
■ **to the chief priests**
and Pharisees; and
■ **they said** unto them,
■ **Why have ye not**
■ **brought him?**
■ 46. **The officers answered,**
■ **Never man spake**
■ **like this man.**
■ 47. **Then answered them the**
■ **Pharisees, Are ye**
■ **also deceived?**
48. Have any of the rulers or of the
Pharisees believed on him?
49. But this people who knoweth not
the law are cursed.
■ 50. **Nicodemus saith** unto
them, (he that came to Jesus by
night, being one of them,)
■ 51. **Doth our law judge**
any man,
■ **before it hear him,**
and know what he doeth?
■ 52. **They answered** and said
unto him, Art thou also of Galilee?
■ **Search,** and look:
■ **for out of Galilee**
■ **ariseth no prophet.**
53. And every man went
unto his own house.

CHAPTER 8

1. Jesus went unto the mount
of Olives.
■ 2. **And early in the morning**
■ **he came again into the**
■ **temple, and all the people**
■ **came** unto him;
■ **and he** sat down, and
■ **taught them.**
■ 3. **And the scribes and**
■ **Pharisees brought** unto him
■ **a woman taken in adultery;**
and when they had
set her in the midst,
■ 4. **They say** unto him,
■ **Master, this woman was**
■ **taken in adultery,**
in the very act.
5. Now Moses in
■ **the law commanded us,**
■ **that such should be**
■ **stoned: but what**
■ **sayest thou?**
6. This they said, tempting him, that
they might have to accuse him. But
■ **Jesus stooped down, and**
■ **with *his* finger wrote**
■ **on the ground,**
as though he heard them not.
■ 7. **So when they continued**
■ **asking him, he**
lifted up himself, and
■ **said** unto them,
■ **He that is without sin**
among you,
■ **let him first cast a stone**
■ **at her.**
■ 8. **And again he**
stooped down, and
■ **wrote on the ground.**
■ 9. **And they** which heard *it,*
■ **being convicted**
by *their own* conscience,
■ **went out** one by one, beginning at
the eldest, *even* unto the last:
■ **and Jesus was left alone,**
■ **and the woman**
standing in the midst.
10. When Jesus had lifted up himself,
and saw none but the woman,
■ **he said unto her, Woman,**
where are those thine accusers?
■ **hath no man**
■ **condemned thee?**
■ 11. **She said, No man, Lord.**
■ **And Jesus said** unto her,
■ **Neither do I** condemn thee:
■ **go, and sin no more.**
■ 12. **Then spake Jesus**
again unto them,
■ **saying, I am the light of the**
■ **world:** he that followeth me shall
not walk in darkness, but shall have
the light of life.
■ 13. **The Pharisees therefore**
■ **said** unto him,
■ **Thou bearest record of**
■ **thyself; thy record**
■ **is not true.**
■ 14. **Jesus answered**
and said unto them,

Though I bear record
of myself,
***yet* my record is true:**
for I know whence I came,
and whither I go;
but ye cannot tell whence I
come, and whither I go.
15. **Ye judge after the flesh; I**
judge no man.
16. **And yet if I judge, my**
judgment is true: for I am not
alone, but I and the Father
that sent me.
17. **It is also written** in your law,
that the testimony of two
men is true.
18. **I** am one that
bear witness of myself,
and the Father that sent me
beareth witness of me.
19. **Then said they** unto him,
Where is thy Father? Jesus
answered, Ye neither know me,
nor my Father:
if ye had known me, ye
should have known my
Father also.
20. These words spake Jesus in the
treasury, as he taught in the temple:
and no man laid hands on him; for his
hour was not yet come.
21. **Then said Jesus** again unto
them, I go my way, and
ye shall seek me, and shall
die in your sins: whither I
go, ye cannot come.
22. **Then said the Jews, Will**
he kill himself? because he
saith, Whither I go, ye cannot come.
23. **And he said** unto them, Ye
are from beneath; I am from above:
ye are of this world; I am
not of this world.
24. I said therefore unto you, that ye
shall die in your sins: for
if ye believe not that I am
***he*, ye shall die in your**
sins.
25. **Then said they** unto him,
Who art thou? And Jesus
saith unto them,
Even *the same* that I said
unto you
from the beginning.
26. I have many things to say and to
judge of you: but
he that sent me is true; and I
speak to the world
those things which I have
heard of him.
27. **They understood not** that
he spake to them of the Father.
28. **Then said Jesus** unto them,
When ye have lifted up the
Son of man,
then shall ye know that I am
he, and *that* I do nothing of myself;
but as my Father hath taught me, I
speak these things.
29. **And** he that sent me is with me:
the Father hath not left me
alone; for I
do always those things that
please him.
30. **As he spake** these words,
many believed on him.
31. **Then said Jesus** to those
Jews which believed on him,
If ye continue in my word,
***then* are ye my disciples**
indeed;
32. **And ye shall know the**
truth, and the truth shall
make you free.
33. **They answered him, We**
be Abraham's seed, and
were never in bondage
to any man:
how sayest thou, Ye shall
be made free?
34. **Jesus answered**
them, Verily, verily, I say unto you,
Whosoever committeth sin
is the servant of sin.
35. And the servant abideth not in the
house for ever: *but* the
Son abideth ever.
36. **If the Son** therefore shall
make you free, ye shall be
free indeed.
37. I know that ye are Abraham's
seed; but ye seek to kill me, because
my word hath no place in you.
38. **I speak that which I have**
seen with my Father: and ye
do that which ye have seen

with your father.
39. **They answered**
and said unto him,
Abraham is our father.
Jesus saith unto them,
If ye were Abraham's
children, ye would do the
works of Abraham.
40. **But now ye seek to kill**
me, a man that hath told you the
truth, which I have heard of God:
this did not Abraham.
41. Ye do the deeds of your father.
Then said they to him, We be not
born of fornication;
we have one Father,
***even* God.**
42. **Jesus said** unto them,
If God were your Father, ye
would love me: for I
proceeded forth and
came from God; neither came I
of myself, but he sent me.
43. Why do ye not understand my
speech? *even* because ye cannot
hear my word.
44. **Ye are of *your* father the**
devil, and the lusts of your father
ye will do.
He was a murderer
from the beginning,
and abode not in the truth,
because there is no truth in him. When
he speaketh a lie, he speaketh
of his own:
for he is a liar, and the
father of it.
45. And because I tell *you* the truth,
ye believe me not.
46. Which of you convinceth me of
sin? And if I say the truth, why do ye
not believe me?
47. **He that is of God heareth**
God's words: ye therefore hear
them not, because
ye are not of God.
48. **Then answered the**
Jews, and said unto him, Say we
not well that
thou art a Samaritan, and
hast a devil?
49. **Jesus answered, I have**
not a devil; but I honour my
Father, and ye do dishonour me.
50. And I seek not mine own glory:
there is one that seeketh and judgeth.
51. Verily, verily, I say unto you,
If a man keep my saying,
he shall never see death.
52. **Then said the Jews** unto
him, Now we know that
thou hast a devil.
Abraham is dead, and the
prophets; and thou sayest, If a man
keep my saying, he shall never taste
of death.
53. **Art thou greater than**
our father
Abraham, which is dead? and the
prophets are dead:
whom makest thou thyself?
54. **Jesus answered,** If I
honour myself, my honour is nothing:
it is my Father that
honoureth me; of whom ye say,
that he is your God:
55. **Yet ye have not known**
him; but I know him: and if I should
say, I know him not, I shall be a liar
like unto you:
but I know him, and keep
his saying.
56. **Your father Abraham**
rejoiced to see my day: and
he saw *it,* and was glad.
57. **Then said the Jews**
unto him,
Thou art not yet fifty years old,
and hast thou
seen Abraham?
58. **Jesus said** unto them, Verily,
verily, I say unto you,
Before Abraham was, I am.
59. **Then took they up stones**
to cast at him: but Jesus hid
himself, and went out of the temple,
going through the midst
of them, and so
passed by.

CHAPTER 9

1. And as *Jesus* passed by,
he saw a man which was
blind from *his* birth.
2. **And his disciples asked**
him, saying, Master,

who did sin, this man, or
his parents,
that he was born blind?
3. **Jesus answered, Neither**
hath this man sinned, nor his parents:
but that the works of God
should be made manifest
in him.
4. **I must work** the works of him
that sent me, while it is day:
the night cometh, when no
man can work.
5. As long as I am in the world,
I am the light of the world.
6. **When he had thus**
spoken, he spat on the
ground, and made clay of
the spittle, and he anointed
the eyes of the blind man
with the clay,
7. **And said** unto him,
Go, wash in the
pool of Siloam,
(which is by interpretation, Sent.)
He went his way therefore,
and washed,
and came seeing.
8. **The neighbours** therefore,
and they which before had seen him
that he was blind,
said, Is not this he that sat
and begged?
9. Some said, This is he: others *said,*
He is like him: *but*
he said, I am *he.*
10. **Therefore said they**
unto him,
How were thine
eyes opened?
11. **He answered**
and said, A man that is called
Jesus made clay, and
anointed mine eyes, and
said unto me,
Go to the pool of
Siloam, and wash:
and I went and washed,
and I received sight.
12. Then said they unto him, Where is
he? He said, I know not.
13. They brought to the Pharisees him
that aforetime was blind.
14. **And it was the sabbath**
day when Jesus made the clay, and
opened his eyes.
15. Then again
the Pharisees also asked
him how he had received
his sight. He said unto them, He
put clay upon mine eyes, and I
washed, and do see.
16. **Therefore said some of**
the Pharisees, This man
is not of God, because he
keepeth not the sabbath
day. Others said, How can
a man that is
a sinner do such miracles?
And there was a division among them.
17. They say unto the blind man
again, What sayest thou of him, that
he hath opened thine eyes? He said,
He is a prophet.
18. **But the Jews did not**
believe concerning him, that he
had been blind,
and received his sight, until they
called the parents of him
that had received his sight.
19. **And they asked**
them, saying,
Is this your son,
who ye say was born blind?
how then doth he now see?
20. **His parents answered**
them and said, We know that
this is our son,
and that he was born blind:
21. **But by what means he**
now seeth, we know not; or
who hath opened his eyes,
we know not:
he is of age; ask him: he shall
speak for himself.
22. These *words* spake his parents,
because they feared the Jews: for the
Jews had agreed already, that if any
man did confess that he was Christ,
he should be put out
of the synagogue.
23. Therefore said his parents, He is
of age; ask him.
24. **Then again called they**
the man that was blind,
and said
unto him, Give God the praise:

we know that this man
is a sinner.
25. **He answered** and said,
Whether he be a sinner *or no,*
I know not: one thing I
know, that, whereas I was
blind, now I see.
26. **Then said they** to him again,
What did he to thee?
how opened he thine eyes?
27. **He answered them, I**
have told you already,
and ye did not hear: wherefore would
ye hear *it* again?
will ye also be his
disciples?
28. **Then they reviled him,**
and said,
Thou art his disciple; but
we are Moses' disciples.
29. We know that God spake unto
Moses:
***as for* this *fellow,* we know**
not from whence he is.
30. **The man answered** and
said unto them, Why herein is a
marvellous thing, that
ye know not from whence he is,
and *yet* he hath opened
mine eyes.
31. **Now we know that God**
heareth not sinners: but if any
man be a worshipper of God, and
doeth his will, him he heareth.
32. Since the world began was it not
heard that any man opened the eyes
of one that was born blind.
33. **If this man were not of**
God, he could do nothing.
34. **They answered** and said
unto him,
Thou wast altogether born
in sins, and dost thou teach us?
And they cast him out.
35. **Jesus heard** that they had
cast him out;
and when he had found
him, he said unto him,
Dost thou believe on the
Son of God?
36. **He answered** and said,
Who is he, Lord, that I might
believe on him?
37. **And Jesus said** unto him,
Thou hast both seen him, and
it is he that talketh
with thee.
38. **And he said, Lord, I**
believe. And he
worshipped him.
39. **And Jesus said, For**
judgment I am come
into this world,
that they which see not
might see; and that they
which see might
be made blind.
40. **And *some* of the**
Pharisees which were with him
heard these words, and
said unto him,
Are we blind also?
41. **Jesus said** unto them,
If ye were blind, ye should
have no sin: but now ye
say, We see; therefore your
sin remaineth.

CHAPTER 10

1. Verily, verily, I say unto you,
He that entereth not by the
door into the sheepfold, but
climbeth up some other way
the same is a thief
and a robber.
2. **But he that entereth in by**
the door is the shepherd
of the sheep.
3. To him the porter openeth;
and the sheep hear his
voice: and he calleth his own sheep
by name, and leadeth them out.
4. And when he putteth forth his own
sheep, he goeth before them,
and the sheep follow
him: for they know his voice.
5. **And a stranger will they**
not follow, but will flee from him:
for they know not the
voice of strangers.
6. This parable spake Jesus unto
them: but they understood not what
things they were which he
spake unto them.
7. **Then said Jesus** unto them
again, Verily, verily, I say unto you,

I am the door of the sheep.
8. All that ever came before me are
thieves and robbers: but the sheep
did not hear them.
9. I am the door:
by me if any man enter in,
he shall be saved, and shall go
in and out, and find pasture.
10. **The thief cometh** not, but for
to steal, and to kill, and to
destroy: I am come that
they might have life,
and that they might have *it*
more abundantly.
11. **I am the good shepherd:**
the good shepherd giveth his life for
the sheep.
12. **But he that is an hireling,**
and not the shepherd, whose own the
sheep are not,
seeth the wolf coming, and
leaveth the sheep, and fleeth:
and the wolf catcheth them,
and scattereth the sheep.
13. The hireling fleeth, because he is
an hireling, and careth
not for the sheep.
14. **I am the good shepherd,**
and know my *sheep,* and
am known of mine.
15. As the Father knoweth me, even
so know I the Father:
and I lay down my life for
the sheep.
16. **And other sheep I have,**
which are
not of this fold: them also I must
bring, and they shall hear my voice;
and there shall be one fold,
***and* one shepherd.**
17. Therefore doth my
Father love me, because
I lay down my life,
that I might take it again.
18. **No man taketh it**
from me, but I lay it down of myself. I
have power to lay it down, and
I have power to take it
again. This commandment have I
received of my Father.
19. There was a division therefore
again among the Jews
for these sayings.
20. **And many** of them
said, He hath a devil,
and is mad; why hear ye him?
21. **Others said,** These are not
the words of him that hath a devil.
Can a devil open the eyes
of the blind?
22. And it was at Jerusalem the feast
of the dedication, and it was winter.
23. **And Jesus walked**
in the temple
in Solomon's porch.
24. **Then came the Jews**
round about him,
and said unto him, How long dost
thou make us to doubt?
If thou be the Christ,
tell us plainly.
25. **Jesus answered** them,
I told you, and ye believed
not: the works that I do in my
Father's name, they
bear witness of me.
26. But ye believe not, because ye
are not of my sheep,
as I said unto you.
27. **My sheep hear my**
voice, and I know them, and they
follow me:
28. **And I give unto them**
eternal life; and they shall
never perish, neither shall
any *man* pluck them out of
my hand.
29. My Father, which gave *them* me, is
greater than all;
and no *man* is able to
pluck *them* out of my
Father's hand.
30. **I and *my* Father are one.**
31. **Then the Jews took up**
stones again to stone him.
32. **Jesus answered** them,
Many good works have I
shewed you from my Father;
for which of those works
do ye stone me?
33. **The Jews answered**
him, saying, For a good work
we stone thee not; but
for blasphemy; and
because that thou,
being a man,

makest thyself God.
34. **Jesus answered** them,
Is it not written in your law, I said,
Ye are gods?
35. If he called them gods, unto whom
the word of God came, and the
scripture cannot be broken;
36. **Say ye of him,** whom the
Father hath sanctified, and sent into
the world,
Thou blasphemest;
because I said, I am the
Son of God?
37. **If I do not the works of**
my Father, believe me not.
38. But if I do, though ye believe not
me, believe the works: that ye may
know, and believe, that the Father *is* in
me, and I in him.
39. **Therefore they sought**
again to take him: but he
escaped out of their hand,
40. And went away again
beyond Jordan into the place
where John at first
baptized; and there he abode.
41. **And many**
resorted unto him, and
said, John did no miracle: but
all things that John spake
of this man were true.
42. **And many believed**
on him there.

CHAPTER 11

1. **Now a certain *man* was**
sick, *named* Lazarus, of
Bethany, the town of Mary and her
sister Martha.
2. (It was *that* Mary which anointed the
Lord with ointment, and wiped his feet
with her hair, whose brother Lazarus
was sick.)
3. **Therefore his sisters sent**
unto him, saying, Lord,
behold, he whom thou
lovest is sick.
4. When Jesus heard *that,*
he said, This sickness is
not unto death, but for the glory
of God, that the Son of God might be
glorified thereby.
5. **Now Jesus loved Martha,**
and her sister,
and Lazarus.
6. **When he had heard**
therefore that
he was sick, he abode two
days still in the same place
where he was.
7. **Then** after that
saith he to *his* disciples,
Let us go into Judaea again.
8. ***His* disciples say**
unto him, Master,
the Jews of late sought to
stone thee;
and goest thou thither again?
9. Jesus answered, Are there not
twelve hours in the day? If any man
walk in the day, he stumbleth not,
because he seeth the
light of this world.
10. But if a man walk in the night, he
stumbleth, because there
is no light in him.
11. These things said he: and
after that he saith unto them,
Our friend Lazarus
sleepeth; but I go, that I
may awake him out of sleep.
12. **Then said his disciples,**
Lord, if he sleep, he shall
do well.
13. Howbeit Jesus spake of his death:
but they thought that he had spoken
of taking of rest in sleep.
14. **Then said Jesus** unto them
plainly, Lazarus is dead.
15. And I am glad for your sakes that I
was not there, to the intent ye may
believe; nevertheless let us
go unto him.
16. Then said Thomas, which is called
Didymus, unto his fellow disciples, Let
us also go, that we may die with him.
17. **Then when Jesus came,**
he found that he had *lain* in
the grave four days already.
18. Now Bethany was nigh unto
Jerusalem, about fifteen furlongs off:
19. And many of the Jews came to
Martha and Mary, to comfort them
concerning their brother.
20. **Then Martha,** as soon as she
heard that Jesus was coming,

went and met him: but Mary sat *still* in the house.
21. **Then said Martha** unto Jesus,
Lord, if thou hadst been here, my brother had not died.
22. **But** I know, that even now,
whatsoever thou wilt ask of God,
God will give *it* **thee.**
23. **Jesus saith** unto her,
Thy brother shall rise again.
24. **Martha saith** unto him,
I know that he shall rise again in the resurrection at the last day.
25. **Jesus said** unto her,
I am the resurrection, and the life: he that believeth in me, though he were dead, yet shall he live:
26. **And whosoever liveth and believeth in me shall never die. Believest thou this?**
27. **She saith** unto him,
Yea, Lord: I believe that thou art the Christ, the Son of God, which should come into the world.
28. And when she had said,
she went her way, and called Mary her sister secretly,
saying, The Master is come, and
calleth for thee.
29. As soon as she heard *that,*
she arose quickly, and came unto him.
30. Now Jesus was not yet come into the town, but was in that place where Martha met him.
31. **The Jews** then which were with her in the house, and comforted her,
when they saw Mary, that she rose up hastily and went out,
followed her, saying, She goeth unto the grave to weep there.
32. **Then when Mary** was come where Jesus was, and
saw him, she fell down at his feet, saying unto him,
Lord, if thou hadst been here, my brother had not died.
33. **When Jesus therefore saw her weeping,** and the Jews also weeping which came with her,
he groaned in the spirit,
and was troubled.
34. **And said, Where have ye laid him? They said** unto him, Lord,
come and see.
35. **Jesus wept.**
36. **Then said the Jews, Behold how he loved him!**
37. And some of them said, Could not this man, which opened the eyes of the blind, have caused that even this man should not have died?
38. **Jesus therefore** again groaning in himself
cometh to the grave. It was a cave, and a stone lay upon it.
39. **Jesus said, Take ye away the stone. Martha,** the sister of him that was dead,
saith unto him,
Lord, by this time he stinketh: for he hath been *dead* four days.
40. **Jesus saith** unto her, Said I not unto thee, that,
if thou wouldest believe, thou shouldest see the glory of God?
41. **Then they took away the stone** *from the place* where the dead was laid.
And Jesus lifted up *his* eyes, and
said, Father, I thank thee that thou hast heard me.
42. **And I knew that thou hearest** me always:
but because of the people which stand by
I said *it,* that they may believe that thou hast sent me.
43. **And** when he thus had spoken,
he cried with a loud voice, Lazarus, come forth.
44. **And he that was dead came forth, bound** hand and foot
with graveclothes: and his

face was bound about with a napkin.
Jesus saith unto them,
Loose him, and let him go.
45. **Then many of the Jews**
which came to Mary, and had seen the
things which Jesus did,
believed on him.
46. **But some** of them
went their ways
to the Pharisees, and told
them what things Jesus had done.
47. **Then gathered** the chief
priests and the Pharisees
a council, and said, What
do we? for this man
doeth many miracles.
48. **If we let him thus alone,**
all *men* will believe on him:
and the Romans shall come and take
away both our place and nation.
49. **And** one of them, *named*
Caiaphas, being the high
priest that same year,
said unto them,
Ye know nothing at all,
50. Nor consider that
it is expedient for us,
that one man should die for
the people, and that the whole
nation perish not.
51. **And this spake he not of**
himself: but
being high priest that year,
he prophesied that Jesus
should die for that nation;
52. And not for that nation only,
but that also he should
gather together in one the
children of God
that were scattered abroad.
53. **Then** from that day forth
they took counsel together for
to put him to death.
54. **Jesus** therefore walked no more
openly among the Jews; but
went thence unto a country near to
the wilderness,
into a city called Ephraim,
and there continued with his
disciples.
55. **And the Jews' passover**
was nigh at hand:
and many went
out of the country up
to Jerusalem
before the passover,
to purify themselves.
56. Then sought they for Jesus, and
spake among themselves, as they
stood in the temple, What think ye,
that he will not come to the feast?
57. Now both the chief priests and the
Pharisees had given a commandment,
that, if any man knew where he were,
he should shew *it*, that they
might take him.

CHAPTER 12

1. **Then Jesus**
six days before the passover
came to Bethany, where
Lazarus was, which had been dead,
whom he raised from the dead.
2. **There they made him a**
supper; and Martha served: but
Lazarus was one of them that sat at
the table with him.
3. **Then took Mary** a pound of
ointment of spikenard,
very costly,
and anointed the feet of
Jesus, and wiped his feet
with her hair: and the house was
filled with the odour of the ointment.
4. **Then saith** one of his disciples,
Judas Iscariot, Simon's *son,*
which should betray him,
5. **Why was not this ointment**
sold for three hundred pence,
and given to the poor?
6. This he said, not that he cared for
the poor; but because he was a thief,
and had the bag, and bare what was
put therein.
7. **Then said Jesus, Let her**
alone: against the day of
my burying hath
she kept this.
8. **For the poor**
always ye have
with you; but me ye have not always.
9. **Much people**
of the Jews therefore
knew that he was there:
and they came not for
Jesus' sake only, but that

■ **they might see Lazarus** also,
whom he had raised from the dead.
■ 10. **But the chief priests**
■ **consulted that they might**
■ **put Lazarus also to death;**
■ 11. **Because that by reason**
■ **of him many**
of the Jews went away, and
■ **believed on Jesus.**
12. On the next day
■ **much people**
that were come to the feast,
■ **when they heard that Jesus**
■ **was coming to Jerusalem,**
■ 13. **Took branches of palm**
■ **trees, and went forth**
to meet him,
■ **and cried, Hosanna:**
■ **Blessed *is* the King of Israel**
that cometh in the name of the Lord.
■ 14. **And Jesus,** when he had
■ **found a young ass, sat**
■ **thereon; as it is written,**
15. Fear not, daughter
of Sion: behold,
■ **thy King cometh, sitting on**
■ **an ass's colt.**
16. These things understood not his
disciples at the first: but when Jesus
was glorified, then remembered they
that these things were written of him,
and *that* they had done these things
unto him.
■ 17. **The people therefore**
■ **that was with him when he**
■ **called Lazarus** out of his grave,
■ **and raised him** from the dead,
■ **bare record.**
■ 18. **For this cause the**
■ **people also met him,**
for that they heard that he had
done this miracle.
19. The Pharisees therefore said
among themselves, Perceive ye how
ye prevail nothing? behold, the world
is gone after him.
■ 20. **And** there were
■ **certain Greeks** among them that
■ **came up to worship**
■ **at the feast:**
■ 21. **The same came**
■ **therefore to Philip,** which was
of Bethsaida of Galilee,
and desired him,
■ **saying, Sir, we would**
■ **see Jesus.**
22. Philip cometh
■ **and** telleth Andrew: and again
■ **Andrew and Philip**
■ **tell Jesus.**
■ 23. **And Jesus answered**
them, saying,
■ **The hour is come, that the**
■ **Son of man should**
■ **be glorified.**
24. Verily, verily, I say unto you,
■ **Except a corn of wheat fall**
■ **into the ground and die, it**
■ **abideth alone: but if it die,**
■ **it bringeth forth much fruit.**
■ 25. **He that loveth his life**
■ **shall lose it;**
and he that hateth his life in this world
shall keep it unto life eternal.
■ 26. **If any man serve me, let**
■ **him follow me;** and where I am,
there shall also my servant be: if any
man serve me,
him will *my* Father honour.
27. Now is my soul troubled; and
■ **what shall I say? Father,**
■ **save me from this hour: but**
■ **for this cause came I unto**
■ **this hour.**
■ 28. **Father, glorify thy name.**
■ **Then came there a voice**
■ **from heaven, *saying,* I**
■ **have** both
■ **glorified *it,* and will glorify**
■ ***it* again.**
■ 29. **The people** therefore,
■ **that** stood by, and
■ **heard *it,* said** that
■ **it thundered: others said,**
■ **An angel spake** to him.
■ 30. **Jesus answered** and said,
■ **This voice came**
not because of me, but
■ **for your sakes.**
■ 31. **Now is the judgment of**
■ **this world: now shall the**
■ **prince** of this world
■ **be cast out.**
■ 32. **And I, if I be lifted up**
from the earth,
■ **will draw all *men* unto me.**

33. This he said, signifying what death
he should die.
34. **The people answered**
him, We have heard out of the law that
Christ abideth for ever:
and how sayest thou, The
Son of man
must be lifted up?
who is this Son of man?
35. **Then Jesus said** unto them,
Yet a little while is the light with you.
Walk while ye have the
light, lest darkness come upon you:
for he that walketh in
darkness knoweth not
whither he goeth.
36. While ye have light,
believe in the light, that ye
may be the children of light.
These things spake Jesus, and
departed, and did hide
himself from them.
37. **But though he had done**
so many miracles before them,
yet they believed not on him:
38. **That** the saying of
Esaias the prophet
might be fulfilled,
which he spake,
Lord, who hath believed
our report? and to whom hath the
arm of the Lord been revealed?
39. Therefore they could not believe,
because that
Esaias said again,
40. **He hath blinded their**
eyes, and hardened their heart;
that they should not see
with *their* eyes,
nor understand with *their* heart,
and be converted,
and I should heal them.
41. These things said Esaias, when
he saw his glory, and spake of him.
42. **Nevertheless among the**
chief rulers also many
believed on him;
but because of the Pharisees they
did not confess *him*, lest they
should be put out of the synagogue:
43. **For they loved the**
praise of men
more than the praise of God.

44. **Jesus cried** and said,
He that believeth on me,
believeth not on me, but
on him that sent me.
45. And he that seeth me seeth him
that sent me.
46. **I am** come a
light into the world, that
whosoever believeth on
me should not abide
in darkness.
47. And if any man hear my words,
and believe not, I judge him not: for
I came not to judge the
world, but to save
the world.
48. **He that rejecteth me,**
and receiveth not my words,
hath one that judgeth him:
the word
that I have spoken, the same
shall judge him in the
last day.
49. **For I have not spoken of**
myself; but the Father
which sent me, he
gave me a commandment,
what I should say,
and what I should speak.
50. And I know that his commandment
is life everlasting: whatsoever I speak
therefore, even as the Father said
unto me, so I speak.

CHAPTER 13

1. **Now before the** feast of the
passover, when Jesus knew that
his hour was come that he should
depart out of this world unto the
Father, having loved his own which
were in the world, he loved them unto
the end.
2. **And supper being ended,**
the devil having now put
into the heart of
Judas Iscariot, Simon's son,
to betray him;
3. **Jesus** knowing that the Father
had given all things into his hands,
and that he was come from God, and
went to God;
4. He riseth from supper, and laid
aside his garments; and

took a towel, and
girded himself.
5. After that he
poureth water into a basin,
and began to wash the
disciples' feet, and to wipe *them*
with the towel wherewith
he was girded.
6. Then cometh he to
Simon Peter: and
Peter saith unto him,
Lord, dost thou
wash my feet?
7. Jesus answered and said unto him,
What I do thou knowest not now; but
thou shalt know hereafter.
8. Peter saith unto him, Thou shalt
never wash my feet.
Jesus answered him,
If I wash thee not, thou hast
no part with me.
9. **Simon Peter saith** unto him,
Lord, not my feet only, but
also
***my* hands and *my* head.**
10. **Jesus saith** to him,
He that is washed needeth
not save to wash
***his* feet,** but is clean every whit:
and ye are clean,
but not all.
11. **For he knew who should**
betray him; therefore said he, Ye
are not all clean.
12. So after he had washed their feet,
and had taken his garments, and was
set down again,
he said unto them,
Know ye what I have done
to you?
13. Ye call me Master and Lord: and
ye say well; for *so* I am.
14. **If** I then,
***your* Lord** and Master,
have washed your feet; ye
also ought to wash one
another's feet.
15. **For** I have given
you an example, that
ye should do as I have
done to you.
16. Verily, verily, I say unto you,
The servant is not greater
than his lord; neither he that is
sent greater than he that sent him.
17. If ye know these things, happy are
ye if ye do them.
18. **I speak not of you all:**
I know whom I have chosen: but that
the scripture may be fulfilled,
He that eateth bread with
me hath lifted up his heel
against me.
19. Now I tell you before it come, that,
when it is come to pass, ye may
believe that I am *he*.
20. Verily, verily, I say unto you, He
that receiveth whomsoever I send
receiveth me; and he that receiveth
me receiveth him that sent me.
21. When Jesus had thus said,
he was troubled in spirit,
and testified, and said, Verily,
verily, I say unto you, that
one of you shall betray me.
22. Then the disciples looked one on
another, doubting of whom he spake.
23. **Now there was leaning**
on Jesus' bosom one of his
disciples, whom Jesus loved.
24. **Simon Peter** therefore
beckoned to him,
that he should
ask who it should be
of whom he spake.
25. **He** then lying on Jesus' breast
saith unto him,
Lord, who is it?
26. **Jesus answered, He it is,**
to whom I shall give a sop,
when I have dipped *it*.
And when he had dipped the sop,
he gave *it* to Judas
Iscariot, *the son* of Simon.
27. **And** after the sop
Satan entered into him.
Then said Jesus unto him,
That thou doest,
do quickly.
28. Now no man at the table knew for
what intent he spake this unto him.
29. For some *of them* thought,
because Judas had the bag, that
Jesus had said unto him, Buy *those*
things that we have need of against
the feast; or that he should give

something to the poor.
30. **He** then having received the sop
went immediately
out: and it was night.
31. Therefore, when he was gone out,
Jesus said, Now is the Son
of man glorified, and God
is glorified in him.
32. If God be glorified in him, God
shall also glorify him in himself, and
shall straightway glorify him.
33. Little children, yet a little while I
am with you. Ye shall seek me: and as
I said unto the Jews, Whither I go, ye
cannot come; so now I say to you.
34. **A new commandment I**
give unto you,
That ye love one another; as
I have loved you, that ye also love
one another.
35. **By this shall all *men***
know that ye are
my disciples,
if ye have love one to another.
36. **Simon Peter said** unto him,
Lord, whither goest thou?
Jesus answered
him, Whither I go,
thou canst not follow me
now; but thou shalt follow
me afterwards.
37. **Peter said** unto him, Lord, why
cannot I follow thee now?
I will lay down my life for
thy sake.
38. **Jesus answered** him, Wilt
thou lay down thy life for my sake?
Verily, verily, I say unto thee,
The cock shall not crow, till
thou hast denied me thrice.

CHAPTER 14

1. **Let not your heart be**
troubled: ye believe in
God, believe also in me.
2. **In my Father's house are**
many mansions: if *it were* not
so, I would have told you.
I go to prepare a
place for you.
3. **And if I go**
and prepare a place for you,
I will come again, and
receive you unto myself;
that where I am, *there* ye
may be also.
4. And whither I go ye know, and the
way ye know.
5. **Thomas saith** unto him, Lord,
we know not whither thou goest; and
how can we know the way?
6. **Jesus saith** unto him,
I am the way, the truth, and
the life: no man cometh
unto the Father, but by me.
7. If ye had known me, ye should have
known my Father also: and from
henceforth ye know him, and have
seen him.
8. **Philip saith** unto him, Lord,
shew us the Father,
and it sufficeth us.
9. **Jesus saith** unto him, Have I
been so long time with you, and yet
hast thou not known me, Philip?
he that hath seen me hath
seen the Father; and how sayest
thou *then,* Shew us the Father?
10. **Believest thou not that I**
am in the Father, and the
Father in me? the words that I
speak unto you
I speak not of myself: but
the Father that dwelleth
in me, he
doeth the works.
11. Believe me that I *am* in the Father,
and the Father in me: or else believe
me for the very works' sake.
12. Verily, verily, I say unto you,
He that believeth on me, the
works that I do shall he do
also; and greater *works*
than these shall he do;
because I go unto my Father.
13. **And whatsoever ye shall**
ask in my name, that will I
do, that the Father may be glorified
in the Son.
14. If ye shall ask any thing in my
name, I will do *it.*
15. **If ye love me, keep my**
commandments.
16. **And I will pray the**
Father, and he shall give
you another Comforter, that

he may abide with you for ever;
17. ***Even* the Spirit of truth;**
whom the world cannot receive,
because it seeth him not, neither
knoweth him: but ye know him; for he
dwelleth with you, and shall be in you.
18. I will not leave you comfortless:
I will come to you.
19. **Yet a little while, and the**
world seeth me no more;
but ye see me: because I
live, ye shall live also.
20. At that day ye shall know that I *am*
in my Father, and ye in me,
and I in you.
21. **He that hath my**
commandments, and
keepeth them, he it is that
loveth me: and he that loveth me
shall be loved of my Father, and
I will love him, and will
manifest myself to him.
22. **Judas saith** unto him,
not Iscariot, Lord,
how is it that thou wilt
manifest thyself
unto us, and not unto the world?
23. **Jesus answered**
and said unto him,
If a man love me, he will
keep my words: and my
Father will love him,
and we will come unto him, and
make our abode with him.
24. He that loveth me not keepeth not
my sayings: and the word which ye
hear is not mine, but the Father's
which sent me.
25. **These things have I**
spoken unto you,
being *yet* present with you.
26. **But the** Comforter, *which is* the
Holy Ghost, whom the Father will
send in my name, he
shall teach you all things,
and bring all things to your
remembrance, whatsoever I
have said unto you.
27. **Peace I leave** with you, my
peace I give unto you: not as the
world giveth, give I unto you.
Let not your heart be
troubled, neither
let it be afraid.
28. Ye have heard how
I said unto you,
I go away, and
come again unto you.
If ye loved me, ye would
rejoice, because I said,
I go unto the Father: for my
Father is greater than I.
29. And now I have told you before it
come to pass, that, when it is come to
pass, ye might believe.
30. **Hereafter I will not talk**
much with you:
for the prince of this world
cometh, and hath nothing in me.
31. But that the world may know that I
love the Father; and as the Father
gave me commandment, even so I do.
Arise, let us go hence.

CHAPTER 15

1. **I am the true vine, and my**
Father is the husbandman.
2. **Every branch** in me
that beareth not fruit he
taketh away: and every
***branch* that beareth fruit,**
he purgeth it, that it may
bring forth more fruit.
3. **Now ye are clean through**
the word which I have
spoken unto you.
4. Abide in me, and I in you. As
the branch cannot bear
fruit of itself,
except it abide
in the vine; no more can ye,
except ye abide in me.
5. **I am the vine,**
ye *are* the branches:
He that abideth in me,
and I in him, the same
bringeth forth much fruit:
for without me ye can do nothing.
6. **If a man abide not in me,**
he is cast forth as a branch,
and is withered; and men gather
them, and cast *them* into the fire,
and they are
burned.
7. **If ye abide in me, and my**
words abide in you, ye shall

ask what ye will, and it
shall be done unto you.
8. Herein is my Father glorified, that
ye bear much fruit; so shall
ye be my disciples.
9. As the Father hath loved me, so
have I loved you:
continue ye in my love.
10. If ye keep my commandments, ye
shall abide in my love; even as I have
kept my Father's commandments, and
abide in his love.
11 **These things have I**
spoken unto you,
that my joy might remain in
you, and *that* your joy
might be full.
12. **This is my command-**
ment, That ye love one
another, as I have loved you.
13. **Greater love hath no**
man than this, that
a man lay down his life for
his friends.
14. Ye are my friends, if ye do
whatsoever I command you.
15. **Henceforth I call you not**
servants; for the servant knoweth
not what his lord doeth:
but I have called you
friends; for all things
that I have heard of my Father
I have made known
unto you.
16. Ye have not chosen me, but
I have chosen you, and
ordained you, that ye
should go and bring forth
fruit, and *that* your fruit should
remain: that
whatsoever ye shall ask of
the Father in my name, he
may give it you.
17. These things I command you, that
ye love one another.
18. **If the world hate you, ye**
know that it hated me before *it*
hated you.
19. If ye were of the world, the world
would love his own: but because ye
are not of the world, but
I have chosen you out of
the world, therefore the world
hateth you.
20. Remember the word that I said
unto you, The servant is not greater
than his lord.
If they have persecuted me,
they will also persecute
you; if they have kept my saying,
they will keep yours also.
21. **But all these things will**
they do unto you for my
name's sake, because they
know not him that sent me.
22. **If I had not come**
and spoken unto them,
they had not had sin: but
now they have no cloak
for their sin.
23. **He that hateth me hateth**
my Father also.
24. If I had not done among them the
works which none other man did, they
had not had sin: but now have they
both seen and hated both
me and my Father.
25. **But** *this cometh to pass,*
that the word might be
fulfilled that is written in their law,
They hated me
without a cause.
26. **But when the Comforter**
is come, whom I will send unto you
from the Father, *even* the Spirit of
truth, which proceedeth
from the Father,
he shall testify of me:
27. **And ye also shall bear**
witness, because ye have been
with me from the beginning.

CHAPTER 16

1. These things have I spoken unto
you, that ye should not be offended.
2. **They shall put you out of**
the synagogues: yea, the
time cometh, that
whosoever killeth you
will think that he doeth
God service.
3. And these things will they do unto
you, because they have not known
the Father, nor me.
4. **But these things have I**
told you, that when the

■ **time shall come,**
■ **ye may remember** that I told
you of them. And these things I said
not unto you at the beginning,
because I was with you.
5. But now I go my way to him that
sent me; and none of you asketh me,
Whither goest thou?
■ 6. **But because I have said**
■ **these things** unto you,
■ **sorrow hath filled**
■ **your heart.**
7. Nevertheless I tell you the truth;
■ **It is expedient** for you
■ **that I go away:**
■ **for if I go not** away,
■ **the Comforter will not come**
unto you; but if I depart,
I will send him unto you.
■ 8. **And** when he is come,
■ **he will reprove the world of**
■ **sin, and of righteousness,**
■ **and of judgment:**
9. Of sin, because they
believe not on me;
10. Of righteousness, because I go to
my Father, and ye see me no more;
11. Of judgment, because the prince
of this world is judged.
■ 12. **I have yet many things to**
■ **say** unto you,
■ **but ye cannot bear**
■ **them now.**
13. Howbeit
■ **when** he,
■ **the Spirit of truth, is come,**
■ **he will guide you into all**
■ **truth:** for he shall not speak of
himself; but whatsoever he shall hear,
that shall he speak:
■ **and he will shew you things**
■ **to come.**
■ 14. **He shall glorify me:** for he
shall receive of mine, and shall shew *it*
unto you.
15. All things that the Father hath are
mine: therefore said I, that he shall
take of mine, and shall
shew *it* unto you.
■ 16. **A little while, and ye**
■ **shall not see me: and**
■ **again, a little while, and ye**
■ **shall see me, because I go**
■ **to the Father.**
■ 17. **Then said *some* of his**
■ **disciples** among themselves,
■ **What is this that he saith**
■ **unto us,** A little while, and ye shall
not see me: and again, a little while,
and ye shall see me: and, Because I
go to the Father?
18. They said therefore, What is this
that he saith, A little while?
■ **we cannot tell**
■ **what he saith.**
■ 19. **Now Jesus knew that**
■ **they were desirous to ask**
■ **him, and said**
unto them, Do ye inquire among
yourselves of that I said, A little while,
and ye shall not see me: and again, a
little while, and ye shall see me?
20. Verily, verily,
■ **I say unto you, That ye**
■ **shall weep and lament,** but
the world shall rejoice:
and ye shall be sorrowful,
■ **but your sorrow shall be**
■ **turned into joy.**
■ 21. **A woman** when she is
■ **in travail hath sorrow,**
because her hour is come:
■ **but as soon as she is**
■ **delivered of the child, she**
■ **remembereth no more the**
■ **anguish,** for joy that a man is born
into the world.
■ 22. **And ye now therefore**
■ **have sorrow: but I will see**
■ **you again,**
and your heart shall rejoice,
■ **and your joy no man taketh**
from you.
23. And in that day ye shall ask me
nothing. Verily, verily, I say unto you,
■ **Whatsoever ye shall ask**
■ **the Father in my name, he**
■ **will give *it* you.**
24. Hitherto have ye asked nothing in
my name:
■ **ask, and ye shall receive,**
■ **that your joy may be full.**
25. These things have I spoken unto
you in proverbs: but the time cometh,
when I shall no more speak unto you
in proverbs, but I shall shew you

plainly of the Father.
26. At that day ye shall ask in my
name: and I say not unto you, that I
will pray the Father for you:
27. **For the Father himself**
loveth you, because ye
have loved me,
and have believed that
I came out from God.
28. I came forth from the Father, and
am come into the world: again,
I leave the world, and go to
the Father.
29. **His disciples said**
unto him, Lo,
now speakest thou plainly,
and speakest no proverb.
30. Now are we sure that
thou knowest all things,
and needest not that any man
should ask thee:
by this we believe that thou
camest forth from God.
31. **Jesus answered**
them, Do ye now believe?
32. **Behold, the hour cometh,**
yea, is now come,
that ye shall be scattered,
every man to his own,
and shall leave me alone:
and yet I am not alone, because the
Father is with me.
33. **These things I have**
spoken unto you,
that in me ye might have
peace. In the world ye shall
have tribulation: but be of
good cheer; I have
overcome the world.

CHAPTER 17

1. These words spake
Jesus, and lifted up his eyes to
heaven, and
said, Father, the hour is
come; glorify thy Son,
that thy Son also may glorify thee:
2. As thou hast given him
power over all flesh,
that he should give eternal
life to as many as thou
hast given him.
3. **And this is life eternal,**
that they might know thee
the only true God,
and Jesus Christ,
whom thou hast sent.
4. I have glorified thee on the earth:
I have finished the work
which thou gavest me to do.
5. **And now, O Father, glorify**
thou me with thine own self with
the glory which I had with
thee before the world was.
6. I have manifested thy name unto
the men which thou gavest me out of
the world: thine they were, and thou
gavest them me; and they have kept
thy word.
7. Now they have known that all things
whatsoever thou hast given
me are of thee.
8. **For I have given unto them**
the words which thou
gavest me;
and they have received *them,* and
have known surely that I came out
from thee, and they have believed
that thou didst send me.
9. I pray for them:
I pray not for the world, but
for them which thou hast
given me; for they are thine.
10. And all mine are thine, and thine
are mine; and I am glorified in them.
11. And now I am no more in the world,
but these are in the world,
and I come to thee.
Holy Father, keep through
thine own name those
whom thou hast given me,
that they may be one,
as we *are*.
12. While I was with them in the world,
I kept them in thy name: those that
thou gavest me I have kept, and none
of them is lost, but the son of
perdition; that the scripture
might be fulfilled.
13. **And now come I to thee;**
and these things I speak in the world,
that they might have my joy
fulfilled in themselves.
14. I have given them thy word; and
the world hath hated them, because
they are not of the world, even as I am

not of the world.
15. **I pray not that thou**
shouldest take them out of
the world, but
that thou shouldest
keep them from the evil.
16. They are not of the world, even as
I am not of the world.
17. **Sanctify them through**
thy truth: thy word is truth.
18. As thou hast sent me into the
world, even so have I also sent them
into the world.
19. And for their sakes I sanctify
myself, that they also might be
sanctified through the truth.
20. **Neither pray I for these**
alone, but for them also
which shall believe on me
through their word;
21. **That they all may be one;**
as thou, Father, *art* in me,
and I in thee,
that they also may be one
in us: that the world may
believe that thou
hast sent me.
22. And the glory which thou gavest
me I have given them; that they may
be one, even as we are one:
23. **I in them, and thou in me,**
that they may be made
perfect in one;
and that the world may know that thou
hast sent me, and hast loved them, as
thou hast loved me.
24. **Father, I will that**
they also, whom thou hast given me,
be with me where I am; that
they may behold my glory,
which thou hast given me:
for thou lovedst me before
the foundation
of the world.
25. O righteous Father, the world hath
not known thee: but I have known
thee, and these have known that thou
hast sent me.
26. **And I have declared**
unto them thy name, and will
declare *it:* that the love wherewith thou
hast loved me may be in them,
and I in them.

CHAPTER 18

1. When Jesus had spoken
these words,
he went forth with his
disciples over the brook Cedron,
where was a garden, into the
which he entered, and his disciples.
2. And Judas also, which betrayed
him, knew the place: for Jesus
ofttimes resorted thither
with his disciples.
3. **Judas then, having**
received a band *of men*
and officers from the chief
priests and Pharisees,
cometh thither with lanterns and
torches and weapons.
4. **Jesus** therefore,
knowing all things that should
come upon him, went forth, and
said unto them,
Whom seek ye?
5. **They answered** him,
Jesus of Nazareth.
Jesus saith unto them,
I am *he.* And Judas
also, which betrayed him,
stood with them.
6. **As soon then as he** had
said unto them,
I am *he,* they went backward, and
fell to the ground.
7. **Then asked he them**
again, Whom seek ye? And
they said, Jesus of Nazareth.
8. **Jesus answered, I have**
told you that I am *he:* if
therefore ye seek me, let
these go their way:
9. **That the saying might be**
fulfilled, which he spake,
Of them
which thou gavest me have
I lost none.
10. Then Simon
Peter having a sword
drew it, and
smote the high priest's
servant, and cut off his
right ear.
The servant's name was Malchus.
11. **Then said Jesus** unto Peter,
Put up thy sword

into the sheath:
the cup which my Father
hath given me, shall I not
drink it?
12. **Then** the band and the captain
and officers of
the Jews took Jesus,
and bound him,
13. **And led him away to**
Annas first; for he was
father in law to Caiaphas,
which was the high priest
that same year.
14. Now Caiaphas was he, which gave
counsel to the Jews, that it was
expedient that one man should die for
the people.
15. **And Simon Peter**
followed Jesus, and
***so did* another disciple:**
that disciple was known unto the high
priest, and went in with Jesus into the
palace of the high priest.
16. But Peter stood
at the door without.
Then went out that other
disciple, which was known unto
the high priest,
and spake unto her that
kept the door, and brought
in Peter.
17. **Then saith the damsel**
that kept the door unto Peter,
Art not thou also *one* of this
man's disciples?
He saith, I am not.
18. **And the servants and**
officers stood there, who had
made a fire
of coals; for it was cold:
and they
warmed themselves: and
Peter stood with them, and
warmed himself.
19. **The high priest then**
asked Jesus
of his disciples, and
of his doctrine.
20. **Jesus answered** him,
I spake openly to the world; I
ever taught in the synagogue, and in
the temple, whither the
Jews always resort;
and in secret have
I said nothing.
21. Why askest thou me?
ask them which heard me,
what I have said unto them:
behold, they know what I said.
22. **And** when he had thus spoken,
one of the officers
which stood by
struck Jesus
with the palm of his hand,
saying, Answerest thou the
high priest so?
23. **Jesus answered** him, If I
have spoken evil, bear witness of the
evil: but if well,
why smitest thou me?
24. **Now Annas had**
sent him bound
unto Caiaphas the
high priest.
25. **And Simon Peter** stood and
warmed himself. They said
therefore unto him,
Art not thou also *one* of his
disciples? He denied *it,* and
said, I am not.
26. **One of the servants of**
the high priest, being *his*
kinsman whose ear Peter cut off,
saith, Did not I see thee in
the garden with him?
27. **Peter then denied again:**
and immediately
the cock crew.
28. **Then led they Jesus from**
Caiaphas unto the hall of
judgment: and it was early; and
they themselves went not into the
judgment hall, lest they should be
defiled; but that they
might eat the passover.
29. **Pilate then**
went out unto them, and
said, What accusation
bring ye against this man?
30. **They answered**
and said unto him,
If he were not a malefactor,
we would not have
delivered him up unto thee.
31. **Then said Pilate**
unto them, Take ye him, and

judge him according to
your law. The Jews therefore
said unto him,
It is not lawful for us to put
any man to death:
32. That the saying of Jesus might be
fulfilled, which he spake, signifying
what death he should die.
33. **Then Pilate** entered into the
judgment hall again, and
called Jesus, and said
unto him,
Art thou the King
of the Jews?
34. **Jesus answered** him,
Sayest thou this thing
of thyself,
or did others tell it thee of me?
35. **Pilate answered, Am I a**
Jew? Thine own nation and the chief
priests have delivered thee unto me:
what hast thou done?
36. **Jesus answered, My**
kingdom is not of this
world: if my kingdom were of this
world, then would my servants fight,
that I should not be delivered to the
Jews: but now is my
kingdom not from hence.
37. **Pilate therefore said**
unto him,
Art thou a king then? Jesus
answered, Thou sayest
that I am a king. To this end
was I born, and for this cause
came I into the world;
that I should bear witness
unto the truth. Every one that is
of the truth heareth my voice.
38. **Pilate saith** unto him,
What is truth? And
when he had said this,
he went out again unto the
Jews, and saith unto them,
I find in him no fault *at all.*
39. **But ye have a custom,**
that I should release unto you
one at the passover: will ye
therefore that I release
unto you
the King of the Jews?
40. **Then cried they**
all again, saying,
Not this man, but
Barabbas. Now Barabbas was
a robber.

CHAPTER 19

1. **Then Pilate**
therefore took Jesus, and
scourged *him.*
2. **And the soldiers platted**
a crown of thorns, and put
***it* on his head, and they put**
on him a purple robe,
3. **And said, Hail, King of the**
Jews! and they smote him
with their hands.
4. **Pilate therefore went forth**
again, and saith unto them,
Behold, I bring him forth to you,
that ye may know that
I find no fault in him.
5. **Then came Jesus forth,**
wearing the crown of thorns, and the
purple robe.
And *Pilate* saith unto them,
Behold the man!
6. **When the chief priests**
therefore
and officers saw him, they
cried out, saying,
Crucify *him,* crucify *him.*
Pilate saith unto them,
Take ye him, and crucify
him: for I find no fault in him.
7. **The Jews answered**
him, We have a law, and by our law
he ought to die, because he
made himself the
Son of God.
8. **When Pilate** therefore
heard that saying, he was
the more
afraid;
9. **And** went again into the judgment
hall, and
saith unto Jesus, Whence
art thou? But Jesus gave
him no answer.
10. **Then saith Pilate** unto him,
Speakest thou not
unto me? knowest thou not that
I have power to
crucify thee,
and have power to release thee?

11. **Jesus answered, Thou**
couldest have no power
at all against me,
except it were given thee
from above:
therefore he that delivered me unto
thee hath the greater sin.
12. And from thenceforth
Pilate sought to release
him: but the Jews cried
out, saying,
If thou let this man go, thou
art not Caesar's friend:
whosoever maketh himself a king
speaketh against Caesar.
13. **When Pilate** therefore
heard that saying,
he brought Jesus forth,
and sat down in the judgment seat in a
place that is called the Pavement, but
in the Hebrew, Gabbatha.
14. And it was the preparation of the
passover, and about the sixth hour:
and he saith unto the Jews,
Behold your King!
15. **But they cried**
out, Away with *him,*
away with *him,* crucify him.
Pilate saith unto them,
Shall I crucify your King?
The chief priests answered,
We have no king
but Caesar.
16. **Then delivered he him**
therefore unto them
to be crucified. And they
took Jesus, and led *him* away.
17. **And he bearing his**
cross went forth into
a place
called *the place* of a skull, which is
called in the Hebrew
Golgotha:
18. **Where they crucified**
him, and two other
with him, on either side one,
and Jesus in the midst.
19. **And Pilate wrote a title,**
and put *it* on the cross.
And the writing was
JESUS OF NAZARETH THE
KING OF THE JEWS.
20. This title then read many of the
Jews: for the place where Jesus was
crucified was nigh to the city: and it
was written in Hebrew,
and Greek, *and* Latin.
21. **Then said the chief**
priests of the Jews to Pilate,
Write not, The King of the
Jews; but that he said, I am
King of the Jews.
22. **Pilate answered, What I**
have written I have written.
23. **Then the soldiers,**
when they had crucified Jesus,
took his garments, and made
four parts, to every soldier a part;
and also *his* coat:
now the coat was
without seam,
woven from the top throughout.
24. **They said**
therefore among themselves,
Let us not rend it, but cast
lots for it, whose it shall be:
that the scripture might be
fulfilled, which saith,
They parted my raiment
among them,
and for my vesture they did
cast lots. These things therefore
the soldiers did.
25. **Now there stood by the**
cross of Jesus his mother,
and his mother's sister, Mary the *wife*
of Cleophas, and Mary Magdalene.
26. **When Jesus therefore**
saw his mother, and the
disciple standing by,
whom he loved, he saith
unto his mother,
Woman, behold thy son!
27. **Then saith he to the**
disciple, Behold thy
mother! And from that hour that
disciple took her unto his own *home.*
28. **After this, Jesus**
knowing that all things were now
accomplished, that the scripture
might be fulfilled,
saith, I thirst.
29. Now there was set a
vessel full of vinegar:
and they filled a sponge
with vinegar,

and put *it* upon hyssop,
and put *it* to his mouth.
30. **When Jesus** therefore had
received the vinegar, he
said, It is finished:
and he bowed his head,
and gave up the ghost.
31. **The Jews** therefore, because it
was the preparation, that the bodies
should not remain upon the cross on
the sabbath day, (for that sabbath
day was an high day,)
besought Pilate that their
legs might be broken,
and *that* they might be taken away.
32. **Then** came
the soldiers, and
brake the legs of the first,
and of the other which was
crucified with him.
33. **But** when they came to
Jesus, and saw that he
was dead already,
they brake not his legs:
34. **But one**
of the soldiers with a spear
pierced his side, and
forthwith came there out
blood and water.
35. And he that saw *it* bare record,
and his record is true: and he knoweth
that he saith true, that ye might
believe.
36. **For these things were**
done, that the scripture
should be fulfilled, A bone
of him shall not be broken.
37. **And** again another
scripture saith,
They shall look on him
whom they pierced.
38. **And** after this
Joseph of Arimathaea, being
a disciple of Jesus, but secretly for
fear of the Jews,
besought Pilate that he
might take away the body
of Jesus:
and Pilate gave *him* leave.
He came therefore,
and took the body of Jesus.
39. **And there came also**
Nicodemus, which at the first
came to Jesus by night,
and brought a mixture of
myrrh and aloes,
about an hundred pound *weight.*
40. **Then took they the body**
of Jesus,
and wound it in linen clothes
with the spices, as the manner
of the Jews is to bury.
41. **Now** in the place
where he was crucified
there was a garden;
and in the garden
a new sepulchre,
wherein was never man yet laid.
42. **There laid they Jesus**
therefore because of the Jews'
preparation *day*; for the sepulchre
was nigh at hand.

CHAPTER 20

1. **The first *day* of the week**
cometh Mary Magdalene
early,
when it was yet dark,
unto the sepulchre,
and seeth the stone taken
away from the sepulchre.
2. **Then she runneth,**
and cometh
to Simon Peter, and to the
other disciple,
whom Jesus loved,
and saith unto them,
They have taken away the
LORD out of the sepulchre, and we
know not where they have laid him.
3. **Peter** therefore went forth,
and that other disciple, and
came to the sepulchre.
4. So they ran both together: and
the other disciple did
outrun Peter,
and came first to the sepulchre.
5. **And he stooping down,**
and looking in,
saw the linen clothes lying,
yet went he not in.
6. **Then cometh Simon Peter**
following him,
and went into the
sepulchre, and seeth the
linen clothes lie,

7. **And the napkin, that was**
about his head,
not lying with the linen clothes,
but wrapped together
in a place by itself.
8. Then went in also that other
disciple, which came first to the
sepulchre, and he saw, and believed.
9. For as yet they knew not the
scripture, that he must rise
again from the dead.
10. **Then the disciples went**
away again unto their own home.
11. **But Mary stood**
without at the sepulchre weeping:
and as she wept, she
stooped down, *and*
***looked* into the sepulchre,**
12. **And seeth two angels** in
white sitting, the one at the head, and
the other at the feet, where the body
of Jesus had lain.
13. **And they say**
unto her, Woman,
why weepest thou? She
saith unto them,
Because they have taken
away my LORD, and I know not
where they have laid him.
14. **And when she had thus**
said, she turned herself back,
and saw Jesus standing,
and knew not that it was
Jesus.
15. **Jesus saith** unto her, Woman,
why weepest thou?
whom seekest thou?
She, supposing him to be
the gardener, saith unto him,
Sir, if thou have borne him hence,
tell me where thou
hast laid him,
and I will take him away.
16. **Jesus saith** unto her,
Mary. She turned herself,
and saith unto him,
Rabboni; which is to say,
Master.
17. **Jesus saith** unto her,
Touch me not; for I am not yet
ascended to my Father:
but go to my brethren, and
say unto them,
I ascend unto my Father, and
your Father; and *to* my God, and your
God.
18. **Mary** Magdalene came and
told the disciples that she
had seen the LORD, and
***that* he had spoken**
these things
unto her.
19. **Then the same day**
at evening,
being the first *day* of the week,
when the doors were shut
where the disciples were
assembled for fear of the Jews,
came Jesus
and stood in the midst,
and saith unto them,
Peace *be* unto you.
20. **And** when he had so said,
he shewed unto them *his*
hands and his side. Then
were the disciples glad, when they
saw the LORD.
21. **Then said Jesus** to them
again, Peace *be* unto you:
as *my* Father hath sent me,
even so send I you.
22. **And** when he had said this,
he breathed on *them,*
and saith unto them,
Receive ye the Holy Ghost:
23. **Whose soever *sins* ye**
remit, they
are remitted unto them;
***and* whose soever sins ye**
retain, they
are retained.
24. **But Thomas,** one of the
twelve, called Didymus,
was not with them
when Jesus came.
25. **The other disciples**
therefore
said unto him, We have
seen the LORD. But he said
unto them,
Except I shall see in his
hands the print of the nails,
and put my finger into the
print of the nails,
and thrust my hand into his
side, I will not believe.

26. **And after eight days again** his disciples were within, and Thomas with them: *then* came **Jesus,** the doors being shut, and **stood in the midst,** and said, Peace *be* unto you.
27. **Then saith he to Thomas, Reach hither thy finger, and behold my hands;** and reach hither thy hand, and thrust *it* into my side: and be not faithless, but believing.
28. **And Thomas answered** and said unto him, **My LORD and my God.**
29. **Jesus saith** unto him, Thomas, **because thou hast seen** me, **thou** hast **believed: blessed** ***are*** **they that have not seen, and** *yet* **have believed.**
30. **And many other signs truly did Jesus** in the presence of his disciples, **which are not written in this book:**
31. **But these are written, that ye might believe that Jesus is the Christ,** the Son of God; and that believing ye might have life through his name.

CHAPTER 21

1. After these things Jesus shewed himself again to the disciples at the sea of Tiberias; and on this wise shewed he *himself.*
2. **There were together Simon Peter, and Thomas** called Didymus, **and Nathanael** of Cana in Galilee, **and the** ***sons*** **of Zebedee, and two other** of his **disciples.**
3. **Simon Peter saith** unto them, **I go a fishing. They say** unto him, **We also go** with thee. **They went forth,** and entered into a ship immediately; **and** that night they **caught nothing.**
4. **But when the morning was** now **come, Jesus stood on the shore:** but the disciples knew not that it was Jesus.
5. **Then Jesus saith** unto them, **Children, have ye any meat? They answered** him, **No.**
6. **And he said** unto them, **Cast** the net **on the right side** of the ship, and ye shall find. **They cast** therefore, **and** now they **were not able to draw** it for **the multitude of fishes.**
7. **Therefore that disciple whom Jesus loved saith** unto Peter, **It is the Lord. Now when** Simon **Peter heard that** it was the Lord, **he** girt *his* fisher's coat *unto him,* (for he was naked,) and did **cast himself into the sea.**
8. **And the other disciples came** in a little ship; (for they were not far from land, but as it were two hundred cubits,) **dragging the net with fishes.**
9. As soon then as they were come to land, **they saw a fire** of coals there, **and fish laid thereon, and bread.**
10. Jesus saith unto them, Bring of the fish which ye have now caught.
11. Simon Peter went up, and drew the net to land full of great fishes, an hundred and fifty and three: and for all there were so many, yet was not the net broken.
12. **Jesus saith** unto them, **Come** ***and*** **dine. And** none of the disciples durst ask him, Who art thou? knowing that it was the Lord.
13. **Jesus** then cometh, and **taketh bread, and giveth them, and fish** likewise.
14. This is now the third time that

Jesus shewed himself to his
disciples, after that he was risen from
the dead.
15. **So when they had dined,**
Jesus saith to
Simon Peter, Simon, *son* of Jonas,
lovest thou me more than
these? He saith unto him,
Yea, Lord;
thou knowest that I love thee.
He saith unto him,
Feed my lambs.
16. **He saith** to him again
the second time, Simon,
son of Jonas,
lovest thou me? He saith
unto him,
Yea, Lord;
thou knowest that I love thee.
He saith unto him,
Feed my sheep.
17. **He saith** unto him the
third time, Simon, *son* of Jonas,
lovest thou me? Peter was
grieved because he said unto him
the third time, Lovest thou me?
And he said unto him,
Lord, thou knowest all things;
thou knowest that I love
thee. Jesus saith unto him,
Feed my sheep.
18. Verily, verily, I say unto thee,
When thou wast young,
thou girdest thyself, and
walkedst whither thou
wouldest: but when
thou shalt be
old, thou shalt stretch
forth thy hands, and
another shall gird thee,
and carry *thee* whither thou
wouldest not.
19. **This spake he, signifying**
by what death he should
glorify God. And when he had
spoken this, he saith unto him,
Follow me.
20. **Then Peter,** turning about,
seeth the disciple whom
Jesus loved following; which also
leaned on his breast at supper, and
said, Lord, which is he
that betrayeth thee?
21. **Peter** seeing him
saith to Jesus,
Lord, and
what *shall* this man *do?*
22. **Jesus saith** unto him,
If I will that he tarry till I
come, what *is that* to thee?
follow thou me.
23. Then went this saying abroad
among the brethren, that that disciple
should not die: yet Jesus said not
unto him, He shall not die; but, If I will
that he tarry till I come,
what *is that* to thee?
24. This is the disciple which testifieth
of these things, and wrote these
things: and we know that his
testimony is true.
25. **And there are also many**
other things which Jesus
did, the which,
if they should be written
every one, I suppose that even
the world itself could not
contain the books that
should be written.
Amen.

THE ACTS OF THE APOSTLES

BACKGROUND INFORMATION

Author – Luke, physician and Gentile companion of Paul.
Date Written – probably **between 60** and **64** A.D.

Number of:
Verses - 1,007
Chapters - 28
Total Words - 24,250
Scan Words - 11,781
Scan Words represent 48 % of Total Words.

Theme – the ministry of the Holy Spirit in the early church as the gospel was spread in fulfillment of the Great Commission.

OUTLINE OF THE ACTS

I. **Christ's commission, the Promise of the Holy Spirit, and His ascension.**
Chapter 1

II. Activities of **Peter, John and the Church at Jerusalem**
Chapter 2—5

III. Activities of **"The Twelve" and** of **Stephen.**
Chapters 5—8

IV. Activities of Philip, Paul, Peter and other Christians. in **taking the Gospel to the Gentiles.**
Chapters 8—12

V. **Activities of Paul,** Barnabas and Silas until Paul's imprisonment in Rome.
Chapters 13—28

CHAPTER 1

1. **The former treatise have I**
made, O Theophilus,
of all that
Jesus began both
to do and teach,
2. **Until** the day in which
he was taken up, after that
he through the Holy Ghost
had given commandments
unto the apostles
whom he had chosen:
3. **To whom also he shewed**
himself alive after his passion
by many infallible proofs,
being seen of them forty days, and
speaking of the things pertaining to
the kingdom of God:
4. **And, being** assembled together
with *them*, commanded
them
that they should not depart
from Jerusalem, but wait
for the promise of the Father,
which, *saith he*, ye have heard of me.
5. For John truly baptized with water;
but ye shall be baptized with
the Holy Ghost
not many days hence.
6. **When they** therefore
were come
together, they asked
of him, saying,
Lord, wilt thou at this
time restore again
the kingdom to Israel?
7. **And he said** unto them
It is not for you to know
the times or the seasons,
which the Father hath put
in his own power.
8. **But ye shall receive**
power, after that the Holy
Ghost is come upon you:
and ye shall be witnesses
unto me both in Jerusalem, and in
all Judaea, and in Samaria, and
unto the uttermost part
of the earth.
9. **And** when he had
spoken these things,
while they beheld,
he was taken up; and
a cloud received him
out of their sight.
10. **And while they looked**
stedfastly toward heaven as he went
up, behold,
two men stood by them
in white apparel;
11. **Which also said,**
Ye men of Galilee,
why stand ye gazing
up
into heaven?
this same Jesus, which is taken
up from you into heaven,
shall so come in like manner
as ye have seen him go
into heaven.
12. **Then returned they unto**
Jerusalem from the mount called
Olivet, which is from Jerusalem a
sabbath day's journey.
13. **And** when they were
come in, they
went up
into an upper room,
where abode both Peter, and James,
and John, and Andrew, Philip, and
Thomas, Bartholomew, and Matthew,
James *the son* of Alphaeus, and
Simon Zelotes, and Judas the brother
of James.
14. **These all continued with**
one accord in prayer and
supplication, with the women,
and Mary the mother of Jesus, and
with his brethren.
15. **And** in those days
Peter stood
up in the midst of the disciples,
and said, (the number of names
together were about an
hundred and twenty,)
16. Men *and* brethren,
this scripture must needs
have been fulfilled,
which the Holy Ghost by the mouth of
David spake before
concerning Judas, which was
guide to them that took Jesus.
17. For he was numbered with us, and
had obtained part of this ministry.
18. **Now this man**
purchased a field with the

reward of iniquity; and
falling headlong, he burst
asunder in the midst,
and all his bowels
gushed out.
19. **And it was known unto**
all the dwellers at
Jerusalem; insomuch as
that field is called
in their proper tongue, Aceldama,
that is to say,
The field of blood.
20. **For it is written**
in the book of Psalms,
Let his habitation
be desolate,
and let no man dwell therein:
and his bishopric let
another take.
21. **Wherefore of these men**
which have companied
with us all the time that the Lord
Jesus went in and out among us,
22. Beginning from the baptism of
John, unto that same day that he was
taken up from us,
must one be ordained to be a
witness with us of his resurrection.
23. **And they appointed two,**
Joseph called Barsabas, who was
surnamed Justus,
and Matthias.
24. **And they prayed,**
and said, Thou,
Lord, which knowest
the hearts of all *men*,
shew whether of these two
thou hast chosen,
25. **That he may take part of**
this ministry and
apostleship, from which
Judas by transgression
fell, that he
might go to his own place.
26. And they gave forth their lots;
and the lot fell upon
Matthias; and he was numbered
with the eleven apostles.

CHAPTER 2

1. **And when** the day of
Pentecost was fully
come, they were all with
one accord in one place.
2. **And suddenly there came**
a sound from heaven
as of a rushing mighty wind,
and it filled all the house
where they were sitting.
3. **And there appeared**
unto them
cloven tongues like as of
fire, and it sat upon each of
them.
4. **And they were all filled**
with the Holy Ghost, and
began to speak with other
tongues, as the Spirit gave
them utterance.
5. **And** there were dwelling
at Jerusalem
Jews, devout men,
out of every nation
under heaven.
6. Now when this was noised abroad,
the multitude
came together,
and were confounded,
because that every man
heard them speak in his
own language.
7. **And they were all amazed**
and marvelled,
saying one to another, Behold,
are not all these which speak
Galilaeans?
8. **And how hear we every**
man in our own tongue,
wherein we were born?
9. Parthians, and Medes, and
Elamites, and the dwellers in
Mesopotamia, and in Judaea, and
Cappadocia, in Pontus, and Asia,
10. Phrygia, and Pamphylia, in Egypt,
and in the parts of Libya about
Cyrene, and strangers of Rome, Jews
and proselytes,
11. Cretes and Arabians, we do hear
them speak in our tongues the
wonderful works of God.
12. **And they were**
all amazed, and were
in doubt, saying one to another,
What meaneth this?
13. **Others mocking said,**
These men are full

■ **of new wine.**
■ 14. **But Peter,**
standing up with the eleven,
■ **lifted up his voice, and**
■ **said** unto them, Ye men of Judaea,
and all *ye* that dwell at Jerusalem, be
this known unto you, and
■ **hearken to my words:**
■ 15. **For these are not**
■ **drunken,** as ye suppose, seeing it
is *but* the third hour of the day.
■ 16. **But this is that** which was
■ **spoken by** the prophet
■ **Joel;**
17. And it shall come to pass
■ **in the last days, saith God,**
■ **I will pour out of my Spirit**
■ **upon all flesh:** and your sons
and your daughters shall prophesy,
and your young men shall see visions,
and your old men shall dream dreams:
18. And on my servants and on my
handmaidens I will pour out in those
days of my Spirit; and they
shall prophesy:
■ 19. **And I will shew wonders**
in heaven above,
■ **and signs** in the earth beneath;
blood, and fire, and vapour of smoke:
20. The sun shall be turned into
darkness, and the moon into blood,
before the great and notable day of
the Lord come:
■ 21. **And** it shall come to pass, *that*
■ **whosoever shall call on**
■ **the name of the Lord shall**
■ **be saved.**
22. Ye men of Israel,
■ **hear these words; Jesus**
of Nazareth,
■ **a man approved of God**
among you
■ **by miracles**
and wonders and signs,
■ **which God did by him**
in the midst of you,
■ **as ye** yourselves also
■ **know:**
■ 23. **Him,** being delivered by the
determinate counsel and foreknowledge of God,
■ **ye have taken, and**
by wicked hands have
■ **crucified** and slain:
■ 24. **Whom God hath raised**
■ **up**, having loosed the pains of death:
because it was not possible that he
should be holden of it.
■ 25. **For David speaketh**
■ **concerning him,** I foresaw the
Lord always before my face, for he is
on my right hand, that I should not
be moved:
26. Therefore did my heart rejoice,
and my tongue was glad; moreover
also my flesh shall rest in hope:
■ 27. **Because thou wilt not**
■ **leave my soul in hell,**
■ **neither wilt thou suffer**
■ **thine Holy One to**
■ **see corruption.**
28. Thou hast made known to me the
ways of life; thou shalt make me full
of joy with thy countenance.
29 Men *and* brethren, let me freely
speak unto you of the patriarch
■ **David**, that he
■ **is both dead and buried,**
■ **and his sepulchre is with**
■ **us** unto this day.
■ 30. **Therefore being a**
■ **prophet, and knowing**
■ **that God had sworn**
with an oath to him,
■ **that of the fruit of his loins,**
according to the flesh,
■ **he would raise up Christ**
to sit on his throne;
■ 31. **He** seeing this before
■ **spake of the resurrection**
■ **of Christ,** that his soul was
not left in hell, neither his flesh
did see corruption.
■ 32. **This Jesus hath God**
■ **raised up,**
whereof we all are witnesses.
■ 33. **Therefore being**
by the right hand of God
■ **exalted,** and having received
of the Father the promise of the
Holy Ghost,
■ **he hath shed forth this,**
■ **which ye now see**
■ **and hear.**
■ 34. **For David is not**
■ **ascended into the**

heavens: but he saith himself,
The Lord said unto my Lord, Sit thou
on my right hand,
35. Until I make thy foes thy footstool.
36. **Therefore** let all the house of
Israel know assuredly, that
God hath made the same
Jesus, whom ye have
crucified, both Lord
and Christ.
37. **Now when they heard**
this,
they were pricked
in their heart,
and said unto Peter and to the
rest of the apostles,
Men *and* brethren,
what shall we do?
38. **Then Peter said** unto them,
Repent, and be baptized
every one of you
in the name of Jesus Christ
for the remission of sins,
and ye shall receive
the gift of
the Holy Ghost.
39. **For the promise is unto**
you, and to your children, and to all
that are afar off, *even*
as many as the LORD our God
shall call.
40. And with many other words did he
testify and exhort, saying, Save
yourselves from this untoward
generation.
41. **Then they that** gladly
received his word were
baptized: and the same day
there were added *unto*
***them* about three**
thousand souls.
42. **And they continued**
stedfastly
in the apostles' doctrine and
fellowship, and in
breaking of
bread, and in
prayers.
43. And fear came upon every soul:
and many wonders
and signs
were done by the apostles.
44. **And all that believed**
were together, and
had all things common;
45. **And sold their**
possessions and goods,
and parted them to all *men,*
as every man had need.
46. **And they, continuing**
daily with one accord
in the temple, and breaking bread
from house to house, did eat their
meat with gladness and singleness
of heart,
47. Praising God, and having favour
with all the people.
And the Lord added to
the church daily
such as should be saved.

CHAPTER 3

1. **Now Peter and John went**
up together
into the temple at the hour
of prayer, *being* the ninth *hour.*
2. **And a certain man lame**
from his mother's womb
was carried, whom they
laid daily at the gate
of the temple which is called
Beautiful, to ask alms
of them that entered into the temple;
3. **Who seeing Peter and**
John about to go into the temple
asked an alms.
4. **And Peter,** fastening his eyes
upon him with John,
said, Look on us.
5. And he gave heed unto them, expecting to receive something of them.
6. Then Peter said,
Silver and gold have I
none; but such as I have
give I thee: In the name of
Jesus Christ of Nazareth
rise up
and walk.
7. **And he took him**
by the right hand,
and lifted *him* up:
and immediately his feet and ankle
bones received strength.
8. **And he leaping up**
stood, and walked, and
entered with them into

the temple, walking, and
leaping, and praising God.
9. **And all the people**
saw him walking and praising God:
10. And they knew that it was he
which sat for alms at the Beautiful
gate of the temple: and they
were filled with wonder
and amazement
at that which had
happened unto him.
11. **And** as the lame man which was
healed held Peter and John, all
the people ran together
unto them in the porch that is called
Solomon's, greatly wondering.
12. **And when Peter saw** *it,*
he answered
unto the people, Ye men of Israel,
why marvel ye at this?
or why look ye so earnestly on us, as
though by our own power or holiness
we had made this man to walk?
13. **The God of Abraham,**
and of
Isaac, and of
Jacob, the God of our fathers,
hath glorified his Son
Jesus; whom ye delivered
up, and denied him in the
presence of Pilate, when he was
determined to let *him* go.
14. **But ye denied the Holy**
One and the Just,
and desired a murderer to
be granted unto you;
15. **And killed the Prince of**
life, whom God hath
raised from the dead;
whereof we are witnesses.
16. **And** his name
through faith in his name
hath made this man strong,
whom ye see and know: yea, the faith
which is by him hath given him this
perfect soundness in the presence of
you all.
17. **And now,** brethren,
I wot that through
ignorance ye did ***it,*** as *did*
also your rulers.
18. **But** those things, which
God before had shewed by
the mouth of all
his prophets, that Christ
should suffer,
he hath so fulfilled.
19. **Repent ye therefore, and**
be converted, that your
sins may be blotted out,
when the times of refreshing shall
come from the presence of the Lord.
20. **And he shall send**
Jesus Christ,
which before was preached unto you:
21. Whom the heaven must receive
until the times of restitution
of all things,
which God hath spoken by
the mouth of all his holy
prophets since the
world began.
22. **For Moses truly said**
unto the fathers,
A prophet shall the Lord
your God
raise up unto you of your brethren,
like unto me; him shall ye hear in
all things whatsoever he shall say
unto you.
23. **And it shall come to**
pass, ***that*** **every soul,**
which will not hear that
prophet, shall
be destroyed
from among the people.
24. Yea, and all the prophets from
Samuel and those that follow after, as
many as have spoken, have likewise
foretold of these days.
25. **Ye are the children**
of the prophets, and
of the covenant which God
made with our fathers, saying
unto Abraham, And in thy seed
shall all the kindreds of the
earth be blessed.
26. **Unto you first God,**
having raised up his Son
Jesus, sent him to bless
you, in turning away every one of
you from his iniquities.

CHAPTER 4

1. **And** as they spake
unto the people,

the priests,
and the captain of the temple,
and the
Sadducees, came
upon them,
2. **Being grieved that they**
taught the people, and
preached through Jesus
the resurrection from the dead.
3. **And they laid hands on**
them, and put *them* in hold
unto the next day:
for it was now eventide.
4. **Howbeit many** of them
which heard the word
believed; and the number
of the
men was about
five thousand.
5. And it came to pass on the morrow,
that their rulers, and elders, and
scribes,
6. **And Annas the high**
priest, and
Caiaphas, and
John, and Alexander,
and as many as were of the kindred of
the high priest,
were gathered together
at Jerusalem.
7. **And when**
they had set them in the midst,
they ask By what power, or
by what
name, have ye done this?
8. **Then Peter, filled with the**
Holy Ghost, said
unto them, Ye rulers of the people,
and elders of Israel,
9. **If we** this day
be examined of the good
deed done to the
impotent man,
by what means he is made whole;
10. **Be it known unto**
you all, and to all the people of
Israel, that by the name of
Jesus Christ of Nazareth,
whom ye crucified, whom
God raised from the dead,
***even* by him doth this man**
stand here before you whole.
11. **This is the stone** which was
set at nought of you builders,
which is become the head
of the corner.
12. **Neither is there**
salvation in any other: for
there is none other name
under heaven given among men,
whereby we must
be saved.
13. **Now when they saw the**
boldness of Peter and
John, and perceived that
they were unlearned and
ignorant men,
they marvelled; and they
took knowledge of them,
that they had been
with Jesus.
14. **And beholding the man**
which was
healed standing with them,
they could say nothing
against it.
15. **But** when they had commanded
them to go aside out of the council,
they conferred among
themselves,
16. **Saying, What shall**
we do
to these men? for that indeed
a notable
miracle hath been done
by them *is* manifest to all them that
dwell in Jerusalem;
and we cannot deny *it.*
17. **But that it spread no**
further among the people,
let us straitly
threaten them, that they speak
henceforth to no man in this name.
18. **And they** called them, and
commanded them not to
speak at all
nor teach in the
name of Jesus.
19. **But Peter and John**
answered and said unto them,
Whether it be right
in the sight of God
to hearken unto you more
than unto God, judge ye.
20. **For we cannot but speak**
the things which we have seen

and heard.
21. **So when they** had
further threatened them,
they let them go, finding
nothing how they might
punish them, because of
the people: for all *men*
glorified God
for that which was done.
22. For the man was above forty years
old, on whom this miracle of healing
was shewed.
23. **And being let go, they**
went to their own company,
and reported all that the
chief priests and elders
had said unto them.
24 **And** when they heard that,
they lifted up their voice to
God with one accord,
and said, Lord, thou *art*
God, which hast made
heaven, and earth, and the sea, and
all that in them is:
25. Who by the mouth of thy servant
David hast said, Why did the heathen
rage, and the people
imagine vain things?
26. The kings of the earth stood up,
and the rulers were gathered
together against the Lord,
and against his Christ.
27. For of a truth against thy holy child
Jesus, whom thou hast anointed,
both Herod, and Pontius Pilate, with
the Gentiles, and the people of Israel,
were gathered together,
28. For to do whatsoever thy hand and
thy counsel determined before
to be done.
29. **And now, Lord, behold**
their threatenings: and
grant unto
thy servants, that with all
boldness they may speak
thy word,
30. By stretching forth thine
hand to heal;
and that signs and
wonders may be done by
the name of thy holy child
Jesus.
31. **And when they had**
prayed, the place was
shaken where they were
assembled together;
and they were all filled with
the Holy Ghost, and they spake
the word of God with boldness.
32. **And the multitude** of them
that believed were of one
heart and of one soul: neither said
any *of them* that aught of the things
which he possessed was his own;
but they
had all things common.
33. **And with great power**
gave the apostles witness
of the resurrection
of the Lord Jesus: and great grace
was upon them all.
34. **Neither was there any**
among them
that lacked: for as many as
were possessors of lands
or houses sold them, and
brought the prices
of the things that were sold,
35. **And laid *them* down at**
the apostles' feet: and
distribution was made
unto every man according
as he had need.
36. And Joses, who by the apostles
was surnamed Barnabas, (which is,
being interpreted, The son of
consolation,) a Levite, *and* of the
country of Cyprus,
37. Having land, sold *it*, and brought
the money, and laid *it* at the
apostles' feet.

CHAPTER 5

1. **But** a certain man named
Ananias, with Sapphira his
wife, sold a possession,
2. **And kept back *part* of the**
price, his wife also being privy *to it*,
and brought a certain
part, and laid *it* at the
apostles' feet.
3. **But Peter said, Ananias,**
why hath Satan filled thine
heart to lie to the Holy
Ghost, and to keep back
***part* of the price** of the land?

4. Whiles it remained, was it not thine
own? and after it was sold, was it not
in thine own power? why hast thou
conceived this thing in thine heart?
thou hast not lied unto men,
but unto God.
5. **And Ananias hearing**
these words fell down, and
gave up the ghost:
and great fear came on all them
that heard these things.
6. **And the young men**
arose, wound him up, and carried
him out, and
buried *him*.
7. **And** it was about the space of
three hours after, when
his wife, not knowing what
was done, came in.
8. **And Peter answered** unto
her, Tell me whether ye sold
the land for so much? And
she said, Yea, for so much.
9. **Then Peter said** unto her,
How is it that ye have
agreed together to
tempt the Spirit of the Lord?
behold, the feet of them which have
buried thy husband *are* at the door,
and shall carry thee out.
10. **Then fell she down**
straightway at his feet,
and yielded up
the ghost: and the young men
came in, and found her dead, and,
carrying *her* forth, buried *her* by
her husband.
11. **And great fear came**
upon all the church, and upon
as many as heard these things.
12. **And by the hands of the**
apostles were many signs
and wonders wrought
among the people; (and they were all
with one accord in Solomon's porch.
13. And of the rest durst no man join
himself to them: but the people
magnified them.
14. **And believers were**
the more
added to the Lord,
multitudes both of men and women.)
15. **Insomuch that they**
brought forth
the sick into the streets,
and laid *them* on beds and couches,
that at the least the shadow
of Peter passing by might
overshadow some of
them.
16. **There came** also
a multitude *out* of the cities
round about unto Jerusalem,
bringing sick folks,
and them which were vexed
with unclean spirits: and
they were healed every one.
17. **Then the high priest**
rose up,
and all they
that were with him, (which is
the sect of the Sadducees,) and
were filled with indignation,
18. **And laid their hands on**
the apostles, and put them
in the common
prison.
19. **But the angel of the Lord**
by night
opened the prison doors,
and brought them forth,
and said,
20. **Go, stand and speak in**
the temple to the people all the
words of this life.
21. **And** when they heard *that*,
they entered into
the temple early in the morning,
and taught. But the high
priest came,
and they that were with him,
and called the council
together, and all the senate of the
children of Israel,
and sent to the prison to
have them brought.
22. **But when the officers**
came, and
found them not in the
prison, they returned
and told,
23. **Saying, The prison** truly
found we shut with all
safety, and the keepers standing
without before the doors:
but when we had opened,

■ **we found no man within.**
24. Now when the high priest and the
captain of the temple and the chief
priests heard these things, they
doubted of them whereunto this
would grow.
■ 25. **Then came one**
and told them,
■ **saying,** Behold,
■ **the men** whom
■ **ye put in prison are**
standing in the temple, and
■ **teaching the people.**
■ 26. **Then went the captain**
with the officers,
■ **and brought them** without
violence: for they feared the people,
lest they should have been stoned.
■ 27. **And** when they had brought
them, they set *them* before the
council: and
■ **the high priest asked them,**
■ 28. **Saying, Did not we** straitly
■ **command you that ye**
■ **should not teach in this**
■ **name?** and, behold, ye have filled
Jerusalem with your doctrine, and
intend to bring this man's blood
upon us.
■ 29 **Then Peter and the *other***
■ **apostles answered** and said,
■ **We ought to obey God**
■ **rather than men.**
■ 30. **The God of our fathers**
■ **raised up Jesus,**
whom ye slew and hanged on a tree.
■ 31. **Him hath God exalted**
with his right hand
■ ***to be* a Prince and a**
■ **Saviour,** for to give repentance to
Israel, and forgiveness of sins.
■ 32. **And we are his**
■ **witnesses** of these things;
■ **and *so is* also the Holy**
■ **Ghost,** whom God hath given to
them that obey him.
■ 33. **When they heard *that*,**
■ **they** were cut *to the heart*, and
■ **took counsel to slay them.**
■ 34. **Then stood**
there up one in the council,
■ **a Pharisee, named**
■ **Gamaliel, a doctor of the**
■ **law,** had
■ **in reputation among all the**
■ **people,** and commanded to put the
apostles forth a little space;
■ 35. **And said unto them,**
Ye men of Israel,
■ **take heed to yourselves**
■ **what ye intend to do**
as touching these men.
■ 36. **For before these days**
■ **rose up Theudas,**
boasting himself to be somebody; to
whom a number of men, about four
hundred, joined themselves:
■ **who was slain; and all, as**
■ **many as obeyed him, were**
■ **scattered,** and brought to nought.
■ 37. **After this man rose** up
■ **Judas of Galilee**
in the days of the taxing, and drew
away much people after him:
■ **he also perished;**
and all, *even* as many as obeyed him,
were dispersed.
■ 38. **And now I say** unto you,
■ **Refrain from these men,**
and let them alone:
■ **for if** this counsel or
■ **this work be of men, it will**
■ **come to nought:**
■ 39. **But if it be of God, ye**
■ **cannot overthrow it; lest**
■ **haply ye** be found even to
■ **fight against God.**
■ 40. **And to him they agreed:**
■ **and when they had called**
■ **the apostles, and beaten**
■ ***them*, they commanded**
■ **that they should not speak**
in the name
■ **of Jesus, and let them go.**
■ 41. **And they departed**
from the presence of the council,
■ **rejoicing that they were**
■ **counted worthy to suffer**
■ **shame for his name.**
■ 42. **And daily in the temple,**
■ **and in every house, they**
■ **ceased not to teach and**
■ **preach Jesus Christ.**

CHAPTER 6

1. And in those days, when the

number of the disciples
was multiplied,
there arose a murmuring of
the
Grecians against the
Hebrews, because their
widows were neglected in
the daily ministration.
2. **Then the twelve**
called the multitude of the disciples
unto them, and
said, It is not reason that we should
leave the word of God,
and serve tables.
3. **Wherefore, brethren, look**
ye out among you
seven men of honest
report, full of the Holy
Ghost and wisdom, whom
we may appoint over
this business.
4. But we will give ourselves
continually to prayer, and to the
ministry of the word.
5. And the saying pleased
the whole multitude:
and they chose Stephen,
a man full of faith and of the
Holy Ghost, and
Philip, and
Prochorus, and
Nicanor, and
Timon, and
Parmenas, and Nicolas
a proselyte of Antioch:
6. **Whom they set before the**
apostles: and when they
had
prayed, they laid
their hands on them.
7. **And the word** of God
increased; and the number
of the
disciples multiplied in
Jerusalem greatly; and a great
company of the priests were obedient
to the faith.
8. **And Stephen, full of faith**
and power, did great
wonders and miracles among
the people.
9. **Then there arose certain**
of the synagogue, which is called
***the synagogue* of the**
Libertines, and Cyrenians,
and Alexandrians,
and of them of Cilicia and of Asia,
disputing with Stephen.
10. **And they were not able**
to resist the wisdom and
the spirit by which
he spake.
11. **Then they**
suborned men, which
said, We have heard him
speak blasphemous
words against Moses,
and *against* God.
12. **And they stirred up the**
people, and the elders, and the
scribes, and came upon *him*, and
caught him,
and brought *him*
to the council,
13. **And set up false**
witnesses, which said,
This man ceaseth not to speak
blasphemous words against this holy
place, and the law:
14. **For we have heard him**
say, that this
Jesus of Nazareth
shall destroy this place,
and shall
change the customs which
Moses delivered us.
15. **And all** that sat in the council,
looking stedfastly on him,
saw his face as it had been
the face of an angel.

CHAPTER 7

1. **Then said the high priest,**
Are these things so?
2. **And he said,** Men, brethren,
and fathers, hearken;
The God of glory appeared
unto our father
Abraham, when he was in
Mesopotamia, before he dwelt
in Charran,
3. **And said**
unto him, Get thee out of thy country,
and from thy kindred, and
come into the land which I
shall shew thee.

4. **Then** came he out of the land of
the Chaldaeans, and dwelt in Charran:
and from thence, when his
father was dead,
he removed him into this
land, wherein
ye now dwell.
5. And he gave him none inheritance
in it, no, not *so much* as to set his foot
on: yet he promised that he would give
it to him for a possession, and to his
seed after him, when *as yet* he
had no child.
6. **And God spake** on this wise,
That his seed should
sojourn in a strange land;
and that they should bring
them into bondage, and
entreat *them* evil four hundred years.
7. And the nation to whom they shall
be in bondage will I judge, said God:
and after that shall they
come forth, and
serve me in this place.
8. **And he gave him the**
covenant of circumcision:
and so *Abraham* begat
Isaac, and circumcised him the
eighth day;
and Isaac *begat*
Jacob; and Jacob *begat*
the twelve patriarchs.
9. **And the patriarchs,**
moved with envy,
sold Joseph into Egypt: but
God was with him,
10. And delivered him out of all his
afflictions, and
gave him favour and
wisdom in the sight of
Pharaoh king of Egypt; and he
made him governor over
Egypt and all his house.
11. **Now there came a**
dearth over all the land of Egypt
and Chanaan, and great affliction: and
our fathers found no sustenance.
12. **But when Jacob heard**
that there was corn in
Egypt, he sent out our
fathers first.
13. And at the second *time* Joseph
was made known to his brethren; and
Joseph's kindred was made known
unto Pharaoh.
14. **Then sent Joseph, and**
called his father Jacob to
***him,* and all his kindred,**
threescore and fifteen souls.
15. **So Jacob**
went down into Egypt, and
died, he,
and our fathers,
16. **And were**
carried over into Sychem, and
laid in the sepulchre that
Abraham bought
for a sum of money of the sons of
Emmor *the father* of Sychem.
17. **But when the time of** the
promise drew nigh,
which God had sworn to Abraham,
the people grew and
multiplied in Egypt,
18. **Till another king arose,**
which knew not Joseph.
19. **The same dealt subtilly**
with our kindred, and evil
entreated our fathers, so that they
cast out their young children, to the
end they might not live.
20. **In which time Moses was**
born, and was exceeding fair, and
nourished up in his father's house
three months:
21. **And** when he was cast out,
Pharaoh's daughter
took him up, and
nourished him for
her own son.
22. **And Moses was learned**
in all the wisdom of the
Egyptians, and was
mighty in words and in deeds.
23. **And when he was** full
forty years old,
it came into his heart to
visit his brethren
the children of Israel.
24. **And seeing one *of them***
suffer wrong, he defended
him, and avenged him
that was oppressed,
and smote the Egyptian:
25. **For he supposed his**
brethren would have

understood how that
God by his hand would
deliver them: but they
understood not.
26. And the next day he shewed
himself unto them as they strove, and
would have set them at one again,
saying, Sirs, ye are brethren; why do
ye wrong one to another?
27. But he that did his neighbour
wrong thrust him away, saying, Who
made thee a ruler and a judge
over us?
28. Wilt thou kill me, as thou diddest
the Egyptian yesterday?
29 **Then fled Moses**
at this saying,
and was a stranger in
the land of
Madian, where he
begat two sons.
30. **And when forty years** were
expired, there appeared to
him in the wilderness of
mount Sina an angel of the
Lord in a flame of fire
in a bush.
31. **When Moses saw *it*,** he
wondered at the sight: and as he drew
near to behold *it*,
the voice of the LORD came
unto him,
32. ***Saying,* I *am* the God**
of thy fathers, the God of
Abraham, and the God of Isaac, and
the God of Jacob. Then Moses
trembled, and durst not behold.
33. **Then said the Lord** to him,
Put off thy shoes from thy feet:
for the place
where thou standest
is holy ground.
34. I have seen,
I have seen the affliction of
my people which is
in Egypt, and I have heard their
groaning, and am come down to
deliver them.
And now come,
I will send thee into Egypt.
35. **This Moses** whom they
refused, saying, Who made thee a
ruler and a judge? the same
did God send *to be* a ruler and a
deliverer by the hand of the
angel which appeared
to him in the bush.
36. **He brought them out,**
after that he had shewed
wonders and signs
in the land of Egypt, and in the Red
sea, and in the wilderness forty years.
37. **This is that Moses, which**
said unto the children of Israel,
A prophet shall the Lord
your God raise up
unto you of your brethren,
like unto me; him
shall ye hear.
38. **This is he,** that was in the
church in the wilderness with the
angel which spake to him in the mount
Sina, and *with* our fathers: who
received the lively oracles to
give unto us:
39. **To whom our fathers**
would not obey,
but thrust *him* from them,
and in their hearts
turned back again into Egypt,
40. **Saying unto Aaron,**
Make us gods to go before
us: for *as for* this
Moses, which brought *us* out of the
land of Egypt, we wot not what is
become of him.
41. **And they made a calf**
in those days,
and offered sacrifice unto
the idol, and rejoiced in the works
of their own hands.
42 **Then God** turned,
and gave them up to
worship the host of
heaven; as it is written in the book
of the prophets, O ye house of Israel,
have ye offered to me slain beasts
and sacrifices *by the space* of forty
years in the wilderness?
43 Yea, ye took up the tabernacle of
Moloch, and the star of your god
Remphan, figures which ye made to
worship them: and I will carry you
away beyond Babylon.
44 **Our fathers had the**
tabernacle of witness in the

wilderness, as he
had appointed, speaking
unto Moses, that he should
make it according to the
fashion that he had seen.
45 Which also our fathers that came
after brought in with Jesus into the
possession of the Gentiles, whom
God drave out before the face of our
fathers, unto the days of
David;
46 Who found favour before God, and
desired to find a
tabernacle for the God
of Jacob.
47 **But Solomon built**
him an house.
48 **Howbeit the most High**
dwelleth not in temples
made with hands;
as saith the prophet,
49 **Heaven *is* my throne,**
and earth *is* my footstool:
what house will ye build
me? saith the Lord: or what *is* the
place of my rest?
50 **Hath not my hand made**
all these things?
51 **Ye stiffnecked and**
uncircumcised in heart
and ears,
ye do always
resist the Holy Ghost: as
your fathers *did, so do* ye.
52 **Which of the prophets**
have not your fathers
persecuted? and they have
slain them which shewed
before of
the coming of the Just One;
of whom ye have been
now the betrayers
and murderers:
53 Who have received the law by the
disposition of angels, and have not
kept *it*.
54 **When they heard these**
things, they were cut to the
heart, and they
gnashed on him with *their* teeth.
55 **But he,**
being full of the Holy Ghost,
looked up stedfastly into
heaven, and saw the glory of God,
and Jesus standing on the right hand
of God,
56 **And said, Behold, I see**
the heavens opened, and the
Son of man
standing on the right hand
of God.
57 **Then they cried out with**
a loud voice,
and stopped their ears,
and ran upon him
with one accord,
58 **And cast *him* out**
of the city, and stoned *him:*
and the witnesses laid
down their clothes at a
young man's feet, whose
name was Saul.
59 **And they stoned**
Stephen, calling upon *God*, and
saying, Lord Jesus, receive my spirit.
60 **And he** kneeled down, and
cried with a loud voice,
Lord, lay not this sin to their
charge. And
when he had said this,
he fell asleep.

CHAPTER 8

1. **And Saul was consenting**
unto his death. And at that
time there was a great
persecution against the
church which was at Jerusalem;
and they were all scattered abroad
throughout the regions of Judaea and
Samaria, except the apostles.
2. And devout men carried Stephen *to*
his burial, and made great
lamentation over him.
3. **As for Saul, he made**
havock of the church,
entering into every house,
and haling men and
women committed
***them* to prison.**
4. Therefore they that were scattered
abroad went every where preaching
the word.
5. **Then Philip went down to**
the city of
Samaria, and preached

Christ unto them.
6. **And the people**
with one accord
gave heed unto those
things which Philip spake,
hearing and seeing the miracles which
he did.
7. **For unclean spirits,**
crying with loud voice,
came out of many
that were possessed *with them*:
and many taken with palsies,
and that were lame,
were healed.
8. **And there was great**
joy in that city.
9. **But** there was a certain
man, called
Simon, which beforetime
in the same city used sorcery, and
bewitched the people of
Samaria, giving out that
himself was some
great one:
10. **To whom they all gave**
heed, from the least to the greatest,
saying, This man is the
great power of God.
11. And to him they had regard,
because that of long time he had
bewitched them with sorceries.
12. **But when they believed**
Philip preaching the things
concerning the
kingdom of God, and
the name of
Jesus Christ, they were
baptized, both men and women.
13. **Then Simon himself**
believed also: and when
he was baptized, he
continued with Philip,
and wondered, beholding the miracles
and signs which were done.
14. **Now when the apostles**
which were at Jerusalem
heard that Samaria had received
the word of God,
they sent unto them Peter
and John:
15. **Who,** when they
were come down
prayed for them,
that they might receive
the Holy Ghost:
16. **(For as yet he was fallen**
upon none of them: only
they were baptized
in the name of the Lord Jesus.)
17. **Then laid they *their***
hands on them, and they
received the Holy Ghost.
18. **And when Simon saw**
that through laying on of the apostles'
hands the Holy Ghost was given,
he offered them money,
19. **Saying, Give me also**
this power,
that on whomsoever I lay hands, he
may receive the Holy Ghost.
20. **But Peter said** unto him,
Thy money perish with thee,
because thou hast thought that the
gift of God may be purchased
with money.
21. **Thou hast neither part**
nor lot in this matter: for thy
heart is not right
in the sight of God.
22. **Repent therefore**
of this thy wickedness,
and pray God, if perhaps
the thought of thine heart
may be forgiven thee.
23. For I perceive that thou art in the
gall of bitterness, and *in* the
bond of iniquity.
24. **Then answered Simon,**
and said,
Pray ye to the LORD for me,
that none of these things
which ye have spoken
come upon me.
25. **And they,**
when they had testified and
preached the word of the Lord,
returned to Jerusalem,
and preached the gospel
in many villages of
the Samaritans.
26. **And the angel of the Lord**
spake unto Philip, saying,
Arise, and
go toward the south unto the way
that goeth down from Jerusalem
unto Gaza, which is desert.

27. **And he arose and went:**
and, behold,
a man of Ethiopia, an
eunuch of great authority
under Candace queen of
the Ethiopians, who had the
charge of all her treasure, and had
come to Jerusalem for to worship,
28. **Was returning, and** sitting
in his chariot read Esaias
the prophet.
29 **Then the Spirit said unto**
Philip, Go near, and join thyself
to this chariot.
30. **And Philip**
ran thither to *him*, and
heard him read the prophet
Esaias, and said,
Understandest thou
what thou readest?
31. **And he said, How can I,**
except some man should
guide me? And he desired Philip
that he would come up
and sit with him.
32. **The** place of the
scripture which he read
was this, He was led as a
sheep to the slaughter;
and like a lamb dumb before his
shearer, so opened he not his mouth:
33. In his humiliation his judgment was
taken away: and who shall declare
his generation? for his life is taken
from the earth.
34. **And the eunuch**
answered Philip, and
said, I pray thee, of whom
speaketh the prophet this?
of himself, or of some other man?
35. **Then Philip** opened his mouth,
and began at the same scripture, and
preached unto him Jesus.
36. **And** as they went on *their* way,
they came unto a certain
water: and the eunuch
said, See, *here is* water;
what doth hinder me
to be baptized?
37. **And Philip said, If thou**
believest with all thine heart,
thou mayest and he
answered and said,
I believe that Jesus Christ
is the Son of God.
38. And he commanded the chariot to
stand still:
and they went down both
into the water, both Philip and
the eunuch;
and he baptized him.
39. **And** when they were come up out
of the water,
the Spirit of the Lord
caught away Philip, that the
eunuch saw him no more:
and he went on his way rejoicing.
40. **But Philip was found at**
Azotus: and passing through
he preached in all the cities,
till he came to Caesarea.

CHAPTER 9

1. **And Saul,** yet breathing out
threatenings and slaughter against
the disciples of the Lord,
went unto the high priest,
2. **And desired** of him
letters to Damascus
to the synagogues,
that if he found any of this
way, whether they were
men or women,
he might bring them
bound unto Jerusalem.
3. **And as** he journeyed,
he came near Damascus:
and
suddenly there shined
round about him
a light from heaven:
4. **And he fell** to the earth,
and heard a voice saying
unto him,
Saul, Saul, why persecutest
thou me?
5. **And he said, Who art**
thou, Lord? And the Lord
said, I am Jesus whom
thou persecutest: *it is* hard for
thee to kick against the pricks.
6. **And he** trembling and astonished
said, Lord, what wilt thou
have me to do? And the
Lord *said* unto him, Arise, and
go into the city, and it shall be

told thee what thou must do.
7. And the men which journeyed with
him stood speechless, hearing a
voice, but seeing no man.
8. **And Saul arose**
from the earth;
and when his eyes were
opened, he saw no man:
but they led him
by the hand, and brought *him*
into Damascus.
9. **And he was three days**
without sight, and neither
did eat nor drink.
10. **And there was a certain**
disciple at Damascus,
named Ananias; and to
him said the Lord in a
vision, Ananias.
And he said, Behold, I *am here*, Lord.
11. And the Lord *said* unto him,
Arise, and go into the street
which is called Straight,
and inquire in the house of Judas
for *one* called Saul, of Tarsus:
for, behold,
he prayeth,
12. **And hath seen in a**
vision a man named
Ananias coming
in, and putting *his* hand on him,
that he might receive
his sight.
13. **Then Ananias answered,**
Lord, I have heard
by many of this man,
how much evil he hath
done to thy saints at Jerusalem:
14. And here he hath authority from
the chief priests to bind all that
call on thy name.
15. **But the Lord said**
unto him, Go thy way: for
he is a chosen vessel
unto me,
to bear my name before the
Gentiles, and kings, and
the children of
Israel:
16. For I will shew him how great
things he must suffer for
my name's sake.
17. **And Ananias**
went his way, and
entered into
the house; and
putting his hands on him
said, Brother Saul, the
Lord, *even* Jesus, that
appeared unto thee
in the way as thou camest,
hath sent me, that thou
mightest receive thy sight,
and be filled with the
Holy Ghost.
18. **And immediately**
there fell from his eyes as it had
been scales: and
he received sight
forthwith, and arose,
and was baptized.
19. And when he had received meat,
he was strengthened.
Then was Saul certain days
with the disciples
which were at Damascus.
20. **And** straightway
he preached Christ in the
synagogues,
that he is the Son of God.
21. **But all** that heard *him*
were amazed, and said; Is
not this he that destroyed
them which called on this
name in Jerusalem, and came
hither for that intent, that he might
bring them bound unto the
chief priests?
22. **But Saul increased**
the more
in strength, and
confounded the Jews
which dwelt at Damascus,
proving that this is
very Christ.
23. **And** after that many
days were fulfilled,
the Jews took counsel
to kill him:
24. But their laying await was known
of Saul. And they watched the gates
day and night to kill him.
25. **Then the disciples took**
him by night, and let *him*
down by
the wall in a basket.

26. **And when Saul was**
come to Jerusalem,
he assayed to join himself to
the disciples: but they
were all afraid of him,
and believed not that he
was a disciple.
27. **But Barnabas** took him, and
brought *him* to the
apostles, and declared
unto them
how he had seen the Lord
in the way, and that he
had spoken to him,
and how he had preached
boldly at Damascus
in the name of Jesus.
28. And he was with them coming in
and going out at Jerusalem.
29. **And he spake boldly in**
the name of the Lord
Jesus, and disputed against
the Grecians: but they went
about
to slay him.
30. ***Which* when the brethren**
knew, they
brought him down to Caesarea, and
sent him forth to Tarsus.
31. **Then had the churches**
rest throughout all Judaea and
Galilee and Samaria, and were edified;
and walking in the fear of the Lord,
and in the comfort of the
Holy Ghost,
were multiplied.
32. **And** it came to pass, as
Peter passed throughout all
quarters, he
came down also
to the saints which dwelt at
Lydda.
33. **And there he found**
a certain man named
Aeneas, which
had kept his bed eight years, and
was sick of the palsy.
34. **And Peter said**
unto him, Aeneas,
Jesus Christ maketh thee
whole: arise, and make thy bed.
And he arose immediately.
35. **And all** that dwelt
at Lydda and Saron saw him, and
turned to the Lord.
36. **Now there was at Joppa**
a certain
disciple named Tabitha,
which by interpretation
is called Dorcas:
this woman was full of
good works
and almsdeeds which she did.
37. **And** it came to pass in those
days, that
she was sick, and
died: whom when they had washed,
they laid *her* in an upper chamber.
38. **And forasmuch as**
Lydda was nigh to Joppa,
and the disciples had
heard that Peter was there,
they sent unto him two men,
desiring *him* that he would
not delay to come to them.
39. **Then Peter** arose and
went with them.
When he was come,
they brought him into the
upper chamber: and all the
widows stood by him
weeping, and shewing the coats
and garments which Dorcas made,
while she was with them.
40. **But Peter** put them all forth, and
kneeled down,
and prayed; and
turning *him* to the body
said, Tabitha, arise. And
she opened her eyes: and
when she saw Peter, she sat up.
41. **And he** gave her *his* hand, and
lifted her up,
and when he had called
the saints and widows,
presented her alive.
42. And it was known throughout
all Joppa;
and many believed in
the Lord.
43. **And** it came to pass, that
he tarried
many days
in Joppa
with one
Simon a tanner.

CHAPTER 10

1. **There was** a certain man
in Caesarea called
Cornelius, a centurion
of the band called the Italian *band,*
2. **A devout *man*, and one**
that feared God with all his
house, which gave much alms to the
people, and prayed to God alway.
3. **He saw in a vision** evidently
about the ninth hour of the day
an angel
of God coming in to him, and
saying unto him,
Cornelius.
4. And when he looked on him, he was
afraid, and said, What is it, Lord?
And he said unto him,
Thy prayers and thine alms
are come up for a
memorial before God.
5. **And now**
send men to Joppa, and
call for *one* Simon, whose
surname is Peter:
6. He lodgeth with one Simon a tanner,
whose house is by the sea side:
he shall tell thee what thou
oughtest to do.
7. **And** when the angel which spake
unto Cornelius was departed,
he called two of his household
servants, and a devout
soldier of them that waited on
him continually;
8. **And** when he had declared all
these things unto them,
he sent them to Joppa.
9. On the morrow,
as they went on their journey, and
drew nigh
unto the city, Peter went up
upon the housetop to pray
about the sixth hour:
10. **And** he became very hungry, and
would have eaten: but while they
made ready,
he fell into a trance,
11. **And saw heaven**
opened, and a certain
vessel descending unto him,
as it had been
a great sheet knit at the four
corners, and let down to the earth:
12. **Wherein were all**
manner of fourfooted
beasts of the earth,
and wild beasts,
and creeping things, and
fowls of the air.
13. **And there came a voice**
to him, Rise, Peter; kill, and
eat.
14. **But Peter said, Not so,**
Lord; for I have never eaten
any thing that is
common or unclean.
15. **And the voice *spake***
unto him again the second time,
What God hath cleansed,
***that* call not** thou
common.
16. This was done thrice: and the
vessel was received up
again into heaven.
17. **Now while Peter doubted**
in himself
what this vision
which he had seen
should mean, behold,
the men which were
sent from Cornelius
had made inquiry for Simon's house,
and stood before the gate,
18. And called, and
asked whether
Simon, which was surnamed
Peter, were lodged there.
19. **While Peter thought on**
the vision, the Spirit said
unto him, Behold,
three men seek thee.
20. **Arise** therefore,
and get thee down,
and go with them,
doubting nothing:
for I have sent them.
21. **Then Peter** went down to the
men which were sent unto him from
Cornelius; and
said, Behold, I am he whom
ye seek: what *is* the cause
wherefore ye are come?
22. **And they said, Cornelius**
the centurion, a just man, and
one that feareth God, and of good

report among all the
nation of the Jews,
was warned from God
by an holy angel
to send for thee into his house,
and to hear words of
thee.
23. Then called he them in, and lodged
them. And on the morrow Peter went
away with them, and certain brethren
from Joppa accompanied him.
24. **And the morrow after**
they entered into
Caesarea. And Cornelius waited
for them, and he had called together
his kinsmen and near friends.
25. **And as Peter was**
coming in,
Cornelius met him,
and fell down at his feet,
and worshipped *him*.
26. **But Peter took him up,**
saying, Stand up; I myself
also am a man.
27. **And as he talked** with him,
he went in, and
found many that were
come together.
28. **And he said** unto them,
Ye know how that it is an
unlawful thing
for a man that is
a Jew to keep company, or
come unto one of another
nation; but God hath
shewed me that I should
not call any man common
or unclean.
29 **Therefore came I *unto***
you without gainsaying, as soon as I
was sent for: I ask therefore for what
intent ye have sent for me?
30. **And Cornelius said,**
Four days ago I was
fasting until this hour; and at the
ninth hour I prayed in my house,
and, behold, a man stood
before me in bright clothing,
31. **And said, Cornelius, thy**
prayer is heard, and thine alms
are had in remembrance in the
sight of God.
32. **Send therefore to**
Joppa, and call hither Simon,
whose surname is
Peter; he is lodged in the house of
one Simon a tanner by the sea side:
who, when he cometh,
shall speak unto thee.
33. Immediately therefore I sent to
thee; and thou hast well done that
thou art come.
Now therefore are we all
here present before God,
to hear all things that are
commanded thee of God.
34. **Then Peter**
opened *his* mouth, and
said, Of a truth I perceive
that God is no respecter
of persons:
35. **But in every nation he**
that feareth him, and
worketh righteousness,
is accepted with him.
36. **The word which *God***
sent unto the children of
Israel, preaching peace by Jesus
Christ: (he is Lord of all:)
37. That word, *I say*, ye know, which
was published throughout all
Judaea, and began from Galilee, after
the baptism which John preached;
38. **How God anointed**
Jesus of Nazareth with the Holy
Ghost and with power: who went about
doing good, and healing all that were
oppressed of the devil; for
God was with him.
39. **And we are witnesses of**
all things which he did both in
the land of the Jews, and in
Jerusalem; whom they slew and
hanged on a tree:
40. **Him God raised up the**
third day, and shewed him openly;
41. Not to all the people, but unto
witnesses chosen before God, *even* to
us, who did eat and drink with him
after he rose from the dead.
42. **And he commanded us**
to preach unto the people,
and to testify that it is he
which was ordained of
God *to be* the Judge of
quick and dead.

43. To him give all the prophets witness, **that through his name whosoever believeth** in him **shall receive remission of sins.**

44. **While Peter yet spake** these words, **the Holy Ghost fell on all** them which heard the word.

45. **And they of the circumcision** which believed **were astonished,** as many as came with Peter, **because that on the Gentiles also was poured out the gift of the Holy Ghost.**

46. **For they heard them speak with tongues,** and magnify God. **Then answered Peter,**

47. **Can any man forbid water, that these should not be baptized, which have received the Holy Ghost** as well as we?

48. **And he commanded them to be baptized** in the name of the Lord. Then prayed they him to tarry certain days

.

CHAPTER 11

1. And the apostles and brethren that were in Judaea heard that the Gentiles had also received the word of God.

2. **And when Peter was come up to Jerusalem, they that were of the circumcision contended with him,**

3. **Saying, Thou wentest in to men uncircumcised, and didst eat with them.**

4. **But Peter rehearsed *the matter* from the beginning, and expounded *it* by order unto them, saying,**

5. I was in the city of Joppa praying: and in a trance I saw a vision, A certain vessel descend, as it had been a great sheet, let down from heaven by four corners; and it came even to me:

6. Upon the which when I had fastened mine eyes, I considered, and saw fourfooted beasts of the earth, and wild beasts, and creeping things, and fowls of the air.

7. And I heard a voice saying unto me, Arise, Peter; slay and eat.

8. But I said, Not so, Lord: for nothing common or unclean hath at any time entered into my mouth.

9. But the voice answered me again from heaven, What God hath cleansed, *that* call not thou common.

10. And this was done three times: and all were drawn up again into heaven.

11. And, behold, immediately there were three men already come unto the house where I was, sent from Caesarea unto me.

12. And the Spirit bade me go with them, nothing doubting. Moreover these six brethren accompanied me, and we entered into the man's house:

13. And he shewed us how he had seen an angel in his house, which stood and said unto him, Send men to Joppa, and call for Simon, whose surname is Peter;

14. Who shall tell thee words, whereby thou and all thy house shall be saved.

15. And as I began to speak, the Holy Ghost fell on them, as on us at the beginning.

16. Then remembered I the word of the Lord, how that he said, John indeed baptized with water; but ye shall be baptized with the Holy Ghost.

17. **Forasmuch then as God gave them the like gift as *he did* unto us, who believed on the Lord Jesus Christ; what was I, that I could withstand God?**

18. **When they heard these things, they held their peace,** and glorified God, **saying, Then hath God also to the Gentiles granted repentance unto life.**

19. **Now they which were**

scattered abroad upon the persecution that arose about Stephen travelled as far as Phenice, and Cyprus, and Antioch, **preaching the word to none but unto the Jews** only.

20. **And some of them** were men of Cyprus and Cyrene, which, when they were come to Antioch, **spake unto the Grecians, preaching the LORD Jesus.**

21. And the hand of the Lord was with them: **and a great number believed,** and turned unto the Lord.

22. **Then tidings** of these things **came unto** the ears of **the church** which was **in Jerusalem: and they sent** forth **Barnabas,** that he should go as far as Antioch.

23. **Who,** when he came, and had seen the grace of God, was glad, and **exhorted them all, that with purpose of heart they would cleave unto the Lord.**

24. **For he was a good man, and full of the Holy Ghost and of faith:** and much people was added unto the Lord.

25. **Then departed Barnabas to Tarsus,** for **to seek Saul:**

26. **And** when he had found him, **he brought him unto Antioch. And** it came to pass, that **a whole year they assembled themselves with the church, and taught much people. And the disciples were called Christians first in Antioch.**

27. **And** in these days **came prophets from Jerusalem** unto Antioch.

28. **And there stood up one** of them **named Agabus, and signified** by the Spirit **that there should be great dearth throughout all the world:** which came to pass in the days of Claudius Caesar.

29. **Then the disciples,** every man according to his ability, **determined to send relief unto the brethren** which dwelt **in Judaea:**

30. Which also they did, and sent it to the elders **by the hands of Barnabas and Saul.**

CHAPTER 12

1. **Now about that time Herod the king stretched forth** *his* hands **to vex certain of the church.**

2. **And he killed James** the brother of John with the sword.

3. **And because** he saw **it pleased the Jews, he proceeded** further **to take Peter** also. (Then were the days of unleavened bread.)

4. **And** when he had apprehended him, **he put *him* in prison,** and delivered *him* to four quaternions of soldiers to keep him; intending after Easter to bring him forth to the people.

5. **Peter therefore was kept in prison: but prayer was made without ceasing of the church** unto God **for him.**

6. **And when Herod would have brought him forth, the same night Peter was sleeping between two soldiers, bound with two chains:** and the keepers before the door kept the prison.

7. **And, behold, the angel of the Lord came** upon *him*, and a light shined in the prison: **and he smote Peter** on the side, **and raised him up, saying, Arise** up quickly. **And his chains fell off** from *his* hands.

8. **And the angel** said unto him,
Gird thyself, and bind on thy sandals.
And so he did. And he
saith unto him,
Cast thy garment about thee, and
follow me.
9. **And he went out,** and followed
him; and wist not that it was true
which was done by the angel;
but thought he
saw a vision.
10. When they were past the first and
the second ward, they came unto
the iron gate that leadeth unto the
city; which opened to them of his
own accord:
and they went out, and
passed on through one
street; and forthwith
the angel departed from him.
11. **And when Peter was**
come to himself, he said,
Now I know of a surety,
that the LORD hath
sent his angel, and hath
delivered me out of the
hand of Herod,
and *from* all the expectation of the
people of the Jews.
12. **And** when he had
considered *the thing,*
he came to the house of
Mary the mother of
John, whose surname was
Mark; where many were gathered
together praying.
13. **And as Peter knocked**
at the door of the gate,
a damsel came to hearken,
named Rhoda.
14. **And when she knew**
Peter's voice, she opened not
the gate for gladness, but ran in, and
told how Peter stood
before the gate.
15. **And they said unto her,**
Thou art mad. But she
constantly affirmed that it was even
so. Then said they, It is his angel.
16. **But Peter continued**
knocking: and when they
had
opened *the door,*
and saw him,
they were astonished.
17. **But he,** beckoning unto them
with the hand to hold their peace,
declared unto them
how the Lord had brought
him out of the prison. And
he said, Go shew these
things unto James,
and to the brethren.
And he departed,
and went into another place.
18. Now as soon as it was day, there
was no small stir among the soldiers,
what was become of Peter.
19. **And when Herod had**
sought for him, and found
him not, he examined
the keepers, and
commanded that *they* should
be put to death. And he
went down from Judaea to
Caesarea, and *there* abode.
20. And Herod was highly displeased
with them of Tyre and Sidon: but
they came with one accord to him,
and, having made Blastus the king's
chamberlain their friend, desired
peace; because their country was
nourished by the king's *country.*
21. **And** upon a set day
Herod, arrayed in
royal apparel,
sat upon his throne, and
made an oration
unto them.
22. **And the people gave a**
shout, *saying, It is* the
voice of a god,
and not of a man.
23. **And immediately the**
angel of the Lord smote
him, because he gave not
God the glory: and he was
eaten of worms, and gave
up the ghost.
24. But the word of God
grew and multiplied.
25. **And Barnabas and Saul**
returned from Jerusalem,
when they had fulfilled *their* ministry,
and took with them
John, whose surname was

Mark.

CHAPTER 13

1. **Now there were in the**
church that was
at Antioch certain prophets
and teachers; as
Barnabas, and Simeon
that was called Niger,
and Lucius of Cyrene,
and Manaen, which had been
brought up with Herod the tetrarch,
and Saul.
2. **As they ministered**
to the Lord, and fasted,
the Holy Ghost said,
Separate me Barnabas
and Saul for the work
whereunto
I have called them.
3. **And when they had fasted**
and prayed,
and laid *their* hands on them,
they sent *them* away.
4. **So they, being sent** forth
by the Holy Ghost, departed
unto Seleucia; and from thence they
sailed to Cyprus.
5. **And** when they were at Salamis,
they preached the word
of God
in the synagogues of the
Jews: and they had also John to
their minister.
6. **And** when they had gone through
the isle unto Paphos,
they found a certain
sorcerer, a false prophet,
a Jew, whose name
***was* Barjesus:**
7. **Which was with the**
deputy of the country,
Sergius Paulus,
a prudent man;
who called for
Barnabas and Saul, and
desired to hear the word
of God.
8. **But Elymas** the sorcerer
(for so is his name by
interpretation) withstood
them, seeking to turn away
the deputy from the faith.
9. **Then Saul,** (who also *is called*
Paul,) filled with the Holy Ghost,
set his eyes on him.
10. **And said,**
O full of all subtilty and all mischief,
***thou* child of the devil,**
thou enemy of all righteousness, wilt
thou not cease to pervert the right
ways of the Lord?
11. And now, behold, the hand of the
Lord *is* upon thee, and
thou shalt be blind,
not seeing the sun
for a season. And
immediately there fell on
him a mist and a
darkness;
and he went about seeking some to
lead him by the hand.
12. **Then the deputy,**
when he saw what was done,
believed, being astonished at the
doctrine of the Lord.
13. **Now when Paul and his**
company loosed from
Paphos, they came to Perga in
Pamphylia: and
John departing from them
returned to Jerusalem.
14. **But** when they
departed from Perga,
they came to Antioch in
Pisidia, and went
into the synagogue
on the sabbath day, and sat down.
15. And after the reading of the law
and the prophets
the rulers of the synagogue
sent unto them, saying,
Ye men *and* brethren,
if ye have any word
of exhortation
for the people, say on.
16. **Then Paul stood up, and**
beckoning with *his* hand
said, Men of Israel, and ye that fear
God, give audience.
17. **The God** of this people
of Israel chose our fathers,
and exalted the people when they
dwelt as strangers in the land of
Egypt, and with an high arm brought
he them out of it.

18. **And about** the time of
forty years suffered he their
manners in the wilderness.
19. **And** when he had destroyed
seven nations in the land of Chanaan,
he divided their land to
them by lot.
20. **And after that he gave**
unto
***them* judges** about the space of
four hundred and fifty years,
until Samuel the prophet.
21. **And afterward they**
desired a king: and God
gave unto them Saul
the son of Cis, a man of the tribe of
Benjamin, by the space
of forty years.
22. **And when he had**
removed him, he raised up
unto them
David to be their king;
to whom also he gave their testimony,
and said, I have found David the *son*
of Jesse, a man after mine own heart,
which shall fulfil all my will.
23. **Of this man's seed hath**
God according to *his* promise
raised unto Israel a
Saviour, Jesus:
24. When John had first preached
before his coming the baptism of
repentance to all the people of Israel.
25. **And as John fulfilled his**
course, he said, Whom
think ye that I am? I am not
***he*. But,** behold,
there cometh one after me,
whose shoes of *his* feet I am not
worthy to loose.
26. **Men *and* brethren,** children
of the stock of Abraham, and
whosoever among you feareth God,
to you is the word of this
salvation sent.
27. **For they that dwell at**
Jerusalem, and their rulers,
because they knew him
not, nor yet the voices of
the prophets which are read
every sabbath day,
they have fulfilled *them* in
condemning *him*.

28. **And though they found**
no cause of death *in him*,
yet desired they Pilate that
he should be slain.
29. **And when they had**
fulfilled all that was written
of him, they
took *him* down from the tree, and
laid *him* in a sepulchre.
30. **But God raised him from**
the dead:
31. And he was seen many days of
them which came up with him from
Galilee to Jerusalem, who are his
witnesses unto the people.
32. **And we declare**
unto you glad tidings, how
that the promise which was
made unto the fathers,
33. **God hath fulfilled**
the same unto us their children,
in that he hath raised up
Jesus again; as it is also written in
the second psalm, Thou art my Son,
this day have I begotten thee.
34. **And as concerning that**
he raised him up from the dead,
***now* no more to return**
to corruption,
he said on this wise, I will give you the
sure mercies of David.
35. **Wherefore he saith** also
in another *psalm*, Thou
shalt not suffer thine Holy
One to see corruption.
36. **For David,** after he had served
his own generation by the will of
God, fell on sleep, and was laid unto
his fathers, and
saw corruption:
37. **But he, whom God**
raised again, saw no
corruption.
38. **Be it known** unto you
therefore, men *and* brethren,
that through this man is
preached unto you the
forgiveness of sins:
39. And by him all that believe are
justified from all things, from which ye
could not be justified by the
law of Moses.
40. **Beware** therefore,

lest that come upon you,
which is spoken of
in the prophets;
41. **Behold, ye despisers,**
and wonder, and perish:
for I work a work in your
days, a work
which ye shall in no wise
believe, though a man declare it
unto you.
42. **And** when the Jews were gone
out of the synagogue,
the Gentiles besought that
these words might be
preached to them
the next sabbath.
43. **Now** when the congregation was
broken up,
many of the Jews
and religious proselytes
followed Paul and
Barnabas: who, speaking to
them, persuaded them to continue in
the grace of God.
44. **And the next sabbath**
day came almost the
whole city together to hear
the word of God.
45. **But when the Jews saw**
the multitudes,
they were filled with envy,
and spake against those
things which were spoken by
Paul, contradicting
and blaspheming.
46. **Then Paul and**
Barnabas waxed bold,
and said, It was necessary
that the word of God
should first have been
spoken to you: but seeing
ye put it from you, and judge
yourselves unworthy
of everlasting life, lo,
we turn to the Gentiles.
47. **For so hath the Lord**
commanded us, *saying*, I
have set thee to be a light
of the Gentiles,
that thou shouldest be for salvation
unto the ends of the earth.
48. **And when the Gentiles**
heard this,
they were glad,
and glorified the word of the Lord:
and as many as were
ordained to eternal
life believed.
49. And the word of the Lord was
published throughout all the region.
50. **But the Jews stirred up**
the devout and honourable women,
and the chief men of the
city, and raised
persecution against Paul
and Barnabas, and
expelled them out of
their coasts.
51. But they shook off the dust of
their feet against them, and came
unto Iconium.
52. And the disciples were filled with
joy, and with the Holy Ghost.

CHAPTER 14

1. And it came to pass
in Iconium, that
they went both together
into the synagogue
of the Jews,
and so spake, that a great
multitude both of the
Jews and also of the
Greeks believed.
2. **But the unbelieving Jews**
stirred up the Gentiles,
and made their minds evil affected
against the brethren.
3. **Long time therefore**
abode they speaking
boldly in the Lord,
which gave testimony unto the word of
his grace, and granted signs and
wonders to be done by their hands.
4. **But the** multitude of the
city was divided:
and part held with the Jews, and part
with the apostles.
5. **And when there was an**
assault made both of the
Gentiles, and also of the
Jews with their rulers,
to use *them* despitefully, and
to stone them,
6. **They were ware of *it*, and**
fled unto Lystra and Derbe,

cities of Lycaonia, and unto the region
that lieth round about:
7. And there they
preached the gospel.
8. **And there sat a certain**
man at Lystra,
impotent in his feet,
being a cripple from his
mother's womb,
who never had walked:
9. **The same heard Paul**
speak: who
stedfastly beholding him, and
perceiving that he had faith
to be healed,
10. **Said with a loud voice,**
Stand upright on thy feet.
And he leaped
and walked.
11. **And when the people**
saw what Paul had done,
they lifted up their
voices, saying
in the speech of Lycaonia,
The gods are come down
to us in the likeness of men.
12. **And they called**
Barnabas, Jupiter; and
Paul, Mercurius,
because he was the chief speaker.
13. Then the priest of Jupiter, which
was before their city, brought oxen
and garlands unto the gates, and
would have done sacrifice
with the people.
14. ***Which*** **when the**
apostles, Barnabas and
Paul, heard *of*, they rent
their clothes, and ran in
among the people,
crying out,
15. And saying,
Sirs, why do ye these things?
We also are men
of like passions with you,
and preach unto you
that ye should turn
from these vanities
unto the living God, which
made heaven, and earth, and the sea,
and all things that are therein:
16. **Who in times past**
suffered all nations to walk
in their own ways.
17. **Nevertheless he left not**
himself without witness,
in that he did good,
and gave us rain from heaven,
and fruitful seasons, filling our
hearts with food and gladness.
18. And with these sayings scarce
restrained they the people, that they
had not done sacrifice unto them.
19. **And there came** thither
certain **Jews from Antioch**
and Iconium,
who persuaded the people,
and having stoned Paul,
drew *him* out of the city,
supposing he had
been dead.
20. **Howbeit,** as the disciples
stood round about him,
he rose up, and came into
the city: and the next day
he departed with Barnabas
to Derbe.
21. **And when they** had
preached the gospel
to that city,
and had taught many,
they returned again to
Lystra, and *to* Iconium,
and Antioch,
22. **Confirming**
the souls of the disciples,
and **exhorting them to**
continue in the faith, and
that we must through much
tribulation enter into
the kingdom of God.
23. **And when they had**
ordained them elders
in every church, and had prayed
with fasting,
they commended them to
the Lord, on whom they believed.
24. And after they had passed
throughout Pisidia, they came
to Pamphylia.
25. And when they had preached the
word in Perga, they went
down into Attalia:
26. And thence sailed to Antioch, from
whence they had been recommended
to the grace of God for the work which

they fulfilled.
27. And when they were come, and
had gathered the church together,
they rehearsed all that God had done
with them, and how he had opened the
door of faith unto the Gentiles.
28. And there they abode long time
with the disciples.

CHAPTER 15

1. **And certain men**
which came down
from Judaea taught the
brethren, *and said*, Except
ye be circumcised
after the manner of Moses,
ye cannot be saved.
2. **When therefore Paul and**
Barnabas had
no small dissension and
disputation with them, they
determined that Paul and
Barnabas, and certain
other of them,
should go up to Jerusalem
unto the apostles and elders
about this question.
3. And being brought on their way by
the church, they passed through
Phenice and Samaria, declaring the
conversion of the Gentiles: and they
caused great joy unto all the brethren.
4. **And when they were come**
to Jerusalem, they were
received of the church,
and *of* the apostles and elders,
and they declared all
things that God had done
with them.
5. **But there rose up**
certain of the sect of the
Pharisees which believed,
saying, That it was needful
to circumcise them,
and to command *them* to keep
the law of Moses.
6. And the apostles and elders came
together for to consider of this matter.
7. **And** when there had
been much disputing,
Peter rose up, and said
unto them, Men *and* brethren,
ye know how
that a good while ago
God made choice
among us,
that the Gentiles by my
mouth should hear the
word of the gospel,
and believe.
8. **And God,**
which knoweth the hearts,
bare them witness, giving
them the Holy Ghost,
even as *he did* unto us;
9. **And put no difference**
between us and them,
purifying their hearts by faith.
10. **Now therefore why tempt**
ye God, to put a yoke upon
the neck of the disciples,
which neither our fathers nor we were
able to bear?
11. But we believe that through the
grace of the LORD Jesus Christ we
shall be saved, even as they.
12. **Then all the multitude**
kept silence, and
gave audience to
Barnabas and Paul, declaring
what miracles and wonders God had
wrought among the Gentiles by them.
13. **And after**
they had held their peace,
James answered, saying, Men
and brethren, hearken unto me:
14. **Simeon hath declared**
how God at the first
did visit the Gentiles, to
take out of them a people
for his name.
15. **And to this agree the**
words of the prophets;
as it is written,
16. **After this I** will return, and
will build again the
tabernacle of David, which is
fallen down; and I will build again the
ruins thereof, and I will set it up:
17. **That the residue of men**
might seek after the Lord,
and all the Gentiles, upon
whom my name is called,
saith the Lord, who doeth
all these things.
18. Known unto God are all his works

from the beginning of the world.
19. **Wherefore my sentence is, that we trouble not them, which from among the Gentiles are turned to God:**
20. **But that we write** unto them, **that they abstain from pollutions** of idols, **and *from* fornication,** and *from* things strangled, **and *from* blood.**
21. For Moses of old time hath in every city them that preach him, being read in the synagogues every sabbath day.
22. **Then pleased it the apostles** and elders with the whole church, **to send chosen men of their own company to Antioch with Paul and Barnabas;** *namely*, Judas surnamed Barsabas and Silas, chief men among the brethren:
23. **And they wrote *letters* by them after this manner;** The apostles and elders and brethren *send* greeting unto the brethren which are of the Gentiles in Antioch and Syria and Cilicia.
24. **Forasmuch as we have heard, that certain which went out from us have troubled you** with words, subverting your souls, **saying, *Ye must* be circumcised,** and keep the law: **to whom we gave no *such* commandment:**
25. **It seemed good unto us,** being assembled with one accord, **to send chosen men** unto you **with our beloved Barnabas and Paul,**
26. Men that have hazarded their lives for the name of our Lord Jesus Christ.
27. **We have sent therefore Judas and Silas,** who shall also tell *you* the same things by mouth.
28. **For it seemed good to the Holy Ghost,** and to us, **to lay upon you no greater burden than these necessary things;**
29. **That ye abstain from meats offered to idols,** and **from blood,** and **from things strangled, and** from **fornication:** from which if ye keep yourselves, ye shall do well. Fare ye well.
30. **So when they were dismissed, they came to Antioch: and** when they had gathered the multitude together, they **delivered the epistle:**
31. ***Which* when they had read, they rejoiced** for the consolation.
32. And Judas and Silas, being prophets also themselves, exhorted the brethren with many words, and confirmed *them*.
33. **And after** they had tarried *there* **a space, they were let go** in peace from the brethren unto the apostles.
34. **Notwithstanding it pleased Silas to abide there still.**
35. **Paul also and Barnabas continued in Antioch,** teaching and preaching the word of the Lord, with many others also.
36. **And** some days after **Paul said unto Barnabas, Let us** go again and **visit** our brethren in **every city where we have preached the word** of the LORD, ***and see* how they do.**
37. **And Barnabas determined to take** with them John, whose surname was **Mark.**
38. **But Paul thought not good to take him** with them, **who departed from them from Pamphylia,** and went not with them to the work.
39. **And the contention was so sharp** between them, **that they departed** asunder **one from the other: and so**

Barnabas took Mark,
and sailed
unto Cyprus;
40. **And Paul chose Silas,**
and departed,
being recommended by the
brethren unto the grace of God.
41. **And he went through**
Syria and Cilicia, confirming
the churches.

CHAPTER 16

1. **Then came he to Derbe**
and Lystra:
and, behold,
a certain disciple was
there, named Timotheus,
the son of a certain woman, which was
a Jewess, and believed; but his father
was a Greek:
2. **Which was well reported**
of by the brethren
that were at Lystra and Iconium.
3. **Him would Paul have to**
go forth with him; and took
and circumcised him
because of the Jews
which were
in those quarters: for they
knew all that his father was a Greek.
4. **And** as they went
through the cities,
they delivered them
the decrees for to keep,
that were ordained of the
apostles and elders which
were at Jerusalem.
5. **And so were the churches**
established in the faith,
and increased in number daily.
6. Now when they had gone
throughout Phrygia and the region of
Galatia, and were forbidden of the
Holy Ghost to preach the
word in Asia,
7. After they were come to Mysia,
they assayed to go into Bithynia: but
the Spirit suffered them not.
8. **And they** passing by Mysia
came down to Troas.
9. **And a vision appeared to**
Paul in the night;
There stood a man of
Macedonia, and prayed him,
saying, Come over into
Macedonia, and help us.
10. **And** after he had seen the vision,
immediately we
endeavoured to go
into Macedonia, assuredly gathering
that the Lord had called us
for to preach
the gospel unto them.
11. **Therefore loosing from**
Troas, we came
with a straight course to Samothracia,
and the next day to Neapolis;
12. And from thence
to Philippi, which is
the chief city of that
part of Macedonia,
and a colony: and we were in that city
abiding certain days.
13. **And on the sabbath we**
went out of the city
by a river side, where prayer was wont
to be made; and we sat down, and
spake unto the women which
resorted *thither.*
14. **And a certain woman**
named Lydia, a seller of purple,
of the city of Thyatira,
which worshipped God,
heard *us*: whose heart the Lord
opened, that she attended unto the
things which were spoken of Paul.
15. **And when she was**
baptized, and her household,
she besought *us*, saying,
If ye have judged me to be
faithful to the Lord,
come into my house, and
abide *there.* And she
constrained us.
16. **And** it came to pass,
as we went to prayer,
a certain damsel
possessed with a spirit of
divination met us, which
brought her masters much
gain by soothsaying:
17. **The same followed Paul**
and us,
and cried, saying,
These men are the servants
of the most high

God, which shew unto us the
way of salvation.
18. **And this did she many**
days. But Paul, being grieved,
turned and said to the
spirit, I command thee in
the name of Jesus Christ
to come out of her.
And he came out
the same hour.
19. **And when her masters**
saw that the hope of their
gains was gone, they
caught Paul and Silas,
and drew *them* into the marketplace
unto the rulers,
20. **And brought them to the**
magistrates, saying, These men,
being Jews, do exceedingly
trouble our city,
21. And teach customs, which are not
lawful for us to receive, neither
to observe, being Romans.
22. **And the multitude rose**
up together
against them: and the
magistrates rent off their
clothes, and
commanded to beat *them*.
23. **And** when they had laid many
stripes upon them,
they cast *them* into prison,
charging the jailor to keep
them safely:
24. Who, having received such a
charge, thrust them into the inner
prison, and made their feet fast
in the stocks.
25. **And at midnight Paul**
and Silas prayed, and
sang praises unto God:
and the prisoners heard them.
26. **And suddenly there was**
a great earthquake,
so that the foundations of the prison
were shaken:
and immediately all the
doors were opened, and
every one's bands were loosed.
27. **And the keeper** of the prison
awaking out of his sleep, and
seeing the prison
doors open, he
drew out
his sword, and would have
killed himself, supposing
that
the prisoners had been
fled.
28. **But Paul cried**
with a loud voice, saying,
Do thyself no harm: for we
are all here.
29. **Then he** called for a light, and
sprang in, and came trembling, and
fell down before
Paul and Silas,
30. **And** brought them out, and
said, Sirs, what must I do to
be saved?
31. **And they said, Believe**
on the Lord Jesus Christ,
and thou shalt be saved,
and thy house.
32. And they spake unto him the word
of the Lord, and to all that were
in his house.
33. **And he took them**
the same hour of the night,
and washed *their* stripes;
and was baptized,
he and all his, straightway.
34. **And when he had**
brought them into his
house, he set meat
before them, and
rejoiced, believing in God
with all his house.
35. **And** when it was day,
the magistrates sent the
sergeants, saying, Let
those men go.
36. **And the keeper** of the prison
told this saying to
Paul, The magistrates have sent
to let you go: now therefore
depart, and go
in peace.
37. **But Paul said** unto them,
They have beaten us
openly uncondemned,
being Romans, and have
cast *us* into prison; and
now do
they thrust us out privily?
nay verily;

but let them come
themselves and fetch us out.
38. **And the sergeants told**
these words unto
the magistrates: and they
feared, when they heard that
they were Romans.
39. **And they came**
and besought them,
and brought *them* out, and
desired *them* to depart
out of the city.
40. **And they**
went out of the prison, and
entered into *the house* of
Lydia: and
when they had seen the brethren,
they comforted them,
and departed.

CHAPTER 17

1. **Now** when they had passed
through Amphipolis and Apollonia,
they came to
Thessalonica, where was a
synagogue of the Jews:
2. **And Paul,** as his manner was,
went in unto them,
and three sabbath days
reasoned with them out of
the scriptures,
3. Opening and
alleging, that Christ must
needs
have suffered, and risen
again from the dead;
and that this
Jesus, whom I preach unto you,
is Christ.
4. **And some of them**
believed, and consorted with
Paul and Silas;
and of the devout Greeks a
great multitude, and of the
chief women not a few.
5. **But the Jews which**
believed not, moved with envy,
took unto them certain lewd fellows of
the baser sort, and gathered a
company, and
set all the city on an
uproar, and assaulted the
house of Jason, and sought to
bring them out to the people.
6. **And** when they found them not,
they drew Jason
and certain brethren
unto the rulers of the city,
crying, These that have turned
the world upside down are come
hither also;
7. **Whom Jason hath**
received: and these all
do contrary to the decrees
of Caesar, saying that
there is another king,
one Jesus.
8. And they troubled the people and
the rulers of the city, when they
heard these things.
9. And when they had taken security
of Jason, and of the other,
they let them go.
10. **And the brethren**
immediately sent away
Paul and Silas
by night unto Berea:
who coming *thither*
went into the synagogue
of the Jews.
11. These were more noble than those
in Thessalonica, in that they
received the word with all readiness
of mind, and searched the scriptures
daily, whether those things were so.
12. **Therefore many of them**
believed; also of honourable
women which were Greeks,
and of men, not a few.
13. **But when the Jews of**
Thessalonica had
knowledge that the word of
God was preached of Paul
at Berea,
they came thither
also, and stirred up the people.
14. **And then immediately**
the brethren sent away
Paul to go as it were to the sea:
but Silas and Timotheus
abode there still.
15. **And they** that conducted Paul
brought him unto
Athens: and
receiving a commandment
unto Silas and Timotheus

for to come to him
with all speed, they departed.
16. **Now while Paul waited**
for them at Athens, his spirit was
stirred in him, when
he saw the city wholly
given to idolatry.
17. **Therefore disputed he**
in the synagogue
with the Jews, and with the
devout persons, and in the
market daily with them
that met with him.
18. **Then certain**
philosophers of the
Epicureans, and of the
Stoics, encountered him.
And some
said, What will this babbler
say? other some, He seemeth to be
a setter forth of strange gods:
because he preached unto them
Jesus, and the resurrection.
19. **And they took him,**
and brought him
unto Areopagus, saying,
May we know what this new
doctrine, whereof thou speakest,
is?
20. For thou bringest certain strange
things to our ears: we would know
therefore what these things mean.
21. **(For all the Athenians**
and strangers which were there
spent their time in nothing
else,
but either to tell, or to hear
some new thing.)
22. **Then Paul stood in the**
midst of Mars' hill, and
said, *Ye* men of Athens, I perceive
that in all things
ye are too superstitious.
23. **For** as I passed by, and beheld
your devotions,
I found an altar with this
inscription, TO THE
UNKNOWN GOD. Whom
therefore ye ignorantly worship,
him declare I unto you.
24. **God that made the world**
and all things therein,
seeing that
he is Lord of heaven and earth,
dwelleth not in temples
made with hands;
25. **Neither is worshipped**
with men's
hands, as though he
needed any thing, seeing
he giveth to all life,
and breath, and all things;
26. **And hath made**
of one blood all nations of
men for to dwell on all the face of the
earth, and hath determined the times
before appointed, and the bounds of
their habitation;
27. **That they should seek**
the Lord, if haply they might feel
after him, and find him,
though he be not far from
every one of us:
28. **For in him we live, and**
move, and have our being;
as certain also of your own poets
have said, For we are also
his offspring.
29. Forasmuch then as we are the
offspring of God,
we ought not to think that
the Godhead is like unto
gold, or silver, or stone,
graven by art and man's device.
30. **And the times of this**
ignorance God winked at;
but now commandeth
all men everywhere
to repent:
31. **Because** he hath appointed a
day, in the which
he will judge the world in
righteousness by *that* man
whom he hath ordained;
whereof he hath given assurance unto
all *men*,
in that he hath raised him
from the dead.
32. **And when they heard of**
the resurrection of the dead,
some mocked: and others
said, We will hear thee
again of this *matter*.
33. **So Paul departed from**
among them.
34. Howbeit certain men clave unto

him, and believed: among the which
was Dionysius the Areopagite, and a
woman named Damaris, and others
with them

CHAPTER 18

1. **After these things Paul**
departed from Athens, and
came to Corinth;
2. **And found a** certain
Jew named Aquila, born in
Pontus, lately come from Italy,
with his wife Priscilla;
(because that Claudius had
commanded all Jews to depart from
Rome:) and came unto them.
3. **And** because he was of
the same craft,
he abode with them,
and wrought:
for by their occupation
they were tentmakers.
4. **And he reasoned in the**
synagogue every sabbath,
and persuaded the Jews
and the Greeks.
5. **And when Silas and**
Timotheus were come
from Macedonia,
Paul was pressed in the spirit, and
testified to the Jews *that*
Jesus *was* Christ.
6. **And when they opposed**
themselves,
and blasphemed, he
shook *his* raiment, and
said unto them,
Your blood *be* upon your
own heads; I *am* clean;
from henceforth I will go
unto the Gentiles.
7. **And he departed** thence,
and entered into a certain
***man's* house, named**
Justus, *one* that worshipped God,
whose house joined hard
to the synagogue.
8. **And Crispus, the chief**
ruler of the synagogue,
believed on the Lord
with all his house;
and many of the
Corinthians hearing
believed, and
were baptized.
9. **Then spake the Lord to**
Paul in the night
by a vision, Be not afraid,
but speak,
and hold not thy peace:
10. **For I am with thee, and**
no man shall set on thee to
hurt thee:
for I have much people in this city.
11. **And he continued *there***
a year and six months,
teaching the word
of God among them.
12. **And when Gallio was the**
deputy of Achaia,
the Jews made
insurrection with one accord
against Paul, and brought
him to the judgment seat,
13. **Saying, This *fellow***
persuadeth men to
worship God contrary
to the law.
14. **And** when Paul was now about to
open *his* mouth,
Gallio said unto the Jews,
If it were a matter of wrong
or wicked lewdness, O *ye* Jews,
reason would that
I should bear with you:
15. **But if it be** a question of words
and names, and
***of* your law,** look ye *to it*; for
I will be no judge
of such *matters*.
16. **And he drave them from**
the judgment seat.
17. **Then all the Greeks took**
Sosthenes,
the chief ruler of the
synagogue, and beat *him*
before the judgment seat. And Gallio
cared for none of those things.
18. **And Paul** *after this* tarried *there*
yet a good while, and then took
his leave of the brethren, and
sailed thence into Syria, and
with him Priscilla and Aquila; having
shorn *his* head in Cenchrea: for he
had a vow
19. **And he came to**

Ephesus, and left them there:
but he himself
entered into the
synagogue, and reasoned with
the Jews.
20. **When they desired *him***
to tarry longer time with them,
he consented not;
21. But bade them farewell, saying,
I must by all means keep this feast
that cometh in Jerusalem: but I will
return again unto you, if God will.
And he sailed from
Ephesus.
22. **And** when he had
landed at Caesarea,
and gone up,
and saluted the church, he
went down
to Antioch.
23. **And after** he had spent some
time *there*, he departed,
and went over *all* the
country of Galatia and
Phrygia in order,
strengthening all
the disciples.
24. **And a** certain
Jew named Apollos,
born at Alexandria,
an eloquent man, *and*
mighty in the
scriptures, came
to Ephesus.
25. **This man** was instructed in the
way of the Lord; and
being fervent in the spirit,
he spake and
taught diligently the things
of the Lord, knowing only
the baptism of John.
26. And he began to speak boldly in
the synagogue: whom
when Aquila and Priscilla
had
heard, they
took him unto *them*, and
expounded unto him the
way of God more perfectly.
27. **And** when he was disposed to
pass into Achaia,
the brethren wrote, exhorting
the disciples to receive
him: who, when he was
come, helped them much
which had believed
through grace:
28. **For he mightily**
convinced the Jews,
and that publicly,
shewing by the scriptures
that Jesus was Christ.

CHAPTER 19

1. And it came to pass, that, while
Apollos was at Corinth,
Paul having passed through the
upper coasts
came to Ephesus: and
finding certain
disciples,
2. **He said** unto them,
Have ye received the Holy
Ghost since ye believed?
And they said unto him,
We have not so much as
heard whether there be
any Holy Ghost.
3. And he said unto them, Unto what
then were ye baptized? And they
said, Unto John's baptism.
4. **Then said Paul, John** verily
baptized with the baptism
of repentance, saying
unto the people,
that they should believe
on him which should come
after him, that is,
on Christ Jesus.
5. **When they heard *this*,**
they were baptized in the
name of the Lord Jesus.
6. **And when Paul** had
laid *his* hands upon them,
the Holy Ghost came on them;
and they spake with
tongues, and prophesied.
7. And all the men were about twelve.
8. **And he** went into the
synagogue, and
spake boldly for the space of
three months, disputing
and persuading the things
concerning the kingdom
of God.
9. **But when divers were**

hardened, and believed not,
but spake evil of that way before
the multitude,
he departed from them, and
separated the disciples,
disputing daily in the school of
one Tyrannus.
10. **And this continued**
by the space of
two years; so that all
they which dwelt
in Asia heard the word of the
Lord Jesus, both Jews and Greeks.
11. **And God wrought** special
miracles by the hands of
Paul:
12. **So that from his body**
were brought unto the sick
handkerchiefs or aprons,
and the diseases departed
from them,
and the evil spirits went
out of them.
13. **Then** certain of the
vagabond Jews, exorcists,
took upon them to call
over them which had evil
spirits the name of the LORD
Jesus, saying, We adjure
you by Jesus whom
Paul preacheth.
14. And there were seven sons of *one*
Sceva, a Jew, *and* chief of the
priests, which did so.
15. **And the evil spirit**
answered and said,
Jesus I know, and Paul I
know; but who are ye?
16. **And the man in whom the**
evil spirit was leaped on
them, and overcame them,
and prevailed against
them, so that they fled out
of that house naked
and wounded.
17. **And this was known to**
all the
Jews and Greeks also dwelling
at Ephesus;
and fear fell on them all,
and the name of the Lord
Jesus was magnified.
18. **And many that believed**
came, and confessed,
and shewed their deeds
19. **Many** of them also
which used curious arts
brought their books together,
and burned them
before all *men*: and they counted the
price of them, and found *it* fifty
thousand *pieces* of silver.
20. **So mightily grew the**
word of God and prevailed.
21. **After these things were**
ended, Paul purposed in the
spirit, when he had passed through
Macedonia and Achaia, to go to
Jerusalem, saying, After I have been
there, I must also see Rome.
22. So he sent into Macedonia two of
them that ministered unto him,
Timotheus and Erastus;
but he himself
stayed in Asia for
a season.
23. And the same time there arose no
small stir about that way.
24. For a certain *man*
named Demetrius,
a silversmith, which made
silver shrines for Diana,
brought no small
gain unto the craftsmen;
25. **Whom he called together**
with the workmen of like occupation,
and said, Sirs, ye know that
by this craft we have
our wealth.
26. **Moreover** ye see and hear,
that not alone at Ephesus, but almost
throughout all Asia, this
Paul hath persuaded
and turned away
much people, saying that
they be no gods, which are
made with hands:
27. **So that not only this our**
craft is in danger
to be set at nought;
but also that
the temple of the great goddess
Diana should be despised, and
her magnificence should be
destroyed, whom all Asia and the
world worshippeth.

28. **And** when they heard
these sayings,
they were full of wrath, and
cried out, saying,
Great *is* Diana of the Ephesians.
29. And the whole city was
filled with confusion:
and having caught Gaius
and Aristarchus,
men of Macedonia,
Paul's companions in travel,
they rushed with one accord
into the theatre.
30. **And when Paul would**
have entered in unto the people,
the disciples suffered
him not.
31. **And certain of the chief**
of Asia, which were his friends,
sent unto him, desiring *him*
that he would not
adventure himself
into the theatre.
32. Some therefore cried one thing,
and some another: for the assembly
was confused: and the more part
knew not wherefore they were
come together.
33. **And they drew**
Alexander out of the
multitude, the Jews
putting him forward.
And Alexander
beckoned with the hand, and
would have made his
defence unto the people.
34. **But when they knew** that
he was a Jew, all with one
voice about the space of
two hours cried out, Great
***is* Diana** of the Ephesians.
35. **And** when
the townclerk
had appeased the people, he
said, *Ye* men of Ephesus,
what man is there that
knoweth not how
that the city of the Ephesians
is a worshipper of
the great goddess
Diana, and of the *image* which
fell down from Jupiter?
36. **Seeing** then
that these things
cannot be spoken against,
ye ought to be quiet,
and to do nothing rashly.
37. **For** ye have brought hither
these men, which
are neither robbers of
churches, nor yet
blasphemers of your goddess.
38. **Wherefore if** Demetrius, and
the craftsmen which are with him,
have a matter against any
man,
the law is open,
and there are deputies:
let them implead
one another.
39. But if ye inquire any thing
concerning other matters, it shall be
determined in a lawful assembly.
40. **For we are in danger to**
be called in question for
this day's uproar, there being
no cause whereby we may give an
account of this concourse.
41. **And** when he had
thus spoken,
he dismissed
the assembly.

CHAPTER 20

1. **And after the uproar**
was ceased,
Paul called unto *him*
the disciples, and
embraced *them*,
and departed
for to go into Macedonia.
2. **And** when he had gone over those
parts, and had given them
much exhortation,
he came into Greece,
3. **And *there* abode three**
months. And when the Jews
laid wait for him,
as he was about to sail into Syria,
he purposed to return
through Macedonia.
4. And there accompanied him into
Asia Sopater of Berea; and of the
Thessalonians, Aristarchus and
Secundus; and Gaius of Derbe, and

Timotheus; and of Asia, Tychicus
and Trophimus.
5. These going before tarried for
us at Troas.
6. **And we sailed away from**
Philippi after the days of
unleavened bread,
and came unto them
to Troas in five days;
where we abode
seven days.
7. **And upon the first *day* of**
the week, when the disciples came
together to break bread,
Paul preached unto them,
ready to depart on the morrow;
and continued his speech
until midnight.
8. And there were many lights in the
upper chamber, where they were
gathered together.
9. **And there sat in a window**
a certain
young man named
Eutychus, being fallen into
a deep sleep: and
as Paul was long
preaching, he sunk down
with sleep,
and fell down
from the third loft, and was
taken up dead.
10. **And Paul**
went down, and fell on him, and
embracing *him* said,
Trouble not yourselves; for
his life is in him.
11. When he therefore was come up
again, and had broken bread, and
eaten, and talked a long while, even
till break of day, so he departed.
12. **And they brought the**
young man alive,
and were not a little comforted.
13. **And we went**
before to ship, and sailed
unto Assos, there intending
to take in
Paul: for so had
he appointed,
minding himself to go afoot.
14. **And** when he met with
us at Assos,
we took him in, and came
to Mitylene.
15. **And we sailed** thence,
and came the next *day* over against
Chios; and the next *day* we arrived at
Samos, and tarried at Trogyllium; and
the next *day* we came to Miletus.
16. **For Paul had determined**
to sail by Ephesus, because he would
not spend the time in Asia: for he
hasted, if it were possible for him,
to be at Jerusalem the day
of Pentecost.
17. **And from Miletus he sent**
to Ephesus, and called the
elders of the church.
18. **And when they were**
come to him,
he said unto them,
Ye know, from the first day that I
came into Asia, after what manner
I have been with you at
all seasons,
19. **Serving the LORD** with all
humility of mind, and
with many tears, and
temptations, which befell me
by the lying in wait of
the Jews:
20. ***And* how I** kept back nothing
that was profitable *unto you*, but have
shewed you, and
have taught you publicly, and
from house to house,
21. **Testifying both to the**
Jews, and also to the
Greeks, repentance
toward God,
and faith toward our Lord
Jesus Christ.
22. **And now, behold, I go**
bound in the spirit unto
Jerusalem, not knowing the
things that shall befall me
there:
23. Save that the Holy Ghost
witnesseth in every city, saying that
bonds and afflictions abide me.
24. **But none of these things**
move me, neither count I
my life dear unto myself,
so that I might finish my
course with joy,

and the ministry, which I have
received of the Lord Jesus, to testify
the gospel of the grace of God.
25. **And now,** behold,
I know that ye
all, among whom I have gone
preaching the kingdom of God,
shall see my face no more.
26. **Wherefore I take you to**
record this day,
that I *am* pure from the
blood of all *men*.
27. **For I have not shunned**
to declare unto you
all the counsel of God.
28. **Take heed therefore**
unto yourselves, and to all the flock,
over the which the Holy Ghost hath
made you overseers,
to feed the church of God,
which he hath
purchased with his
own blood.
29. **For I know** this, that
after my departing shall
grievous
wolves enter in among you,
not sparing the flock.
30. **Also of your own selves**
shall men arise, speaking
perverse things, to draw away
disciples after them.
31. **Therefore** watch, and
remember, that
by the space of three years
I ceased not to warn every
one night and day
with tears.
32. **And now, brethren, I**
commend you to God, and
to the word of his grace,
which is able to build you
up, and to give you an inheritance
among all them which are sanctified.
33. **I have coveted no man's**
silver, or
gold, or apparel.
34. Yea, ye yourselves know, that
these hands have ministered unto my
necessities, and to them that were
with me.
35. I have shewed you all things, how
that so labouring
ye ought to support the
weak, and to remember
the words of the Lord
Jesus, how he said,
It is more blessed to give
than to receive.
36. **And** when he had thus spoken,
he kneeled down,
and prayed with them all.
37. **And they all wept** sore,
and fell on Paul's neck,
and kissed him,
38. Sorrowing most of all for the words
which he spake, that they should
see his face no more. And they
accompanied him unto the ship.

CHAPTER 21

1. **And** it came to pass, that
after we were gotten from
them, and had launched, we came
with a straight course unto Coos, and
the *day* following unto Rhodes, and
from thence unto Patara:
2. And finding a ship sailing
over unto Phenicia,
we went aboard, and set forth.
3. Now when we had discovered
Cyprus, we left it on the left hand,
and sailed into Syria, and
landed at Tyre: for there the
ship was to unlade her burden.
4. **And finding disciples, we**
tarried there seven days:
who said to Paul through
the Spirit, that he should
not go up to Jerusalem.
5. And when we had accomplished
those days, we departed and went our
way; and they all brought us on our
way, with wives and children, till *we*
were out of the city: and we kneeled
down on the shore, and prayed.
6. And when we had taken our leave
one of another, we took ship; and
they returned home again.
7. **And** when we had finished *our*
course from Tyre,
we came to Ptolemais, and
saluted the brethren,
and abode with them one day.
8. **And the next *day* we**
that were of Paul's company

departed, and came
unto Caesarea: and we
entered into the house of
Philip the evangelist, which
was *one* of the seven; and
abode with him.
9. And the same man had four
daughters, virgins, which
did prophesy.
10. **And** as we tarried
there many days,
there came down from Judaea
a certain prophet,
named Agabus.
11. **And** when he was come unto us,
he took Paul's girdle, and
bound his own hands and
feet, and said, Thus saith
the Holy Ghost, So shall the
Jews at Jerusalem bind the
man that owneth this girdle,
and shall deliver *him* into
the hands of
the Gentiles.
12. **And when we heard**
these things, both
we, and they of that place,
besought him not to go
up to Jerusalem.
13. **Then Paul answered,**
What mean ye to weep
and to break mine heart?
for I am ready not to be
bound only, but also to die
at Jerusalem
for the name of
the Lord Jesus.
14. And when he would not be
persuaded, we ceased, saying, The
will of the Lord be done.
15. **And** after those days
we took up our carriages, and
went up to Jerusalem.
16. There went with us also *certain* of
the disciples of Caesarea, and
brought with them one Mnason of
Cyprus, an old disciple, with whom we
should lodge.
17. **And** when we were
come to Jerusalem,
the brethren received
us gladly.
18. **And** the *day* following
Paul went in with us
unto James; and all the
elders were present.
19. **And** when he had saluted them,
he declared particularly
what things God had
wrought among the
Gentiles by his ministry.
20. **And when they heard** *it,*
they glorified the Lord, and
said unto him,
Thou seest, brother,
how many thousands of
Jews there are which
believe; and
they are all zealous of the law:
21. **And they are informed of**
thee, that thou teachest all
the Jews which are among
the Gentiles
to forsake Moses, saying
that
they ought not to
circumcise *their* children, neither
to walk after the customs.
22. What is it therefore?
the multitude must needs
come together: for they will
hear that thou art come.
23. **Do therefore this**
that we say to thee:
We have four men which
have a vow on them;
24. Them take, and
purify thyself with them,
and be at charges with
them, that they may
shave *their* heads:
and all may know that those
things, whereof they were informed
concerning thee, are nothing; but
***that* thou thyself**
also walkest orderly, and
keepest the law
25. As touching the Gentiles which
believe, we have written *and*
concluded that they observe no such
thing, save only that they keep
themselves from *things* offered to
idols, and from blood, and from
strangled, and from fornication.
26. **Then Paul**
took the men, and the next day

■ **purifying himself with them**
■ **entered into the temple, to**
■ **signify the accomplish-**
■ **ment** of the days of purification, until
that an offering should be offered for
every one of them.
■ 27. **And** when the seven days were
almost ended,
■ **the Jews** which were
■ **of Asia, when they saw him**
in the temple,
■ **stirred up all the people,**
■ **and laid hands on him,**
■ 28. **Crying out,** Men of Israel,
■ **help: This is the man, that**
■ **teacheth** all *men* every where
■ **against** the people, and
■ **the law,** and this place:
■ **and further brought Greeks**
also
■ **into the temple, and hath**
■ **polluted this holy place.**
29. (For they had seen before with
him in the city Trophimus an
Ephesian, whom they supposed that
Paul had brought into the temple.)
■ 30. **And all the city**
■ **was moved,**
and the people ran together:
■ **and they took Paul, and**
■ **drew him out of the temple:**
and forthwith the doors were shut.
■ 31. **And as they went** about
■ **to kill him, tidings came**
■ **unto the chief captain**
of the band,
■ **that all Jerusalem was in**
■ **an uproar.**
■ 32. **Who immediately took**
■ **soldiers** and centurions,
■ **and ran** down
■ **unto them: and when they**
■ **saw** the chief captain and
■ **the soldiers, they left**
■ **beating of Paul.**
■ 33. **Then the chief captain**
came near, and took him, and
■ **commanded *him* to be**
■ **bound** with two chains;
■ **and demanded who he**
■ **was, and what he**
■ **had done.**
34. And some cried one thing, some
another, among the multitude:
■ **and when he could not**
■ **know the certainty for the**
■ **tumult, he commanded him**
■ **to be carried into**
■ **the castle.**
35. And when he came upon the
stairs, so it was, that he was borne
of the soldiers for the violence
of the people.
■ 36. **For the multitude**
of the people
■ **followed after, crying,**
■ **Away with him.**
■ 37. **And as Paul was** to be
■ **led** into the castle,
■ **he said unto the chief** captain,
May I speak unto thee? Who said,
Canst thou speak Greek?
38. Art not thou that Egyptian, which
before these days madest an
uproar, and leddest out into the
wilderness four thousand men that
were murderers?
39. But Paul said,
■ **I am** a man *which am*
■ **a Jew of Tarsus,** *a city* in
Cilicia, a citizen of no mean city: and,
■ **I beseech thee, suffer me to**
■ **speak unto the people.**
■ 40. **And** when he had
given him licence,
■ **Paul stood on the stairs,**
and beckoned with the hand unto
the people.
■ **And when there was**
made a great
■ **silence, he spake** unto *them*
■ **in the Hebrew tongue,**
■ **saying,**

CHAPTER 22

1. Men, brethren, and fathers,
■ **hear ye my defence**
which I make now unto you.
■ 2. **(And when they heard**
that he spake in
■ **the Hebrew tongue** to them,
■ **they kept the more silence:**
and he saith,)
■ 3. **I am** verily a man *which am*
■ **a Jew, born in Tarsus,**
a city in Cilicia,

yet brought up in this city at
the feet of Gamaliel, ***and***
taught according to
the perfect manner of the
law of the fathers, and was
zealous toward God,
as ye all are this day.
4. **And I persecuted this way**
unto the death,
binding and delivering into prisons
both men and women.
5. **As also the high priest**
doth bear me witness,
and all the estate of the elders:
from whom also
I received letters
unto the brethren,
and went to Damascus, to
bring them which were there
bound unto Jerusalem, for
to be punished.
6. **And** it came to pass, that,
as I made my journey,
and was come nigh unto
Damascus about noon,
suddenly there shone
from heaven
a great light round about me.
7. **And I fell unto the ground,**
and heard a voice saying
unto me,
Saul, Saul, why persecutest
thou me?
8. **And I answered, Who art**
thou, Lord? And he said
unto me,
I am Jesus of Nazareth,
whom thou persecutest.
9. And they that were with me saw
indeed the light, and were afraid; but
they heard not the voice of him that
spake to me.
10. **And I said, What shall I**
do, LORD? And the Lord
said unto me, Arise, and
go into Damascus; and there it
shall be told thee of all things
which are appointed for thee to do.
11. **And** when I could not see for the
glory of that light,
being led by the hand
of them that were with me,
I came into Damascus.
12. **And one Ananias,**
a devout man according to the law,
having a good report of all the Jews
which dwelt *there*,
13. **Came unto me,** and stood,
and said unto me,
Brother Saul, receive thy
sight. And the same hour I looked
up upon him.
14. **And he said, The God of**
our fathers hath chosen
thee, that thou shouldest
know his will, and see that
Just One, and shouldest
hear the voice of
his mouth.
15. **For thou shalt be his**
witness unto all men of what thou
hast seen and heard.
16. **And now**
why tarriest thou? arise, and
be baptized,
and wash away thy sins,
calling on the name
of the Lord.
17. **And** it came to pass, that, when I
was come again to Jerusalem, even
while I prayed in the temple,
I was in a trance;
18. **And saw him saying**
unto me, Make haste, and
get thee quickly
out of Jerusalem:
for they will not receive thy
testimony concerning me.
19. **And I said, Lord, they**
know that I imprisoned
and beat in every synagogue
them that believed on thee:
20. **And when the blood of**
thy martyr Stephen was
shed, I also
was standing by, and
consenting unto his death,
and kept the raiment of them that
slew him.
21. **And he said** unto me,
Depart: for I will send thee
far hence
unto the Gentiles.
22. **And they gave him**
audience unto this word,
and ***then***

lifted up their voices, and
said, Away with such a
fellow from the earth: for
it is not fit that he
should live.
23. And as they cried out, and cast off
their clothes, and threw dust
into the air,
24. **The chief captain**
commanded him to be brought
into the castle, and bade that he
should be examined by scourging;
that he might know wherefore
they cried so against him.
25. **And as they bound him**
with thongs,
Paul said unto the centurion
that stood by,
Is it lawful for you to
scourge a man that is
a Roman, and uncondemned?
26. **When the centurion**
heard *that,*
he went and told the chief
captain,
saying, Take heed
what thou doest:
for this man is a Roman.
27. **Then the chief captain**
came, and
said unto him, Tell me,
art thou a Roman?
He said, Yea.
28. **And the chief captain**
answered, With a great
sum obtained I this
freedom. And Paul said, But
I was *free* born.
29. **Then** straightway they departed
from him which should have examined
him: and
the chief captain also was
afraid, after he knew that he was a
Roman, and
because he had
bound him.
30. **On the morrow,**
because he would have known the
certainty wherefore he was accused
of the Jews,
he loosed him from *his* bands,
and commanded the chief
priests and all
their council to appear,
and brought Paul
down, and set him
before them.

CHAPTER 23

1. **And Paul,**
earnestly beholding the council,
said, Men *and* brethren,
I have lived in all good
conscience before God
until this day.
2. **And the high priest**
Ananias commanded them
that stood by him
to smite him on the mouth.
3. **Then said Paul unto him,**
God shall smite thee,
thou whited wall:
for sittest thou to judge me
after the law, and
commandest me to be
smitten contrary to
the law?
4. **And they** that stood by
said, Revilest thou God's
high priest?
5. **Then said Paul, I wist not,**
brethren, that he was
the high priest:
for it is written, Thou shalt not speak
evil of the ruler of thy people.
6. **But when Paul perceived**
that the one part were
Sadducees, and the
other Pharisees, he cried
out in the council, Men *and* brethren,
I am a Pharisee,
the son of a Pharisee:
of the hope and
resurrection of the dead
am called in question.
7. **And** when he had so said,
there arose a dissension
between the Pharisees and
the
Sadducees: and the multitude
was divided.
8. **For the Sadducees say**
that
there is no resurrection,
neither angel, nor spirit:
but the Pharisees

confess both.
9. **And** there arose a great cry: and
the scribes *that were* of
the Pharisees' part arose,
and strove,
saying, We find no evil in
this man: but if a spirit or an angel
hath spoken to him, let us not fight
against God.
10. **And** when there arose
a great dissension,
the chief captain, fearing
lest Paul should have been
pulled in pieces of them,
commanded the soldiers
to go down, and to
take him by force
from among them,
and to
bring *him* into the castle.
11. **And the night following**
the Lord stood by him, and
said, Be of good cheer,
Paul: for as thou hast
testified of me in
Jerusalem, so must thou
bear witness also
at Rome.
12. **And** when it was day,
certain of the
Jews banded together, and
bound themselves under a curse,
saying that they would neither eat nor
drink till they had killed Paul.
13. And they were more than forty
which had made this conspiracy.
14. **And they came to the**
chief priests and elders,
and said, We have bound
ourselves under a great curse,
that we will eat nothing until
we have slain Paul.
15. **Now therefore**
ye with the council
signify to the chief captain
that he bring him down unto
you to-morrow, as though ye would
inquire something more perfectly
concerning him:
and we, or ever he come near,
are ready to kill him.
16. **And when Paul's sister's**
son heard of their lying in wait,
he went
and entered into the castle,
and told Paul.
17. **Then Paul called one of**
the centurions unto *him,*
and said, Bring this young
man unto the chief captain:
for he hath a certain thing to tell him.
18. So he took him, and brought *him* to
the chief captain, and said, Paul
the prisoner called me unto *him*, and
prayed me to bring this young man
unto thee, who hath something to say
unto thee.
19. **Then the chief captain**
took him by the hand, and went
with him aside privately,
and asked *him,*
What is that thou hast
to tell me?
20. **And he said, The Jews**
have agreed to
desire thee
that thou wouldest bring
down
Paul to-morrow
into the council,
as though they would inquire
somewhat of him more perfectly.
21. **But do not** thou
yield unto them: for there lie
in wait for him of them more than
forty men, which have
bound themselves
with an oath, that they will
neither eat nor drink till
they have killed him:
and now are they ready, looking for a
promise from thee.
22. **So the chief captain** *then*
let the young man depart,
and charged *him, See thou* tell no man
that thou hast shewed these
things to me.
23. **And he called** unto *him*
two centurions, saying,
Make ready two hundred
soldiers to go to
Caesarea, and horsemen
threescore and ten, and spearmen
two hundred, at the third hour
of the night;
24. And provide *them* beasts,

that they may set Paul on,
and bring *him* safe unto
Felix the governor.
25. **And he wrote a letter**
after this manner:
26. Claudius Lysias
unto the most excellent governor
Felix *sendeth* greeting.
27. This man was taken of the Jews,
and should have been killed of them:
then came I with an army, and
rescued him, having understood that
he was a Roman.
28. And when I would have known the
cause wherefore they accused him, I
brought him forth into their council:
29. Whom I perceived to be accused
of questions of their law, but to
have nothing laid to his charge worthy
of death or of bonds.
30. And when it was told me how that
the Jews laid wait for the man, I
sent straightway to thee, and gave
commandment to his accusers also to
say before thee what *they had* against
him. Farewell.
31. **Then the soldiers,**
as it was commanded them,
took Paul, and brought *him* by
night to Antipatris.
32. On the morrow they left the
horsemen to go with him, and returned
to the castle:
33. Who, when they came
to Caesarea and
delivered the epistle
to the governor,
presented Paul also before him.
34. **And when the governor**
had read *the letter*, he
asked of what province
he was. And when he understood
that *he was* of Cilicia;
35. **I will hear thee, said he,**
when thine accusers are also
come. And he commanded him to
be kept in Herod's
judgment hall.

CHAPTER 24

1. **And after five days**
Ananias the high priest
descended with the elders, and
***with* a** certain
orator *named* Tertullus, who
informed the governor against Paul.
2. **And** when he was called forth,
Tertullus began to accuse
***him*, saying,** Seeing that by thee
we enjoy great quietness, and that
very worthy deeds are
done unto this nation by
thy providence,
3. **We accept *it* always,**
and in all places,
most noble Felix, with
all thankfulness.
4. Notwithstanding, that I be not
further tedious unto thee,
I pray thee
that thou wouldest hear us
of thy clemency a few words.
5. **For we have found this**
man *a* pestilent *fellow*, and
a mover of sedition among
all the
Jews throughout the world,
and a ringleader of the sect
of the Nazarenes:
6. Who also hath gone about to
profane the temple:
whom we took, and
would have judged
according to our law.
7. **But the chief captain**
Lysias came *upon us*, and with
great violence
took *him* away
out of our hands,
8. **Commanding his**
accusers to come unto
thee: by examining of whom
thyself mayest take knowledge of all
these things, whereof we accuse him.
9. And the Jews also assented,
saying that these things were so.
10. **Then Paul,** after that the
governor had beckoned
unto him to speak,
answered, Forasmuch as I
know that thou hast been of
many years a judge unto
this nation, I do
the more cheerfully
answer for myself:
11. **Because that thou**

mayest understand, that
there are yet
but twelve days
since I went up
to Jerusalem for to worship.
12. **And they neither found**
me in the temple
disputing with any man,
neither raising up the people, neither
in the synagogues,
nor in the city:
13. Neither can they prove the things
whereof they now accuse me.
14. **But this I confess** unto thee,
that after the way which
they call heresy, so
worship I the God of my
fathers, believing
all things which are written
in the law and in
the prophets:
15. **And have hope** toward God,
which they themselves also allow,
that there shall be a
resurrection of the dead,
both of the just and unjust.
16. And herein do I exercise myself,
to have always a conscience void to
offence toward God, and *toward* men.
17. **Now** after many years
I came to bring alms to my
nation, and offerings.
18. **Whereupon certain Jews**
from Asia found me
purified in the temple,
neither with multitude, nor with tumult.
19. **Who ought to have been**
here before thee, and object,
if they had aught
against me.
20. **Or** else
let these same *here*
say, if they have found any
evil doing in me,
while I stood before the council,
21. **Except it be** for this one voice,
that I cried standing among them,
Touching the resurrection
of the dead I am called in
question by you this day.
22. **And when Felix heard**
these things, having more perfect
knowledge of *that* way,
he deferred them, and
said, When Lysias
the chief captain
shall come down,
I will know the uttermost
of your matter.
23. **And he commanded a**
centurion to keep Paul,
and to
let *him* have liberty, and
that he should forbid none
of his acquaintance
to minister or
come unto him.
24. **And after certain days,**
when Felix came with his
wife Drusilla,
which was a Jewess,
he sent for Paul, and heard
him concerning the faith in
Christ.
25. **And as he reasoned of**
righteousness,
temperance, and judgment
to come,
Felix trembled, and
answered, Go thy way
for this time;
when I have a
convenient season, I will
call for thee.
26. He hoped also that money should
have been given him of Paul, that he
might loose him: wherefore he sent for
him the oftener, and
communed with him.
27. **But after two years** Porcius
Festus came into Felix'
room: and Felix, willing to
shew the Jews a pleasure,
left Paul bound.

CHAPTER 25

1. **Now when Festus was**
come into the province, after three
days he ascended from Caesarea
to Jerusalem.
2. Then the high priest and the chief of
the Jews informed him
against Paul, and besought him,
3. **And desired**
favour against him,
that he would send for him

to Jerusalem, laying wait
in the way
to kill him.
4. **But Festus answered, that**
Paul should be kept at
Caesarea, and that he himself
would depart shortly *thither.*
5. **Let them** therefore, said he,
which among you are able,
go down with *me,*
and accuse this man, if there
be any wickedness in him.
6. And when he had tarried among
them more than ten days,
he went down unto Caesarea;
and the next day sitting on
the judgment seat
commanded Paul
to be brought.
7. **And** when he was come,
the Jews which came down from
Jerusalem stood round about, and
laid many and grievous
complaints against Paul,
which they
could not prove.
8. **While he answered**
for himself,
Neither against the law
of the Jews, neither against
the temple, nor yet against
Caesar, have I offended
any thing at all.
9. **But Festus, willing to do**
the Jews a
pleasure, answered Paul, and
said, Wilt thou go up
to Jerusalem, and there be
judged of these things
before me?
10. **Then said Paul, I stand**
at Caesar's judgment seat,
where I ought to be judged:
to the Jews have I done no wrong,
as thou very well
knowest.
11. **For if I be an offender,**
or have committed any thing
worthy of death,
I refuse not to die: but if
there be none of these
things whereof these
accuse me, no man may
deliver me unto them.
I appeal unto Caesar.
12. **Then Festus,** when he had
conferred with the council,
answered, Hast thou appealed
unto Caesar?
unto Caesar shalt thou go.
13. **And** after certain days
king Agrippa and Bernice
came unto Caesarea
to salute Festus.
14. **And** when they had been there
many days,
Festus declared Paul's
cause unto the king,
saying, There is a certain man left
in bonds by Felix:
15. About whom,
when I was at Jerusalem,
the chief priests
and the elders of
the Jews informed *me*,
desiring *to have* judgment
against him.
16. To whom I answered, It is not the
manner of the Romans to deliver
any man to die, before that he which is
accused have the accusers face to
face, and have licence to answer for
himself concerning the crime
laid against him.
17. Therefore,
when they were come
hither, without any
delay on the morrow
I sat on the judgment seat, and
commanded the man to be
brought forth.
18. Against whom
when the accusers stood
up, they brought none
accusation of such things
as I supposed:
19. **But had** certain
questions against him
of their own superstition,
and of one Jesus, which
was dead, whom Paul
affirmed to be alive.
20. **And** because I doubted of such
manner of questions,
I asked *him* whether he
would go to Jerusalem,

and there
be judged of these matters.
21. **But when Paul** had
appealed to be reserved
unto the hearing of
Augustus, I commanded
him to be kept till I might
send him to Caesar.
22. **Then Agrippa said**
unto Festus,
I would also hear the man
myself. To-morrow, said he, thou
shalt hear him.
23. **And on the morrow,**
when Agrippa was come,
and Bernice, with great pomp,
and was entered into the place of
hearing, with the chief captains, and
principal men of the city,
at Festus' commandment
Paul was brought forth.
24. **And Festus said, King**
Agrippa, and all men which are
here present with us,
ye see this man, about
whom all the multitude
of the Jews
have dealt with me,
both at Jerusalem, and *also* here,
crying that he ought not to
live any longer.
25. But when I found that he had
committed nothing worthy of death,
and that he himself hath appealed to
Augustus, I have determined
to send him.
26. Of whom I have no certain thing to
write unto my lord.
Wherefore I have brought
him forth before you,
and specially before thee,
O king Agrippa,
that, after examination had, I might
have somewhat to write.
27. For it seemeth to me unreasonable
to send a prisoner, and not withal
to signify the crimes *laid* against him.

CHAPTER 26

1. **Then Agrippa said unto**
Paul, Thou art permitted to
speak for thyself.
Then Paul
stretched forth the hand, and
answered for himself:
2. **I think myself happy, king**
Agrippa, because I shall
answer for myself
this day before thee
touching all the things
whereof I am accused
of the Jews:
3. **Especially *because I***
***know* thee to be expert in**
all customs
and questions which are
among the Jews: wherefore I
beseech thee to hear me patiently.
4. **My manner of life from** my
youth, which was at the first among
mine own nation at Jerusalem,
know all the Jews;
5. Which knew me from the beginning,
if they would testify, that after the
most straitest sect
of our religion
I lived a Pharisee.
6. **And now I** stand and
am judged for the hope of
the promise made of God, unto
our fathers:
7. Unto which *promise* our twelve
tribes, instantly serving *God* day and
night, hope to come. For which hope's
sake, king Agrippa, I am accused
of the Jews.
8. **Why should it be thought**
a thing
incredible with you,
that God should raise
the dead?
9. **I verily thought** with myself,
that I ought to do many things
contrary to the name of
Jesus of Nazareth.
10. **Which thing I** also
did in Jerusalem:
and many of the
saints did I shut up in
prison, having received authority
from the chief priests;
and when they were put to
death, I gave my voice
against *them*.
11. And I punished them oft in every
synagogue, and compelled *them* to

blaspheme; and being exceedingly
mad against them,
I persecuted *them* even
unto strange cities.
12. **Whereupon as I went to**
Damascus with authority and
commission from the chief priests,
13. At midday, O king,
I saw in the way
a light from heaven, above the
brightness of the sun, shining round
about me and them which
journeyed with me.
14. **And when we were all**
fallen to the earth,
I heard a voice
speaking unto me, and
saying in the Hebrew tongue, Saul,
Saul, why persecutest thou
me? *it is* hard for thee to kick
against the pricks.
15. **And I said, Who art thou,**
Lord? And he said, I am
Jesus whom thou
persecutest
16. But rise, and stand
upon thy feet: for
I have appeared unto thee
for this purpose,
to make thee a minister and a
witness both of these things which
thou hast seen, and of those things in
the which I will appear unto thee;
17. Delivering thee from the people,
and *from* the Gentiles, unto whom
now I send thee,
18. To open their eyes, *and*
to turn *them*
from darkness to light, and
from the power of Satan
unto God, that they may receive
forgiveness of sins, and inheritance
among them which are sanctified by
faith that is in me.
19. **Whereupon,** O king Agrippa,
I was not disobedient unto
the heavenly
vision:
20. **But shewed first** unto
them of Damascus, and at
Jerusalem, and
throughout all the coasts of
Judaea, and *then* to the
Gentiles, that they should repent
and turn to God, and do works meet
for repentance.
21. **For these causes the**
Jews caught me in the temple, and
went about to kill *me*.
22. **Having therefore**
obtained help of God, I
continue unto this day,
witnessing both
to small and great,
saying none other things
than those which the
prophets and Moses did
say should come
23. **That Christ should suffer,**
and that he should be the first that
should rise from the dead,
and should shew light unto
the people, and to
the Gentiles.
24. **And** as he
thus spake for himself,
Festus said with a loud voice,
Paul, thou art beside thyself;
much learning doth
make thee mad.
25. **But he said, I am not**
mad, most noble
Festus; but speak forth the
words of truth and soberness.
26. **For the king knoweth** of
these things, before whom also I
speak freely: for I am persuaded that
none of these things are hidden
from him; for
this thing was not done
in a corner.
27. **King Agrippa, believest**
thou
the prophets? I know that
thou believest.
28. **Then Agrippa said**
unto Paul,
Almost thou persuadest
me to be a Christian
29. **And Paul said, I would**
to God,
that not only thou, but also
all that hear me this day,
were both almost, and
altogether such
as I am, except these bonds.

30. And when he had thus spoken, the
king rose up, and the governor, and
Bernice, and they that sat with them:
31. And when they were gone aside,
they talked between themselves,
saying, This man doeth nothing
worthy of death or of bonds.
32. **Then said Agrippa unto**
Festus, This man might
have been set at liberty, if
he had not appealed
unto Caesar.

CHAPTER 27

1. **And when it was**
determined that we should
sail into Italy, they
delivered Paul
and certain other prisoners
unto *one* named
Julius, a centurion
of Augustus' band.
2. And entering into a ship of
Adramyttium, we launched, meaning
to sail by the coasts of Asia; *one*
Aristarchus, a Macedonian of
Thessalonica, being with us.
3. And the next *day* we touched at
Sidon. And Julius courteously
entreated Paul, and gave *him* liberty
to go unto his friends to
refresh himself.
4. And when we had launched from
thence, we sailed under Cyprus,
because the winds were contrary.
5. **And when we had sailed**
over the sea of Cilicia
and Pamphylia,
we came to Myra,
a city of Lycia.
6. **And there the centurion**
found a ship of Alexandria
sailing into Italy; and he
put us therein.
7. And when we had sailed slowly
many days, and scarce were come
over against Cnidus, the wind not
suffering us, we sailed under Crete,
over again Salmone;
8. And, hardly passing it, came unto a
place which is called The fair
havens; nigh whereunto was the city
of Lasea.
9. Now when much time was spent,
and when sailing was now
dangerous, because the
fast was now
already past, Paul
admonished *them*,
10. **And said** unto them, Sirs,
I perceive that this voyage
will be with hurt and much
damage, not only of the
lading and
ship, but also of
our lives.
11. **Nevertheless the**
centurion believed the
master and the owner
of the ship, more than
those things which were spoken by
Paul.
12. **And because the haven**
was not commodious to
winter in, the more part
advised to depart thence
also, if by any means they might
attain to Phenice, *and there* to winter;
which is an haven of Crete,
and lieth toward the south-west
and north-west.
13. **And when the south wind**
blew softly,
supposing that they had obtained *their*
purpose, loosing *thence*,
they sailed close by Crete.
14. **But** not long after
there arose against it
a tempestuous wind,
called Euroclydon.
15. **And when the ship was**
caught, and could not bear
up into the wind,
we let *her* drive.
16. **And running under a**
certain
island which is
called Clauda, we had
much work to come by the boat:
17. Which when they had taken up,
they used helps, undergirding the
ship; and, fearing lest they should fall
into the quicksands, strake
sail, and so were driven.
18. **And we being** exceedingly
tossed with a tempest, the

next *day* they
lightened the ship;
19. And the third *day* we
cast out with our own hands
the tackling of the ship.
20. And when neither sun
nor stars in many days
appeared, and no small
tempest lay on *us*,
all hope that we should be saved
was then taken away.
21. But after long abstinence
Paul stood forth in
the midst of them,
and said, Sirs, ye should have
hearkened unto me, and not have
loosed from Crete, and to have gained
this harm and loss.
22. And now I exhort you to
be of good cheer: for there
shall be no loss of *any man's*
life among you, but
of the ship.
23. For there stood by me
this night the angel of God,
whose I am, and whom I serve,
24. Saying, Fear not,
Paul; thou must be brought
before Caesar: and, lo,
God hath given thee all
them that sail with thee.
25. Wherefore, sirs,
be of good cheer: for
I believe God, that it shall
be even as it was told me
26. Howbeit we must be cast
upon a certain island.
27. But when the fourteenth
night was come, as we
were driven up and down in Adria,
about midnight
the shipmen deemed that
they drew near to
some country;
28. And sounded, and
found *it* twenty fathoms:
and when they had gone
a little further, they
sounded again, and found
it fifteen fathoms.
29. Then fearing lest we
should have fallen upon
rocks, they cast four
anchors out of the stern,
and wished for the day.
30. And as the shipmen
were about to flee out of the
ship, when they had let down the boat
into the sea, under colour as though
they would have cast anchors
out of the foreship,
31. Paul said to
the centurion and to
the soldiers, Except these
abide in the ship, ye
cannot be saved.
32. Then the soldiers cut off
the ropes of the
boat, and let her fall off.
33. And while the
day was coming on,
Paul besought *them*
all to take meat,
saying, This day
is the fourteenth day that ye
have tarried and
continued fasting,
having taken nothing.
34. Wherefore I pray you to
take *some* meat: for this is
for your health: for there
shall not an hair fall from
the head of
any of you.
35. And when he had thus spoken,
he took bread, and gave
thanks to God
in presence of them all:
and when he had broken *i t*, he
began to eat.
36. Then were they all of
good cheer, and they also
took *some* meat.
37. And we were in all in the ship two
hundred threescore and
sixteen souls.
38. And when they had
eaten enough,
they lightened the ship, and
cast out the wheat into the sea.
39. And when it was day,
they knew not the land: but
they discovered a certain
creek with a shore,
into the
which they were minded,

if it were possible,
to thrust in
the ship.
40. **And** when they had
taken up the anchors,
they committed *themselves*
unto the sea, and loosed the
rudder bands, and hoised up the
mainsail to the wind, and made
toward shore.
41. **And** falling into a place where
two seas met,
they ran the ship
aground; and the forepart
stuck fast,
and remained unmoveable,
but the hinder
part was broken
with the violence of the waves.
42. **And the soldiers'**
counsel was to kill the
prisoners, lest any of them
should swim out, and escape.
43. **But the centurion,**
willing to save Paul,
kept them from *their*
purpose; and commanded
that they which could swim
should cast *themselves* first *into*
the sea , and
get to land:
44. **And the rest,** some
on boards, and some on
broken pieces of the ship.
And so it came to pass, that they
escaped all safe
to land.

CHAPTER 28

1. **And** when they were escaped,
then they knew that
the island was
called Melita.
2. **And the barbarous**
people shewed us no little
kindness: for they
kindled a fire, and
received us every one,
because of the present
rain, and because of the
cold.
3. **And when Paul** had
gathered a bundle of
sticks, and laid *them* on the
fire, there came a viper
out of the heat,
and fastened on his hand.
4. **And when the barbarians**
saw the *venomous* beast
hang on his hand, they
said among themselves, No doubt
this man is a murderer,
whom, though he hath
escaped the sea, yet
vengeance suffereth
not to live.
5. **And he shook off the**
beast into the fire,
and felt no harm.
6. **Howbeit they looked** when
he should have swollen, or fallen down
dead suddenly: but after they had
looked a great while,
and saw no harm come to
him, they changed their minds,
and said that he was
a god.
7. In the same quarters were
possessions of
the chief man of the island,
whose name was Publius;
who received us, and
lodged us three days
courteously.
8. **And** it came to pass,
that the father of Publius
lay sick of a fever and of a
bloody flux: to whom Paul
entered in, and prayed,
and laid his
hands on him,
and healed him.
9. **So** when this was done,
others also,
which had diseases
in the island,
came, and were healed:
10. Who also honoured us with many
honours; and when we departed, they
laded *us* with such things as
were necessary.
11. **And after three months**
we departed in a ship of
Alexandria, which had wintered in the
isle, whose sign was
Castor and Pollux.

12. **And landing at**
Syracuse, we tarried *there*
three days.
13. **And from thence**
we fetched a compass, and
came to Rhegium: and after
one day the south wind blew,
and we came the
next day
to Puteoli:
14. **Where we found**
brethren, and were
desired to tarry with them
seven days: and so we
went toward Rome.
15. **And** from thence,
when the brethren heard of
us, they came to meet us
as far as Appii forum,
and The three taverns: whom when
Paul saw, he thanked God,
and took courage.
16. **And when we came to**
Rome, the centurion
delivered the prisoners
to the captain of the guard: but
Paul was suffered
to dwell by himself with a
soldier that kept him.
17. **And** it came to pass, that
after three days Paul
called the chief of the Jews
together: and
when they were come together, he
said unto them,
Men *and* brethren,
though I have committed
nothing against the people,
or customs of our fathers,
yet was I delivered
prisoner from Jerusalem
into the hands
of the Romans.
18. **Who,** when they
had examined me,
would have let *me* go,
because there was no cause
of death in me.
19. **But** when
the Jews spake against *it*, I
was constrained to appeal
unto Caesar; not that I had
ought to accuse my nation of.

20. **For this cause**
therefore have
I called for you,
to see *you* , and to speak with *you* :
because that
for the hope of Israel I am
bound with this chain.
21. **And they said** unto him,
We neither received letters
out of Judaea concerning thee,
neither any of the brethren
that came shewed or
spake any harm of thee.
22. **But we desire to hear**
of thee
what thou thinkest: for as
concerning this sect, we know that
every where it is spoken against.
23. **And** when they had
appointed him a day,
there came many to him into
his lodging; to whom he
expounded and
testified the kingdom of
God, persuading them
concerning Jesus, both out
of the law of Moses, and
out of
the prophets, from
morning till evening.
24. **And some believed**
the things which were spoken,
and some
believed not.
25. **And** when they agreed not
among themselves,
they departed, after that
Paul had spoken one word,
Well spake the Holy Ghost
by Esaias the prophet
unto our fathers,
26. **Saying, Go unto this**
people, and say, Hearing
ye shall hear, and shall not
understand; and seeing ye shall
see, and not perceive:
27. **For the heart of this**
people is waxed gross,
and their ears are dull
of hearing, and their eyes have
they closed; lest they should see with
their eyes, and hear with *their* ears,
and understand with *their* heart,

and should be converted,
and I should heal them.
28. **Be it known therefore**
unto you,
that the salvation of God is
sent unto the Gentiles,
and *that* they will hear it.
29. **And when he had said**
these words, the Jews
departed, and had great
reasoning among themselves.

30. **And Paul dwelt two** whole
years in his own hired
house, and received
all that came in unto him,
31. **Preaching the kingdom**
of God,
and teaching
those things which concern
the Lord Jesus Christ, with
all confidence,
no man forbidding him.

THE EPISTLE TO THE ROMANS

BACKGROUND INFORMATION

Author – Paul, an Apostle.
Date Written – probably **between 58** and **60** A.D.

Number of:
Verses - 433
Chapters - 16
Total Words - 9,447
Scan Words - 4,700
Scan Words represent 49 % of Total Words.

Theme – the righteousness of God revealed and accomplished **in Jesus Christ** and how believers should live in light of God's righteousness.

OUTLINE OF THE EPISTLE

Prologue
Chapter 1—1:15

I. The righteousness of God revealed in the **judgment of sin.** Chapters 1—3
II. The righteousness of God revealed in **justification by faith.** Chapters 3—4
III. The righteousness of God revealed in **salvation.** Chapters 5—8
IV. The righteousness of God revealed in **history.** Chapters 9—12
V. The righteousness of God revealed in **Christian living.** Chapters 12—16.

CHAPTER 1

1. **Paul,** a servant of Jesus Christ,
called *to be* an apostle,
separated unto the gospel of God,
2. (Which he had promised afore by
his prophets in the holy scriptures,)
3. **Concerning** his Son Jesus
Christ our Lord, which was made of
the seed of David
according to the flesh;
4. And declared *to be*
the Son of God with power,
according to the spirit of holiness,
by the resurrection
from the dead:
5. By whom we have received grace
and apostleship, for obedience to the
faith among all nations, for his name:
6. Among whom are ye also the called
of Jesus Christ:
7. **To all that be in Rome,**
beloved of God,
called *to be* saints: Grace
to you and peace
from God our Father,
and the Lord Jesus Christ.
8. **First, I thank my God**
through Jesus Christ for you all,
that your faith is spoken
of throughout the
whole world.
9. **For God is my witness,**
whom I serve with my spirit in the
gospel of his Son, that
without ceasing I make
mention of you always
in my prayers;
10. Making request, if by any means
now at length I might have a
prosperous journey by the will of God
to come unto you.
11. **For I long to see you, that**
I may impart unto you
some spiritual gift, to the end
ye may be established;
12. That is, that I may be comforted
together with you by the mutual faith
both of you and me.
13. Now I would not have you
ignorant, brethren, that oftentimes I
purposed to come unto you, (but was
let hitherto,) that I might have some
fruit among you also, even as among
other Gentiles.
14. **I am debtor both to the**
Greeks, and to the
Barbarians; both to the wise,
and to the unwise.
15. **So,** as much as in me is,
I am ready to preach the
gospel to you
that are at Rome also.
16. **For I am not ashamed of**
the gospel of Christ:
for it is the power of
God unto salvation to
every one that believeth; to
the Jew first, and also to the Greek.
17. **For therein is the**
righteousness of God
revealed from faith to faith:
as it is written, The just
shall live by faith.
18. **For the wrath of God is**
revealed from heaven
against all ungodliness and
unrighteousness of men,
who hold the truth in
unrighteousness;
19. Because that which may be known
of God is manifest in them; for God
hath shewed *it* unto them.
20. **For the invisible things**
of him from the creation
of the world
are clearly seen,
being understood
by the things that are
made, *even* his eternal
power and Godhead; so
that they are
without excuse:
21. **Because that, when they**
knew God, they glorified
***him* not**
as God, neither were thankful;
but became vain in their
imaginations, and their foolish heart
was darkened.
22. **Professing themselves**
to be wise, they
became fools,
23. **And changed the glory**
of the uncorruptible God
into an image made
like to corruptible man, and to birds,

and fourfooted beasts,
and creeping things.
24. **Wherefore God also**
gave them up to
uncleanness through the
lusts of their own hearts,
to dishonour their own
bodies between
themselves:
25. **Who changed the truth of**
God into a lie, and
worshipped and served
the creature more than the
Creator, who is blessed
for ever. Amen.
26. For this cause God gave them up
unto vile affections:
for even their women did
change the natural use into
that which is
against nature:
27. **And likewise also the**
men, leaving the
natural use of the woman,
burned in their
lust one toward another;
men with men working that which is
unseemly, and
receiving in themselves
that recompence of their
error which was meet.
28. **And** even as they did not like to
retain God in *their* knowledge,
God gave them over to a
reprobate mind, to do those
things which are not convenient;
29. **Being filled with all**
unrighteousness, fornication,
wickedness, covetousness,
maliciousness; full of envy, murder,
debate, deceit, malignity; whisperers,
30. Backbiters, haters of God,
despiteful, proud, boasters, inventors
of evil things, disobedient to parents,
31. Without understanding, covenant
breakers, without natural affection,
implacable, unmerciful:
32. **Who knowing the**
judgment of God, that they
which commit such things
are worthy of death, not
only do the same, but have
pleasure in them
that do them.

CHAPTER 2

1. **Therefore thou art**
inexcusable, O man,
whosoever thou art that judgest:
for wherein thou judgest
another, thou condemnest
thyself; for thou that judgest doest
the same things.
2. **But** we are sure that
the judgment of God is
according to truth against
them which commit such things.
3. **And thinkest thou**
this, O man,
that judgest them which do
such things, and doest the
same, that thou shalt
escape the judgment of God?
4. **Or despisest thou**
the riches of
his goodness
and forbearance and longsuffering;
not knowing that the
goodness of
God leadeth thee
to repentance?
5. **But after thy** hardness and
impenitent heart treasurest
up unto thyself
wrath against the day of
wrath and
revelation of the righteous
judgment of God;
6. **Who will render to every**
man according to
his deeds:
7. **To them who** by patient
continuance in well-doing
seek for glory and honour
and immortality,
eternal life:
8. **But unto them that** are
contentious, and
do not obey the truth,
but obey unrighteousness,
indignation and wrath,
9. **Tribulation and anguish,**
upon every soul of man that doeth
evil, of the Jew first,
and also of the Gentile;
10. But glory, honour, and peace, to

every man that worketh good, to the
Jew first, and also to the Gentile:
11. **For there is no respect of**
persons with God.
12. **For as many as have**
sinned without law shall also
perish without law:
and as many as have
sinned in the law shall be
judged by the law;
13. **(For not the hearers** of the
law *are* just before God,
but the doers of the law
shall be justified.
14. **For when the Gentiles,**
which have not the law, do
by nature the
things contained
in the law, these,
having not the law,
are a law unto themselves:
15. **Which shew the work of**
the law written in their
hearts, their conscience also
bearing witness, and *their* thoughts
the mean while accusing or else
excusing one another;)
16. **In the day when God**
shall judge the secrets of
men by Jesus Christ according
to my gospel.
17. **Behold, thou art called a**
Jew, and restest in the law, and
makest thy boast of God,
18. And knowest *his* will, and
approvest the things that are more
excellent, being instructed
out of the law;
19. And art confident that thou thyself
art a guide of the blind, a light of them
which are in darkness,
20. **An instructor** of the foolish, a
teacher of babes, which hast the form
of knowledge and of the truth
in the law.
21. **Thou therefore which**
teachest another, teachest
thou not thyself?
thou that preachest a man should not
steal, dost thou steal?
22. **Thou that sayest a man**
should not commit
adultery, dost thou commit
adultery? thou that abhorrest
idols, dost thou commit sacrilege?
23. Thou that makest thy boast of the
law, through breaking the law
dishonourest thou God?
24. For the name of God is
blasphemed among the Gentiles
through you, as it is written.
25. **For circumcision** verily
profiteth, if thou keep the
law: but if thou be a
breaker of the law,
thy circumcision is made
uncircumcision.
26. **Therefore if the**
uncircumcision keep the
righteousness of the
law, shall not his
uncircumcision be counted
for circumcision?
27. **And shall not**
uncircumcision which is by
nature, if it
fulfil the law, judge thee,
who by the letter and circumcision
dost transgress the law?
28. **For he is not a Jew,**
which is one outwardly;
neither *is that* circumcision, which is
outward in the flesh:
29. **But he *is* a Jew, which is**
one inwardly; and
circumcision *is* *that*
of the heart,
in the spirit, *and* not in the
letter; whose praise *is* not of
men, but of God.

CHAPTER 3

1. **What advantage then**
hath the Jew? or what profit *is*
there of circumcision?
2. **Much** every way: chiefly,
because that
unto them were committed
the oracles of God.
3. **For what if some did not**
believe? shall their
unbelief make the faith of
God without effect?
4. **God forbid:** yea,
let God be true, but every
man a liar; as it is written, That

thou mightest be justified in thy
sayings, and mightest overcome
when thou art judged.
5. **But if our unrighteousness
commend the righteous-
ness of God,** what shall we say?
***Is* God unrighteous who
taketh vengeance?**
(I speak as a man)
6. **God forbid: for then how
shall God judge the world?**
7. **For if the truth** of God hath more
**abounded through my lie
unto his glory; why** yet
am I also
judged as
a sinner?
8. And not *rather,* (as we be slander-
ously reported, and as some affirm
that we say,) Let us do evil, that good
may come? whose damnation is just.
9. **What then? are we better
than they? No,** in no wise: for
we have before
**proved both Jews and
Gentiles,** that they
are all
under sin;
10. **As it is written, There is
none righteous,** no, not one:
11. **There is none**
that understandeth, there is none
that seeketh after God.
12. They are all gone out of
the way, they are together
become unprofitable;
**there is none that
doeth good,** no, not one.
13. Their throat *is* an open sepulchre;
with their tongues they have used
deceit; the poison of asps *is* under
their lips:
14. Whose mouth *is* full of cursing
and bitterness:
15. Their feet *are* swift to shed blood:
16. Destruction and misery
are in their ways:
17. And the way of peace have they
not known:
18. There is no fear of God before
their eyes.
19. **Now we know that**
what things soever
the law saith, it saith
to them who are
**under the law: that every
mouth** may
be stopped, and all the world
**may become guilty
before God.**
20. **Therefore by the**
deeds of the
law there
shall no flesh be justified
in his sight:
**for by the law *is* the
knowledge of sin.**
21. **But now the righteousness of God without the law
is manifested,** being witnessed
by the law and the prophets;
22. Even the righteousness of God
***which is* by faith of Jesus
Christ unto all** and upon all them
**that believe: for there
is no difference:**
23. **For all have sinned, and
come short of the
glory of God;**
24. **Being justified** freely
by his grace through the
redemption that is
in Christ Jesus:
25. **Whom God hath set forth
to be a propitiation
through faith in his
blood, to** declare his
righteousness for
the remission of sins that are
past, through the forbearance of God;
26. To declare, *I say,* at this time his
righteousness: that he might be
just, and the justifier of him which
believeth in Jesus.
27. **Where is boasting then?
It is excluded.** By what law? of
works? Nay: but by the law of faith.
28. **Therefore we conclude
that a man is justified by
faith without the deeds of
the law.**
29. *Is he* the God of the Jews only? *is
he* not also of the Gentiles? Yes,
of the Gentiles also:
30. **Seeing *it is* one God,
which shall justify the**

■ **circumcision** by faith,
■ **and uncircumcision**
■ **through faith.**
■ 31. **Do we then make void**
■ **the law through faith? God**
■ **forbid:** yea,
■ **we establish the law.**

CHAPTER 4

■ 1. **What shall we say** then
■ **that Abraham** our father, as
pertaining to the flesh,
■ **hath found?**
■ 2. **For if Abraham were**
■ **justified by works, he hath**
■ ***whereof* to glory; but**
not before God.
3. For what saith the scripture?
■ **Abraham believed God,**
■ **and it was counted**
unto him for
■ **righteousness.**
■ 4. **Now to him that worketh**
■ **is the reward not** reckoned
■ **of grace,** but of debt.
■ 5. **But to him that worketh**
■ **not, but believeth on him**
■ **that justifieth the ungodly,**
■ **his faith is counted** for
■ **righteousness.**
■ 6. **Even** as
■ **David** also
■ **describeth** the blessedness of
the man, unto whom God imputeth
righteousness without works,
■ 7. ***Saying*, Blessed *are* they**
■ **whose iniquities are**
■ **forgiven,** and whose sins
are covered.
8. Blessed *is* the man to whom the
Lord will not impute sin.
■ 9. ***Cometh* this blessedness**
■ **then upon the circumcision**
■ ***only*, or upon the**
■ **uncircumcision also? for**
we say that
■ **faith was reckoned to**
■ **Abraham for**
■ **righteousness.**
■ 10. **How was it then**
■ **reckoned?** when he was in
circumcision, or in uncircumcision?
■ **Not in circumcision, but in**
■ **uncircumcision.**
11. And he received the sign of
circumcision, a seal of the
righteousness of the faith which *he*
had yet being uncircumcised:
■ **that he might be the**
■ **father of all** them
■ **that believe, though they be**
■ **not circumcised;**
that righteousness might be imputed
unto them also:
■ 12. **And the father of**
circumcision to
■ **them who** are not of the
circumcision only, but who also
■ **walk in** the steps of that
■ **faith** of our father
Abraham, which *he had*
■ **being *yet* uncircumcised.**
■ 13. **For the promise,** that he
should be the heir of the world,
■ ***was* not to Abraham,**
or to his seed,
■ **through the law, but**
■ **through the righteousness**
■ **of faith.**
■ 14. **For if they** which are
■ **of the law *be* heirs,**
■ **faith is** made
■ **void,** and the promise
made of none effect:
15. Because the law worketh wrath:
for where no law is, *there is* no
transgression.
■ 16. **Therefore *it is* of faith,**
■ **that *it might be* by grace;** to
the end the promise might be sure to
all the seed; not to that only which is
of the law, but to that also which is of
the faith of
■ **Abraham; who is the father**
■ **of us all,**
17. (As it is written, I have made thee
a father of many nations,)
■ **before** him whom he believed, *even*
■ **God, who quickeneth the**
■ **dead, and calleth those**
■ **things which be not as**
■ **though they were.**
■ 18. **Who against hope**
■ **believed** in hope,
■ **that he might become the**
■ **father of many nations,**

according to that which was spoken,
So shall thy seed be.
19. **And being not**
weak in faith, he
considered not his
own body now dead, when he was
about an hundred years old,
neither yet
the deadness of
Sarah's womb:
20. **He staggered not at the**
promise of God
through unbelief;
but was strong in faith,
giving glory to God;
21. And being fully
persuaded that, what he
had promised, he was
able also
to perform.
22. **And therefore it was**
imputed to him for
righteousness.
23. **Now it was not written for**
his sake alone,
that it was imputed to him;
24. **But for us also, to whom**
it shall be imputed, if we
believe on him that raised
up Jesus our Lord from the dead;
25. Who was delivered for our
offences, and was raised again
for our justification.

CHAPTER 5

1. **Therefore being justified**
by faith, we have peace
with God through
our Lord Jesus
Christ:
2. **By whom also we have**
access by faith into this grace
wherein we stand, and rejoice in hope
of the glory of God.
3. And not only *so*,
but we glory in tribulations
also: knowing that
tribulation worketh
patience;
4. **And patience,**
experience; and
experience, hope:
5. **And hope maketh not**
ashamed; because the
love of God is shed abroad
in our hearts by the Holy
Ghost which is given unto us.
6. **For when we were** yet
without strength, in due time
Christ died for the ungodly.
7. **For scarcely for a**
righteous man will one die:
yet peradventure for a good man
some would even dare to die.
8. **But God commendeth his**
love toward us,
in that, while we were yet
sinners, Christ died for us.
9. Much more then,
being now justified by his
blood, we shall be saved
from wrath through him.
10. **For if, when we were**
enemies, we were
reconciled to God
by the death of his Son,
much more, being
reconciled, we shall be
saved by his life.
11. And not only *so*, but
we also joy in God through
our Lord Jesus
Christ, by whom we have now
received the atonement.
12. **Wherefore, as by one**
man sin entered into the world,
and death by sin; and so
death passed upon all
men, for that all have sinned:
13. **(For until the law sin was**
in the world: but sin is not
imputed when there is
no law.)
14. **Nevertheless death**
reigned from Adam to
Moses, even over them that
had not sinned
after the similitude of
Adam's transgression, who
is the figure of him that was to come.
15. But not as the offence, so also *is*
the free gift. For if through the
offence of one many be dead, much
more the grace of God, and the gift by
grace, *which is* by one man, Jesus
Christ, hath abounded unto many.

16. And not as *it was* by one that
sinned, *so is* the gift: for the judgment
was by one to condemnation, but the
free gift *is* of many offences
unto justification.
17. For if by one man's offence death
reigned by one; much more they
which receive abundance of grace
and of the gift of righteousness shall
reign in life by one, Jesus Christ.)
18. **Therefore as by the
offence of one *judgment*
*came*** upon all men
to condemnation;
**even so by the righteous-
ness of one *the free gift*
*came*** upon all men unto
justification of life.
19. **For as by one man's
disobedience many were
made sinners, so by the
obedience of one shall
many be made righteous.**
20. **Moreover the law
entered, that the offence
might abound. But where
sin abounded, grace did
much more abound:**
21. That as sin hath reigned unto
death, even so might grace reign
through righteousness unto eternal
life by Jesus Christ our Lord.

CHAPTER 6

1. What shall we say then?
**Shall we continue in sin,
that grace may abound?**
2. **God forbid.**
How shall we, that are dead to sin, live
any longer therein?
3. **Know ye not, that so
many of us as were
baptized into Jesus Christ
were baptized into
his death?**
4. **Therefore we are buried
with him by baptism into
death: that** like
as Christ was raised
up from the dead by the glory of the
Father, even
**so we also should walk in
newness of life.**
5. For if we have been planted
together in the likeness of his death,
we shall be also *in the likeness* of *his*
resurrection:
6. Knowing this, that
**our old man is crucified
with *him*, that the body of
sin might be destroyed,
that** henceforth
we should not serve sin.
7. For he that is dead is freed from sin.
8. **Now if we be dead with
Christ,** we believe that
we shall also live with him:
9. **Knowing that Christ** being
raised from the dead
dieth no more; death hath no
more dominion over him.
10. **For** in that he died,
**he died unto sin once:
but** in that he liveth,
he liveth unto God.
11. **Likewise reckon** ye also
yourselves to be dead
indeed
**unto sin, but alive unto God
through Jesus** Christ our Lord.
12. **Let not sin** therefore
reign in your mortal body,
that ye should obey it in the lusts
thereof.
13. Neither yield ye your members *as*
instruments of unrighteousness unto
sin:
**but yield yourselves unto
God,** as those that are
alive from the dead,
**and your members *as*
instruments of
righteousness** unto God.
14. **For sin shall not have
dominion over you:** for ye are
not under the law, but under grace.
15. **What then? shall we sin,
because we are**
not under the law, but
under grace? God forbid.
16. **Know ye not, that** to whom
ye yield yourselves servants to obey,
**his servants ye are to
whom ye obey;** whether of sin
unto death, or of obedience
unto righteousness?

17. But God be thanked, that ye were
the servants of sin, but ye have
obeyed from the heart that form of
doctrine which was delivered you.
18. **Being then made free**
from sin, ye became the
servants of righteousness.
19. I speak after the manner of men
because of the infirmity of your
flesh: for
as ye have yielded
your members servants
to uncleanness
and to iniquity unto iniquity;
even so now yield
your members servants
to righteousness
unto holiness.
20. For when ye were the servants of
sin, ye were free from righteousness.
21. What fruit had ye then in those
things whereof ye are now ashamed?
for the end of those things *is* death.
22. **But now** being made
free from sin, and become
servants to God, ye have
your fruit unto holiness,
and the end
everlasting life.
23. **For the wages of sin *is***
death; but the gift of God *is*
eternal life through
Jesus Christ our Lord.

CHAPTER 7

1. **Know ye not,** brethren, (for I
speak to them that know the law,) how
that the law hath dominion
over a man as long
as he liveth?
2. **For the woman**
which hath an husband
is bound by the law to *her*
husband so long as he
liveth; but if the husband be
dead, she is loosed from the
law of *her* husband.
3. So then if, while *her* husband liveth,
she be married to another man, she
shall be called an adulteress: but if
her husband be dead, she is free
from that law; so that she is no
adulteress, though she be married to
another man.
4. Wherefore, my brethren,
ye also are become dead
to the law by the body of
Christ; that ye should be
married to another, *even*
to him who is raised
from the dead,
that we should bring forth
fruit unto God.
5. For when we were in the flesh, the
motions of sins, which were by the
law, did work in our members to bring
forth fruit unto death.
6. **But now we are delivered**
from the law, that being dead
wherein we were held;
that we should serve in
newness of spirit,
and not *in* the oldness of the letter.
7. What shall we say then?
***Is* the law sin?** God forbid.
Nay, I had not known sin,
but by the law: for I had not
known lust, except the law had said,
Thou shalt not covet.
8. **But sin,** taking occasion
by the commandment,
wrought in me all manner of
concupiscence.
For without the law sin *was* dead.
9. **For I was alive without the**
law once: but when the
commandment came, sin
revived, and I died.
10. **And the commandment,**
which *was ordained* to life,
I found *to be* unto death.
11. **For sin,** taking occasion
by the commandment,
deceived me, and by it
slew *me*.
12. **Wherefore the law *is***
holy, and the commandment
holy, and just,
and good.
13. Was then that which is good made
death unto me? God forbid. But sin,
that it might appear sin, working death
in me by that which is good; that sin
by the commandment might become
exceeding sinful.
14. **For** we know that

the law is spiritual: but I am
carnal, sold under sin.
15. For that which I do I
allow not: for what I would,
that do I not; but what I
hate, that do I.
16. If then I do that which I would not,
I consent unto the law that *it is* good.
17. Now then it is no more I that do it,
but sin that dwelleth in me.
18. For I know that in me (that is,
in my flesh,) dwelleth no
good thing:
for to will is present with me; but
how to perform that which
is good I find not.
19. For the good that I would
I do not: but the evil
which I would not, that
I do.
20. Now if I do that I would
not, it is no more I that do it,
but sin that dwelleth in me.
21. I find then a law, that, when I
would do good, evil is present
with me.
22. For I delight in the law of
God after the inward man:
23. But I see another law
in my members,
warring against the law of
my mind, and bringing me into
captivity to the law of sin which is in
my members.
24. O wretched man that I
am! who shall deliver me
from the body of
this death?
25. I thank God through
Jesus Christ our Lord. So then
with the mind I myself serve the law of
God; but with the flesh the law of sin.

CHAPTER 8

1. *There is* therefore now no
condemnation to them
which are
in Christ Jesus,
who walk not after the
flesh, but after the Spirit.
2. For the law of the Spirit
of life in Christ Jesus
hath made me free
from the law of sin and
death.
3. For what the law could
not do, in that it was weak through
the flesh,
God sending his own Son
in the likeness of sinful
flesh, and for sin,
condemned sin in the flesh:
4. That the righteousness of
the law might be fulfilled in
us, who walk not after the flesh, but
after the Spirit.
5. For they that are after the flesh do
mind the things of the flesh; but
they that are after the Spirit the things
of the Spirit.
6. For to be carnally minded
is death; but to be spiritually minded *is* life and peace.
7. Because the carnal mind
is enmity against God:
for it is not subject to the law of God,
neither indeed can be.
8. So then they that are in the
flesh cannot please God.
9. But ye are not in the flesh, but
in the Spirit, if so be that the Spirit
of God dwell in you. Now if any man
have not the Spirit of Christ, he
is none of his.
10. And if Christ *be* in you,
the body *is* dead because
of sin; but the Spirit *is* life
because of righteousness.
11. But if the Spirit of him
that raised up Jesus
from the dead
dwell in you, he that raised
up Christ from the dead
shall also quicken your
mortal bodies by his Spirit
that dwelleth in you.
12. Therefore, brethren, we are
debtors, not to the flesh,
to live after the flesh.
13. For if ye live after the flesh, ye
shall die: but if ye through the Spirit do
mortify the deeds of the body,
ye shall live.
14. For as many as are led
by the Spirit of God, they
are the sons of God.

15. **For ye** have not received the
spirit of bondage again to fear; but ye
have received the Spirit of
adoption, whereby we cry,
Abba, Father.
16. **The Spirit itself beareth**
witness with our spirit, that
we are the children of God:
17. **And if children,** then heirs;
heirs of God, and joint-
heirs with Christ; if so be
that we suffer with *him*, that
we may be also
glorified together.
18. **For** I reckon that
the sufferings of this
present time *are* not worthy
***to be compared* with the**
glory which shall be
revealed in us.
19. **For** the earnest expectation of
the creature waiteth for the
manifestation of the sons
of God.
20. For the creature was made subject
to vanity, not willingly, but by reason
of him who hath subjected
the same in hope,
21. **Because the creature**
itself also shall be
delivered from the bondage of
corruption into the
glorious liberty
of the children of God.
22. **For we know that the**
whole creation groaneth
and travaileth in pain
together until now.
23. **And** not only *they*, but
ourselves also,
which have the first fruits of the Spirit,
even we ourselves
groan within ourselves,
waiting for the adoption, *to wit*,
the redemption of our
body.
24. **For we are saved by**
hope:
but hope that is seen is not hope: for
what a man seeth, why doth he yet
hope for?
25. **But if we hope for that we**
see not, *then* do we with
patience wait for *it*.
26. **Likewise the Spirit** also
helpeth our infirmities: for
we know not what we
should pray for as we ought:
but the Spirit itself maketh
intercession for us with
groanings which cannot be uttered.
27. **And** he that searcheth the hearts
knoweth what *is* the mind of
the Spirit, because he
maketh intercession
for the saints
according to *the will*
***of* God.**
28. **And we know that all**
things work together for
good to them that love
God, to them who are the
called according to
***his* purpose.**
29. **For whom he did**
foreknow, he also
did predestinate *to be*
conformed to the image of
his Son, that he might be the
firstborn among many brethren.
30. Moreover whom he did
predestinate,
them he also called:
and whom he called,
them he also justified:
and whom he justified,
them he also glorified.
31. What shall we then say to
these things?
If God *be* for us, who *can*
***be* against us?**
32. **He that spared not his**
own Son, but delivered him up
for us all, how
shall he not with him also
freely give us all things?
33. **Who shall lay any thing**
to the charge of God's
elect? It *is* God
that justifieth.
34. Who *is* he that condemneth?
***It is* Christ that died,**
yea rather,
that is risen again, who is even at
the right hand of God,
who also maketh

intercession for us.

35. **Who shall separate us from the love of Christ? *shall* tribulation,** or distress, or persecution, or famine, or nakedness, or peril, **or sword?**

36. **As it is written, For thy sake we are killed all the day long;** we are accounted as sheep for the slaughter.

37. **Nay, in all these things we are more than conquerors through him that loved us.**

38. **For I am persuaded, that neither death, nor life, nor angels,** nor principalities, nor powers, nor things present, nor things to come,

39. Nor height, nor depth, **nor any other creature, shall** be able to **separate us from the love of God,** which is **in Christ** Jesus our Lord.

CHAPTER 9

1. **I say the truth in Christ,** I lie not, my conscience also bearing me witness in the Holy Ghost,

2. **That I have** great heaviness and continual **sorrow in my heart.**

3. **For I could wish that myself were accursed from Christ for my brethren,** my kinsmen according to the flesh:

4. **Who are Israelites;** to whom *pertaineth* the adoption, and the glory, and the covenants, and the giving of the law, and the service *of God*, and the promises;

5. Whose *are* the fathers, **and of whom as concerning the flesh Christ *came*,** who is over all, God blessed for ever. Amen.

6. **Not as though the word** of God **hath** taken **none effect. For they *are* not all Israel, which are of Israel:**

7. **Neither, because they are** the seed **of Abraham, *are they* all children:** but, In Isaac shall thy seed be called.

8. **That is, They** which are the children **of the flesh,** these ***are* not the children of God: but the children of the promise are counted** for the seed.

9. **For this *is* the word of promise,** At this time will I come, and **Sarah shall have a son.**

10. **And** not only *this*; but when **Rebecca also had conceived by** one, *even* by our father **Isaac;**

11. **(For *the children* being not yet born, neither having done any good or evil, that the purpose of God** according to election **might stand, not of works, but of him that calleth;)**

12. **It was said unto her, The elder shall serve the younger.**

13. **As it is written, Jacob have I loved, but Esau have I hated.**

14. **What shall we say then? *Is there* unrighteousness with God?** God forbid.

15. **For he saith to Moses, I will have mercy on whom I will** have mercy, **and I will have compassion on whom I will** have compassion.

16. **So then *it is* not of him that willeth,** nor of him that runneth, **but of God** that sheweth mercy.

17. For the scripture saith unto Pharaoh, Even for this same purpose have I raised thee up, that I might shew my power in thee, and that my name might be declared throughout all

the earth.
18. **Therefore hath he mercy on whom he will** *have mercy*, **and whom he will he hardeneth.**
19. **Thou wilt say then unto me, Why doth he yet find fault? For who hath resisted his will?**
20. Nay but, O man, **who art thou that repliest against God? Shall the thing formed say to him that formed** ***it*****, Why hast thou made me thus?**
21. **Hath not the potter power over the clay,** of the same lump to make one vessel unto honour, and another unto dishonour?
22. *What* if God, willing to shew *his* wrath, and to make his power known, endured with much longsuffering the vessels of wrath fitted to destruction:
23. And that he might make known the riches of his glory on the vessels of mercy, which he had afore prepared unto glory,
24. Even us, whom he hath called, not of the Jews only, but also of the Gentiles?
25. **As he saith also in Osee, I will call them my people, which were not my people;** and her beloved, which was not beloved.
26. And it shall come to pass, *that* in the place where it was said unto them, Ye *are* not my people; there shall they be called the children of the living God.
27. Esaias also crieth concerning Israel, Though the number of the children of Israel be as the sand of the sea, a remnant shall be saved:
28. For he will finish the work, and cut *it* short in righteousness: because a short work will the Lord make upon the earth.
29. And as Esaias said before, Except the Lord of Sabaoth had left us a seed, we had been as Sodoma, and been made like unto Gomorrha.
30. **What shall we say then? That the Gentiles, which followed not after righteousness, have attained** to righteousness, even **the righteousness** which is **of faith.**
31. **But Israel, which followed after the law of righteousness, hath not attained** to the law of **righteousness.**
32. **Wherefore? Because** ***they sought it*** **not by faith, but** as it were **by the works of the law.** For they stumbled at that stumblingstone;
33. As it is written, Behold, I lay in Sion a stumblingstone and rock of offence: and whosoever believeth on him shall not be ashamed.

CHAPTER 10

1. **Brethren, my heart's desire** and prayer to God **for Israel is, that they might be saved.**
2. **For** I bear them record that **they have a zeal of God, but not according to knowledge.**
3. **For they being ignorant of God's righteousness, and going about to establish their own righteousness, have not submitted** themselves **unto the righteousness of God.**
4. **For Christ** ***is*** **the end of the law for righteousness to every one that believeth.**
5. **For Moses describeth the righteousness** which is **of the law,** That the man which doeth those things shall live by them.
6. **But the righteousness** which is **of faith speaketh on this wise,** Say not in thine heart, Who shall ascend into heaven? (that is, to bring Christ down *from above:*)
7. Or, Who shall descend into the

deep? (that is, to bring up Christ
again from the dead.)
8. But what saith it? The word is nigh
thee, *even* in thy mouth, and in
thy heart: that is, the word of faith,
which we preach;
9. **That if thou shalt confess**
with thy mouth the Lord
Jesus, and shalt believe in
thine heart that God hath
raised him from the dead,
thou shalt be saved.
10. **For with the heart man**
believeth unto
righteousness; and with the
mouth confession is made
unto salvation.
11. **For the scripture saith,**
Whosoever believeth on
him shall not be ashamed.
12. For there is no difference between
the Jew and the Greek: for the
same Lord over all is rich unto all that
call upon him.
13. **For whosoever shall call**
upon the name of the Lord
shall be saved.
14. **How then shall they call**
on him in
whom they have not
believed? and how shall
they believe in him of whom
they have not heard? and
how shall they
hear without a preacher?
15. **And how shall they**
preach, except they be
sent? as it is written,
How beautiful are the feet
of them that preach the
gospel of peace, and bring
glad tidings of good things!
16. But they have not all obeyed the
gospel. For Esaias saith, Lord, who
hath believed our report?
17. **So then faith *cometh* by**
hearing, and hearing by the
word of God.
18. But I say, Have they not heard?
Yes verily, their sound went into all
the earth, and their words unto the
ends of the world.
19. **But I say, Did not Israel**
know? First Moses saith,
I will provoke you to jealousy by *them*
that are no people, *and*
by a foolish nation I will
anger you.
20. **But Esaias** is very bold, and
saith, I was found of them
that sought me not;
I was made manifest unto them that
asked not after me.
21. **But to Israel he saith,** All
day long
I have stretched forth
my hands unto a
disobedient and gainsaying
people.

CHAPTER 11

1. **I say then, Hath God cast**
away his people? God
forbid. For I also am
an Israelite, of the seed of
Abraham, *of* the tribe of Benjamin.
2. **God hath not cast away**
his people which he foreknew.
Wot ye not what
the scripture saith of Elias?
how he maketh
intercession to God
against Israel saying,
3. **Lord, they have killed thy**
prophets, and digged down thine
altars; and I am left alone,
and they seek my life.
4. **But what saith** the answer of
God unto him?
I have reserved to myself
seven thousand men,
who have not bowed the knee to *the*
image of Baal.
5. **Even so then at this**
present time also there is a
remnant according
to the election of grace.
6. **And if by grace, then *is it***
no more of works: otherwise
grace is no more grace. But if *it be* of
works, then it is no more grace:
otherwise work is no more work.
7. **What then? Israel hath**
not obtained that which he
seeketh for;
but the election hath

obtained it, and the rest
were blinded.
8. (According as it is written, God hath
given them the spirit of slumber, eyes
that they should not see, and ears
that they should not hear;)
unto this day.
9. And David saith, Let their table be
made a snare, and a trap, and a
stumblingblock, and a recompence
unto them:
10. Let their eyes be darkened, that
they may not see, and bow down
their back alway.
11. **I say then, Have they**
stumbled that they should
fall? God forbid: but *rather*
through their fall salvation
***is come* unto the Gentiles,**
for to provoke them to jealousy.
12. Now if the fall of them *be* the riches
of the world, and the
diminishing of them the riches of the
Gentiles; how much more their
fulness?
13. **For** I speak to you Gentiles,
inasmuch
as I am the apostle of the
Gentiles, I magnify mine
office:
14. **If by any means I may**
provoke to emulation *them*
***which are* my flesh, and**
might save some of them.
15. For if the casting away of them *be*
the reconciling of the world,
what *shall* the receiving *of them be*, but
life from the dead?
16. **For if the firstfruit *be***
holy, the lump *is* also
***holy*: and if the**
root *be* holy, so *are*
the branches.
17. **And if some** of the
branches be broken off,
and thou, being a wild
olive tree, wert grafted in
among them, and with them
partakest of the root
and fatness of the olive tree;
18. **Boast not against the**
branches. But if thou boast,
thou bearest not the root,
but the root thee.
19. **Thou wilt say** then,
The branches were
broken off,
that I might be
grafted in.
20. **Well; because of**
unbelief they were
broken off,
and thou standest by
faith. Be not highminded,
but fear:
21. **For if God spared not the**
natural branches, *take*
***heed* lest he also**
spare not thee.
22. **Behold therefore the**
goodness and severity of
God: on them which fell,
severity; but toward thee,
goodness, if thou continue in *his*
goodness: otherwise thou
also shalt be cut off.
23. **And they also, if they**
abide not still
in unbelief, shall be grafted
in: for God is able to graft them in
again.
24. For if thou wert cut out of the olive
tree which is wild by
nature, and wert grafted contrary to
nature into a good olive tree: how
much more shall these, which be the
natural *branches*, be grafted into their
own olive tree?
25. **For** I would not, brethren, that ye
should be ignorant of this mystery,
lest ye should be wise in your own
conceits; that
blindness in part is
happened to Israel, until
the fulness of the Gentiles
be come in.
26. **And so all Israel shall**
be saved: as it is written,
There shall come out of Sion the
Deliverer, and shall turn away
ungodliness from Jacob:
27. **For this *is* my covenant**
unto them, when
I shall take away their sins.
28. **As concerning the**
gospel, *they are* enemies

for your sakes: but as
touching the election, *they*
***are* beloved for the**
father's sakes.
29. For the gifts and calling of God *are*
without repentance.
30. **For as ye** in times past have
not believed God, yet have now
obtained mercy through
their unbelief:
31. **Even so** have these also
now not believed, that
through your mercy
they also may obtain
mercy.
32. For God hath concluded them all in
unbelief, that he might have mercy
upon all.
33. **O the depth** of the riches both
of the wisdom and
knowledge of God!
how unsearchable *are* his
judgments, and his ways past
finding out!
34. **For who hath known the**
mind of the Lord? or who hath
been his counsellor?
35. Or who hath first given to him, and
it shall be recompensed unto him
again?
36. **For of him, and through**
him, and to him, *are* all
things: to whom *be* glory for ever.
Amen.

CHAPTER 12

1. **I beseech you**
therefore, brethren,
by the mercies of God, that
ye present your bodies a
living sacrifice, holy,
acceptable unto God,
which is your reasonable service.
2. **And be not conformed to**
this world: but be ye
transformed by the
renewing of your mind, that
ye may prove what *is* that good, and
acceptable, and perfect, will of God.
3. **For I say,** through the grace
given unto me,
to every man
that is among you,
not to think *of himself* more
highly than he ought to think;
but to think soberly,
according as God hath dealt to every
man the measure of faith.
4. **For as we have many**
members in one body, and all
members have not the same office:
5. **So we, *being* many, are**
one body in Christ, and every
one members one of another.
6. **Having then gifts differing**
according to the grace that is
given to us, whether prophecy, *let*
us prophesy according to the
proportion of faith;
7. Or ministry, *let us wait* on *our*
ministering: or he that teacheth, on
teaching;
8. Or he that exhorteth, on
exhortation: he that giveth, *let him do*
it with simplicity; he that ruleth, with
diligence; he that sheweth mercy, with
cheerfulness.
9. ***Let* love be without**
dissimulation. Abhor that
which is evil; cleave
to that which is good.
10. ***Be* kindly affectioned**
one to another
with brotherly love; in honour
preferring one another;
11. **Not slothful in business;**
fervent in spirit;
serving the Lord;
12. **Rejoicing in hope;**
patient in tribulation;
continuing instant
in prayer;
13. **Distributing to the**
necessity of saints;
given to hospitality.
14. **Bless them which**
persecute you:
bless, and curse not.
15. **Rejoice with them that do**
rejoice, and weep with
them that weep.
16. *Be* of the same mind
one toward another.
Mind not high things, but
condescend to men of low
estate. Be not wise in your

own conceits.
17. **Recompense to no man**
evil for evil. Provide things
honest in the sight of all men.
18. **If it be possible,**
as much as lieth in you,
live peaceably with
all men.
19. **Dearly beloved, avenge**
not yourselves,
but *rather* give place unto wrath:
for it is written, Vengeance
***is* mine;** I will repay,
saith the Lord.
20. **Therefore if thine enemy**
hunger, feed him;
if he thirst, give him drink: for
in so doing thou shalt heap
coals of fire on his head.
21. **Be not overcome of evil,**
but overcome evil
with good.

CHAPTER 13

1. **Let every soul be subject**
unto the higher powers. For
there is no power but
of God: the powers
that be are
ordained of God.
2. **Whosoever therefore**
resisteth the power,
resisteth the ordinance of
God: and they that resist
shall receive to themselves
damnation.
3. **For rulers are not a terror**
to good works, but to the
evil. Wilt thou then not be afraid of
the power? do that which is good, and
thou shalt have praise of the same:
4. **For he is the minister of**
God to thee for good. But if
thou do that which is
evil, be afraid; for he beareth
not the sword in vain:
for he is the minister of God,
a revenger to *execute*
wrath upon him that
doeth evil.
5. **Wherefore *ye* must needs**
be subject, not only for wrath,
but also for conscience sake.
6. For for this cause
pay ye tribute also: for they
are God's ministers,
attending continually upon
this very thing.
7. **Render therefore to all**
their dues: tribute to whom tribute
is due; custom to whom custom; fear
to whom fear; honour to whom honour.
8. **Owe no man any thing,**
but to love one another: for
he that loveth another hath
fulfilled the law.
9. For this, Thou shalt not commit
adultery, Thou shalt not kill, Thou
shalt not steal, Thou shalt not bear
false witness, Thou shalt not
covet; and
if *there be* any other
commandment, it is
briefly comprehended
in this saying, namely,
Thou shalt love thy
neighbour as thyself.
10. Love worketh no ill to his
neighbour: therefore love *is* the
fulfilling of the law.
11. And that, knowing the time, that
now *it is* high time to awake out of
sleep: for now is our salvation nearer
than when we believed.
12. The night is far spent,
the day is at hand:
let us therefore
cast off the works of
darkness, and let us
put on the armour of light.
13. **Let us walk honestly,**
as in the day; not in rioting and
drunkenness, not in chambering and
wantonness, not in strife
and envying.
14. **But put ye on the Lord**
Jesus Christ, and make not
provision for the flesh,
to *fulfil* the lusts *thereof*.

CHAPTER 14

1. **Him that is weak in the**
faith receive ye,
***but* not to** doubtful
disputations.
2. **For one believeth that he**

may eat all things: another,
who is weak, eateth herbs.
3. **Let not him that eateth**
despise him that eateth
not; and let not him
which eateth not judge him
that eateth: for God hath
received him.
4. **Who art thou that judgest**
another man's servant?
to his own master he standeth or
falleth. Yea, he shall be holden up: for
God is able to make him stand.
5. **One man esteemeth one**
day above another:
another esteemeth every
day *alike*. Let every
man be fully
persuaded in his
own mind.
6. He that regardeth the day,
regardeth *it* unto the Lord; and he that
regardeth not the day, to the Lord he
doth not regard *it*.
He that eateth, eateth to the
Lord, for he giveth God thanks;
and he that eateth not, to
the Lord he eateth not,
and giveth God thanks.
7. **For none of us liveth**
to himself,
and no man dieth
to himself.
8. For whether we live, we live unto the
Lord; and whether we die, we die unto
the Lord:
whether we live therefore,
or die, we are the Lord's.
9. **For to this end Christ both**
died, and rose, and revived,
that he might be Lord both
of the dead and living.
10. **But why dost thou judge**
thy brother? or why dost thou set
at nought thy brother?
for we shall all stand
before the judgment
seat of Christ.
11. For it is written,
***As* I live, saith the Lord,**
every knee shall bow to me,
and every tongue shall
confess to God.
12. **So then every one** of us
shall give account
of himself to God.
13. **Let us not therefore**
judge one another
any more: but judge this rather,
that no man put
a stumblingblock
or an occasion to fall
in *his* brother's way.
14. **I know,** and am persuaded
by the Lord Jesus, that
***there is* nothing unclean of**
itself: but to him that
esteemeth any thing to be
unclean, to him
***it is* unclean.**
15. **But if thy brother be**
grieved with *thy* meat,
now walkest thou not charitably.
Destroy not him with thy
meat, for whom Christ died.
16. **Let not then your good**
be evil spoken of:
17. **For the kingdom** of God
is not meat and drink; but
righteousness, and peace, and
joy in the Holy Ghost.
18. For he that in these things serveth
Christ *is* acceptable to God, and
approved of men.
19. **Let us therefore follow**
after the
things which make for
peace, and things
wherewith one may
edify another.
20. For meat destroy not
the work of God.
All things indeed *are* pure;
but *it is* evil for that man
who eateth with offence.
21. ***It is* good neither to eat**
flesh, nor to drink wine, nor
***any thing* whereby thy**
brother stumbleth,
or is offended, or is made weak.
22. Hast thou faith? have *it* to thyself
before God.
Happy *is* he that condem-
neth not himself in that thing
which he alloweth.
23. **And he that doubteth is**

damned if he eat,
because *he eateth* not of faith:
for whatsoever *is* not of
faith is sin.

CHAPTER 15

1. **We then that are strong**
ought to bear the infirmities of
the weak, and not to
please ourselves.
2. Let every one of us please *his*
neighbour for *his* good to edification.
3. **For even Christ pleased**
not himself; but, as it is written,
The reproaches of them that
reproached thee fell on me.
4. **For whatsoever things**
were written aforetime were
written for our learning, that
we through
patience and comfort of
the scriptures might
have hope.
5. Now the God of patience and
consolation grant you to be
likeminded one toward another
according to Christ Jesus:
6. **That ye may with one**
mind *and* one mouth glorify
God, even the Father of our Lord
Jesus Christ.
7. Wherefore receive ye one another,
as Christ also received us to the
glory of God.
8. **Now I say that Jesus**
Christ was a minister of the
circumcision for the truth of God,
to confirm the promises
***made* unto the fathers:**
9. **And that the Gentiles**
might glorify God for *his*
mercy; as it is written,
For this cause
I will confess to thee
among the Gentiles,
and sing unto thy name.
10. And again he saith, Rejoice, ye
Gentiles, with his people.
11. **And again, Praise the**
Lord, all ye Gentiles;
and laud him, all ye people.
12. **And again, Esaias saith,**
There shall be a root of
Jesse, and he that
shall rise to reign over the Gentiles;
in him shall the
Gentiles trust.
13. **Now the God of hope fill**
you with all joy and peace
in believing,
that ye may abound in hope,
through the power of
the Holy Ghost.
14. **And I myself** also
am persuaded
of you, my brethren,
that ye also are
full of goodness,
filled with all knowledge,
able also to admonish
one another.
15. **Nevertheless, brethren, I**
have written the more
boldly unto you in some sort, as
putting you in mind,
because of the grace that
is given to me of God,
16. **That I should be the**
minister of Jesus Christ to
the Gentiles,
ministering the gospel of God,
that the offering up of the Gentiles
might be acceptable, being sanctified
by the Holy Ghost.
17. **I have therefore whereof**
I may glory through Jesus
Christ in those things which pertain
to God.
18. **For I will not dare to**
speak of any of those
things which Christ hath not
wrought by me, to make the
Gentiles obedient,
by word and deed,
19. **Through mighty signs**
and wonders, by the power
of the Spirit of God; so
that from Jerusalem, and round about
unto Illyricum,
I have fully preached
the gospel of Christ.
20. Yea, so have I strived to preach
the gospel,
not where Christ was
named, lest I should build upon
another man's foundation:

21. **But as it is written, To
whom he was not spoken
of, they shall see:** and they that
have not heard shall understand.
22. **For which cause** also
**I have been much hindered
from coming to you.**
23. **But** now having no more place in
these parts, and
having a great desire
these many years
to come unto you;
24. **Whensoever I take my
journey into Spain, I will
come to you:** for I trust to see
you in my journey, and to be brought
on my way thitherward by you, if first I
be somewhat filled with your *company*.
25. **But now I go
unto Jerusalem**
to minister unto the saints.
26. **For it hath pleased them
of Macedonia and Achaia
to make a certain
contribution for the poor
saints** which are
at Jerusalem.
27. It hath pleased them verily; and
their debtors they are. For if the
Gentiles have been made partakers of
their spiritual things, their duty is
also to minister unto them in carnal
things.
28. When therefore I have performed
this, and have sealed to them this
fruit, I will come by you into Spain.
29. And I am sure that, when I come
unto you, I shall come in the fulness
of the blessing of the gospel of Christ.
30. **Now I beseech you,
brethren, for** the Lord Jesus
Christ's sake, and
for the love of the Spirit,
that ye strive together with me
**in *your* prayers to
God for me;**
31. **That I may be delivered
from them that do not
believe in Judaea; and
that my service** which *I have*
**for Jerusalem may be
accepted of the saints;**
32. That I may come unto you with joy
by the will of God, and may with you
be refreshed.
33. Now the God of peace *be* with you
all. Amen.

CHAPTER 16

1. I commend unto you Phoebe our
sister, which is a servant of the
church which is at Cenchrea:
2. That ye receive her in the Lord, as
becometh saints, and that ye
assist her in whatsoever business
she hath need of you: for she hath
been a succourer of many, and of
myself also.
3. Greet Priscilla and Aquila my
helpers in Christ Jesus:
4. Who have for my life laid down their
own necks: unto whom not only I
give thanks, but also all the churches
of the Gentiles.
5. Likewise *greet* the church that is in
their house. Salute my well-beloved
Epaenetus, who is the firstfruits of
Achaia unto Christ.
6. Greet Mary, who bestowed much
labour on us.
7. Salute Andronicus and Junia, my
kinsmen, and my fellow-prisoners,
who are of note among the apostles,
who also were in Christ before me.
8. Greet Amplias my beloved
in the Lord.
9. Salute Urbane, our helper in Christ,
and Stachys my beloved.
10. Salute Apelles approved in Christ.
Salute them which are of Aristobulus'
household.
11. Salute Herodion my kinsman.
Greet them that be of the *household* of
Narcissus, which are in the Lord.
12. Salute Tryphena and Tryphosa,
who labour in the Lord. Salute the
beloved Persis, which laboured much
in the Lord.
13. Salute Rufus chosen in the Lord,
and his mother and mine.
14. Salute Asyncritus, Phlegon,
Hermas, Patrobas, Hermes, and the
brethren which are with them.
15. Salute Philologus, and Julia,
Nereus, and his sister, and Olympas,
and all the saints which are with them.

16. **Salute one another with**
an holy kiss. The churches of
Christ salute you.
17. **Now I beseech you,**
brethren, mark them which
cause divisions
and offences contrary to the doctrine
which ye have learned;
and avoid them.
18. **For they** that are such
serve not our Lord
Jesus Christ,
but their own belly; and
by good words and fair speeches
deceive the hearts
of the simple.
19. For your obedience is come
abroad unto all *men*. I am glad
therefore on your behalf: but yet
I would have you wise unto
that which is good,
and simple concerning evil.
20. **And the God of peace**
shall bruise Satan under
your feet shortly.
The grace of our Lord Jesus Christ *be*
with you. Amen.
21. Timotheus my workfellow, and
Lucius, and Jason, and Sosipater, my
kinsmen, salute you.
22. I Tertius, who wrote *this* epistle,
salute you in the Lord.
23. Gaius mine host, and of the whole
church, saluteth you. Erastus the
chamberlain of the city saluteth you,
and Quartus a brother.
24. The grace of our Lord Jesus Christ
be with you all. Amen.
25. **Now to him that is of**
power to stablish you
according to my gospel, and the
preaching of Jesus
Christ, according to the
revelation of the mystery,
which was kept
secret since the
world began,
26. **But now is made**
manifest, and
by the scriptures
of the prophets,
according to the
commandment of
the everlasting
God, made known to all nations
for the obedience of faith:
27. **To God only wise, *be***
glory through Jesus Christ
for ever.
Amen.

THE EPISTLE TO THE ROMANS

The bridge between the Gospels, the Acts, and the New Testament

Paul's Epistle to the **Romans is** recognized as **one of the great masterpieces of literature,** both sacred **and** secular. Addressed to Christians living in Rome – the city which was the center of the ancient world – Romans **is the only book in the New Testament,** with the possible exception of Hebrews, **which was written as a Theological Treatise** rather than an encouraging or correcting letter.

In Romans, Paul forcefully **presents the entire scope of Christian doctrine and** provides an authoritative theology as well as expresses the universality of the Gospel. Romans **gives a comprehensive interpretation of the Incarnation and the ministry of Christ, showing** with convincing logic and supported by Old Testament scriptures, **that God has made a radical breakthrough** into human history **in the life, death, and resurrection of His Son. The** dilemma of the **human condition, sinfulness, is met with** a profound solution – **the righteousness of God made real** for the individual **by faith.** Many of the great revivals began with a study of Romans.

Augustine, Luther and Wesley, credit Romans as the source from which they gained an understanding of the Gospel. Christian theology has never had a higher expression than presented by Paul in Romans under the inspiration of the Holy Spirit.

The Epistle has another significance for the student of the Bible. **It interprets the life of Jesus as seen in the Gospels, and** finally, it **forms a bridge between the Acts and the rest of the New Testament.**

THE FIRST EPISTLE TO THE CORINTHIANS

BACKGROUND INFORMATION

Author – Paul, an Apostle.
Date Written – probably **between 55** and **60** A.D.

Number of:
Verses - 437
Chapters - 16
Total Words - 9,489
Scan Words - 4,543
Scan Words represent 47 % of Total Words.

Theme – written to reveal the new life believers have in Christ and **how believers should conduct themselves individually and as members of the Church.**

OUTLINE OF THE EPISTLE

I. Paul denounces factions and stresses **the need for Church discipline.** Chapters 1—6

II. Paul answers questions **concerning marriage and** the Christian's **influence upon others.** Chapters 6—10

III. Paul contrasts **disorderly worship** with **the way of love and** explains **the** meaning of the **resurrection.** Chapter 11—16

CHAPTER 1

1. **Paul** called *to be* an apostle of
Jesus Christ through the will
of God,
and Sosthenes *our* brother,
2. **Unto the church of God**
which is
at Corinth, to them that are
sanctified in Christ Jesus, called *to be*
saints, with all that in every place call
upon the name of Jesus Christ our
Lord, both theirs and ours:
3. **Grace** ***be*** **unto you,** and
peace, from God our Father, and *from*
the Lord Jesus Christ.
4. **I thank** my
God always on your behalf,
for the grace of God which is
given you by Jesus Christ;
5. **That in every thing ye are**
enriched by him, in all
utterance, and *in* all knowledge;
6. Even as the testimony of Christ
was confirmed in you:
7. **So that ye come behind in**
no gift; waiting for the
coming of our Lord Jesus
Christ:
8. **Who shall also confirm**
you unto the end,
that ye may be **blameless**
in the day of our Lord Jesus Christ.
9. God *is* faithful, by whom ye were
called unto the fellowship of his Son
Jesus Christ our Lord.
10. **Now I beseech you,**
brethren,
by the name of
our Lord Jesus Christ, that ye all
speak the same thing, and
that **there be no divisions**
among you; but *that* ye be
perfectly joined together in the same
mind and in the same judgment.
11. **For it hath been**
declared unto me of you, my
brethren, by them *which are of the*
house of Chloe,
that there are contentions
among you.
12. Now this I say, that
every one of you saith, I am
of Paul; and
I of Apollos; and
I of Cephas; and I of Christ.
13. **Is Christ divided? was**
Paul crucified for you? or
were ye baptized in the
name of Paul?
14. **I thank God that I**
baptized none of you, but
Crispus and Gaius;
15. **Lest any should say**
that I had
baptized in mine
own name.
16. And I baptized also the household
of Stephanas: besides, I know not
whether I baptized any other.
17. **For Christ sent me not to**
baptize, but to preach
the gospel:
not with wisdom of words,
lest the cross of Christ should
be made of none effect.
18. **For** the preaching of
the cross is to them that
perish foolishness; but
unto us which are saved it
is the power of God.
19. **For it is written, I will**
destroy the wisdom of the
wise, and will bring to nothing the
understanding of the prudent.
20. Where *is* the wise? where *is* the
scribe? where *is* the disputer
of this world?
hath not God made foolish
the wisdom of this world?
21. **For after**
that in the wisdom of God
the world by wisdom knew
not God, it pleased God by
the foolishness of
preaching to save them
that believe.
22. **For the Jews require a**
sign, and the Greeks
seek after
wisdom:
23. **But we preach Christ**
crucified, unto the Jews a
stumblingblock, and unto the
Greeks foolishness;
24. But unto them which are called,
both Jews and Greeks, Christ

the power of God, and the
wisdom of God.
25. **Because the foolishness**
of God is wiser than men;
and the weakness of God is
stronger than men.
26. For ye see your calling, brethren,
how that not many wise men after the
flesh, not many mighty, not many
noble, *are called:*
27. **But God hath chosen the**
foolish things of the world
to confound the wise;
and God hath chosen the weak things
of the world to confound the things
which are mighty;
28. **And base things** of the
world, and things which are despised,
hath God chosen, *yea,* and
things which are not, to bring to
nought things that are:
29. **That no flesh should**
glory in his presence.
30. **But** of him are ye
in Christ Jesus, who of
God is made unto us
wisdom, and
righteousness, and
sanctification, and
redemption:
31. That, according as it is written,
He that glorieth, let him
glory in the Lord.

CHAPTER 2

1. **And I,**
brethren, when I came to you,
came not with excellency
of speech or of
wisdom, declaring unto you the
testimony of God.
2. **For I determined not to**
know any thing among you,
save Jesus
Christ, and him crucified.
3. And I was with you in weakness,
and in fear, and in much trembling.
4. **And my speech**
and my preaching
***was* not** with enticing words
of man's wisdom, but in
demonstration of the Spirit
and of power:
5. **That your faith should**
not stand in the
wisdom of men,
but in the power of God.
6. Howbeit we speak wisdom among
them that are perfect: yet not the
wisdom of this world, nor of the
princes of this world,
that come to nought:
7. **But we speak the wisdom**
of God in a mystery, *even*
the hidden *wisdom,* which God
ordained before the world
unto our glory:
8. Which none of the princes of this
world knew: for had they known *it,*
they would not have crucified the Lord
of glory.
9. **But as it is written, Eye**
hath not seen, nor ear heard,
neither have entered into the heart
of man,
the things which God hath
prepared for them
that love him.
10. **But God hath revealed**
them unto us
by his Spirit: for the Spirit
searcheth all things, yea,
the deep things of God.
11. For what man knoweth the things
of a man, save the spirit of man which
is in him? even so the things of God
knoweth no man, but the Spirit
of God.
12. **Now we have received,**
not the spirit of the world, but
the spirit which is of God;
that we might know the
things that are freely given to us
of God.
13. **Which things** also we speak,
not in the words which man's wisdom
teacheth, but which
the Holy Ghost teacheth;
comparing spiritual things
with spiritual.
14. **But the natural man**
receiveth not the things of
the Spirit of God: for they are
foolishness unto him:
neither can he know *them,*
because they are

spiritually discerned.
15. **But he that is spiritual**
judgeth all things,
yet he himself is judged
of no man.
16. **For who hath known the**
mind of the Lord,
that he may instruct him?
But we have the mind
of Christ.

CHAPTER 3

1. **And I,** brethren, could not
speak unto you as unto
spiritual, but as unto carnal, *even*
as unto babes in Christ.
2. **I have fed you with milk,**
and not with meat: for hitherto
ye were not able *to bear it*,
neither yet now are ye able.
3. **For ye are yet carnal:**
for whereas
there is among you
envying, and
strife, and divisions,
are ye not carnal, and walk as men?
4. **For while one saith, I am**
of Paul; and another, I *am*
of Apollos; are ye
not carnal?
5. **Who then is Paul, and**
who *is*
Apollos, but ministers
by whom ye believed, even as the
Lord gave to every man?
6. **I have planted, Apollos**
watered; but God gave
the increase.
7. So then neither is he that planteth
any thing, neither he that watereth;
but God that giveth the increase.
8. **Now he that planteth and**
he that watereth are one:
and every man shall receive his own
reward according to his own labour.
9. **For we are labourers**
together with God:
ye are God's husbandry,
***ye are* God's building.**
10. According to the grace of God
which is given unto me, as a wise
masterbuilder,
I have laid the foundation,
and another buildeth thereon.
But let every man take heed
how he buildeth thereupon.
11. **For other foundation can**
no man lay than
that is laid, which is
Jesus Christ.
12. **Now if any man build**
upon this foundation gold,
silver, precious stones,
wood, hay, stubble;
13. **Every man's work shall**
be made
manifest: for the day
shall declare it,
because it shall be revealed
by fire; and
the fire shall try every
man's work of what sort it is.
14. **If any man's work abide**
which he hath built thereupon,
he shall receive a reward.
15. **If any man's work shall**
be burned, he shall suffer
loss: but he himself shall
be saved; yet so as by fire.
16. **Know ye not that ye are**
the temple of God, and *that*
the Spirit of God
dwelleth in you?
17. **If any man defile the**
temple of God,
him shall God destroy:
for the temple of God is holy, which
temple ye are.
18. **Let no man deceive**
himself. If any man among you
seemeth to be wise in this world, let
him become a fool, that he
may be wise
19. **For the wisdom of this**
world is foolishness with
God. For it is written, He taketh the
wise in their own craftiness.
20. And again, The Lord knoweth the
thoughts of the wise,
that they are vain.
21. **Therefore let no man**
glory in men. For all things
are yours;
22. Whether Paul, or Apollos, or
Cephas, or the world, or life, or death,
or things present, or things to come;

all are yours;
23. **And ye are Christ's; and**
Christ *is* God's.

CHAPTER 4

1. **Let a man so account** of
us, as of the
ministers of Christ,
and stewards of the mysteries
of God.
2. **Moreover it is required in**
stewards, that a
man be found
faithful.
3. But with me
it is a very small thing
that I should
be judged of you, or
of man's judgment:
yea, I judge not mine own self.
4. **For** I know nothing by myself; yet
am I not hereby justified: but
he that judgeth me
is the Lord.
5. **Therefore judge nothing**
before the time,
until the Lord come, who both
will bring to light the hidden things of
darkness, and will make manifest the
counsels of the hearts: and then shall
every man have praise of God.
6. **And these things,**
brethren, I have in a figure
transferred to myself and *to*
Apollos for your sakes;
that ye might learn in us
not to think *of men*
above that which is written, that no
one of you be puffed up for one
against another.
7. For who maketh thee to differ *from*
another? and
what hast thou that thou didst not
receive? now if thou didst receive *it*,
why dost thou glory, as if thou hadst
not received *it*?
8. Now ye are full, now ye are rich,
ye have reigned as kings
without us: and I would to
God ye did reign,
that we also might reign with you.
9. **For I think that God hath**
set forth us
the apostles last,
as it were appointed to death: for we
are made a spectacle unto the world,
and to angels, and to men.
10. **We *are* fools for Christ's**
sake, but ye *are* wise in Christ; we
are weak, but ye *are* strong; ye *are*
honourable, but we *are* despised.
11. **Even unto this** present
hour we both
hunger, and
thirst, and are naked,
and are buffeted,
and have no certain
dwellingplace;
12. **And labour,** working
with our own hands:
being reviled, we bless; being
persecuted, we suffer it:
13. Being defamed, we entreat:
we are made as the filth of
the world, *and are* the offscouring
of all things unto this day.
14. **I write not these things to**
shame you, but as my
beloved sons
I warn *you*.
15. **For though ye have ten**
thousand instructors in
Christ, yet *have ye* not
many fathers:
for in Christ Jesus I have begotten
you through the gospel.
16. **Wherefore** I beseech you,
be ye
followers of me.
17. **For this cause have I**
sent unto you
Timotheus, who is my beloved
son, and faithful in the Lord,
who shall bring you into
remembrance of my ways
which be
in Christ, as I teach every where in
every church.
18. **Now some are puffed**
up, as though I would not
come to you.
19. **But I will come** to you shortly,
if the Lord will, and will know, not
the speech of them which are puffed
up, but the power.
20. For the kingdom of God *is* not in

word, but in power.
21. **What will ye? shall I**
come unto you
with a rod, or in love,
and *in* the spirit of meekness?

CHAPTER 5

1. **It is reported** commonly
***that there is* fornication**
among you, and
such fornication as is not so much as
named among the Gentiles,
that one should have his
father's wife.
2. **And ye** are puffed up, and
have not rather
mourned, that he that hath
done this deed might be
taken away from among you.
3. **For I** verily, as absent in body,
but present in spirit,
have judged already,
as though I were present, *concerning*
him that hath so
done this deed,
4. In the name of our Lord Jesus
Christ, when ye are gathered
together, and my spirit, with the power
of our Lord Jesus Christ,
5. **To deliver such an one**
unto Satan for the
destruction of the flesh,
that the spirit may be
saved in the day of the
Lord Jesus.
6. Your glorying *is* not good.
Know ye not that a little
leaven leaveneth
the whole lump?
7. **Purge out therefore the**
old leaven, that ye may be a new
lump, as ye are unleavened. For even
Christ our passover is
sacrificed for us:
8. **Therefore let us keep the**
feast, not with old leaven,
neither with the leaven of
malice and wickedness;
but with the unleavened *bread* of
sincerity and truth.
9. **I wrote unto you** in an epistle
not to company
with fornicators:
10. **Yet not altogether with**
the fornicators of this
world, or with the covetous,
or extortioners, or with idolaters;
for then must ye needs go
out of the world.
11. **But now I have written**
unto you
not to keep company, if
any man that is called a
brother be a fornicator,
or covetous, or an idolater, or a railer,
or a drunkard, or an extortioner;
with such an one
no not to eat.
12. For what have I to do to judge
them also that are without? do not ye
judge them that are within?
13. But them that are
without God judgeth.
Therefore put away from
among yourselves that
wicked person.

CHAPTER 6

1. **Dare any** of you, having a
matter against another,
go to law before the unjust,
and not before the saints?
2. **Do ye not know that the**
saints shall judge the
world? and
if the world shall be judged by you,
are ye unworthy to judge
the smallest matters?
3. **Know ye not that we shall**
judge angels? how much more
things that pertain to this life?
4. **If then ye have judgments**
of things pertaining to this life,
set them to judge who are
least esteemed
in the church.
5. I speak to your shame.
Is it so, that there
is not a wise man among
you? no, not one that shall be
able to judge between his
brethren?
6. **But brother goeth to law**
with brother, and that
before the unbelievers.
7. Now therefore there is utterly a fault

among you, because ye go to law one with another.
Why do ye
not rather take wrong? why
do ye
not rather *suffer yourselves to*
be defrauded?
8. Nay, ye do wrong, and defraud, and that *your* brethren.
9. **Know ye not that the**
unrighteous shall not
inherit the kingdom of God?
Be not deceived: neither
fornicators, nor
idolaters, nor
adulterers, nor
effeminate, nor
abusers of themselves
with mankind,
10. **Nor thieves,** nor
covetous, nor
drunkards, nor
revilers, nor extortioners,
shall inherit the kingdom
of God
11. **And such were some of**
you: but ye are washed,
but ye are sanctified,
but ye are justified in the
name of the Lord
Jesus, and by the Spirit
of our God.
12. **All things are lawful**
unto me,
but all things are not
expedient: all things are lawful for me, but I will not be brought under the power of any.
13. Meats for the belly, and the belly for meats: but God shall destroy both it and them. Now
the body ***is*** **not for**
fornication, but for the
Lord; and the Lord for the body.
14. **And God** hath both
raised up the Lord, and will
also raise up us
by his own power.
15. **Know ye not that your**
bodies are the members of
Christ? shall I then
take the members of Christ, and
make ***them*** **the members of**
an harlot? God forbid.
16. What? know ye not that he which is joined to an harlot is one body? for two, saith he, shall be one flesh.
17. But he that is joined unto the Lord is one spirit.
18. **Flee fornication.** Every sin that a man doeth is without the body; but he that committeth fornication sinneth against his own body.
19. **What? know ye not that**
your body is the temple of
the Holy Ghost
which is in you, which ye have of God,
and ye are not your own?
20. **For ye are bought with a**
price: therefore glorify God
in your body,
and in your spirit, which are God's.

CHAPTER 7

1. Now concerning the things whereof ye wrote unto me:
It is **good for a man not to**
touch a woman.
2. **Nevertheless,** ***to avoid***
fornication, let every man
have his own wife, and let
every woman have
her own husband.
3. **Let the husband render**
unto the wife
due benevolence: and
likewise also
the wife unto the husband.
4. **The wife hath not power of**
her own body,
but the husband: and
likewise also the husband
hath not power of his own
body, but the wife.
5. **Defraud ye not one the**
other, except
it be with consent for a time,
that ye may give
yourselves to fasting and
prayer; and come together again, that Satan tempt you not for your incontinency.
6. **But I speak this by**
permission, ***and*** **not of**
commandment.
7. **For I would that all men**

were even
as I myself. But every man
hath his proper gift of God,
one after this manner,
and another after that.
8. **I say therefore to the**
unmarried and widows, It
is good for them
if they abide even
as I.
9. **But if they cannot contain,**
let them marry:
for it is better to marry than to burn.
10. **And unto the married I**
command, *yet* not I, but the
Lord, Let not the wife depart
from *her* husband:
11. **But and if she depart, let**
her remain unmarried or be
reconciled to *her* husband: and
let not the husband put
away *his* wife.
12. But to the rest speak I,
not the Lord:
If any brother hath a wife
that believeth not, and she
be pleased to dwell with
him, let him not put
her away.
13. And the woman which hath an
husband that believeth not, and if he
be pleased to dwell with her, let her
not leave him.
14. **For the unbelieving**
husband is sanctified by
the wife, and the
unbelieving wife is sanctified
by the husband:
else were your children unclean;
but now are they holy.
15. **But if the unbelieving**
depart, let him depart. A
brother or a sister is not
under bondage in such
***cases*:** but God hath
called us to peace.
16. **For** what
knowest thou, O wife,
whether thou shalt save *thy*
husband? or how knowest thou,
O man, whether thou shalt save
***thy* wife?**
17. **But** as God hath distributed to
every man,
as the Lord hath called
every one, so let him walk.
And so ordain I in all churches.
18. **Is any man called being**
circumcised? let him not
become uncircumcised. Is
any called in
uncircumcision? let him not
be circumcised.
19. **Circumcision** is nothing,
and uncircumcision is
nothing, but the keeping of
the commandments
of God.
20. Let every man abide in the same
calling wherein he was called.
21. Art thou called *being* a servant?
care not for it: but if thou mayest be
made free, use *it* rather.
22. **For he that is called**
in the Lord,
***being* a servant, is the**
Lord's freeman: likewise
also
he that is called, *being*
free, is Christ's servant.
23. **Ye are bought with a**
price; be not ye the
servants of men.
24. Brethren, let every man, wherein
he is called, therein abide with God.
25. **Now concerning virgins I**
have no commandment of
the Lord: yet I give my
judgment, as one that hath
obtained mercy of the Lord
to be faithful.
26. **I suppose** therefore that this
is good for the present distress,
I say,
that *it is* good for a man so
to be.
27. Art thou bound unto a wife? seek
not to be loosed. Art thou loosed
from a wife? seek not a wife.
28. **But and if thou marry,**
thou hast not sinned; and if a
virgin marry, she hath not sinned.
Nevertheless such shall have trouble
in the flesh: but I spare you.
29. **But** this I say,
brethren, the time *is* short: it

■ **remaineth, that** both
■ **they that have wives be as**
■ **though they had none;**
30. And they that weep, as though
they wept not; and they that rejoice,
as though they rejoiced not; and they
that buy, as though they
possessed not;
31. And they that use this world, as
not abusing *it*: for the fashion of
this world passeth away.
32. But I would have you
without carefulness.
■ **He that is unmarried careth**
■ **for the things that belong**
■ **to the Lord,**
how he may please the Lord:
■ 33. **But he that is married**
■ **careth for the things that**
■ **are of the world,**
how he may please *his* wife.
■ 34. **There is difference *also***
■ **between a wife and a**
■ **virgin. The unmarried**
■ **woman careth for the**
■ **things of the Lord,** that she may
be holy both in body and in spirit:
■ **but she that is married**
■ **careth for the things**
■ **of the world,**
how she may please *her* husband.
35. And this I speak for your own
profit; not that I may cast a snare
upon you, but for that which is
comely, and that ye may attend upon
the Lord without distraction.
■ 36. **But if any man** think that he
■ **behaveth himself**
■ **uncomely toward his**
■ **virgin, if she pass the**
■ **flower of *her* age,**
and need so require,
■ **let him do what he will, he**
■ **sinneth not: let them marry.**
37. Nevertheless he that standeth
stedfast in his heart, having no
necessity, but hath power over his
own will, and hath so decreed in his
heart that he will keep his virgin,
doeth well.
■ 38. **So then he that giveth *her***
■ **in marriage doeth well; but**
■ **he that giveth *her* not**
in marriage
■ **doeth better.**
■ 39. **The wife** is bound by the law as
long as her husband liveth; but
■ **if her husband be dead,** she
■ **is at liberty to be married**
to whom she will; only
■ **in the Lord.**
■ 40. **But she is happier if**
■ **she so abide,**
after my judgment: and I think also
that I have the Spirit of God.

CHAPTER 8

1. Now as touching things offered
unto idols, we know that we all have
knowledge. Knowledge puffeth up, but
charity edifieth.
2. And if any man think that he
knoweth any thing, he knoweth
nothing yet as he ought to know.
3. But if any man love God, the same
is known of him.
■ 4. **As concerning** therefore the
■ **eating** of those
■ **things** that are
■ **offered** in sacrifice
■ **unto idols, we know** that
■ **an idol *is* nothing** in the world,
■ **and** that
■ ***there is* none other**
■ **God but one.**
5. For though there be that are called
gods, whether in heaven or in earth,
(as there be gods many,
and lords many,)
6. But to us *there is but* one God, the
Father, of whom *are* all things,
and we in him;
■ **and one Lord Jesus Christ,**
by whom *are* all things, and we by him.
■ 7. **Howbeit *there* is not in**
■ **every man that knowledge:**
■ **for some** with conscience of the
idol unto this hour
■ **eat *it* as a thing offered**
■ **unto an idol; and their**
■ **conscience** being weak
■ **is defiled.**
8. But meat commendeth
us not to God:
■ **for neither, if we eat, are we**
■ **the better; neither, if we eat**

not, are we the worse.
9. **But take heed lest**
by any means
this liberty of yours
become a stumblingblock
to them that are weak.
10. For if any man see thee which hast
knowledge sit at meat in the
idol's temple, shall not the conscience
of him which is weak be emboldened
to eat those things which are offered
to idols;
11. And through thy knowledge shall
the weak brother perish, for whom
Christ died?
12. But when ye sin so against the
brethren, and wound their weak
conscience, ye sin against Christ.
13. **Wherefore, if meat make**
my brother to offend, I will
eat no flesh
while the world standeth, lest I make
my brother to offend.

CHAPTER 9

1. **Am I not an apostle? am I**
not free? have I not seen
Jesus Christ our Lord?
are not ye my work in the Lord?
2. If I be not an apostle unto others,
yet doubtless I am to you: for the
seal of mine apostleship
are ye in the Lord.
3. **Mine answer to them that**
do examine me is this,
4. **Have we not power to eat**
and to drink?
5. **Have we not power to**
lead about a sister,
a wife, as well as other
apostles, and *as* the brethren of
the Lord, and Cephas?
6. Or I only and Barnabas,
have not we power to
forbear working?
7. Who goeth a warfare any time at his
own charges? who planteth a
vineyard, and eateth not of the fruit
thereof? or
who feedeth a flock, and
eateth not of the milk
of the flock?
8. Say I these things as a man? or
saith not the law the same also?
9. For it is written in the law of Moses,
Thou shalt not muzzle the mouth of
the ox that treadeth out the corn. Doth
God take care for oxen?
10. Or saith he *it* altogether
for our sakes?
For our sakes, no doubt,
***this* is written: that he that**
ploweth should plow in
hope; and
that he that thresheth in hope
should be partaker
of his hope.
11. **If we have sown** unto you
spiritual things, *is it* a great
thing if we shall reap your
carnal things?
12. If others be partakers of *this*
power over you, *are* not we rather?
Nevertheless we have not
used this power; but suffer
all things, lest we should
hinder the gospel of Christ.
13. **Do ye not know that they**
which minister about holy things
live *of the things* of the
temple? and they which wait at the
altar are partakers with the altar?
14. **Even so hath the Lord**
ordained that they which
preach the gospel
should live of the gospel.
15. **But I have used none of**
these things:
neither have I written these things,
that it should be so done unto me:
for *it were* better for me to
die, than that any man should
make my glorying void.
16. **For though I preach**
the gospel,
I have nothing to glory of:
for necessity is laid upon me; yea,
woe is unto me, if I preach
not the gospel!
17. For if I do this thing willingly, I
have a reward: but if against my
will, a dispensation *of the gospel* is
committed unto me.
18. **What is my reward then?**
***Verily* that, when I preach**
the gospel, I may make the gospel of

Christ without charge,
that I abuse not my power
in the gospel.
19. **For though I be free**
from all *men*,
yet have I made myself
servant unto all,
that I might gain the more.
20. **And unto the Jews I**
became as a Jew, that I
might gain the Jews;
to them that are under the law, as
under the law, that I might gain them
that are under the law;
21. **To them that are without**
law, as without law,
(being not without law to God, but
under the law to Christ,)
that I might gain them
that are without law.
22. To the weak became I as weak,
that I might gain the weak:
I am made all things to all
***men*, that I might by all**
means save some.
23. And this I do for the gospel's
sake, that I might be partaker thereof
with *you*.
24. **Know ye not that they**
which run in a race run all,
but one receiveth the prize?
So run, that ye may obtain.
25. And every man that striveth for
the mastery is temperate in all
things. Now they *do it* to obtain a
corruptible crown;
but we an incorruptible.
26. **I therefore** so
run, not as uncertainly; so
fight I, not as one that beateth the air:
27. **But I keep under my**
body, and bring *it* into
subjection: lest
that by any means,
when I have preached
to others,
I myself should be a
castaway.

CHAPTER 10

1. **Moreover, brethren, I**
would not that ye should
be ignorant, how that all our
fathers were under the cloud, and all
passed through the sea;
2. And were all baptized unto Moses in
the cloud and in the sea;
3. And did all eat the
same spiritual meat;
4. And did all drink the same spiritual
drink: for they drank of that
spiritual Rock that followed them: and
that Rock was Christ.
5. But with many of them God was not
well pleased: for they were
overthrown in the wilderness.
6. Now these things were our
examples, to the intent
we should not lust after evil
things, as they also lusted.
7. **Neither be ye idolaters,** as
were some of them; as it is written,
The people sat down to eat and drink,
and rose up to play.
8. **Neither let us commit**
fornication, as some of them
committed, and fell in one day three
and twenty thousand.
9. **Neither let us tempt**
Christ, as some of them also
tempted, and were
destroyed of serpents.
10. **Neither murmur ye,** as
some of them also murmured, and
were destroyed of the destroyer.
11. Now all these things happened
unto them for ensamples: and they
are written for our admonition, upon
whom the ends of the world are come.
12. **Wherefore let him that**
thinketh he standeth take
heed lest he fall.
13. **There hath no temptation**
taken you but such as is
common to man: but
God *is* faithful, who will not
suffer you to be tempted
above that ye are able;
but will with the temptation also
make a way to escape,
that ye may be able to bear *it*.
14. **Wherefore,**
my dearly beloved,
flee from idolatry.
15. I speak as to wise men;
judge ye what I say.

16. **The cup of blessing which we bless, is it not the communion of the blood of Christ? The bread** which we break, **is it not the communion of the body of Christ?**

17. **For we *being* many are** one bread, *and* **one body: for we are all partakers of that one bread.**

18. Behold Israel after the flesh: are not they which eat of the sacrifices partakers of the altar?

19. **What** say I then? that the idol is any thing, or that which is offered in sacrifice to idols is any thing?

20. But *I say*, that **the things which the Gentiles sacrifice, they sacrifice to devils,** and not to God: **and I would not that ye should have fellowship with devils.**

21. **Ye cannot drink the cup of the Lord, and** the cup **of devils:** ye cannot be partakers of the Lord's table, and of the table of devils.

22. Do we provoke the Lord to jealousy? are we stronger than he?

23. **All things are lawful for me, but all things are not expedient:** all things are lawful for me, but all things edify not.

24. **Let no man seek his own, but every man another's *wealth*.**

25. **Whatsoever is sold** in the shambles, ***that* eat, asking no question for conscience sake:**

26. **For the earth *is* the Lord's, and the fulness thereof.**

27. **If any** of them **that believe not bid you *to a feast*,** and ye be disposed to go; **whatsoever is set before you, eat, asking no question** for conscience sake.

28. **But if any man say** unto you, **This is offered** in sacrifice **unto idols, eat not for his sake** that shewed it, **and for conscience sake:** for the earth *is* the Lord's, and the fulness thereof:

29. Conscience, I say, not thine own, but of the other: for why is my liberty judged of another *man's* conscience?

30. For if I by grace be a partaker, why am I evil spoken of for that for which I give thanks?

31. **Whether therefore ye eat, or drink, or whatsoever ye do, do all to the glory of God.**

32. **Give none offence,** neither to the Jews, nor to the Gentiles, nor to the church of God:

33. **Even as I please all *men*** in all *things*, **not seeking mine own profit, but the *profit* of many, that they may be saved.**

CHAPTER 11

1. Be ye followers of me, even as I also *am* of Christ.

2. Now I praise you, brethren, that ye remember me in all things, and keep the ordinances, as I delivered *them* to you.

3. **But I would have you know, that the head of every man is Christ; and the head of the woman *is* the man; and the head of Christ *is* God.**

4. **Every man** praying or prophesying, **having *his* head covered, dishonoureth his head.**

5. **But every woman that prayeth** or prophesieth **with *her* head uncovered dishonoureth her head:** for that is even all one

as if she were shaven.
6. **For if the woman be not**
covered, let her also be
shorn: but if it be a shame for a
woman to be shorn or shaven, let her
be covered.
7. **For a man indeed ought**
not to cover *his* head,
forasmuch
as he is the image and glory
of God: but the woman is
the glory of the man.
8. **For** the
man is not of the
woman: but the
woman of the
man.
9. Neither was the man created for the
woman; but the woman for the man.
10. For this cause ought the woman to
have power on *her* head because
of the angels.
11. Nevertheless neither is the man
without the woman, neither the woman
without the man, in the Lord.
12. **For as the woman *is* of**
the man, even so *is* the man
also by the
woman; but all things
of God.
13. Judge in yourselves: is it comely
that a woman pray unto
God uncovered?
14. **Doth not even nature** itself
teach you, that, if a man
have long hair, it is a
shame unto him?
15. **But if a woman have long**
hair, it is a glory to her: for
her hair is given her for a covering.
16. But if any man seem to be
contentious, we have no such
custom, neither the churches of God.
17. **Now in this**
that I declare *unto you*
I praise *you* not, that ye
come together not for the
better, but for
the worse.
18. For first of all,
when ye come together in
the church, I hear that
there be divisions among
you; and I partly believe it.
19. **For there must be also**
heresies among you,
that they which are approved may be
made manifest among you.
20. **When ye come together**
therefore into one place,
***this* is not to eat the**
Lord's supper.
21. **For in eating every one**
taketh before *other* his own supper:
and one is hungry, and
another is drunken.
22. **What? have ye not**
houses to eat and to drink
in? or despise ye the
church of God, and shame them
that have not? What shall I say to
you? shall I praise you in this?
I praise *you* not.
23. **For** I have received of the Lord
that which also
I delivered unto you, That
the Lord Jesus the *same* night in
which he was betrayed
took bread:
24. **And when he had given**
thanks, he brake *it*, and
said, Take, eat: this is my
body, which is
broken for you: this do in
remembrance of me.
25. After the same manner
also *he took* the cup,
when he had supped,
saying, This cup is the new
testament in my blood: this
do ye, as oft as ye drink *it*,
in remembrance of me.
26. **For as** often as
ye eat this bread, and
drink this cup, ye do shew
the Lord's death
till he come.
27. Wherefore whosoever shall eat
this bread, and drink *this* cup of the
Lord, unworthily, shall be guilty of the
body and blood of the Lord.
28. **But let a man examine**
himself, and so let him eat of *that*
bread, and drink of *that* cup.
29. **For he that eateth and**
drinketh unworthily, eateth

and drinketh damnation to
himself, not discerning
the Lord's body.
30. **For this cause many *are***
weak and
sickly among you,
and many sleep.
31. For if we would judge ourselves,
we should not be judged.
32. But when we are judged, we are
chastened of the Lord, that we should
not be condemned with the world.
33. **Wherefore,** my brethren,
when ye come together to
eat, tarry one for another.
34. **And if any man hunger,**
let him eat at home; that ye
come not together
unto condemnation. And the
rest will I set in order when I come.

CHAPTER 12

1. **Now concerning spiritual**
gifts, brethren, I would not
have you ignorant.
2. Ye know that ye were Gentiles,
carried away unto these dumb idols,
even as ye were led.
3. Wherefore I give you to
understand, that
no man speaking by the
Spirit of God calleth Jesus
accursed: and *that*
no man can say that
Jesus is the Lord, but by
the Holy Ghost.
4. **Now there are diversities**
of gifts, but the same Spirit.
5. And there are differences of
administrations, but the same Lord.
6. And there are diversities of
operations, but it is the same God
which worketh all in all.
7. But the manifestation of the Spirit is
given to every man to profit withal.
8. **For to one is given by the**
Spirit the word of wisdom;
to another the word of
knowledge by the same Spirit;
9. **To another faith**
by the same Spirit;
to another the gifts of
healing by the same Spirit;
10. **To another** the working of
miracles; to another
prophecy; to another
discerning of spirits; to
another *divers* kinds of
tongues; to another the
interpretation of tongues:
11. **But all these worketh**
that one and
the selfsame Spirit, dividing to
every man severally as he will.
12. For as the body is one, and hath
many members, and all the members
of that one body, being many, are one
body: so also *is* Christ.
13. **For by one Spirit are we**
all baptized into one body,
whether *we be* Jews or Gentiles,
whether *we be* bond or free; and have
been all made to drink into one Spirit.
14. **For the body is not one**
member, but many.
15. **If the foot shall say,**
Because I am not the hand,
I am not of the body; is it
therefore not of the body?
16. And if the ear shall say, Because I
am not the eye, I am not of the
body; is it therefore not of the body?
17. **If the whole body *were***
an eye, where *were* the
hearing? If the whole *were* hearing,
where *were* the smelling?
18. But now hath God set the
members every one of them in the
body, as it hath pleased him.
19. And if they were all one member,
where *were* the body?
20. **But now *are they* many**
members, yet
but one body.
21. And the eye cannot say unto the
hand, I have no need of thee: nor
again the head to the feet, I have no
need of you.
22. Nay, much more
those members of the body,
which seem to be
more feeble,
are necessary:
23. **And those *members***
of the body,
which we think to be

less honourable,
upon these we
bestow more abundant
honour; and our uncomely *parts*
have more abundant comeliness.
24. For our comely *parts* have
no need:
but God hath tempered the
body together, having
given more
abundant honour to that
part which lacked.
25. That there should be no
schism in the body; but *that* the
members should have the same care
one for another.
26. And whether one
member suffer, all the
members suffer with it; or
one member be honoured, all the
members rejoice with it.
27. Now ye are the body of
Christ, and members
in particular.
28. And God hath set some
in the church, first
apostles, secondarily
prophets, thirdly teachers,
after that miracles, then
gifts of healings,
helps, governments,
diversities of tongues.
29. *Are* all apostles? *are* all
prophets? *are* all teachers? *are* all
workers of miracles?
30. Have all the gifts of healing? do all
speak with tongues? do all interpret?
31. But covet earnestly
the best
gifts: and yet shew I unto you
a more excellent way.

CHAPTER 13

1. Though I speak with the
tongues of men and of
angels, and have not
charity, I am become *as*
sounding brass, or
a tinkling cymbal.
2. And though I have *the gift*
of prophecy, and
understand all mysteries,
and all knowledge; and
though I
have all faith, so
that I could remove
mountains, and have not
charity, I am nothing.
3. And though I
bestow all my goods to
feed *the poor*, and though I
give my body to be burned,
and have not charity, it
profiteth me nothing.
4. Charity suffereth long,
and is kind; charity envieth
not; charity vaunteth not itself,
is not puffed up,
5. Doth not behave itself
unseemly, seeketh not her
own, is not easily
provoked, thinketh no evil;
6. Rejoiceth not in iniquity, but
rejoiceth in the truth;
7. Beareth all things, believeth all things, hopeth all
things, endureth all things.
8. Charity never faileth: but
whether *there be*
prophecies, they
shall fail; whether *there be*
tongues, they
shall cease; whether *there be*
knowledge, it
shall vanish away.
9. For we know in part,
and we prophesy in part.
10. But when that which is
perfect is come, then
that which is
in part shall be
done away.
11. When I was a child, I
spake as a child,
I understood as a child,
I thought as a child: but
when I became a man, I put
away childish things.
12. For now we see through
a glass, darkly; but then
face to face: now I know in
part; but then shall I know
even as also
I am known.
13. And now abideth faith,
hope, charity, these three;

but the greatest of
these *is* charity.

CHAPTER 14

1. **Follow after charity,**
and desire spiritual *gifts*, but rather
that ye may prophesy.
2. **For he that speaketh** in
an *unknown* tongue
speaketh not unto men, but
unto God: for no man
understandeth *him* ;
howbeit in the spirit
he speaketh mysteries.
3. **But he that prophesieth**
speaketh unto men
***to* edification,**
and exhortation, and comfort.
4. **He that speaketh in an**
***unknown* tongue edifieth**
himself; but he that
prophesieth edifieth the church.
5. **I would that ye all spake**
with tongues but rather that
ye prophesied: for greater *is* he
that prophesieth than he that
speaketh with tongues, except he
interpret, that the church may
receive edifying.
6. **Now, brethren, if I come**
unto you
speaking with tongues,
what shall I profit you,
except I shall
speak to you either
by revelation, or by know-
ledge, or by prophesying,
or by doctrine?
7. And even things without life giving
sound, whether pipe or harp,
except they give a distinction in the
sounds, how shall it be known what is
piped or harped?
8. For if the trumpet give an uncertain
sound, who shall prepare himself
to the battle?
9. So likewise ye,
except ye utter by the
tongue words easy to be
understood, how shall it be
known what is spoken?
for ye shall speak into the air.
10. There are, it may be, so many
kinds of voices in the world, and none
of them *is* without signification.
11. Therefore if I know not the
meaning of the voice, I shall be unto
him that speaketh a barbarian, and he
that speaketh *shall be* a barbarian
unto me.
12. Even so ye,
forasmuch as ye are
zealous of spiritual *gifts*,
seek that ye may excel to
the edifying of the church.
13. **Wherefore let him that**
speaketh in an *unknown*
tongue pray that he
may interpret.
14. **For if I pray in an**
***unknown* tongue, my spirit**
prayeth, but my
understanding is unfruitful.
15. What is it then?
I will pray with the spirit,
and I will pray
with the understanding also: I
will sing with the spirit, and I will sing
with the understanding also.
16. Else when thou shalt bless with
the spirit, how shall he that occupieth
the room of the unlearned say Amen
at thy giving of thanks, seeing
he understandeth not what
thou sayest?
17. For thou verily givest thanks well,
but the other is not edified.
18. **I thank my God, I speak**
with tongues more than
ye all:
19. **Yet in the church I had**
rather speak five words
with my
understanding, that
by my voice
I might teach others also,
than ten thousand words in
an *unknown* tongue.
20. **Brethren, be not children**
in understanding: howbeit in malice be
ye children,
but in understanding
be men.
21. In the law it is written, With *men of*
other tongues and other lips
will I speak unto this people; and yet

for all that will they not hear me, saith the LORD.
22. **Wherefore tongues are for a sign,** not to them that believe, but **to them that believe not: but prophesying *serveth*** not for **them that believe** not, but for them which believe.
23. **If therefore the** whole **church be come together** into one place, **and all speak with tongues, and there come** in ***those that are*** **unlearned, or unbelievers, will they not say** that **ye are mad?**
24. **But if all prophesy, and there come in one that believeth not,** or *one* unlearned, he is convinced of all, he is judged of all:
25. **And thus are the secrets of his heart made manifest;** and so falling down on *his* face **he will worship God,** and report that God is in you of a truth.
26. **How is it then,** brethren? **when ye come together, every one of you hath a psalm,** hath **a doctrine,** hath **a tongue,** hath **a revelation,** hath **an interpretation.** Let all things be done unto edifying.
27. **If any man speak in an *unknown* tongue,** *let it be* by two, or at the most *by* three, and *that* by course; and **let one interpret.**
28. **But if there be no interpreter, let him keep silence** in the church; and let him speak to himself, and to God.
29. **Let the prophets speak** two or three, **and let the other judge.**
30. **If *any thing* be revealed to another** that sitteth by, **let the first hold his peace.**
31. For ye may all prophesy one by one, that all may learn, and all may be comforted.
32. And the spirits of the prophets are subject to the prophets.
33. **For God is not *the author* of confusion, but of peace,** as in all churches of the saints.
34. **Let your women keep silence in the churches:** for it is not permitted unto them to speak; but *they are commanded* to be under obedience as also saith the law.
35. **And if they will learn any thing, let them ask their husbands at home:** for it is a shame for women to speak in the church.
36. What? came the word of God out from you? or came it unto you only?
37. **If any man think himself to be a prophet, or spiritual, let him acknowledge that the things that I write** unto you **are the commandments of the Lord.**
38. But if any man be ignorant, let him be ignorant.
39. Wherefore, brethren, **covet to prophesy, and forbid not to speak with tongues.**
40. **Let all things be done** decently and **in order.**

CHAPTER 15

1. Moreover, brethren, **I declare** unto you **the gospel** which I preached unto you, which also ye have received, and wherein ye stand;
2. **By which also ye are saved,** if ye keep in memory what I preached unto you, **unless ye have believed in vain.**
3. **For I delivered** unto you **first** of all that which I also received, how **that Christ died for our sins according to the scriptures;**

4. And that he was buried, and
that he rose again the third
day according to the scriptures:
5. **And that he was seen of**
Cephas, then of the twelve:
6. **After that, he was seen of**
above five hundred
brethren at once; of whom the greater
part remain unto this present, but
some are fallen asleep.
7. **After that, he was seen**
of James; then of all
the apostles.
8. **And last** of all
he was seen of me also, as of
one born out of due time.
9. **For I am the least of the**
apostles, that am not meet to be
called an apostle,
because I persecuted the
church of God.
10. **But by the grace of God I**
am what I am: and his
grace which *was bestowed* upon me
was not in vain; but I
laboured more abundantly
than they all: yet not I, but
the grace of God which was
with me.
11. Therefore whether *it were* I or they,
so we preach, and so ye believed.
12. **Now if Christ**
be preached that he
rose from the dead, how
say some among you that
there is no resurrection
of the dead?
13. But if there be no resurrection of
the dead, then is Christ not risen:
14. **And if Christ be not**
risen, then *is* our preaching
vain, and your faith *is* also vain.
15. **Yea, and we are** found
false witnesses of God;
because we have
testified of God that he
raised up
Christ: whom he raised not up, if so
be that the dead rise not.
16. For if the dead rise not, then is not
Christ raised
17. **And if Christ be not**
raised, your faith *is* vain;
ye are yet in your sins.
18. Then they also which are fallen
asleep in Christ are perished.
19. **If in this life only we have**
hope in Christ, we are of all
men most miserable.
20. **But now is Christ risen**
from the dead, *and* become the
firstfruits of them that slept.
21. **For since by man *came***
death, by man *came* also
the resurrection of the dead.
?? **For as in Adam all die,**
even so in Christ shall all
be made alive.
23. But every man in his own order:
Christ the firstfruits; afterward they
that are Christ's at his coming.
24. **Then *cometh* the end,**
when he shall have delivered up the
kingdom to God, even the Father;
when he shall have put
down all rule and all
authority and power.
25. **For he must reign,**
till he hath put all enemies
under his feet.
26. **The last enemy *that* shall**
be destroyed *is* death.
27. For he hath put all things under his
feet. But when he saith all things are
put under *him, it is* manifest that he is
excepted, which did put all things
under him.
28. **And when all things shall**
be subdued unto him, then
shall the Son also himself
be subject unto him
that put all things under him,
that God may be all in all.
29. **Else what shall they do**
which are baptized for the
dead, if the dead rise not
at all? why are they then baptized for
the dead?
30. **And why stand** we
in jeopardy every hour?
31. I protest by your rejoicing which I
have in Christ Jesus our LORD,
I die daily.
32. **If after the manner of**
men I have fought with
beasts at Ephesus,

what advantageth it me, if the dead rise not? let us eat and drink; for to-morrow we die.

33. **Be not deceived: evil communications corrupt good manners.**

34. **Awake to righteousness, and sin not;** for some have not the knowledge of God: I speak *this* to your shame.

35. **But some *man* will say, How are the dead raised up?** and with what body do they come?

36. ***Thou* fool, that which thou sowest is not quickened, except it die:**

37. And that which thou sowest, thou sowest not that body that shall be, but bare grain, it may chance of wheat, or of some other *grain*:

38. But God giveth it a body as it hath pleased him, and to every seed his own body.

39. All flesh *is* not the same flesh: but *there is* one *kind of* flesh of men, another flesh of beasts, another of fishes, *and* another of birds.

40. *There are* also celestial bodies, and bodies terrestrial: but the glory of the celestial *is* one, and the *glory* of the terrestrial *is* another.

41. *There is* one glory of the sun, and another glory of the moon, and another glory of the stars: for *one* star differeth from *another* star in glory.

42. **So also *is* the resurrection** of the dead.
It is sown in corruption; it is raised in incorruption:

43. It is sown in dishonour; it is raised in glory: it is sown in weakness; it is raised in power:

44. **It is sown a natural body; it is raised a spiritual body.**
There is a natural body, and there is a spiritual body.

45. And so it is written,
The first man Adam was made a living soul; the last Adam *was made* a quickening spirit.

46. Howbeit that *was* not first which is spiritual, but that which is natural; and afterward that which is spiritual.

47. **The first man *is* of the earth,** earthy;
the second man *is* the Lord from heaven.

48. As *is* the earthy, such *are* they also that are earthy: and as *is* the heavenly, such *are* they also that are heavenly.

49. And as we have borne the image of the earthy, we shall also bear the image of the heavenly.

50. **Now** this I say, brethren, that **flesh and blood cannot inherit the kingdom of God; neither doth corruption inherit incorruption.**

51. **Behold, I shew you a mystery; We shall not all sleep, but we shall all be changed,**

52. **In a moment,**
in the twinkling of an eye,
at the last trump:
for the trumpet shall sound, and
the dead shall be raised incorruptible, and we shall be changed.

53. **For** this corruptible must put on incorruption, and
this mortal *must* put on immortality.

54. **So when this corruptible shall have put on incorruption, and this mortal** shall have put on **immortality, then shall be brought to pass the saying** that is written,
Death is swallowed up in victory.

55. **O death, where *is* thy sting? O grave, where *is* thy victory?**

56. **The sting of death *is* sin; and the strength of sin *is* the law.**

57. **But thanks *be* to God, which giveth us** the **victory through** our Lord Jesus

Christ.
58. **Therefore,**
my beloved brethren,
be ye stedfast, unmoveable,
always abounding in the work of
the Lord,
forasmuch as ye know that
your labour is not in vain in
the Lord.

CHAPTER 16

1. **Now concerning the**
collection for the saints,
as I have given order to the churches
of Galatia, even so do ye.
2. **Upon the first *day* of the**
week let every one of you
lay by him in store, as *God*
hath prospered him, that
there be no gatherings when I come.
3. And when I come,
whomsoever ye shall
approve by *your* letters,
them will I send to bring
your liberality
unto Jerusalem.
4. And if it be meet that I go also, they
shall go with me.
5. **Now I will come unto you,**
when I shall pass through Macedonia:
for I do pass through Macedonia.
6. **And it may be that I will**
abide, yea,
and winter with you,
that ye may bring me on my journey
whithersoever I go.
7. For I will not see you now
by the way; but
I trust to tarry a while with
you, if the Lord permit.
8. **But I will tarry at Ephesus**
until Pentecost.
9. **For a great door**
and effectual
is opened unto me,
and *there are*
many adversaries.
10. **Now if Timotheus come,**
see that he may be with you
without fear: for he worketh the
work of the Lord, as I also *do*.
11. Let no man therefore despise him:
but conduct him forth in peace, that
he may come unto me: for I look for
him with the brethren.
12. **As touching** *our* brother
Apollos, I greatly
desired him to come unto
you with the brethren:
but his will was not at all
to come at this time;
but he will come when he shall have
convenient time.
13. **Watch ye, stand fast**
in the faith,
quit you like men,
be strong.
14. **Let all your things be**
done with charity.
15. I beseech you, brethren, (ye know
the house of Stephanas, that it is
the firstfruits of Achaia, and *that* they
have addicted themselves to the
ministry of the saints,)
16. That ye submit yourselves unto
such, and to every one that helpeth
with *us*, and laboureth.
17. I am glad of the coming of
Stephanas and Fortunatus and
Achaicus: for that which was lacking
on your part they have supplied.
18. For they have refreshed my spirit
and yours: therefore acknowledge
ye them that are such.
19. The churches of Asia salute you.
Aquila and Priscilla salute you much in
the Lord, with the church that is in
their house.
20. **All the brethren greet**
you. Greet ye one another with an
holy kiss.
21. The salutation of *me* Paul with
mine own hand.
22. **If any man love not the**
Lord Jesus Christ,
let him be Anathema
Maranatha.
23. The grace of our Lord Jesus Christ
be with you.
24. My love *be* with you all in Christ
Jesus.
Amen.

THE SECOND EPISTLE TO THE CORINTHIANS

BACKGROUND INFORMATION

Author – Paul, an Apostle of Jesus Christ.
Date Written – probably **between 55** and **60** A.D.

Number of:
Verses - 257
Chapters - 13
Total Words - 6,092
Scan Words - 2,646
Scan Words represent 47 % of Total Words.

Theme – written by Paul to recount his perils in the service of Christ **and to lay claim on the Corinthians as his children in Christ.**

OUTLINE OF THE EPISTLE

I. **Paul's** personal **Testimony.** Chapters 1:1—2:13
II. **Paul's** account of his **ministry.** Chapters 2:14—6:10
III. **Paul's plea** for reconciliation. Chapters 6:11—7:16
IV. **Paul's appeal for** an offering for **the poor.** Chapters 8—9
V. **Paul's** defense of his **Apostleship.** Chapters 10:1—13:10
VI. **Paul's closing words** to the Corinthian Church. Chapters 13:11—14

CHAPTER 1

1. **Paul,** an apostle of Jesus Christ
by the will of God,
and Timothy *our* brother,
unto the church of God which is
at Corinth, with all the saints
which are in all Achaia:
2. **Grace *be* to you and**
peace from God our Father,
and *from* the Lord Jesus
Christ.
3. **Blessed *be*** God, even
the Father of our Lord
Jesus Christ, the Father of
mercies, and the God of all comfort;
4. **Who comforteth us**
in all our tribulation,
that we may be able to
comfort them which are
in any
trouble, by the comfort wherewith
we ourselves are comforted of God.
5. For as the sufferings of Christ
abound in us, so our consolation also
aboundeth by Christ.
6. **And whether we be**
afflicted, *it is* for your
consolation and
salvation, which is effectual in
the enduring of the same sufferings
which we also suffer: or whether we be
comforted, *it is* for your consolation
and salvation.
7. And our hope of you *is* stedfast,
knowing, that as ye are
partakers of the sufferings,
so *shall ye be* also
of the consolation.
8. **For** we would not, brethren, have
you ignorant of our trouble which
came to us in Asia, that
we were pressed out of
measure, above strength,
insomuch that we
despaired even of life:
9. **But we had the sentence**
of death in ourselves,
that we should not trust in
ourselves, but in God
which raiseth the dead:
10. **Who delivered us**
from so great a death,
and doth deliver:
in whom we trust
that he will yet deliver *us*;
11. Ye also helping together by prayer
for us, that for the gift *bestowed*
upon us by the means of many
persons thanks may be given by
many on our behalf.
12. **For our rejoicing is** this,
the testimony of our conscience, *that*
in simplicity and
godly sincerity, not with fleshly
wisdom, but by the grace of God,
we have had our conversation in the
world, and more abundantly
to you-ward.
13. For we write none other things
unto you, than what ye read or
acknowledge; and I trust ye shall
acknowledge even to the end;
14. **As** also
ye have acknowledged
us in part,
that we are your rejoicing,
even as ye also
***are* our's in the day of the**
Lord Jesus.
15. And in this confidence
I was minded to come unto
you before, that ye might have a
second benefit;
16. **And to pass by you into**
Macedonia, and to come again
out of Macedonia unto you, and of you
to be brought on my
way toward Judaea.
17. When I therefore was thus
minded, did I use lightness? or the
things that I purpose, do I purpose
according to the flesh, that with me
there should be yea yea,
and nay nay?
18. But *as* God *is* true,
our word toward you was
not yea and nay.
19. **For the Son of God,**
Jesus Christ,
who was preached among
you by us, *even* by me and Silvanus
and Timotheus,
was not yea and nay, but
in him was
yea.
20. **For all the promises**

of God
in him *are* yea, and in him Amen,
unto the glory of God by us.
21. **Now he which**
stablisheth us with you in
Christ, and hath anointed us,
***is* God;**
22. Who hath also sealed us, and
given the earnest of the Spirit in
our hearts.
23. Moreover I call God for a record
upon my soul, that to spare you I
came not as yet unto Corinth.
24. **Not** for
that we have dominion
over your faith,
but are helpers of your joy:
for by faith ye stand.

CHAPTER 2

1. **But** I determined
this with myself, that
I would not come again to
you in heaviness.
2. For if I make you sorry, who is he
then that maketh me glad, but the
same which is made sorry by me?
3. And I wrote this same unto you,
lest, when I came, I should have
sorrow from them of whom I ought to
rejoice; having confidence in you all,
that my joy is *the joy* of you all.
4. For out of much affliction and
anguish of heart I wrote unto you with
many tears; not that ye should be
grieved, but that ye might know the
love which I have more abundantly
unto you.
5. **But if any have caused**
grief, he hath not grieved
me, but in part: that I may not
overcharge you all.
6. **Sufficient to such a man *is***
this punishment, which *was*
inflicted of many.
7. So that contrariwise
ye *ought* rather
to forgive *him*, and comfort *him*,
lest perhaps
such a one should
be swallowed up
with overmuch
sorrow.
8. Wherefore I beseech
you that ye would
confirm *your* love
toward him.
9. For to this end also did I write, that I
might know the proof of you,
whether ye be obedient in all things.
10. **To whom ye forgive**
any thing,
I *forgive* also: for if I forgave any
thing, to whom I forgave *it*, for your
sakes *forgave I it* in the
person of Christ;
11. **Lest Satan should get an**
advantage of us:
for we are not ignorant of
his devices.
12. **Furthermore, when I**
came to Troas
to *preach* Christ's gospel, and
a door was opened unto me
of the Lord,
13. **I had no rest** in my spirit,
because I found not Titus
my brother: but taking my leave of
them, I went from thence
into Macedonia.
14. **Now thanks *be* unto**
God, which always
causeth us to triumph in
Christ, and maketh manifest the
savour of his knowledge by
us in every place.
15. **For we are unto God a**
sweet savour of Christ,
in them that are saved, and in
them that perish:
16. **To the one *we are* the**
savour of death unto death;
and to the other the savour
of life unto life. And who *is* sufficient
for these things?
17. **For we are not as many,**
which corrupt the word
of God: but as of sincerity, but as of
God, in the sight of God speak
we in Christ.

CHAPTER 3

1. Do we begin again to commend
ourselves? or need we, as some
others, epistles of commendation to
you, or *letters* of commendation

from you?
2. **Ye are our epistle**
written in our hearts,
known and read of all men:
3. *Forasmuch as ye are* manifestly
declared to be the epistle of Christ
ministered by us,
written not with ink, but with
the Spirit of the living God; not in
tables of stone, but in fleshy tables of
the heart.
4. **And such trust have we**
through Christ to God ward:
5. **Not that we are sufficient**
of ourselves to think any thing
as of ourselves;
but our sufficiency
***is* of God;**
6. **Who also hath made us**
able ministers of the new
testament; not of the letter, but
of the spirit: for the letter
killeth, but the spirit
giveth life.
7. **But if the ministration**
of death,
written *and* engraven
in stones, was glorious,
so that the children of Israel could not
stedfastly behold the face of Moses
for the glory of his countenance;
which *glory* was to be done away:
8. **How shall not the**
ministration of the spirit be
rather glorious?
9. For if the ministration of
condemnation *be* glory, much more
doth the ministration of righteousness
exceed in glory.
10. For even that which was made
glorious had no glory in this respect,
by reason of the glory that excelleth.
11. **For if that which is done**
away *was* glorious, much
more that which remaineth
***is* glorious.**
12. **Seeing then that we have**
such hope, we use great
plainness of speech:
13. **And not as Moses,**
***which* put a vail over his**
face, that the children of Israel
could not stedfastly look to the end of
that which is abolished:
14. But their minds were blinded:
for until this day remaineth
the same vail untaken away in
the reading of the old testament;
which *vail* is done
away in Christ.
15. **But even unto this day,**
when Moses is read, the
vail is upon their heart.
16. Nevertheless when it shall turn to
the Lord, the vail shall be taken away.
17. **Now the Lord is that**
Spirit: and where the Spirit
of the Lord
***is*, there *is* liberty.**
18. **But we all, with open**
face beholding as in a glass
the glory of the Lord, are
changed into the same
image from glory to glory, *even* as
by the Spirit of the LORD.

CHAPTER 4

1. **Therefore** seeing we have this
ministry, as we have received mercy,
we faint not;
2. **But have renounced the**
hidden things of
dishonesty, not walking in
craftiness, nor handling the
word of God
deceitfully; but by
manifestation of the truth
commending ourselves to every
man's conscience
in the sight of God.
3. **But if our gospel be hid, it**
is hid to them that are lost:
4. **In whom the god of this**
world hath blinded the
minds of them which
believe not, lest the light of the
glorious gospel of Christ, who is the
image of God, should shine
unto them.
5. For we preach not ourselves, but
Christ Jesus the Lord; and ourselves
your servants for Jesus' sake.
6. **For God,** who commanded the
light to shine out of darkness,
hath shined in our hearts,
to *give* the light

of the knowledge
of the glory of God in the
face of Jesus Christ.
7. **But we have this treasure**
in earthen vessels, that
the excellency of
the power may
be of God, and not of us.
8. ***We are* troubled**
on every side,
yet not distressed; *we are*
perplexed, but not in despair;
9. Persecuted, but not forsaken;
cast down,
but not destroyed;
10. **Always bearing about in**
the body the dying of the Lord
Jesus, that the life also
of Jesus might be made
manifest in our body.
11. For we which live are alway
delivered unto death for Jesus' sake,
that the life also of Jesus might be
made manifest in our mortal flesh.
12. So then death worketh in us,
but life in you.
13. **We having the same**
spirit of faith, according as
it is written, I believed, and
therefore have I spoken;
we also
believe, and
therefore speak;
14. **Knowing that he which**
raised up the Lord
Jesus shall raise up
us also
by Jesus,
and shall present *us* with you.
15. For all things *are* for your sakes,
that the abundant grace might
through the thanksgiving of many
redound to the glory of God.
16. For which cause
we faint not; but though our
outward man perish, yet
the inward *man*
is renewed day by day.
17. For our light affliction, which is but
for a moment, worketh for us a
far more exceeding *and* eternal
weight of glory;
18. **While we look not at** the
things which are
seen, but at the
things which are
not seen: for the
things which are
seen *are* temporal; but the
things which are
not seen *are* eternal.

CHAPTER 5

1. **For we know that if our**
earthly house of *this*
tabernacle were
dissolved, we have a
building of God, an house not
made with hands, eternal
in the heavens.
2. **For** in this
we groan, earnestly
desiring to be clothed upon with
our house which is
from heaven:
3. If so be that being clothed we shall
not be found naked.
4. For we that are in *this* tabernacle do
groan, being burdened: not for that we
would be unclothed, but clothed upon,
that mortality might be
swallowed up of life.
5. **Now he that hath wrought**
us for the selfsame thing
***is* God, who** also
hath given unto us
the earnest of
the Spirit.
6. **Therefore**
we are always confident,
knowing that, whilst we are
at home in the body, we are
absent from the Lord:
7. (For we walk by faith, not by sight:)
8. **We are** confident, *I say*, and
willing rather to be absent
from the body, and to be
present with the Lord.
9. **Wherefore we labour,**
that, whether present or absent,
we may be accepted of him.
10. **For we must all appear**
before the judgment seat of
Christ; that every one may receive
the things *done* in *his* body, according
to that he hath done, whether *it be*

good or bad.
11. **Knowing therefore the terror of the Lord, we persuade men;** but we are made manifest unto God; and I trust also are made manifest in your consciences.
12. For we commend not ourselves again unto you, but give you occasion to glory on our behalf, that ye may have somewhat to *answer* them which glory in appearance, and not in heart.
13. For whether we be beside ourselves, *it is* to God: or whether we be sober, *it is* for your cause.
14. **For the love of Christ** constraineth us; because we thus judge, that if one died for all, then were all dead:
15. And *that* he died for all, that **they which live should not** henceforth **live unto themselves, but unto him which died** for them, **and rose** again.
16. Wherefore henceforth know we no man after the flesh: yea, though we have known Christ after the flesh, yet now henceforth know we *him* no more.
17. **Therefore if any man *be* in Christ, *he is* a new creature: old things are passed away; behold, all things are become new.**
18. **And** all things *are* of **God,** who **hath reconciled us** to himself **by Jesus** Christ, **and** hath **given** to **us the ministry of reconciliation;**
19. **To wit, that God was in Christ, reconciling the world** unto himself, not imputing their trespasses unto them; **and hath committed unto us the word of reconciliation.**
20. **Now then we are ambassadors** for Christ, as though God did beseech *you* by us: we pray *you* **in Christ's stead,** be ye reconciled to God.
21. **For he hath made him** *to be* **sin** for us, **who knew no sin; that we might be made the righteousness of God in him.**

CHAPTER 6

1. **We** then, *as* workers together *with him,* **beseech *you*** also **that ye receive not the grace of God in vain.**
2. **(For he saith,** I have heard thee in a time accepted, and in the day of salvation have I succoured thee: **behold, now *is* the accepted time;** behold, **now *is* the day of salvation.)**
3. **Giving no offence** in any thing, **that the ministry be not blamed:**
4. **But** in all *things* **approving ourselves as** the **ministers** of God, **in much patience,** in afflictions, in necessities, in distresses,
5. **In stripes, in imprisonments,** in tumults, in labours, in watchings, **in fastings;**
6. **By pureness, by knowledge,** by longsuffering, by kindness, **by the Holy Ghost,** by love unfeigned,
7. **By the word** of truth, **by the power of God,** by the armour of righteousness on the right hand and on the left,
8. By honour and dishonour, by evil report and good report: as deceivers, and *yet* true;
9. As unknown, and *yet* well known; **as dying, and, behold, we live;** as chastened, and not killed;
10. **As sorrowful, yet alway**

rejoicing; as poor, yet
making many rich; as
having nothing, and *yet*
possessing all things.
11. **O ye Corinthians,**
our mouth is open unto you,
our heart is enlarged.
12. Ye are not straitened in us, but ye
are straitened in your own bowels.
13. Now for a recompence in the
same, (I speak as unto my children,)
be ye also enlarged.
14. **Be ye not unequally**
yoked together
with unbelievers: for what
fellowship hath righteousness with
unrighteousness? and
what communion hath
light with darkness?
15. And what concord hath Christ
with Belial?
or what part hath he that
believeth with an infidel?
16. **And what agreement**
hath the temple of God with
idols? for ye are the temple
of the living
God; as God hath said,
I will dwell in them,
and walk in *them*; and I will be their
God, and they shall be my people.
17. **Wherefore come out**
from among them,
and be ye
separate, saith the Lord, and
touch not the unclean *thing*;
and I will receive you.
18. **And will be a Father unto**
you, and ye shall be my sons and
daughters, saith the Lord Almighty.

CHAPTER 7

1. **Having therefore these**
promises, dearly beloved,
let us cleanse ourselves
from all
filthiness of the flesh and spirit,
perfecting holiness in the
fear of God.
2. **Receive us; we have**
wronged no man,
we have corrupted no man, we have
defrauded no man.
3. **I speak not *this* to**
condemn *you:* for
I have said before, that
ye are in our hearts
to die and live with *you*.
4. **Great *is* my boldness of**
speech toward you,
great *is* my glorying of you: I am filled
with comfort, I am exceeding joyful in
all our tribulation.
5. **For,** when we were come into
Macedonia, our flesh had no rest, but
we were troubled on every
side; without *were* fightings,
within *were* fears.
6. **Nevertheless God,** that
comforteth those that are cast down,
comforted us by the
coming of Titus;
7. **And** not by his coming only, but
by the consolation wherewith
he was comforted in you,
when he told us
your earnest desire, your mourning,
your fervent mind toward
me; so that I rejoiced the more.
8. **For though I made you**
sorry with a letter, I do not
repent, though I did repent: for I
perceive that the same epistle hath
made you sorry, though *it were* but for
a season.
9. **Now I rejoice,**
not that ye were made sorry, but
that ye sorrowed to
repentance: for ye were made
sorry after a godly manner, that ye
might receive damage
by us in nothing.
10. **For godly sorrow**
worketh repentance to
salvation not to be repented of:
but the sorrow of the world
worketh death.
11. **For** behold this self
same thing, that
ye sorrowed after a godly
sort, what carefulness it wrought in
you, yea, *what* clearing of yourselves,
yea, *what* indignation, yea, *what* fear,
yea, *what* vehement desire, yea, *what*
zeal, yea, *what* revenge!
In all *things* ye have

approved yourselves to be
clear in this matter.
12. **Wherefore,** though
I wrote unto you,
I did it not for his cause that had done
the wrong, nor for his cause that
suffered wrong, but
that our care for you
in the sight of God
might appear unto you.
13. **Therefore we were**
comforted in your comfort:
yea, and exceedingly the more joyed
we for the joy of Titus, because his
spirit was refreshed by you all.
14. **For** if I have boasted any thing to
him of you, I am not ashamed;
but as
we spake all things to you
in truth, even so
our boasting, which *I made*
before Titus, is found a truth.
15. **And his inward affection**
is more abundant toward
you, whilst he remembereth
the obedience of you all,
how with fear and trembling
ye received him.
16. I rejoice therefore that I have
confidence in you in all *things*.

CHAPTER 8

1. **Moreover,** brethren,
we do you to wit of the grace
of God bestowed on
the churches
of Macedonia;
2. How that
in a great trial of affliction
the abundance of their joy
and their deep
poverty abounded unto
the riches of their
liberality.
3. **For** to *their* power, I bear record,
yea, and beyond *their* power
***they were* willing**
of themselves;
4. **Praying** us with much entreaty
that we would receive the
gift, and *take upon us* the fellowship
of the ministering to the saints.
5. And *this they did*, not as we hoped,
but first gave their own
selves to the Lord,
and unto us by the will of God.
6. **Insomuch that we desired**
Titus, that as he had begun, so
he would also finish in you
the same grace also.
7. **Therefore, as ye abound**
in every *thing,* *in* faith, and
utterance, and knowledge, and *in* all
diligence, and *in* your love to us,
see that ye abound in this
grace also.
8. I speak not by commandment, but
by occasion of the forwardness of
others, and to prove the sincerity of
your love.
9. **For ye know the grace of**
our Lord Jesus Christ,
that, though he was rich,
yet for your sakes he
became poor, that ye
through his poverty
might be rich.
10. And herein I give *my* advice: for
this is expedient for you, who have
begun before, not only to do, but also
to be forward a year ago.
11. **Now therefore perform**
the doing *of it* ; that as *there was*
a readiness to will, so *there may be* a
performance also out of that
which ye have.
12. For if there be first a willing mind,
***it is* accepted according to**
that a man hath, *and* not
according to that
he hath not.
13. **For *I mean* not that other**
men be eased,
and ye burdened:
14. **But by an equality, *that***
now at this time
your abundance *may be a*
***supply* for their want, that**
their abundance also
may be *a supply* for your
want: that there may be equality:
15. **As it is written, He that** *had*
***gathered* much had**
nothing over; and he
that *had*
***gathered* little had no lack.**

16. **But thanks *be* to God,**
which put the same earnest
care into the heart of Titus
for you.
17. For indeed he accepted the
exhortation; but being more forward,
of his own accord he went unto you.
18. **And we have sent with**
him the brother, whose
praise *is* in the gospel
throughout all the churches;
19. **And** not *that* only, but
who was also
chosen of the churches to
travel with us with this grace,
which is administered by us to the
glory of the same Lord, and
declaration of your ready mind:
20. Avoiding this, that no man should
blame us in this abundance which is
administered by us:
21. Providing for honest things, not
only in the sight of the Lord, but
also in the sight of men.
22. **And we have sent**
with them
our brother, whom we have
oftentimes proved diligent
in many things, but now much more
diligent, upon the great confidence
which *I have* in you.
23. **Whether *any do inquire***
of Titus, *he is* my partner
and fellow-helper
concerning you: or our
brethren *be inquired of,*
***they are* the messengers**
of the churches,
and the glory of Christ.
24. **Wherefore shew ye to**
them and before the churches,
the proof of your love,
and of our boasting on your behalf.

CHAPTER 9

1. **For as touching the**
ministering to the saints, it
is superfluous for me
to write to you:
2. **For I know the**
forwardness of your mind,
for which I boast of you to them
of Macedonia, that Achaia was ready
a year ago;
and your zeal hath
provoked very
many.
3. **Yet have I sent the**
brethren, lest our boasting
of you should
be in vain in this behalf; that, as I
said, ye may be ready:
4. Lest haply if they of Macedonia
come with me, and find you
unprepared, we (that we say not, ye)
should be ashamed in this same
confident boasting.
5. **Therefore I thought it**
necessary to exhort the
brethren, that they would
go before unto you,
and make up beforehand
your bounty, whereof ye had
notice before, that the same might be
ready, as *a matter of* bounty, and not
as *of* covetousness.
6. **But this *I say*, He which**
soweth sparingly shall
reap also
sparingly; and he which
soweth bountifully shall
reap also
bountifully.
7. **Every man according as**
he purposeth in his heart,
***so let him give*; not**
grudgingly, or of necessity:
for God loveth a
cheerful giver.
8. **And God *is* able to make**
all grace abound toward
you; that ye, always having all
sufficiency in all *things*, may abound
to every good work:
9. **(As it is written,**
He hath dispersed abroad;
he hath given to the poor:
his righteousness
remaineth for ever.
10. **Now he that ministereth**
seed to the sower both
minister bread for *your*
food, and multiply your
seed sown, and increase the
fruits of your righteousness;)
11. Being enriched in every thing to all

bountifulness, which causeth
through us thanksgiving to God.
12. **For** the administration of
this service not only
supplieth the want of
the saints, but is abundant
also by many
thanksgivings unto God;
13. **Whiles** by the experiment
of this ministration
they glorify God for your
professed
subjection unto the gospel
of Christ,
and for *your* liberal
distribution unto them, and
unto all *men*;
14. **And by their prayer**
for you, which long after you
for the exceeding
grace of God in you.
15. **Thanks *be* unto God for**
his unspeakable gift.

CHAPTER 10

1. Now I Paul myself beseech you by
the meekness and gentleness of
Christ, who in presence *am* base
among you, but being absent am bold
toward you:
2. **But I beseech *you*, that I**
may not be bold when I am
present with that confidence,
wherewith I think to be bold
against some, which think
of us as if we walked
according to the flesh.
3. For though we walk in the flesh,
we do not war
after the flesh:
4. **(For the weapons of our**
warfare *are* not carnal, but
mighty through God to the
pulling down of
strong holds;)
5. **Casting down**
imaginations, and every
high thing that exalteth itself
against the knowledge of
God, and bringing into
captivity every thought
to the obedience of Christ;
6. **And having in a**
readiness to revenge all
disobedience,
when your obedience is fulfilled.
7. Do ye look on things after the
outward appearance?
If any man trust
to himself
that he is Christ's,
let him of himself think this again,
that, as he *is* Christ's,
even so *are* we Christ's.
8. **For though I should boast**
somewhat more
of our
authority, which the Lord
hath given us
for edification, and not
for your
destruction,
I should not be ashamed:
9. **That I may not seem as if I**
would
terrify you by letters.
10. **For *his* letters, say they,**
***are* weighty** and powerful;
but *his* bodily
presence *is* weak, and *his*
speech contemptible.
11. Let such an one
think this, that, such
as we are in word
by letters when we are
absent, such *will we be* also
in deed when we are
present.
12. **For we dare not**
make ourselves of the number, or
compare ourselves
with some that commend
themselves: but they measuring
themselves by themselves, and
comparing themselves
among themselves,
are not wise.
13. **But we will not boast of**
things without
***our* measure, but**
according to the measure
of the rule which
God hath distributed to us,
a measure to reach even unto
you.
14. For we stretch not ourselves

beyond *our measure*, as though we reached not unto you: for we are come as far as to you also in *preaching* the gospel of Christ:
15. **Not boasting of** things without *our* measure, *that is*, of **other men's labours; but having hope,** when your faith is increased, **that we shall be enlarged by you** according to our rule abundantly,
16. To preach the gospel in the *regions* beyond you, ***and* not to boast in another man's line of things** made ready to our hand.
17. But he that glorieth, let him glory in the Lord.
18. **For not he that commendeth himself is approved, but whom the Lord commendeth.**

CHAPTER 11

1. Would to God ye could bear with me a little in *my* folly: and indeed bear with me.
2. **For I am jealous over you with godly jealousy: for I have espoused you** to one husband, that I may present *you* ***as* a** chaste **virgin to Christ.**
3. **But I fear,** lest by any means, **as the serpent beguiled Eve** through his subtilty, **so your minds should be corrupted from the simplicity** that is **in Christ.**
4. **For if he that cometh preacheth another Jesus,** whom we have not preached, or *if* ye receive another spirit, which ye have not received, **or another gospel,** which ye have not accepted, **ye might** well **bear with *him*.**
5. For I suppose **I was not** a whit **behind the** very **chiefest apostles.**
6. **But though *I be* rude in speech,** yet not in knowledge; but we have been throughly made manifest among you in all things.
7. Have I committed an offence in abasing myself that ye might be exalted, because **I have preached** to you **the gospel** of God **freely?**
8. **I robbed other churches,** taking wages *of them*, **to do you service.**
9. **And when I was present with you,** and wanted, I was chargeable to no man: for that which was lacking to me the brethren which came from Macedonia supplied: and in all *things* **I** have **kept myself from being burdensome** unto you, and *so* will I keep *myself*.
10. **As the truth of Christ is in me, no man shall stop** me of **this boasting** in the regions of Achaia.
11. Wherefore? because I love you not? God knoweth.
12. But what I do, that I will do, **that I may cut off occasion from them which desire occasion;** that wherein they glory, they may be found even as we.
13. **For such *are* false apostles,** deceitful workers, **transforming themselves into the apostles of Christ.**
14. **And no marvel; for Satan** himself **is transformed into an angel of light.**
15. **Therefore *it is* no great thing if his ministers** also **be transformed** as the ministers of righteousness; whose end shall be according to their works.
16. **I say again, Let no man think me a fool;** if otherwise, yet as a fool receive me, that I may boast myself a little.
17. That which I speak, I speak *it* not

after the Lord, but as it were foolishly,
in this confidence of boasting.
18. Seeing that many glory after the
flesh, I will glory also.
19. For ye suffer fools gladly, seeing
ye *yourselves* are wise.
20. For ye suffer, if a man bring you
into bondage, if a man devour *you*, if a
man take *of you*, if a man exalt himself, if a man smite you on the face.
21. I speak as concerning reproach,
as though we had been weak.
Howbeit whereinsoever
any is bold, (I speak
foolishly,) I am bold also.
22. **Are they Hebrews? so**
***am* I.** Are they Israelites? so am I.
Are they the seed of
Abraham? so *am* I.
23. **Are they ministers of**
Christ? (I speak as a fool)
I *am* more; in labours more
abundant, in stripes above measure,
in prisons more frequent,
in deaths oft.
24. **Of the Jews five times**
received I forty *stripes*
save one.
25. **Thrice was I beaten with**
rods, once was I stoned,
thrice I suffered shipwreck,
a night and a day
I have been in the deep;
26. *In* journeyings often,
in perils of waters,
***in* perils of robbers,** *in* perils
by *mine own* countrymen, *in* perils by
the heathen, *in* perils in the city, *in*
perils in the wilderness, *in* perils in the
sea, *in* perils among false brethren;
27. **In weariness and**
painfulness, in watchings often,
in hunger and thirst,
in fastings often,
in cold and nakedness.
28. Beside those things that are
without, that which cometh upon me
daily, the care of all the churches.
29. Who is weak, and I am not weak?
who is offended, and I burn not?
30. **If I must needs glory, I**
will glory of the things
which concern
mine infirmities.
31. **The God and Father of**
our Lord Jesus Christ, which is
blessed for evermore,
knoweth that I lie not.
32. **In Damascus the**
governor under Aretas the king
kept the city of the Damascenes with
a garrison,
desirous to apprehend me:
33. **And through a window**
in a basket was
I let down by the wall, and
escaped his hands.

CHAPTER 12

1. It is not expedient for me
doubtless to glory.
I will come to visions and
revelations of the Lord.
2. **I knew a man in Christ**
above fourteen years ago,
(whether in the
body, I cannot tell; or whether
out of the body, I cannot tell:
God knoweth;) such an one
caught up to the
third heaven.
3. And I knew such a man, (whether in
the body, or out of the body, I cannot
tell: God knoweth;)
4. **How that he was caught**
up into paradise, and
heard unspeakable
words, which it is
not lawful for a man
to utter.
5. **Of such an one will I**
glory: yet of myself I will not glory,
but in mine infirmities.
6. For though I would desire to glory, I
shall not be a fool; for I will say the
truth: but *now* I forbear, lest any man
should think of me above that which
he seeth me *to be*, or *that* he heareth
of me.
7. **And lest I should be**
exalted above measure
through the abundance of
the revelations, there was
given to me a thorn
in the flesh,
the messenger of Satan to

■ **buffet me,** lest I should be exalted
above measure.
8. For this thing
■ **I besought the Lord thrice,**
■ **that it might depart** from me.
■ 9. **And he said** unto me,
■ **My grace is sufficient** for thee:
for my strength is made perfect
in weakness.
■ **Most gladly therefore will I**
rather
■ **glory in my infirmities, that**
■ **the power of Christ may**
■ **rest upon me.**
■ 10. **Therefore I take pleas-**
■ **ure in** infirmities, in reproaches, in
necessities, in persecutions, in
■ **distresses for Christ's**
■ **sake: for when I am**
■ **weak, then am I strong.**
11. I am become a fool in glorying; ye
have compelled me: for I ought to
have been commended of you: for
■ **in nothing am I behind the**
very
■ **chiefest apostles,**
though I be nothing.
■ 12. **Truly the signs of an**
■ **apostle were wrought**
■ **among you**
in all patience, in signs, and wonders,
and mighty deeds.
13. For what is it wherein ye were
inferior to other churches, except *it*
be that I myself was not burdensome
to you? forgive me this wrong.
■ 14. **Behold, the third time I**
■ **am ready to come to you;**
■ **and I will not be burden-**
■ **some** to you: for I seek not your's
but you: for the children ought not
to lay up for the parents, but the
parents for the children.
■ 15. **And I will very gladly**
■ **spend and be spent for**
■ **you;** though the more
abundantly I love you, the less I
be loved.
16. But be it so, I did not burden you:
nevertheless, being crafty,
I caught you with guile.
17. Did I make a gain of you by any of
them whom I sent unto you?
18. I desired Titus, and with *him* I sent
a brother. Did Titus make a gain of
you? walked we not in the same spirit?
walked we not in the same steps?
19. Again, think ye that we excuse
ourselves unto you? we speak before
God in Christ: but
■ ***we do* all things,**
dearly beloved,
■ **for your edifying.**
■ 20. **For I fear, lest, when I**
■ **come,** I shall not find you such as I
would, and *that* I shall be found unto
you such as ye would not: lest
■ ***there be* debates,**
envyings, wraths, strifes,
■ **backbitings, whisperings**
swellings, tumults:
■ 21. ***And* lest, when I come**
■ **again,** my God will humble me
among you, and *that*
■ **I shall bewail many which**
■ **have sinned** already,
■ **and have not repented**
■ **of the uncleanness** and
fornication and lasciviousness
■ **which they have**
■ **committed.**

CHAPTER 13

1. This *is* the third *time* I am coming to
you. In the mouth of two or three
witnesses shall every
word be established.
2. I told you before, and foretell you,
as if I were present, the second
time; and being absent now
■ **I write to them which**
heretofore
■ **have sinned,** and to all other,
■ **that, if I come again,**
■ **I will not spare:**
■ 3. **Since ye seek a proof of**
■ **Christ speaking in me,**
■ **which to you-ward is not**
■ **weak, but is mighty in you.**
■ 4. **For though he was**
■ **crucified through weak-**
■ **ness, yet he liveth by the**
■ **power of God. For we** also
■ **are weak in him, but we**
■ **shall live with him by the**
■ **power of God** toward you.

5. **Examine yourselves,**
whether ye be in the faith;
prove your own selves. Know ye not
your own selves, how that Jesus
Christ is in you, except
ye be reprobates?
6. But I trust that ye shall know that
we are not reprobates.
7. **Now I pray to**
God that ye
do no evil; not that we should
appear approved,
but that ye should
do that which
is honest,
though we be as reprobates.
8. For we can do nothing against the
truth, but for the truth.
9. For we are glad, when we are weak,
and ye are strong: and this also we
wish, *even* your perfection.
10. **Therefore I write**
these things
being absent, lest being
present I should use
sharpness, according to
the power which the Lord
hath given me to edifica-
tion, and not to destruction.
11. **Finally,** brethren, farewell.
Be perfect,
be of good comfort, be of one mind,
live in peace; and the
God of love and peace
shall be with you.
12. Greet one another
with an holy kiss.
13. All the saints salute you.
14. **The grace of the Lord**
Jesus Christ,
and the love of God, and
the communion of the Holy
Ghost, *be* with you all.
Amen.

THE EPISTLE TO THE GALATIANS

BACKGROUND INFORMATION

Author – Paul, an Apostle.
Date Written – probably **between 45** and **56** A.D.

Number of:
Verses - 149
Chapters - 6
Total Words - 3,098
Scan Words - 1,496
Scan Words represent 48 % of Total Words.

Theme – written to show that we are **justified** by God **through faith** and not through keeping laws.

OUTLINE OF THE EPISTLE

I. **Paul's vindication of his Apostleship** and of our redemption through Christ. Chapter 1
II. Paul's rebuke of Peter, and **a defense of justification by faith.** Chapters 2—3:9
III. Paul's explanation of **the curse of the law,** and Christ's power to redeem. Chapters 3:9—4
IV. Paul's exposition of our **freedom and benefits as sons of God.** Chapters 4—5:13
V. Paul's teaching on **subjecting the flesh to the Holy Spirit.** Chapters 5:15—6

CHAPTER 1

1. **Paul,** an apostle, (not of men,
neither by man, but by Jesus Christ,
and God the Father, who raised him
from the dead;)
2. And all the brethren which are
with me,
unto the churches
of Galatia:
3. **Grace *be* to you and**
peace from God the Father,
and *from* our Lord
Jesus Christ,
4. **Who gave himself for our**
sins, that he might deliver
us from this present evil
world, according to the will
of God and our Father:
5. To whom *be* glory for ever and ever.
Amen.
6. **I marvel that ye are so**
soon removed from him that
called you into the grace of Christ
unto another gospel:
7. **Which is not another; but**
there be some that
trouble you, and would
pervert the gospel
of Christ.
8. **But though we, or an**
angel from heaven,
preach any other gospel
unto you than that which we have
preached unto you,
let him be accursed.
9. As we said before,
so say I now again, if any
***man* preach any other**
gospel unto you than that ye
have received,
let him be accursed.
10. For do I now persuade men, or
God? or do I seek to please men? for
if I yet pleased men, I should not be
the servant of Christ.
11. But I certify you, brethren, that
the gospel which was
preached of me is not
after man.
12. For I neither received it of man,
neither was I taught *it*,
but by the revelation of
Jesus Christ.
13. **For ye have heard**
of my conversation in time past
in the Jews' religion,
how that beyond measure
I persecuted the church
of God,
and wasted it:
14. **And profited in the Jews'**
religion above many my equals in
mine own nation,
being more exceedingly
zealous of the traditions
of my fathers.
15. **But when it pleased God,**
who separated me from my mother's
womb, and called *me* by his grace,
16. **To reveal his Son in me,**
that I might preach him among
the heathen;
immediately I conferred
not with flesh and blood:
17. Neither went I up to Jerusalem to
them which were apostles before me;
but I went into Arabia, and
returned again
unto Damascus.
18. **Then after three years I**
went up to Jerusalem
to see Peter, and abode with him
fifteen days.
19. **But other of the apostles**
saw I none, save James
the Lord's brother.
20. Now the things which I write unto
you, behold, before God, I lie not.
21. **Afterwards I came into**
the regions of
Syria and Cilicia;
22. **And was unknown by**
face unto the churches of Judaea
which were in Christ:
23. **But they had heard only,**
That he which persecuted
us in times past
now preacheth the faith
which once he destroyed.
24. And they glorified God in me.

CHAPTER 2

1. **Then fourteen years after I**
went up again to
Jerusalem with Barnabas, and
took Titus with *me* also.

2. And I went up
by revelation, and
communicated unto them
that gospel which I preach
among the Gentiles,
but privately to them which were of
reputation, lest by any means I should
run, or had run, in vain.
3. **But neither Titus,**
who was with me,
being a Greek, was com-
pelled to be circumcised:
4. **And** that because of
false brethren
unawares brought in, who
came in privily to spy out
our liberty which we have
in Christ Jesus, that they
might bring us
into bondage:
5. **To whom we gave place**
by subjection, no,
not for an hour; that the
truth of the gospel
might continue with you.
6. But of these who seemed to be
somewhat, (whatsoever they were, it
maketh no matter to me: God
accepteth no man's person:) for they
who seemed *to be somewhat* in
conference added nothing to me:
7. **But** contrariwise, when
they saw that the gospel of
the uncircumcision was
committed unto me, as
the gospel of
the circumcision *was*
unto Peter;
8. (For he that wrought effectually in
Peter to the apostleship of the
circumcision, the same was mighty in
me toward the Gentiles:)
9. **And when James,**
Cephas, and John,
who seemed to be pillars,
perceived
the grace that was
given unto
me, they gave to me and
Barnabas the right
hands of fellowship; that
we *should go* unto the
heathen, and they unto the
circumcision.
10. Only *they would* that we should
remember the poor; the same which I
also was forward to do.
11. **But when Peter was**
come to Antioch, I
withstood him to the face,
because he was to be
blamed.
12. **For before**
that certain came from James,
he did eat with the Gentiles:
but when they were come,
he withdrew and
separated himself, fearing
them which were
of the circumcision.
13. **And the other Jews**
dissembled likewise
with him; insomuch that
Barnabas also was
carried away
with their dissimulation.
14. **But when I saw that they**
walked not uprightly
according to
the truth of
the gospel, I said unto Peter
before *them* all,
If thou, being a Jew,
livest after the manner of
Gentiles, and not as do the
Jews, why compellest
thou the
Gentiles to live as do the
Jews?
15. We *who are* Jews by nature, and
not sinners of the Gentiles,
16. Knowing that a
man is not justified by the
works of the law, but by
the faith of Jesus Christ,
even we have believed in Jesus
Christ, that we might be justified by
the faith of Christ, and not by the
works of the law:
for by the works of the law
shall no flesh be justified.
17. But if, while we seek to be justified
by Christ, we ourselves also are found
sinners, *is* therefore Christ the
minister of sin? God forbid.
18. For if I build again the things which

I destroyed, I make myself
a transgressor.
19. **For I through the law am**
dead to the law,
that I might live unto God.
20. **I am crucified with**
Christ: neverthless I live;
yet not I, but Christ liveth in
me: and the life which I now
live in the flesh I live by the
faith of the Son of God, who
loved me, and gave
himself for me.
21. I do not frustrate the
grace of God: for
if righteousness *come* by
the law, then Christ is dead
in vain.

CHAPTER 3

1. **O foolish Galatians, who**
hath bewitched you,
that ye should not obey the truth,
before whose eyes Jesus Christ hath
been evidently set forth, crucified
among you?
2. This only would I learn of you,
Received ye the Spirit by the works
of the law, or by the hearing of faith?
3. **Are ye so foolish? having**
begun in the Spirit, are ye
now made perfect by
the flesh?
4. Have ye suffered so many things in
vain? if *it be* yet in vain.
5. **He therefore that**
ministereth to you
the Spirit, and worketh
miracles among you,
***doeth he it* by** the works of
the law, or by the hearing of
faith?
6. **Even as Abraham**
believed God, and it was
accounted to him for
righteousness.
7. Know ye therefore that
they which are
of faith, the same
are the children
of Abraham.
8. **And the scripture,**
foreseeing that God would
justify the heathen through
faith, preached before
the gospel
unto Abraham, *saying,* In
thee shall all nations
be blessed.
9. So then they which be of faith are
blessed with faithful Abraham.
10. **For as many as are of**
the works of the
law are under the curse:
for it is written, Cursed *is* every one
that continueth not in all things which
are written in the book of the law to
do them.
11. **But that no man is**
justified by the law
in the sight of God, *it*
***is* evident: for, The just shall**
live by faith.
12. And the law is not of faith: but, The
man that doeth them shall live in them.
13. **Christ hath redeemed us**
from the curse of the law,
being made a curse for us:
for it is written, Cursed *is* every one
that hangeth on a tree:
14. **That the blessing of**
Abraham might come on
the Gentiles through Jesus
Christ; that we might receive the
promise of the Spirit through faith.
15. Brethren, I speak after the manner
of men; Though *it be* but a man's
covenant, yet *if it be* confirmed, no
man disannulleth, or addeth thereto.
16. **Now to Abraham and his**
seed were the promises
made. He saith not, And to
seeds, as of many;
but as of one, And to thy
seed, which is Christ.
17. And this I say, *that* the covenant,
that was confirmed before of God in
Christ, the law, which was four
hundred and thirty years after, cannot
disannul, that it should make the
promise of none effect.
18. For if the inheritance *be* of the law,
it is no more of promise: but
God gave *it* to Abraham
by promise.
19. **Wherefore then *serveth***

the law? It was added
because of
transgressions, till the
seed should come to
whom the promise was
made; *and it was* ordained by
angels in the hand of a mediator.
20. Now a mediator is not a *mediator* of
one, but God is one.
21. ***Is* the law then against**
the promises of God? God
forbid: for if there had been
a law given which
could have given life, verily
righteousness should
have been by the law.
22. **But the scripture hath**
concluded all under sin,
that the promise by
faith of Jesus Christ might
be given to them that believe.
23. But before faith came, we were
kept under the law, shut up unto the
faith which should afterwards be
revealed.
24. **Wherefore the law was**
our schoolmaster *to bring*
***us* unto Christ,**
that we might be justified by faith.
25. **But after** that
faith is come, we
are no longer under
a schoolmaster.
26. **For ye are all the**
children of God by faith in
Christ Jesus.
27. **For** as many of
you as have been
baptized into Christ have
put on Christ.
28. **There is neither Jew nor**
Greek, there is neither
bond nor free, there is
neither male nor female: for
ye are all one in
Christ Jesus.
29. And if ye *be* Christ's, then are ye
Abraham's seed,
and heirs according to
the promise.

CHAPTER 4

1. Now I say, *That*
the heir, as long as he is
a child, differeth nothing
from a servant,
though he be lord of all;
2. **But is under tutors**
and governors
until the time appointed of
the father.
3. **Even so we, when we were**
children, were in bondage
under the elements
of the world:
4. **But** when the fulness of
the time was come,
God sent forth
his Son, made of a woman,
made under the law,
5. **To redeem them** that were
under the law, that we might
receive the adoption of sons.
6. **And because ye are**
sons, God hath
sent forth
the Spirit of his Son into
your hearts, crying,
Abba, Father.
7. **Wherefore thou art no**
more a servant, but a son;
and if a son, then
an heir of God
through Christ.
8. Howbeit then, when ye knew not
God, ye did service unto them which
by nature are no gods.
9. **But now, after that ye**
have known God,
or rather are known of God,
how turn ye again
to the weak and beggarly elements,
whereunto ye desire again
to be in bondage?
10. Ye observe days, and months,
and times, and years.
11. **I am afraid of you, lest I**
have bestowed upon you
labour in vain.
12. Brethren, I beseech you, be as I
am; for I *am* as ye *are*: ye have not
injured me at all.
13. Ye know how
through infirmity of the flesh
I preached the gospel
unto you at the first.

14. **And** my temptation which was in
my flesh
ye despised not, nor
rejected; but received me
as an angel of God, *even*
as Christ Jesus.
15. Where is then the blessedness ye
spake of? for I bear you record, that,
if *it had been* possible,
ye would have plucked out
your own eyes, and have
given them to me.
16. **Am I therefore** become
your enemy, because I tell
you the truth?
17. They zealously affect you, *but* not
well; yea, they would exclude you,
that ye might affect them.
18. But *it is* good to be zealously
affected always in *a* good *thing*, and
not only when I am present with you.
19. **My little children, of**
whom I travail in birth again
until Christ be formed
in you,
20. I desire to be present with you
now, and to change my voice; for I
stand in doubt of you.
21. Tell me, ye that desire
to be under the law,
do ye not hear the law
22. For it is written, that
Abraham had two sons,
the one by a bondmaid, the
other by a freewoman.
23. **But he** *who was*
of the bondwoman was
born after the flesh; but he
of the freewoman *was*
by promise.
24. **Which things are an**
allegory: for these are the
two covenants; the
one from the mount Sinai, which
gendereth to bondage,
which is Agar.
25. For this Agar is mount Sinai in
Arabia, and answereth to Jerusalem
which now is, and is in bondage with
her children.
26. **But Jerusalem**
which is above
is free, which is the mother
of us all.
27. For it is written, Rejoice, *thou*
barren that bearest not; break forth
and cry, thou that travailest not: for
the desolate hath many more children
than she which hath an husband.
28. **Now we,** brethren,
as Isaac was,
are the children
of promise.
29. **But** as then
he that was born after the
flesh persecuted him *that was*
***born* after the Spirit,**
even so *it is* now.
30. **Nevertheless what saith**
the scripture? Cast out the
bondwoman and her son:
for the son of the
bondwoman shall not be
heir with the son of the freewoman.
31. So then, brethren,
we are not
children of the bondwoman, but
of the free.

CHAPTER 5

1. **Stand fast**
therefore in the liberty wherewith
Christ hath made us
free, and be not entangled
again with the yoke
of bondage.
2. Behold, I Paul say unto you, that
if ye be circumcised, Christ
shall profit you nothing.
3. For I testify again to
every man that is
circumcised, that he
is a debtor to do the
whole law.
4. Christ is become of
no effect unto you,
whosoever of you are
justified by the law; ye are
fallen from grace.
5. For we through the Spirit wait for the
hope of righteousness by faith.
6. **For in Jesus Christ neither**
circumcision availeth any
thing, nor uncircumcision;
but faith which worketh
by love.

7. Ye did run well;
who did hinder you that ye should not obey the truth?
8. **This persuasion *cometh* not of him that calleth you.**
9. A little leaven leaveneth the whole lump.
10. **I have confidence** in you through the Lord, **that ye will be none otherwise minded: but he that troubleth you shall bear his judgment,** whosoever he be.
11. And I, brethren, if I yet preach circumcision, why do I yet suffer persecution? then is the offence of the cross ceased.
12. I would they were even cut off which trouble you.
13. For, brethren, **ye have been called unto liberty; only *use* not liberty** for an occasion **to the flesh,** but by love serve one another.
14. **For all the law is fulfilled in one word,** *even* in this; **Thou shalt love thy neighbour as thyself.**
15. But if ye bite and devour one another, take heed that ye be not consumed one of another.
16. *This* I say then, **Walk in the Spirit, and ye shall not fulfil the lust of the flesh.**
17. **For the flesh** lusteth against the Spirit, **and the Spirit** against the flesh: and these **are contrary the one to the other:** so that ye cannot do the things that ye would.
18. But if ye be led of the Spirit, ye are not under the law.
19. **Now the works of the flesh are manifest, which are *these*; Adultery, fornication, uncleanness, lasciviousness,**
20. **Idolatry, witchcraft, hatred, variance, emulations, wrath, strife, seditions, heresies,**
21. **Envyings, murders, drunkenness, revellings,** and such like: of the which I tell you before, as I have also told *you* in time past, that **they which do such things shall not inherit the kingdom** of God.
22. **But the fruit of the Spirit is love, joy, peace, long-suffering, gentleness, goodness, faith,**
23. **Meekness, temperance: against such there is no law.**
24. And they that are Christ's have crucified the flesh with the affections and lusts.
25. **If we live in the Spirit, let us also walk in the Spirit.**
26. Let us not be desirous of vain glory, provoking one another, envying one another.

CHAPTER 6

1. **Brethren, if a man be overtaken in a fault,** ye which are spiritual, **restore such an one in the spirit of meekness;** considering thyself, lest thou also be tempted.
2. **Bear one another's burdens,** and so fulfil the law of Christ.
3. **For if a man think himself to be something, when he is nothing, he deceiveth himself.**
4. But let every man prove his own work, and then shall he have rejoicing in himself alone, and not in another.
5. For every man shall bear his own burden.
6. Let him that is taught in the word communicate unto him that teacheth in all good things.
7. **Be not deceived; God is not mocked: for whatsoever a man soweth, that shall he also reap.**

8. **For he that soweth to his flesh shall** of the flesh **reap corruption; but he that soweth to the Spirit shall** of the Spirit **reap life everlasting.**
9. And let us not be weary in well-doing: for in due season we shall reap, if we faint not.
10. **As we have** therefore **opportunity, let us do good unto all *men*,** especially unto them who are of the household of faith.
11. Ye see how large a letter I have written unto you with mine own hand.
12. As many as desire to make a fair shew in the flesh, they constrain you to be circumcised; only lest they should suffer persecution for the cross of Christ.
13. **For neither they themselves who are circumcised keep the law; but desire to have you circumcised, that they may glory in your flesh.**
14. **But God forbid that I should glory, save in the cross of our Lord Jesus Christ,** by whom the world is crucified unto me, and I unto the world.
15. **For in Christ Jesus neither circumcision availeth** any thing, **nor uncircumcision, but a new creature.**
16. And as many as walk according to this rule, peace *be* on them, and mercy, and upon the Israel of God.
17. From henceforth let no man trouble me: for I bear in my body the marks of the Lord Jesus.
18. Brethren, the grace of our Lord Jesus Christ *be* with your spirit. **Amen.**

THE EPISTLE TO THE EPHESIANS

BACKGROUND INFORMATION

Author – Paul, an Apostle.
Date Written – probably **between 60** and **65** A.D.

Number of:
Verses - 155
Chapters - 6
Total Words - 3,039
Scan Words - 1,486
Scan Words represent 48 % of Total Words.

Theme – written to show that **the Church is the Body of Christ, and** the quality of **Christian conduct** which should follow.

OUTLINE OF THE EPISTLE

I. **The supremacy of Christ,** God's gift of salvation to both Jew and Gentile and Paul's mission to the Gentiles. Chapters 1—3

II. **The ministry of the Church** in God's plan of reconciliation through Christ, the unity of the Church despite its variety of gifts and his instructions to the family. Chapters 4—6

III. A discourse to Christians on **the full armor of Christ** and the responsibility of the believer to the Church. Chapter 6

CHAPTER 1

1. **Paul,** an apostle of Jesus Christ
by the will of God,
to the saints
which are
at Ephesus, and to the
faithful in Christ Jesus:
2. Grace *be* to you, and peace, from
God our Father, and *from* the Lord
Jesus Christ.
3. **Blessed *be* the God**
and Father
of our Lord
Jesus Christ,
who hath blessed us with all
spiritual blessings in
heavenly *places* in Christ:
4. **According as he hath**
chosen us in him before the
foundation of the world,
that we should be holy and without
blame before him in love:
5. **Having predestinated us**
unto the adoption of
children by Jesus Christ
to himself, according to the good
pleasure of his will,
6. To the praise of the glory of his
grace, wherein he hath made us
accepted in the beloved.
7. **In whom we have**
redemption through his
blood, the forgiveness of
sins, according to
the riches of
his grace;
8. **Wherein he hath**
abounded toward us in all
wisdom and prudence;
9. **Having made known unto**
us the mystery of his will,
according to his good pleasure which
he hath purposed in himself:
10. **That in** the dispensation of
the fulness of times he
might gather together in one
all things in Christ, both
which are
in heaven, and which are on
earth; *even* in him:
11. **In whom also**
we have obtained
an inheritance, being
predestinated
according to the purpose
of him who worketh all
things after the counsel
of his own will:
12. **That we should be to the**
praise of his glory, who
first trusted in Christ.
13. **In whom** ye also *trusted,* after
that ye heard the word of truth, the
gospel of your salvation: in whom also
after that ye believed,
ye were sealed with that
holy Spirit of promise,
14. **Which is the earnest of**
our inheritance until the
redemption of the
purchased possession,
unto the praise of his glory.
15. **Wherefore I** also, after I heard
of your faith in the Lord Jesus, and
love unto all the saints,
16. **Cease not to give thanks**
for you, making mention of
you in my prayers;
17. **That the God of our Lord**
Jesus Christ, the Father of glory,
may give unto
you the spirit of
wisdom and revelation in
the knowledge of him:
18. The eyes of your understanding
being enlightened;
that ye may know what is
the hope of his calling, and
what the riches of
the glory of his
inheritance in the saints,
19. **And what *is* the** exceeding
greatness of his power to
us-ward who believe,
according to the working of
his mighty
power,
20. Which he wrought
in Christ, when he raised
him from the dead,
and set *him* at his own
right hand in the heavenly *places,*
21. **Far above all**
principality, and power, and
might, and dominion, and every name
that is named, not only in this world,

but also in that which is to come:
22. **And hath put all *things***
under his feet, and gave
him *to be* the head over all
***things* to the church,**
23. **Which is his body,** the
fulness of him that filleth all in all.

CHAPTER 2

1. **And you *hath he***
***quickened*, who were dead**
in trespasses and
sins;
2. **Wherein in time past ye**
walked according to
the course of
this world, according to the
prince of the power of
the air, the spirit that now worketh
in the children of disobedience:
3. **Among whom also we all**
had our conversation
in times past
in the lusts of our flesh,
fulfilling the desires of the flesh and of
the mind; and were by nature the
children of wrath, even as others.
4. **But God, who is rich in**
mercy, for his great love
wherewith he loved us,
5. **Even when we were dead**
in sins, hath quickened us
together with Christ,
(by grace ye are saved;)
6. **And hath raised *us* up**
together, and made *us* sit together
in heavenly *places* in Christ Jesus:
7. **That in the ages to come**
he might shew the
exceeding riches of his
grace in *his* kindness
toward us through Christ Jesus.
8. **For by grace are ye**
saved through faith; and
that
not of yourselves:
***it is* the gift of God:**
9. **Not of works, lest any**
man should boast.
10. **For we are his**
workmanship, created in
Christ Jesus unto good
works, which God hath before
ordained that we should walk in them.
11. **Wherefore remember,**
that ye *being* in time past
Gentiles in the flesh,
who are called Uncircumcision by that
which is called the Circumcision in the
flesh made by hands;
12. **That at that time ye were**
without Christ, being aliens
from the commonwealth of Israel, and
strangers from the
covenants of promise,
having no hope,
and without God in the world:
13. **But now in Christ Jesus**
ye who sometimes were far off
are made nigh by the
blood of Christ.
14. **For he is our peace,** who
hath made both one,
and hath broken down the
middle wall of partition
between us;
15. Having abolished in his flesh the
enmity, *even* the law of
commandments *contained* in
ordinances; for to make in himself of
twain one new man, *so* making peace;
16. **And that he might**
reconcile both unto God in
one body by the cross,
having slain the enmity thereby:
17. And came and preached peace to
you which were afar off, and to them
that were nigh.
18. **For through him we both**
have access by one Spirit
unto the Father.
19. **Now therefore ye are** no
more strangers and foreigners, but
fellow-citizens with the
saints, and of the household
of God;
20. **And are built upon the**
foundation of the apostles
and prophets, Jesus
Christ himself being the
chief corner *stone*;
21. In whom all the building fitly
framed together groweth unto an holy
temple in the Lord:
22. **In whom ye also are**
builded together

■ **for an habitation of God**
through the Spirit.

CHAPTER 3

1. For this cause I Paul, the prisoner
of Jesus Christ for you Gentiles,
■ 2. **If ye have heard of the**
■ **dispensation of the grace**
■ **of God which is given me to**
■ **you-ward:**
■ 3. **How that by revelation he**
■ **made known** unto me
■ **the mystery;**
(as I wrote afore in few words,
4. Whereby, when ye read, ye may
understand my knowledge in the
mystery of Christ)
5. Which in other ages was not made
known unto the sons of men, as it is
now revealed unto his holy apostles
and prophets by the Spirit;
■ 6. **That the Gentiles should**
■ **be fellow heirs, and**
of the same body, and
■ **partakers of his promise in**
■ **Christ** by the gospel:
■ 7. **Whereof I was made a**
■ **minister,** according to the gift of
the grace of God given unto me by the
effectual working of his power.
8. Unto me, who am less than the
least of all saints, is this
grace given,
■ **that I should preach**
■ **among the Gentiles**
the unsearchable riches of Christ;
■ 9. **And to make all *men* see**
■ **what *is* the fellowship of the**
■ **mystery, which**
from the beginning of the world
■ **hath been hid in God, who**
■ **created all things by**
■ **Jesus Christ:**
10. To the intent that now unto the
principalities and powers in heavenly
places might be known by the church
the manifold wisdom of God,
11. According to the eternal purpose
which he purposed in Christ Jesus
our Lord:
■ 12. **In whom we have**
■ **boldness and access**
with confidence
■ **by the faith of him.**
■ 13. **Wherefore I desire that**
■ **ye faint not at my**
■ **tribulations for you,**
which is your glory
■ 14. **For this cause I bow**
my knees
■ **unto** the Father of
■ **our Lord Jesus Christ,**
15. Of whom the whole family in
heaven and earth is named,
■ 16. **That he would grant you,**
according to the riches of his glory,
■ **to be strengthened with**
■ **might by his Spirit**
in the inner man;
■ 17. **That Christ may dwell in**
■ **your hearts by faith;** that ye,
being rooted and grounded in love,
18. May be able to comprehend with
all saints what *is* the breadth, and
length, and depth, and height;
■ 19. **And to know the love of**
■ **Christ,** which passeth knowledge,
that ye might be filled with all the
fulness of God.
■ 20. **Now unto him that is**
■ **able to do** exceeding abundantly
■ **above all that we ask or**
■ **think,** according to the power that
worketh in us,
■ 21. **Unto him *be* glory**
in the church by Christ Jesus
■ **throughout all ages,**
world without end. Amen.

CHAPTER 4

■ 1. **I therefore,**
the prisoner of the Lord,
■ **beseech you that ye walk**
■ **worthy of the vocation**
■ **wherewith ye are called,**
■ 2. **With all lowliness and**
meekness, with longsuffering,
■ **forbearing one another**
■ **in love;**
■ 3. **Endeavouring to keep the**
■ **unity of the Spirit**
in the bond of peace.
■ 4. ***There is* one body,**
and one Spirit, even as ye are called
in one hope of your calling;
■ 5. **One Lord, one faith,**

one baptism,
6. **One God and Father of**
all, who *is* above all, and through all,
and in you all.
7. **But unto every one of us is**
given grace according to the
measure of the gift of Christ.
8. Wherefore he saith, When he
ascended up on high, he led captivity
captive, and gave gifts unto men.
9. (Now that he ascended, what is it
but that he also descended first
into the lower parts of the earth?
10. He that descended is the same
also that ascended up far above all
heavens, that he might fill all things.)
11. **And he gave some,**
apostles; and
some, prophets; and
some, evangelists;
and some, pastors
and teachers;
12. **For the perfecting of the**
saints, for the work of the ministry,
for the edifying of the body
of Christ:
13. **Till we all come** in the unity
of the faith, and of the knowledge
of the Son of God, unto a perfect man,
unto the measure of the
stature of the
fulness of Christ:
14. **That we *henceforth* be**
no more children,
tossed to and fro, and
carried about with every
wind of doctrine, by the sleight
of men, *and* cunning craftiness,
whereby they lie in wait to deceive;
15. **But speaking the truth in**
love, may grow up into him in all
things, which is the head, *even* Christ:
16. From whom the whole body fitly
joined together and compacted by
that which every joint supplieth,
according to the effectual working in
the measure of every part, maketh
increase of the body unto the edifying
of itself in love.
17. **This I say therefore,**
and testify in the Lord,
that ye henceforth
walk not as other Gentiles
walk,
in the vanity of their mind,
18. **Having the**
understanding darkened,
being alienated from the life of God
through the ignorance that is in them,
because of the
blindness of
their heart:
19. **Who being past feeling**
have given themselves
over unto lasciviousness,
to work all uncleanness
with greediness.
20. **But ye have not so**
learned Christ;
21. If so be that
ye
have heard him, and
have been taught by him, as
the truth is in Jesus:
22. **That ye put off**
concerning the former
conversation the old man,
which is corrupt according to the
deceitful lusts;
23. **And be renewed in the**
spirit of your mind;
24. **And that ye put on**
the new man,
which after God is created in
righteousness and true holiness.
25. **Wherefore putting away**
lying, speak every man
truth with his neighbour:
for we are members one of another.
26. Be ye angry, and sin not:
let not the sun go down
upon your wrath:
27. **Neither give place to**
the devil.
28. **Let him that stole steal**
no more: but rather let him
labour, working with *his* hands the
thing which is good, that he may have
to give to him that needeth.
29. **Let no corrupt**
communication proceed
out of your mouth,
but that which is good to the use of
edifying, that it may minister grace
unto the hearers.
30. **And grieve not the holy**

Spirit of God, whereby ye are
sealed unto the day of redemption.
31. **Let all bitterness,** and
wrath, and
anger, and clamour,
and evil speaking, be put
away from you, with all malice:
32. **And be ye kind**
one to another,
tenderhearted, forgiving
one another, even as God for
Christ's sake hath forgiven you.

CHAPTER 5

1. **Be ye therefore followers**
of God, as dear children;
2. **And walk in love, as**
Christ also hath loved us,
and hath given himself
for us an offering and a
sacrifice to God
for a sweet smelling savour.
3. But fornication, and all
uncleanness, or covetousness, let it
not be once named among you, as
becometh saints;
4. Neither filthiness, nor foolish
talking, nor jesting, which are not
convenient: but rather giving
of thanks.
5. **For this ye know, that no**
whoremonger, nor
unclean person, nor
covetous man, who is an idolater,
hath any inheritance in the
kingdom of Christ and of God.
6. **Let no man deceive you**
with vain words: for because of
these things cometh the wrath of God
upon the children of disobedience.
7. **Be not ye therefore**
partakers with them.
8. **For ye were sometimes**
darkness, but now
are ye light in the Lord:
walk as children of light:
9. (For the fruit of the Spirit *is* in all
goodness and righteousness
and truth;)
10. Proving what is acceptable unto
the Lord.
11. **And have no fellowship**
with the unfruitful works of
darkness, but rather
reprove *them.*
12. For it is a shame even to speak of
those things which are done of
them in secret.
13. **But all things that are**
reproved are made
manifest by the light:
for whatsoever doth make manifest
is light.
14. **Wherefore he saith,**
Awake thou that sleepest, and
arise from the dead, and
Christ shall give thee light.
15. See then that ye walk circum-
spectly, not as fools, but as wise,
16. Redeeming the time, because the
days are evil.
17. **Wherefore be ye not**
unwise, but understanding
what the will of the Lord *is.*
18. **And be not drunk with**
wine, wherein is excess;
but be filled with the Spirit;
19. **Speaking to yourselves**
in psalms and hymns and
spiritual songs, singing
and making melody
in your heart to the Lord;
20. **Giving thanks always**
for all things unto God
and the Father in the name of our Lord
Jesus Christ;
21. **Submitting yourselves**
one to another in the fear
of God.
22. **Wives, submit** yourselves
unto your own
husbands, as unto the Lord.
23. **For the husband is the**
head of the wife, even as
Christ is the head
of the church:
and he is the saviour of the body.
24. **Therefore as the church**
is subject unto Christ, so
***let* the wives *be* to their own**
husbands in every thing.
25. **Husbands, love your**
wives, even as Christ also
loved the church, and
gave himself for it;
26. That he might sanctify and

cleanse it with the washing of water by
the word,
27. That he might present it to himself
a glorious church, not having spot, or
wrinkle, or any such thing; but that it
should be holy and without blemish.
28. **So ought men to love
their wives as their own
bodies.** He that loveth
his wife loveth himself.
29. **For no man ever yet
hated his own flesh; but**
nourisheth and
cherisheth it,
even as the Lord the church:
30. For we are members of his body,
of his flesh, and of his bones.
31. **For this cause shall a
man leave his father and
mother, and shall be
joined unto his wife, and
they two shall be one flesh.**
32. **This is a great mystery:
but I speak concerning
Christ and the church.**
33. Nevertheless let every one of you
in particular so love his wife even
as himself; and the wife *see* that she
reverence *her* husband.

CHAPTER 6

1. **Children, obey your
parents** in the Lord:
for this is right.
2. **Honour thy father and
mother;** which is the first
commandment with promise;
3. **That it may be well with
thee, and thou mayest live
long** on the earth.
4. **And, ye fathers, provoke
not your children to wrath:
but bring them up in the
nurture and admonition of
the Lord.**
5. **Servants, be obedient to**
them that are
***your* masters** according to the
flesh, with fear and trembling, in
singleness of your heart, as
unto Christ;
6. Not with eye service, as men
pleasers; but as the servants of
Christ, doing the will of God from
the heart;
7. **With good will doing
service, as to the Lord, and
not to men:**
8. **Knowing that whatsoever
good thing any man doeth,
the same shall he receive
of the Lord, whether** *he be*
bond or free.
9. **And, ye masters, do the
same** things unto them, forbearing
threatening: knowing that your Master
also is in heaven; neither is there
respect of persons with him.
10. **Finally,** my brethren,
be strong in the Lord,
and in the power of his might.
11. **Put on the whole armour
of God,** that ye may be able
**to stand against the wiles
of the devil.**
12. **For we wrestle not
against flesh** and blood,
but against principalities, against
powers, against
**the rulers of the darkness
of this world, against
spiritual wickedness in
high *places.***
13. Wherefore take unto you the
whole armour of God, that ye may be
able to withstand in the evil day, and
having done all, to stand.
14. **Stand therefore, having
your loins girt about with
truth, and having on the
breastplate of
righteousness;**
15. **And your feet shod with
the** preparation of the
gospel of peace;
16. **Above all, taking the
shield of faith,**
wherewith ye shall be able
**to quench all the fiery darts
of the wicked.**
17. **And take the helmet of
salvation, and the sword of
the Spirit, which is the word
of God:**
18. **Praying always with all
prayer and supplication in**

the Spirit, and watching thereunto
with all perseverance and supplication
for all saints;
19. **And for me,** that utterance
may be given unto me,
that I may open my mouth
boldly, to make known
the mystery of
the gospel,
20. **For which I am an**
ambassador in bonds:
that therein I may speak boldly, as I
ought to speak.
21. But that ye also may know my
affairs, *and* how I do, Tychicus, a
beloved brother and faithful minister in
the Lord, shall make known to you
all things:
22. Whom I have sent unto you for the
same purpose, that ye might know
our affairs, and *that* he might comfort
your hearts.
23. **Peace** *be* to the brethren,
and love with faith, from
God the Father
and the Lord Jesus Christ.
24. **Grace *be* with all them**
that love our Lord Jesus Christ
in sincerity.
Amen.

THE EPISTLE TO THE PHILIPPIANS

BACKGROUND INFORMATION

Author – Paul, an Apostle.
Date Written – probably **between 60** and **65** A.D.

Number of:
Verses - 104
Chapters - 4
Total Words - 2,002
Scan Words - 1,055
Scan Words represent 52 % of Total Words.

Theme – written to show the **radiant joy** which the believer possesses even **in the** stresses and **storms of life.**

OUTLINE OF THE EPISTLE

I. **Paul's call to live worthy of the gospel** and to follow Christ's example of humility. Chapters 1—3:2

II. **Paul's warning against the Judaizers** and his appeal for harmony and joy. Chapter 3—4:17

III. **Paul's caution about worldliness** and his appeal for steadfastness. Chapters 3:18—4

CHAPTER 1

1. **Paul and Timotheus,**
the servants of Jesus Christ,
to all the saints
in Christ Jesus which are
at Philippi,
with the bishops and deacons:
2. Grace *be* unto you, and peace, from
God our Father, and *from* the Lord
Jesus Christ.
3. **I thank** my
God upon every
remembrance of you,
4. **Always in** every
prayer of mine for you all
making request with joy,
5. **For your fellowship in the**
gospel from the first day until now;
6. **Being confident**
of this very thing,
that he which hath begun a
good work in you will
perform *it*
until the day of Jesus Christ:
7. Even as it is meet for me to think
this of you all, because
I have you in my heart;
inasmuch as both
in my bonds, and in the
defence and confirmation
of the gospel, ye all are
partakers of my grace.
8. For God is my record, how greatly
I long after you all in the bowels
of Jesus Christ.
9. And this I pray,
that your love may abound
yet more and more
in knowledge and *in* all
judgment;
10. **That ye** may
approve things that are
excellent; that ye may
be sincere and without
offence till the day of Christ;
11. **Being filled with** the fruits of
righteousness, which are
by Jesus Christ,
unto the glory and praise of God.
12. **But** I would ye should
understand, brethren,
that the things *which*
***happened* unto me have**
fallen out rather
unto the furtherance of
the gospel;
13. **So that my bonds in**
Christ are manifest in all the
palace, and in all other *places;*
14. **And** many of
the brethren in the Lord,
waxing confident by my
bonds, are much more
bold to speak the word
without fear.
15. **Some** indeed
preach Christ even
of envy and
strife; and some also
of good will:
16. **The one preach Christ**
of contention,
not sincerely, supposing to add
affliction to my bonds:
17. **But the other of love,**
knowing that I am set for the defence
of the gospel.
18. **What then?** notwithstanding,
every way, whether
in pretence, or in truth,
Christ is preached; and I
therein do rejoice, yea, and will
rejoice.
19. For I know that
this shall turn to my
salvation through your
prayer, and the supply of
the Spirit of Jesus Christ,
20. According to my earnest
expectation and
***my* hope, that in nothing I**
shall be ashamed, but *that*
with all
boldness, as always, *so* now also
Christ shall be magnified
in my body, whether *it be*
by life, or by death.
21. **For to me to live *is* Christ,**
and to die *is* gain.
22. But if I live in the flesh, this *is* the
fruit of my labour: yet what I shall
choose I wot not.
23. **For I am** in a strait
betwixt two, having a
desire to depart, and to be
with Christ; which is far better:

24. **Nevertheless to abide**
in the flesh
is more
needful for you.
25. And having this confidence,
I know that
I shall abide and continue
with you all
for your furtherance and joy
of faith;
26. That your rejoicing may be more
abundant in Jesus Christ for me by my
coming to you again.
27. **Only let your**
conversation be
as it becometh the gospel
of Christ: that whether I come
and see you, or else be absent,
I may hear of your affairs,
that ye stand fast
in one spirit, with one mind
striving together
for the faith of the
gospel;
28. **And in nothing terrified**
by your adversaries:
which is to them an evident token of
perdition, but to you of salvation, and
that of God.
29. For unto you
it is given in the behalf of
Christ, not only to believe
on him, but also to suffer
for his sake;
30. Having the same conflict which ye
saw in me, and now hear *to be* in me.

CHAPTER 2

1. **If *there be*** therefore
any consolation in Christ,
if any comfort of love, if any fellowship
of the Spirit, if any bowels
and mercies,
2. **Fulfil ye my joy,**
that ye be like-minded,
having the same love,
being of one accord,
of one mind.
3. ***Let* nothing *be done***
through strife or vainglory;
but in lowliness of mind let each
esteem other better than themselves.
4. **Look not every man on**
his own things, but
every man also
on the things of others.
5. **Let this mind be in you,**
which was also
in Christ Jesus:
6. **Who, being in the form of**
God, thought it not robbery
to be equal with God:
7. **But** made himself of no reputation,
and took upon him the form of a
servant, and
was made in the likeness
of men:
8. **And** being found in fashion
as a man, he humbled
himself, and became
obedient unto death,
even the death of the cross.
9. **Wherefore God** also
hath highly
exalted him, and given him
a name which is
above every name:
10. **That at the name of**
Jesus every knee should
bow, of *things* in heaven, and *things*
in earth, and *things* under the earth;
11. **And** *that*
every tongue should
confess that Jesus Christ
***is* Lord,** to the glory of
God the Father.
12. **Wherefore,** my beloved, as ye
have always obeyed, not as in my
presence only, but now much more in
my absence,
work out your own
salvation with fear
and trembling.
13. **For it is God which**
worketh in you both to will
and to do of
***his* good pleasure.**
14. **Do all things without**
murmurings and
disputings:
15. **That ye may be**
blameless and harmless, the
sons of God, without rebuke,
in the midst of
a crooked and
perverse nation, among

whom ye shine as lights
in the world;
16. **Holding forth the word**
of life;
that I may rejoice in the day
of Christ, that I have not run in
vain, neither laboured in vain.
17. Yea, and if I be offered upon the
sacrifice and service of your faith, I
joy, and rejoice with you all.
18. For the same cause also do ye
joy, and rejoice with me.
19. **But I trust in the Lord**
Jesus to send Timotheus
shortly unto you, that I also may be of
good comfort, when I know
your state.
20. For I have no man like minded,
who will naturally care for your state.
21. **For all seek their own,**
not the things which are
Jesus Christ's.
22. **But ye know the proof of**
him, that, as a son
with the father,
he hath served with me
in the gospel.
23. Him therefore I hope to send
presently, so soon as I shall see how
it will go with me.
24. But I trust in the Lord that
I also myself shall come
shortly.
25. **Yet I** supposed it necessary to
send to you
Epaphroditus, my brother,
and companion in labour,
and fellow-soldier, but
your messenger, and he that
ministered to my wants.
26. **For he longed after you**
all, and was full of heaviness,
because that
ye had heard that
he had been sick.
27. **For indeed he was sick**
nigh
unto death: but God had
mercy on him; and
not on him only, but
on me also, lest I should
have sorrow upon sorrow.
28. **I sent him therefore**
the more carefully,
that, when ye see him again,
ye may rejoice, and that
I may
be the
less sorrowful.
29. **Receive him**
therefore in the Lord
with all
gladness; and hold
such in reputation:
30. **Because for** the work of
Christ he was nigh
unto death, not regarding
his life, to supply your lack of
service toward me.

CHAPTER 3

1. **Finally,** my brethren,
rejoice in the Lord.
To write the same things
to you, to me indeed
***is* not grievous,** but for you
***it is* safe.**
2. Beware of dogs,
beware of evil workers,
beware of the concision.
3. **For we are the**
circumcision, which
worship God in the spirit,
and rejoice in Christ Jesus,
and have no confidence in
the flesh.
4. Though I might also have
confidence in the flesh.
If any other
man thinketh that
he hath whereof he might
trust in the flesh, I more:
5. Circumcised the eighth day,
of the stock of Israel, *of* the
tribe of Benjamin,
an Hebrew of the Hebrews;
as touching the law,
a Pharisee;
6. **Concerning** zeal, persecuting
the church; touching the
righteousness which is in
the law, blameless.
7. **But what things were gain**
to me, those I counted loss
for Christ
8. Yea doubtless, and

I count all things *but* loss
for the excellency of
the knowledge of Christ
Jesus my Lord:
for whom I have
suffered the loss of all
things, and do
count them *but* dung, that I
may win Christ,
9. And be found in him,
not having mine own
righteousness, which is
of the law, but that which is
through the faith of Christ,
the righteousness which is
of God by faith:
10. **That I may know him,**
and the power of his
resurrection, and
the fellowship of
his sufferings, being made
conformable unto
his death;
11. If by any means I might attain unto
the resurrection of the dead.
12. **Not as though I**
had already attained, either
were already
perfect: but I follow after, if
that I may apprehend that
for which also
I am apprehended of
Christ Jesus.
13. **Brethren,** I count not myself to
have apprehended: but
this* one thing *I do,
forgetting those things
which are
behind, and reaching forth
unto those things which are before,
14. **I press toward**
the mark for the prize of
the high calling of God in
Christ Jesus.
15. **Let us therefore,**
as many as be perfect,
be thus minded: and if
in any thing
ye be otherwise minded,
God shall reveal even
this unto you.
16. **Nevertheless, whereto**
we have already
attained, let us walk by the
same rule,
let us mind the same thing.
17. Brethren, be followers together of
me, and mark them which walk so as
ye have us for an ensample.
18. **(For many walk,**
of whom I have told you often, and
now tell you even weeping,
***that* they**
are the
enemies of the cross
of Christ:
19. **Whose end**
***is* destruction,**
whose God *is their* belly, and *whose*
glory *is* in their shame,
who mind earthly things.)
20. **For our conversation is**
in heaven; from whence
also we look for the
Saviour, the Lord Jesus Christ:
21. **Who shall change our**
vile body, that it may be
fashioned
like unto
his glorious body,
according to the working whereby he
is able even to subdue all things
unto himself.

CHAPTER 4

1. **Therefore,** my brethren dearly
beloved and longed for, my joy and
crown, so stand fast in the Lord, *my*
dearly beloved.
2. I beseech Euodias, and beseech
Syntyche, that they be of the same
mind in the Lord.
3. And I entreat thee also, true yoke-
fellow, help those women which
laboured with me in the gospel, with
Clement also, and *with* other my
fellow-labourers, whose names *are* in
the book of life.
4. **Rejoice in the Lord alway:**
and again I say, Rejoice.
5. **Let your moderation be**
known unto all men.
The Lord *is* at hand.
6. **Be careful for nothing; but**
in every thing by prayer
and supplication with

■ **thanksgiving let your**
■ **requests be made known**
■ **unto God.**
■ 7. **And the peace of God,**
which passeth all understanding,
■ **shall keep your hearts and**
■ **minds through**
■ **Christ Jesus.**
■ 8. **Finally, brethren,**
■ **whatsoever things are true,**
whatsoever things *are*
■ **honest,** whatsoever things *are*
■ **just,** whatsoever things *are*
■ **pure,** whatsoever things *are*
■ **lovely,** whatsoever things *are*
■ **of good report; if *there be***
■ **any virtue, and** if *there be* any
■ **praise, think on**
■ **these things.**
■ 9. **Those things, which ye**
■ **have** both learned,
and received, and heard, and
■ **seen in me, do: and the**
■ **God of peace shall be**
■ **with you.**
10. But I rejoiced in the Lord greatly,
that now at the last your care of me
hath flourished again; wherein ye were
also careful, but ye
lacked opportunity.
11. Not that I speak in respect of
want: for
■ **I have learned, in**
■ **whatsoever state I am,**
■ ***therewith* to be content.**
12. I know both how to be abased,
and I know how to abound:
■ **every where and in all**
■ **things I am instructed**
■ **both to be full and**
■ **to be hungry,**
both to abound and to suffer need.
■ 13. **I can do all things**
■ **through Christ which**
■ **strengtheneth me.**
■ 14. **Notwithstanding ye have**
■ **well done, that ye did**
■ **communicate with**
■ **my affliction.**
15. Now ye Philippians know also, that
in the beginning of the gospel, when I
departed from Macedonia, no church
communicated with me as concerning
giving and receiving, but ye only.
16. For even in Thessalonica ye sent
once and again unto my necessity.
■ 17. **Not because I desire a**
■ **gift: but I desire fruit**
■ **that may abound to**
■ **your account.**
■ 18. **But** I have all, and abound:
■ **I am full, having received**
of Epaphroditus
■ **the things** *which were*
■ ***sent* from you,**
an odour of a sweet smell,
■ **a sacrifice** acceptable,
■ **well-pleasing to God.**
■ 19. **But my God shall supply**
■ **all your need according to**
■ **his riches in glory by**
■ **Christ Jesus.**
20. Now unto God and our Father *be*
glory for ever and ever. Amen.
21. Salute every saint in Christ Jesus.
The brethren which are with me
greet you.
22. All the saints salute you, chiefly
they that are of Caesar's household.
23. The grace of our Lord Jesus Christ
be with you all.
■ **Amen.**

THE EPISTLE TO THE COLOSSIANS

BACKGROUND INFORMATION

Author – Paul, an Apostle.
Date Written – probably **between 60** and **65** A.D.

Number of:
Verses - 95
Chapters - 4
Total Words - 1,998
Scan Words -844
Scan words represent 42 % of total words.

Theme – written to show **the pre-eminence of Christ** over all competing systems, and how believers should conduct their lives.

OUTLINE OF THE EPISTLE

I. Paul describes **the pre-eminence of Christ,** our reconciliation in Christ and his own service for Christ. Chapters 1—2:3

II. Paul warns against false teaching, explains **the new life in Christ,** Christian virtues and gives advice for domestic life. Chapters 2:4—4

CHAPTER 1

1. **Paul,** an apostle of Jesus Christ
by the will of God,
and Timotheus *our* brother,
2. **To the saints** and faithful
brethren in Christ which are
at Colosse: Grace *be* unto you,
and peace, from God our Father and
the Lord Jesus Christ.
3. **We give thanks to God** and
the Father of our Lord Jesus Christ,
praying always for you,
4. **Since we heard of your**
faith in Christ Jesus, and of
the love *which ye have* to
all the saints,
5. For the hope which is laid up for you
in heaven, whereof ye heard before in
the word of the truth of the gospel;
6. Which is come unto you, as *it is* in
all the world; and bringeth forth
fruit, as *it doth* also in you, since the
day ye heard *of it*, and knew the
grace of God in truth:
7. As ye also learned of Epaphras our
dear fellow-servant, who is for you
a faithful minister of Christ;
8. Who also declared unto us your
love in the Spirit.
9. **For this cause we**
also, since the day we heard *it*,
do not cease to pray for
you, and to desire
that ye might be filled with
the knowledge of his
will in all wisdom
and spiritual
understanding;
10. **That ye might walk**
worthy of the Lord
unto all pleasing,
being fruitful in every good work,
and increasing in the
knowledge of God;
11. **Strengthened** with all might,
according to his glorious
power, unto all
patience and longsuffering
with joyfulness;
12. **Giving thanks unto the**
Father, which hath made us meet to
be partakers of the inheritance of the
saints in light:
13. **Who hath delivered us**
from the power of
darkness, and hath
translated *us* into the
kingdom of his dear Son:
14. **In whom we have**
redemption through
his blood,
even the forgiveness of sins:
15. **Who is the image of the**
invisible God,
the firstborn of every creature:
16. **For by him were all**
things created, that are in
heaven, and that are in earth,
visible and invisible, whether
they be thrones, or dominions, or
principalities, or powers: all things
were created by him, and for him:
17. **And he is before all**
things, and by him all
things consist.
18. **And he is the**
head of the body,
the church:
who is the beginning,
the firstborn from the dead;
that in all *things* he might
have the preeminence.
19. **For it pleased *the Father***
that in him should all
fulness dwell;
20. **And, having made**
peace through the blood of
his cross, by him to
reconcile all things unto
himself; by him, *I say*, whether *they*
be things in earth, or things in heaven.
21. **And you,** that were sometime
alienated and enemies in *your* mind by
wicked works, yet now
hath he reconciled
22. **In** the body of
his flesh through death, to
present you holy and
unblameable and unreproveable
in his sight:
23. **If ye continue in the faith**
grounded and settled,
and *be* not moved away
from the hope of
the gospel, which ye have heard,
and which was preached to every

creature which is
under heaven; whereof
I Paul am made a minister;
24. **Who now rejoice in my**
sufferings for you, and fill up
that which is behind of the afflictions
of Christ in my flesh for his body's
sake, which is the church:
25. **Whereof I am made a**
minister, according to the
dispensation of God which is given to
me for you,
to fulfil the word of God;
26. ***Even* the mystery which**
hath been hid from ages and
from generations, but now
is made manifest
to his saints:
27. To whom God would make known
what *is* the riches of the glory of this
mystery among the Gentiles; which is
Christ in you, the hope of glory:
28. **Whom we preach,**
warning every man,
and teaching every man
in all wisdom;
that we may present every
man perfect in Christ Jesus:
29. Whereunto I also labour, striving
according to his working, which
worketh in me mightily.

CHAPTER 2

1. For I would that ye knew what great
conflict I have for you, and *for*
them at Laodicea, and *for* as many as
have not seen my face in the flesh;
2. That their hearts might be
comforted, being knit together in love,
and unto all riches of the full
assurance of understanding, to the
acknowledgement of the mystery of
God, and of the Father, and of Christ;
3. In whom are hid all the treasures of
wisdom and knowledge.
4. **And this I say, lest any**
man should
beguile you with enticing words.
5. **For though I be absent in**
the flesh, yet am I with you
in the spirit, joying and beholding
your order, and the stedfastness of
your faith in Christ.
6. **As ye have** therefore
received Christ Jesus the Lord,
***so* walk ye in him:**
7. **Rooted and built up in**
him, and stablished in the
faith, as ye have been taught,
abounding therein with thanksgiving.
8. **Beware lest any man**
spoil you through
philosophy and vain deceit,
after the tradition of men,
after the rudiments of the world,
and not after Christ.
9. **For in him dwelleth**
all the fulness of the
Godhead bodily.
10. **And ye are complete in**
him, which is the head of all
principality and power:
11. **In whom also ye are**
circumcised with the
circumcision made without hands,
in putting off the body of the
sins of the flesh
by the circumcision
of Christ:
12. **Buried with him in**
baptism, wherein also ye
are risen with *him*
through the
faith of the operation of God, who
hath raised him from the dead.
13. **And you, being**
dead in your
sins and the uncircumcision
of your flesh,
hath he quickened
together with him,
having forgiven you
all trespasses;
14. **Blotting out** the handwriting of
ordinances that was
against us,
which was contrary to us,
and took it out of the way,
nailing it to his cross;
15. ***And* having spoiled**
principalities and powers,
he made a shew of them openly,
triumphing over them in it.
16. **Let no man therefore**
judge you in meat, or in
drink, or in respect of an

holyday, or of the new moon, or of the sabbath *days*:
17. Which are a shadow of things to come; but the body *is* of Christ.
18. **Let no man beguile you** of your reward **in a voluntary humility and worshipping of angels,** intruding into those things which he hath not seen, **vainly puffed up by his fleshly mind,**
19. **And not holding the Head, from which all the body by joints** and bands **having nourishment** ministered, **and knit together, increaseth** with the increase of God.
20. **Wherefore if ye be dead with Christ** from the rudiments of the world, **why, as though living in the world, are ye subject to** ordinances,
21. (Touch not; taste not; handle not;
22. Which all are to perish with the using;) after **the** commandments and **doctrines of men?**
23. **Which things have indeed a shew of wisdom in** will-worship, and humility, and **neglecting** of **the body; not in any honour to the satisfying of the flesh.**

CHAPTER 3

1. **If ye then be risen with Christ, seek** those **things** which are **above,** where Christ sitteth on the right hand of God.
2. Set your affection on things above, **not** on **things on the earth.**
3. For ye are dead, and your life is hid with Christ in God.
4. When Christ, *who is* our life, shall appear, then shall ye also appear with him in glory.
5. **Mortify therefore your members** which are **upon the earth;** fornication, uncleanness, inordinate affection, evil concupiscence, and covetousness, which is idolatry:
6. For which things' sake the wrath of God cometh on the children of disobedience:
7. In the which ye also walked some time, when ye lived in them.
8. But now ye also put off all these; anger, wrath, malice, blasphemy, filthy communication out of your mouth.
9. **Lie not one to another, seeing that ye have put off the old man with his deeds;**
10. **And have put on the new *man*,** which is renewed in knowledge **after the image of him that created him:**
11. **Where there is neither Greek nor Jew, circumcision nor uncircumcision,** Barbarian, Scythian, **bond *nor* free: but Christ *is* all, and in all.**
12. **Put on therefore, as the elect of God,** holy and beloved, bowels of mercies, **kindness, humbleness of mind,** meekness, **longsuffering;**
13. **Forbearing** one another, **and forgiving one another,** if any man have a quarrel against any: even as Christ forgave you, so also *do* ye.
14. **And above all** these things ***put on* charity, which is the bond of perfectness.**
15. **And let the peace of God rule in your hearts,** to the which also ye are called in one body; **and be ye thankful.**
16. **Let the word of Christ dwell in you** richly in all wisdom; **teaching and admonishing one another in psalms** and

hymns and spiritual songs,
singing with grace in your
hearts to the Lord.
17. **And whatsoever ye do in**
word or deed, *do* all in the
name of the Lord Jesus,
giving thanks to God and the Father
by him.
18. **Wives, submit**
yourselves unto your own
husbands, as it is fit in the Lord.
19. **Husbands, love *your***
wives, and be not bitter
against them.
20. **Children, obey *your***
parents in all things: for this is well
pleasing unto the Lord.
21. **Fathers, provoke not**
your children *to anger*, lest
they be discouraged.
22. **Servants, obey** in all things
***your* masters** according to the
flesh; not with eye-service, as men
pleasers; but in singleness of heart,
fearing God:
23. **And whatsoever ye do,**
do *it* heartily, as to the
Lord, and not unto men;
24. Knowing that of the Lord ye shall
receive the reward of the inheritance:
for ye serve the Lord Christ.
25. But he that doeth wrong shall
receive for the wrong which he hath
done: and there is no
respect of persons.

CHAPTER 4

1. **Masters, give** unto
***your* servants that which is**
just and equal; knowing that ye also
have a Master in heaven.
2. **Continue in prayer, and**
watch in the same
with thanksgiving;
3. **Withal praying also for**
us, that God would open
unto us
a door of utterance,
to speak the mystery
of Christ, for which I am
also in bonds:
4. That I may make it manifest, as I
ought to speak.
5. **Walk in wisdom toward**
them that are without,
redeeming the time.
6. **Let your speech *be* alway**
with grace, seasoned with salt,
that ye may know how ye ought to
answer every man.
7. **All my state shall**
Tychicus declare unto you,
who is a beloved brother, and a
faithful minister and fellow-servant
in the Lord:
8. Whom I have sent unto you for the
same purpose, that he might know
your estate, and comfort your hearts;
9. **With Onesimus,** a faithful and
beloved brother, who is *one* of you.
They shall make known unto you all
things which *are done* here.
10. **Aristarchus**
my fellow prisoner
saluteth you, and Marcus,
sister's son to Barnabas,
(touching whom ye received
commandments: if he come unto you,
receive him;)
11. **And** Jesus, which is called
Justus, who are of the
circumcision.
These only *are my* fellow-
workers unto the kingdom
of God, which have been a
comfort unto me.
12. **Epaphras,** who is *one* of you,
a servant of Christ,
saluteth you, always
labouring fervently
for you in prayers,
that ye may stand perfect and
complete in all the will of God.
13. For I bear him record, that he hath
a great zeal for you, and them
that are in Laodicea, and
them in Hierapolis.
14. **Luke, the beloved**
physician, and Demas,
greet you.
15. Salute the brethren which are in
Laodicea, and Nymphas, and the
church which is in his house.
16. **And when this epistle is**
read among you,
cause that it be read also

■ **in the church** of the Laodiceans;
and that ye likewise read the *epistle*
from Laodicea.
17. And say to Archippus, Take heed
to the ministry which thou hast
received in the Lord, that thou fulfil it.
■ 18. **The salutation by the**
■ **hand of me Paul.**
■ **Remember my bonds.**
Grace *be* with you.
■ **Amen.**

THE FIRST EPISTLE TO THE THESSALONIANS

BACKGROUND INFORMATION

Author – Paul, an Apostle.
Date Written – probably **between 50** and **52** A.D.

Number of:
Verses - 89
Chapters - 5
Total Words - 1,857
Scan Words - 878
Scan Words represent 48 % of Total Words.

Theme – written to instruct the church in practical Christian living and **how Christians should respond to the Second Coming.**

OUTLINE OF THE EPISTLE

I. **Paul** gives thanks for the Thessalonian's spiritual progress and **defends his message.** Chapters 1—2

II. Paul sends Timothy to the Thessalonians and **Paul's prayer** for them. Chapter 3

III. Paul outlines Christian doctrine concerning morality, **the Second Coming and church life.** Chapters 4—5

CHAPTER 1

1. **Paul,** and **Silvanus, and Timotheus, unto the church of the Thessalonians** *which is* in God the Father and *in* the Lord Jesus Christ: Grace *be* unto you, and peace, from God our Father, and the Lord Jesus Christ.

2. **We give thanks** to God always **for you** all, making mention of you **in our prayers;**

3. **Remembering** without ceasing **your** work of **faith,** and labour of **love, and patience** of hope **in our Lord** Jesus Christ, in the sight of God and our Father;

4. **Knowing,** brethren beloved, **your election** of God.

5. **For our gospel came not** unto you **in word only, but** also **in power,** and **in the Holy Ghost, and in** much **assurance;** as ye know what manner of men we were among you for your sake.

6. **And ye became followers of us, and** of **the Lord, having received the word in** much **affliction, with joy of the Holy Ghost:**

7. **So that ye were ensamples** to all that believe in Macedonia and Achaia.

8. **For from you sounded out the word** of the Lord **not only in Macedonia and Achaia, but also in every place your faith** to God-ward **is spread** abroad; so that we need not to speak any thing.

9. **For they themselves shew** of us what manner of entering in we had unto you, and **how ye turned** to God **from idols to serve the** living and **true God;**

10. **And to wait for his Son** from heaven, **whom he raised** from the dead, ***even* Jesus, which delivered us from the wrath to come.**

CHAPTER 2

1. For yourselves, brethren, know our entrance in unto you, that it was not in vain:

2. **But even after that we had suffered** before, and were shamefully entreated, as ye know, **at Philippi, we were bold** in our God **to speak** unto you **the gospel** of God with much contention.

3. For our exhortation *was* not of deceit, nor of uncleanness, nor in guile:

4. **But as we were** allowed of God to be **put in trust with the gospel,** even so **we speak; not as pleasing men, but God,** which trieth our hearts.

5. **For neither** at any time **used we flattering words,** as ye know, nor a cloak of covetousness; God *is* witness:

6. **Nor** of men **sought we glory,** neither of you, nor *yet* of others, when we might have been burdensome, as the apostles of Christ.

7. **But we were gentle among you,** even as a nurse cherisheth her children:

8. So being affectionately desirous of you, **we were willing to have imparted** unto you, **not the gospel** of God **only, but also our own souls,** because ye were dear unto us.

9. **For ye remember, brethren, our labour and travail:** for labouring night and day,

because we would not be
chargeable unto any of
you, we preached unto you
the gospel of God.
10. **Ye *are* witnesses, and**
God *also*, how
holily and justly and
unblameably we behaved
ourselves
among you that believe:
11. **As ye know how we**
exhorted and comforted
and charged every one of
you, as a father *doth* his children,
12. **That ye would walk**
worthy of God, who hath called
you unto his kingdom and glory
13. **For this cause also**
thank we God without ceasing,
because, when ye
received the word of God
which ye heard of us,
ye received *it* not *as* the word
of men, but as it is
in truth, the word of God, which
effectually worketh also in
you that believe.
14. **For ye,** brethren,
became followers of the
churches of God which
in Judaea are in Christ Jesus:
for ye also have suffered
like things
of your own countrymen,
even as they *have* of the Jews:
15. **Who both killed the Lord**
Jesus, and their own
prophets, and have
persecuted us; and they please
not God, and are contrary to all men:
16. **Forbidding us to speak**
to the Gentiles that they might be
saved, to fill up their sins alway: for
the wrath is come upon them
to the uttermost.
17. **But we, brethren, being**
taken from you for a short time
in presence, not in heart,
endeavoured
the more abundantly
to see your face
with great desire.
18. **Wherefore we would**
have come unto you,
even I Paul, once and again;
but Satan hindered us.
19. For what *is* our hope, or joy, or
crown of rejoicing? *Are* not even ye
in the presence of our Lord Jesus
Christ at his coming?
20. For ye are our glory and joy.

CHAPTER 3

1. Wherefore when we could
no longer forbear,
we thought it good to be
left at Athens alone;
2. **And sent Timotheus,** our
brother, and minister of God, and our
fellow-labourer in the gospel of Christ,
to establish you,
and to comfort you
concerning your faith:
3. **That no man should be**
moved by these
afflictions: for yourselves know
that we are appointed thereunto.
4. For verily, when we were with you,
we told you before that we
should suffer tribulation;
even as it came to pass, and ye know.
5. **For this cause,** when I could
no longer forbear,
I sent to know your faith,
lest by some means the
tempter have tempted you,
and our labour be in vain.
6. **But** now when
Timotheus came from
you unto us, and
brought us good tidings
of your faith and charity, and that ye
have good remembrance of us
always, desiring greatly to see us, as
we also *to see* you:
7. **Therefore, brethren, we**
were comforted over you in all
our affliction and distress
by your faith:
8. For now we live, if ye stand
fast in the Lord.
9. For what thanks can we
render to God again for you, for
all the joy wherewith
we joy for your sakes
before our God;

10. **Night and day praying**
exceedingly that we might
see your face, and might perfect
that which is lacking in your faith?
11. **Now God himself** and our
Father, and our Lord Jesus Christ,
direct our way unto you.
12. **And the Lord make you**
to increase and abound in
love one toward another, and toward
all *men*, even as we *do* toward you:
13. **To the end he may**
stablish your hearts
unblameable in holiness before
God, even our Father,
at the coming of our Lord Jesus
Christ with all his saints.

CHAPTER 4

1. **Furthermore then we**
beseech you, brethren, and
exhort *you* by the Lord Jesus,
that as ye have received
of us how
ye ought to walk and to
please God, *so* ye would abound
more and more.
2. For ye know what commandments
we gave you by the Lord Jesus.
3. **For this is the will of God,**
***even* your sanctification,**
that ye should
abstain from fornication:
4. **That every one of you**
should
know how to possess his
vessel in sanctification
and honour;
5. Not in the lust of concupiscence,
even as the Gentiles which
know not God:
6. **That no *man*** go beyond and
defraud his brother in *any*
matter: because that the Lord *is* the
avenger of all such, as we also have
forewarned you and testified.
7. **For God hath not called**
us unto uncleanness,
but unto holiness.
8. **He therefore that**
despiseth, despiseth not
man, but God, who hath also
given unto us his holy Spirit

9. **But as touching brotherly**
love ye need not that
I write unto you: for
ye yourselves are taught of
God to love one another.
10. **And indeed ye do**
it toward all the brethren which are
in all Macedonia:
but we beseech you, brethren,
that ye increase more
and more;
11. **And that ye study to be**
quiet, and to do your own
business, and to work with
your own hands,
as we commanded you;
12. **That ye may walk**
honestly toward them
that are without,
and *that* ye may
have lack of nothing.
13. **But I would not have you**
to be ignorant, brethren,
concerning them which are
asleep, that ye sorrow not,
even as others which have no hope.
14. **For** if we believe that Jesus died
and rose again, even so
them also
which sleep in Jesus will
God bring with him.
15. **For** this we say unto you by the
word of the Lord, that
we which are alive *and* remain
unto the coming of the Lord
shall not prevent them
which are
asleep.
16. **For the Lord himself**
shall descend from heaven
with a shout, with the voice
of the archangel, and with
the trump of God: and the
dead in Christ shall
rise first:
17. **Then we which** are alive *and*
remain shall be caught up
together
with them in the clouds, to
meet the Lord in the air:
and so shall we ever be
with the Lord.
18. **Wherefore comfort one**

another with these words.

CHAPTER 5

1. **But of the times**
and the seasons, brethren,
ye have no need that I write
unto you.
2. **For** yourselves know perfectly that
the day of the Lord so
cometh as a thief
in the night.
3. **For when they shall say,**
Peace and safety; then
sudden destruction
cometh upon them, as travail upon
a woman with child; and they
shall not escape.
4. **But ye, brethren, are not in**
darkness, that that day
should overtake you
as a thief.
5. **Ye are all the children of**
light, and the children of the day: we
are not of the night, nor of darkness.
6. **Therefore** let us not sleep, as *do*
others; but
let us watch and be sober.
7. For they that sleep sleep in the
night; and they that be drunken are
drunken in the night.
8. But let us, who are of the
day, be sober,
putting on the breastplate
of faith and love;
and for an helmet,
the hope
of salvation.
9. **For God hath not**
appointed us to wrath, but
to obtain salvation by
our Lord Jesus
Christ,
10. **Who died for us, that,**
whether we wake or sleep,
we should live together
with him.
11. Wherefore comfort yourselves
together, and edify one another, even
as also ye do.
12. And we beseech you,
brethren, to know
them which labour among
you, and are over you in
the Lord, and admonish you;
13. And to
esteem them very highly
in love
for their work's sake. *And* be at peace
among yourselves.
14. Now we exhort you, brethren,
warn them that are unruly,
comfort the feebleminded,
support the weak, be
patient toward all *men*.
15 . **Seeing that none render**
evil for evil unto any *man*; but
ever follow that which is good, both
among yourselves, and to all *men*.
16. Rejoice evermore.
17. **Pray without ceasing.**
18. **In every thing give**
thanks: for this is the will of
God in Christ Jesus
concerning you.
19. **Quench not the Spirit.**
20. **Despise not**
prophesyings.
21. Prove all things; hold fast that
which is good.
22. **Abstain from all**
appearance of evil.
23. And the very God of peace
sanctify you wholly;
and *I pray God* your
whole spirit and
soul and body be
preserved blameless unto
the coming of our Lord
Jesus Christ.
24. Faithful *is* he that calleth you,
who also will do *it*.
25. Brethren, pray for us.
26. Greet all the brethren
with an holy kiss.
27. I charge you by the Lord that this
epistle be read unto all the
holy brethren.
28. The grace of our Lord Jesus Christ
be with you.
Amen.

THE SECOND EPISTLE TO THE THESSALONIANS

BACKGROUND INFORMATION

Author – Paul, an apostle.
Date Written – probably between 50 and **52** A.D.

Number of:
Verses - 47
Chapters - 3
Total Words - 1,042
Scan Words - 487
Scan Words represent 46 % of Total Words.

Theme – written to instruct Christians in **practical conduct and the** continued **need for industry in light of the Second Coming.**

OUTLINE OF THE EPISTLE

I. Paul offers **encouragement in persecution and instruction** concerning the day of the Lord.
Chapters 1—2.

II. Paul gives confession of confidence and **commandments to work.**
Chapter 3

CHAPTER 1

1. **Paul, and Silvanus, and**
Timotheus, unto the church
of the Thessalonians in God
our Father and the Lord Jesus Christ:
2. Grace unto you, and peace,
from God our Father and the
Lord Jesus Christ.
3. **We** are bound to
thank God always for you,
brethren, as it is meet,
because that
your faith groweth
exceedingly, and the charity of every
one of you all toward each
other aboundeth;
4. **So that we** ourselves
glory in you
in the churches of God
for your patience and faith
in all your
persecutions and
tribulations that ye endure:
5. ***Which is* a manifest token**
of the righteous judgment
of God, that ye may be
counted worthy of the
kingdom of God, for
which ye also suffer:
6. **Seeing *it is* a righteous**
thing with God to
recompense tribulation
to them that trouble you;
7. And to you who are
troubled rest with us,
when the Lord
Jesus shall be revealed
from heaven with his
mighty angels,
8. **In flaming fire taking**
vengeance on them that
know not God, and that
obey not the gospel
of our Lord Jesus Christ:
9. **Who shall be punished**
with everlasting
destruction from the presence
of the Lord, and from the
glory of his power;
10. **When he shall come to**
be glorified in his saints,
and to be admired in all them that
believe (because our testimony
among you was believed) in that day.
11. **Wherefore also we pray**
always for you,
that our
God would
count you worthy of *this*
calling, and fulfil all the good
pleasure of *his* goodness, and
the work of faith with power:
12. **That** the name of our Lord
Jesus Christ may be
glorified in you, and ye in
him, according to the grace of our
God and the Lord Jesus Christ.

CHAPTER 2

1. **Now we beseech you,**
brethren, by the coming of our Lord
Jesus Christ, and *by* our gathering
together unto him,
2. **That ye be not soon**
shaken in mind, or be troubled,
neither by spirit, nor by word, nor by
letter as from us, as that the day of
Christ is at hand.
3. **Let no man deceive you**
by any means:
for *that day shall not come*,
except there come a falling
away first, and that man of
sin be revealed,
the son of perdition;
4. **Who opposeth and**
exalteth himself above all
that is called God,
or that is worshipped; so that he as
God sitteth in the temple of God,
shewing himself that
he is God.
5. Remember ye not, that, when I was
yet with you, I told you these things?
6. And now ye know what withholdeth
that he might be revealed in his time.
7. **For the mystery of iniquity**
doth already work: only he
who now letteth *will let*,
until he be taken out
of the way.
8. **And then shall that**
Wicked be revealed, whom
the Lord shall consume
with the spirit of his mouth,
and shall destroy with the

brightness of
his coming:
9. ***Even him*, whose coming**
is after the working
of Satan with all power and
signs and lying wonders,
10. **And with all**
deceivableness
of unrighteousness
in them that perish;
because they received not
the love of
the truth, that they might be saved.
11. **And for this cause God**
shall send them strong
delusion, that they
should believe a lie:
12. **That they** all might
be damned who believed
not the truth, but had pleasure
in unrighteousness.
13. **But** we are bound to give thanks
alway to God for you, brethren
beloved of the Lord, because
God hath from the beginning
chosen you to salvation
through sanctification of
the Spirit and belief of the truth:
14. Whereunto he called you by our
gospel, to the obtaining of the glory
of our Lord Jesus Christ.
15. **Therefore, brethren,**
stand fast, and hold the traditions
which ye have been taught, whether
by word, or our epistle.
16. **Now our Lord** Jesus Christ
himself, and God, even our Father,
which hath loved us, and hath given
us everlasting consolation and good
hope through grace,
17. **Comfort your hearts,**
and stablish you in every
good word and work.

CHAPTER 3

1. **Finally, brethren, pray for**
us, that the word of the Lord
may have *free* course, and
be glorified, even as *it is* with you:
2. **And that we may be**
delivered from
unreasonable and wicked
men: for all *men* have not faith.
3. **But the Lord is faithful,**
who shall stablish you, and
keep *you* from evil.
4. **And we have confidence**
in the Lord touching you, that ye
both do and will do the things which we
command you.
5. **And the Lord direct your**
hearts into the love of God,
and into the patient waiting
for Christ.
6. Now we command you, brethren,
in the name of our Lord
Jesus Christ, that ye
withdraw yourselves from
every brother that walketh
disorderly, and not after the
tradition which he received of us.
7. **For yourselves know how**
ye ought to follow us: for
we behaved not ourselves disorderly
among you;
8. **Neither did we eat any**
man's bread for nought;
but wrought with labour
and travail night and day,
that we might not be
chargeable to any of you:
9. Not because we have
not power, but
to make ourselves an
ensample unto you to follow us.
10. **For** even when
we were with you, this
we commanded you, that if
any would not work,
neither should he eat.
11. **For we hear that** there are
some which
walk among you
disorderly, working not at
all, but are busybodies.
12. Now them that are such we
command and exhort by our Lord
Jesus Christ, that with quietness they
work, and eat their own bread.
13. **But ye, brethren, be not**
weary in well-doing.
14. **And if any** man
obey not our word
by this epistle, note that man, and
have no company with him,
that he may be ashamed.

15. **Yet count *him* not as an
enemy, but admonish *him*
as a brother.**
16. Now the Lord of peace himself
give you peace always by all means.
The Lord *be* with you all.
17. The salutation of Paul with mine
own hand, which is the token in
every epistle: so I write.
18. The grace of our Lord Jesus
Christ *be* with you all.
Amen.

THE FIRST EPISTLE TO TIMOTHY

BACKGROUND INFORMATION

Author – Paul, an Apostle.
Date Written – probably **between 60** and **65** A.D.

Number of:
Verses - 113
Chapters - 6
Total Words - 2,269
Scan Words - 1,059
Scan Words represent 46 % of Total Words.

Theme – written to encourage a young minister and instruct him in the proper conduct of his ministry.

OUTLINE OF THE EPISTLE

I. **Paul** greets Timothy and **warns about false teachers.**
Chapter 1:1—11

II. **Paul declares the apostolic commission.**
Chapter 1:12—20

III. **Paul outlines rules for public worship and qualifications for church leaders.**
Chapters 2—3

IV. **Paul gives Timothy personal advice.**
Chapters 4—6.

CHAPTER 1

1. **Paul,** an apostle of Jesus Christ by the commandment of God our Saviour, and Lord Jesus Christ, *which is* our hope;

2. **Unto Timothy,** *my* own son in the faith: Grace, mercy, *and* peace, from God our Father and Jesus Christ our Lord.

3. **As I besought thee to abide still at Ephesus,** when I went into Macedonia, **that thou mightest charge some that they teach no other doctrine,**

4. **Neither give heed to fables and** endless **genealogies,** which minister questions, **rather than godly edifying** which is in faith: *so do.*

5. **Now the end of the commandment is charity out of a pure heart, and** *of* a good conscience, and ***of* faith unfeigned:**

6. **From which some** having swerved **have turned aside** unto vain jangling;

7. **Desiring to be teachers of the law;** understanding neither what they say, nor whereof they affirm.

8. But we know that **the law *is* good, if a man use it lawfully;**

9. **Knowing this, that the law is not made for a righteous man, but for the lawless** and disobedient, for the ungodly and for sinners, for unholy and profane, for murderers of fathers and murderers of mothers, for manslayers,

10. For whoremongers, for them that defile themselves with mankind, for menstealers, for liars, for perjured persons, and if there be any other thing that is contrary to sound doctrine;

11. According to the glorious gospel of the blessed God, which was committed to my trust.

12. **And I thank Christ** Jesus our Lord, who hath enabled me, **for** that he counted me faithful, **putting me into the ministry;**

13. **Who was before a blasphemer,** and a **persecutor, and injurious: but I obtained mercy, because I did *it* ignorantly in unbelief.**

14. And the grace of our Lord was exceeding abundant with faith and love which is in Christ Jesus.

15. **This *is* a faithful saying,** and worthy of all acceptation, **that Christ Jesus came into the world to save sinners; of whom I am chief.**

16. Howbeit for this cause **I obtained mercy, that in me** first Jesus **Christ might shew** forth all **longsuffering, for a pattern to them which should** hereafter **believe** on him to life everlasting.

17. Now unto the King eternal, immortal, invisible, the only wise God, *be* honour and glory for ever and ever. Amen.

18. **This charge I commit unto thee,** son Timothy, **according to the prophecies** which went before **on thee, that thou** by them **mightest war a good warfare;**

19. **Holding faith, and a good conscience;** which some having put away concerning faith have made shipwreck:

20. Of whom is Hymenaeus and Alexander; whom I have delivered unto Satan, that they may learn not to blaspheme.

CHAPTER 2

1. **I exhort therefore, that,** first of all, **supplications, prayers, intercessions, *and* giving of thanks, be made for all men;**

2. **For kings, and *for* all**
that are
in authority; that we may
lead a quiet and
peaceable life
in all godliness and honesty.
3. **For this *is* good**
and acceptable
in the sight of God
our Saviour;
4. **Who will have all men to**
be saved, and to come unto the
knowledge of the truth.
5. **For *there is* one God, and**
one mediator between God
and men, the man
Christ Jesus;
6. **Who gave himself a**
ransom for all,
to be testified in due time.
7. **Whereunto I am**
ordained a preacher, and
an apostle, (I speak the truth
in Christ, *and* lie not;)
a teacher of the Gentiles
in faith and verity.
8. **I will therefore that men**
pray every where,
lifting up holy hands,
without wrath and doubting.
9. **In like manner also, that**
women adorn themselves
in modest apparel, with
shamefacedness and
sobriety; not with
broided hair, or gold, or pearls, or
costly array;
10. **But** (which becometh women
professing godliness)
with good works.
11. **Let the woman learn in**
silence with all subjection.
12. **But I suffer not a woman**
to teach, nor
to usurp authority over the
man, but to be in silence.
13. **For Adam was first**
formed, then Eve.
14. **And Adam was not**
deceived, but the woman
being deceived was in
the transgression.
15. Notwithstanding she shall be
saved in childbearing, if they continue
in faith and charity and holiness
with sobriety.

CHAPTER 3

1. This *is* a true saying,
If a man desire the office of
a bishop, he desireth a
good work.
2. **A bishop then must be**
blameless, the husband of one
wife, vigilant, sober, of good
behaviour, given to hospitality,
apt to teach;
3. Not given to wine, no striker, not
greedy of filthy lucre; but patient, not
a brawler, not covetous;
4. One that ruleth well his own house,
having his children in subjection
with all gravity;
5. (For if a man know not how to rule
his own house, how shall he take
care of the church of God?)
6. Not a novice, lest being lifted up
with pride he fall into the
condemnation of the devil.
7. **Moreover he must have a**
good report of them which
are without; lest he fall into
reproach and the snare of the devil.
8. **Likewise *must* the**
deacons *be* grave, not
double-tongued, not given to
much wine, not greedy of filthy lucre;
9. Holding the mystery of the faith in a
pure conscience.
10. **And let these also first**
be proved; then let them use
the office of a deacon, being
found blameless.
11. **Even so *must their* wives**
***be* grave, not slanderers,**
sober, faithful in all things.
12. **Let the deacons be the**
husbands of one wife,
ruling their children and their
own houses well.
13. **For they that have used**
the office of a deacon well
purchase to themselves
a good degree,
and great boldness in the faith
which is in Christ Jesus.

14. These things write I unto thee,
hoping to come unto thee shortly:
15. **But if I tarry** long, that
thou mayest know how
thou oughtest to behave
thyself
in the house of God,
which is the church of the living God,
the pillar and ground of the truth.
16. And without controversy
great is the mystery of
godliness: God was
manifest in the flesh,
justified in the Spirit, seen
of angels, preached unto
the Gentiles, believed on in
the world, received up
into glory.

CHAPTER 4

1. **Now the Spirit speaketh**
expressly,
that in the latter times some
shall depart from the faith,
giving heed to seducing
spirits, and doctrines of devils;
2. **Speaking lies in**
hypocrisy; having their
conscience seared with a hot iron;
3. **Forbidding to marry, *and***
***commanding* to abstain**
from meats, which God
hath created to be
received with thanksgiving
of them which believe and know
the truth.
4. **For every creature of God**
***is* good, and nothing to be**
refused, if it be received
with thanksgiving:
5. **For it is sanctified by the**
word of God and prayer.
6. **If thou put the brethren in**
remembrance of these
things, thou shalt be a
good minister
of Jesus Christ, nourished up in the
words of faith and of good doctrine,
whereunto thou hast attained.
7. **But refuse** profane and
old wives' fables, and
exercise thyself *rather*
unto godliness.
8. **For bodily exercise**
profiteth little: but
godliness is profitable
unto all things, having
promise of the life that now
is, and of that which is
to come.
9. This *is* a faithful saying and worthy
of all acceptation.
10. For therefore
we both
labour and suffer reproach,
because we trust in the living
God, who is the Saviour of all
men, specially of those that believe.
11. **These things command**
and teach.
12. **Let no man despise thy**
youth; but be thou an
example of the believers, in word,
in conversation, in charity, in spirit, in
faith, in purity.
13. **Till I come, give**
attendance to reading, to
exhortation, to doctrine.
14. **Neglect not the gift**
that is in thee, which was
given thee by prophecy,
with the laying on of the
hands of the presbytery.
15. **Meditate upon these**
things; give thyself wholly
to them; that thy profiting may
appear to all.
16. **Take heed unto thyself,**
and unto
the doctrine; continue in them:
for in doing this thou shalt both save
thyself, and them that hear thee.

CHAPTER 5

1. **Rebuke not an elder,** but
entreat *him* as a father; *and*
the younger men
as brethren;
2. **The elder women as**
mothers; the younger as
sisters, with all purity.
3. **Honour widows**
that are widows indeed.
4. **But if any widow have**
children or nephews,
let them learn

first to shew piety at home, and
to requite their parents:
for that is good and acceptable
before God.
5. **Now she that is a widow**
indeed,
and desolate, trusteth in
God, and continueth in
supplications and prayers
night and day.
6. **But she that liveth in**
pleasure is dead
while she liveth.
7. And these things give in charge,
that they may be blameless.
8. **But if any provide not for**
his own, and specially for those of
his own house,
he hath denied the faith, and
is worse than an infidel.
9. **Let not a widow be taken**
into the number under
threescore years old, having
been the wife of one man,
10. Well reported of for good works; if
she have brought up children, if
she have lodged strangers, if she
have washed the saints' feet, if she
have relieved the afflicted, if she have
diligently followed every good work.
11. **But the younger widows**
refuse: for when they have begun
to wax wanton against Christ,
they will marry;
12. Having damnation, because they
have cast off their first faith.
13. **And withal they learn *to***
***be* idle,** wandering about from
house to house;
and not only idle, but
tattlers also and
busybodies, speaking things
which they ought not.
14. **I will therefore that the**
younger women marry,
bear children, guide the house, give
none occasion to the adversary to
speak reproachfully.
15. For some are already turned aside
after Satan.
16. **If any man**
or woman that believeth
have widows, let them
relieve them, and let not the
church be charged; that it may
relieve them that are widows indeed.
17. **Let the elders that rule**
well be counted worthy of
double honour, especially they
who labour in the word and doctrine.
18. For the scripture saith, Thou shalt
not muzzle the ox that treadeth out
the corn. And, The labourer *is* worthy
of his reward.
19. **Against an elder receive**
not an accusation,
but before two or
three witnesses.
20. **Them that sin rebuke**
before all,
that others also may fear.
21. **I charge *thee*** before God,
and the Lord Jesus Christ,
and the elect angels,
that thou observe these
things without preferring
one before another,
doing nothing by partiality.
22. **Lay hands suddenly on**
no man, neither be partaker of
other men's sins:
keep thyself pure.
23. **Drink no longer water,**
but use a little
wine for thy stomach's
sake and thine often infirmities.
24. **Some men's sins are**
open beforehand, going
before to judgment; and
some *men* they
follow after.
25. **Likewise also the good**
works *of some* are manifest
beforehand; and they that are
otherwise cannot be hid.

CHAPTER 6

1. **Let** as many
servants as are under the yoke
count their own masters
worthy of all honour,
that the name of God and *his* doctrine
be not blasphemed.
2. **And** they that have
believing masters,
let them not despise *them*,

because they are brethren; but rather
do *them* service, because they are
faithful and beloved, partakers of the
benefit. These things teach
and exhort.
3. **If any man teach**
otherwise, and consent not to
wholesome words, *even* the words of
our Lord Jesus Christ, and to the
doctrine which is according
to godliness;
4. **He is proud, knowing**
nothing, but doting about
questions and strifes of words,
whereof cometh envy, strife, railings,
evil surmisings,
5. Perverse disputings of men of
corrupt minds, and destitute of the
truth, supposing that
gain is godliness:
from such withdraw thyself.
6. **But godliness with**
contentment is great gain.
7. **For we brought nothing**
into *this* world, *and it is*
certain we can carry
nothing out.
8. **And having food and**
raiment let us be therewith
content.
9. **But they that will be rich**
fall into temptation
and a snare,
and *into* many
foolish and hurtful
lusts, which drown men in
destruction and perdition.
10. **For the love of money is**
the root of all evil: which while
some coveted after, they have erred
from the faith, and pierced themselves through with many sorrows.
11. **But thou, O man of God,**
flee these things; and
follow after righteousness,
godliness, faith, love,
patience, meekness.
12. **Fight the good fight of**
faith, lay hold on eternal
life, whereunto thou art also called,
and hast professed a good profession
before many witnesses.
13. **I give thee charge**
in the sight of God, who quickeneth all
things, and *before* Christ Jesus, who
before Pontius Pilate witnessed a
good confession;
14. **That thou keep**
***this* commandment**
without spot, unrebukable,
until the appearing of our
Lord Jesus Christ:
15. Which in his times he shall shew,
***who is* the blessed and**
only Potentate, the King of
kings, and Lord of lords;
16. **Who only hath**
immortality, dwelling in the
light which no man can
approach unto;
whom no man hath seen,
nor can see: to whom *be* honour and
power everlasting. Amen.
17. **Charge them that are**
rich in this world,
that they be not
highminded, nor trust in
uncertain
riches, but in the living
God, who giveth us richly all things
to enjoy;
18. **That they** do good, that they
be rich in good works,
ready to distribute,
willing to communicate;
19. **Laying up** in store
for themselves a
good foundation
against the time to come,
that they may lay hold on
eternal life.
20. **O Timothy, keep that**
which is
committed to thy trust,
avoiding profane *and* vain
babblings, and
oppositions of science
falsely so called:
21. Which some professing have
erred concerning the faith. Grace *be*
with thee.
Amen.

THE SECOND EPISTLE TO TIMOTHY

BACKGROUND INFORMATION

Author – Paul, an Apostle.
Date Written – probably **between 64** and **65** A.D.

Number of:
Verses - 83
Chapters - 4
Total Words - 1,703
Scan Words - 782
Scan Words represent 45 % of Total Words.

Theme – written to challenge a young minister to **hold fast to the truths of the Gospel.**

OUTLINE OF THE EPISTLE

I. **Paul gives thanks** for Timothy, exhorts him to endurance, and offers advice on personal conduct and relationships.
Chapters 1—2

II. **Paul speaks of the coming apostasy** and the reliability of the scriptures.
Chapter 3

III. **Paul charges Timothy to preach** and Paul presents his own Last Testament.
Chapter 4

CHAPTER 1

■ 1. **Paul,** an apostle of Jesus Christ
by the will of God, according to the
promise of life which is in
Christ Jesus,
■ 2. **To Timothy,** *my* dearly beloved
son: Grace, mercy, *and* peace, from
God the Father and Christ Jesus
our Lord.
3. I thank God, whom I serve from *my*
forefathers with pure conscience,
that without ceasing I have
remembrance of thee in my prayers
night and day;
4. Greatly desiring to see thee, being
mindful of thy tears, that I may
be filled with joy;
5. When I call to remembrance the
unfeigned faith that is in thee, which
dwelt first in thy grandmother Lois,
and thy mother Eunice; and I am
persuaded that in thee also.
6. Wherefore I put thee in
remembrance that thou
■ **stir up the gift of God,**
which is
■ **in thee by the putting on of**
■ **my hands.**
■ 7. **For God hath not given us**
■ **the spirit of fear; but of**
■ **power,** and of
■ **love, and of a sound mind.**
■ 8. **Be not** thou therefore
■ **ashamed** of the testimony
■ **of our Lord, nor of me**
his prisoner:
■ **but be thou partaker of the**
■ **afflictions of the gospel**
■ **according to the power**
■ **of God;**
■ 9. **Who hath saved us, and**
■ **called *us*** with an holy calling,
■ **not according to** our
■ **works, but according to his**
■ **own purpose and grace,**
which was
■ **given us in Christ** Jesus
■ **before the world began,**
■ 10. **But is now made**
■ **manifest by**
the appearing of our Saviour Jesus
■ **Christ, who** hath
■ **abolished death, and** hath
■ **brought life** and immortality to
light through the gospel:
11. Whereunto
■ **I am appointed a**
■ **preacher,** and an
■ **apostle, and** a
■ **teacher of the Gentiles.**
■ 12. **For** the
■ **which cause I** also
■ **suffer** these things:
■ **nevertheless I am not**
■ **ashamed: for I know whom**
■ **I have believed, and am**
■ **persuaded that he is able**
■ **to keep that which I have**
■ **committed unto him**
■ **against that day.**
■ 13. **Hold fast the form of**
■ **sound words,** which thou hast
heard of me, in faith and love which is
in Christ Jesus.
■ 14. **That good thing which**
■ **was committed unto thee**
■ **keep by the Holy Ghost**
which dwelleth in us.
■ 15. **This thou knowest,** that
■ **all** they which are
■ **in Asia be turned away**
■ **from me;** of whom are Phygellus
and Hermogenes.
■ 16. **The Lord give mercy unto**
■ **the house of Onesiphorus;**
■ **for he oft refreshed me,**
and was not ashamed of my chain:
17. But, when he was in Rome, he
sought me out very diligently, and
found *me.*
18. The Lord grant unto him that he
may find mercy of the Lord in that
day: and in how many things he
ministered unto me at Ephesus, thou
knowest very well.

CHAPTER 2

■ 1. **Thou therefore,** my son,
■ **be strong in** the
■ **grace** that is in Christ Jesus.
■ 2. **And the things** that thou hast
■ **heard of me among many**
■ **witnesses, the same**
■ **commit thou to faithful men,**
who shall be able to teach others also.
3. Thou therefore

endure hardness, as a
good soldier of Jesus Christ.
4. **No man that warreth**
entangleth himself with the
affairs of *this* life;
that he may please him who hath
chosen him to be a soldier.
5. **And if a man also strive**
for masteries, *yet* is he not
crowned, except he
strive lawfully.
6. The husbandman that laboureth
must be first partaker of the fruits.
7. **Consider what I say; and**
the Lord give thee
understanding in all things.
8. **Remember that Jesus**
Christ of the seed of David
was raised from the dead
according to my gospel:
9. **Wherein I suffer**
trouble, as an evildoer,
***even* unto bonds; but the**
word of God
is not bound.
10. **Therefore I endure all**
things
for the elect's sakes, that they
may also obtain the salvation which is
in Christ Jesus with eternal glory.
11. *It is* a faithful saying:
For if we be dead with *him*,
we shall also live with *him:*
12. **If we suffer, we shall**
also reign with *him:* if we
deny *him*, he also
will deny us:
13. If we believe not, *yet* he abideth
faithful: he cannot deny himself.
14. Of these things put *them* in
remembrance, charging *them* before
the Lord that they strive not about
words to no profit, *but* to the
subverting of the hearers.
15. **Study to shew thyself**
approved unto God,
a workman that needeth not
to be ashamed,
rightly dividing the word
of truth.
16. **But shun profane *and***
vain babblings: for they will
increase unto more ungodliness.
17. **And their word will eat**
as doth a
canker: of whom is
Hymenaeus and Philetus;
18. **Who** concerning the truth have
erred, saying that the
resurrection is past
already; and overthrow the faith
of some.
19. **Nevertheless the**
foundation of God
standeth sure, having this
seal, The Lord knoweth
them that are his. And, Let
every one that nameth the name
of Christ depart from iniquity.
20. **But in a great house**
there are not only vessels
of gold and of
silver, but also
of wood and of
earth; and some to honour,
and some to dishonour.
21. If a man therefore purge himself
from these, he shall be a vessel
unto honour, sanctified, and meet for
the master's use, *and* prepared unto
every good work.
22. **Flee also youthful lusts:**
but follow righteousness,
faith, charity, peace, with them that
call on the Lord out of a pure heart.
23. **But foolish and**
unlearned questions
avoid, knowing that they do
gender strifes.
24. **And the servant of the**
Lord must not strive; but
be gentle unto all *men*, apt to
teach, patient,
25. **In meekness instructing**
those that oppose
themselves; if God
peradventure
will give them repentance
to the acknowledging of the truth;
26. And *that* they may recover
themselves out of the snare of the
devil, who are taken captive by him at
his will.

CHAPTER 3

1. **This know also, that in the**

last days perilous times
shall come.
2. **For men shall be lovers of**
their own selves, covetous,
boasters, proud, blas-
phemers, disobedient to
parents, unthankful,
unholy,
3. **Without natural affection,**
trucebreakers, false
accusers, incontinent,
fierce, despisers of those
that are good,
4. **Traitors,** heady,
highminded, lovers of pleasures
more than lovers of God;
5. **Having a form of**
godliness, but denying the
power thereof: from such
turn away.
6. **For** of
this sort are they which creep into
houses, and
lead captive silly women
laden with sins,
led away with divers lusts,
7. **Ever learning, and never**
able to come to
the knowledge of
the truth.
8. Now as Jannes and Jambres
withstood Moses, so do these also
resist the truth: men of corrupt minds,
reprobate concerning the faith.
9. **But they shall proceed no**
further: for their folly shall
be manifest unto all *men*, as
theirs also was.
10. **But thou hast** fully
known my doctrine,
manner of life, purpose,
faith, longsuffering,
charity, patience,
11. **Persecutions,** afflictions,
which came unto me at Antioch, at
Iconium, at Lystra; what persecutions
I endured: but out of *them* all the
Lord delivered me.
12. **Yea, and all that will live**
godly in Christ Jesus
shall suffer persecution.
13. **But evil men** and seducers
shall wax worse and worse,
deceiving, and
being deceived.
14. **But continue** thou
in the things which thou hast
learned and hast been assured of,
knowing of whom
thou hast learned *them;*
15. And that
from a child thou hast
known the holy scriptures,
which are able to
make thee wise unto salvation
through faith which is in Christ Jesus.
16. **All scripture *is* given by**
inspiration of God, and *is*
profitable for doctrine, for
reproof, for correction, for
instruction in
righteousness:
17. **That the man of God may**
be perfect, throughly furn-
ished unto all good works.

CHAPTER 4

1. **I charge *thee*** therefore before
God, and the Lord Jesus Christ, who
shall judge the quick and the dead at
his appearing and his kingdom;
2. **Preach the word; be**
instant in season, out of
season; reprove, rebuke,
exhort with all
longsuffering and doctrine.
3. **For the time will come**
when they will not endure
sound doctrine; but after their own
lusts shall they heap to themselves
teachers, having itching ears;
4. **And they shall turn away**
their ears
from the truth, and shall be
turned unto fables.
5. **But watch thou in all**
things, endure afflictions, do the
work of an evangelist, make full proof
of thy ministry.
6. **For I am now ready to be**
offered, and the time of my
departure is at hand.
7. **I have fought a good fight,**
I have finished *my* course,
I have kept the faith:
8. **Henceforth there is laid**

up for me a crown of
righteousness, which the
Lord, the righteous judge,
shall give me at that day:
and not to me only, but
unto all them also
that love his appearing.
9. Do thy diligence to
come shortly unto me:
10. **For Demas hath**
forsaken me, having loved this
present world, and is departed unto
Thessalonica, Crescens to Galatia,
Titus unto Dalmatia.
11. **Only Luke is with me.**
Take Mark, and bring him
with thee: for he is profitable to me
for the ministry.
12. And Tychicus have I sent
to Ephesus.
13. The cloak that I left at Troas with
Carpus, when thou comest, bring
with thee, and the books, *but*
especially the parchments.
14. Alexander the coppersmith
did me much evil: the Lord
reward him according
to his works:
15. Of whom be thou ware also; for he
hath greatly withstood our words.
16. **At my first answer no**
man stood with me, but all *men*
forsook me: *I pray God* that it may not
be laid to their charge.
17. **Notwithstanding the**
Lord stood with me,
and strengthened me;
that by me the preaching might be
fully known, and *that* all
the Gentiles might hear:
and I was delivered out of the mouth
of the lion.
18. **And the Lord shall**
deliver me from every evil
work, and will preserve *me* unto his
heavenly kingdom: to whom *be* glory
for ever and ever. Amen.
19. Salute Prisca and Aquila, and the
household of Onesiphorus.
20. Erastus abode at Corinth: but
Trophimus have I left at Miletum sick.
21. Do thy diligence to come before
winter. Eubulus greeteth thee, and
Pudens, and Linus, and Claudia, and
all the brethren.
22. The Lord Jesus Christ *be* with thy
spirit. Grace *be* with you.
Amen.

THE EPISTLE TO TITUS

BACKGROUND INFORMATION

Author – Paul, an Apostle.
Date Written – probably **between 62** and **65** A.D.

Number of:
Verses - 46
Chapters - 3
Total Words - 921
Scan Words - 466
Scan Words represent 50 % of Total Words.

Theme – written **to instruct a** young **minister in the** proper **conduct and role of believers in the Church.**

OUTLINE OF THE EPISTLE

I. Paul presents **the qualifications of elders and bishops** and warns against false teachers. Chapter 1

II. Paul describes **domestic regulations** and the Christian life. Chapter 2

III. Paul tells Timothy the bases of **Christian ethics and** advises him on how to **discipline** factious men. Chapter 3

CHAPTER 1

1. **Paul,** a servant of God, and
an apostle of Jesus Christ,
according to the faith of God's elect,
and the acknowledging of the truth
which is after godliness;
2. **In hope of eternal life,**
which God, that cannot lie,
promised before the
world began;
3. But hath in due times manifested
his word through preaching, which is
committed unto me according to the
commandment of God our Saviour;
4. **To Titus, *mine* own son**
after the common
faith: Grace, mercy, *and* peace,
from God the Father and the Lord
Jesus Christ our Saviour.
5. **For this cause left I thee in**
Crete, that thou shouldest
set in order the things that
are wanting, and ordain
elders in every city, as I had
appointed thee:
6. If any be blameless, the husband of
one wife, having faithful children not
accused of riot or unruly.
7. **For a bishop must**
be blameless,
as the steward of God;
not selfwilled, not soon
angry, not given to wine,
no striker, not given to filthy lucre;
8. **But a lover of hospitality,**
a lover
of good men, sober, just,
holy, temperate;
9. **Holding fast the faithful**
word as he hath been taught,
that he may be able by
sound doctrine both to
exhort and to convince the
gainsayers.
10. **For there are many**
unruly and
vain talkers and
deceivers, specially they of
the circumcision:
11. **Whose mouths must be**
stopped, who subvert
whole houses, teaching things
which they ought not, for filthy
lucre's sake
12. **One of** themselves, *even* a
prophet of
their own, said, The
Cretians *are* alway liars,
evil beasts, slow bellies.
13. **This witness is true.**
Wherefore rebuke them
sharply, that they may be
sound in the faith;
14. **Not giving heed to**
Jewish fables, and
commandments of men, that turn
from the truth.
15. **Unto the pure all things**
***are* pure: but unto them that**
are defiled and unbelieving
***is* nothing pure;** but even their
mind and conscience is defiled.
16. **They profess that they**
know God; but in works
they deny *him*, being
abominable, and disobedient, and
unto every good work reprobate.

CHAPTER 2

1. **But speak thou the**
things which become
sound doctrine:
2. **That the aged men be**
sober, grave, temperate,
sound in faith, in charity,
in patience.
3. **The aged women**
likewise, that *they be* in behaviour
as becometh holiness, not false
accusers, not given to much wine,
teachers of good things;
4. **That they may teach the**
young women to be sober,
to love their husbands, to
love their children,
5. ***To be* discreet, chaste,**
keepers at home, good,
obedient to their own
husbands, that the word of God
be not blasphemed.
6. **Young men likewise**
exhort to be
sober minded.
7. **In all things shewing**
thyself a pattern of
good works: in doctrine

***shewing* uncorruptness,**
gravity, sincerity,
8. **Sound speech, that**
cannot be condemned;
that he that is of the contrary part may
be ashamed, having no evil thing to
say of you.
9. ***Exhort* servants to be**
obedient unto their own masters,
and to please *them* well in all *things;*
not answering again;
10. **Not purloining, but**
shewing all good
fidelity; that they may adorn the
doctrine of God our Saviour
in all things.
11. **For the grace of God that**
bringeth salvation hath
appeared to all men,
12. **Teaching us that,**
denying ungodliness
and worldly
lusts, we should live
soberly, righteously,
and godly, in this present
world;
13. **Looking for**
that blessed hope, and
the glorious appearing of
the great God and
our Saviour Jesus Christ;
14. **Who gave himself** for us,
that he might redeem us
from all iniquity, and purify
unto himself
a peculiar people, zealous
of good works.
15. **These things speak,**
and exhort, and rebuke
with all authority. Let no
man despise thee.

CHAPTER 3

1. **Put them in mind to be**
subject to principalities
and powers,
to obey magistrates,
to be ready to every good work,
2. **To speak evil of no man,**
to be no brawlers, *but* gentle, shewing
all meekness unto all men.
3. **For we ourselves also**
were sometimes foolish,
disobedient, deceived,
serving divers lusts
and pleasures, living in malice
and envy, hateful,
***and* hating one another.**
4. **But** after that
the kindness and
love of God our Saviour
toward man
appeared,
5. **Not by works of**
righteousness which we
have done, but according
to his mercy he saved us,
by the washing of regen-
eration, and renewing of
the Holy Ghost;
6. Which he shed on us abundantly
through Jesus Christ our Saviour;
7. **That being justified by his**
grace, we should be made
heirs according to the hope
of eternal life.
8. ***This is* a faithful saying,**
and these things I will that thou
affirm constantly,
that they which have
believed in God might be
careful to maintain good
works. These things are good and
profitable unto men.
9. **But avoid foolish**
questions, and
genealogies, and
contentions, and strivings
about the law; for they are
unprofitable and vain.
10. **A man that is an heretic**
after the first and second
admonition reject;
11. Knowing that he that is such is
subverted, and sinneth, being
condemned of himself.
12. When I shall send Artemas unto
thee, or Tychicus, be diligent to come
unto me to Nicopolis: for I have
determined there to winter.
13. Bring Zenas the lawyer and
Apollos on their journey diligently, that
nothing be wanting unto them.
14. And let ours also learn to maintain
good works for necessary uses,
that they be not unfruitful.

15. **All that are with me salute thee.** Greet them that love us in the faith. Grace *be* with you all. **Amen.**

THE EPISTLE TO PHILEMON

BACKGROUND INFORMATION

Author – Paul, an Apostle.
Date Written – probably **between 60** and **65** A.D.

Number of:
Verses - 25
Chapters - 1
Total Words - 445
Scan Words - 214
Scan Words represent 48 % of Total Words.

Theme – written to show that **relationships** between people **take on a new dimension when** they become **Christians.**

OUTLINE OF THE EPISTLE

I. **Paul's greeting** to Philemon.
Verses 1—3
II. **Paul's** offer of **thanksgiving.**
Verses 4—7
III. **Paul's appeal for Onesimus,** a slave.
Verses 8—21
IV. **Paul's conclusion.**
Verses 22—25

CHAPTER 1

1. **Paul, a prisoner of** Jesus
Christ, and Timothy *our* brother,
unto Philemon our dearly
beloved, and fellow-labourer,
2. And to *our* beloved Apphia, and
Archippus our fellow-soldier, and to
the church in thy house:
3. Grace to you, and peace, from God
our Father and the Lord Jesus Christ.
4. **I thank my God,** making
mention of thee always in my prayers,
5. **Hearing of thy love and**
faith, which thou hast
toward the Lord Jesus, and
toward all saints;
6. That the communication of thy faith
may become effectual by the
acknowledging of every good thing
which is in you in Christ Jesus.
7. **For we have great joy**
and consolation in thy love,
because the bowels of
the saints are refreshed by
thee, brother.
8. **Wherefore, though I might**
be much
bold in Christ to enjoin thee that
which is convenient,
9. **Yet for love's sake I**
rather beseech *thee*, being
such an one as
Paul the aged, and now also
a prisoner of Jesus Christ.
10. **I beseech thee for my**
son Onesimus,
whom I have
begotten in
my bonds:
11. **Which in time past was**
to thee unprofitable, but
now profitable to thee
and to me:
12. **Whom I have sent again:**
thou therefore receive him,
that is, mine own bowels:
13. **Whom I would have**
retained
with me, that in thy stead he might
have ministered unto me in the bonds
of the gospel:
14. **But without thy mind**
would I do nothing; that thy
benefit should not be as it were of
necessity, but willingly.
15. **For perhaps he** therefore
departed for a season,
that thou shouldest
receive him for ever;
16. **Not now as a servant,**
but above a servant,
a brother beloved, specially to
me, but how much more unto thee,
both in the flesh, and in the Lord?
17. **If thou count me** therefore
a partner, receive him
as myself.
18. **If he hath wronged thee,**
or oweth *thee* aught,
put that on mine account;
19. **I Paul have written *it***
with mine own hand,
I will repay *it*: albeit I do not say
to thee how thou owest unto me even
thine own self besides.
20. **Yea, brother, let me**
have joy of thee in the Lord:
refresh my bowels in the Lord.
21. **Having confidence in thy**
obedience I wrote unto thee,
knowing that thou wilt also
do more than I say.
22. But withal
prepare me also a lodging:
for I trust that through your
prayers I shall be given
unto you.
23. There salute thee Epaphras, my
fellow-prisoner in Christ Jesus;
24. Marcus, Aristarchus, Demas,
Lucas, my fellow-labourers.
25. The grace of our Lord Jesus Christ
be with your spirit.
Amen.

THE EPISTLE TO THE HEBREWS

BACKGROUND INFORMATION

Author – Unknown
Date Written – probably **between 65** and **85** A.D.

Number of:
Versus - 303
Chapters - 13
Total Words - 6,913
Scan Words - 3,493
Scan Words represent 50 % of Total Words.

Theme – written to encourage believers, especially Jewish believers, to endure persecution and remain faithful to the Lord, **showing the superiority of Jesus Christ.**

OUTLINE OF THE EPISTLE

I. **Christ as superior to angels.**
Chapters 1—2

II. **Christ as superior to Moses and Joshua.**
Chapters 3—4

III. **Christ's superiority as the High Priest.**
Chapters 5—10

IV. **Christ and the superiority of the new covenant**
Chapters 10:19—13

CHAPTER 1

1. **God,** who at sundry times and in
divers manners spake in time past
unto the fathers by the prophets,
2. **Hath in these last days**
spoken unto us
by *his* Son, whom he hath
appointed heir of all
things, by whom also he
made the worlds;
3. **Who being**
the brightness of *his* glory, and
the express
image of his person,
and upholding all things
by the word of his power,
when he had by himself
purged our sins, sat down
on the right hand of the
Majesty on high;
4. **Being made** so much
better than the
angels, as
he hath by inheritance
obtained a more
excellent name than they.
5. **For unto which of the**
angels said he at any time,
Thou art my Son, this day
have I begotten thee?
And again, I will be to him a Father,
and he shall be to me a Son?
6. **And again,** when he bringeth in
the first begotten into the world,
he saith, And
let all the angels of God
worship him.
7. **And of the angels he**
saith, Who maketh his
angels spirits,
and his ministers a flame of fire.
8. **But unto the Son *he saith,***
Thy throne, O God,
***is* for ever**
and ever: a sceptre of righteousness
is the sceptre of thy kingdom.
9. Thou hast loved righteousness,
and hated iniquity;
therefore God, *even* thy God, hath
anointed thee with the oil of gladness
above thy fellows.
10. **And, Thou,**
Lord, in the beginning
hast laid the foundation of
the earth; and the heavens
are the works
of thine hands:
11. **They shall perish;**
but thou remainest; and they all shall
wax old as doth a garment;
12. And as a vesture shalt thou fold
them up, and they shall be changed:
but thou art the same, and
thy years shall not fail.
13. **But to which of the**
angels said he at any time,
Sit on my right hand,
until I make thine enemies
thy footstool?
14. Are they not all ministering spirits,
sent forth to minister for them who
shall be heirs of salvation?

CHAPTER 2

1. **Therefore** we ought to
give the more
earnest heed to the things
which we have
heard, lest at any time
we should let *them* slip.
2. **For if the word spoken by**
angels was stedfast, and
every transgression
and disobedience
received a just
recompence of reward;
3. **How shall we escape, if**
we neglect so great
salvation; which
at the first began to be
spoken by the Lord, and
was confirmed unto us by
them that heard *him;*
4. **God also bearing *them***
witness, both
with signs and
wonders, and with divers
miracles, and gifts of the
Holy Ghost,
according to his own will?
5. For unto the angels hath he not put
in subjection the world to come,
whereof we speak.
6. **But one** in a certain place
testified, saying,
What is man,

■ **that thou art mindful**
■ **of him?**
or the son of man,
that thou visitest him?
■ 7. **Thou madest him a little**
■ **lower than the angels;** thou
crownedst him with glory and honour,
■ **and** didst
■ **set him over the works**
■ **of thy hands:**
■ 8. **Thou hast put all things**
in subjection
■ **under his feet.**
For in that he put all
in subjection under him, he left
nothing *that is* not put under him.
■ **But** now
■ **we see not yet all** things
■ **put under him.**
■ 9. **But we see Jesus, who**
■ **was made a little lower**
■ **than** the
■ **angels for the suffering**
■ **of death,**
crowned with glory and honour;
■ **that he by** the
■ **grace** of God
■ **should taste death for**
■ **every man.**
■ 10. **For it became him,**
for whom *are* all things, and by whom
are all things, in bringing many sons
unto glory,
■ **to make the captain of** their
■ **salvation perfect**
■ **through sufferings.**
■ 11. **For both he**
■ **that sanctifieth**
■ **and they** who are
■ **sanctified** ***are*** all of
■ **one: for which cause**
■ **he is not ashamed to**
■ **call them brethren,**
12. Saying, I will declare thy
name unto my brethren,
in the midst of the church will
I sing praise unto thee.
13. And again, I will put my trust in
him. And again, Behold I and the
children which God hath given me.
■ 14. **Forasmuch then as the**
■ **children are** partakers of
■ **flesh and blood, he also**
himself likewise
■ **took part of the same;**
■ **that through death he might**
■ **destroy** him that had
the power of death, that is,
■ **the devil;**
■ 15. **And deliver them who**
through fear of death
■ **were** all their lifetime
■ **subject to bondage.**
16. For verily he took not on *him*
the nature of angels; but he took on
him the seed of Abraham.
17. Wherefore in all things
■ **it behoved him to be made**
■ **like unto** ***his*** **brethren, that**
■ **he might be a**
merciful and faithful
■ **high priest**
in things *pertaining* to God,
■ **to make reconciliation for**
■ **the sins of the people.**
18. For in that he himself
hath suffered being tempted, he is
able to succour them that
are tempted.

CHAPTER 3

■ 1. **Wherefore,** holy brethren,
partakers of the heavenly calling,
■ **consider** the Apostle and High
Priest of our profession,
■ **Christ Jesus;**
2. Who was faithful to him that
appointed him, as also
Moses *was faithful* in all his house.
■ 3. **For this** ***man*** **was** counted
■ **worthy of more glory than**
■ **Moses, inasmuch as**
■ **he who hath builded the**
■ **house hath more honour**
■ **than the house.**
4. For every house is builded
by some *man;* but
■ **he that built all things**
■ ***is*** **God.**
■ 5. **And Moses verily**
■ ***was*** **faithful** in all his house,
■ **as a servant,**
for a testimony of those things which
were to be spoken after;
■ 6. **But Christ as a son**
over his own house;

■ **whose house are we, if we**
■ **hold fast** the confidence and the
rejoicing of the hope firm
■ **unto the end.**
■ 7. **Wherefore (as the Holy**
■ **Ghost saith, To-day if ye**
■ **will hear his voice,**
■ 8. **Harden not your hearts,**
as in the provocation, in the day of
temptation in the wilderness:
9. When your fathers tempted me,
proved me, and saw
my works forty years.
10. Wherefore I was grieved with that
generation, and said, They do alway
err in *their* heart; and they
have not known my ways.
11. So I sware in my wrath, They shall
not enter into my rest.)
■ 12. **Take heed, brethren,**
■ **lest there be**
in any of you an evil heart of
■ **unbelief,** in departing
from the living God.
■ 13. **But exhort one another**
daily, while it is called To-day;
■ **lest any** of you
■ **be hardened through the**
■ **deceitfulness of sin.**
■ 14. **For we are made**
■ **partakers of Christ, if we**
■ **hold** the beginning of
our confidence
■ **stedfast unto the end;**
15. While it is said,
■ **To-day if ye** will
■ **hear his voice, harden not**
■ **your hearts,**
as in the provocation.
■ 16. **For some, when they had**
■ **heard, did provoke:**
■ **howbeit not all** that
■ **came out of Egypt** by Moses.
■ 17. **But** with whom was he grieved
forty years? *was it* not
with them that had sinned,
■ **whose carcases fell**
■ **in the wilderness?**
18. And to whom sware he that they
should not enter into his rest, but
to them that believed not?
19. So we see that
■ **they could not enter in**
■ **because of unbelief.**

CHAPTER 4

■ 1. **Let us therefore fear, lest,**
a promise being left *us* of
■ **entering into his rest, any**
of you should seem to
■ **come short** of it.
■ 2. **For** unto us was the gospel
preached, as well as unto them: but
■ **the word preached**
■ **did not profit them, not**
■ **being mixed with faith**
in them that heard *it*.
■ 3. **For we which have**
■ **believed do enter into rest,**
as he said, As I have sworn in my
wrath, if they shall enter into my rest:
■ **although the works were**
■ **finished from the**
■ **foundation of the world.**
■ 4. **For** he spake in a certain place of
the seventh *day* on this wise, And
■ **God did rest the seventh**
■ **day from all his works.**
5. And in this *place* again, If
they shall enter into my rest.
■ 6. **Seeing therefore** it remaineth
■ **that some**
must enter therein, and they
■ **to whom it was first**
■ **preached entered not in**
■ **because of unbelief:**
■ 7. **Again,** he limiteth a certain day,
■ **saying in David,** To-day, after
so long a time; as it is said,
■ **To-day if ye will hear**
■ **his voice, harden**
■ **not your hearts.**
■ 8. **For if Jesus had given**
■ **them rest, then would he**
■ **not afterward have spoken**
■ **of another day.**
■ 9. **There remaineth therefore**
■ **a rest to the people of God.**
10. For he that is entered into his rest,
he also hath ceased from his own
works, as God *did* from his.
■ 11. **Let us labour therefore**
■ **to enter into that rest,**
lest any man fall after the same
example of unbelief.
■ 12. **For the word of God *is***

quick, and powerful, and sharper than any two edged **sword,** piercing **even to the dividing** asunder **of soul and spirit,** and of the joints and marrow, **and *is* a discerner of the thoughts and intents of the heart.**

13. Neither is there any creature that is not manifest in his sight: but **all things *are* naked and opened unto** the eyes of **him** with whom we have to do.

14. **Seeing then that we have a great high priest,** that is passed into the heavens, **Jesus the Son of God, let us hold** fast ***our* profession.**

15. **For we have not an high priest which cannot be touched with** the feeling of **our infirmities; but was** in all points **tempted** like **as *we are, yet* without sin.**

16. **Let us therefore come boldly unto the throne of grace, that we may obtain mercy, and find grace to help in time of need.**

CHAPTER 5

1. **For every high priest** taken from among men **is ordained** for men in things *pertaining* to God, **that he may offer** both gifts and **sacrifices for sins:**

2. **Who can have compassion** on the ignorant, and **on them that are out of the way; for** that **he** himself **also is compassed with infirmity.**

3. And by reason hereof he ought, as for the people, so also for himself, to offer for sins.

4. **And no man taketh this honour** unto himself, **but he that is called** of God, **as *was* Aaron.**

5. **So also Christ glorified not himself to be made an high priest; but he that said unto him, Thou art my Son,** to-day have I begotten thee.

6. As he saith also in another *place*, **Thou *art* a priest for ever after the order of Melchisedec.**

7. **Who in** the days of **his flesh,** when he had **offered up prayers** and supplications **with** strong crying and **tears unto him that was able to save him from death,** and was heard in that he feared;

8. **Though he were a Son, yet learned he obedience** by the things which he suffered;

9. **And being made perfect, he became the author of eternal salvation** unto all them that obey him;

10. Called of God an high priest after the order of Melchisedec.

11. **Of whom we have many things to say, and hard to be uttered, seeing ye are dull** of hearing.

12. **For** when for the time ye ought to be teachers, **ye have need that one teach you again** which *be* **the first principles of the oracles of God; and** are become such as **have need of milk, and not** of **strong meat.**

13. **For every one that useth milk** *is* unskilful in the word of righteousness: for he **is a babe.**

14. **But strong meat belongeth to them** that are **of full age, *even* those who**

by reason of use have
their senses exercised to
**discern both good
and evil.**

CHAPTER 6

1. **Therefore** leaving the principles
of the doctrine of Christ,
**let us go on unto
perfection; not laying
again the foundation of
repentance** from dead works,
and of faith toward God,
2. **Of** the doctrine of
**baptisms, and of laying on
of hands, and of
resurrection** of the dead,
and of eternal
judgment
3. And this will we do, if God permit.
4. **For *it is* impossible for
those who were once
enlightened, and have
tasted of the heavenly gift,
and were made partakers
of the Holy Ghost,**
5. **And have tasted the
good word** of God,
and the powers of the world
to come,
6. **If they shall fall away, to
renew them** again
**unto repentance; seeing
they crucify** to themselves
the Son of God afresh,
and put *him* to an open shame.
7. For the earth which drinketh in the
rain that cometh oft upon it, and
bringeth forth herbs meet for them by
whom it is dressed, receiveth
blessing from God:
8. But that which beareth thorns and
briers *is* rejected, and *is* nigh unto
cursing; whose end *is* to be burned.
9. **But, beloved, we are
persuaded better things
of you,**
and things that accompany salvation,
though we thus speak.
10. **For God *is* not
unrighteous to forget
your** work and
**labour of love, which ye
have shewed** toward his name,
**in that ye have ministered
to the saints,** and do minister.
11. **And** we desire that
every one of you do
shew the same diligence
to the full assurance of hope
unto the end:
12. That ye
be not slothful, but
followers of them who
**through faith and patience
inherit the promises.**
13. **For when God made
promise to Abraham,**
because he could
swear by no greater,
he sware by himself,
14. **Saying,** Surely blessing
I will bless thee,
and multiplying I will multiply thee.
15. **And so, after he had
patiently endured,
he obtained** the promise.
16. For men verily swear by the
greater: and an oath for confirmation
is to them an end of all strife.
17. **Wherein God,**
willing more abundantly
to shew unto the heirs of promise
**the immutability of his
counsel, confirmed *it*
by an oath:**
18. That by two immutable things,
**in which *it was* impossible
for God to lie,** we might have a
strong consolation, who have
fled for refuge to lay hold upon the
hope set before us:
19. **Which *hope* we have
as an anchor** of the soul,
both sure and stedfast, and
which entereth into that within
the veil;
20. **Whither the forerunner is**
for us entered, *even*
**Jesus, made an high
priest for ever after the
order of Melchisedec.**

CHAPTER 7

1. **For this Melchisedec,**
king of Salem, priest of the

most high God, who
met Abraham returning
from the slaughter of the kings,
and blessed him;
2. **To whom also Abraham**
gave a tenth part of all; first
being by interpretation
King of righteousness,
and after that also King of Salem,
which is, King of peace;
3. **Without father,**
without mother, without descent,
having neither beginning
of days,
nor end of life; but made
like unto the Son of God;
abideth a
priest continually.
4. **Now consider how great**
this man *was*, unto whom
even the patriarch
Abraham gave the tenth
of the spoils.
5. And verily they that are of
the sons of Levi, who receive
the office of the priesthood,
have a commandment to
take tithes of the people
according to the law, that is,
of their brethren, though they
come out of the loins of Abraham:
6. **But he whose descent is**
not counted from them
received tithes of
Abraham, and blessed
him that had the promises.
7. **And** without all contradiction
the less is blessed
of the better.
8. And here men that die receive
tithes; but there he *receiveth them*, of
whom it is witnessed that he liveth.
9. And as I may so say,
Levi also, who receiveth
tithes, payed tithes
in Abraham.
10. For he was yet in the loins of his
father, when Melchisedec met him.
11. **If therefore**
perfection were by the
Levitical priesthood, (for
under it the people received the law,)
what further
need *was there* that
another priest should rise
after the order of
Melchisedec, and not be called
after the order of Aaron?
12. For the priesthood being changed,
there is made of necessity a change
also of the law.
13. **For he of whom these**
things are spoken
pertaineth to another tribe,
of which no man gave
attendance at the altar.
14. **For** *it is* evident that
our Lord sprang out of
Juda; of which tribe
Moses spake nothing
concerning priesthood.
15. **And** it is yet
far more evident: for that
after the similitude of
Melchisedec there
ariseth another priest,
16. **Who is made, not**
after the law
of a carnal commandment,
but after the power of an
endless life.
17. **For he testifieth, Thou *art***
a priest for ever after the
order of Melchisedec.
18. For there is verily a disannulling of
the commandment going before
for the weakness and
unprofitableness thereof.
19. **For the law made**
nothing perfect, but
the bringing in of
a better hope *did;* by the
which we draw nigh
unto God.
20. **And** inasmuch as
not without an oath
he was made priest:
21. (For those priests were made
without an oath; but this with an oath
by him that said unto him,
The Lord sware
and will not repent,
Thou *art* a priest for
ever after the order
of Melchisedec:)
22. By so much was

■ **Jesus made a surety of a**
■ **better testament.**
23. And they truly
were many priests, because they
were not suffered to continue
by reason of death:
24. But this *man*,
■ **because he** continueth ever,
■ **hath an unchangeable**
■ **priesthood.**
■ 25. **Wherefore he is able**
■ **also to save them**
to the uttermost
■ **that come unto God by him,**
■ **seeing he ever liveth to**
■ **make intercession** for them.
■ 26. **For such an high priest**
■ **became us, *who is* holy,**
harmless, undefiled,
■ **separate from sinners,**
■ **and** made
■ **higher than the heavens;**
■ 27. **Who needeth not daily,**
as those high priests,
■ **to offer up sacrifice,** first
■ **for his own sins, and** then for
■ **the people's: for this he did**
■ **once, when he offered**
■ **up himself.**
28. For the law maketh men high
priests which have infirmity; but the
word of the oath, which was since the
law, *maketh* the Son, who is
consecrated for evermore.

CHAPTER 8

■ 1. **Now** of the things which we have
spoken *this is* the sum:
■ **We have** such
■ **an high priest,** who is
■ **set on the right hand of the**
■ **throne of the Majesty**
in the heavens;
■ 2. **A minister of**
the sanctuary, and of
■ **the true tabernacle,** which
■ **the Lord pitched,**
■ **and not man.**
3. For every high priest is ordained to
offer gifts and sacrifices: wherefore *it*
is of necessity that this man have
somewhat also to offer.
■ 4. **For if he were on earth, he**
■ **should not be a priest,**
■ **seeing that there are**
■ **priests** that offer gifts
■ **according to the law:**
■ 5. **Who serve unto the**
■ **example** and shadow
■ **of heavenly things, as**
■ **Moses was admonished of**
■ **God** when he was
about to make the tabernacle:
■ **for, See, saith he,** *that* thou
■ **make all things**
■ **according to the pattern**
■ **shewed** to thee
■ **in the mount.**
■ 6. **But now hath he obtained**
■ **a more excellent ministry,**
by how much
■ **also he is the mediator of a**
■ **better covenant,** which was
established upon better promises.
■ 7. **For if that first *covenant***
■ **had been faultless, then**
■ **should no place have been**
■ **sought for the second.**
■ 8. **For** finding fault with them,
■ **he saith,** Behold,
■ **the days** come, saith the Lord,
■ **when I will make a new**
■ **covenant with** the house of
■ **Israel and** with the house of
■ **Judah:**
9. Not according to the covenant that
I made with their fathers in the day
when I took them by the hand to lead
them out of the land of Egypt;
because they continued not in my
covenant, and I regarded them not,
saith the Lord.
■ 10. **For this *is* the covenant**
■ **that I will make**
with the house of Israel after those
days, saith the Lord;
■ **I will put my laws into their**
■ **mind, and write them in**
■ **their hearts: and I will be to**
■ **them a God, and they shall**
■ **be to me a people:**
11. And they shall not teach every
man his neighbour, and every man his
brother, saying, Know the Lord: for all
shall know me, from the
least to the greatest.

12. **For I will be merciful**
to their unrighteousness,
and their sins and their
iniquities will I remember
no more.
13. In that he saith, A new *covenant*,
he hath made the first old. Now that
which decayeth and waxeth old *is*
ready to vanish away.

CHAPTER 9

1. **Then verily the first**
***covenant* had**
also ordinances
of divine service,
and a worldly sanctuary.
2. **For there was a**
tabernacle made; the first,
wherein *was* the candlestick, and the
table, and the shewbread;
which is called
the sanctuary.
3. **And after the**
second veil, the
tabernacle which is called the
Holiest of all;
4. **Which had**
the golden censer, and
the ark of the covenant
overlaid round about with gold,
wherein *was* the golden
pot that had manna,
and Aaron's rod that budded,
and the
tables of the covenant;
5. **And over it the cherubims**
of glory
shadowing the mercyseat;
of which we cannot now
speak particularly.
6. **Now** when these things
were thus ordained,
the priests went always
into the first tabernacle,
accomplishing the service
of God.
7. **But into the second *went***
the high priest alone once
every year, not without
blood, which he
offered for himself, and
***for* the errors of**
the people:
8. **The Holy Ghost this**
signifying, that the way into
the holiest of all
was not yet made
manifest, while as
the first tabernacle was yet
standing:
9. Which *was* a figure for the time then
present, in which were offered
both gifts and sacrifices, that could
not make him that did the service
perfect, as pertaining to
the conscience;
10. *Which stood* only in meats and
drinks, and divers washings, and
carnal ordinances, imposed *on them*
until the time of reformation.
11. **But Christ being**
come an high priest
of good things to come,
by a greater and more
perfect tabernacle,
not made with hands,
that is to say, not of this building;
12. **Neither by the blood of**
goats and calves, but by
his own blood he entered in
once into
the holy place, having
obtained eternal
redemption *for us.*
13. **For if the blood of bulls**
and of goats, and the ashes of
an heifer sprinkling the unclean,
sanctifieth to the purifying of
the flesh:
14. **How much more shall**
the blood of Christ,
who through the eternal Spirit
offered himself without
spot to God, purge your
conscience from dead works
to serve the living
God?
15. **And** for this cause
he is the mediator of the
new testament, that by means of
death, for the redemption of the
transgressions *that were* under the
first testament, they which are called
might receive the promise of
eternal inheritance.
16. **For where a testament *is*,**

there must also of necessity
be the death of the testator.
17. **For a testament** ***is*** **of**
force after men are dead:
otherwise it is of no strength at all
while the testator liveth.
18. **Whereupon neither the**
first ***testament*** **was**
dedicated without blood.
19. **For when Moses had**
spoken every precept to all the
people according to the law,
he took the blood of calves
and of goats, with water, and
scarlet wool, and hyssop, and
sprinkled both the book,
and all the people,
20. **Saying, This** ***is*** **the blood**
of the testament which God
hath enjoined unto you.
21. **Moreover he sprinkled**
with blood
both the tabernacle, and
all the vessels
of the ministry.
22. **And almost**
all things are by the law
purged with blood;
and without shedding of
blood is no remission.
23. *It was* therefore necessary that
the patterns of things in the heavens
should be purified with these; but the
heavenly things themselves with
better sacrifices than these.
24. **For Christ** is not
entered into the holy places
made with hands, *which are* the figures
of the true; but into heaven itself,
now to appear in
the presence of God for us:
25. **Nor** yet that he should offer
himself often,
as the high priest entereth
into the holy place every
year with blood of others;
26. For then must he often have
suffered since the foundation
of the world:
but now
once in the end of the world hath
he appeared to put away
sin by the sacrifice
of himself.
27. **And as it is appointed**
unto men once to die, but
after this the judgment:
28. **So Christ was once**
offered to bear the sins of
many; and unto them
that look for him shall he
appear the second time
without sin unto salvation.

CHAPTER 10

1 **For the law** having a shadow of
good things to come, *and* not the very
image of the things,
can never with those
sacrifices which they
offered year by year
continually
make the comers
thereunto perfect.
2. **For then would they not**
have ceased to be offered?
because that
the worshippers once
purged should have had
no more conscience
of sins.
3. **But in those** ***sacrifices***
there is **a remembrance**
again *made*
of sins every year.
4. **For** ***it is*** **not possible that**
the blood of bulls and of
goats should take
away sins.
5. **Wherefore when he**
cometh into the world,
he saith, Sacrifice and
offering thou wouldest not,
but a body hast thou
prepared me:
6. In burnt offerings and *sacrifices* for
sin thou hast had no pleasure.
7. Then said I, Lo, I come (in the
volume of the book it is written of
me,) to do thy will, O God.
8. Above when he said, Sacrifice and
offering and burnt offerings and
offering for sin thou wouldest not,
neither hadst pleasure *therein;* which
are offered by the law;
9. **Then said he, Lo, I come**

to do thy will, O God.
He taketh away the first, that he may
establish the second.
10. **By the which will we are**
sanctified through the
offering of the body of
Jesus Christ once *for all.*
11. And every priest standeth daily
ministering and offering oftentimes
the same sacrifices, which can never
take away sins:
12. **But this man, after he**
had offered one sacrifice
for sins for ever,
sat down on the right hand
of God;
13. From henceforth expecting
till his enemies be made
his footstool.
14. **For by one offering he**
hath perfected for ever
them that are sanctified.
15. ***Whereof* the**
Holy Ghost also
is a witness to us:
for after that
he had said before,
16. **This *is* the covenant that I**
will make with them after those
days, saith the Lord,
I will put my laws into their
hearts, and in their
minds will I write them;
17. **And their sins** and iniquities
will I remember no more.
18. **Now where remission**
of these
***is, there is* no more**
offering for sin.
19. **Having therefore,** brethren,
boldness to enter into the
holiest by the blood
of Jesus,
20. **By a new and living way,**
which he hath consecrated for us,
through the veil, that is
to say,
his flesh;
21. **And *having* an high**
priest over the house of God;
22. **Let us draw near with a**
true heart in full assurance
of faith, having our hearts sprinkled
from an evil conscience, and our
bodies washed with pure water.
23. **Let us hold fast the**
profession of *our* faith
without wavering;
(for he *is* faithful that promised;)
24. **And let us consider one**
another to provoke unto love and
to good works:
25. **Not forsaking the**
assembling of
ourselves together, as the
manner of some *is;*
but exhorting *one another*: and so
much the more, as ye see the
day approaching.
26. **For if we sin**
wilfully after that
we have received
the knowledge of the truth,
there remaineth no more
sacrifice for sins,
27. **But a certain**
fearful looking for of
judgment and fiery
indignation, which shall devour
the adversaries.
28. **He that despised Moses'**
law died without mercy
under two or
three witnesses:
29. **Of how much sorer**
punishment, suppose ye,
shall he be thought
worthy, who hath trodden
under foot the Son of God,
and hath counted the
blood of the covenant,
wherewith he was sanctified,
an unholy thing, and hath
done despite unto
the Spirit of grace?
30. **For we know him that** hath
said, Vengeance
belongeth unto me,
I will recompense,
saith the Lord. And again, The Lord
shall judge his people.
31. ***It is* a fearful thing to fall**
into the hands of the
living God.
32. But call to remembrance the
former days, in which, after ye were

illuminated, ye endured a great
fight of afflictions;
33. Partly, whilst ye were made a
gazingstock both by reproaches and
afflictions; and partly, whilst ye
became companions of them that
were so used.
34. For ye had compassion of me in
my bonds, and took joyfully the
spoiling of your goods, knowing in
yourselves that ye have in heaven a
better and an enduring substance.
■ 35. **Cast not away therefore**
■ **your confidence,** which hath
great recompence of reward.
■ 36. **For** ye have need
of patience, that,
■ **after ye have done the will**
■ **of God, ye might receive**
■ **the promise.**
37. For yet a little while, and he that
shall come will come, and
will not tarry.
■ 38. **Now the just shall live by**
■ **faith: but if *any man* draw**
■ **back, my soul shall have**
■ **no pleasure** in him.
■ 39. **But we are not of them**
who draw back unto perdition;
■ **but of them that believe to**
■ **the saving of the soul.**

CHAPTER 11

■ 1. **Now faith is the**
■ **substance of things hoped**
■ **for, the evidence of things**
■ **not seen.**
2. For by it the elders
obtained a good report.
■ 3. **Through faith**
we understand that
■ **the worlds were framed**
■ **by the word of God, so that**
■ **things** which are
■ **seen were not made of**
■ **things which do appear.**
■ 4. **By faith Abel offered**
unto God
■ **a more excellent sacrifice**
than Cain, by which he obtained
witness that he was righteous, God
testifying of his gifts: and by it he
being dead yet speaketh.
■ 5. **By faith Enoch was**
■ **translated** that he should not see
death; and was not found, because
God had translated him:
■ **for before his translation**
he had this testimony, that
■ **he pleased God.**
■ 6. **But without faith *it is***
■ **impossible to please**
him: for he that cometh to
■ **God** must believe that he is, and
that he is a rewarder of them that
diligently seek him.
■ 7. **By faith Noah,**
being warned of God of things not
seen as yet, moved with fear,
■ **prepared an ark to the**
■ **saving of his house;** by the
which he condemned the world,
■ **and became heir of the**
■ **righteousness** which is
■ **by faith.**
■ 8. **By faith Abraham,** when he
was called to go out into a place which
he should after receive for an
inheritance, obeyed; and he
■ **went out, not knowing**
■ **whither he went.**
■ 9. **By faith he sojourned in**
■ **the land of promise,**
as *in* a strange country, dwelling
in tabernacles
■ **with Isaac and Jacob,**
■ **the heirs with him**
of the same promise:
■ 10. **For he looked for a city**
■ **which hath foundations,**
■ **whose builder** and maker
■ ***is* God.**
■ 11. **Through faith also**
■ **Sara** herself
■ **received strength to**
■ **conceive** seed, and was
delivered of a child
■ **when she was past age,**
because she judged him faithful
who had promised.
■ 12. **Therefore sprang**
there even
■ **of one,** and him
■ **as good as dead,**
■ ***so many* as the stars**
of the sky in multitude,

and as
the sand which is
by the sea shore innumerable.
13. **These all died in faith,**
not having received the
promises, but having seen
them afar off, and were
persuaded of *them*,
and embraced *them*,
and confessed that they
were strangers
and pilgrims on the earth.
14. **For** they that say such things
declare plainly that
they seek a country.
15. And truly, if they had been mindful
of that *country* from whence they
came out, they might have had
opportunity to have returned.
16. But now they desire
a better *country*,
that is, an
heavenly: wherefore God
is not ashamed to be
called
their God: for he hath
prepared for them a city.
17. **By faith Abraham,**
when he was tried,
offered up Isaac; and he that
had received the promises offered up
his only begotten *son*,
18.**Of whom it was said,**
That in Isaac shall thy
seed be called:
19. **Accounting that God**
was* able to raise *him
up, even
from the dead; from whence
also he received him in a figure.
20. **By faith Isaac blessed**
Jacob and Esau
concerning things to come.
21. **By faith Jacob,**
when he was a-dying,
blessed both
the sons of Joseph;
and worshipped, *leaning* upon
the top of his staff.
22. **By faith Joseph,**
when he died,
made mention of
the departing of the children of
Israel; and gave commandment
concerning his bones.
23. **By faith Moses,**
when he was born,
was hid three months of his
parents, because they saw *he was*
a proper child; and they were not
afraid of the king's commandment.
24. **By faith Moses,**
when he was come to years,
refused to be called the
son of Pharaoh's daughter;
25. **Choosing rather to**
suffer affliction with the
people of God, than to
enjoy the pleasures of sin
for a season;
26. **Esteeming the reproach**
of Christ greater riches
than the treasures in Egypt:
for he had respect unto the
recompence of the reward.
27. **By faith he forsook**
Egypt, not fearing the wrath of the
king: for he endured, as
seeing him who
is invisible.
28. **Through faith he kept the**
passover, and the sprinkling of
blood, lest he that destroyed the
firstborn should touch them.
29. **By faith they passed**
through the Red sea as by dry
land: which the Egyptians assaying to
do were drowned.
30. **By faith the walls of**
Jericho fell down, after they were
compassed about seven days.
31. **By faith the harlot**
Rahab perished not
with them that believed not,when she
had received the spies with peace.
32. **And what shall I more**
say? for the
time would fail me to tell of
Gedeon, and *of*
Barak, and *of*
Samson, and *of*
Jephthae; *of*
David also, and
Samuel, and *of*
the prophets:
33. **Who through faith**

subdued kingdoms,
wrought righteousness,
obtained promises,
stopped the mouths
of lions.
34. **Quenched** the violence of
fire, escaped the edge of the
sword, out of weakness were made
strong, waxed valiant in fight,
turned to flight the
armies of the aliens.
35. **Women received their**
dead raised to life again:
and others were tortured,
not accepting deliverance;
that they might obtain a
better resurrection:
36. **And others had**
trial of *cruel*
mockings and scourgings,
yea, moreover of bonds
and imprisonment:
37. They were stoned,
they were sawn asunder,
were tempted, were
slain with the sword: they wandered
about in sheepskins and
goatskins; being
destitute, afflicted,
tormented;
38. **(Of whom the world was**
not worthy:) they wandered in
deserts, and *in* mountains, and *in* dens
and caves of the earth.
39. **And these all, having**
obtained a good report
through faith, received not
the promise:
40. **God having provided**
some better thing for us,
that they without us should
not be made perfect.

CHAPTER 12

1. **Wherefore seeing we also**
are compassed about with
so great a cloud of
witnesses, let us lay aside
every weight, and the
sin which doth so easily beset *us*,
and let us
run with patience
the race that is set
before us,
2. **Looking unto Jesus the**
author and finisher of ***our***
faith; who for the joy
that was set before him
endured the cross,
despising the shame,
and is set down at the right
hand of the throne of
God.
3. **For consider him that**
endured such contradiction of
sinners against himself,
lest ye be wearied and
faint in your minds.
4. **Ye have not yet resisted**
unto blood, striving against sin.
5. **And ye have forgotten**
the exhortation which speaketh
unto you as unto children,
My son, despise not thou
the chastening of the Lord,
nor faint when thou art rebuked of him:
6. **For whom the Lord loveth**
he chasteneth, and scourgeth
every son whom he receiveth.
7. **If ye endure chastening,**
God dealeth with you as
with sons; for what son is he
whom the father chasteneth not?
8. **But if ye be without**
chastisement,
whereof all are partakers,
then are ye bastards,
and not sons.
9. **Furthermore we have had**
fathers of our flesh
which corrected ***us,***
and we gave *them* reverence:
shall we not much rather be
in subjection unto the
Father of spirits, and live?
10. **For they verily** for a few days
chastened ***us*** **after their** own
pleasure; but he for *our* profit,
that ***we*** **might be partakers**
of his holiness.
11. Now no chastening
for the present seemeth to be joyous,
but grievous: nevertheless afterward
it yieldeth the peaceable fruit of
righteousness unto them which are
exercised thereby.

12. **Wherefore lift up the**
hands which hang down,
and the feeble knees;
13. And make straight paths for your
feet, lest that which is lame be turned
out of the way; but let it rather
be healed.
14. **Follow peace with all**
***men*, and holiness, without**
which no man shall
see the Lord:
15. **Looking diligently lest**
any man fail of the grace of
God; lest any root of bitterness
springing up trouble *you*, and thereby
many be defiled;
16. **Lest there *be* any**
fornicator, or profane
person, as Esau, who
for one morsel of meat
sold his birthright.
17. **For** ye know how that
afterward, when he would have
inherited the blessing,
he was rejected:
for he found no place of
repentance, though he
sought it carefully with tears.
18. **For ye are not come unto**
the mount that might
be touched, and that burned with
fire, nor unto blackness, and
darkness, and tempest,
19. And the sound of a trumpet, and
the voice of words; which *voice* they
that heard entreated that the word
should not be spoken
to them any more:
20. **(For they could not**
endure that which was
commanded, And if so much as
a beast touch the mountain, it shall be
stoned, or thrust through with a dart:
21. **And so terrible was the**
sight, *that* Moses said, I
exceedingly fear and quake:)
22. **But ye are come unto**
mount Sion, and unto
the city of the living
God, the heavenly
Jerusalem, and to
an innumerable company of
angels,
23. **To the** general assembly and
church of the firstborn,
which are written in
heaven, and to God the
Judge of all,
and to the spirits of just
men made perfect,
24. **And to Jesus the**
mediator of the new
covenant, and to the blood
of sprinkling,
that speaketh better things
than *that of* Abel.
25. **See that ye refuse not**
him that speaketh.
For if they escaped not who
refused him that spake on
earth, much more *shall not*
we *escape*, if we turn away
from him that *speaketh*
from heaven:
26. Whose voice then
shook the earth: but now he hath
promised, saying, Yet once more
I shake not the earth only,
but also heaven.
27. And this *word*, Yet once more,
signifieth the removing of those
things that are shaken, as of
things that are made, that those
things which cannot be
shaken may remain.
28. **Wherefore we receiving**
a kingdom which cannot
be moved, let us have grace,
whereby we may
serve God acceptably
with reverence and godly
fear:
29. **For our God *is* a**
consuming fire.

CHAPTER 13

1. **Let brotherly**
love continue.
2. Be not forgetful to
entertain strangers: for
thereby some
have entertained
angels unawares.
3. **Remember them** that are
in bonds, as bound with them;
***and* them which suffer**

adversity,
as being yourselves
also in the body.
4. **Marriage *is* honourable**
in all,
and the bed undefiled:
but whoremongers and
adulterers God will judge.
5. *Let your* conversation
be without covetousness;
***and be* content with such**
things as ye have:
for he hath
said, I will never leave thee, nor
forsake thee.
6. **So that we may boldly**
say, The Lord *is* my helper,
and I will not fear what
man shall do unto me.
7. **Remember them which**
have the rule over you, who
have spoken unto you the word of
God: whose faith follow, considering
the end of *their* conversation.
8. **Jesus Christ the same**
yesterday, and
to-day, and for ever.
9. **Be not carried about with**
divers and
strange doctrines. For *it is* a
good thing that the heart be
established with grace; not
with meats, which have not
profited them that have been
occupied therein.
10. We have an altar,
whereof they have no right to eat
which serve the tabernacle.
11. **For the bodies of**
those beasts, whose
blood is brought
into the sanctuary
by the high priest
for sin, are burned
without the camp.
12. **Wherefore Jesus also,**
that he might sanctify the
people with his own blood,
suffered without the gate.
13. **Let us go** forth therefore
unto him without the camp,
bearing his reproach.
14. **For here have we no**
continuing city, but we seek
one to come.
15. **By him**
therefore let us
offer the sacrifice of praise
to God continually,
that is, the fruit of *our* lips
giving thanks to his name.
16. But to do good and to
communicate forget not:
for with such sacrifices
God is well pleased.
17. Obey them that have the rule over
you, and submit yourselves: for they
watch for your souls, as they that
must give account, that they may do
it with joy, and not with grief: for that *is*
unprofitable for you.
18. **Pray for us:** for we trust we
have a good conscience, in all things
willing to live honestly.
19. But I beseech *you* the rather to do
this, that I may be restored
to you the sooner.
20. **Now the God of peace,**
that brought again
from the dead our Lord
Jesus, that great shepherd
of the sheep,
through the blood of the
everlasting covenant,
21. **Make you perfect**
in every good work to do his will,
working in you that which is
well-pleasing in his sight,
through Jesus Christ; to whom
be glory for ever and ever. Amen.
22. And I beseech you, brethren,
suffer the word of exhortation:
for I have written a letter
unto you in few words.
23. Know ye that *our* brother Timothy
is set at liberty; with whom, if he come
shortly, I will see you.
24. Salute all them that have the rule
over you, and all the saints.
They of Italy salute you.
25. Grace *be* with you all.
Amen.

THE EPISTLE OF JAMES

BACKGROUND INFORMATION

Author – James, a pastor in Jerusalem.
Date Written – probably **between 45** and **60** A.D.

Number of:
Verses - 108
Chapters - 5
Total Words - 2,309
Scan Words - 1,129
Scan Words represent 48 % of Total Words.

Theme – written to instruct believers of the necessity of **demonstrating faith through** the conduct of their lives, through practical **Christian living.**

OUTLINE OF THE EPISTLE

I. James instructs **believers on facing trials, hearing and doing the word,** impartiality **and faith that works.** Chapters 1—2

II. James warns of **the dangers of the tongue,** true and **false wisdom, worldliness and** pride, inconsideration and **unchristian conduct.** Chapters 3—4

III. James exhorts the believer to have **patience in affliction and** to save **an erring brother.** Chapter 5

CHAPTER 1

1. **James,** a servant of God and of
the Lord Jesus Christ,
to the twelve tribes which are
scattered abroad, greeting.
2. **My brethren, count it all**
joy when ye fall into
divers temptations;
3. **Knowing** *this,*
that the trying of your faith
worketh patience.
4. **But let patience**
have *her* perfect
work, that ye may be
perfect and entire,
wanting nothing.
5. **If any of you lack**
wisdom, let him
ask of God, that giveth to all *men*
liberally, and upbraideth not;
and it shall be given him.
6. **But let him ask in faith,**
nothing wavering.
For he that wavereth
is like a wave of the sea driven with
the wind and tossed.
7. For let not that man think that he
shall receive any thing of the Lord.
8. A double-minded man
is **unstable in all his ways.**
9. **Let the brother of low**
degree rejoice in that
he is exalted:
10. **But the rich,** in that he
is made low: because as
the flower of the grass
he shall pass away.
11. For the sun is no sooner risen with
a burning heat, but it withereth the
grass, and the flower thereof falleth,
and the grace of the fashion of it
perisheth: so also shall the rich man
fade away in his ways.
12. **Blessed** *is* **the man that**
endureth temptation: for
when he is tried,
he shall receive the crown
of life, which the Lord hath promised
to them that love him.
13. **Let no man say**
when he is tempted,
I am tempted of God: for God
cannot be tempted with evil, neither
tempteth he any man:
14. **But every man is**
tempted, when he is drawn away
of his own lust, and enticed.
15. Then when
lust hath conceived, it
bringeth forth sin: and sin,
when it is finished,
bringeth forth death.
16. Do not err, my beloved brethren.
17. **Every good gift and**
every perfect gift is
from above, and cometh down
from the Father of lights,
with whom is no
variableness, neither
shadow of turning.
18. **Of his own will begat he**
us with the word of truth,
that we should be a kind of
firstfruits of his creatures.
19. **Wherefore,** my beloved
brethren, let every man
be swift to hear, slow to
speak, slow to wrath:
20. **For the wrath of man**
worketh not the
righteousness of God.
21. Wherefore lay apart all filthiness
and superfluity of
naughtiness, and
receive with meekness
the engrafted word, which
is able to save your souls.
22. **But be ye doers of the**
word, and not hearers
only, deceiving your own selves.
23. **For** if any be
a hearer of the word,
and not a doer, he
is like unto
a man beholding his natural
face in a glass:
24. For he beholdeth himself,
and goeth his way,
and straightway
forgetteth what manner of
man he was.
25. **But whoso looketh into**
the perfect law of liberty, and
continueth *therein,* he
being not a forgetful hearer, but
a doer of the work, this man

shall be blessed in his deed.
26. **If any man** among you
seem to be religious, and
bridleth not his tongue,
but deceiveth his own heart,
this man's religion *is* vain.
27. **Pure religion** and undefiled
before God and the Father
is this, To visit the
fatherless and widows
in their affliction,
***and* to keep himself**
unspotted from the world.

CHAPTER 2

1. **My brethren, have not the**
faith of our Lord Jesus Christ,
the Lord of glory,
with respect of persons.
2. **For if there come**
unto your assembly
a man with a gold ring,
in goodly apparel,
and there come in
also a poor man
in vile raiment;
3. **And ye have respect to**
him that weareth the gay
clothing, and say unto him, Sit
thou here in a good place; and say to
the poor, Stand thou there, or sit here
under my footstool:
4. **Are ye not then partial**
in yourselves, and are become
judges of evil thoughts?
5. Hearken, my beloved brethren,
Hath not God chosen the
poor of this world
rich in faith, and heirs of the
kingdom which he hath promised
to them that love him?
6. **But ye have despised the**
poor. Do not rich men
oppress you, and draw you
before the judgment seats?
7. Do not they
blaspheme that worthy
name by the which ye are called?
8. **If** ye fulfil the royal law according to
the scripture,
Thou shalt love thy
neighbour as thyself,
ye do well:
9. **But if ye have respect to**
persons, ye commit sin,
and are convinced of the law
as transgressors.
10. **For whosoever shall**
keep the whole law, and
yet offend in one *point*, he
is guilty of all.
11. For he that said, Do not commit
adultery, said also, Do not kill.
Now if thou commit no
adultery, yet if thou
kill, thou art become
a transgressor of the law.
12. So speak ye, and so do,
as they that shall be judged
by the law of liberty.
13. For he shall have judgment without
mercy, that hath shewed no mercy;
and mercy rejoiceth against judgment.
14. **What *doth it* profit,**
my brethren,
though a man say he hath
faith, and have
not works? can faith
save him?
15. **If a brother or sister be**
naked, and destitute of
daily food,
16. **And** one of
you say unto them,
Depart in peace,
be *ye* warmed and filled;
notwithstanding ye give
them not those things which
are needful to the body;
what *doth it* profit?
17. **Even so faith, if it hath**
not works, is dead,
being alone.
18. Yea, a man may say, Thou hast
faith, and I have works:
shew me thy faith without
thy works, and I will shew
thee my faith by my works.
19. **Thou believest that there**
is one God; thou doest well:
the devils also believe,
and tremble.
20. But wilt thou know, O vain man,
that faith without works is dead?
21. **Was not Abraham**
our father

justified by works,
when he had
offered Isaac
his son upon the altar?
22. **Seest thou how** faith wrought
with his works,
and by works
was faith made perfect?
23. And the scripture was fulfilled
which saith,
Abraham believed God,
and it was imputed unto him
for righteousness: and he
was called the Friend
of God.
24. Ye see then how that
by works a man is justified,
and not by faith only.
25. Likewise also was not Rahab the
harlot justified by works, when she
had received the messengers, and
had sent *them* out another way?
26. **For as the body without**
the spirit is dead, so faith
without works is dead also.

CHAPTER 3

1. **My brethren, be not many**
masters, knowing that we shall
receive the greater condemnation.
2. For in many things we offend all.
If any man offend not in
word, the same *is*
a perfect man, *and*
able also to bridle the
whole body.
3. **Behold, we put bits in the**
horses' mouths,
that they may obey us;
and we turn about their
whole body.
4. **Behold also the ships,**
which though *they be* so great, and *are*
driven of fierce winds, yet
are they
turned about with a very
small helm, whithersoever the
governor listeth.
5. **Even so the tongue is a**
little member, and boasteth
great things. Behold, how great a
matter a little fire kindleth!
6. And the tongue *is* a fire, a world of
iniquity: so is the tongue among
our members, that
it defileth the whole body,
and setteth on fire the course
of nature;
and it is set on fire of hell.
7. **For every kind of beasts,**
and of birds, and of serpents, and of
things in the sea, is tamed, and
hath been tamed
of mankind:
8. **But the tongue can no**
man tame; *it is* an unruly evil, full
of deadly poison.
9. **Therewith bless we God,**
even the Father;
and therewith
curse we
men, which are made after the
similitude of God.
10. **Out of the same mouth**
proceedeth blessing and
cursing. My brethren, these things
ought not so to be.
11. **Doth a fountain send**
forth at the same place sweet *water*
and bitter?
12. Can the fig tree, my brethren, bear
olive berries? either a vine, figs?
so *can* no fountain
both yield
salt water and fresh.
13. **Who *is* a wise man**
and endued with knowledge
among you? let him shew
out of a good conversation
his works
with meekness of wisdom.
14. **But if ye have bitter**
envying and strife in your
hearts, glory not, and lie not
against the truth.
15. This wisdom descendeth not from
above, but *is* earthly,
sensual, devilish.
16. For where envying and strife *is*,
there *is* confusion and
every evil work.
17. **But the wisdom** that is
from above is first pure,
then peaceable, gentle, *and* easy to
be entreated,
full of mercy and good fruits,

without partiality, an
without
hypocrisy.
18. And the fruit of righteousness is
sown in peace of them that
make peace.

CHAPTER 4

1. **From whence *come* wars**
and fightings among you?
***come they* not hence,**
***even* of your lusts**
that war in your members?
2. **Ye lust,** and have not: ye kill,
and desire to have,
and cannot obtain:
ye fight and war,
yet ye have not, because
ye ask not.
3. **Ye ask,** and receive not,
because ye ask
amiss, that ye may
consume *it* upon
your lusts.
4. Ye adulterers and adulteresses,
know ye not that the
friendship of the world is enmity
with God? whosoever therefore will
be a friend
of the world is the enemy
of God.
5. Do ye think that
the scripture saith in vain,
The spirit that dwelleth in us
lusteth to envy?
6. **But he giveth more grace.**
Wherefore he saith, God resisteth the
proud, but giveth grace
unto the humble.
7. **Submit yourselves**
therefore to God. Resist the
devil, and he will flee
from you.
8. **Draw nigh to God, and he**
will draw nigh to you. Cleanse
your hands, *ye* sinners; and purify
your hearts, *ye* double-minded.
9. Be afflicted, and mourn, and weep:
let your laughter be turned to
mourning, and *your* joy to heaviness.
10. **Humble yourselves**
in the sight of the Lord,
and he shall lift you up.

11. Speak not evil one of
another brethren.
He that speaketh evil of *his*
brother, and judgeth
his brother,
speaketh evil of the law,
and judgeth the law: but if thou judge
the law, thou art not a doer of the law,
but a judge.
12. **There is one lawgiver,**
who is able to save and to destroy:
who art thou that judgest
another?
13. Go to now,
ye that say, To-day or to-
morrow we will go into such a
city, and continue there a year, and
buy and sell, and get gain:
14. **Whereas ye know not**
what *shall be* on the
morrow. For what *is*
your life? It
is even a vapour, that
appeareth for a little time,
and then vanisheth away.
15. **For that ye *ought* to say,**
If the Lord will, we shall
live, and
do this, or that.
16. But now ye rejoice in your
boastings: all such rejoicing is evil.
17. **Therefore to him that**
knoweth to do good, and
doeth *it* not, to him it is sin.

CHAPTER 5

1. Go to now,
***ye* rich men,**
weep and howl for your
miseries that shall come upon *you*.
2. **Your riches are**
corrupted, and your garments
are motheaten.
3. Your gold and silver is cankered;
and the rust of them shall
be a witness against you,
and shall eat your flesh as it were fire.
Ye have heaped treasure
together for the last days.
4. Behold, the hire of the labourers
who have reaped down your fields,
which is of you kept back by fraud,
crieth: and the cries of them which

have reaped are entered into the ears
of the Lord of sabaoth.
5. **Ye have lived in pleasure**
on the earth,
and been wanton;
ye have nourished your hearts,
as in a day of slaughter.
6. **Ye have condemned *and***
killed the just; *and* he doth
not resist you.
7. **Be patient** therefore, brethren,
unto the coming of
the Lord. Behold,
the husbandman waiteth
for the precious fruit of the
earth, and hath long patience for it,
until he receive the early and
latter rain.
8. Be ye also patient; stablish your
hearts: for
the coming of the Lord
draweth nigh.
9. **Grudge not one against**
another, brethren, lest ye be
condemned: behold, the judge
standeth before the door.
10. **Take,** my brethren,
the prophets, who have spoken
in the name of the Lord,
for an example of suffering
affliction, and of patience.
11. **Behold, we count them**
happy which endure. Ye have
heard of the patience of Job, and
have seen the end of the Lord; that
the Lord is very pitiful, and of
tender mercy.
12. **But above all things,**
my brethren,
swear not, neither by heaven,
neither by the earth,
neither by any other oath:
but let your yea be yea;
and *your* nay, nay;
lest ye fall into condemnation.
13. Is any among you afflicted? let
him pray. Is any merry?
let him sing psalms.
14. **Is any sick** among you?
let him call for
the elders of the church;
and let them
pray over him,
anointing him with oil in the
name of the Lord:
15. **And the prayer of faith**
shall save the sick, and the
Lord shall raise him up; and
if he have committed sins, they shall
be forgiven him.
16. **Confess *your* faults**
one to another,
and pray one for another,
that ye may be healed.
The effectual fervent prayer
of a righteous man
availeth much.
17. **Elias** was a man subject to like
passions as we are, and he
prayed earnestly
that it might not rain:
and it rained not on the earth
by the space of three years
and six months.
18. **And he prayed again,**
and the heaven gave rain,
and the earth brought forth her fruit.
19. **Brethren, if any** of you do
err from the truth,
and one convert him;
20. **Let him know, that he**
which converteth the sinner
from the error of his way,
shall save a soul from
death, and shall hide
a multitude of sins.

THE FIRST EPISTLE OF PETER

BACKGROUND INFORMATION

Author – Peter, an Apostle.
Date Written – probably **between 60** and **70** A.D.

Number of:
Verses - 105
Chapters - 5
Total Words - 2,482
Scan Words - 1,201
Scan Words represent 48 % of Total Words.

Theme – written to show believers that **in spite of persecution, there is** living hope and **ultimate triumph in Jesus Christ.**

OUTLINE OF THE EPISTLE

I. **Peter explains** that **salvation** is wrought by the Father, the Son and the Holy Spirit **and** he **gives a call for Christian dedication.** Chapters 1—2:10

II. **Peter outlines** the nature of **Christian** social **relationships,** sufferings, rewards, **and explains the ministry** of the elders and the flock. Chapters 2:11—5

CHAPTER 1

1. **Peter,** an apostle of Jesus Christ,
to the strangers scattered
throughout Pontus,
Galatia, Cappadocia,
Asia, and Bithynia,
2. **Elect** according to the
foreknowledge of God the Father,
through sanctification of
the Spirit, unto obedience
and sprinkling of
the blood of Jesus Christ:
Grace unto you, and peace,
be multiplied.
3. **Blessed *be* the God**
and Father of our Lord Jesus Christ,
which according to his
abundant mercy hath
begotten us
again unto a lively hope
by the resurrection of
Jesus Christ from the dead,
4. **To an inheritance**
incorruptible, and undefiled,
and that fadeth not away,
reserved in heaven
for you,
5. **Who are kept by the**
power of God through faith
unto salvation ready to be
revealed in the last time.
6. Wherein ye greatly rejoice,
though now for a season,
if need be,
ye are in heaviness
through manifold
temptations:
7. **That the trial of your faith,**
being much more precious
than of
gold that perisheth,
though it be tried with fire,
might be found unto praise
and honour and glory
at the appearing of
Jesus Christ:
8. **Whom having not seen,**
ye love; in whom,
though now
ye see *him* not, yet
believing, ye rejoice with
joy unspeakable
and full of glory:
9. **Receiving the end of your**
faith, *even* the salvation of
***your* souls.**
10. **Of which** salvation
the prophets have
inquired and searched
diligently, who prophesied
of the grace *that should*
***come* unto you:**
11. **Searching what,**
or what manner of time
the Spirit of Christ which was in
thom did signify, when it
testified beforehand the
sufferings of Christ,
and the glory that should follow.
12. **Unto whom it was**
revealed, that not unto
themselves, but unto us they
did minister the things, which
are now reported unto you
by them that have
preached the gospel
unto you with the Holy Ghost sent
down from heaven; which things the
angels desire to look into.
13. **Wherefore** gird up the
loins of your mind,
be sober, and hope
to the end
for the grace that is
to be brought unto you at
the revelation of
Jesus Christ;
14. **As obedient children,** not
fashioning yourselves according to
the former lusts in your ignorance:
15. But as he which hath called
you is holy, so
be ye holy in all manner
of conversation;
16. **Because it is written, Be**
ye holy; for I am holy.
17. And if ye call on the Father, who
without respect of persons judgeth
according to every man's work, pass
the time of your sojourning
here in fear:
18. **Forasmuch as ye know**
that ye were not redeemed
with corruptible things,
as silver and gold, from your vain
conversation *received* by tradition

from your fathers;
19. **But with the precious**
blood of Christ, as of a lamb
without blemish and without spot:
20. **Who verily was**
foreordained before the
foundation of the world,
but was manifest in these last times
for you,
21. **Who** by him do believe in
God, that raised him up
from the dead,
and gave him glory;
that your faith and hope
might be in God.
22. **Seeing ye have purified**
your souls in obeying the truth
through the Spirit
unto unfeigned love of the brethren,
see that ye
love one another
with a pure heart
fervently:
23. **Being born again,** not of
corruptible seed, but of incorruptible,
by the word of God, which
liveth and abideth for ever.
24. **For all flesh *is* as grass,**
and all the glory of man
as the flower of grass. The grass
withereth, and
the flower thereof
falleth away:
25. **But the word of the Lord**
endureth for ever.
And this is the word which by the
gospel is preached unto you.

CHAPTER 2

1. **Wherefore** laying aside all
malice, and all guile, and hypocrisies,
and envies, all evil speakings,
2. **As newborn babes,**
desire the sincere milk of
the word, that ye may
grow thereby:
3. If so be ye have tasted that the
Lord *is* gracious.
4. To whom coming, *as unto* a living
stone, disallowed indeed of men, but
chosen of God, *and* precious,
5. **Ye also,** as lively stones, are
built up a spiritual house, an holy
priesthood, to
offer up spiritual
sacrifices, acceptable to
God by Jesus Christ.
6. **Wherefore also it is**
contained in the scripture,
Behold,
I lay in Sion a chief corner
stone, elect, precious:
and he that believeth on
him shall not be
confounded.
7. Unto you therefore which
believe *he is* precious:
but unto them which be disobedient,
the stone which the
builders disallowed,
the same
is made the head of
the corner,
8. **And a stone of stumbling,**
and a rock of offence, *even*
***to them* which stumble at**
the word, being disobedient:
whereunto also they were appointed.
9. **But ye *are* a chosen**
generation, a royal
priesthood, an holy nation,
a peculiar people;
that ye should shew forth the praises
of him who hath
called you out of darkness
into his marvellous light:
10. Which in time past *were* not a
people, but *are* now the people of God:
which had not obtained mercy, but
now have obtained mercy.
11. **Dearly beloved,** I beseech
you as strangers and pilgrims,
abstain from fleshly lusts,
which war against the soul;
12. **Having your conver-**
sation honest among the
Gentiles: that, whereas they
speak against you as evildoers,
they may by *your* good
works, which they shall behold,
glorify God in the day
of visitation.
13. **Submit yourselves to**
every ordinance of man for
the Lord's sake: whether it
be to the king, as supreme;

14. **Or unto governors, as** unto **them** that are **sent by him for the punishment of evildoers,** and for the praise of them that do well.
15. **For so is the will of God, that** with well-doing **ye may put to silence the ignorance of foolish men:**
16. As free, and not using *your* liberty for a cloak of maliciousness, but as the servants of God.
17. **Honour all *men*.** Love the brotherhood. Fear God. Honour the king.
18. **Servants, *be* subject to *your* masters** with all fear; not only to the good and gentle, but also to the froward.
19. **For this *is* thankworthy, if a man for conscience toward God endure grief, suffering wrongfully.**
20. For what glory *is it*, if, when ye be buffeted for your faults, ye shall take it patiently? but if, when ye do well, and suffer *for it*, ye take it patiently, this *is* acceptable with God.
21. For even hereunto were ye called: because **Christ also suffered for us, leaving us an example,** that ye should follow his steps:
22. **Who did no sin,** neither was guile found in his mouth:
23. Who, when he was reviled, reviled not again; when he suffered, he threatened not; **but committed *himself* to him that judgeth righteously:**
24. **Who** his own self **bare our sins in his own body on the tree, that we,** being dead to sins, **should live unto righteousness: by whose stripes ye were healed.**
25. **For ye were as sheep going astray; but are now returned unto the Shepherd and Bishop of your souls.**

CHAPTER 3

1. **Likewise, ye wives, *be* in subjection to your own husbands; that,** if any obey not the word, **they also may** without the word **be won by** the conversation of the wives;
2. While they behold **your chaste conversation *coupled* with fear.**
3. **Whose adorning let it not be** that **outward** *adorning* of plaiting the hair, and of wearing of gold, or of putting on of apparel;
4. **But *let it be* the hidden man of the heart,** in that which is not corruptible, *even the ornament* of a meek and quiet spirit, which is in the sight of God of great price.
5. **For after this manner in the old time the holy women** also, who trusted in God, **adorned themselves, being in subjection unto their own husbands:**
6. **Even as Sara obeyed Abraham, calling him lord:** whose daughters ye are, as long as ye do well, and are not afraid with any amazement.
7. **Likewise, ye husbands,** dwell with *them* according to knowledge, giving **honour** unto **the wife, as** unto **the weaker vessel, and as being heirs together of the grace of life; that your prayers be not hindered.**
8. **Finally,** *be ye* all of one mind, **having compassion one of another,** love as brethren, *be* pitiful, *be* courteous:
9. Not rendering evil for evil, or railing for railing: but contrariwise blessing; **knowing that ye are thereunto called,**

that ye should inherit a blessing.
10. **For he that will love life,**
and see good days,
let him refrain his tongue
from evil, and his lips that they
speak no guile:
11. Let him eschew evil, and do good;
let him seek peace, and ensue it.
12. **For the eyes of the Lord**
***are* over the righteous, and**
his ears *are open* unto
their prayers: but the face of the
Lord *is* against them that do evil.
13. **And who *is* he that will**
harm you, if ye be followers of
that which is good?
14. **But and if ye suffer for**
righteousness' sake,
happy *are ye:* and be not afraid
of their terror, neither be troubled;
15. **But sanctify the Lord**
God in your hearts: and *be*
ready always to *give* an
answer to every man that
asketh you a reason of the
hope that is in you
with meekness and fear:
16. Having a good conscience;
that, whereas they speak evil of
you, as of evildoers,
they may be ashamed that
falsely accuse your good
conversation in Christ.
17. **For *it is* better,**
if the will of God be so,
that ye suffer for well-
doing, than for evil-doing.
18. **For Christ also hath**
once suffered for sins,
the just for the unjust,
that he might bring us to
God, being put to death
in the flesh,
but quickened by the Spirit:
19. By which also
he went and preached unto
the spirits in prison;
20. **Which sometime were**
disobedient, when
once the longsuffering of
God waited in the days of
Noah, while the ark was a-
preparing, wherein
few, that is,
eight souls were saved
by water.
21. The like figure whereunto *even*
baptism doth also now
save us (not the putting away of
the filth of the flesh, but the answer of
a good conscience toward God,)
by the resurrection of
Jesus Christ:
22. **Who is gone into**
heaven, and is on the right
hand of God; angels and
authorities and powers
being made subject
unto him.

CHAPTER 4

1. **Forasmuch then as Christ**
hath suffered for us
in the flesh,
arm yourselves likewise
with the same mind: for he
that hath suffered in the flesh
hath ceased from sin;
2. **That he** no longer
should live the rest of *his*
time in the flesh to the lusts of
men, but
to the will of God.
3. **For the time past**
of *our* life may suffice us to have
wrought the will of the Gentiles, when
we walked in
lasciviousness, lusts, excess
of wine, revellings, banquetings,
and abominable
idolatries:
4. **Wherein they think it**
strange that ye run not with
***them* to the same excess**
of riot, speaking evil of *you*:
5. Who shall give account to him that
is ready to judge the quick and
the dead.
6. **For** for
this cause was the gospel
preached also to them that
are dead,
that they might be judged
according to men in the flesh, but
live according to God in
the spirit.

7. **But the end** of all things
is at hand:
be ye therefore sober, and
watch unto prayer.
8. **And above all things**
have fervent charity
among yourselves:
for charity shall cover the
multitude of sins.
9. Use hospitality one to another
without grudging.
10. **As every man hath**
received the gift, *even so*
minister the same one to
another, as good stewards of
the manifold grace of God.
11. If any man speak, *let him speak* as
the oracles of God; if any man
minister, *let him do it* as of the ability
which God giveth:
that God in all things may
be glorified through Jesus
Christ, to whom be praise and
dominion for ever and ever. Amen.
12. **Beloved, think it not**
strange concerning the
fiery trial which is to
try you, as though some strange
thing happened unto you:
13. **But rejoice, inasmuch as**
ye are partakers of Christ's
sufferings; that, when his glory
shall be revealed, ye may be glad also
with exceeding joy.
14. **If ye be reproached for**
the name of Christ, happy
***are ye;* for the spirit**
of glory and
of God resteth upon you:
on their part he is evil spoken of, but
on your part he is glorified.
15. **But let none** of you
suffer as
a murderer, or *as* a thief, or *as*
an evildoer, or as a busybody in
other men's matters.
16. **Yet if *any man suffer*** as
a Christian,
let him not be ashamed; but
let him glorify God
on this behalf.
17. **For** the time *is come* that
judgment must begin at the
house of God:
and if *it* first *begin* at us,
what shall the end *be* of
them that obey not the
gospel of God?
18. And if the righteous scarcely be
saved, where shall the ungodly and
the sinner appear?
19. **Wherefore let them that**
suffer according to the will
of God commit
the keeping of
their souls *to him* in well doing,
as unto a faithful Creator.

CHAPTER 5

1. **The elders** which are among you
I exhort, who am also an elder, and
a witness of the sufferings of Christ,
and also a partaker of the glory that
shall be revealed:
2. **Feed the flock of God**
which is among you, taking the
oversight *thereof,*
not by constraint, but
willingly; not for filthy lucre,
but of a ready mind;
3. Neither as being lords over *God's*
heritage, but
being ensamples to
the flock.
4. **And when the chief**
Shepherd shall appear, ye
shall receive a crown of
glory that fadeth not away.
5. **Likewise, ye younger,**
submit yourselves
unto the elder.
Yea, all *of you* be subject one to
another, and be clothed with humility:
for God resisteth the
proud, and giveth grace to
the humble.
6. **Humble yourselves**
therefore under the mighty
hand of God,
that he may exalt you
in due time:
7. **Casting all your care**
upon him; for he careth
for you.
8. **Be sober,** be vigilant;
because your adversary

■ **the devil,** as a roaring lion,
■ **walketh about, seeking**
■ **whom he may devour:**
9. Whom resist stedfast in the faith,
knowing that the same afflictions
are accomplished in your brethren
that are in the world.
■ 10. **But the God of all grace,**
who hath called us unto his eternal
glory by Christ Jesus, after that ye
have suffered a while,
■ **make you perfect,**
stablish, strengthen, settle *you.*
■ 11. **To him *be* glory** and
dominion for ever and ever. Amen.
12. By Silvanus, a faithful brother
unto you, as I suppose, I have
written briefly, exhorting, and
testifying that this is the true grace of
God wherein ye stand.
13. The *church that is* at Babylon,
elected together with *you,* saluteth
you; and *so doth* Marcus my son.
14. Greet ye one another with a kiss
of charity. Peace *be* with you all
that are in Christ Jesus.
■ **Amen.**

THE SECOND EPISTLE OF PETER

BACKGROUND INFORMATION

Author – Peter, an Apostle.
Date Written – unknown.

Number of:
Verses - 61
Chapters - 3
Total Words - 1,559
Scan Words - 758
Scan Words represent 48 % of Total Words.

Theme – written to urge believers to defeat false teachings by practicing Christian virtues **and** to **prepare for the coming of the Lord.**

OUTLINE OF THE EPISTLE

I. **Peter's salutation,** advice for growing in grace, and being grounded in the truth.
Chapter 1

II. **Peter's warning** about false teachers.
Chapter 2

III. **Peter's admonition** as to how believers must live **in hope of the second coming** of Christ.
Chapter 3

CHAPTER 1

1. **Simon Peter,** a servant and an
apostle of Jesus Christ,
to them that have obtained
like precious
faith with us through the
righteousness of God and
our Saviour Jesus Christ:
2. **Grace and peace be**
multiplied unto you through
the knowledge of God,
and of Jesus our Lord,
3. **According as his divine**
power hath given unto us
all things that *pertain* unto life and
godliness, through the
knowledge of him that hath
called us to glory
and virtue:
4. Whereby are given unto us
exceeding great and
precious promises:
that by these
ye might be partakers of
the divine nature, having
escaped the corruption that is in the
world through lust.
5. **And** beside this, giving
all diligence,
add to your faith virtue;
and to virtue
knowledge;
6. **And** to knowledge
temperance; and
to temperance
patience; and to patience
godliness;
7. **And** to godliness
brotherly kindness; and
to brotherly kindness
charity.
8. **For if these things be in**
you, and abound,
they make *you that*
***ye shall* neither *be* barren**
nor unfruitful in the know-
ledge of our Lord Jesus Christ.
9. **But he that lacketh these**
things is blind, and
cannot see afar off, and
hath forgotten that he was
purged from his old sins.
10. **Wherefore**
the rather, brethren,
give diligence to make
your calling and election
sure: for if ye do these things, ye
shall never fall:
11. For so an entrance shall be
ministered unto you abundantly into
the everlasting kingdom of our Lord
and Saviour Jesus Christ.
12. Wherefore I will not be negligent to
put you always in remembrance of
these things, though ye know *them*,
and be established in the
present truth.
13. **Yea, I think it meet,**
as long as I am in this tabernacle,
to stir you up by putting
***you* in remembrance;**
14. **Knowing** that shortly
I must put off *this* my
tabernacle, even as our Lord
Jesus Christ hath shewed me.
15. Moreover I will endeavour that ye
may be able after my decease to
have these things
always in remembrance.
16. **For we have not**
followed cunningly devised
fables, when we made
known unto you
the power and coming of
our Lord Jesus Christ,
but were eyewitnesses
of his majesty.
17. **For he received**
from God the Father
honour and glory, when
there came such a voice to
him from the excellent glory,
This is my beloved Son, in
whom I am well pleased.
18. **And this voice**
which came from heaven
we heard, when we were with him
in the holy mount.
19. **We have also a more**
sure word of prophecy;
whereunto ye do well that ye take
heed, as unto a light that shineth in a
dark place, until the day dawn, and
the day star arise in your hearts:
20. **Knowing** this first,
that no prophecy

of the scripture
is of any
private interpretation.
21. **For the prophecy came**
not in old time
by the will of man: but holy
men of God spake *as they*
***were* moved by the**
Holy Ghost.

CHAPTER 2

1. **But there were false**
prophets also among the people,
even as there shall be false
teachers among you,
who privily shall
bring in damnable
heresies, even denying the
Lord that bought them,
and bring upon themselves
swift destruction.
2. **And many shall follow**
their pernicious ways;
by reason of whom the way of truth
shall be evil spoken of.
3. **And through**
covetousness shall they
with feigned words
make merchandise of you:
whose judgment
now of a long time
lingereth not, and their
damnation slumbereth not.
4. **For if God spared not the**
angels that sinned, but
cast *them* down to hell,
and delivered *them* into chains
of darkness, to be reserved
unto judgment;
5. **And spared not the old**
world, but saved Noah
the eighth *person*, a preacher
of righteousness,
bringing in the flood upon
the world of the
ungodly;
6. **And turning the cities of**
Sodom and Gomorrha into
ashes condemned
them with an overthrow,
making *them* an ensample
unto those that after
should live ungodly;
7. **And delivered just Lot,**
vexed with the filthy conversation
of the wicked:
8. (For that righteous man dwelling
among them, in seeing and hearing,
vexed *his* righteous soul from day to
day with *their* unlawful deeds;)
9. **The Lord knoweth how to**
deliver the godly out of
temptations, and to
reserve the unjust unto the
day of judgment to
be punished:
10. **But chiefly them that**
walk after the flesh
in the lust of
uncleanness, and despise
government. Presumptuous *are*
they, self-willed, they are not afraid to
speak evil of dignities.
11. **Whereas angels,**
which are greater in power and might,
bring not railing
accusation against them
before the Lord.
12. **But these,**
as natural brute beasts, made to be
taken and destroyed,
speak evil of the things that
they understand not; and shall
utterly perish in their own corruption;
13. And shall receive the reward of
unrighteousness,
as they that count it pleasure to riot in
the day time. Spots *they are* and
blemishes, sporting themselves with
their own deceivings while
they feast with you;
14. **Having eyes full of**
adultery, and that cannot cease
from sin; beguiling unstable souls: an
heart they have exercised with
covetous practices; cursed children:
15. **Which have forsaken the**
right way, and are gone
astray, following
the way of Balaam
the son of Bosor,
who loved the wages of
unrighteousness;
16. **But was rebuked**
for his iniquity:
the dumb ass speaking

■ **with man's voice** forbad the
madness of the prophet.
■ 17. **These are wells without**
■ **water,** clouds that are carried
with a tempest;
■ **to whom** the mist of
■ **darkness is reserved**
■ **for ever.**
18. For when they speak great
swelling *words* of vanity, they allure
through the lusts of the flesh, *through*
much wantonness, those that were
clean escaped from
them who live in error.
■ 19. **While they promise them**
■ **liberty, they themselves**
■ **are the servants of**
■ **corruption:** for of whom a man is
overcome, of the same is he brought
in bondage.
■ 20. **For if after they have**
■ **escaped** the pollutions of
■ **the world through the**
■ **knowledge of**
the Lord and Saviour Jesus
■ **Christ, they are again**
■ **entangled therein,**
■ **and** overcome,
■ **the latter end is worse**
with them
■ **than the beginning.**
■ 21. **For it had been better for**
■ **them not to have known the**
■ **way of righteousness,**
■ **than,** after they have known *it*,
■ **to turn from the holy**
■ **commandment**
delivered unto them.
■ 22. **But it is happened**
unto them
■ **according to the** true
■ **proverb, The dog *is* turned**
■ **to his own vomit**
again; and the sow that was washed
to her wallowing in the mire.

CHAPTER 3

■ 1. **This second epistle,**
beloved,
■ **I now write**
unto you; in *both* which I stir up your
pure minds by way of remembrance:
■ 2. **That ye may be mindful of**
■ **the words** which were
■ **spoken** before
■ **by the holy prophets, and**
■ **of the commandment of us**
■ **the apostles**
of the Lord and Saviour:
■ 3. **Knowing** this first,
■ **that there shall come**
in the last days
■ **scoffers,** walking after their
own lusts,
■ 4. **And saying, Where is the**
■ **promise of his coming? for**
since the fathers fell asleep,
■ **all things continue as *they***
■ ***were* from the beginning**
of the creation.
■ 5. **For** this they willingly are ignorant
of, that
■ **by the word of God the**
■ **heavens were of old,**
and the earth standing out of the
water and in the water:
■ 6. **Whereby the world**
that then was,
■ **being overflowed with**
■ **water, perished:**
■ 7. **But the heavens and the**
■ **earth,** which are now,
■ **by the same word are**
kept in store,
■ **reserved unto fire against**
■ **the day of judgment**
and perdition of ungodly men.
■ 8. **But,** beloved, be not ignorant of
this one thing, that one day *is* with
the Lord as a thousand years, and a
thousand years as one day.
■ 9. **The Lord** is not slack concerning
his promise, as some men count
slackness; but
■ **is longsuffering to us-**
■ **ward, not willing that any**
■ **should perish,** but that all
should come to repentance.
■ 10. **But** the day of
■ **the Lord will come as a**
■ **thief in the night; in the**
■ **which the heavens shall**
■ **pass** away with a great noise,
■ **and the elements shall**
■ **melt** with fervent heat,
■ **the earth also and the**

■ **works** that are
■ **therein shall be burned up.**
■ 11. ***Seeing*** then *that* all
■ **these things** shall be dissolved,
■ **what manner *of persons***
■ **ought ye to be in *all***
holy conversation and
■ **godliness,**
■ 12. **Looking for** and hasting unto
■ **the coming of the day of**
■ **God, wherein** the heavens being
on fire shall be dissolved, and
■ **the elements shall melt**
■ **with fervent heat?**
■ 13. **Nevertheless we,**
according to his promise,
■ **look for new heavens and**
■ **a new earth, wherein**
■ **dwelleth righteousness.**
■ 14. **Wherefore,** beloved, seeing
that ye look for such things,
■ **be diligent that ye may be**
■ **found** of him in peace,
■ **without spot,**
■ **and blameless.**
■ 15. **And account *that* the**
■ **longsuffering of our Lord *is***
■ **salvation; even**
as our beloved brother
■ **Paul** also according to the
wisdom given unto him
■ **hath written** unto you;
16. As also in all *his* epistles,
speaking in them of these things; in
which are some
■ **things hard to be**
■ **understood,** which they that are
unlearned and unstable wrest, as *they*
do also the other scriptures, unto their
own destruction.
■ 17. **Ye therefore,** beloved,
seeing ye know *these things*
■ **before, beware lest ye**
■ **also,** being led away with the
error of the wicked,
■ **fall from your**
■ **own stedfastness.**
■ 18. **But grow in grace, and *in***
■ **the knowledge of our Lord**
and Saviour Jesus Christ. To him *be*
glory both now and for ever.
■ **Amen.**

THE FIRST EPISTLE OF JOHN

BACKGROUND INFORMATION

Author – John, one of the twelve disciples.
Date Written – probably **between 90** and **96** A.D.

Number of:
Verses- 105
Chapters- 5
Total Words- 2,523
Scan Words- 1,234
Scan Words represent 48 % of Total Words.

Theme – written to show that **through** personal experience with
Jesus Christ, The Word, **one has passed from death to life.**

OUTLINE OF THE EPISTLE

I. **John's testimony concerning Christ,** his tests of fellowship with God and his declaration of the importance of love.
Chapters 1—2:17

II. **John's warning concerning Antichrists** and his explanation of righteousness and God's children.
Chapter 2:17—3

III. **John's teaching concerning the trying of spirits,** the nature of God and the victory of faith.
Chapters 4—5

CHAPTER 1

1. **That which was from the beginning, which we have heard, which we have seen** with our eyes, which we have looked upon,
and our hands have handled, of the Word of life;
2. **(For the life was manifested, and we** have seen *it*, and **bear witness,**
and shew unto you that eternal life, which was with the Father, and was manifested unto us;)
3. That which we have seen and heard declare we unto you,
that ye also may have fellowship with us: and truly our fellowship *is* **with the Father, and with his Son** Jesus Christ.
4. **And these things write we** unto you,
that your joy may be full.
5. **This then is the message which we** have heard of him, and **declare** unto you,
that God is light, and in him is no darkness at all.
6. **If we say that we have fellowship with him, and walk in darkness, we lie,** and do not the truth:
7. **But if we walk in the light,** as he is in the light,
we have fellowship one with another,
and the blood of Jesus Christ his Son **cleanseth us from all sin.**
8. If we say that we have no sin, we deceive ourselves, and the truth is not in us.
9. **If we confess our sins, he is faithful** and just **to forgive us** *our* sins,
and to cleanse us from all unrighteousness.
10. **If we say that we have not sinned,** we make him a liar, and **his word is not in us.**

CHAPTER 2

1. **My little children,** these things write I unto you, that ye sin not. And
if any man sin, we have an advocate with the Father, Jesus Christ the righteous:
2. **And he is the propitiation** for our sins: and not for ours only, but also **for *the sins of* the whole world.**
3. **And hereby** we do know that **we know him, if we keep his commandments.**
4. He that saith, I know him, and keepeth not his commandments, is a liar, and the truth is not in him.
5. **But whoso keepeth his word, in him** verily **is the love of God perfected:** hereby know we that we are in him.
6. **He that saith he abideth in him ought** himself also so **to walk, even as he walked.**
7. Brethren, I write no new commandment unto you, but an old commandment which ye had from the beginning. The old commandment is the word which ye have heard from the beginning.
8. **Again, a new commandment I write** unto you, which thing is true in him and in you:
because the darkness is past, and **the true light now shineth.**
9. **He that saith he is in the light, and hateth his brother, is in darkness** even until now.
10. He that loveth his brother abideth in the light, and there is none occasion of stumbling in him.
11. But he that hateth his brother is in darkness, and walketh in darkness, and knoweth not whither he goeth, because that darkness hath blinded his eyes.
12. **I write unto you, little**

children, because your
sins are forgiven
you for his name's sake.
13. I write unto you, fathers, because
ye have known him *that is* from the
beginning. I write unto you, young
men, because ye have overcome the
wicked one. I write unto you, little
children, because ye have known
the Father.
14. **I have written unto you,**
fathers, because ye have
known him *that is* from the
beginning. I have written
unto you, young men,
because ye are strong, and the
word of God abideth in you, and
ye have overcome the
wicked one.
15. **Love not** the world, neither
the things *that are* in the
world. If any man love the world,
the love of the Father is not in him.
16. **For all that *is* in the**
world, the lust of the flesh,
and the lust
of the eyes, and the pride
of life, is not of the Father,
but is of the world.
17. **And the world passeth**
away, and the lust thereof:
but he that doeth the will of
God abideth for ever.
18. **Little children,**
it is the last time: and as
ye have heard that
antichrist shall come, even
now are there many antichrists;
whereby we know that it is
the last time.
19. **They went out from us,** but
they were not of us; for if they had
been of us, they would *no doubt* have
continued with us: but *they went out,*
that they might be made
manifest that they were not
all of us.
20. **But ye have an unction**
from the Holy One, and
ye know all things.
21. I have not written unto you
because ye
know not the truth, but
becaue ye know it, and that no lie is of
the truth.
22. Who is a liar but
he that denieth that Jesus
is the Christ? He is
antichrist, that denieth the Father
and the Son.
23. **Whosoever denieth the**
Son, the same
hath not the Father:
he that acknowledgeth the Son hath
the Father also.
24. **Let that** therefore abide in you,
which ye have heard
from the beginning. If that which ye
have heard from the beginning shall
remain in you, ye also shall
continue in the Son, and in the Father.
25. **And** this is the promise that
he hath promised us, *even*
eternal life.
26. These *things* have I written unto
you concerning them that
seduce you.
27. **But the anointing which**
ye have received of him
abideth in you,
and ye need not that any man teach
you: but as the same anointing
teacheth you of
all things, and is truth,
and is no lie, and even as it hath
taught you, ye shall abide in him.
28. **And now,** little children,
abide in him; that,
when he shall appear,
we may have confidence, and
not be ashamed before him
at his coming.
29. If ye know that he is righteous,
ye know that
every one that doeth right-
eousness is born of him.

CHAPTER 3

1. **Behold, what manner of**
love the Father hath
bestowed upon us, that we
should be called the sons
of God: therefore the
world knoweth us not,
because it knew him not.
2. Beloved, now are we the sons

of God,
and it doth not yet appear what
we shall be: but
we know that, when he
shall appear, we shall be
like him; for we shall see
him as he is.
3. **And every man that hath**
this hope in him purifieth
himself, even as he is pure.
4. Whosoever committeth sin
transgresseth also the law: for sin is
the transgression of the law.
5. **And ye know that he was**
manifested to take away
our sins; and in him is no sin.
6. **Whosoever abideth in**
him sinneth not:
whosoever sinneth hath not seen him,
neither known him.
7. Little children, let no man
deceive you:
he that doeth righteous-
ness is righteous,
even as he is righteous.
8. **He that committeth sin is**
of the devil; for the devil sinneth
from the beginning.
For this purpose
the Son of God was
manifested, that he might
destroy the works of
the devil.
9. **Whosoever is born of**
God doth not commit sin;
for his seed remaineth in
him: and he cannot sin,
because he is born of God.
10. **In this the children of**
God are manifest,
and the children of the devil:
whosoever doeth not
righteousness is not of
God, neither he that
loveth not
his brother.
11. **For this is the message**
that ye heard from the
beginning, that
we should love
one another.
12. **Not as Cain,** ***who***
was of that wicked one, and
slew his brother.
And wherefore slew he him?
Because his own works
were evil,
and his brother's righteous.
13. Marvel not, my brethren, if the
world hate you.
14. **We know that we have**
passed from death unto
life, because we love the
brethren. He that loveth not *his*
brother abideth in death.
15. **Whosoever hateth his**
brother is a murderer: and
ye know that
no murderer hath eternal
life abiding in him.
16. **Hereby perceive we the**
love ***of God*****, because he**
laid down his life for us:
and we ought to lay down
our **lives for the brethren.**
17. **But whoso hath this**
world's good, and seeth
his brother have need, and
shutteth up his bowels *of*
compassion **from him, how**
dwelleth the love of God
in him?
18. **My little children, let us**
not love in word,
neither in tongue;
but in deed and in truth.
19. And hereby we know that we are of
the truth, and shall assure our hearts
before him.
20. For if our heart condemn us, God
is greater than our heart, and
knoweth all things.
21. **Beloved, if our heart**
condemn us not, ***then***
have we confidence
toward God.
22. **And whatsoever we ask,**
we receive of him, because
we keep his commandments, and do
those things that
are pleasing in his sight.
23. **And this is his**
commandment, That we
should believe on the
name of his Son Jesus Christ,
and love one another, as he

gave us commandment.
24. And he that keepeth his
commandments dwelleth in him,
and he in him.
■ **And hereby we know that**
■ **he abideth in us, by the**
■ **Spirit** which he hath given us.

CHAPTER 4

■ 1. **Beloved, believe not**
■ **every spirit, but try the**
■ **spirits** whether they are of God:
because many false prophets are
gone out into the world.
2. Hereby know ye the Spirit of God:
■ **Every spirit that confesseth**
■ **that Jesus Christ is come in**
■ **the flesh is of God:**
■ 3. **And every spirit that**
■ **confesseth not** that Jesus Christ
is come in the flesh is not of God:
and this
■ **is that *spirit* of antichrist,**
whereof ye have heard that it
should come;
■ **and even now already is it**
■ **in the world.**
■ 4. **Ye** are of God, little children, and
■ **have overcome** them:
■ **because greater is he that**
■ **is in you, than he that is in**
■ **the world.**
5. They are of the world: therefore
speak they of the world, and the
world heareth them.
■ 6. **We are of God: he that**
■ **knoweth God heareth us;**
he that is not of God heareth not us.
■ **Hereby know we the spirit**
■ **of truth, and** the spirit of
■ **error.**
■ 7. **Beloved,** let us love one
another: for
■ **love is of God;** and every one
that loveth is born of God, and
knoweth God.
8. He that loveth not knoweth not
God; for God is love.
■ 9. **In this was manifested the**
■ **love of God toward us,**
because that
■ **God sent his only begotten**
■ **Son into the world,**
that we might live through him.
10. Herein is love, not that we loved
God, but that he loved us, and sent
his Son
■ ***to be* the propitiation for**
■ **our sins.**
11. Beloved, if God so loved us, we
ought also to love one another.
12. No man hath seen
God at any time.
■ **If we love one another, God**
■ **dwelleth in us,**
and his love is perfected in us.
13. Hereby know we that we dwell in
him, and he in us, because he hath
given us of his Spirit.
■ 14. **And we have seen and**
■ **do testify that the Father**
■ **sent the Son *to be* the**
■ **Saviour of the world.**
■ 15. **Whosoever shall**
■ **confess that Jesus is the**
■ **Son** of God,
■ **God dwelleth in him,**
and he in God.
■ 16. **And** we have known and believed
the love that God hath to us. God is
love; and
■ **he that dwelleth in love**
■ **dwelleth in God, and God**
■ **in him.**
■ 17. **Herein is our love made**
■ **perfect, that we may have**
■ **boldness in the day of**
■ **judgment:** because as he is, so
are we in this world.
■ 18. **There is no fear in love;**
■ **but perfect love casteth out**
■ **fear:** because fear hath torment. He
that feareth is not made perfect
in love.
■ 19. **We love him, because he**
■ **first loved us.**
■ 20. **If a man** say, I love God, and
hateth his brother, he is a liar: for
he that
■ **loveth not his brother**
■ **whom he hath seen, how**
■ **can he love God whom he**
■ **hath not seen?**
21. And this commandment have we
from him, That he who loveth God love
his brother also.

CHAPTER 5

1. **Whosoever believeth that**
Jesus is the Christ is born
of God: and every one that loveth
him that begat loveth him also that is
begotten of him.
2. **By this we know that we**
love the children of God,
when we love God, and
keep his commandments.
3. For this is the love of God, that we
keep his commandments:
and his commandments
are not grievous.
4. **For whatsoever is born of**
God overcometh the world:
and this is the victory that
overcometh the world, *even* our faith.
5. Who is he that overcometh the
world, but
he that believeth that Jesus
is the Son of God?
6. **This is he that came by**
water and blood, *even*
Jesus Christ; not by water only,
but by water and blood.
And it is
the Spirit that
beareth witness,
because the Spirit is truth.
7. **For there are three that**
bear record in heaven, the
Father, the Word, and the
Holy Ghost:
and these three are one.
8. **And there are three that**
bear witness in earth, the
Spirit, and the water, and
the blood:
and these three agree in one.
9. **If we receive the witness**
of men, the witness of God
is greater:
for this is the witness of God which he
hath testified of his Son.
10. He that believeth on the Son of
God hath the witness in himself: he
that believeth not God hath made him
a liar; because he believeth not the
record that God gave of his Son.
11. **And this is the record,**
that God hath given to
us eternal life, and this life is
in his Son.
12. **He that hath the Son hath**
life; *and* he that hath not the Son of
God hath not life.
13. **These things have I**
written unto you that believe on the
name of the Son of God;
that ye may know that ye
have eternal life,
and that ye may believe on the name
of the Son of God.
14. **And this is the**
confidence that we have in
him, that, if we ask any
thing according to his will,
he heareth us:
15. **And** if we know that he hear us,
whatsoever we ask, we know that
we have the petitions that
we desired of him.
16. **If any man see his**
brother sin a sin *which is*
not unto death, he shall
ask, and he shall give him
life for them that sin not unto death.
There is a sin unto death:
I do not say that he shall pray for it.
17. **All unrighteousness is**
sin: and there is a
sin not unto death.
18. We know that whosoever is born
of God sinneth not; but he that is
begotten of God keepeth himself, and
that wicked one toucheth him not.
19. ***And* we know**
that we are of God, and
the whole world lieth
in wickedness.
20. **And we know that the**
Son of God is come,
and hath given us an understanding,
that we may know him
that is true,
and we are in him that is true,
***even* in his Son** Jesus Christ.
This is the true God, and eternal life.
21. **Little children, keep**
yourselves
from idols. Amen.

THE SECOND EPISTLE OF JOHN

BACKGROUND INFORMATION

Author – John, one of the twelve disciples.
Date Written – probably **between 90** and **99** A.D.

Number of:
Verses - 13
Chapters - 1
Total Words - 303
Scan Words - 151
Scan Words represent 49 % of Total Words

Theme – written to show **the importance of** Christian **truth and** the necessity to practice Christian **love.**

OUTLINE OF THE EPISTLE

I. **John's greeting.**
Verses 1—3
II. **John's teachings on love.**
Verses 4—6
III. **John's warning concerning deceivers.**
Verses 7—11
IV. **John's final greeting.**
Verses 12, 13

CHAPTER 1

1. **The elder unto the elect**
lady and her children,
whom I love in the truth; and not I
only, but also all they that have
known the truth;
2. For the truth's sake, which dwelleth
in us, and shall be with us for ever.
3. **Grace** be with you,
mercy, *and* peace, from
God the Father, and from
the Lord Jesus Christ, the
Son of the Father, in truth and love.
4. **I rejoiced greatly that I**
found of
thy children
walking in truth,
as we have received a commandment
from the Father.
5. **And now I beseech thee,**
lady, not as though I wrote a new
commandment unto thee, but that
which we had from the beginning,
that we love one another.
6. **And this is love, that we**
walk after his command-
ments. This is the commandment,
That, as ye have heard from the
beginning, ye should walk in it.
7. **For many deceivers**
are entered into the world, who
confess not
that Jesus
Christ is come in the flesh.
This is a deceiver and an
antichrist.
8. **Look to yourselves,**
that we lose not those
things which we have
wrought, but that we
receive a full reward.
9. **Whosoever** transgresseth, and
abideth not in the doctrine of
Christ, hath not God. He
that abideth in the
doctrine of Christ,
he hath both the
Father and the Son.
10. **If** there come
any unto you, and
bring not this doctrine,
receive him not into *your* house,
neither bid him God speed:
11. **For he that biddeth him**
God speed
is partaker of his
evil deeds.
12. Having many things to write
unto you, I would not *write* with
paper and ink: but
I trust to come unto you,
and speak face to face,
that our joy may be full.
13. The children of thy elect sister
greet thee.
Amen.

THE THIRD EPISTLE OF JOHN

BACKGROUND INFORMATION

Author – John, one of the twelve disciples.
Date Written – probably **between 90** and **99** A.D.

Number of:
Verses - 14
Chapters - 1
Total Words - 299
Scan Words - 154
Scan Words represent 51 % of Total Words.

Theme – written to show that **error must be challenged to maintain Christian purity** and fellowship.

OUTLINE OF THE EPISTLE

I. **John offers greeting,** tells believers to serve others, and rebukes Diotrephes.
Verses 1—10

II. **John implores believers to have a good testimony.**
Verses 11—14

CHAPTER 1

1. **The elder unto**
the well-beloved
Gaius, whom I love in the truth.
2. **Beloved, I wish**
above all things
that thou mayest
prosper and be in
health, even
as thy soul prospereth.
3. **For I rejoiced** greatly, when the
brethren came and testified
of the truth that is in thee,
even as thou walkest in the truth.
4. **I have no greater joy than**
to hear that my children
walk in truth.
5. **Beloved, thou doest**
faithfully whatsoever thou doest
to the brethren, and to
strangers;
6. **Which have borne**
witness of thy charity
before the church: whom if thou bring
forward on their journey after a godly
sort, thou shalt do well:
7. Because that for his name's sake
they went forth, taking nothing
of the Gentiles.
8. **We therefore ought to**
receive such, that we might
be fellow-helpers
to the truth.
9. **I wrote unto the church:**
but Diotrephes, who loveth
to have the
preeminence among them,
receiveth us not.
10. Wherefore, if I come,
I will remember his deeds
which he doeth, prating against us
with malicious words: and not
content therewith,
neither doth he himself
receive the brethren,
and forbiddeth them that would,
and casteth *them* out of
the church.
11. **Beloved, follow not**
that which is
evil, but that which is good.
He that doeth good is of
God: but he that doeth evil
hath not seen God.
12. **Demetrius hath good**
report of all *men*,
and of the truth itself: yea, and we
also bear record; and ye know that our
record is true.
13. **I had many things to**
write, but I will not with ink
and pen write unto thee:
14. **But I trust I shall shortly**
see thee,
and we shall speak face to face.
Peace *be* to thee.
Our friends salute thee.
Greet the friends by name.

THE GENERAL EPISTLE OF JUDE

BACKGROUND INFORMATION

Author – Jude, probably the brother of James.
Date Written – probably **between 70** and **100** A.D.

Number of:
Verses - 25
Chapters - 1
Total Words - 613
Scan Words - 288
Scan Words represent 46 % of Total Words.

Theme – written to warn Christians **against false** teachers and their **doctrines.**

OUTLINE OF THE EPISTLE

I. **Jude offers** a salutation and a **warning against false teachers.** Verses 1—16
II. **Jude presents exhortations** to Christians and a benediction. Verses 16—25

CHAPTER 1

1. **Jude,** the servant of Jesus
Christ, and brother of James,
to them that are sanctified
by God the Father,
and preserved in Jesus
Christ, *and* called:
2. Mercy unto you, and peace, and
love, be multiplied.
3. **Beloved,** when
I gave all diligence to
write unto you
of the common salvation,
it was needful for me to write unto you,
and exhort ***you*** **that ye**
should earnestly
contend for the faith
which was
once delivered
unto the saints.
4. **For there are** certain men crept
in unawares, who were before of old
ordained to this condemnation,
ungodly men, turning the
grace of our God into
lasciviousness, and
denying the only Lord God, and
our Lord Jesus Christ.
5. I will therefore put you in
remembrance, though
ye once knew this,
how that the Lord, having
saved the people out
of the land
of Egypt, afterward
destroyed them that
believed not.
6. **And the angels which**
kept not their first estate,
but left their own habitation,
he hath reserved in everlasting
chains under darkness
unto the judgment
of the great day.
7. **Even as Sodom and**
Gomorrha, and the cities about
them in like manner, giving
themselves over to fornication, and
going after strange flesh,
are set forth for an
example, suffering the
vengeance of eternal fire.
8. Likewise also these *filthy* dreamers
defile the flesh, despise
dominion, and speak evil of dignities.
9. **Yet Michael**
the archangel, when
contending with the devil
he disputed
about the body of Moses,
durst not bring against him
a railing accusation,
but said, The Lord
rebuke thee.
10. **But these speak evil of**
those things which they
know not: but what
they know naturally, as brute beasts,
in those things they
corrupt themselves.
11. **Woe unto them! for they**
have gone in the way of
Cain, and ran greedily after the
error of Balaam for reward, and
perished in the gainsaying of Core.
12. **These are spots in your**
feasts of charity,
when they feast with you, feeding
themselves without fear:
clouds *they are*
without water,
carried about of winds;
trees whose fruit withereth,
without fruit, twice dead,
plucked up by the roots;
13. **Raging waves** of the sea,
foaming out their own shame;
wandering stars,
to whom is reserved
the blackness of
darkness for ever.
14. **And Enoch**
also, the seventh from Adam,
prophesied of these, saying,
Behold, the Lord cometh
with ten thousands of
his saints,
15. **To execute judgment**
upon all, and to convince all that
are ungodly among them of all their
ungodly deeds which they have
ungodly committed, and of all their
hard *speeches* which
ungodly sinners
have spoken against him.
16. **These are**

murmurers, complainers,
walking after their own
lusts; and their mouth speaketh
great swelling *words*, having men's
persons in admiration
because of advantage.
17. **But, beloved, remember**
ye the words which were spoken
before of the apostles of our Lord
Jesus Christ;
18. **How that** they told you
there should be mockers in
the last time, who should walk
after their own ungodly lusts.
19. **These be they** who separate
themselves, sensual,
having not the Spirit.
20. **But ye,** beloved, building up
yourselves on your most holy faith,
praying in the Holy Ghost,
21. **Keep yourselves in the**
love of God, looking for
the mercy of our Lord Jesus
Christ unto eternal life.
22. **And of some**
have compassion,
making a difference:
23. **And others save with**
fear, pulling *them* out of the
fire; hating even the garment
spotted by the flesh.
24. **Now unto him that is**
able to keep you from
falling, and to present
***you* faultless** before the
presence of his glory with
exceeding joy,
25. **To** the only wise
God our Saviour, *be* glory
and majesty,
dominion and power,
both now and ever. Amen.

THE REVELATION OF JESUS CHRIST TO JOHN

BACKGROUND INFORMATION

Author – John, one of the twelve Apostles.
Date Written – probably **between 90** and **99** A.D.

Number of:
Verses - 404
Chapters - 22
Total Words - 12,000
Scan Words - 5,973
Scan Words represent 49 % of Total Words.

Theme – written to reveal that in spite of adverse world events,
Jesus Christ will triumph over all the enemies of God.

OUTLINE OF THE REVELATION

I. The revelation of the Son of Man, **the letters to the seven Churches** and the open door in heaven.
Chapters 1—5

II. The revelation of the **seven seals, the seven trumpets and the war in heaven.**
Chapters 6—14

III. The revelation of **the seven vials and the fall of Babylon.**
Chapters 14—19

IV. The revelation of **the millennium and the Holy City.**
Chapters 20—22

THE REVELATION OF JESUS CHRIST TO JOHN

The Conclusion Of History

The first book of the Bible, ***Genesis, is a revelation of the beginnings of history,*** *both the beginning of the created order, and human beings. The final book of the Bible,* ***Revelation, is a revelation of the conclusion of history*** *– the end of time, the created order as we know it today, and of man in his fallen state.* ***Revelation,*** *in essence,* ***shows what will occur when*** *God in* ***Christ concludes*** *human* ***history and ushers in a New Order.*** *For centuries now, Bible scholars have studied the Book of Revelation. There has been a wide variety of interpretations.* ***Some Bible students give a literal interpretation to the Revelation. At the other extreme,*** *there are* ***scholars*** *who* ***attempt to show that the Revelation is totally symbolic.*** *There is, of course, a great deal of symbolism in the book,* ***but for the*** *Bible* ***student*** *who is* ***committed to the Scripture as the*** *authoritative, written* ***word of God, the symbolism points to a deeper reality. That reality,*** *regardless of one's interpretations of specific verses or chapters in the Revelation,* ***is that*** *God in* ***Christ will*** *ultimately* ***triumph over all the enemies of the truth*** *– sin, satan, political systems,* ***and all*** *that stands* ***in opposition to the*** *purposes and* ***will of God. Evil will be defeated,*** *the saints of God will be sustained,* ***persecution*** *and tribulation* ***shall end, and a new creation,*** *a new heaven and a new earth –* ***without sorrows,*** *tears, suffering, heartache,* ***and death – shall be established by*** *a direct act of* ***God. The Eden*** *which was* ***lost*** *by the first Adam,* ***shall be restored*** *by the second Adam, Jesus Christ.* ***What seems plain*** *in the Revelation* ***is that man, through his own*** *ingenuity or* ***effort, cannot solve his problems,*** *he cannot save himself individually, socially, or politically.* ***But God in sheer grace, shall finish all that was accomplished in the death and resurrection of His Son, and in that new beginning, He,*** *the Alpha and Omega,* ***shall be All in All.***

CHAPTER 1

1. **The Revelation of Jesus**
Christ, which God gave
unto him,
to shew unto his servants
things which must shortly
come to pass; and he
sent and signified
it by his angel
unto his servant
John:
2. Who bare record of the word of
God, and of the testimony of Jesus
Christ, and of all things that he saw.
3. **Blessed *is* he that**
readeth, and they that hear
the words of
this prophecy, and keep
those
things which are
written therein:
for the time *is* at hand.
4. **John to the seven**
churches which are
in Asia: Grace *be* unto you,
and peace,
from him which is, and which was,
and which is to come; and from the
seven Spirits which are before
his throne;
5. And from Jesus
Christ, *who is* the faithful
witness, *and* the first begotten of the
dead, and the
prince of the kings of the earth.
Unto him
that loved us, and washed
us from our sins in his
own blood
6. **And hath made us kings**
and priests unto God and his
Father; to him *be* glory and dominion
for ever and ever. Amen.
7. **Behold, he cometh**
with clouds;
and every eye shall see
him, and they *also* which pierced
him: and all kindreds of the earth shall
wail because of him. Even so, Amen.
8. **I am** Alpha and Omega,
the beginning and the
ending, saith the Lord,
which is, and which was, and which is
to come, the Almighty.
9. **I John,** who also am your brother,
and companion in tribulation, and in
the kingdom and patience of
Jesus Christ,
was in the isle that is
called Patmos, for the word of
God, and for the testimony of
Jesus Christ.
10. **I was in the Spirit on the**
Lord's day, and heard
behind me
a great voice, as of a trumpet,
11. **Saying,** I am Alpha and Omega,
the first and the last: and,
What thou seest, write
in a book,
and send *it* unto the seven
churches which are
in Asia; unto Ephesus, and unto
Smyrna, and unto Pergamos, and
unto Thyatira, and unto Sardis, and
unto Philadelphia, and unto Laodicea.
12. And I turned to see the voice that
spake with me.
And being turned,
I saw seven golden
candlesticks;
13. **And in the midst**
of the seven candlesticks
***one* like unto the**
Son of man,
clothed with a garment down to the
foot, and girt about the paps with a
golden girdle.
14. His head and *his* hairs *were* white
like wool, as white as snow; and
his eyes *were* as a flame of fire;
15. And his feet like unto fine brass,
as if they burned in a furnace;
and his voice as the sound of
many waters.
16. **And he had in his right**
hand seven stars: and out of
his mouth went a sharp two-edged
sword: and his countenance *was* as
the sun shineth in his strength.
17. **And when I saw him, I fell**
at his feet as dead. And he
laid his right hand upon
me, saying unto me,
Fear not; I am the first
and the last:

18. **I *am* he that liveth, and**
was dead; and, behold,
I am alive for evermore,
Amen;
and have the keys of hell
and of death.
19. **Write the things**
which thou hast seen, and the things
which are, and the things which
shall be hereafter;
20. The mystery of the seven stars
which thou sawest in my right hand,
and the seven golden candlesticks.
The seven stars are the
angels of the seven
churches: and the seven
candlesticks which thou sawest
are the seven churches.

CHAPTER 2

1. **Unto the angel of the**
church of Ephesus write;
These things saith he that holdeth the
seven stars in his right hand, who
walketh in the midst of the seven
golden candlesticks;
2. **I know thy works,**
and thy labour, and thy patience,
and how thou canst not
bear them which are evil:
and thou
hast tried them which say
they are apostles, and
are not, and hast
found them liars:
3. **And** hast borne, and hast
patience, and
for my name's sake
hast laboured, and
hast not fainted.
4. **Nevertheless** I have *somewhat*
against thee, because
thou hast left thy first love.
5. Remember therefore from whence
thou art fallen, and
repent, and do the first works;
or else I will come
unto thee quickly,
and will
remove thy candlestick
out of his place, except thou repent.
6. **But this thou hast,** that
thou hatest the deeds
of the Nicolaitanes,
which I also hate.
7. He that hath an ear,
let him hear what
the Spirit saith unto the
churches; To him that
overcometh will I give to
eat of the tree of life, which is
in the midst of the paradise of God.
8. **And unto the angel of the**
church in Smyrna write;
These things saith the first and the
last, which was dead, and is alive;
9. **I know thy works,**
and tribulation,
and poverty, (but thou art rich)
and *I know*
the blasphemy of them
which say they are Jews,
and are not,
but *are* the synagogue
of Satan.
10. Fear none of those things which
thou shalt suffer: behold,
the devil shall cast *some* of
you into prison,
that ye may be tried;
and ye shall have
tribulation ten days: be
thou faithful unto death,
and I will give thee a
crown of life.
11. He that hath an ear, let him hear
what the Spirit saith unto
the churches;
He that overcometh shall
not be hurt of the
second death.
12. **And to the angel of the**
church in Pergamos write;
These things saith he which hath the
sharp sword with two edges;
13. I know thy works, and where
thou dwellest, *even* where
Satan's seat *is:* and thou
holdest fast my name, and
hast not denied my faith,
even in those days wherein Antipas
was my faithful martyr, who was slain
among you, where Satan dwelleth.
14. **But I have** a few
things against thee,
because thou hast there

them that hold the doctrine
of Balaam, who taught Balac to
cast a stumblingblock before the
children of Israel,
to eat things sacrificed
unto idols, and to
commit fornication.
15. So hast thou also them that hold
the doctrine of the Nicolaitanes,
which thing I hate.
16. **Repent; or else I will**
come unto thee quickly,
and will
fight against
them with the sword
of my mouth.
17. He that hath an ear,
let him hear what the Spirit saith
unto the churches;
To him that overcometh
will I give to eat of
the hidden manna, and
will give him
a white stone, and in the
stone a new name written,
which no man knoweth saving he that
receiveth *it.*
18. **And unto the angel of the**
church in Thyatira write;
These things saith the Son of God,
who hath his eyes like unto a flame of
fire, and his feet *are* like fine brass;
19. **I know thy works,**
and charity, and service,
and faith,
and thy patience, and thy works; and
the last *to be* more than the first.
20. **Notwithstanding I have**
a few
things against thee,
because thou sufferest that
woman Jezebel,
which calleth herself a prophetess,
to teach and
to seduce my servants to
commit fornication, and to
eat things sacrificed
unto idols.
21. And I gave her space to
repent of her fornication;
and she repented not.
22. **Behold, I will cast her**
into a bed,
and them that commit
adultery with her into great
tribulation, except they
repent of their deeds.
23. **And I will kill her children**
with death; and all the churches shall
know that
I am he which searcheth the
reins and
hearts: and I will
give unto every one of you
according to your
works.
24. **But** unto you I say, and
unto the rest in Thyatira,
as many as have not this
doctrine, and which have not
known the depths of Satan,
as they speak;
I will put upon you none
other burden.
25. But that which ye have *already*
hold fast till I come.
26. **And he that overcometh,**
and keepeth my works unto the end,
to him
will I give power over
the nations:
27. **And he shall rule** them with
a rod of iron; as the vessels of a
potter shall they be broken to shivers:
even as I received of my Father.
28. **And I will give him the**
morning star.
29. He that hath an ear,
let him hear what the Spirit
saith unto the churches.

CHAPTER 3

1. **And unto the angel of the**
church in Sardis write; These
things saith he that hath the seven
Spirits of God, and the seven stars; I
know thy works, that
thou hast a name that thou
livest, and art dead.
2. Be watchful, and
strengthen the things
which remain, that are
ready to die: for I have not
found thy works perfect
before God.
3. Remember therefore how thou hast

received and heard, and hold fast,
and repent. If therefore
thou shalt not watch, I will
come on thee
as a thief, and thou shalt
not know what hour
I will come upon thee.
4. **Thou hast a few**
names even in Sardis
which have not defiled their
garments; and they shall
walk with me
in white: for they
are worthy.
5. **He that overcometh,**
the same shall be clothed in white
raiment; and
I will not blot out his name
out of the book of life, but I
will confess his name
before my Father,
and before his angels.
6. He that hath an ear,
let him hear what the Spirit
saith unto the churches.
7. **And to the angel of the**
church in Philadelphia
write; These things saith he that is
holy, he that is true, he that hath the
key of David, he that openeth, and no
man shutteth; and shutteth, and no
man openeth;
8. I know thy works: behold,
I have set before thee an
open door,
and no man can shut it:
for thou hast a little
strength, and hast kept my word,
and hast not denied
my name.
9. Behold, I will make
them of the synagogue of
Satan, which say they are
Jews, and are not,
but do lie; behold,
I will make them
to come and
worship before thy feet,
and to know that I have loved thee.
10. **Because thou hast kept**
the word of my patience,
I also will keep thee from
the hour of temptation,
which shall come
upon all the world, to try them
that dwell upon the earth.
11. Behold, I come quickly:
hold that
fast which thou hast,
that no man take thy crown.
12. **Him that overcometh**
will I make a pillar in the temple of
my God, and he shall go no more out:
and I will
write upon him the name of my
God, and the name of the city of my
God, *which is* new Jerusalem, which
cometh down out of heaven from my
God: and *I will write upon him*
my new name.
13. He that hath an ear,
let him hear what the Spirit
saith unto the churches.
14. **And unto the angel of the**
church of the Laodiceans
write; These things saith the Amen,
the faithful and true witness, the
beginning of the creation of God;
15. I know thy works, that
thou art neither cold nor
hot: I would thou wert cold or hot.
16. **So then because thou**
art lukewarm,
and neither cold nor hot,
I will spue thee out
of my mouth.
17. **Because thou sayest, I**
am rich, and increased with goods,
and have need of nothing;
and knowest not that thou
art wretched, and miserable, and
poor, and
blind, and naked:
18. **I counsel thee to buy of**
me gold tried in the fire, that
thou mayest be rich; and
white raiment, that thou
mayest be clothed,
and *that* the shame of thy nakedness
do not appear;
and anoint thine eyes with
eye-salve, that thou
mayest see.
19. **As many as I love, I**
rebuke and chasten: be zealous
therefore, and

repent.
20. **Behold, I stand at the**
door, and knock: if any
man hear my voice, and
open the door,
I will come in to him,
and will
sup with him, and he with me.
21. **To him that overcometh**
will I grant to sit with me in
my throne, even as I also
overcame, and am set down with my
Father in his throne.
22. **He that hath an ear, let**
him hear what the Spirit saith unto
the churches.

CHAPTER 4

1. **After this** I looked, and, behold,
a door *was* opened in
heaven: and the
first voice which
I heard *was* as it were of a trumpet
talking with me; which
said, Come up hither,
and I will shew thee things
which must be hereafter.
2. **And immediately I was in**
the spirit; and, behold,
a throne was set
in heaven, and *one* sat on
the throne.
3. And he that sat was to look upon
like a jasper and a sardine stone: and
there was a rainbow round about the
throne, in sight like unto an emerald.
4. **And round about the**
throne *were* four and
twenty seats: and
upon the seats I saw
four and twenty elders
sitting, clothed in white raiment;
and they had on their heads
crowns of gold.
5. And out of the throne proceeded
lightnings and thunderings
and voices:
and *there were* seven
lamps of fire burning
before the throne, which
are the seven Spirits
of God.
6. And before the throne *there was* a
sea of glass like unto crystal:
and in the midst of the throne, and
round about the throne,
***were* four beasts full of**
eyes before and behind.
7. **And the first beast *was***
like a lion, and
the second beast
like a calf, and
the third beast
had a face as a man, and
the fourth beast
***was* like a flying eagle.**
8. And the four beasts had each of
them six wings about *him*; and *they*
were full of eyes within:
and they rest not day and
night, saying, Holy, holy,
holy, LORD God Almighty,
which was, and
is, and is to come.
9. And when those beasts give glory
and honour and thanks to him that sat
on the throne, who liveth
for ever and ever,
10. **The four and twenty**
elders fall down
before him that sat on the throne,
and worship him that liveth
for ever and ever, and cast their
crowns before the throne,
saying,
11. **Thou art worthy, O Lord,**
to receive glory
and honour and power:
for thou hast created all
things, and
for thy pleasure
they are and were created.

CHAPTER 5

1. **And I saw in the right**
hand of him
that sat on the throne
a book written within and on the
backside, sealed
with seven seals.
2. **And I saw a strong angel**
proclaiming with a loud voice,
Who is worthy to
open the book,
and to loose the seals thereof?
3. **And no man in heaven,**

nor in earth,
neither under the earth,
was able to open the book,
neither to look thereon.
4. **And I wept much,** because no
man was found worthy to open and to
read the book, neither to
look thereon.
5. **And one of the elders**
saith unto me,
Weep not: behold, the Lion
of the tribe of Juda,
the Root of David,
hath prevailed to
open the book,
and to loose the seven seals thereof.
6. **And** I beheld, and, lo,
in the midst of the throne and of
the four beasts, and in the midst of
the elders,
stood a Lamb as it had
been slain, having seven horns
and seven eyes, which are the seven
Spirits of God sent forth
into all the earth.
7. **And he came and took**
the book out of the right hand of
him that sat upon the throne.
8. **And** when he had taken the book,
the four beasts and four
***and* twenty elders fell down**
before the Lamb, having every
one of them harps, and golden vials
full of odours, which are the
prayers of saints.
9. **And they sung a new**
song, saying, Thou art
worthy to take the book,
and to open the seals thereof:
for thou wast slain, and
hast redeemed us to God
by thy blood
out of every kindred, and tongue,
and people, and nation;
10. **And hast made us unto**
our God kings and priests:
and we shall reign
on the earth.
11. And I beheld,
and I heard the
voice of many
angels round about the
throne and the
beasts and the
elders: and the number of them
was ten thousand times ten thousand,
and thousands of thousands;
12. **Saying with a loud**
voice, Worthy is the Lamb
that was slain to receive
power, and
riches, and
wisdom, and
strength, and
honour, and
glory, and blessing.
13. **And every creature**
which is in heaven, and on the earth,
and under the earth, and such as are
in the sea, and all that are in them,
heard I
saying, Blessing,
and honour, and
glory, and power, *be* unto him
that sitteth upon the throne, and
unto the Lamb for ever and ever.
14. And the four beasts said, Amen.
And the four *and* twenty elders fell
down and worshipped him that liveth
for ever and ever.

CHAPTER 6

1. **And** I saw when
the Lamb opened one of
the seals, and I heard,
as it were the noise of thunder,
one of the four
beasts saying,
Come and see.
2. **And I saw,** and behold
a white horse: and he that
sat on him had a bow; and a crown
was given unto him: and he
went forth conquering,
and to conquer.
3. **And when he had opened**
the second seal, I heard the
second beast say, Come and see.
4. **And there went out**
another horse *that was*
red: and *power* was given
to him that sat thereon
to take peace from the
earth, and that they should
kill one another: and there was
given unto him a great sword.

5. **And when he had opened the third seal,** I heard the third beast say, Come and see. And **I beheld,** and lo **a black horse; and he that sat on him had** a pair of **balances** in his hand.
6. **And I heard a voice** in the midst of the four beasts **say, A measure of wheat for a penny, and three measures of barley for a penny; and** *see* thou **hurt not the oil and** the **wine.**
7. **And when he** had **opened the fourth seal,** I heard the voice of the fourth beast say, Come and see.
8. And I looked, and **behold a pale horse: and his name that sat on him was Death, and Hell** followed with him. **And power was given** unto **them over the fourth** part **of the earth, to kill** with sword, and with hunger, and with death, and with the beasts of the earth.
9. **And when he had opened the fifth seal, I saw** under the altar **the souls** of them that were **slain for the word of God,** and for the testimony which they held:
10. **And they cried** with a loud voice, saying, **How long, O Lord,** holy and true, **dost thou not** judge and **avenge our blood** on them that dwell on the earth?
11. **And white robes were given unto** every one of **them; and** it was said unto them, that **they should rest** yet for a little season, **until their fellow-servants** also and their brethren, that **should be killed as they *were*,** should be fulfilled.
12. And I beheld **when he** had **opened the sixth seal,** and, lo, **there was a great earthquake; and the sun became black** as sackcloth of hair, **and the moon** became **as blood;**
13. **And the stars** of heaven **fell** unto the earth, even as a fig tree casteth her untimely figs, when she is shaken of a mighty wind.
14. **And the heaven departed** as a scroll when it is rolled together; **and every mountain and island were moved** out of their places.
15. **And the kings** of the earth, and the **great men,** and the **rich men,** and the **chief captains,** and the **mighty men,** and **every bondman, and** every **free man, hid** themselves **in the dens and** in the **rocks of** the **mountains;**
16. **And said to the mountains and rocks, Fall on us, and hide us** from the face of him that sitteth on the throne, and from the wrath of the Lamb:
17. **For the great day of his wrath is come; and who shall be able to stand?**

CHAPTER 7

1. **And** after these things **I saw four angels** standing on the four corners of the earth, **holding the four winds** of the earth, **that the wind should not blow on the earth,** nor on the sea, nor on any tree.
2. **And I saw another angel ascending** from the east, **having the seal of** the living **God: and he cried**

with a loud voice
■ **to the four angels,**
to whom it was given to hurt the
earth and the sea,
■ 3. **Saying, Hurt not the earth,**
neither the sea, nor the trees,
■ **till we have sealed the**
■ **servants of our God in**
■ **their foreheads.**
4. And I heard the number of them
which were sealed:
■ ***and there were* sealed an**
■ **hundred *and* forty *and* four**
■ **thousand of** all
■ **the tribes of** the children of
■ **Israel.**
5. Of the tribe of Juda *were* sealed
twelve thousand. Of the tribe of
Reuben *were* sealed twelve thousand.
Of the tribe of Gad *were* sealed
twelve thousand.
6. Of the tribe of Aser *were* sealed
twelve thousand. Of the tribe of
Nephthalim *were* sealed twelve
thousand. Of the tribe of Manasses
were sealed twelve thousand.
7. Of the tribe of Simeon *were* sealed
twelve thousand. Of the tribe of Levi
were sealed twelve thousand. Of the
tribe of Issachar *were* sealed twelve
thousand.
8. Of the tribe of Zabulon *were* sealed
twelve thousand. Of the tribe of
Joseph *were* sealed twelve thousand.
Of the tribe of Benjamin *were* sealed
twelve thousand.
■ 9. **After this** I beheld, and, lo,
■ **a great multitude,** which no man
could number, of all nations, and
kindreds, and people, and tongues,
■ **stood before the throne,**
■ **and before the Lamb,**
■ **clothed with white robes,**
and palms in their hands;
■ 10. **And cried**
with a loud voice, saying,
■ **Salvation to our God**
which sitteth upon the throne,
■ **and** unto
■ **the Lamb.**
■ 11. **And all the angels** stood
round about the throne, and *about* the
elder and the four beasts, and fell
before the throne on their faces, and
■ **worshipped God,**
■ 12. **Saying, Amen: Blessing,**
and
■ **glory,** and
■ **wisdom,** and
■ **thanksgiving,** and
■ **honour,** and
■ **power, and might, *be***
■ **unto our God for ever**
and ever. Amen.
■ 13. **And one of the elders**
■ **answered,** saying unto me,
■ **What are these** which are
■ **arrayed in white robes?**
and whence came they?
■ 14. **And I said** unto him,
■ **Sir, thou knowest.**
■ **And he said** to me,
■ **These** are they which
■ **came out of great**
■ **tribulation, and have**
■ **washed their robes,**
and made them white
■ **in the blood of the Lamb.**
■ 15. **Therefore are they**
■ **before** the throne of
■ **God,** and serve him day
and night in his temple:
■ **and he** that sitteth on the throne
■ **shall dwell among them.**
16. They shall hunger no more, neither
thirst any more; neither shall the sun
light on them, nor any heat.
■ 17. **For the Lamb** which is in the
midst of the throne
■ **shall feed them, and** shall
■ **lead them unto living**
■ **fountains** of waters:
■ **and God shall wipe away**
■ **all tears from their eyes.**

CHAPTER 8

■ 1. **And when he had opened**
■ **the seventh seal, there was**
■ **silence** in heaven about the space
of half an hour.
2. And I saw
■ **the seven angels**
which stood before God; and to them
■ **were given seven trumpets.**
■ 3. **And another angel**
came and stood at the altar,

having a golden censer;
and there was
given unto him
much incense, that he
should offer *it* with the
prayers of all saints
upon the golden altar which was
before the throne.
4. **And the smoke of the**
incense, *which came* with the
prayers of the saints,
ascended up before God
out of the angel's hand.
5. **And the angel took the**
censer, and
filled it
with fire of the altar, and
cast *it* into the earth: and there
were voices, and thunderings, and
lightnings, and an earthquake.
6. **And the seven angels**
which had the seven
trumpets prepared
themselves
to sound.
7. **The first angel sounded,**
and there followed hail
and fire mingled
with blood, and they were cast
upon the earth: and the
third part of trees
was burnt up,
and all green
grass was burnt up.
8. **And the second angel**
sounded, and as it were a great
mountain burning with fire was cast
into the sea:
and the third part of the sea
became blood;
9. **And the third part of the**
creatures which were
in the sea, and had life,
died; and the third part of
the ships were destroyed.
10. **And the third angel**
sounded, and there fell
a great star from heaven,
burning as it were a lamp, and it
fell upon the third part of
the rivers, and upon the
fountains of waters;
11. And the name of
the star is called
Wormwood: and the third part
of the waters became wormwood;
and many men died of the
waters, because they were
made bitter.
12. **And the fourth angel**
sounded, and the third part
of the sun was smitten, and
the third part of
the moon, and the third part of
the stars; so as the third part of
them was darkened,
and the day shone not for a
third part of it, and the
night likewise.
13. **And I** beheld, and
heard an angel flying
through the midst of
heaven, saying
with a loud voice, Woe, woe,
woe, to the inhabiters of the
earth by reason of the
other voices of the trumpet of the
three angels, which are
yet to sound!

CHAPTER 9

1. **And the fifth angel**
sounded, and I saw a star
fall from heaven
unto the
earth: and to him was given
the key of the
bottomless pit.
2. **And he opened the**
bottomless
pit; and there arose a smoke out of
the pit, as the smoke of a great
furnace; and the sun and the air
were darkened by reason of the
smoke of the pit.
3. **And there came out**
of the smoke
locusts upon the earth:
and unto them was given
power, as the scorpions
of the earth
have power.
4. **And it was commanded**
them
that they should
not hurt the grass

of the earth, neither any green thing,
neither any tree; but only those
men which have not the
seal of God in
their foreheads.
5. **And** to them it was given that
they should not kill them,
but that
they should be tormented
five months: and their torment *was* as the torment of a scorpion, when he striketh a man.
6. **And** in those days shall
men seek death, and shall not find it; and
shall desire to die, and
death shall flee from them.
7. **And the shapes of the**
locusts *were* like unto
horses prepared unto
battle; and on their heads *were* as it were crowns like gold, and
their faces *were*
as the faces of
men.
8. **And they had hair as** the hair of
women, and their teeth were
as *the teeth* of
lions.
9. **And they had** breastplates, as it were
breastplates of iron; and
the sound of their wings *was*
as the sound of
chariots of many horses running to battle.
10. **And they had tails like** unto
scorpions, and there were
stings in their tails:
and their
power *was*
to hurt men five months.
11. **And they had a king** over them,
***which is* the angel of the** bottomless
pit, whose name in the
Hebrew tongue
***is* Abaddon, but in** the
Greek tongue hath *his* name
Apollyon.
12. One woe is past; *and*, behold, there come two woes more hereafter.
13. **And the sixth angel**
sounded, and I heard a
voice from the four horns of the golden altar which is before God,
14. **Saying to the sixth angel** which had the trumpet,
Loose the four angels which are
bound in the great
river Euphrates.
15. **And the four angels were**
loosed, which were prepared for an hour, and a day, and a month, and a year, for
to slay the third part
of men.
16. And the number of
the army of the
horsemen *were* two
hundred thousand
thousand: and I heard the number of them.
17. **And thus I saw the**
horses in the vision, and
them that sat on them, having breastplates of fire, and of jacinth, and brimstone:
and the heads of the
horses *were*
as the heads of lions; and
out of their mouths
issued fire and smoke
and brimstone.
18. **By these three was the**
third part of men killed, by the fire, and by the smoke, and by the brimstone, which issued out of their mouths.
19. **For their power is in their**
mouth, and in their
tails: for their tails *were* like unto serpents, and had heads, and with them they do hurt.
20. **And the rest** of the men
which were not killed by these plagues
yet repented not of the works of their hands,
that they should not
worship devils, and idols

of gold, and silver, and brass, and
stone, and of wood: which neither can
see, nor hear, nor walk:
21. **Neither repented they of**
their murders, nor of their
sorceries, nor of their
fornication, nor of their
thefts.

CHAPTER 10

1. **And I saw another mighty**
angel come down from heaven,
clothed with a cloud: and a rainbow
was upon his head, and his face *was*
as it were the sun, and his feet as
pillars of fire:
2. **And he had** in his hand
a little book open: and he set
his right foot upon the sea, and *his* left
foot on the earth,
3. And cried with a loud voice,
as *when* a lion roareth:
and when he had
cried, seven thunders
uttered their voices.
4. **And** when the seven thunders had
uttered their voices,
I was about to write: and I
heard a voice from heaven
saying unto me,
Seal up those things
which the seven thunders
uttered, and write them
not.
5. **And the angel which I saw**
stand upon the sea and
upon the earth
lifted up his hand to heaven,
6. **And sware by him that**
liveth for ever and ever, who
created heaven, and the things that
therein are, and the earth, and the
things that therein are, and the sea,
and the things which are therein,
that there should be time
no longer:
7. **But in the days of the**
voice of the seventh angel,
when he shall begin to sound,
the mystery of God should
be finished, as he hath declared
to his servants the prophets.
8. **And the voice which I**
heard from heaven spake
unto me again, and
said, Go *and*
take the little book
which is open in the hand of the angel
which standeth upon the sea and
upon the earth.
9. **And I went unto the angel,**
and said unto him,
Give me the little book.
And he said unto me,
Take *it*, and eat it up; and it
shall make thy belly bitter, but it shall
be in thy mouth sweet as honey.
10. **And I** took the little book out of
the angel's hand, and
ate it up;
and it was in my mouth
sweet as honey: and
as soon as I had eaten it,
my belly was bitter.
11. **And he said** unto me,
Thou must prophesy again
before many peoples, and nations,
and tongues, and kings.

CHAPTER 11

1. **And there was given me**
a reed like unto
a rod: and the angel stood,
saying, Rise, and measure
the temple of God,
and the altar, and them that
worship therein.
2. **But the court** which is without
the temple leave out, and
measure it not; for it is
given unto the Gentiles: and
the holy city shall they tread under
foot forty *and* two months.
3. **And I will give *power* unto**
my two witnesses, and they
shall prophesy a thousand
two hundred *and*
threescore days,
clothed in sackcloth.
4. These are the two olive trees, and
the two candlesticks standing
before the God of the earth.
5. **And if any man will hurt**
them, fire proceedeth out of their
mouth, and devoureth their enemies:
and if any man will hurt them,

he must in this manner
be killed.
6. **These have power to shut**
heaven, that it rain not
in the days of their prophecy:
and have power
over waters to turn them to
blood, and to smite the
earth with all
plagues, as often as
they will.
7. **And when they** shall
have finished their
testimony, the beast
that ascendeth
out of the bottomless
pit shall make war against
them, and shall overcome them,
and kill them.
8. **And their dead bodies**
***shall lie* in** the street of
the great city, which spiritually is
called Sodom and Egypt,
where also our Lord
was crucified.
9. **And they of the people** and
kindreds and tongues and nations
shall see their dead
bodies three days and an
half, and shall not suffer
their dead
bodies to be put in graves.
10. **And they** that dwell
upon the earth shall rejoice
over them, and make merry, and shall
send gifts one to another;
because these two
prophets tormented them
that dwelt on the earth.
11. **And after three days and**
an half the Spirit of life from God
entered into
them, and they stood
upon their feet;
and great fear fell
upon them which saw them.
12. **And they heard a great**
voice from heaven saying
unto them,
Come up hither.
And they ascended up
to heaven in a cloud; and their
enemies beheld them.

13. **And the same hour was**
there a great earthquake,
and the tenth part of the city fell,
and in the earthquake were
slain of men
seven thousand: and
the remnant were
affrighted, and gave glory
to the
God of heaven.
14. The second woe is past;
***and,* behold, the third woe**
cometh quickly.
15. **And the seventh angel**
sounded; and there were
great
voices in heaven,
saying, The kingdoms of
this world are become *the*
***kingdoms* of our Lord, and**
of his Christ; and he shall reign
for ever and ever.
16. **And the four and twenty**
elders, which sat before God on
their seats, fell upon their faces, and
worshipped God,
17. **Saying, We give** thee
thanks, O LORD God Almighty,
which art, and
wast, and art to come;
because thou hast taken
to thee thy
great power, and
hast reigned.
18. And the nations were angry, and
thy wrath is come, and
the time of the dead, that
they should be judged, and
that thou shouldest give
reward unto thy servants the
prophets, and to the saints, and
them that fear thy name,
small and great;
and shouldest destroy
them which destroy
the earth.
19. **And the temple of God**
was opened in heaven,
and there was
seen in his temple
the ark of his testament:
and there were lightnings, and voices,
and thunderings, and an earthquake,

and great hail.

CHAPTER 12

1. **And there appeared**
a great wonder
in heaven; a woman
clothed with the sun, and the moon
under her feet, and upon her head a
crown of twelve stars:
2. **And she being with child**
cried, travailing in birth, and pained
to be delivered.
3. **And there appeared**
another wonder in heaven; and behold
a great
red dragon, having seven heads
and ten horns, and seven crowns
upon his heads.
4. And his tail drew the third part of the
stars of heaven, and did cast them to
the earth:
and the dragon stood
before the woman which was
ready to be delivered, for
to devour her child as
soon as it was born.
5. **And she brought forth a**
man child, who was to rule
all nations with a rod of iron:
and her child was caught
up unto God, and *to* his throne.
6. **And the woman fled into**
the wilderness, where she hath
a place prepared of God,
that they should feed her there a
thousand two hundred *and*
threescore days.
7. **And there was war in**
heaven: Michael and his
angels fought against the
dragon; and the dragon
fought and his angels,
8. And
prevailed not;
neither was their place found any
more in heaven.
9. **And the great dragon**
was cast out, that old serpent,
called the Devil, and
Satan, which deceiveth the
whole world: he
was cast out into the earth,
and his angels were cast
out with him.
10. **And I heard a loud voice**
saying in heaven,
Now is come salvation,
and strength, and the kingdom of our
God, and the power of his Christ:
for the accuser of our
brethren is cast down,
which accused them before our God
day and night.
11. **And they overcame him**
by the blood of the Lamb,
and by the word of
their testimony; and they loved
not their lives unto the death.
12. Therefore rejoice, *ye* heavens,
and ye that dwell in them.
Woe to the inhabiters of the
earth and of the
sea! for the devil is come
down unto you,
having great wrath,
because he knoweth that
he hath but a short time.
13. **And when the dragon**
saw that he
was cast unto the
earth, he persecuted the
woman which brought forth the
man *child.*
14. **And to the woman were**
given two wings
of a great eagle,
that she might fly
into the wilderness,
into her place,
where she is nourished
for a time,
and times, and half a time,
from the face of
the serpent.
15. **And the serpent cast**
out of his mouth
water as a flood
after the woman,
that he might cause her to
be carried away of the flood.
16. **And the earth**
helped the woman, and the earth
opened her mouth, and
swallowed up the flood
which the dragon cast out
of his mouth.

17. **And the dragon**
was wroth with the woman, and
went to make
war with the remnant of
her seed, which keep the
commandments of God,
and have the testimony of
Jesus Christ.

CHAPTER 13

1. **And I** stood upon the
sand of the sea, and
saw a beast rise up
out of the sea, having
seven heads and ten
horns, and upon his horns
ten crowns,
and upon his heads the
name of blasphemy.
2. And the beast which I saw was like
unto a leopard, and his feet were as
the feet of a bear, and his mouth as
the mouth of a lion: and the dragon
gave him his power, and his seat, and
great authority.
3. **And I saw one of his**
heads as it were
wounded to death; and his
deadly
wound was healed: and all
the world wondered after
the beast.
4. **And they worshipped the**
dragon which gave power
unto the beast: and they
worshipped the beast,
saying, Who *is* like unto the
beast? who is able to
make war with him?
5. **And there was given** unto
him a mouth speaking
great things and
blasphemies; and power
was given unto him
to continue forty *and*
two months.
6. **And he opened his mouth**
in blasphemy
against God, to
blaspheme his name,
and his tabernacle, and them that
dwell in heaven.
7. **And it was given** unto
him to make war with the
saints, and to
overcome them: and
power was given him
over all kindreds, and
tongues, and
nations.
8. **And** all that dwell upon
the earth shall worship
him, whose names are
not written
in the book of life of the
Lamb slain from the
foundation of the world.
9. If any man have an ear,
let him hear.
10. He that leadeth into captivity shall
go into captivity: he that killeth with
the sword must be killed with the
sword. Here is the patience
and the faith of the saints.
11. **And I beheld another**
beast coming up out of the earth;
and he had two horns like
a lamb, and he spake as
a dragon.
12. **And he** exerciseth all the power
of the first beast before him, and
causeth the earth and them
which dwell
therein to worship the first
beast, whose deadly
wound was healed.
13. **And he doeth great**
wonders, so that he maketh fire
come down from heaven on the earth
in the sight of men,
14. **And deceiveth**
them that dwell on the earth
by *the*
means of those
miracles which he had power to do
in the sight of the beast;
saying to them
that dwell on the earth,
that they should make an
image to the beast, which
had the wound by a sword,
and did live.
15. **And he had power to**
give life unto the image of
the beast, that the image of the
beast should both speak,

and cause that as many as
would not worship the
image of the beast should
be killed.
16. **And he causeth all,**
both small and great, rich and poor,
free and bond,
to receive a mark in their
right hand, or in their
foreheads:
17. **And that no man might**
buy or sell, save he that
had the mark, or the
name of the beast,
or the number of his name.
18. **Here is wisdom.** Let him that
hath understanding
count the number of the
beast: for it is the number of a
man; and his number *is*
Six hundred threescore
***and* six.**

CHAPTER 14

1. And I looked, and, lo,
a Lamb stood on the mount
Sion, and
with him
an hundred forty *and*
four thousand, having his
Father's name written in
their foreheads.
2. **And I heard a voice from**
heaven, as the voice of many
waters, and as the voice of a
great thunder:
and I heard the voice of
harpers harping
with their harps:
3. **And they sung** as it were
a new song before the throne,
and before the four beasts,
and the elders:
and no man could learn
that song but the hundred
and
forty *and*
four thousand, which were
redeemed from the earth.
4. These are they which were not
defiled with women;
for they are virgins.
These are they which
follow the Lamb whithersoever
he goeth. These were redeemed from
among men,
***being* the firstfruits unto**
God and to the Lamb.
5. And in their mouth was found
no guile:
for they are without fault
before the throne of God.
6. **And I saw another angel**
fly in the midst of heaven,
having the everlasting
gospel to preach unto
them that dwell on the earth, and to
every nation, and
kindred, and
tongue, and people,
7. **Saying** with a loud voice,
Fear God, and give glory to him;
for the hour of
his judgment is come: and
worship him that made heaven,
and earth, and the sea, and the
fountains of waters.
8. **And** there followed
another angel, saying,
Babylon is fallen,
is fallen, that great city,
because she made all
nations drink of
the wine of the wrath of
her fornication.
9. **And the third angel**
followed them,
saying with a loud voice,
If any man worship the
beast and his image,
and receive *his* mark
in his forehead, or in his hand,
10. **The same shall drink** of
the wine of the wrath of
God, which is poured out without
mixture into the cup of his indignation;
and he shall be tormented
with fire and brimstone
in the presence of the holy
angels, and in the presence of
the Lamb:
11. **And the smoke of their**
torment ascendeth up for
ever and ever:
and they have no rest
day nor night,

■ **who worship the beast and**
his image, and whosoever
■ **receiveth the mark**
of his name.
12. Here is the patience of the saints:
here *are* they that keep the
commandments of God, and the faith
of Jesus.
■ 13. **And I heard a voice**
from heaven
■ **saying** unto me,
■ **Write, Blessed *are* the dead**
■ **which die in the Lord**
from henceforth:
■ **Yea, saith the Spirit,** that
■ **they may rest** from their labours;
■ **and their works** do
■ **follow** them.
■ 14. **And I looked, and**
■ **behold a white cloud, and**
■ **upon the cloud *one* sat like**
unto
■ **the Son of man, having**
on his head
■ **a golden crown, and**
in his hand
■ **a sharp sickle.**
■ 15. **And another angel came**
out of the temple,
■ **crying** with a loud voice
■ **to him** that sat on the cloud,
■ **Thrust** in
■ **thy sickle, and reap:** for the
time is come for thee to reap;
■ **for the harvest** of the earth
■ **is ripe.**
■ 16. **And he** that sat on the cloud
■ **thrust** in
■ **his sickle** on the earth;
■ **and** the earth was
■ **reaped.**
■ 17. **And another angel came**
■ **out of the temple**
which is in heaven, he also
■ **having a** sharp
■ **sickle.**
■ 18. **And another angel**
came out from the altar,
■ **which had power over fire;**
and
■ **cried** with a loud cry
■ **to him** that had the sharp
sickle, saying,
■ **Thrust in thy** sharp
■ **sickle, and gather the**
■ **clusters of the vine**
of the earth;
■ **for her grapes are** fully
■ **ripe.**
■ 19. **And the angel** thrust in his
sickle into the earth, and
■ **gathered the vine** of the earth,
■ **and cast *it* into the** great
■ **winepress of the wrath**
■ **of God.**
20. And the winepress was trodden
without the city,
■ **and blood came out of the**
■ **winepress,** even unto the horse
bridles, by the space of a thousand
and six hundred furlongs.

CHAPTER 15

■ 1. **And I saw** another sign in
heaven, great and marvellous,
■ **seven angels having the**
■ **seven last plagues;** for in
them is filled up the wrath of God.
■ 2. **And I saw as it were a sea**
■ **of glass** mingled
■ **with fire: and them that had**
■ **gotten the victory over the**
■ **beast,** and over his image,
and over his mark, *and* over the
number of his name,
■ **stand on the sea** of glass,
having the harps of God.
■ 3. **And they sing the song of**
■ **Moses** the servant of God,
■ **and the song of the Lamb,**
■ **saying, Great** and marvellous
■ ***are* thy works, Lord**
God Almighty;
■ **just and true *are* thy ways,**
■ **thou King of saints.**
■ 4. **Who shall not fear**
thee, O Lord,
■ **and glorify thy name? for**
■ ***thou* only *art* holy: for all**
■ **nations shall** come and
■ **worship** before
■ **thee;** for thy judgments
are made manifest.
5. And after that I looked, and,
behold, the temple of the tabernacle
of the testimony in heaven

was opened:
6. **And the seven angels**
came out of the temple,
having the seven plagues, clothed in
pure and white linen, and having their
breasts girded with golden girdles.
7. **And one of the four**
beasts gave unto the seven
angels seven golden vials
full of the wrath of God,
who liveth for ever and ever.
8. And the temple was filled with
smoke from the glory of God, and from
his power; and no man was able to
enter into the temple, till the seven
plagues of the seven angels
were fulfilled.

CHAPTER 16

1. **And I heard a great voice**
out of the temple
saying to the seven
angels, Go your ways, and
pour out the vials of the
wrath of God upon the earth.
2. **And the first** went, and
poured out his vial upon the
earth; and there fell a
noisome and
grievous sore upon the
men which had the mark
of the beast, and *upon* them which
worshipped his image.
3. **And the second** angel
poured out
his vial upon the sea; and it
became as the
blood of a dead *man;*
and every living
soul died in the sea.
4. **And the third** angel
poured out his vial upon the
rivers and fountains of
waters; and they
became blood.
5. **And I heard the angel of**
the
waters say, Thou art
righteous, O Lord,
which art, and wast, and shalt be,
because thou hast
judged thus.
6. **For they have shed the**
blood of saints and prophets,
and thou hast given them blood to
drink; for they are worthy.
7. And I heard another out of the altar
say, Even so, Lord God Almighty, true
and righteous *are* thy judgments.
8. **And the fourth** angel
poured out his vial upon
the sun; and power was
given unto
him to scorch men
with fire.
9. **And men were scorched**
with great heat,
and blasphemed the name of
God, which hath power
over these plagues:
and they
repented not to give him glory.
10. **And the fifth** angel
poured out his vial upon
the seat of
the beast; and his kingdom
was full of darkness;
and they gnawed their
tongues for pain,
11. **And blasphemed** the
God of heaven
because of their
pains and their
sores, and repented not
of their deeds.
12. **And the sixth** angel
poured out his vial upon
the great river
Euphrates; and the water
thereof was
dried up, that the way of the
kings of the east might
be prepared.
13. **And I saw three unclean**
spirits like frogs
***come* out of the mouth**
of the dragon,
and out of the mouth of
the beast, and
out of the mouth of
the false prophet.
14. **For they are the spirits of**
devils, working miracles,
***which* go forth unto the**
kings of the earth
and of the whole world,

to gather them to the battle
of that great day of God Almighty.
15. Behold, I come as a thief. Blessed
is he that watcheth, and keepeth his
garments, lest he walk naked, and
they see his shame.
16. **And he gathered them**
together
into a place called in the
Hebrew tongue
Armageddon.
17. **And the seventh** angel
poured out
his vial into the air; and
there came a great voice
out of the temple of heaven,
from the throne, saying,
It is done.
18. And there were voices, and
thunders, and lightnings; and there
was a great earthquake, such as was
not since men were upon the earth, so
mighty an earthquake, *and* so great.
19. **And the great city was**
divided into three parts,
and the cities of the nations
fell: and great Babylon
came in remembrance
before God, to give unto
her the cup of the wine of the
fierceness of his wrath.
20. **And every island fled**
away,
and the
mountains were not found.
21. **And there fell**
upon men a great
hail out of heaven, *every stone*
about the weight of a talent:
and men blasphemed God
because of the plague of
the hail; for the plague thereof
was exceeding great.

CHAPTER 17

1. And there came
one of the seven
angels which had the seven
vials, and
talked with me, saying
unto me,
Come hither;
I will shew unto the
judgment of the great
whore that sitteth
upon many waters:
2. **With whom the**
kings of the earth
have committed
fornication, and the
inhabitants of the earth
have been made drunk
with the wine of
her fornication.
3. **So he carried me** away
in the spirit into the wilderness:
and I saw a woman sit
upon a scarlet coloured
beast, full of names of
blasphemy, having seven
heads and ten horns.
4. And the woman was arrayed in
purple and scarlet colour, and decked
with gold and precious stones and
pearls, having a golden cup in her
hand full of abominations and
filthiness of her fornication
5. **And upon her forehead**
was a name
written, MYSTERY, BABYLON
THE GREAT, THE MOTHER OF
HARLOTS AND
ABOMINATIONS OF
THE EARTH.
6. **And I saw the woman**
drunken with the blood of
the saints, and with the blood of
the martyrs of Jesus:
and when I saw her, I wondered with
great admiration.
7. **And the angel said** unto me,
Wherefore didst thou marvel?
I will tell thee the mystery of
the woman, and of the
beast that carrieth her, which hath
the seven heads and ten horns.
8. **The beast** that thou sawest
was, and is
not; and shall ascend out
of the bottomless pit, and
go into perdition: and they that
dwell on the earth shall wonder, whose
names were not written in the book of
life from the foundation of the world,
when they behold the beast that was,
and is not, and yet is.

9. And here *is* the mind which
hath wisdom.
The seven heads are seven
mountains, on which the
woman sitteth.
10. And there are seven
kings: five are fallen, and
one is, *and* the other is not
yet come; and when he
cometh, he must continue a
short space.
11. And the beast that was, and
is not, even he is the eighth, and
is of the seven, and goeth
into perdition.
12. And the ten horns
which thou sawest
are ten kings, which have
received no kingdom as
yet; but receive power
as kings
one hour with the beast.
13. These have one mind, and
shall give their power
and strength
unto the beast.
14. These shall make war
with the Lamb, and the
Lamb shall overcome
them: for he is Lord of
lords, and King of kings:
and they that are with him *are* called,
and chosen, and faithful.
15. And he saith unto me,
The waters which thou sawest,
where the whore sitteth, are
peoples, and
multitudes, and nations,
and tongues.
16. And the ten horns which
thou sawest upon the beast, these
shall hate the whore, and
shall
make her desolate
and naked, and shall eat her flesh,
and burn her with fire.
17. For God hath put in their
hearts to fulfil his will,
and to agree,
and give their kingdom
unto the beast, until the words of
God shall be fulfilled.
18. And the woman
which thou sawest
is that great city, which
reigneth over the kings
of the earth.

CHAPTER 18

1. And after these things
I saw another angel
come down from heaven, having great
power; and the earth was lightened
with his glory.
2. And he cried mightily with a
strong voice, saying,
Babylon the great
is fallen, is fallen,
and is become
the habitation of devils,
and the hold of every foul
spirit, and a cage of every
unclean and hateful
bird.
3. For all nations have
drunk of the wine of
the wrath of her fornication,
and the kings of the earth have
committed fornication with her,
and the merchants of the earth
are waxed
rich through the abundance of
her delicacies.
4. And I heard another
voice from heaven, saying,
Come out of her, my
people, that ye be not partakers of
her sins, and that ye receive not of
her plagues.
5. For her sins have
reached unto
heaven, and God hath
remembered her iniquities.
6. Reward her even as she
rewarded you, and double unto
her double according to her works: in
the cup which she hath filled
fill to her double.
7. How much she hath
glorified herself,
and lived deliciously, so much
torment and sorrow give
her: for she saith in her heart,
I sit a queen, and am no widow,
and shall see no sorrow.
8. Therefore shall her

plagues come in one day,
death, and mourning, and famine;
and she shall be utterly
burned with fire: for strong *is*
the Lord God who
judgeth her.
9. **And the kings** of the earth, who
have committed fornication and lived
deliciously with her,
shall bewail her, and
lament for her, when they shall
see the smoke of her burning,
10. Standing afar off for the fear
of her torment,
saying, Alas, alas that great city
Babylon, that mighty city! for
in one hour is thy
judgment come.
11. **And the merchants**
of the earth
shall weep and mourn
over her; for no man buyeth
their merchandise
any more:
12. The merchandise of gold, and
silver, and precious stones, and of
pearls, and fine linen, and purple, and
silk, and scarlet, and all thyine wood,
and all manner vessels of ivory, and
all manner vessels of most precious
wood, and of brass, and iron,
and marble,
13. And cinnamon, and odours, and
ointments, and frankincense, and
wine, and oil, and fine flour, and
wheat, and beasts, and sheep, and
horses, and chariots, and slaves, and
souls of men.
14. **And the fruits that thy**
soul lusted after are
departed from thee,
and all things
which were dainty and
goodly are departed
from thee, and thou shalt find
them no more at all.
15. **The merchants**
of these things, which were
made rich by her, shall
stand afar off for the fear of
her torment, weeping and wailing,
16. **And saying, Alas, alas**
that great city, that was clothed
in fine linen, and purple, and scarlet,
and decked with gold, and precious
stones, and pearls!
17. **For in one hour so great**
riches is come to nought.
And every shipmaster, and
all the company in
ships, and sailors,
and as many as trade by sea,
stood afar off,
18. And cried when they saw the
smoke of her burning, saying, What
city is like unto this great city!
19. **And they**
cast dust on their heads, and
cried, weeping and wailing,
saying, Alas, alas
that great city, wherein
were made rich all that had
ships in the sea by reason
of her costliness!
for in one hour is she
made desolate.
20. **Rejoice** over her,
thou heaven, and
***ye* holy apostles and**
prophets; for God hath
avenged you on her.
21. **And a mighty angel took**
up a stone like a great millstone,
and cast *it* into the sea,
saying, Thus
with violence shall that
great city Babylon
be thrown down, and shall be
found no more at all.
22. And the voice of harpers, and
musicians, and of pipers, and
trumpeters, shall be heard no more at
all in thee; and no craftsman, of
whatsoever craft *he be,* shall be found
any more in thee; and the sound of a
millstone shall be heard no more at all
in thee;
23. And the light of a candle shall
shine no more at all in thee; and the
voice of the bridegroom and of the
bride shall be heard no more at all in
thee: for thy merchants were the great
men of the earth; for by thy sorceries
were all nations deceived.
24. **And in her was found the**
blood of prophets, and of

saints, and of
all that were
slain upon the earth.

CHAPTER 19

1. And after these things
I heard a great voice of
much people in heaven,
saying, Alleluia;
Salvation, and
glory, and
honour, and power, unto
the Lord our God:
2. **For true and righteous**
***are* his judgments: for he**
hath judged the great
whore, which did corrupt
the earth with her fornication, and
hath avenged the blood of his
servants at her hand.
3. And again they said, Alleluia. And
her smoke rose up for ever and ever.
4. **And the four and twenty**
elders and the four beasts
fell down and
worshipped God
that sat on the throne,
saying, Amen; Alleluia.
5. **And a voice came out of**
the throne, saying, Praise
our God, all ye his
servants, and ye that fear him,
both small and great.
6. **And I heard as it were the**
voice of a great multitude, and as the
voice of many waters, and
as the voice of mighty
thunderings, saying,
Alleluia: for
the Lord God
omnipotent reigneth.
7. **Let us** be glad and
rejoice, and give honour to
him: for the marriage of the
Lamb is come, and his wife
hath made herself ready.
8. **And to her was granted**
that she should be arrayed in
fine linen, clean and white:
for the fine linen is the
righteousness of saints.
9. **And he saith** unto me,
Write, Blessed *are* they
which are
called unto the marriage
supper of the Lamb.
And he saith unto me, These are the
true sayings of God.
10. **And I fell** at his feet
to worship him. And he
said unto me,
See *thou do it* not: I am thy
fellow-servant,
and of thy brethren that have the
testimony of Jesus:
worship God: for the
testimony of Jesus is the
spirit of prophecy.
11. **And I saw heaven**
opened, and behold a
white horse; and he that sat
upon him *was* called
Faithful and True, and in
righteousness he doth
judge and make war.
12. His eyes *were* as a flame of fire,
and on his head *were* many crowns;
and he had a name written, that no
man knew, but he himself.
13. **And he *was* clothed with**
a vesture dipped in blood:
and his name is called The
Word of God.
14. **And the armies** *which were*
in heaven followed him
upon white horses,
clothed in fine linen,
white and clean.
15. **And out of his mouth**
goeth a sharp sword, that
with it he should smite the
nations: and he shall rule
them
with a rod of iron:
and he treadeth the winepress of
the fierceness and wrath of
Almighty God.
16. **And he hath**
on *his* vesture and
on his thigh a name written,
KING OF KINGS, AND
LORD OF LORDS.
17. **And I saw an angel**
standing in the sun;
and he cried
with a loud voice, saying

to all the fowls
that fly in the midst of heaven,
Come and gather
yourselves together
unto the supper of the
great God;
18. That ye may
eat the flesh of kings,
and the flesh of
captains, and the flesh of
mighty men, and the flesh of
horses, and of them
that sit on them,
and the flesh of all *men,*
both free and bond,
both small and great.
19. **And I saw the beast,** and
the kings of the earth,
and their armies, gathered
together
to make war against him
that sat
on the horse, and against
his army.
20. **And the beast was**
taken, and with him
the false prophet
that wrought miracles before him,
with which he deceived them that
had received the mark of the beast,
and them that worshipped his
image. These
both were cast alive into a
lake of fire
burning with brimstone.
21. **And the remnant were**
slain with the sword of him
that sat
upon the horse, which *sword*
proceeded out of his mouth:
and all the fowls were filled
with their flesh.

CHAPTER 20

1. **And I saw an angel**
come down from heaven,
having the key of the
bottomless pit and a great
chain in his hand.
2. **And he laid hold on**
the dragon, that old serpent, which is
the Devil, and
Satan, and bound him a
thousand years,
3. **And cast him into the**
bottomless pit, and shut him up,
and set a seal upon him,
that he should deceive the
nations no more, till the
thousand years should be
fulfilled: and after that he
must be loosed a
little season.
4. And I saw thrones, and they sat
upon them, and judgment was given
unto them:
and *I saw* the souls of
them that were beheaded
for the witness of
Jesus, and for
the word of God, and which had
not worshipped the beast, neither his
image, neither had received *his* mark
upon their foreheads,
or in their hands;
and they lived
and reigned with Christ a
thousand years.
5. **But the rest** of the dead
lived not again
until the thousand years
were finished. This *is* the
first resurrection.
6. **Blessed** and holy
***is* he that hath part in the**
first resurrection: on such
the second death hath no
power, but they shall be
priests of God and of Christ,
and shall reign with him a
thousand years.
7. **And when the thousand**
years are expired, Satan
shall be loosed
out of his prison,
8. **And shall go out to**
deceive the nations
which are in the four quarters of the
earth, Gog, and Magog,
to gather them together
to battle: the number of whom *is* as
the sand of the sea.
9. **And they** went up on the breadth
of the earth, and
compassed the camp
of the saints

about, and the beloved city:
and fire came down from
God out of heaven,
and devoured them.
10. **And the devil and fire**
came down from God
out of heaven,
and devoured them.
10. **And the devil**
that deceived them
was cast into the lake of
fire and brimstone,
where the beast and the
false prophet *are,* and
shall be tormented
day and night
for ever and ever.
11. **And I saw a great white**
throne, and him that sat
on it, from whose face the earth and
the heaven fled away; and there was
found no place for them.
12. **And I saw the dead,**
small and great,
stand before God; and the
books were opened: and
another book was opened,
which is *the book* of life:
and the dead were judged
out of those things which were
written in the books,
according to their works.
13. **And the sea gave up the**
dead which were in it;
and death and hell
delivered up the dead
which were in them:
and they were judged
every man
according to their works.
14. **And death and hell were**
cast into the lake of fire.
This is the second death.
15. **And whosoever was not**
found written in the book of
life was cast into the lake
of fire.

CHAPTER 21

1. **And I saw a new heaven**
and a new earth:
for the first heaven and the first earth
were passed away; and there was
no more sea.
2. **And I John saw the holy**
city, new Jerusalem,
coming down
from God out of heaven,
prepared as a bride adorned
for her husband.
3. **And I heard a great voice**
out of heaven
saying, Behold,
the tabernacle of God *is*
with men, and he will dwell with
them, and they shall be his people,
and God himself shall be
with them, *and be*
their God.
4. **And God shall wipe away**
all tears from their eyes;
and there shall be no more
death, neither sorrow, nor crying,
neither shall there be any more
pain: for the former things are
passed away.
5. **And he that sat upon the**
throne said, Behold,
I make all things new.
And he said unto me,
Write: for these words are
true and faithful.
6. And he said unto me,
It is done. I am Alpha and
Omega, the beginning and the end.
I will give unto him that is
athirst of the fountain of
the water of life freely.
7. **He that overcometh shall**
inherit all things; and I will be his
God, and he shall be my son.
8. **But the** fearful, and
unbelieving, and the abominable,
and murderers, and whoremongers,
and sorcerers, and idolaters,
and all liars,
shall have their part in the
lake which burneth with fire
and brimstone:
which is the second death.
9. **And there came** unto me
one of the seven angels
which had the seven vials full of the
seven last plagues, and
talked with me,
saying, Come hither,

I will shew thee the bride,
the Lamb's wife.
10. **And he**
carried me away in the spirit to a
great and high mountain, and
shewed me that great city,
the holy Jerusalem,
descending out of heaven
from God,
11. **Having the glory of God:**
and her light *was* like unto a
stone most precious,
even like a jasper stone,
clear as crystal;
12. **And had a wall**
great and high,
and had
twelve gates, and at the
gates twelve angels, and
names written thereon,
which are *the names* of the
twelve tribes of the children
of Israel:
13. On the east three gates; on the
north three gates; on the south three
gates; and on the west three gates.
14. **And the wall** of the city
had twelve foundations,
and in them the names of
the twelve apostles
of the Lamb.
15. And he that talked with me had a
golden reed to measure the city,
and the gates thereof,
and the wall thereof.
16. **And the city lieth**
foursquare, and the length is
as large as the breadth: and he
measured the city with the reed,
twelve thousand furlongs.
The length and the
breadth and the
height of it
are equal.
17. **And he measured the**
wall thereof,
an hundred *and*
forty *and*
four cubits,
according to the measure of a man,
that is, of the angel.
18. **And** the building of
the wall of it
was *of*
jasper: and the city *was*
pure gold, like unto clear
glass.
19. **And the foundations**
of the wall of the city
were garnished with all manner
of precious stones.
The first foundation *was* jasper; the
second, sapphire; the third, a
chalcedony; the fourth, an emerald;
20. The fifth, sardonyx; the sixth,
sardius; the seventh, chrysolyte; the
eighth, beryl; the ninth, a topaz; the
tenth, a chrysoprasus; the eleventh,
a jacinth; the twelfth, an amethyst.
21. **And the twelve gates**
***were* twelve pearls:** every
several gate was of one pearl:
and the street of the city *was*
pure gold,
as it were transparent glass.
22. **And I saw no temple**
therein:
for the Lord God Almighty
and the Lamb are the
temple of it.
23. **And the city had no need**
of the sun, neither of
the moon, to shine in it:
for the glory of God
did lighten it,
and the Lamb *is* the
light thereof.
24. And the nations of them which are
saved shall walk in the light of it: and
the kings of the earth do bring their
glory and honour into it.
25. **And the gates** of it
shall not be shut at all by day:
for there shall be
no night there.
26. And they shall bring the glory and
honour of the nations into it.
27. **And there shall in no**
wise enter into
it any thing
that defileth, neither *whatsoever*
worketh abomination, or *maketh* a lie:
but they which are
written in
the Lamb's
book of life.

CHAPTER 22

1. And he shewed me
a pure river of water of life,
clear as crystal,
proceeding out of the
throne of God and of
the Lamb.
2. In the midst of the street of it,
and on either side of the
river, *was* *there*
the tree of life, which bare twelve
manner of fruits, *and* yielded
her fruit every month:
and the leaves of the tree
***were* for the healing of**
the nations.
3. **And there shall be no**
more curse: but the throne of
God and of the Lamb shall be in it;
and his servants shall
serve him:
4. **And they shall see his**
face; and his name *shall be*
in their foreheads.
5. **And there shall be no**
night there; and they need no
candle, neither light of the sun;
for the Lord God
giveth them
light: and they shall reign
for ever and ever.
6. **And he said** unto me,
These sayings *are* faithful and
true: and the Lord God of the holy
prophets sent his angel to shew unto
his servants the things which must
shortly be done.
7. **Behold, I come quickly:**
blessed *is* he that keepeth
the sayings of
the prophecy of this book.
8. **And I John** saw these things,
and heard *them*. And when I had heard
and seen, I
fell down to worship
before the feet of
the angel
which shewed me these things.
9. **Then saith he** unto me,
See *thou do it* not: for I am thy
fellow-servant, and of thy brethren the
prophets, and of them which keep the
sayings of this book:
worship God.
10. **And he saith** unto me,
Seal not the sayings of
the prophecy of this book:
for the time is at hand.
11. **He that is unjust, let him**
be unjust still: and he which is
filthy, let him be filthy still: and he that
is righteous, let him be righteous still:
and he that is holy, let him
be holy still.
12. **And, behold, I come**
quickly; and my reward *is*
with me, to give every man
according as his work shall be.
13. **I am Alpha and Omega,**
the beginning and the end, the first
and the last.
14. **Blessed *are* they that do**
his commandments, that
they may have right to the tree of
life, and
may enter in through the gates
into the city.
15. For without *are* dogs, and
sorcerers, and whoremongers, and
murderers, and idolaters, and
whosoever loveth and maketh a lie.
16. **I Jesus have sent mine**
angel to testify unto you these
things in the churches.
I am the root and the offspring
of David, *and* the bright
and morning star.
17. **And the Spirit and the**
bride say, Come. And let him
that heareth say, Come. And let him
that is athirst come.
And whosoever will, let him
take the water of life freely.
18. **For I testify** unto every man
that heareth the words of the
prophecy of this book,
If any man shall add unto
these things, God shall
add unto him the plagues
that are written
in this book:
19. **And if any man shall**
take away from
the words of the book of
this prophecy, God shall
take away his part out of

the book of life, and out
of the holy city, and *from* the
things which are written in this book.
20. **He** which testifieth these things
saith, Surely I come
quickly. Amen.
Even so, come, Lord Jesus.
21. The grace of our Lord Jesus Christ
be with you all.
Amen.